INTERNATIONAL TRADE

INTERNATIONAL TRADE

An Approach to the Theory

Akira Takayama

Purdue University

Holt, Rinehart and Winston, Inc.

New York   Chicago   San Francisco   Atlanta
Dallas   Montreal   Toronto   London   Sydney

To my parents

Preface

This book is intended to provide a complete and systematic treatment of international trade theory, a field that has progressed enormously in recent decades. It will discuss and extend existing theories in the field in a unified manner. The author adopts the viewpoint that the theory of international trade should be treated as a *part* of general economic theory. The approach of general equilibrium analysis is used throughout to present a unified treatment of trade theory.

In discussing each topic, the author has made a special effort to specify explicitly the model, the assumptions, and the scope of the analysis as well as to make the logic precise and clear. In other words, he has a critical bias against the traditional verbal or diagrammatical school of economic theory, in which the model and the logic are often very unclear, confusing the authors as well as the readers. Although an intuitive understanding of each topic or problem is important and hence is also stressed in this book, theory is useless or at best confusing without the clear specification of a model. With this viewpoint, the author attempts to clarify and simplify many diversified theories in the literature of international trade, as well as to generalize the results obtained from them. Students in related fields of economic theory will find that the methodology employed here will be useful when applied to problems in their own interest such as public finance, monetary theory, and growth theory.

Few fields of economics have enjoyed as much interaction with actual policy questions of the real world as has international trade theory. Adam Smith loudly advocated freedom from mercantilistic bondages, and David Ricardo considered a theoretical background for free trade. Trade policy in the nineteenth century is full of tariff problems. The controversy concerning the Corn Laws is a famous one. In the twentieth century, there are, for example, the departure from the gold standard, concern with exchange stability in the 1930s, the reparation problem after World War I and World War II, the Great Depression and the Keynesian Revolution, the problems of underdeveloped countries and a strong interest in the problem of economic growth after World War II, the European Common Market, and the problem of flexible and fixed exchange rates in connection with the Canadian experiences in the 1950s and 1960s. In other words, international trade theory has developed under a strong demand and stimulus from problems in the real world, and many first-class economists have participated in the development of the field. Hence, it may be dangerous to separate the "theory" from a more general body, called international economics. Hence, we should discuss each topic under a rich vision of the real world with a full understanding of the institutional framework of the problem. However, it is also important to find the basic logical structure of the problem and obtain a unified and transparent theoretical understanding of the problem. This is particularly clear when we realize that the analysis is often obscured by a large number of policy viewpoints based on the vested interests to a particular policy and that the theory for each policy question has become very complex and diversified. Actually, the motive in writing this book arises from such a concern.

In order to accomplish the above purposes and to facilitate the above-stated approach, the use of mathematics is very useful and often a matter of necessity. It is a language that facilitates honest presentation of the theory developed, by making the assumptions explicit and by making each step of the logical deductions clear. Thus it provides a basis for further developments and extensions. Although the author realizes that economics is a complex subject and involves many things which cannot be readily expressed in terms of mathematics, he does not hesitate to use mathematics in this book.

The mathematical prerequisites are, however, kept at a minimum. This book (except the fourth section of Chapter 7 and the second section of Chapter 17) requires only a knowledge of elementary calculus and elementary matrix theory (say, the rule of matrix multiplication). This level of mathematical preparation has recently become the standard requirement for entering graduate work in economics in major universities in the United States and Canada. Hence, there should be no reason to lower the mathematical prerequisite.

No preliminary knowledge of international trade theory is required, although the reader who has such a knowledge has an obvious advantage. Chapter 1 summarizes some important preparations necessary to those who have no knowledge of the field. International trade theory is a part of economic theory and it is not a field which should be made distinct from general economic theory. Many works in the field of trade theory have been written without this explicit recognition, and thus their real significance is often very obscure.

In spite of the rather elementary mathematical prerequisite, this book is designed to bring the reader to the frontiers of international trade theory so that he will be able to read articles in the field without difficulty. It is not an introduction to a higher-level book. Rather, it starts at a rather elementary level and brings the reader to the frontiers of economic knowledge. It will be useful as a reference book for professional economists who wish to become familiar with some of the topics and techniques of international trade theory. It is also suitable for use as a textbook for a graduate course in international trade theory (or for an advanced undergraduate course in those institutions where undergraduates receive substantial instruction in economic theory).

This book is a record of the author's lectures on international trade theory given at Purdue University and the University of Rochester during the past five years. These lectures are a revision of the author's lectures given to advanced undergraduate students in Tokyo during 1962–1964, which are published in the form of a book in Japanese [*International Economics* (Tokyo: Toyo Keizai Shimpo-sha), 1963]. This latter, in turn, has its origin in his Ph.D. dissertation at the University of Rochester, in which he attempted to coordinate many diversified trade theories by clarifying their logical structures.

An earlier version of this study is much indebted to Meade (*The Theory of International Economic Policy*, Vol. 1, 1951, and Vol. 2, 1956) and Johnson (*International Trade and Economic Growth*, 1958). In addition, credit must be given to a) Chipman, J. S., "A Survey of International Trade" (Parts 1, 2, 3), in *Econometrica*, July, Oct. 1965, and Jan. 1966, b) Kemp, M. C., *The Pure Theory of International Trade and Investment*, 1969 (1st ed., 1964), c) Mundell, R. A., *International Economics*, 1968, and d) various works on trade theory by Takashi Negishi, for the subsequent revision of this earlier version.

I am indebted to Professors Ronald W. Jones, Lionel W. McKenzie, S. C. Tsiang, and H. G. Johnson for many helpful comments on my Ph.D. dissertation which is the original source of much of this present study. I am also grateful to Lionel McKenzie for allowing me to use the material of a joint work with him, which has its origin in his lecture given at Harvard in 1957. (See Chapter 10, third section, and Chapter 12.)

In addition, I would like to thank a number of people who read a portion or the whole of the manuscript of this book. To those students who read my lectures in note form, offering their invaluable assistance, I would like to express my gratitude. I would also like to thank Edward Sieper, Takashi Negishi, James C. Moore, Murray C. Kemp, Ajit Sabharwal, Michihiro Ohyama, Yasuo Uekawa, and Nancy Baggott.

I am also indebted to the capable research assistance provided by Erik Haites, Gene Warren, Frank Maris, Robert Parks, and Kenneth Avio and to the excellent secretarial services of Mrs. Gladys Cox, Mrs. Helen Antonienko, and others, most of which was provided by Purdue University. Finally, thanks are due to the editors and publishers of the *Australian Economic Papers*, the *Canadian Journal of Economics*, and the *Review of Economic Studies* for permission to include in this book the articles originally published in them. A part of the research for this book was supported by the Krannert Summer Research

Grant of Purdue University in 1969. I am grateful to Deans Emanuel T. Weiler, John S. Day, and Rene P. Manes of the Krannert School of Industrial Administration of Purdue University, who have provided me with generous encouragement as well as unusually favorable research conditions.

Lafayette, Indiana   A.T.
November 1971.

Contents

10 A Keynesian Theory of International Trade—Simple Multipliers, Exchange Devaluation, and the Transfer Problem   279

11 The Effects of Fiscal and Monetary Policies under Flexible and Fixed Exchange Rates   327

PART IV Economic Growth, International Trade, and Factor Mobility   367

Some Notations

1 Sets

$x \in X$ x belongs to X (x is a member of X)

$x \notin X$ x does not belong to X (x is not a member of X)

$\{x: \text{properties of } x\}$ set notation

$\emptyset$ the empty set

R the set of real numbers

R^n the n-dimensional real space

$X \subset Y$ X is contained in Y (X is a subset of Y)

$X = Y$ X is equal to Y (that is, $X \subset Y$ and $Y \subset X$)

$X \cap Y$ the intersection of X and Y

$X \cup Y$ the union of X and Y

$\bigotimes\limits_{i=1}^{n} X_i$ the Cartesian product of the X_is (similarly $X \otimes Y$)

2 Vectors

Latin letters are used to denote vectors as well as scalars. However, note

$x \cdot y$ the inner product of x and y. Thus the dot ($\cdot$) here signifies that x and y are vectors.

Given two vectors x and y in R^n

1. $x \geqq y$ means $x_i \geqq y_i$ for all i
2. $x \geq y$ means $x_i \geqq y_i$ for all i *and* with strict inequality for at least one i
3. $x > y$ means $x_i > y_i$ for all i

3 Multiplication of matrix and vector

Let A be an $m \times n$ matrix

$A \cdot x$ (or simply Ax) means x is an n-column vector

$x \cdot A$ (or simply xA) means x is an m-row vector

$x \cdot A \cdot y$ (or simply xAy) means x is an m-row vector and y is an n-column vector

That is, we do not use any transpose notation for vectors. The matrices are denoted by capital Latin letters.

4 Operations

$\sum$ (addition)   that is, $\displaystyle\sum_{i=1}^{m} x_i = x_1 + x_2 + \cdots + x_m$

$\prod$ (multiplication)   that is, $\displaystyle\prod_{i=1}^{m} x_i = x_1 x_2 x_3 \ldots x_m$

dF/dx (or $F'(x)$ or F')   the (total) derivative of F with respect to x

$\partial F/\partial x$ (or F_x)   the partial derivative of F with respect to x

The time derivatives are often denoted by dot such as $\dot{P} = dP/dt$. In Chapters 10, 12, and 13, small Latin letters are used to denote infinitesimal change such as $dX \equiv x$.

INTERNATIONAL TRADE

INTRODUCTION

SCOPE OF THE BOOK

There is an enormous amount of literature on the theory of international trade. In the 1930s, there appeared two important works, one by Haberler (*The Theory of International Trade*) and the other by Viner (*Studies in the Theory of International Trade*), in which the authors accomplished the task of clarifying and coordinating the contributions and the many diversified advances of their contemporaries and predecessors. They thus raised tremendously the status of international trade theory as a unified academic discipline in economics. However, the progress of the field since their contributions has been enormous. A list of some of the important topics which have attracted the special attention of economists in the last three decades would include, for example: the Heckscher-Ohlin theorem, the Leontief paradox, the factor price equalization theorem, the Stolper-Samuelson theorem, the problem of exchange stability and exchange devaluation, the impact of the Keynesian Revolution upon international trade theory, international trade multipliers, the development of the theory of transfer payments, the impact of new welfare economics, the gains from trade and the compensation principle, the theory of economic integration and the theory of second best, economic growth and international trade, especially those works after Hicks' "Inaugural Lecture," and so on. To illustrate the enormous amount of progress in the field, it will suffice to call attention to the thick bibliography contained in the survey work by R. E. Caves, *Trade and Economic Structure*, which itself is becoming obsolete.

The present book is not intended to be a history of doctrines or a survey of developments in the field. More precisely, it is preferable to avoid a mere listing, whether systematic or non-systematic, of the doctrines and theories. Such a work very often gives the reader only a superficial knowledge and fragmentary memories of the topics covered in the work. Rather, this book proceeds in a

1

direction which facilitates a unified understanding of the diversified topics of international trade theory. More specifically, we shall build several important models and see that the logical structure and the basic set of assumptions of most of the works in the literature belong to one of these relatively few models, and that the major conclusions in the literature are often simple corollaries of the results obtained from these models.

This approach will thus clarify and simplify the logical structure of many diversified theories in the literature, as well as generalize the results obtained from them. This will facilitate further developments in the theories. The traditional approach to graduate education in economics, including the theory of international trade, is that of assigning many books and articles for the students to read. This book does *not* use this approach, both because of the size and complexity of the field and because it fails to provide students with the knowledge of the unifying analytical structure in trade theory. Instead, the book attempts to provide the material usually obtained from a multitude of books and articles with a systematic framework while requiring a minimum of outside reading. It should be noted that the reader should be able to recognize the importance of the construction of an explicit model for the arguments and the basic method of model-building in economic theory as well as to be able to generalize the models in whatever direction interests him. The importance of this recognition is stressed, for, as in other fields of economic theory, what is important in international trade theory is *not* the collection of theorems, but the method of analysis and the way of developing a certain explicit model which is relevant to some specific problem in the real world. The actual problems in the economy are too complex to allow immediate application of ready-made theorems. Recall here the famous words, ascribed to J. M. Keynes: "The theory of economics does not furnish a body of settled conclusions immediately applicable to policy. It is a method rather than a doctrine, an apparatus of the mind, a technique of thinking, which helps its possessor to draw conclusions." ("Introduction" to *Cambridge Economic Handbooks*.)

OUTLINE OF THE BOOK

We shall outline the contents of this book in the order of Chapter 1 (Preliminaries), Part I (Chapters 2 and 3), Part III (Chapters 8, 9, 10, and 11), Part IV (Chapters 12, 13, and 14), Part II (Chapters 4, 5, 6, and 7), Part V (Chapters 15, 16, and 17), and Part VI (Chapter 18).

This book starts with Chapter 1, intended to give the reader the preparation necessary for the main body of the work. It consists of a geometrical exposition of some essential problems involved in the theory of international trade, a simple mathematical model with its diagrammatical counterpart which will clarify the mathematical structure involved in a simple model of trade, and certain concepts which will be useful in the analysis of international trade, such as the techniques of comparative statics, "hat" calculus, and production functions with constant returns to scale. Those readers who are sufficiently well-trained in economic theory can skim through this chapter.

An important part of the theory of international trade is the analysis based on the model of a two-country, two-commodity trading world. In fact, most analysis in trade theory, carried out diagrammatically, is based on such a model. In Chapter 2, we shall construct a mathematical model of a two-commodity economy. It will serve as a basic model from which most of the traditional results for a two-sector economy can be obtained as simple corollaries without requiring the special ingenuity inherent in diagrammatical analysis. Such a straightforward analysis will point the way to further applications of the model —applications which are not confined to the theory of international trade. At the end of Chapter 2 we shall give examples of such applications.

Chapter 3 formally opens this book of trade theory by discussing the theory of comparative advantage based on the Heckscher-Ohlin trade model. This is an extremely important topic in trade theory. We shall develop it in a clear and straightforward manner as an application of the model developed in Chapter 2.

Traditionally, the emphasis on diagrammatical techniques in trade theory is so great that the analysis often becomes messy, and important assumptions are frequently concealed by the usual way in which the curves are drawn. The Appendix to Chapter 3 is a warning to such an overemphasis of diagrammatical technique. In particular, we shall point out that the usual convention in the literature to draw the contract curve concave to the diagonal is incorrect.

The analytical technique employed in Chapters 2 and 3 is basically that of comparative statics. This technique is known to be very useful in international trade theory and is, in fact, commonly used. In Parts III and IV, we shall make heavy use of this technique, and the model developed in Chapter 2 will again be useful in much of these latter two parts.

Part III is the analysis of trade policy. Here major policy tools such as tariffs, transfer payments, domestic taxes, exchange rates, and so on, are taken as the shift parameters in the comparative statics analysis. We discuss the effect of these policies under both a neoclassical and Keynesian framework.

Part III opens with the effects of tariffs, transfer payments, and domestic taxes, all treated within a neoclassical framework (Chapter 10). It is well-known that the stability condition plays a crucial role in any comparative statics analysis. We shall obtain the Marshall-Lerner condition as such a stability condition for a neoclassical model before we enter the analysis of the above-stated policy questions. It will then be seen that, in the discussion of these policy questions, the Marshall-Lerner condition as a stability condition plays an important role.

In Chapter 9, we introduce money explicitly into the neoclassical analysis. Here, money serves as a store of value as well as a means of payments and as the unit of account. That is, the asset aspect of money is emphasized. The role of the exchange rate in the neoclassical economy is clear only with the explicit introduction of the demand for money. We shall discuss such topics as exchange devaluation and exchange stability. It will be argued, for example, that if all goods are "gross substitutes" and none of the goods are inferior and if a complete sterilization policy is adopted in the devaluing country, then devaluation will always improve the balance of payments of the devaluing country. The importance of the separability between real goods and money in connection with our analysis of Chapter 8 will also be discussed.

Chapter 10 summarizes a Keynesian theory of international trade. In the first section of the chapter we shall summarize the essence of the Keynesian macroeconomic theory. The second section deals with the theory of international trade multipliers. We shall make the assumptions of this theory specific so that we understand the scope and the limitation of such a theory. The next section is the main section of Chapter 10. In it we shall discuss the Keynesian theory of exchange devaluation. Here, such well-known conditions as the Laursen-Metzler condition and the Harberger condition are the major matters of concern. Next we shall make two important remarks on the Keynesian theory of devaluation. One concerns the very important distinction between the exchange stability problem and the exchange devaluation problem. The other deals with the role of money in the Keynesian devaluation analysis. The last section treats the transfer problem from the Keynesian framework of analysis.

Chapter 11 is the last chapter of Part III. Here we shall discuss a topic which has recently attracted great attention: the effects of fiscal and monetary policies under flexible and fixed exchange rates in an economy in which both international trade and international capital mobility are present. There is a great deal of literature on this topic including several important articles by Mundell. We shall build a clearly stated, general model from which the major results in the literature appear as simple corollaries. In view of the complexities of the subject, we shall give a simple diagrammatical account of the essence of the topic in the beginning of Chapter 11. In the course of the discussion of Chapter 11, we shall need the relations between comparative statics analysis, the stability condition, and the correspondence principle for an open economy. We shall carry out our discussion of this problem in the Appendix to Chapter 11. One important distinction between the analysis in Chapter 11 and that of the previous two chapters is that the former is based on the assumption that the country concerned is small compared to the rest of the world, whereas the latter does not have such an assumption. This restrictive assumption of Chapter 11, however, enables us to generalize the analysis considerably in other directions.

Part IV deals with the problem of economic growth and international trade (and factor mobility). This is again a topic which has attracted a great deal of attention from economists. The discussion was heated, especially after Hicks' "Inaugural Lecture" at Oxford with many contributions by Johnson, Mishan, Asimakopulos, Kemp, Bhagwati, Findlay, Grubert, Takayama, and others. In Chapters 12 and 13, we shall build a general model from which all the major conclusions can be obtained as simple corollaries. The analysis is basically a neoclassical one. The major distinction between these two chapters is that Chapter 13 is based on a model with two factors of production, while in the model of Chapter 12 the actual number of the factors is not explicitly specified. The model of Chapter 13 is basically that of Chapter 2 and the model of Chapter 12 is basically well-known due to Meade. Although the model in Chapter 13 may be superior to that of Chapter 12, it is important to become familiar with the important model by Meade to understand the literature. We may also point out that essentially the same model as used in Chapter 12 was used in analyzing completely different problems in Chapter 10; that is, exchange devaluation and transfer payments under the Keynesian framework. We may also note that the models of Chapters 12 and 13 can also be used to analyze the effect of factor mobility (as well as the effect of economic growth).

As remarked before, the analytical technique used in Chapters 12 and 13 is that of comparative statics. The importance of an explicitly dynamic model for the topic of trade and growth was recently pointed out. Although the discussion here is more or less academic at present, it is very important that the reader become acquainted with such a dynamic technique. In Chapter 14, we shall re-examine the important study by Oniki and Uzawa on this topic. We shall revise their result as well as obtain more definite results than they obtained.

Part II of the book is rather distinct from Parts I, III, and IV in the sense that the basic analytical technique employed in Part II is that of linear and nonlinear programming. The importance of this programming technique in economic theory is well-known. However, we can also see applications of this remarkable technique in such ancient topics as the Ricardian theory of comparative advantage and J. S. Mill's extension of the Ricardian theory. We shall discuss these topics from the programming point of view in Chapters 4 and 5. Chapter 4 also contains an exposition of the duality theorem in linear programming (with its applications to the Ricardian theory). The Appendix to Chapter 5 contains a concise summary of the theory of nonlinear programming.

Chapter 6 is the extension of the two-country, two-commodity classical model to a multi-country, multi-commodity model. Such an extension is obviously very difficult as long as we employ a diagrammatical technique. We shall carry out this extension explicitly from the mathematical programming viewpoint. Such important topics as Kuhn's theorem and the McKenzie-Jones theorem will also be discussed in the chapter.

Chapter 7 discusses a more general international trade model with an optimality characterization and the proof of the existence of equilibrium. To make this book sufficiently self-contained, we add the expository account of the elements of activity analysis and vector maximum analysis (beginning of Chapter 7). After reading Part II, the reader will have become familiar with the mathematical programming technique, a very important technique in modern economic theory, as well as become familiar with the topics of international trade theory discussed in the chapters of Part II.

The technique of mathematical programming again becomes important and useful in Part V, where we discuss the question of trade and welfare. Part V opens with a discussion of the question of optimal tariff and investment (Chapter 15). The optimal tariff question is an age-old question and the results are well-known. This topic was recently combined with the topic of optimal foreign investment by Kemp, Jones, and others. We shall clarify the logical structure of their argument. We shall also attempt to clarify the basic methodology involved so that the reader can apply a similar methodology to other problems of international trade theory. Therefore, we include a discussion on the question of deterministic versus optimization models in the chapter. The theory of optimal tariffs and foreign investment is treated explicitly as an optimization problem in this context. The mathematical technique used is that of mathematical programming.

Chapter 16 discusses the problem of economic integration or customs union. In the first section of this chapter we shall summarize some of the major theoretical problems that have occurred in the literature. This problem opened a new realm of economic theory in the literature, called the *theory of second best*. Although this problem is not yet fully solved, a new approach, called the *piecemeal approach*, seems to give a fruitful result. We shall treat the *theory of economic integration* from this viewpoint. For example, we shall show that free trade within the union is, after all, desirable from the viewpoint both of the union and of the world as a whole. We shall also show that the duty which the union will impose on the import from the third country will follow the well-known optimal tariff formula, as we would normally expect. The crucial mathematical technique in this chapter is again that of mathematical programming.

Chapter 17 deals with the theory of the compensation principle. When a certain economic policy (say, the repeal of the Corn Law) changes an economic situation from one situation to another and when there are losers as well as gainers, can we say that this policy is beneficial to the society? This is again a very difficult question which is not quite solved. However, we shall attempt to clarify the problems involved and to straighten out the logical structure of the problem. This is again a field in which mathematical programming can be an important technique. In the Appendix to Chapter 17, we shall illustrate some of the concepts developed in the chapter. In particular we shall investigate the implication of a welfare criterion, the "Hicks-Samuelson criterion," under the compensation principle when the economy is organized in a competitive way. We shall then give a unified treatment of various subjects such as gains from trade, the welfare effect of price divergence, gains from economic growth, and so on.

Part VI contains only Chapter 18. In this chapter we shall summarize recent discussions on the multi-commodity, multi-factor extension of the factor price equalization theorem and the Stolper-Samuelson theorem. This topic goes beyond the traditional Heckscher-Ohlin model. It requires a separate treatment because it involves some conspicuous and complicated questions which are important in the modern treatment of trade theory. The mathematical techniques, especially the one developed in connection with the subject matter of this chapter by Gale and Nikaido, also deserve special attention.

1

PRELIMINARIES

A DIAGRAMMATICAL ANALYSIS OF INTERNATIONAL TRADE

Consider a country which produces two commodities, good X and good Y. Suppose that the production transformation curve of the two commodities is drawn as illustrated in Figure 1-1, that is, concave to the origin. Suppose that the price ratio of the two commodities is illustrated by the slope of the α-line in Figure 1-1. Then the production point of a country under a competitive situation is given by point A in Figure 1-1. It is important to note that point A,

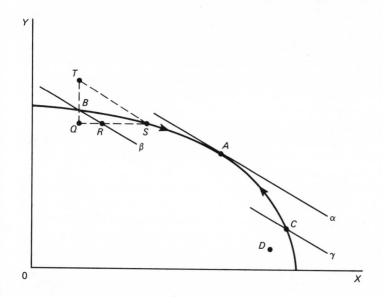

Figure 1-1   Production Transformation Curve

on the above "concave" transformation curve, is a "stable" point in the sense that if the actual production takes place at any other points (such as B, C, and so on) on the production transformation curve, then there is a mechanism which brings these production points to A. To see this, consider, for example, that the actual production takes place at point B. In Figure 1-1, the β-line is parallel to the α-line so that its slope represents the price ratio of the two commodities. Let BQ represent one unit of good Y. By shifting productive resources from good Y to good X, thus reducing the output of good Y and increasing the output of good X, the economy moves along the production transformation curve towards point A. If one unit of good Y's output is reduced in this way, there is an increase in output of good X, measured by QS. However, if the two goods are exchanged in the market under the price ratio represented by the slope of the β-line, then a one-unit sacrifice of good Y, that is, QB, will obtain the amount QR of good Y. If, on the other hand, an amount of good X, QS, is offered, QT of Y may be obtained, where the TS line is parallel to the β-line. Hence, as long as the price line, represented by the β-line, prevails, and as long as the market is competitive in the sense that traders cannot affect the price ratio which prevails in the market, producers can obtain a "profit" in terms of good Y in the amount of TB per unit reduction of output of good Y. In other words, producers obtain good X in the amount of QS by a per unit sacrifice of good Y's output, and then, exchanging the obtained good X in the market, they can obtain good Y in the amount of QT. $TB = (QT - BQ)$ measures the profit in terms of good Y per unit sacrifice of good Y.

Hence the production point moves towards point A as long as a constant price ratio prevails. Similarly, if the actual production point happens to be at point C, there is an analogous mechanism which brings the production point towards point A. It is important to note the two assumptions that are crucial in the above argument: one is that the production transformation curve is concave to the origin; the other is that the market is competitive. Note also that the money price of each good is irrelevant to the above discussion. Only the relative price of the two commodities (that is, the exchange ratio of the two commodities) is important. Also note that any point inside the production transformation curve is inefficient in the sense that one can find a point on the transformation curve at which more of at least one good can be produced without decreasing the output of the other good. For example, at point D, we can find such a point C. At point C more of both goods are produced compared to point D. Then producers would move from a point such as D to a point such as C. If the "competitive situation" prevails so that inefficient producers are driven out of the market by their competitors, such a movement from the inside of the transformation curve to a point on the transformation curve is inevitable. After a point on the transformation curve is realized, then the movement along the transformation curve towards point A will occur under the mechanism described above.

Assume now that international trade occurs. The introduction of trade implies the introduction of foreign consumers and foreign producers into our consideration. Due to the introduction of this new sphere of demand and supply conditions, the price ratio which would prevail in the market would, in general, be different from the one which prevails under the state of no international trade (isolation). As the price ratio of the two commodities changes, the production point moves. This is illustrated in the following diagram (Figure 1-2) as a movement from point A to point B. Here we assume, for the sake of simplicity, that the country in question is small enough compared with the rest of the world in the sense that the volume of her import and export will not affect the price line to any significant degree. (For the case in which this assumption is discarded, see Baldwin [1].)

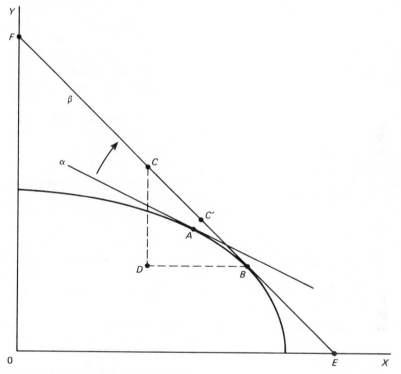

Figure 1-2　Opening of Trade

The actual consumption point is somewhere on the price line (the β-line, in Figure 1-2) which is tangent to the transformation curve at point B, that is, a point such as C or C'. The precise location of the consumption point clearly depends on the demand conditions of the two goods. Suppose point C is the consumption point of the country, then BD represents the amount of export and CD represents the amount of import of the country.

Is a point such as C or C', which is reached after the opening of trade, any "better" than point A which is both the production and consumption point before the opening of trade? We may reject the argument which in effect says that the society chose point C (or C') when it could have chosen a point such as A. This argument is unsatisfactory as long as the society is organized individualistically.

However, if the point after trade is C', then we may claim that the society is better off compared with point A in the sense that more of each good is available for consumption. Although this argument is very convincing, we have to realize that there are at least two loose points in the argument. One is that it presupposes the assumptions of free disposability of the goods and of non-satiation. In other words, sometimes more of a good may be less desirable than less of that good unless it can be thrown away with negligible cost when it is undesired. The second loose point in the argument above is that it pays no attention to the problem of redistribution of income. Any shift of the production point usually is accompanied by a redistribution of income among the owners of various factors of production. Hence, the shift of production from A to B must usually be accompanied by a redistribution of income. Also, the income effect due to the price change would cause an income redistribution among consumers. If an individual's satisfaction is non-measurable, how can we conclude that the satisfaction of the gainers in these processes is greater than the satisfaction of the losers?

The situation is more complicated if the consumption point achieved after trade is C instead of C'. Then less of good X is available for consumption after trade, compared with the pre-trade situation, although more of good Y is available for consumption. Then even abstracting from the problem of free disposability and non-satiation and the problem of the redistribution of income, this creates another serious problem. In what sense can we say that point C is better than point A, when less amount of one of the goods becomes available for consumption at C?

This problem, together with the problem of income redistribution, caused a serious debate, especially in the 1940s and 1950s, which is now known as the debate on the *compensation principle*. Postponing a full discussion of this problem to a later chapter (Chapter 17), we may point out one argument (assuming free disposability and non-satiation) which is possible here about the welfare comparison of two situations. We can say that situation C' is better than situation A in the sense that the losers in connection with the redistribution of income due to a shift in production can be compensated because more of each good is available at C'. Similarly we can also say that situation C is better than A in the sense that the losers in connection with a shift from A to C can be compensated by an approximate redistribution of income.[1] Note also that the losers cannot compensate the gainers *not* to move from situation A to either of situations C and C'. In Chapter 17, we shall point out that these arguments can best be illustrated in terms of Samuelson's utility possibility curves (see Samuelson [11] and [12]). After pointing out the weaknesses involved in the above arguments, we shall then argue that either situation C or C' is still better than situation A under the compensation principle. Here we simply point out

[1] It is not necessary that income actually be redistributed so that everybody is in fact made better off than before. That is, compensation is a hypothetical question rather than an actual one. In the argument it is sufficient that everybody *could* be better off. More practical questions, such as how the compensation could be instituted or what are the costs of such a redistribution of income and wealth, are not asked.

that the set of points in the triangle OEF determined by the β-line (Figure 1-2) and the set of points in the production block, respectively, signify the sets of available consumptions before and after trade. That the former set is larger than the latter, signifies the welfare improvement due to the opening of trade under the compensation principle.

In traditional trade theory, the above difficulty involved in welfare comparison is often avoided by assuming that the society possesses a utility indicator which represents the utility indicators of all members of the society. This is clearly an extremely heroic assumption (especially when it is applied to a normative analysis), as can be seen in view of Arrow's Impossibility Theorem.[2] However, this is a very useful assumption (especially when it is applied to a positive analysis) in the sense that it focuses our attention on some important problems without putting ourselves in the position of being led astray in the heavy jungle of welfare economics. Such a simplifying practice is known to be very useful in economics. For example, nobody believes that there are such things as an aggregate commodity or the "general price level," but macroeconomic analysis deals precisely with these things and they are known to be very useful.[3]

Suppose, then, that there is such a utility indicator in the society and assume that it can be represented by indifference curves (called the community indifference curves) like the individual's. Assume also that these indifference curves, like each individual's indifference curves, are convex to the origin and never intersect each other. Then, the opening of trade as illustrated in Figure 1-2 can be re-illustrated by the well-known diagram in Figure 1-3.[4] Here point C is better than point B in the sense that it represents a point on a higher indifference curve.

Although there is an extremely difficult problem involved in "gains from trade" as discussed above, the positive aspect of the opening of trade is easier to understand. As remarked before, it simply says that as long as the post-trade price ratio is different from the pre-trade price ratio prevailing at the opening of trade, the country reaches a consumption and a production point which is different from the original consumption and production point under a competitive mechanism. This change will naturally determine the volume of export

---

[2] This theorem asserts that under a certain axiom system it is impossible to find a mechanism in the society which generates the society's utility indicator which reflects the utility indicator of every member of the society accurately.

[3] For a good critical review of such concepts as community indifference (or social welfare function) and representative citizen, see Chipman [2]. A sharp distinction must, however, be made with regard to the concept of the social welfare function, depending whether it is used to describe the welfare level of the society or to describe the behavior of the society. The latter is the question of whether the society acts as if it were single "rational" unit. The former question is a very difficult one as illustrated in Arrow's Impossibility Theorem and the Compensation Principle debate, while a much stronger statement can be obtained in the latter question. Therefore the use of a diagram such as Figure 1–3 for the purpose of welfare analysis is to be questioned, although its "positive" use may be accepted.

[4] The first use of community indifference curves to clarify the basic problem of international trade is due to Leontief [7].

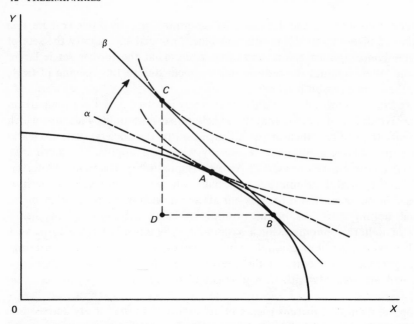

Figure 1-3 Community Indifference Curve and the Opening of Trade

and import (such as *BD* and *CD* in Figure 1-2). As is clear from the diagram, the volume of export and of import will vary with the post-trade price ratio. Note also that this commodity price ratio is accompanied by the determination of which country is the exporter and which the importer of good *X*. As the post-trade price ratio changes due to changes in demand and supply conditions, the country can move from exporting good *X* to exporting good *Y*. Moreover, the pattern of production will be different depending upon the commodity price ratio. This is illustrated in Figure 1-4.

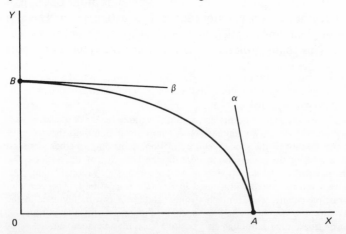

Figure 1-4 Patterns of Production

In Figure 1-4, the α-line and the β-line respectively represent the price lines which are tangent to the transformation curve at A and B. Let p_x and p_y, respectively, be the price of good X and good Y. Let $p \equiv p_x/p_y$. Let p_{max} and p_{min} respectively be the values of p which correspond to the slopes of the α- and β-line. Then we have

1. $p \geqq p_{max}$: Only good X is produced,

2. $p \leqq p_{min}$: Only good Y is produced,

3. $p_{min} < p < p_{max}$: Both goods are produced.

When $p \geqq p_{max}$, clearly this country exports good X and imports good Y as long as there is trade. Also when $p \leqq p_{min}$, this country exports good Y and imports good X as long as there is trade. When $p_{min} < p < p_{max}$, this country can either export or import the same good (say, good X). Case 1 or 2 are called cases of *complete specialization* and case 3 is called the case of *incomplete specialization*. Note that if the production transformation curve is a straight line, then complete specialization is more likely, for the only case of incomplete specialization is the case in which the price ratio is equal to the cost ratio which is represented by the production transformation *line*. Such a case is well-known in connection with the classical Ricardo-Mill theory of comparative advantage, which will be discussed in Chapters 4 and 5.

What then determines the post-trade price ratio? The answer is obvious: It depends on the world demand and supply of each good. Assuming away such complications as transport costs, institutional impediments on trade, and tariffs and international factor mobility, J. S. Mill first established such a theory based on the Ricardian theory of comparative advantage. Then, we have a more recent formulation of the same problem, known as the Heckscher-Ohlin theorem. These theories offer us the understanding of the crucial factors involved in the determination of international equilibrium price ratio. J. S. Mill's model will be discussed in Chapter 5 and the Heckscher-Ohlin theorem will be discussed in Chapter 3. In the Heckscher-Ohlin theorem, the production transformation curve is one which is concave to the origin, as illustrated in the three diagrams above. In the Ricardo-Mill classical model, the production transformation curve is the straight line signifying "constant costs." Although the two-country, two-commodity formulation, together with the various assumptions such as no international factor mobility and no transport costs, will be very useful to sharpen the results, we may also be interested in establishing a more general model. Such a task will be attempted in Chapter 7.

The question of the determinants of the pattern of trade among countries is treated in the theory of "comparative advantage." A corollary of this problem is that of which commodities will be produced in each country before and after trade. There are clearly two aspects in this problem of determination of the pattern of trade and production. One is that of asking what will be the "optimal" patterns of trade and production from the point of view of the world or each country. The second is that of asking what will be the actual pattern of trade and production when trade is opened and when certain market conditions (such as free trade and perfect competition) are imposed.

The theory that answers the first type of question is known as normative. The classical theory of trade has a strong flavor of this type. The second question is dealt with in a positive type of theory; in trade, the Heckscher-Ohlin theory. In Chapter 7, we shall show that these two theories are closely related in the sense that free-trade equilibrium realizes a certain optimum for the world and that such an optimum can be supported by free-trade equilibrium. An earlier version of this theory can be discovered in classical Ricardo-Mill theory of comparative advantage as we shall see in Chapters 4 and 5. In Chapter 6, we shall discuss the multi-country, multi-commodity version of the classical theory.

Here we explore the basic nature of the "positive" theory of comparative advantage. Assume a two-country, two-commodity trading world with negligible international transport costs. Our question is what determines the patterns of specialization when trade is opened between the countries and free trade and perfect competition prevail in every market? Clearly it depends on the price ratio which prevails in each country before trade. To illustrate our argument, we assume that each country produces both goods before trade.[5] Let p_i be the price ratio (the price of good X vis-à-vis the price of good Y) which prevails in Country i, $(i = 1, 2)$ before trade. Then if $p_1 < p_2$, Country 1 will export good X and import good Y, when trade is opened. (Thus Country 2 will export good Y and import good X.) Similarly, if $p_1 > p_2$, Country 1 imports good X and exports good Y. After trade, without international transport costs, the commodity price ratio of the two countries will be equalized (which is called the international equilibrium price ratio).[6] What then determines the pre-trade price ratio? This question has already been answered. It is determined by the demand and supply conditions of each country. It is important to note that any difference in these conditions can create a difference in pre-trade price ratios of the two countries. For example, the pre-trade price ratios can be different even if the production transformation curves of the two countries are identical. This will be the case if the demand conditions of the two countries are different. This is illustrated in Figure 1-5, Case a.[7] Here, $a_1, b_1, \cdots (a_2, b_2, \cdots)$ represent the indifference curves of Country 1 (Country 2). The pre-trade price ratio which prevails in Country 1 (Country 2) is represented by the α_1-line (the α_2-line). The pre-trade price ratios of the two countries can be different even if

---

[5] The reader should be able to analyze, in a manner analogous to the subsequent analysis, the case in which the two countries specialize in the production of a different good before trade (say, good X for Country 1 and good Y for Country 2) and the case in which both countries specialize in the production of the same good before trade.

[6] It is not necessarily the case that each country produces both goods *after* trade. It is possible that one or both countries specialize in the production of one good after trade. It depends on the international equilibrium price ratio.

[7] In both Case a and Case b in Figure 1-5, the α_1-line is steeper than the α_2-line so that $p_1 > p_2$. Hence, after trade, Country 1 will export good Y and import good X. The reader can easily construct a diagram in which $p_1 < p_2$.

the demand conditions of the two countries are identical. This will be the case if there is a difference in the production conditions between the countries. This is illustrated in Figure 1-5, Case *b*. Here the identical demand conditions of the two countries are represented by the same community indifference curves and the differences in the production conditions are represented by a difference in the production transformation curve of the two countries.

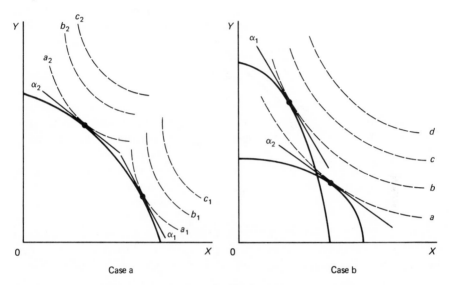

Case a   Case b

Figure 1-5   Determinants of Pre-Trade Price Ratios

THE OFFER CURVE

Suppose a certain commodity price ratio prevails. Then, assuming a competitive market, both the production point and the consumption point are determined. The individualistic basis of such a determination is profit maximization for the producers and maximization of satisfaction for the consumers. In Figure 1-3, we illustrated the production and the consumption point, when the price line β prevails, by point B and point C respectively. Under this situation this country exports good X in the amount of BD and imports good Y in the amount of CD.

I is important to note that for this country BD signifies the amount of excess supply of good X, and CD signifies the amount of excess demand for good Y, when the price line β prevails. When the price ratio changes, the amount of the export or the import also changes. The *offer curve* is the locus of the points which relate the price ratio to the volume of the export and the import. It is illustrated in the following diagram:

In Figure 1-6, point A signifies the export-import configuration when the price ratio is represented by the slope of the α-line. In other words, when this price ratio prevails, the amount of excess demand (import demand) for good Y

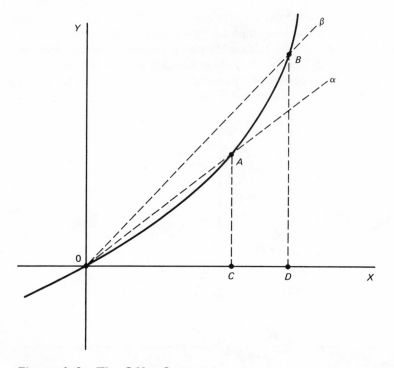

Figure 1-6   The Offer Curve

is equal to AC and the amount of excess supply (export supply) of good X is equal to $0C$.

When the price line moves from α to β in Figure 1-6, good X becomes more expensive relative to good Y. The country's export supply changes to $0D$ and the import demand changes to BD. The locus of points A, B, and so on, is the *offer curve* of the country. *It is the locus of combinations of excess demand (import demand) and excess supply (export supply) corresponding to various levels of the commodity price ratio.* In the third quadrant of Figure 1-6, we measure the configuration of excess supply of good Y (instead of X) and excess demand for good X (instead of Y). Then the offer curve in the first quadrant is extended to the third quadrant. Thus in the first quadrant this country is the exporter of good X and the importer of good Y, while in the third quadrant she is the exporter of good Y and the importer of good X.

The above concept of the offer curve is often known as the *Mill-Marshall offer curve*, as they were the economists who conceived or explicitly introduced it into economic analysis for the first time.[8]

The construction and the implications of the offer curve under the classical constant cost assumption will be discussed in Chapter 5. Here we show its construction for a more difficult case, that is, the case in which the transformation curve is concave to the origin. Our construction here is due to Meade [9].

[8] See Marshall [8].

We may note that in Chapter 5 the emphasis of the argument is not on the construction of the offer curve.

In Figure 1-7, the a-curve shows the locus of the corner T of the production transformation block RST of a certain country, when it moves along a certain community indifference curve, say, the a'-curve. The RS curve is moved so that the a'-curve is always tangent to it (and the ST line is parallel to the X-axis). The a-curve thus constructed is called the *trade indifference curve*. When the production transformation block, RST, is slid along a different community indifference curve, then we obtain a different trade indifference curve. Thus corresponding to the family of the community indifference curves, we obtain the family of trade indifference curves.

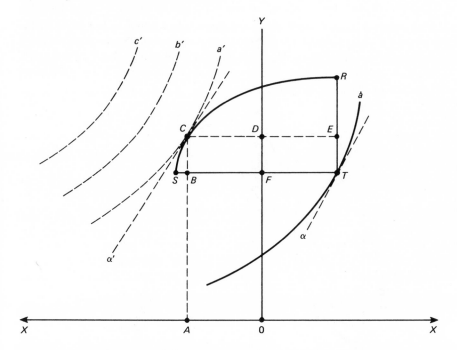

Figure 1-7   A Trade Indifference Curve

In Figure 1-7, the production transformation block RST is tangent to the community indifference curve a' at point C. The α'-line denotes the common tangency line at C. Suppose that the country can trade an amount FT of good X for an amount $F0$ of good Y, then it can achieve the level of consumption represented by point C. That is, if it produces good X in the amount of CE and good Y in the amount of CB, then by exporting good X in the amount of DE ($= FT$) to the rest of the world it can obtain good Y (that is, imports) in the amount of $F0$ in exchange. Thus it can consume good X in the amount of CD and good Y in the amount of CA. Note that point T signifies the export-import combination in the first quadrant.

It is easy to see that the trade indifference curves are upward sloping and convex shaped as illustrated in the diagram, as long as the community indifference curves are convex to the origin 0, and sloped as in the direction illustrated in the diagram, and as long as the production transformation curve, RCS, is concave to the corner T. Let α be the line tangent to the trade indifference curve at T. Then it can be shown that the slope of the α-line is equal to the slope of the α'-line.[9]

In general, the α-line does not pass through the origin, for it is the line tangent to an arbitrary trade indifference curve at an arbitrary point of the trade indifference curve. Hence the value of the volume of export (FT) is not in general equal to the value of the volume of import ($0F$).

However, if the α-line happens to pass through the origin, 0, then the value of the country's import demand, $0F$ (of good Y), is equal to the value of the export supply, FT (of good X). In other words, this country can indeed acquire an amount $0F$ of good Y in the world market in exchange for an amount FT of good X (without violating the "budget condition"), when the price ratio represented by the α-line prevails.

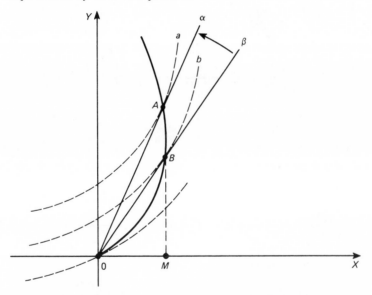

Figure 1-8   Trade Indifference Curves and the Offer Curve

Since the slope of the α-line is equal to the slope of the α'-line, and since the α'-line is tangent to both the production transformation curve and the community indifference curve (here a'), the commodity price ratio represented by the α-line can in this case support the production point C on the country's transformation curve as well as the consumers' equilibrium of the country represented by point C.

9 For the proof of this statement, see Meade [9], pp. 13–14.

In Figure 1-8, we draw the family of this country's trade indifference curves (*a, b, c,* and so on). Clearly, as the trade indifference curve moves to the left, it reflects a higher level of consumers' satisfaction for this country. For example, the *a*-curve represents a higher consumers' satisfaction of this country than the *b*-curve. Let *A, B,* and so on, be the points at which the rays from the origin are tangent to these trade indifference curves. The locus of these points defines the offer curve of the country.

For example, if the price ratio β prevails in the world market, then this country would export good *X* in the amount of $0M$ and import good *Y* in the amount of BM and thus achieve the level of consumption on the community indifference curve associated with the trade indifference curve *b*. $0M$ signifies the volume of excess supply of good *X* and BM signifies the volume of excess demand for good *Y*, when the price line β prevails. Thus the locus of these points *A, B,* and so on, is the offer curve of the country.

In Figure 1-9 we now describe an international equilibrium. The slope of the ray passing through the intersection of the offer curves (*e* and *g*) of the two

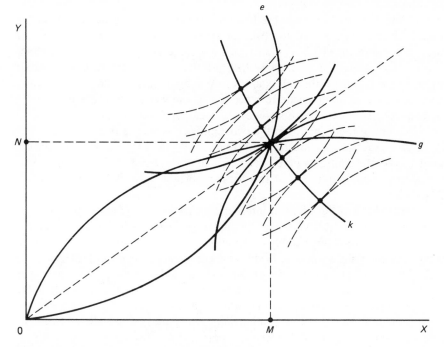

Figure 1-9 International Equilibrium

countries (say, *E* and *G*), signifies the international equilibrium commodity price ratio. Note that $0M$ equals the volume of excess supply of good *X* for Country *E* which equals the volume of excess demand for good *X* for Country *G*, and that $0N$ equals the volume of excess demand for good *Y* for Country *E* which equals the volume of excess supply of good *Y* for Country *G*.

In Figure 1-9 it is tacitly assumed that the transportation costs of the commodities are negligible and that there are no institutional impediments such as tariffs. That is, point T denotes the point of free-trade equilibrium. It is also assumed that there is no international mobility of productive factors, for if there were such a mobility the introduction of the other country and international trade would, in general, shift the offer curve of each country by changing the shape of each country's production transformation curve. Note that, if there is perfect mobility of factors, then the problems of international trade, at least its non-monetary real aspect, would essentially be the same as those in ordinary economic theory. It was a contribution of the classical economists such as Ricardo which clarified this crucial role of international factor immobility in the theory of international trade. These assumptions may be too extreme. For example, there is some international mobility of factors in the real world. However, these assumptions are very useful in sharpening the analysis and the conclusions. We may note that we can always relax these assumptions and examine the results after the analysis until such assumptions are completed.

In Figure 1-9, the k-curve is the locus of the common tangency points of the trade indifference curves of the two countries. Hence, it signifies the *contract curve*, the curve in which a country cannot increase the level of its welfare without decreasing the level of welfare of the other country, given a fixed supply of the factors in the two countries. As long as each country's community indifference curve is the accurate reflection of the welfare of every member of the country, the k-curve also signifies the locus of Pareto optimal points from the viewpoint of the *members* of the two countries as well as from the viewpoint of the two countries. As illustrated in Figure 1-9, the international equilibrium point T is on the contract curve k. Hence, free trade signifies a Pareto optimum. A more rigorous foundation of this very important thesis will be discussed in Chapter 7.

In the traditional literature in international trade theory, many problems of international trade policy, especially under the neoclassical framework, are solved by using the above concept of the offer curve. Hence, it is important to obtain a precise understanding of this concept. Many problems of international trade policy are reduced to shifts of the offer curve due to changes in the policy parameters such as the tariff rate. However, it is very tedious to analyze the changes of every such policy parameter in terms of the trade indifference curves (and the equilibrium of consumption and production) as we did above. The diagrams would, in general, become very complicated even for a simple analysis. Hence, we shall avoid such an analysis. Mathematically, as we shall see in Chapter 8, this becomes an exercise in elementary calculus, that is, comparative statics.

An important concept associated with the offer curve is that of the *elasticity of the offer curve*, which is defined as the percentage change of the amount of import demand divided by a percentage change in the exchange ratio (or the price ratio). Let p_x, p_y, and y denote, respectively, the price of good X, the price of good Y, and the volume of the import demand for good Y of the country. Then the elasticity of the offer curve (η_E) of this country (say, Country E) can be defined as

$$\eta_E \equiv -\frac{dy}{y} \bigg/ \frac{d(p_y/p_x)}{(p_y/p_x)} = -\frac{dy}{d(p_y/p_x)} \frac{p_y/p_x}{y}. \qquad (1\text{-}1)$$

Consider the following diagram (Figure 1-10) where the line PT is tangent to the offer curve e at point P, and the line PM is orthogonal to the X axis. Marshall [8] showed that the value of η_E at the point P is equal to the ratio $0M/0T$.

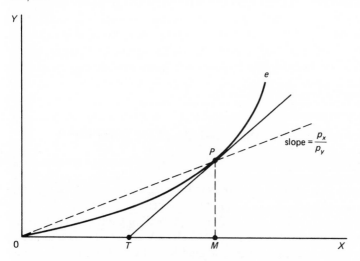

Figure 1-10   The Elasticity of the Offer Curve

To prove this statement, first write the coordinates of point P as (x, y), that is, $x = 0M$ and $y = PM$. Then the price ratio p_y/p_x at point P can be written as x/y. Hence the value of η_E at point P can be computed as

$$\eta_E = -\frac{dy}{d(x/y)}\frac{x/y}{y} = \frac{-dy}{(ydx-xdy)/y^2}\cdot\frac{x}{y^2} = \frac{x}{x-y(dx/dy)} = \frac{0M}{0T}. \qquad (1\text{-}2)$$

Note that the value of η_E depends on the location of the offer curve. If the offer curve bends back, then the value of η_E of the ratio $0M/0T$ becomes less than unity. In Figure 1-11 points A, B, and C respectively illustrate the points at which $\eta_E > 1$, $\eta_E = 1$, and $\eta_E < 1$.

It is important to note that the concept of the elasticity of the offer curve is a reflection of the interactions of two kinds of economic behavior—consumption and production. This can be seen easily from the above construction of the offer curve. Later we shall show that the elasticity of the offer curve can be written as the sum of the *consumer's elasticity of substitution*, the *marginal propensity to consume*, and the *elasticity of export supply* (Chapter 8).

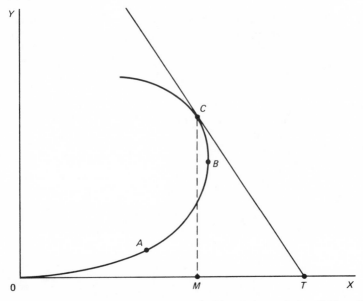

Figure 1-11   The Values of the Elasticity of the Offer Curve

A MATHEMATICAL MODEL

In the previous two sections we presented a diagrammatic model of international trade equilibrium. Here we present a mathematical formulation of the same model. We shall conclude this section by presenting another version of the offer curve. Our mathematical model and the construction of this alternative offer curve will enhance the reader's understanding of the diagrammatic model presented in the previous sections.

Consider a country which is capable of producing two commodities (X and Y). Let the production transformation curve of the country be represented by

$$Y = \varphi(X), \quad \text{where } X \geqq 0 \quad \text{and} \quad Y \geqq 0. \tag{1-3}$$

We assume that this production transformation curve is concave to the origin, reflecting the diminishing marginal rate of transformation. In other words,

$\varphi' < 0$ and $\varphi'' < 0$ for all levels of X,

where $\varphi' \equiv d\varphi/dX$ and $\varphi'' \equiv d^2\varphi/dX^2$. $\tag{1-4}$

Let p_x and p_y respectively be the price of good X and Y, and let $p \equiv p_x/p_y$ be the relative price of the two commodities. Producer's equilibrium under a competitive situation, as explained in the first section, can be described by

$$p = -\varphi'. \tag{1-5}$$

In other words, given p, this equation determines the output of good X, which then determines the output of good Y by (1-3). Equation (1-5) specifies a point on the production transformation curve. Clearly, there are many things that are implicit in relations (1-3), (1-4), and (1-5). For example, such things as the production functions of the commodities, the allocative principle of the factors of production, and the role of factor prices are implicit. We shall postpone the construction of a model which makes these things explicit to Chapter 2.

Let C_x and C_y respectively be the consumption of good X and good Y in a country. Let $u(C_x, C_y)$ be the community utility function (indicator). It is assumed that an individual's utility function is capable of being aggregated and that the aggregation is u. In other words, it is assumed that the country behaves as if it were a single "rational" unit (which maximizes u). A sufficient condition for aggregation is that each individual has the same homothetic utility function. Eisenberg's theorem [3] provides a case in which individuals' utility functions are not necessarily identical (see Chipman [2]). If price ratio p prevails in the market, then consumers' equilibrium of a country can be described by

$$p = \frac{u_x}{u_y}, \quad \text{where } u_x \equiv \partial u/\partial X \text{ and } u_y \equiv \partial u/\partial Y. \tag{1-6}$$

This equation signifies that the community indifference curve is tangent to the price line. Write $v \equiv u_x/u_y$. Then v is a function of C_x and C_y. We may rewrite (1-6) as

$$p = v(C_x, C_y). \tag{1-7}$$

Note that this relation is invariant to any monotone increasing transformation of $u(C_x, C_y)$, that is, $U[u(C_x, C_y)]$, where $dU/du > 0$ everywhere. In other words, only the ordinality of the utility function is required in (1-7).

Let E_x be the excess demand for (excess supply of) good X of the country if $E_x > 0$ ($E_x < 0$). E_y is defined similarly. Then we have

$$C_x = X + E_x \tag{1-8}$$

$$C_y = Y + E_y. \tag{1-9}$$

Note that (1-8) and (1-9) are the definitional equations for E_x and E_y. Note that E_x signifies the import demand for good X if $E_x > 0$ and export supply for good X if $E_x < 0$. E_y can be interpreted analogously. Using E_x and E_y, we can write the budget equation of the country as follows:

$$p_x E_x + p_y E_y = 0, \quad \text{or} \quad pE_x + E_y = 0. \tag{1-10}$$

There are now seven variables to be determined, X, Y, C_x, C_y, E_x, E_y, and p. There are six equations, (1-3), (1-5), (1-7), (1-8), (1-9), and (1-10): We then assume that we can write each of X, Y, C_x, C_y, E_x, and E_y as a function of price ratio p. If p is given to a country from outside, then we can completely specify the values of X, Y, C_x, C_y, E_x, and E_y. This will be the case if a country is small enough compared to the rest of the world so that it cannot affect the commodity price ratio which prevails in the market. In this case, p is determined by the rest of the world.

If a country is not small enough, then p shall be determined by an interaction of the demand and productive conditions of this country and the rest of the world. We now call this country, Country 1, and the rest of the world, Country 2. We then have the world consisting of two countries. In the literature of international trade, various alternative names are used for these two countries. Examples are: a) England and Portugal, b) England and Germany, c) the home country and the foreign country, and d) the home country and the rest of the world. Clearly, it is more realistic to consider the world as consisting of more than two countries and to analyze the various interactions of the demand and supply conditions of these countries. However, it is also known that this two-country-world assumption (like the two-commodity assumption) is very useful in sharpening our analysis and focusing our attention on the specific problems to be considered.

With the introduction of the second country, how should we then modify our model? This can most easily be done by first putting a suffix i, which denotes Country i, to each variable, that is, X_i, Y_i, C_{xi}, C_{yi}, E_{xi}, and E_{yi}, where $i = 1, 2$. Assuming free trade and no transport costs, the commodity price ratio of the two countries will be the same. p denotes this common price ratio. So, now there are 13 variables to be determined in the system. Note that the following equations must hold definitionally at equilibrium.

$$E_{x1} + E_{x2} = 0 \quad \text{and} \quad E_{y1} + E_{y2} = 0 . \tag{1-11}$$

This states that, at equilibrium, the world excess demand for each good is equal to zero. At equilibrium, therefore, both countries' import plans can be jointly realized, making the export supply of one country equal to the import demand of the other (that is, $E_{x1} = -E_{x2}$, $E_{y1} = -E_{y2}$).

Note that the two equations of (1-11) are not independent of each other (one can be obtained from the other) in view of the two budget equations $pE_{x1} + E_{y1} = 0$ and $pE_{x2} + E_{y2} = 0$. Now we can count the number of equations. Equations (1-3), (1-5), (1-7), (1-8), (1-9), and (1-10) give 12 equations with $i = 1, 2$, and, with one of the equations in (1-11), we have 13 equations. Equivalently we may consider that one of the budget equations, say, $pE_{x2} + E_{y2} = 0$, is derived in view of the other together with (1-11). Then equations (1-3), (1-5), (1-7), (1-8), (1-9), (1-11), and $pE_{x1} + E_{y1} = 0$ give the 13 equations of the model. We may note that (1-10) in view of (1-11) can yield the equation $pE_{x2} - E_{y1} = 0$, which is often known to be the one signifying the "balance of payments equilibrium relation."

We now consider a diagrammatical representation of this international equilibrium. The essential idea here is to recall that X_i, Y_i, C_{xi}, C_{yi}, E_{xi}, and E_{yi} are all expressed as a function of p for each $i = 1, 2$. Then $pE_{x1}(p) + E_{y1}(p) = 0$ determines the international equilibrium commodity price ratio, say, p^*, which in turn determines the equilibrium values for the rest of the variables, that is, values $X_i(p^*)$, $Y_i(p^*)$, $C_{xi}(p^*)$, $C_{yi}(p^*)$, $i = 1, 2$, and $E_{x1}^* = -E_{x2}(p^*)$, $E_{y2}^* = -E_{y1}(p^*)$. Hence our task is focused on obtaining a diagrammatical representation of $E_{x2}(p)$ and $E_{y1}(p)$. In the Mill-Marshall offer curve, such a diagram is depicted by representing p as a ray from the origin (recall Figure 1-6). In Figure 1-6, the first (respectively the third) quadrant is the region in which $E_{y1} > 0$ and $E_{x2} > 0$ (respectively $E_{y1} < 0$ and $E_{x2} < 0$).

Here we would like to introduce an alternative method to draw the offer curve. Such an offer curve is constructed by Oniki-Uzawa [10] in connection with their dynamic analysis of international trade. We shall postpone the description of the Oniki-Uzawa model to Chapter 13, but we shall construct the Oniki-Uzawa type offer curve in connection with the present model, in order to illustrate international equilibrium.[10]

To construct such an offer curve for one country, we do not need to attach a subscript i. Hence, for the time being, we omit i for the sake of notational simplicity. The equations which are relevant here are (1-3), (1-5), (1-7), (1-8), (1-9), and (1-10). First rewrite (1-8), (1-9), and (1-10) as

$$C_x = X + E_x \tag{1-12}$$

$$C_y = Y - pE_x . \tag{1-13}$$

If $E_x > 0$, then good X is imported in the country concerned (say, Country 2) and if $E_x < 0$, good X is exported. It is also important to recall that the sign of E_x is not given a priori.

From a certain shape of the production transformation curve it is easy to suppose that there exist certain values of p, $p_{\max}$, and $p_{\min}$, such that the following patterns of production are implied, as we remarked in the first section.

$p \geqq p_{\max}$: Only good X is produced. $\tag{1-14a}$

$p \leqq p_{\min}$: Only good Y is produced. $\tag{1-14b}$

$p_{\min} < p < p_{\max}$: Both goods are produced. $\tag{1-14c}$

Hence, in view of (1-3), we may rewrite these relations as

$p \geqq p_{\max}$: $X = \overline{X}$, $Y = \varphi(\overline{X}) = 0$, $\tag{1-15a}$

$p \leqq p_{\min}$: $X = 0$, $Y = \overline{Y} = \varphi(0)$, $\tag{1-15b}$

$p_{\min} < p < p_{\max}$: $Y = \varphi(X)$, $X > 0, Y > 0$. $\tag{1-15c}$

Note that (1-15) imposed the restriction on the function, φ, such that $\varphi(\overline{X}) = 0$ and $\varphi(0) = \overline{Y}$.

In order to illustrate the concept of the Oniki-Uzawa type offer curve, let us assume that the community utility indicator is represented by the following "Cobb-Douglas" function.[11]

$$u = C_x^{\alpha} C_y^{\beta} , \quad \text{where } \alpha > 0 \quad \text{and} \quad \beta > 0 . \tag{1-16}$$

---

[10] In the Oniki-Uzawa model, it is assumed that one of the two goods is the capital good, while in our presentation here both goods are assumed to be consumption goods.

[11] The main conclusion below with (1-16) follows when u is replaced by any given monotone-increasing transformation curve such as $u = U(C_x^{\alpha} C_y^{\beta})$, where $U' > 0$.

Then we have $u_x = \alpha C_x^{\alpha-1} C_y^{\beta}$ and $u_y = \beta C_x^{\alpha} C_y^{\beta-1}$ so that $v(C_x, C_y) \equiv u_x/u_y = (\alpha C_y)/(\beta C_x)$. Hence equation (1-7) may be rewritten as

$$C_y = apC_x, \quad \text{where } a \equiv \beta/\alpha. \tag{1-17}$$

This is a well-known result. Under the Cobb-Douglas utility function, the income consumption path is a straight line from the origin. That is, with a fixed p, the ratio in which these goods are demanded, C_y/C_x, is constant. Note that this shape of the utility function implies that in consumer's equilibrium $C_x > 0$ and $C_y > 0$ as long as $\infty > p > 0$.

Combining (1-17) with (1-12) and (1-13) we obtain

$$E_x = \frac{1}{(a+1)p} [Y - apX]. \tag{1-18}$$

Hence, in view of (1-15a) and (1-15b), we obtain

$$E_x = \frac{-a}{(a+1)} \overline{X} < 0 \quad \text{if} \quad p \geqq p_{\max}; \tag{1-19}$$

$$E_x = \frac{1}{(a+1)p} \overline{Y} > 0 \quad \text{if} \quad p \leqq p_{\min}.^{12} \tag{1-20}$$

For the case $p_{\min} < p < p_{\max}$, we recall the equilibrium conditions for the producers, equation (1-5). Since relation (1-4) holds, the relation between p and X (or Y) is one-to-one for $p_{\min} < p < p_{\max}$. Hence, from (1-4) we may obtain

$$X = X(p) \quad \text{and} \quad Y = Y(p) \quad (= \varphi[X(p)]). \tag{1-21}$$

We then have

$$X' > 0 \quad \text{and} \quad Y' < 0 \quad \text{for all } p \text{ such that } p_{\min} < p < p_{\max}$$
$$\text{where } X' \equiv dX/dp \quad \text{and} \quad Y' \equiv dY/dp.^{13} \tag{1-22}$$

Then combining (1-21) with (1-18) we obtain

$$E_x = \frac{1}{(a+1)p} [Y(p) - apX(p)], \quad \text{if} \quad p_{\min} < p < p_{\max}. \tag{1-23}$$

Equations (1-19), (1-20), and (1-23) relate E_x to p and they describe the equations for our offer curve. In view of (1-19), it is clear that $E_x = \text{constant} < 0$ if $p \geqq p_{\max}$ and that $E_x > 0$ and $dE_x/dp < 0$ if $p \leqq p_{\min}$. From (1-23) we obtain, for $p_{\min} < p < _{\max}$

$$\frac{dE_x}{dp} = \frac{-1}{(a+1)p} (Y/p + apX' - Y'), \tag{1-24}$$

---

[12] Note that, for $p \leqq p_{\min}$, $E_x \to \infty$ as $p \to 0$.
[13] Clearly $Y' = \varphi'X'$, which in turn shows $Y' < 0$ for all p.

which is negative in view of (1-22). In other words, if $p_{min} < p < p_{max}$, X is a decreasing function with respect to p. We can now illustrate the relation between E_x and p in the following diagram, which is the offer curve we are seeking.

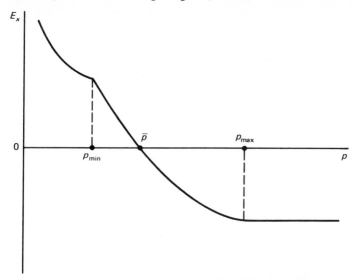

Figure 1-12   The Oniki-Uzawa Type Offer Curve

We should stress that we assumed a specific form of the utility function. When the utility function does not have this form, then we cannot, in general, ascertain $dE_x/dp < 0$ for $p_{min} < p < p_{max}$. Then, in the region of p in which $p_{min} < p < p_{max}$, the offer curve may oscillate (for example, the case of Giffen's paradox) and intersect the p-axis several times.[14]

In order to increase our understanding of the remark on the possible oscillation of the offer curve, it may be useful to recall some elementary economics. The effect of a change of p on the excess demands E_x and E_y can be decomposed into two parts, a production (or supply) effect and a consumption (or demand) effect. An increase in p, that is, an increase in the relative price of good X, would unambiguously increase the output of X and decrease the output of Y (if $p_{min} < p < p_{max}$), as long as the production transformation curve is concave to the origin. In other words, the production effect is such that it tends to lower E_x and raise E_y. The demand effect is rather ambiguous. It can, as is well-known, be decomposed into an income effect and a pure substitution effect. Although the substitution effect is always negative, that is, an increase in p tends to lower (raise) the demand for good X (Y), the income effect can be either negative or positive. If it is positive, then there is a possibility of the income effect outweighing the substitution effect. If this happens (say, for commodity X) then the demand effect of an increase in p is such that it tends to increase the demand for

---

[14] Note that this is the case even if we have an aggregate social utility function. When we do not have such a function, the offer curve may oscillate anyway, for a change in it will, in general, cause a change in income distribution among the people in the society.

commodity X and, hence, also E_x. In an extreme case this income effect may outweigh both the substitution effect and the production effect, so that an increase in p would cause an increase (decrease) in the excess demand for commodity X (Y), that is, E_x (E_y). This may not be the case over the entire range of p, but may occur only within certain ranges of p, causing the offer curve to oscillate. In the above we have shown that if the utility function is of the Cobb-Douglas type, this will not happen anywhere over the *entire* range of p. It should also be stressed, however, that the flat portion of the offer curve in Figure 1-12 is also a result of the specification of the utility function as Cobb-Douglas. The possible oscillations of the offer curve are illustrated in Figure 1-13.

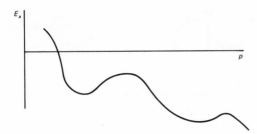

Figure 1-13   Oscillations of the Offer Curve

Although oscillations are possible, it is impossible for the offer curve to intersect more than once with the p-axis, under the usual circumstances that the production transformation curve is (strictly) concave to the origin and the social indifference curves are (strictly) convex to the origin. In other words, multiple autarkic equilibria are ruled out under such circumstances. This can be seen easily, for it is impossible to have more than one common tangency point of the production transformation curve and the social indifference curve under the usual circumstances. We should note, however, that this crucially depends on the existence of a social welfare function, or social indifference curves. If this is not the case, a change, for example, in income distribution among people due to a price change can produce many autarkic equilibria. In this book, unless otherwise specified, we assume a unique autarkic equilibrium.

In order to illustrate the international equilibrium in terms of the above offer curve, we recall from (1-11) the basic equilibrium relation,

$$E_{x1} + E_{x2} = 0 . \tag{1-25}$$

Then, superimposing the offer curves of the two countries in Figure 1-14, the international equilibrium commodity price ratio is obtained as p^* at which condition (1-25) is satisfied.

It is important to note that the pattern of production and the question of which country exports which good is determined as a result of the interaction of the offer curves of two countries. In Figure 1-14, the case illustrated is one in which p^* is such that each country produces both goods (incomplete specialization). Country 2 imports good X and Country 1 imports good Y

$$E_{x2} > 0 , \quad E_{x1} < 0 .$$

It is important to note that the relation $[dE_{xi}/dp < 0$ for all p, $p < p_{max}]$ is sufficient to guarantee the uniqueness of international equilibrium. If the utility function u takes a more general form, then multiple international equilibria are possible. Note that p^* in Figure 1-14 is a globally stable equilibrium price in the sense that if p deviates from p^* there exists a mechanism which brings p to p^* (how large the deviation of p from p^* may be). Such a mechanism is provided if p increases or decreases according to whether $(E_{x1} + E_{x2}) \lessgtr 0$.[15]

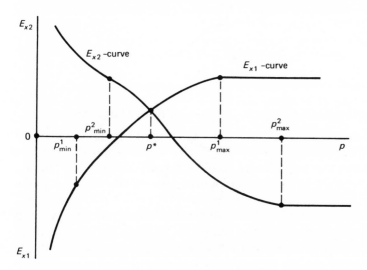

Figure 1-14 International Equilibrium

Figure 1-15 may also be useful to illustrate some of the above points. The reader may note that the above diagram corresponds to the familiar excess demand curve in elementary price theory. In connection with the concept of international equilibrium, it is important to remind our assumption that for each country autarkic equilibrium is unique. For, otherwise, the following seemingly obvious statement does not necessarily hold. "If $p_1 < p_2$, where p_i is the pre-trade price ratio of the ith country ($i = 1, 2$), Country 1 will export good X and import good Y."

It should be noted, however, that if one or both of two countries' offer curves oscillate, then the world excess demand curve, $E_{x1} + E_{x2}$, may also oscillate. This is illustrated in Figure 1-16. In this case there can be more than one equilibrium point, that is, there can be more than one point in which $E_{x1} + E_{x2} = 0$. In Figure 1-16, A, B, C, D, and E denote such points. Note that the

[15] This means that if the excess demand for good X in the world ($E_{x1} + E_{x2}$) is positive (negative) then the price of good X vis-à-vis good Y (p) increases (decreases). In terms of the Samuelsonian dynamic adjustment equation we may write it as $dp/dt = k(E_{x1} + E_{x2})$, where t refers to time and $k > 0$ represents the speed of adjustment of the world market. In Figure 1-13, note that, if $p < p^*$, then $(E_{x1} + E_{x2}) > 0$ and if $p > p^*$, then $(E_{x1} + E_{x2}) < 0$, which proves the global stability of p^*. See Chapter 8, second section, for a more detailed discussion.

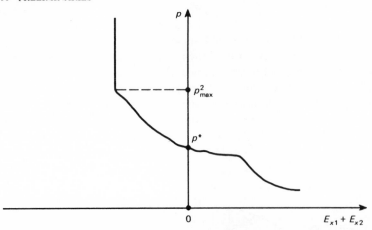

Figure 1-15   Another Illustration of International Equilibrium

equilibrium points A, C, and E are locally stable while equilibrium points B and D are unstable. Here the term "locally" refers to the assumption that our attention is restricted to a sufficiently small neighborhood about the relevant equilibrium point. For example, A is a locally stable equilibrium point in the sense that if p is in a sufficiently small neighborhood of point A, it converges to A.

There are many complications when multiple equilibria occur compared with the case in which equilibrium is unique and stable. Hence, in this book we shall, unless otherwise specified, restrict our attention either to the case in which the equilibrium is unique or to a sufficiently small neighborhood of an equilibrium point.

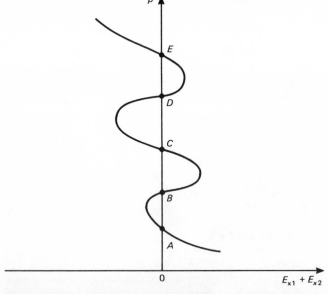

Figure 1-16   Multiple Equilibria

EULER'S THEOREM AND PRODUCTION FUNCTIONS WITH CONSTANT RETURNS TO SCALE

Euler's Theorem

In much of the economic literature, Euler's theorem, a mathematical theorem concerning the nature of homogeneous functions, often plays an important role.

DEFINITION   A real-valued function,[16] $f(x)$, on R^n is called *homogeneous of degree m* if and only if for any real number $\lambda \neq 0$,

$$f(\lambda x) = \lambda^m f(x) \quad \text{for all } x \equiv (x_1, x_2, \cdots, x_n). \tag{1-26}$$

In economics, the domain of f is often restricted to the non-negative orthant of R^n. In this case λ should also be restricted to be positive. The definition of a homogeneous function for such a case is strictly analogous to the above. In order to emphasize this non-negativity, and especially the positivity of λ, the phrase "*positively* homogeneous of degree m" is often used. Since such a non-negativity of the domain or the positivity of λ is usually obvious from the context, we shall not worry about such phraseology.

With the above definition, we are now able to state Euler's theorem for homogeneous functions.

THEOREM   Let $f(x)$ be a differentiable real-valued function on R^n (or its non-negative orthant). Then f is homogeneous of degree m if and only if

$$mf(x) = \frac{\partial f}{\partial x_1} x_1 + \frac{\partial f}{\partial x_2} x_2 + \cdots + \frac{\partial f}{\partial x_n} x_n, \quad \text{for all } x \equiv (x_1, x_2, \cdots, x_n).$$

$$\tag{1-27}$$

PROOF   First we prove that the homogeneity implies (1-27). Fix x and define $g(\lambda)$ by $g(\lambda) \equiv f(\lambda x)$. Then

$$g'(\lambda) = \sum_{i=1}^{n} \frac{\partial f(\lambda x)}{\partial(\lambda x_i)} x_i \quad \text{so that} \quad g'(1) = \sum_{i=1}^{n} \frac{\partial f}{\partial x_i} x_i. \tag{1-28}$$

But the homogeneity of f means that $\lambda^m f(x) = f(\lambda x)$ so that $g'(\lambda) = m\lambda^{m-1} f(x)$ or $g'(1) = mf(x)$. Hence we obtain (1-27). Since the choice of x is arbitrary, (1-27) holds for all x.

Now we prove the converse, that is, that (1-27) implies the homogeneity of f. Define $g(\lambda)$ as above. Then, in view of (1-27) and (1-28), $\lambda g'(\lambda) = mf(\lambda x)$. Then $d[g(\lambda)\lambda^{-m}]/d\lambda = g'(\lambda)\lambda^{-m} - mg(\lambda)\lambda^{-m-1} = \lambda^{-m-1}[\lambda g'(\lambda) - mg(\lambda)] = \lambda^{-m-1}[mf(\lambda x) - mf(\lambda x)] = 0$. Hence $g(\lambda)\lambda^{-m} = $ constant $(= c$, say). Thus, $g(\lambda) = \lambda^m c$. Then $f(x) = g(1) = c$, so that $f(\lambda x) = g(\lambda) = \lambda^m f(x)$. This is true for any λ. (Q.E.D.)

---

[16] This definition of a homogeneous function can be extended for a vector-valued function. Note that a vector-valued function is homogeneous of degree m if each of its component functions is homogeneous of degree m.

Important examples of homogeneous functions in economics can be seen in demand functions and production functions. Let x_i be an individual's demand for ith good $(i = 1, 2, \cdots, n)$, which is assumed to be expressed as

$$x_i = f_i(p_1, p_2, \cdots, p_n, M), \tag{1-29}$$

where p_i $(i = 1, 2, \cdots, n)$ is the price of the ith good and M is money income. It is usually assumed that f_i is a homogeneous function of degree zero with respect to all its argument, for, otherwise, it would not be independent of the monetary units which are used to measure the p_is and M. In other words,

$$x_i = f_i(\lambda p_1, \lambda p_2, \cdots, \lambda p_n, \lambda M), \quad \text{for any } \lambda > 0. \tag{1-30}$$

Euler's theorem implies that this is equivalent to

$$\sum_{j=1}^{n} \frac{\partial f_i}{\partial p_j} p_j + \frac{\partial f_i}{\partial M} M = 0 \quad \text{for all } p_j \text{s and } M. \tag{1-31}$$

Another example of a homogeneous function can be seen in the production function. Let y be the maximum amount of output of good Y which can be produced by employing m productive factors, $v_1, v_2, \cdots, v_m$. We may then write the production function of Y as

$$y = f(v_1, v_2, \cdots, v_m). \tag{1-32}$$

f is said to exhibit *constant returns to scale* if f is homogeneous of degree one. If f is homogeneous of degree one (also called *linear homogeneous*), then Euler's equation (1-27) means

$$y = \frac{\partial f}{\partial v_1} v_1 + \frac{\partial f}{\partial v_2} v_2 + \cdots + \frac{\partial f}{\partial v_m} v_m. \tag{1-33}$$

Since $\partial f/\partial v_i$ is the marginal physical product of the ith factor, equation (1-33) means the total output is distributed to all the factors without any surplus or shortage when each factor is rewarded according to its marginal physical product.

Still another example can be seen in the monetary equilibrium equation in macroeconomic theory. Let M, Y, and i be the supply of money, national income, and the interest rate, respectively. Writing the demand function for money as $L(Y, i)$, the monetary equilibrium equation is expressed as

$$M = L(Y, i). \tag{1-34}$$

L is taken to be homogeneous of degree one, with respect to Y, since otherwise it would not be independent of the monetary units which are used to measure Y and M. That is,

$$\lambda M = L(\lambda Y, i) \quad \text{for any } \lambda > 0. \tag{1-35}$$

Let p be the general price level. Then choosing $\lambda = 1/p$, we have

$$\frac{M}{p} = L(X, i) \quad \text{where } X \text{ is real national income (that is, } X \equiv Y/p). \tag{1-36}$$

Production Functions with Constant Returns to Scale

Let the production function of a certain good (say, Y) be expressed by equation (1-32). An important classification of the production function can be done according to whether, for any $\lambda > 0$, 1 and $(v_1, v_2, \cdots, v_m)$,

$$\lambda y \gtreqqless f(\lambda v_1, \lambda v_2, \cdots, \lambda v_m), \tag{1-37}$$

which is called a production function with *diminishing returns to scale, constant returns to scale*, and *increasing returns to scale*, for $>$, $=$, $<$, respectively. An example is the Cobb-Douglas type production function, that is,

$$y = AL^\alpha K^\beta, \quad \alpha > 0, \quad \beta > 0, \tag{1-38}$$

exhibits diminishing returns to scale, constant returns to scale, and increasing returns to scale according to whether $\alpha + \beta < 1, \alpha + \beta = 1$, and $\alpha + \beta > 1$, respectively. In much of the economic literature the production function is assumed to exhibit constant returns to scale. This rather restrictive looking assumption has several important justifications. We now turn to a discussion of the rationale for the use of the constant returns to scale production function.

If the production function of a certain good exhibits increasing returns to scale, then the producers of this good who succeed in expanding the scale of their production prior to the other producers of the same good can produce the good with less cost and thus can drive the other producers out of the market. Therefore, the market for such a good will be characterized by either oligopoly or complete monopoly. In other words, the production function with increasing returns to scale is inconsistent with a perfectly competitive market.

If the production function of a certain good exhibits diminishing returns to scale at certain levels of output (which are greater than zero), then the producer of the good can simply avoid the accompanying increasing costs by increasing the number of plants. If the producer does not do this then he will be driven out of the market, if the market is competitive.

To analyze many economic problems, formulation of the model under the assumption of perfect competition is known to be useful and sometimes essential. Then, as long as we adopt such a competitive assumption, the production function which is to be used in the model has to be that of constant returns to scale in order to preserve the logical consistency of the model.

Another rationale for the use of the constant returns to scale production function can be found in the marginal productivity theory. The marginal productivity theory of distribution has an established importance in economics. Its history is well explained in Stigler [14], for example. One of the important problems in marginal productivity theory is whether or not the output is distributed to all the participating factors without either surplus or shortage when each factor is rewarded according to its marginal productivity. This question, known as the *exhaustion of product problem*, can be solved trivially when the production function exhibits constant returns to scale, thanks to Euler's theorem. This point was already explained in connection with equation

(1-33). For a historical sketch of the exhaustion problem, the reader is referred to Stigler [14], Chapter XII.

Another rationale for the use of the constant returns to scale production function (especially for an industry) is found in the contention that under perfect competition the profit of the firm would be driven to zero in the long run through the exit and entry of firms in the market. That is, under a competitive situation, those firms which have negative profits will be driven out of the market, and if a firm's profits are positive, profits will be reduced to zero by entry of new firms. If the production function exhibits constant returns to scale it can be easily shown that, under a competitive situation, the maximum profit for the industry is zero. Let p be the price of the output and w_i be the price of the ith factor. The p and w_is are given constants to each firm under perfect competition. Profit maximization means the maximization of

$$pf(v_1, v_2, \cdots, v_m) - \sum_{i=1}^{m} w_i v_i .$$

The first order conditions for the optimal values of the v_is are $\partial f / \partial v_i = w_i / p$. Then, if f is homogeneous of degree one (constant returns to scale), we have

$$pf(v_1, v_2, \cdots, v_m) = \sum_{i=1}^{m} p \frac{\partial f}{\partial v_i} v_i = \sum_{i=1}^{m} w_i v_i , \qquad (1\text{-}39)$$

which implies profit is zero for optimal values of the v_is.

The last rationale for the use of a constant returns to scale production function is found in the very fact that it simplifies the analysis considerably. Mathematically, the source of the simplification can be found in Euler's equation (1-33). In the two dimensional diagrammatical analysis in which the number of factors is restricted to two (say, $y = f(v_1, v_2)$), the source of the simplification is found in the fact that the marginal rate of transformation and the marginal product of each factor depend only on the ratio of the two factors employed, that is, v_1 / v_2, and not on the absolute magnitude of each factor. This means, for example, that the slopes of the various production isoquants are the same as long as they are measured from the origin along the same ray.

One methodological remark is in order here. Any economic theory consists of assumptions, logical deductions, and conclusions. Assuming that the logical deduction of a particular theory is correct, there are possibly two tests for the theory to be a good one. One is concerned with whether the assumptions are realistic and the other is concerned with the explanatory and predictive power of the conclusions. Milton Friedman [4] argued that any set of assumptions is an abstraction from reality and hence the real test of a good theory must be on the explanatory and predictive power of the conclusions. Galileo's law of a falling body is a good theory since it explains the movement of certain falling bodies very well in spite of the fact that it is based on the unrealistic assumption that our world is characterized by a vacuum. He then argued that Chamberlin's theory of monopolistic competition is a bad theory, for it produces almost no definite conclusions compared with the theory of perfect competition. In spite of the fact there can be many arguments against Friedman's contention, we should grant that there is an element of truth in this, and we find an important rationale for simplifying assumptions in economics such as perfect competition and production functions with constant returns to scale.

There are at least two corollaries to the above methodological remarks. One is that those assumptions which are unnecessary to obtain conclusions (which should be abandoned). The second is that there is a type of assumptions which are used to focus the analysis and sharpen the conclusions. The assumptions of aggregate commodity and general price level in the usual macro theory belong to such a type.

COMPARATIVE STATICS AND "HAT" CALCULUS

One of the most important analytical techniques in economic theory and in international trade theory is that of comparative statics. It is concerned with changes in the equilibrium values of economic variables when there is a shift in one or more of the economic parameters. The list of economic parameters includes the variables which are exogenous to the system, such as policy parameters, and the indicators which represent autonomous shifts of behavioral and technological functions.

Let the system of an economic equilibrium be represented by

$$f_i(x_1, x_2, \cdots, x_n; \alpha, \beta, \gamma, \cdots) = 0, \quad i = 1, 2, \cdots, n, \tag{1-40}$$

where the x_is are the variables to be determined within the system and $\alpha, \beta, \gamma, \cdots$ are the shift parameters. Notice that the values of the x_is are determined only when the values of $\alpha, \beta, \cdots$ are specified. Hence the comparative statics analysis presupposes that f_is are somewhat nicely shaped so that the equilibrium values of the x_is can be expressed as functions of the shift parameters alone, that is, $x_i = x_i(\alpha, \beta, \cdots)$. Thus when the values of $\alpha, \beta, \cdots$ change, then the equilibrium values of the x_is change. The comparative statics analysis is concerned with obtaining the values of $dx_i/d\alpha, dx_i/d\beta, \cdots, i = 1, 2, \cdots, n$, which can simply be accomplished by totally differentiating both sides of (1-40).

To illustrate this process, differentiate both sides of (1-40) with respect to α keeping the other shift parameters $\beta, \gamma, \cdots$ constant. Then, writing $f_{ij} \equiv \partial f_i/\partial x_j, f_{i\alpha} \equiv \partial f_i/\partial \alpha$, and $z_j \equiv dx_j/d\alpha$, we obtain[17]

$$\sum_{j=1}^{n} f_{ij}z_j = -f_{i\alpha}, \quad i = 1, 2, \cdots, n. \tag{1-41}$$

Here note that the f_{ij}s and $f_{i\alpha}$ are evaluated at the original values of $\alpha, \beta, \cdots$, and the corresponding equilibrium values of the x_is. Let F be an $n \times n$ matrix where f_{ij} is the jth element in the ith row, and let a be an n vector whose ith

---

[17] Strictly speaking, z_j should be written as $\partial x_j/\partial \alpha$ instead of $dx_j/d\alpha$, signifying that the other parameters $\beta, \gamma, \cdots$ are kept constant (recall $x_i = x_i(\alpha, \beta, \cdots)$). However, in economics, the notation $dx_j/d\alpha$ is very often used. This is probably due to the fact that the assumption of the constancy of the other parameters (here $\beta, \gamma, \cdots$) is usually obvious from the context.

element is $f_{i\alpha}$ and z be an n vector whose jth element is z_j, then we can rewrite (1-41) as

$$Fz = -a. \tag{1-42}$$

Hence, assuming that F is non-singular, we obtain the desired result of the present comparative statics analysis as follows:

$$z = -F^{-1}a. \tag{1-43}$$

Simple but important illustrations of this analysis can be found in Samuelson [13], Chapter 3. In this book we shall also observe many applications of this technique. Notable examples are those chapters which explicitly deal with the policy questions such as Chapters 8, 9, and 10. Here, the policy variables such as taxes, tariffs, transfer payments, exchange rates, government expenditures, and so on, are the shift parameters of the system. The effect of economic growth on international trade can also be treated as a shift of production transformation curves or the production functions of countries. Chapters 10 and 11 are examples of such analysis. Even the question of comparative advantage, that is, the question of the determinants of the trade pattern of a country, can be considered from the point of view of comparative statics analysis, by viewing the differences of the two countries as due to a shift of the demand and production conditions of one of the countries.

As remarked above, the mathematics involved in the comparative statics analysis is simple differentiation. Although this is simple conceptually, it can be very tedious computationally. Hence, it is sometimes useful to invent some rule of simplification. One such rule is concerned with the rate of change of the variables, which we now present as *hat calculus*.

Consider the equation [18]

$$z = xy. \tag{1-44}$$

Now take the logarithm of both sides of this equation and differentiate both sides. Thus we obtain

$$dz/z = dx/x + dy/y. \tag{1-45}$$

Then, denoting these percentage rates of change by the "^" (hat), that is, $\hat{z} \equiv dz/z$, $\hat{x} \equiv dx/x$, and $\hat{y} \equiv dy/y$, we can rewrite (1-45) as

$$\hat{z} = \hat{x} + \hat{y}. \tag{1-46}$$

Thus the multiplication in (1-44) is transformed into a simple addition in (1-46).

Similarly, if we have

$$z = x/y, \tag{1-47}$$

then by logarithmic differentiation, we obtain

$$\hat{z} = \hat{x} - \hat{y}. \tag{1-48}$$

---

[18] z, x, and y are all real numbers.

An example is if x and y denote national income and population, respectively, then the percentage rate of change of per capital income, $\hat{z}$, is obtained as the difference of the percentage rate of change of income ($\hat{x}$) and the percentage rate of change of population ($\hat{y}$).

If we are given the functional relationship[19]

$$z = f(x_1, x_2, \cdots, x_n),\tag{1-49}$$

then totally differentiating both sides of (1-49) and dividing both sides by z, we obtain

$$\hat{z} = \eta_1 \hat{x}_1 + \eta_2 \hat{x}_2 + \cdots + \eta_n \hat{x}_n,\tag{1-50}$$

where the η_is are defined by

$$\eta_i \equiv \frac{\partial f}{\partial x_i} \frac{x_i}{z}, \quad i = 1, 2, \cdots, n.\tag{1-51}$$

In economics, η_i is known as the *elasticity of z with respect to x_i*. It signifies the percentage rate of change of z per unit percentage rate of change of x_i with the other variables ($x_j, j \neq i$) being kept constant. An example is if the demand, z, of a certain commodity is a function of price p and income y, that is,

$$z = f(p, y),\tag{1-52}$$

then we have

$$\hat{z} = -\eta_p \hat{p} + \eta_y \hat{y},\tag{1-53}$$

where

$$\eta_p \equiv -\frac{\partial f}{\partial p} \frac{p}{z} \quad \text{and} \quad \eta_y \equiv \frac{\partial f}{\partial y} \frac{y}{z}.\tag{1-54}$$

Here the minus sign is attached to follow the convention in economics which prefers to keep the positivity in elasticities. η_p is the price elasticity of demand for z, and η_y is the income elasticity of demand for z.

Two remarks should be made in connection with the above concept of elasticity. First, it is a concept which does not depend on the unit of measurement of these variables. This is obvious from the definitional equation (1-51). Second, the elasticity is a local concept. In the definitional equation (1-51), the partial derivative $\partial f / \partial x_i$ is evaluated at the original value of $(x_1, x_2, \cdots, x_n)$ for which equation (1-49) holds. Hence, the η_is are all evaluated at this value of $(x_1, x_2, \cdots, x_n)$. Corresponding to a different value of $(x_1, x_2, \cdots, x_n)$, we, in general, have a different value of η_i. However, we may also remark that the case in which η_i is indeed constant for all values of $(x_1, x_2, \cdots, x_n)$, often plays an important role in economics. A notable example is the production function in which the elasticity of factor substitution is constant.

[19] z and x_is are again all real numbers.

Another rule of hat calculus is given when the original relation of the variables is given by

$$z = a_1x_1 + a_2x_2 + \cdots + a_nx_n ,$$ (1-55)

where a_is are positive constants.

Totally differentiating both sides of (1-55), we obtain

$$\hat{z} = \theta_1\hat{x}_1 + \theta_2\hat{x}_2 + \cdots + \theta_n\hat{x}_n , \quad \text{where } \theta_i > 0 ,$$

$$i = 1, 2, \cdots, n \quad \text{and} \quad \sum_{i=1}^{n} \theta_i = 1 .$$ (1-56)

the θ_is are obviously defined by

$$\theta_i \equiv a_ix_i/z , \quad i = 1, 2, \cdots, n .$$ (1-57)

An example is if the total supply of labor, L, is allocated to the two industries X and Y so that we have $L = L_x + L_y$, then the rule which corresponds to (1-56) can be written as

$$\hat{L} = \theta\hat{L}_x + (1 - \theta)\hat{L}_y, \quad \theta > 0 .$$ (1-58)

That is, a change in the percentage rate of the total supply of labor is a weighted average of the percentage rate of change of labor allocated to each industry. The weight is determined by the initial proportion of the allocation of L to each industry ($\theta = L_x/L$ and $(1 - \theta) = L_y/L$).

We have thus assembled four rules of hat calculus—(1-46), (1-48), (1-50), and (1-56). The reader will find many useful applications of these rules. Finally, we should note that the derivatives which are involved in the hat ($\hat{}$) are most naturally to be interpreted as the ones which are involved in the comparative statics as described above.

REFERENCES

1. Baldwin, R. E., "The New Welfare Economics and Gains in International Trade," *Quarterly Journal of Economics*, LXVI, February 1952.
2. Chipman, J. S., "A Survey of the Theory of International Trade: Part 2, The Neoclassical Theory," *Econometrica*, 33, October 1965.
3. Eisenberg, E., "Aggregation of Utility Functions," *Management Science*, 7, July 1961.
4. Friedman, M., "The Methodology of Positive Economics," in his *Essays in Positive Economics* (Chicago: University of Chicago Press), 1953.
5. Haberler, G., "Some Problems in the Pure Theory of International Trade," *Economic Journal*, LX, June 1950, revised and reprinted in *Readings in International Economics*, ed. by Caves and Johnson (Homewood, Ill.: Richard D. Irwin), 1968.
6. Hicks, J. R., *Value and Capital*, 2nd ed. (London: Oxford University Press), 1946.

7. Leontief, W. W., "The Use of Indifference Curves in the Analysis of Foreign Trade," *Quarterly Journal of Economics*, XLVII, May 1933.
8. Marshall, A., "The Pure Theory of International Trade," (1879) *Reprints of Scarce Tracts on Political Economy* (London: London School of Economics), 1930. Also revised and reprinted in Marshall, A., *Money Credit and Commerce* (London: Macmillan & Co., Ltd.), 1923, Appendix J.
9. Meade, J. E., *A Geometry of International Trade* (London: George Allen and Unwin), 1952.
10. Oniki, T. and Uzawa, H., "Patterns of Trade and Investment in a Dynamic Model of International Trade," *Review of Economic Studies*, XXXII, January 1965.
11. Samuelson, P. A., "The Gains from International Trade," *Canadian Journal of Economics and Political Science*, 5, May 1939.
12. ———, "Evaluation of Real National Income," *Oxford Economic Papers*, n.s., 2, January 1950.
13. ———, *Foundations of Economic Analysis* (Cambridge, Mass.: Harvard University Press), 1947, especially Chapter 2.
14. Stigler, G., *Production and Distribution Theories* (New York: Crowell-Collier and Macmillan, Inc.), 1959.
15. Takayama, A., *International Economics* (Tokyo: Toyo Keizai Shimposha), 1963, especially Chapter 2, Section 2.
16. Vanek, J., *International Trade, Theory and Economic Policy* (Homewood, Ill.: Richard D. Irwin), 1962, especially Chapters 13, 14, and 15.

PART I

THE HECKSCHER-OHLIN THEOREM AND RELATED TOPICS

2

THE MATHEMATICAL
MODEL OF A
TWO-SECTOR ECONOMY

INTRODUCTION

The essence of the international trade problem is the exchange of goods. In order to have an exchange of goods, there must be at least two goods in the world. In the traditional analysis of international trade problems, the number of goods is usually restricted to two, with each country being able to produce one or both of these goods. This restriction of the number of goods to two has at least two great virtues. One is that the simplicity of the model sharpens the analysis considerably and enables us to obtain a wide variety of important results. The other is that it facilitates the use of diagrammatical techniques. In fact, almost all the analysis of international trade problems, until very recently, was carried out in terms of diagrammatical techniques such as production isoquants, box diagrams, production transformation curves, and utility indifference curves, if not in terms of strictly verbal arguments. Although the diagrammatical technique is very useful for understanding the essential points of the problem being considered, it is also well-known that one is very prone to make mistakes because of the way in which the diagram is usually drawn and that diagrams can become unmanageably complicated even for fairly simple analyses. Furthermore, we cannot, in general, obtain any rigorous or quantitative results from diagrams. We may quote the following penetrating comments by Koopmans [7] on the weaknesses of the diagrammatical technique.

> Diagrammatic representation, by its nature most suitable as a tool of exposition, has long occupied a dominant position among tools of analysis in spite of the availability of more reliable tools. . . . But the eye is essentially an organ of perception rather than of reasoning. Nothing in the process of reading a diagram forces the full statement of assumptions and the stepwise advance through successive implications to conclusions that are characteristic of logical reasoning. Assumptions may be

concealed in the manner in which the curves are "usually" drawn, and conclusions may be accepted unconditionally although they actually depend on such unstated assumptions. (p. 174)

In view of the abundance of literature, in international trade theory as well as in other fields of economics, involving an economy which produces two goods, it is natural to proceed with the mathematical construction of the general equilibrium of a two-sector economy.[1] Since the major tool of analysis in economics is comparative statics, we will then be interested in obtaining various relations among the changes in the variables of the model. This can easily and rigorously be done after we have constructed the mathematical model. Once this has been done, not only shall we be able to understand the precise meaning of the model, but we shall also be able to re-examine, restate in precise fashion, and generalize (if correct) many of the results obtained in the past from diagrammatical or verbal arguments. Surprisingly enough, this seemingly simple task was not attempted until recently. In the theory of international trade, an energetic attempt was made by Meade [8] [9] in the 1950s. This work was extended by Jones [3] in connection with the Heckscher-Ohlin theorem. In this process many properties of the two-sector economy, especially of its supply side, have become well-known to trade theorists.[2] This task of building the two-sector model and finding out what its basic relations are was finally more or less completed by Takayama [13], [14], and [15]. He has since shown some applications of this model to problems in international trade and in other areas such as growth and development (for example, [15] and [16]).[3]

The purpose of this chapter is to present this mathematical model of a two-sector economy. The model will be stated and the various basic relations obtained in the next section.[4] The results of the second section will be used repeatedly in later chapters. In particular, we shall find that they are basic to the Heckscher-Ohlin model of international trade presented in the next chapter. In this chapter we shall also present some immediate applications of these results to illustrate their power. In particular, we shall discuss in the third section: a) the elasticity of production, b) variable factor supplies, c) Rybczynski's theorem, d) Mishan's theorem, and e) Jones' "magnification effect." Finally, in the Appendix to Chapter 2, we will summarize: a) Jones' proof of Rybczynski's theorem and b) the two-sector model of economic growth.

[1] In international trade theory the two sectors are naturally the sector producing the exportable good and the sector producing the importable good. But the two sectors can be interpreted in many ways. For example: (a) the consumption good industry and the capital good industry in [15], (b) the two industries both produce consumption goods in [16], and (c) the corporate sector and the non-corporate sector in [1].

[2] For a remarkable application of this model to the problem of public finance, see Harberger [1].

[3] For a recent exposition of the mathematical model of a two-sector economy and some applications, see Kemp [5].

[4] The statement and the derivation of these results were first systematically shown in the English literature by Takayama [15].

THE BASIS OF THE MODEL AND VARIOUS RELATIONS

Consider an economy producing two goods, X and Y, with inputs labor (L) and capital (K). Write the production function for each good as follows:

$$X = F(L_x, K_x), \tag{2-1}$$

$$Y = G(L_y, K_y), \tag{2-2}$$

where L_i $(i = x, y)$ and K_i $(i = x, y)$ denote the labor and capital input respectively in the ith industry. Assuming constant returns to scale for each industry (the linear homogeneity of the production function), we rewrite equations (2-1) and (2-2) as

$$X = L_x f(k_x) \quad \text{where } k_x \equiv K_x/L_x, \tag{2-3}$$

$$Y = L_y g(k_y) \quad \text{where } k_y \equiv K_y/L_y. \tag{2-4}$$

k_i $(i = x, y)$ is called the *factor-intensity* or the *capital-labor ratio* of the ith industry. We assume f and g are twice differentiable.

Assuming perfect competition and adopting the marginal productivity theory, we can conclude that the price of each factor (service) will be equated to the value of its marginal product and that the price of each factor (service) will be the same in each industry.[5] We express this relation by the following equations:

$$w = p_x \mu_x = p_y \mu_y, \tag{2-5}$$

$$r = p_x v_x = p_y v_y. \tag{2-6}$$

Here p_i is the price of the ith good $(i = x, y)$; w, the money wage rate; r, the rent for capital service; μ_i, the marginal physical product of labor in the ith industry $(i = x, y)$; and v_i, the marginal physical product of capital in the ith industry $(i = x, y)$. Clearly we have

$$\mu_x \equiv \frac{\partial X}{\partial L_x}, \quad v_x \equiv \frac{\partial X}{\partial K_x}, \quad \text{and so on.} \tag{2-7}$$

We assume $\mu_i > 0$ and $v_i > 0$ $(i = x, y)$. We also assume the law of diminishing returns,[6] that is,

$$\frac{\partial \mu_i}{\partial L_i} < 0, \quad \frac{\partial v_i}{\partial K_i} < 0 \quad (i = x, y). \tag{2-8}$$

The reader should recall the basic fact that the law of diminishing returns is,

---

[5] Profit maximization by the producers and the free mobility of factors are assumed. The proposition thus stated is at the heart of traditional economic theory. See any elementary textbook on price theory. For the historical background to marginal productivity theory, see G. Stigler, *Production and Distribution Theories*, New York, 1941.

[6] This is also called the *law of decreasing marginal productivity* or the *law of variable proportions*. This law has been well-known to economists since the nineteenth century English classical economists.

in principle, a phenomenon independent of the returns to scale.[7] A well-known example of a production function with constant returns to scale which exhibits the law of diminishing returns is the following Cobb-Douglas production function.

$$X = L_x{}^a K_x{}^{1-a}, \quad 1 > a > 0.$$ (2-9)

Recalling the assumption of the linear homogeneity of the production function and using equations (2-3) and (2-4), we can obtain the following expressions for the marginal physical product of each factor:[8]

$$\mu_x = f - k_x f', \quad \mu_y = g - k_y g';$$ (2-10)

$$v_x = f', \qquad v_y = g';$$ (2-11)

where $f' = df/dk_x$ and $g' = dg/dk_y$.

Using (2-10) and (2-11), we can easily prove that the law of diminishing returns [relation (2-8)] is equivalent to the following relation.[9]

$$f'' < 0 \quad \text{and} \quad g'' < 0,$$ (2-12)

where

$$f'' \equiv \frac{df'}{dk_x} \quad \text{and} \quad g'' \equiv \frac{dg'}{dk_y}.$$

Let L be the total supply of labor (service) and let K be the total supply of capital (service). Assume the full employment of each factor. Then we obtain

$$L_x + L_y = L,$$ (2-13)

$$K_x + K_y = K.$$ (2-14)

The left-hand side of (2-13) [respectively (2-14)] denotes the total amount of labor (capital) employed in production so that those equations denote the equilibrium relations (demand = supply) for each factor market.

Equations (2-1), (2-2), (2-5), (2-6), (2-13), and (2-14) (eight equations altogether) describe the production side of the economy. Our system is closed by adding the two demand equations (one for X and the other for Y). One equation

---

[7] This apparently obvious fact is often confusing to economists. A well-known elementary textbook on economic theory by Stonier and Hague (*A Textbook of Economic Theory*, London, 1957, 2nd ed., p. 229) made the mistake of stating that the homogeneity of the production function implies diminishing returns. There are lengthy discussions in the *American Economic Review* about this rather obvious point (for example, Nutter, 1963, 1964, 1965; Rowe, 1964, 1965; Sato, 1964; Schneider, 1964; Moeseke, 1965; Chattopadhyay, 1966; Piron, 1966; and so on). If a certain assumption (such as concavity) is imposed on the production function, then there can be a definite relation between these two phenomena (for example, Eichhorn, *American Economic Review*, March 1968).

[8] See Chapter 1.

[9] That is, we can show that $\partial \mu_x / \partial L_x < 0$ if, and only if, $f'' < 0$, and $\partial v_x / \partial K_x < 0$, if, and only if, $f'' < 0$. Similar statements hold for $g'' < 0$. See Chapter 1.

can be eliminated from these 10 equations by Walras' law,[10] thus there are nine independent equations. There are nine variables to be determined in the system: L_x, L_y, K_x, K_y, X, Y, w/p_x, r/p_x, and p_x/p_y.[11] Therefore, our system is consistent in the sense that there are the same number of equations and (endogenous) variables. Leaving a more sophisticated discussion of the existence of a solution to the reader[12] and assuming the existence of a *unique positive* solution, we now proceed with our analysis. In particular, we shall obtain the important relations which can be implied from the above description of the production side of our economy. These relations have their own immediate applications and will be important in later chapters. They will be stated and proved as *lemmas* and their immediate applications will be discussed in the next section.

DEFINITION (labor's relative share)

$$\Gamma_x \equiv \mu_x L_x / X ; \quad \Gamma_y \equiv \mu_y L_y / Y . \tag{2-15}$$

REMARK   Given the competitive situation, we have $\mu_x = w/p_x$ and $\mu_y = w/p_y$ [equation (1-5)]. Hence Γ_i ($i = x, y$) is called *labor's relative share* in the ith industry. It can be considered as the *elasticity of output with respect to labor input*, since $\Gamma_x = \cdot(dX/X)/(dL_x/L_x)$, and so on. When the production function is of the Cobb-Douglas variety we have a simple expression for Γ_i. For example, if $X = L_x{}^a K_x{}^{1-a}$, $1 > a > 0$, we can easily show that $\Gamma_x = a$.

LEMMA 1 $\Gamma_x \gtreqless \Gamma_y$ according to whether $k_x \lesseqgtr k_y$.

PROOF   Using Euler's equation for a linear homogeneous function, we obtain from (2-1) and (2-2)

$$X = \mu_x L_x + v_x K_x , \tag{2-16}$$

$$Y = \mu_y L_y + v_y K_y . \tag{2-17}$$

From equations (2-5) and (2-6) we have

$$q \equiv \frac{w}{r} = \frac{\mu_i}{v_i}, \quad i = x, y . \tag{2-18}$$

[10] Walras' law states that the total value of goods purchased in the economy is equal to the total value of the income earned in the economy. In our model, $p_x X + p_y Y = wL + rK$. Note that this equation, often called the "exhaustion equation," holds in our model due to the linear homogeneity of the production functions.

[11] k_x and k_y are obtained from K_x/L_x and K_y/L_y respectively, as defined. The absolute prices p_x and p_y are indeterminate in our model since money is not explicitly introduced.

[12] To check the existence for the present model is not too difficult, see E. Burmeister and A. R. Dobell, *Mathematical Theories of Economic Growth* (New York: The Macmillan Company, 1970), Chapter 4. We shall later discuss this question of the existence of a positive solution for a more general model. See Part II of this book.

Combining (2-16) and (2-18), we obtain

$$X = \mu_x L_x + \frac{\mu_x}{q} K_x .$$

Dividing both sides of this equation by X, we obtain

$$1 = \Gamma_x + \frac{1}{q} \Gamma_x k_x = \Gamma_x \frac{q + k_x}{q} . \tag{2-19}$$

Hence,

$$\Gamma_x = q/(q + k_x) . \tag{2-20}$$

Similarly from (2-17), we obtain

$$\Gamma_y = q/(q + k_y) . \tag{2-21}$$

Therefore,

$$\Gamma_x - \Gamma_y = \frac{q}{q + k_x} - \frac{q}{q + k_y} = \frac{q(k_y - k_x)}{(q + k_x)(q + k_y)} . \tag{2-22}$$

From this the statement of the lemma follows immediately.   (Q.E.D.)

REMARK   When $k_x > k_y$, we say that X is *more capital intensive than Y, and Y is more labor intensive than X.* Similarly, X is more labor intensive than Y and Y is more capital intensive than X if $k_x < k_y$.

LEMMA 2

$$\hat{p} = (\Gamma_x - \Gamma_y)\hat{q} , \quad \text{where } p \equiv p_x/p_y, \, q \equiv w/r , \quad \text{and } \hat{p} \equiv dp/p, \hat{q} \equiv dq/q . \tag{2-23}$$

PROOF   By dividing both sides of (2-16) by X, we have

$$\Gamma_x + \tilde{\Gamma}_x = 1 , \quad \text{where } \tilde{\Gamma}_x \equiv v_x K_x/X . \tag{2-24}$$

Similarly, from (2-17) we have

$$\Gamma_y + \tilde{\Gamma}_y = 1 , \quad \text{where } \tilde{\Gamma}_y \equiv v_y K_y/Y . \tag{2-25}$$

Since $v_x = r/p_x$ and $v_y = r/p_y$, $\tilde{\Gamma}_i$ is capital's relative share in the ith industry $(i = x, y)$.

Now, differentiating the production functions, (2-1) and (2-2), we obtain

$$dX = \mu_x \, dL_x + v_x \, dK_x , \tag{2-26}$$

$$dY = \mu_y \, dL_y + v_y \, dK_y . \tag{2-27}$$

Dividing both sides of (2-26) [respectively (2-27)] by X (respectively Y), and recalling the definition of labor's relative share together with equations (2-24) and (2-25), we obtain from (2-26) and (2-27)

$$\hat{X} = \Gamma_x \hat{L}_x + (1 - \Gamma_x)\hat{K}_x , \tag{2-28}$$

$$\hat{Y} = \Gamma_y \hat{L}_y + (1 - \Gamma_y)\hat{K}_y , \tag{2-29}$$

where $\hat{X} \equiv dX/X$, $\hat{Y} \equiv dY/Y$, $\hat{L}_i \equiv dL_i/L_i$, and $\hat{K}_i \equiv dK_i/K_i$ $(i = x, y)$.

Differentiating equations (2-16) and (2-17) and recalling the definition of labor's relative share, together with (2-24) and (2-25), we obtain

$$\hat{X} = \Gamma_x \hat{L}_x + (1 - \Gamma_x)\hat{K}_x + \Gamma_x \hat{\mu}_x + (1 - \Gamma_x)\hat{v}_x, \tag{2-30}$$

$$\hat{Y} = \Gamma_y \hat{L}_y + (1 - \Gamma_y)\hat{K}_y + \Gamma_y \hat{\mu}_y + (1 - \Gamma_y)\hat{v}_y, \tag{2-31}$$

where $\hat{\mu}_x \equiv d\mu_x/\mu_x$, $\hat{v}_x \equiv dv_x/v_x$, and so on.
Then, combining these equations with (2-28) and (2-29), we have

$$\Gamma_x \hat{\mu}_x + (1 - \Gamma_x)\hat{v}_x = 0, \tag{2-32}$$

$$\Gamma_y \hat{\mu}_y + (1 - \Gamma_y)\hat{v}_y = 0. \tag{2-33}$$

Since equations (2-5) and (2-6) imply $p\mu_x = \mu_y$, $pv_x = v_y$, and $q = \mu_x/v_x = \mu_y/v_y$, we obtain

$$\hat{p} + \hat{\mu}_x = \hat{\mu}_y, \tag{2-34a}$$

$$\hat{p} + \hat{v}_x = \hat{v}_y, \tag{2-34b}$$

$$\hat{q} = \hat{\mu}_x - \hat{v}_x = \hat{\mu}_y - \hat{v}_y. \tag{2-35}$$

Combining (2-32) and (2-33) with (2-35), we get

$$\Gamma_x \hat{q} + \hat{v}_x = 0, \tag{2-36}$$

$$\Gamma_y \hat{q} + \hat{v}_y = 0. \tag{2-37}$$

Or, $(\Gamma_x - \Gamma_y)\hat{q} = \hat{v}_y - \hat{v}_x$.

Hence, using (2-34b), we obtain the statement of the lemma [equation (2-23)].

(Q.E.D.)

COROLLARY   If $k_x > k_y$, then

$\hat{p} \gtreqless 0$ according to whether $\hat{q} \lesseqgtr 0$;   that is,

$\dfrac{dq}{dp} \lesseqgtr 0$ according to whether $k_x \gtreqless k_y$.

PROOF   Combine lemma 2 with lemma 1.   (Q.E.D.)

REMARK   When $k_x < k_y$, then $\hat{p} \gtreqless 0$ according to whether $\hat{q} \gtreqless 0$. This remark and the above corollary can be illustrated by Figure 2-1.

REMARK   In terms of plain English, the above corollary can be explained as: "If capital becomes more expensive than labor, there will be a substitution of labor for capital in each industry. So, to keep the equality between the factor prices and the marginal value products in each industry, the price of the labor

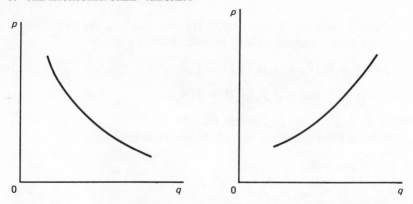

Figure 2-1 **The Relation between the Good Price Ratio and the Factor Price Ratio**

intensive good will decline relative to the price of the capital intensive good, provided there is full employment of labor and capital."[13]

LEMMA 3

$$\hat{v}_x = -\Gamma_x \hat{q} ; \tag{2-38a}$$

$$\hat{v}_y = -\Gamma_y \hat{q} . \tag{2-38b}$$

PROOF Obvious from equations (2-36) and (2-37). (Q.E.D.)

REMARK In terms of plain English, this simply means that the marginal productivity of capital in each industry increases if capital becomes more expensive than labor. The same process as described in the above remark for Lemma 2 also holds here.

LEMMA 4 q is a monotone increasing function with respect to k_i ($i = x, y$). That is, an increase in the capital labor ratio (factor intensity), k_i, will increase the marginal productivity of labor relative to that of capital.

PROOF By equations (2-5) and (2-6), and using (2-10) and (2-11), we have

$$q = \frac{f(k_x)}{f'(k_x)} - k_x = \frac{g(k_y)}{g'(k_y)} - k_y . \tag{2-39}$$

Write (2-39) as

$$q = h(k_x) = \tilde{h}(k_y). \tag{2-40}$$

---

[13] Johnson ([2] p. 19) has the following remark:

> If the capital:labour ratios in the two industries remained constant as the relative price of labour was increased, the relative cost of the labour intensive good would obviously increase; and the effect on relative costs of the substitution of capital for labour in both industries induced by the increase in the relative price of labour can be neglected, since in the neighbourhood of the minimum cost point substitution of one factor for the other does not alter cost.

A straightforward differentiation yields

$$\frac{dh}{dk_x} = \frac{-ff''}{(f')^2} , \tag{2-41a}$$

$$\frac{d\tilde{h}}{dk_y} = \frac{-gg''}{(g')^2} . \tag{2-41b}$$

By (2-12) (the law of diminishing returns), we have $dh/dk_x > 0$ and $d\tilde{h}/dk_y > 0$.

(Q.E.D.)

REMARK Note that lemma 4 also says that if factor prices change, factor proportions alter in the same direction in *both* industries. Lemma 4 can be illustrated by Figure 2-2.

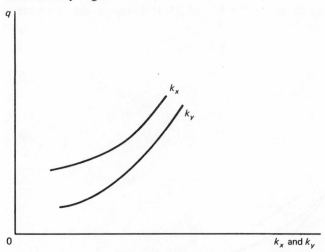

Figure 2-2 The Relation between the Factor Intensity and the Factor Price Ratio

COROLLARY r/p_x, r/p_y, and r/w all move in the same direction. In other words, if $r/p_x = \Phi(1/q)$ and $r/p_y = \psi(1/q)$, where $1/q = r/w$, then $\Phi' > 0$ and $\psi' > 0$.

PROOF From equation (2-11), $r/p_x = f'(k_x)$. And, due to the diminishing returns, $f'' < 0$. That is, $d(r/p_x)/dk_x < 0$. By the above lemma, $dk_x/dq > 0$. Hence $\Phi' = -[d(r/p_x)/dq]q^2 = -[d(r/p_x)/dk_x][dk_x/dq]q^2 > 0$. Similarly $\psi' = -[d(r/p_y)/dq]q^2 > 0$.   (Q.E.D.)

REMARK This corollary says that the *real* returns to capital (rent) move in the same direction regardless of the numéraire (X, Y, or labor).[14]

DEFINITION The percentage rate change of the factor intensity per unit percentage change of the marginal rate of transformation (equals the factor price

[14] A similar corollary can be proved with regard to the real wage rate.

ratio here) is called the *elasticity of factor substitution*. Or, more explicitly, we define the elasticity of factor substitution in the ith industry by

$$\sigma_i = \left(\frac{dk_i}{k_i}\right)\Big/\left(\frac{dq}{q}\right), \quad i = x, y. \tag{2-42}$$

REMARK Note

$$\sigma_i = \left(\frac{q}{k_i}\right)\left(\frac{dk_i}{dq}\right).$$

Clearly, in view of Lemma 4, σ_is are well-defined and positive. It can be shown that if the production function is of the Cobb-Douglas type, the elasticity of factor substitution is constant and equal to one. If the production isoquants are L-shaped, then it is equal to zero. The concept of the elasticity of factor substitution can be illustrated by the Figure 2-3. It represents the curvature of the production isoquant.

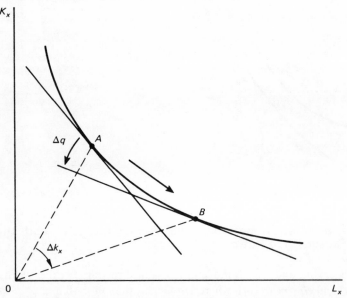

Figure 2-3 An Illustration of the Elasticity of Factor Substitution

LEMMA 5 (Takayama [15][15]) Under the assumption $k_x \neq k_y$, we have the following relations:

$$\hat{X} = A\left(\hat{K} - \frac{k_y}{k}\hat{L}\right) - B\hat{q}, \tag{2-43}$$

$$\hat{Y} = -\bar{A}\left(\hat{K} - \frac{k_x}{k}\hat{L}\right) + \bar{B}\hat{q}, \quad \text{where } k \equiv K/L; \tag{2-44}$$

$$\hat{X} - \hat{Y} = C(\hat{K} - \hat{L}) - D\hat{q}. \tag{2-45}$$

[15] Also [13] and [14].

A, B, $\bar{A}$, $\bar{B}$, C, and D are defined as follows:

$$A \equiv \frac{1}{k_x - k_y} \frac{K}{L_x}, \quad \text{and} \quad \bar{A} \equiv \frac{1}{k_x - k_y} \frac{K}{L_y}; \tag{2-46}$$

$$B \equiv \frac{1}{k_x - k_y} \{[\Gamma_x k_x + (1 - \Gamma_x)k_y]\sigma_x + K_y\sigma_y/L_x\}; \tag{2-47}$$

$$\bar{B} \equiv \frac{1}{k_x - k_y} \{[(1 - \Gamma_y)k_x + \Gamma_y k_y]\sigma_x + K_x\sigma_x/L_y\}; \tag{2-48}$$

$$C \equiv \frac{1}{k_x - k_y} \frac{LK}{L_x L_y}, \quad \text{and} \quad D \equiv B + \bar{B}. \tag{2-49}$$

PROOF   From the definition of σ_i in equation (2-42), we obtain

$$\hat{K}_i = \sigma_i \hat{q} + \hat{L}_i, \quad i = x, y. \tag{2-50}$$

From equations (2-13) and (2-14), we have

$$\frac{L_x}{L} \hat{L}_x + \frac{L_y}{L} \hat{L}_y \doteq \hat{L}, \tag{2-51}$$

$$\frac{K_x}{K} \hat{K}_x + \frac{K_y}{K} \hat{K}_y = \hat{K}. \tag{2-52}$$

From the four equations (2-50), (2-51), and (2-52) we obtain expressions for $\hat{L}_x$, $\hat{L}_y$, $\hat{K}_x$, and $\hat{K}_y$ in terms of the others. Then substitute these into (2-28) and (2-29). After a somewhat complicated computation lemma 5 is obtained.[16]

(Q.E.D.)

APPLICATIONS

In this section we shall illustrate various immediate applications of the relations established in the previous section. This will indicate the power of the lemmas in the previous sections and also enhance the reader's understanding of these lemmas.

The (Price) Elasticity of Production

Suppose that the endowments of factors (capital and labor) in a particular economy are fixed. Then the output of each of the two goods (X and Y) can be written as a function of the relative price ratio of the goods, $p \equiv p_x/p_y$. A change in this price ratio will change the (equilibrium) level of each output. The percentage rate of change of output per unit percentage change in the relative price is known as the (price) elasticity of production. Mathematically,

[16] Alternatively we can prove this lemma as follows. Consider (2-28), (2-29), (2-50), (2-51), and (2-52) as simultaneous linear equations with $\hat{L}_x$, $\hat{L}_y$, $\hat{K}_x$, $\hat{K}_y$, $\hat{X}$, and $\hat{Y}$ as the variables. Then apply Cramer's rule.

the elasticity of production for the ith industry, denoted by ε_i ($i = x, y$), is defined by

$$\varepsilon_x \equiv \left(\frac{dX}{X}\right)\bigg/\left(\frac{dp}{p}\right) = \hat{X}/\hat{p}\,, \tag{2-53}$$

$$\varepsilon_y \equiv -\left(\frac{dY}{Y}\right)\bigg/\left(\frac{dp}{p}\right) = -\hat{Y}/\hat{p}\,. \tag{2-54}$$

The minus sign is used for ε_y to keep ε_y, in general, positive. This concept of the elasticity of production is best illustrated in terms of the following diagram with the production possibility curve.

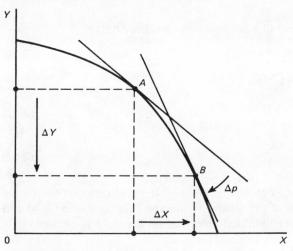

Figure 2-4   The Elasticity of Production

The above concept of the elasticity of production is quite a neat concept and is often used in the literature. But the exact meaning of the underlying mechanism of this concept is not clear from the above definition. Using the model and lemmas of the previous section, we can easily obtain expressions for the ε_is in terms of more basic concepts and understand the exact meaning of the mechanism underlying the ε_is.

Recall that lemma 2 gives a relationship between $\hat{p}$ and $\hat{q}$ and that lemma 5 gives a relationship between $\hat{q}$ and $\hat{X}$ (or $\hat{Y}$) ($\hat{K} = \hat{L} = 0$ by the assumption of constant factor endowments). Then, using equations (2-23) and (2-43) [or (2-44)], we immediately obtain the following expressions for the ε_is:

$$\varepsilon_x = \frac{-1}{(k_x - k_y)(\Gamma_x - \Gamma_y)} \left\{[\Gamma_x k_x + (1 - \Gamma_x)k_y]\sigma_x + K_y\sigma_y/L_x\right\}, \tag{2-55}$$

$$\varepsilon_y = \frac{-1}{(k_x - k_y)(\Gamma_x - \Gamma_y)} \left\{[(1 - \Gamma_y)k_x + \Gamma_y k_y]\sigma_y + K_x\sigma_x/L_y\right\}. \tag{2-56}$$

Note that $(k_x - k_y)(\Gamma_x - \Gamma_y)$ is always negative due to *lemma* 1, hence, ε_x and ε_y are always positive. We may also note that if $k_x = k_y$ (or $\Gamma_x = \Gamma_y$) the above ε_is are not defined.

It should be clear that an increase in the output of one good is bound to cause a decrease in the output of the other good (see Figure 2-4). In other words, if $\hat{X} > 0$, then $\hat{Y} < 0$, and vice versa. The tangency condition (of the price line and the production transformation curve) with respect to an equilibrium output requires that

$$\frac{dY}{dX} = -\frac{p_x}{p_y}. \tag{2-57}$$

Suppose we choose the unit of measurement for each good in such a way that $p_x/p_y = 1$ initially. Then we must have $dX + dY = 0$. (That is, $dX > 0$ implies $dY < 0$, and vice versa.) Under the assumption of the initial $p = 1$, $\varepsilon_x X - \varepsilon_y Y = dX/dp + dY/dp$. Hence, in view of (2-57), we obtain

$$\varepsilon_x X = \varepsilon_y Y. \tag{2-58}$$

This equation can also be obtained from equation (2-55) with reference to lemmas 5 and 2 (in a much more tedious way). Equation (2-58) gives a very simple relation between ε_x and ε_y. This will be useful when we attempt more complicated analyses using the concepts of ε_x and ε_y. (See later chapters.)

Variable Factor Supplies

In the above concept of the elasticity of production we assumed that the amounts of the factor endowments were constant. This assumption is, in reality, not true. For example, the amount of labor supply would naturally depend on the real wage rate, and the amount of capital supply may depend on the real rent. Let us now suppose that the real wage rate is measured in terms of the price of capital (service), r (that is, r is taken as a numéraire), and real rent is measured in terms of w. A similar consideration as the corollary of lemma 4 will immediately tell us that the choice of numéraire will not alter the subsequent analysis. Then we obtain the following expressions for the factor supply function:

$$L = L(q), \tag{2-59}$$

$$K = K(1/q). \tag{2-60}$$

Let α and β be the *elasticity of labor and capital supply*, that is,

$$\alpha \equiv \left(\frac{dL}{L}\right) \bigg/ \left(\frac{dq}{q}\right) = \hat{L}/\hat{q}, \tag{2-61}$$

$$\beta \equiv \left(\frac{dK}{K}\right) \bigg/ \frac{d\left(\frac{1}{q}\right)}{\left(\frac{1}{q}\right)} = -\hat{K}/\hat{q}, \tag{2-62}$$

where we set $q = 1$ initially. Substituting these expressions into (2-43) and (2-44) of lemma 5, we obtain

$$\hat{X} = -[A(\beta + \alpha k_y/k) + B]\hat{q}\,, \tag{2-63}$$

$$\hat{Y} = [\bar{A}(\beta + \alpha k_x/k) + \bar{B}]\hat{q}\,, \tag{2-64}$$

where A, $\bar{A}$, B, and $\bar{B}$ are as defined in lemma 5.

Using this relation and lemma 2, we can obtain the expressions for the "generalized" elasticity of production

$$\varepsilon_x = \frac{-1}{(k_x - k_y)(\Gamma_x - \Gamma_y)}$$
$$\times \{(\beta K/L_x + \alpha k_y/k) + [\Gamma_x k_x + (1 - \Gamma_x)k_y]\sigma_x + K_y\sigma_y/L_x\}\,, \tag{2-65}$$

$$\varepsilon_y = \frac{-1}{(k_x - k_y)(\Gamma_x - \Gamma_y)}$$
$$\times \{(\beta K/L_y + \alpha k_x/k) + [(1 - \Gamma_y)k_x + \Gamma_y k_y]\sigma_y + K_x\sigma_x/L_y\}\,. \tag{2-66}$$

Note that if $\alpha > 0$ and $\beta > 0$, then ε_x and ε_y are positive due to lemma 1 and that the magnitudes of ε_x and ε_y for the present case ((2-63) and (2-64)) are larger than those for the fixed supply case [(2-55) and (2-56), that is, the case of $\alpha = 0$ and $\beta = 0$]. This remark about the magnitudes of ε_x and ε_y is simply the observation of a special case of a general principle, known as Samuelson's *Le Chatelier Principle*.[17]

Now suppose that our assumption of $\alpha > 0$ and $\beta > 0$ does not hold. For example, we know from elementary wage theory that the labor supply curve can be backward bending. In this case α is clearly negative. If α is negative and its absolute value is large enough, then ε_x and ε_y can be negative. Kemp and Jones [6] considered a similar case, the case in which the capital supply is fixed and only the labor supply is flexible. Note that we have made this consideration as a simple corollary of the basic lemmas of the previous section. As Kemp and Jones [6] pointed out, the case of negative ε_x and ε_y will upset many results in the literature. In the subsequent analyses of the book we will simply assume that ε_x and ε_y are positive. The reader can easily determine how the results should be modified when ε_x and ε_y are negative.

An implicit assumption in the above analysis is that the flexibility of labor and capital supplies does not upset the basic premise, the stationary state. In general this is not true. An increase in capital supply will lead us to a dynamic economy with capital accumulation, and a rise in the real wage rate may induce an increase in the birth rate and consequently the population. The complications due to such a dynamization are all neglected. In other words, we are assuming that such effects of dynamization are second order small so that the basic stationary state assumptions are approximately true.

[17] See Samuelson, P. A., *Foundations of Economic Analysis*, Cambridge, Mass.: Harvard University Press, 1947, and Samuelson, P. A., "An Extension of the LeChatelier Principle," *Econometrica*, 28, April 1960.

Rybczynski's Theorem

In an article which considered the effect of a change in the supply of a factor [11], Rybczynski proved the following theorem, now well-known as *Rybczynski's theorem.*

> If the supply of one factor increases with the supply of the other factor constant, the absolute output of the good which uses the increased factor relatively less "intensively" should diminish in order to keep the relative price of the goods constant.

The proof of this theorem is now almost trivial in view of our lemma 5. Due to lemma 2, we can assert immediately that $\hat{q} = 0$ when $\hat{p} = 0$. Then inserting this $\hat{q} = 0$ into lemma 5, we obtain

$$\hat{X} = A \left(\hat{K} - \frac{k_y}{k} \hat{L} \right) \quad \text{and} \quad \hat{Y} = - \bar{A} \left(\hat{K} - \frac{k_x}{k} \hat{L} \right), \tag{2-67}$$

where A and $\bar{A}$ are as defined in lemma 5 and $k_x \neq k_y$.

Suppose that X is more capital intensive than Y (that is, $k_x > k_y$), then $A > 0$ and $\bar{A} > 0$. Thus, in view of (2-67), we obtain

$$\text{if} \qquad \hat{K} > \frac{k_x}{k} \hat{L}, \quad \text{then } \hat{X} > 0, \quad \text{and} \quad \hat{Y} < 0, \tag{2-68a}$$

$$\text{if} \qquad \hat{K} < \frac{k_y}{k} \hat{L}, \quad \text{then } \hat{X} < 0, \quad \text{and} \quad \hat{Y} > 0, \tag{2-68b}$$

$$\text{if} \quad \frac{k_x}{k} \hat{L} > \hat{K} > \frac{k_y}{k} \hat{L}, \quad \text{then } \hat{X} > 0, \quad \text{and} \quad \hat{Y} > 0. \tag{2-68c}$$

Rybczynski's theorem can be obtained by setting $\hat{K} > 0$, $\hat{L} = 0$; *or* $\hat{K} = 0$, $\hat{L} > 0$ in this relation (2-68). Hence our relation (2-68) is considered as a *generalized Rybczynski's theorem.* Rybczynski proved his theorem using a diagrammatical technique. We obtained a more general result rigorously as a *simple* corollary of our analysis in the previous section.

Rybczynski's theorem has various important applications other than the original purpose as stated in [11]. The following consideration may enhance our understanding of the theorem. Consider a country which is small enough so that the goods price ratio of this country is equal to that of the rest of the world. Then we can immediately apply the theorem to the case in which there are factor movements (immigration and emigration of labor, and the movement of capital), as well as the case where there are changes in factor supplies due to growth.

Mishan's Theorem

In an article [10] commenting on the above article by Rybczynski, Mishan proved the following theorem using a diagrammatical technique. "An increase in the output of the capital (labor) intensive good will result in a decrease (increase) in the wage:rent ratio." The proof of this theorem follows trivially from lemma 5. In other words, put $\hat{K} = 0$ and $\hat{L} = 0$ in equations (2-43) and (2-44) of lemma 5. Then we obtain

$$\hat{X} = -B\hat{q} \quad \text{and} \quad \hat{Y} = \bar{B}\hat{q}, \tag{2-69}$$

where B and $\bar{B}$ are as defined in lemma 5. Suppose that X is more capital intensive than Y (that is, $k_x > k_y$). Then $B > 0$ and $\bar{B} > 0$. This finishes the proof of the theorem. Note that (2-69) gives a more precise statement of Mishan's theorem.

Magnification Effect (Jones)

In his article [4], Jones obtained the following remarkable relation:

$$\hat{X} > \hat{K} > \hat{L} > \hat{Y}, \quad \text{if } k_x > k_y, \quad \hat{p} = 0 \quad \text{and} \quad \hat{K} > \hat{L}. \tag{2-70}$$

Similarly,

$$\hat{Y} > \hat{L} > \hat{K} > \hat{X}, \quad \text{if } k_x > k_y, \quad \hat{p} = 0 \quad \text{and} \quad \hat{L} > \hat{K}. \tag{2-71}$$

Jones expresses these relations as follows ([4], p. 561).

> If factor endowments expand at different rates, the commodity intensive in the use of the fastest growing factor expands at a greater rate than either factor, and the other commodity grows (if at all) at a slower rate than either factor.

He called this the *Magnification Effect*. Here we note that the proofs of these relations (2-70) and (2-71) do not require the extensive arguments, not all of them are explicit, as used by Jones. Instead, we shall show that they can be obtained as a simple corollary of our analysis.

Note first that the assumption $\hat{p} = 0$ yields equation (2-67) in view of lemmas 2 and 5. Then carry out the following straightforward manipulations.

$$\hat{X} - \hat{K} = A\left(\hat{K} - \frac{k_y}{k}\hat{L}\right) - \hat{K}, \quad \left(\text{where } A \equiv \frac{1}{k_x - k_y} \cdot \frac{K}{L_x}\right)$$

$$= \frac{1}{k_x - k_y} \cdot \left\{\left[\frac{K}{L_x} - (k_x - k_y)\right]\hat{K} - \frac{k_y}{k}\frac{K}{L_x}\hat{L}\right\}.$$

But

$$\frac{K}{L_x} - (k_x - k_y) = \frac{1}{L_x}[K - (k_x - k_y)L_x] = \frac{1}{L_x}(K - K_x + k_yL_x)$$

$$= \frac{1}{L_x}(K_y + k_yL_x) = \frac{k_y}{L_x}(L_y + L_x) = \frac{k_y}{L_x}L..$$

Hence

$$\left[\frac{K}{L_x} - (k_x - k_y)\right]\hat{K} - \frac{k_y}{k}\frac{K}{L_x}\hat{L} = \frac{k_y}{L_x}L\hat{K} - \frac{k_y}{k}\frac{K}{L_x}\hat{L} = k_y\frac{L}{L_x}(\hat{K} - \hat{L}).$$

Therefore, we have

$$\hat{X} - \hat{K} = \frac{1}{k_x - k_y}\frac{k_y}{L_x}L(\hat{K} - \hat{L}). \tag{2-72}$$

Hence, under the assumptions of $\hat{K} > \hat{L}$ and $k_x > k_y$, we obtain $\hat{X} > \hat{K}$.

Similarly, from $\hat{L} - \hat{Y} = \hat{L} + \bar{A}\left(\hat{K} - \frac{k_x}{k}\hat{L}\right)$, we obtain

$$\hat{L} - \hat{Y} = \frac{1}{k_x - k_y}\frac{K}{L_y}(\hat{K} - \hat{L}). \tag{2-73}$$

Therefore, if $\hat{K} > \hat{L}$ and $k_x > k_y$, then $\hat{L} > \hat{Y}$. This finishes the proof of relation (2-70). Relation (2-71) follows immediately from (2-70) by switching the notation.

Jones [4] also considered the following magnification effect of commodity prices on factor prices as a *dual* of the above magnification effect of factor supplies on outputs:

$$\hat{r} > \hat{p}_x > \hat{p}_y > \hat{w}, \quad \text{if } k_x > k_y \quad \text{and} \quad \hat{p}_x > \hat{p}_y. \tag{2-74}$$

The proof of this magnification effect is also a simple corollary of the analysis of the previous section. First, note that equation (2-6) implies $\hat{r} - \hat{p}_x = \hat{v}_x$. But lemma 3 says $\hat{v}_x = -\Gamma_x\hat{q}$. Hence $\hat{r} - \hat{p}_x = -\Gamma_x\hat{q}$. If $k_x > k_y$, then by the corollary of lemma 2, $\hat{q} < 0$, if and only if $\hat{p} > 0$. Therefore, $\hat{r} - \hat{p}_x > 0$ if and only if $\hat{p} = \hat{p}_x - \hat{p}_y > 0$.

Also, from equation (2-5) we obtain $\hat{w} - \hat{p}_y = \hat{\mu}_y$. Then, using equation (2-35) and lemma 3 successively, we obtain

$$\hat{w} - \hat{p}_y = \hat{\mu}_y = (\hat{v}_y + \hat{q}) = \hat{q} - \Gamma_y\hat{q}.$$

Note that $\Gamma_y < 1$, and under the assumption $k_x > k_y$, $\hat{q} < 0$ if and only if $\hat{p} > 0$. Hence, $\hat{w} - \hat{p}_y < 0$ if and only if $\hat{p} = \hat{p}_x - \hat{p}_y > 0$. This finishes the proof of relation (2-74).

By switching the notations, we can obtain the following relation immediately:

$$\hat{r} < \hat{p}_y < \hat{p}_x < \hat{w}, \quad \text{if } k_x < k_y \text{ and } \hat{p}_x > \hat{p}_y. \tag{2-75}$$

Verbally, (2-74) may be restated as "If good X is relatively more capital intensive than good Y, and if the price of X increases relative to the price of Y, then the price of capital increases relative to the price of labor in a "magnified" fashion.

Samuelson's Reciprocity Relation

In an important article [12], Samuelson presented the following remarkable relation, which he called the *Reciprocity Relation*.[18]

$$\frac{\partial X}{\partial K} = \frac{\partial r}{\partial p_x}, \quad \frac{\partial X}{\partial L} = \frac{\partial w}{\partial p_x}, \quad \frac{\partial Y}{\partial K} = \frac{\partial r}{\partial p_y}, \quad \frac{\partial Y}{\partial L} = \frac{\partial w}{\partial p_y}. \tag{2-76}$$

The precise understanding of these partial derivatives is important. On the left-hand side of each equation we are concerned with a change in output when the endowments of one of the two factors in the economy changes with the relative goods price ratio (p_x/p_y) being fixed. For example, $\partial X/\partial K$ means the change in output per unit of change in the capital stock with the stock of labor and the relative price p kept constant. On the right-hand side of each equation we are concerned with the change in a factor price (in money terms) when *one* of the goods prices (p_x or p_y) has changed. For example, $\partial r/\partial p_x$ means the change in the money rate of return on capital (rent) per unit change in the price of X when the price of Y is fixed.

To prove the above relations we first note that they can easily be derived from the following interesting relations.[19]

$$\frac{\partial X}{\partial K} = \frac{d(r/p_y)}{d(p_x/p_y)}, \quad \frac{\partial X}{\partial L} = \frac{d(w/p_y)}{d(p_x/p_y)}, \quad \frac{\partial Y}{\partial K} = \frac{d(r/p_x)}{d(p_y/p_x)}, \quad \frac{\partial Y}{\partial L} = \frac{d(w/p_x)}{d(p_y/p_x)}. \tag{2-77}$$

Note that the right-hand side of each of the above equations is now written in *real* terms and the partial derivatives are replaced by total derivatives (since we are no longer assuming that the other price is fixed).

We now want to show that the above relations can be obtained as a simple corollary of our discussion in the previous section. We illustrate the proof of only the first of the above relations, that is, $\dfrac{\partial X}{\partial K} = \dfrac{d(r/p_y)}{d(p_x/p_y)}$. The rest can be proved analogously.

Due to lemma 5 [equation (2-43)], we can easily obtain the following expression for $\partial X/\partial K$:

$$\frac{\partial X}{\partial K} = \frac{1}{k_x - k_y} \frac{X}{L_x}. \tag{2-78}$$

---

[18] Samuelson presented this in a more general context of n goods and r factors. Writing the production function of the ith good as $X_i = X_i(V_1, V_2, \cdots, V_r)$, and writing p_i for the price of good i and w_j for the price of factor j, Samuelson's reciprocity relation is elegantly written as $(\partial X_i/\partial V_j) = (\partial w_j/\partial p_i)$. See Samuelson [12], p. 10. He obtained this in a remarkably short way by observing the equality between the national product and the national expenditure. Samuelson's own explanation of this relation is useful in this context. "If an increase in a given factor such as land will cause a good like food to be increased in production within a country facing fixed international prices, then an increase in the relative price of food can be expected to raise the rent of that kind of land" ([12] p. 10).

[19] Since w/p_i and r/p_i ($i = x, y$) are monotone functions with respect to k_i due to (2-10) and (2-11) with $f'' < 0$ and $g'' < 0$, k_i can be expressed as a function of w/p_i or r/p_i. Since $p = g'/f'$, i.e., a function of k_i, p is expressed as a function of w/p_i or r/p_i only.

To obtain the expression for $d(r/p_y)/dp$, we note that this is equal to dv_y/dp. Using lemma 3 and lemma 2 successively, we obtain

$$\hat{v}_y = -\Gamma_y \hat{q} = -\Gamma_y \hat{p}/(\Gamma_x - \Gamma_y) . \tag{2-79}$$

Hence,

$$\frac{dv_y}{dp} = \frac{-\Gamma_y v_y}{p(\Gamma_x - \Gamma_y)} . \tag{2-80}$$

But from equations (2-20) and (2-21) in the proof of lemma 1, we can obtain

$$\frac{-\Gamma_y}{\Gamma_x - \Gamma_y} = \frac{q}{(k_x - k_y)\Gamma_x} . \tag{2-81}$$

Substituting this into (2-80) and recalling that $q = \mu_y/v_y$ and $p = \mu_y/\mu_x$, we have

$$\frac{dv_y}{dp} = \frac{1}{k_x - k_y} \cdot \frac{X}{L_x} . \tag{2-82}$$

Combining (2-82) and (2-78) completes the proof of the reciprocity relation.

We may note that this reciprocity relation plays an important role in the recent discussions by Kemp and Jones on the optimal tariff and direct investment.[20] Kemp remarked that in Samuelson [12], "the proof was barely sketched and is, in any case, embedded in an especially difficult article" (Kemp, *ibid.*, p. 807). Kemp has since shown his proof, but it is also very sketchy, with the tedious part of the computation hidden.

REFERENCES

1. Harberger, A. C., "The Incidence of the Corporation Income Tax," *Journal of Political Economy*, LXX, June 1962.

2. Johnson, H. G., *International Trade and Economic Growth* (Cambridge, Mass.: Harvard University Press), 1958, Chapter 1.

3. Jones, R. W., "Factor Proportions and the Heckscher-Ohlin Model," *Review of Economic Studies*, XXIV, 1956–57.

4. ———, "The Structure of Simple General Equilibrium Models," *Journal of Political Economy*, LXXIII, December 1965.

5. Kemp, M. C., *The Pure Theory of International Trade and Investment* (Englewood Cliffs, N.J.: Prentice-Hall), 1969 (1st ed. 1964).

6. ———, and Jones, R. W., "Variable Labor Supply and the Theory of International Trade," *Journal of Political Economy*, LXX, February 1962.

7. Koopmans, T. C., *Three Essays on the State of Economic Science* (New York: McGraw Hill), 1957.

8. Meade, J. E., *The Balance of Payments: Mathematical Supplement* (London: Oxford University Press), 1951.

[20] See Kemp, M. C., "Gains from International Trade and Investment," *American Economic Review*, LVI, September 1966, and Jones, R. W., "International Capital Movements and The Theory of Tariffs and Trade," *Quarterly Journal of Economics*, LXXXI, February 1967. We shall discuss this topic later.

9. Meade, J. E., *Trade and Welfare: Mathematical Supplement* (London: Oxford University Press), 1955.

10. Mishan, E. J., "Factor Endowment and Relative Commodity Prices: A Comment," *Economica*, XXIII, November 1956.

11. Rybczynski, T. M., "Factor Endowment and Relative Commodity Prices," *Economica*, XXII, November 1955.

12. Samuelson, P. A., "Prices of Factors and Goods in General Equilibrium," *Review of Economic Studies*, XXI, 1953–54.

13. Takayama, A., *Economic Growth and International Trade*, Ph.D. Dissertation, University of Rochester, March 1962.

14. ———, *International Economics* (Tokyo: Toyo Keizai Shimpo-Sha), 1963.

15. ———, "On a Two-Sector Model of Economic Growth—A Comparative Statics Analysis," *Review of Economic Studies*, XXX, June 1963.

16. ———, "Reconsideration of the Nurkse Balanced Growth Thesis," *International Economic Review*, 8, February 1967.

Appendix to Chapter 2

A Geometric Proof of Rybczynski's Theorem

In his article [A8], Jones proposed a geometric proof of Rybczynski's theorem, as an alternative to Rybczynski's original geometric proof.[21] Since the technique developed by Jones will be useful for other problems, and since his proof is remarkably simple, we shall present his technique and recapitulate his proof rigorously here.

Rybczynski's basic premise is that the goods price ratio is constant (that is, $\hat{p} = 0$). This implies that the factor price ratio is constant (recall lemma 2). It is well-known that if the production function exhibits constant returns to scale, the marginal rate of substitution of the factors (which is equal to the factor price ratio) is constant as long as the capital:labor ratio is constant. Note that the formal proof of this statement is obvious from our lemma 4 (that is, $\hat{q} = 0$ if and only if k_x (or k_y) is constant). This can be illustrated by Figure 2-5.

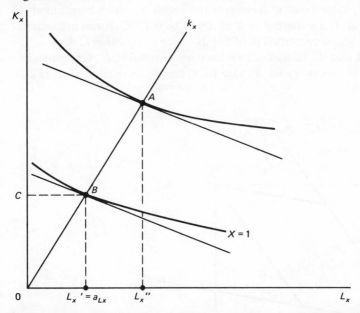

Figure 2-5   Production Isoquants with Constant Returns to Scale

[21] For the other diagrammatical proofs, which use the box diagram technique, see Amano [A1] and Guha [A4].

In Figure 2-5 the slope of the k_x line represents the value of the capital:labor ratio k_x. The factor price lines, which are tangent to the production isoquants at the different points (for example, A, B) of the same ray from the origin, are all parallel. Since $X = L_x f(k_x)$ and $f(k_x) =$ constant along the same ray from the origin, the amount of output (of X) can be measured along the ray. For example, if $L_x'' = 2L_x'$, then point A represents an output of X twice as big as that at B. Suppose this economy produces two goods, X and Y, and let $a_{Lx} \equiv L_x/X$, $a_{Kx} \equiv K_x/X$, $a_{Ly} \equiv L_y/Y$, and $a_{Ky} \equiv K_y/Y$. Then we have

$$a_{Lx}X + a_{Ly}Y = L, \tag{2-83a}$$

$$a_{Kx}X + a_{Ky}Y = K. \tag{2-83b}$$

Or, in vector notation

$$a_x X + a_y Y = E, \quad \text{where}$$

$$a_x \equiv \begin{bmatrix} a_{Lx} \\ a_{Kx} \end{bmatrix}, \quad a_y \equiv \begin{bmatrix} a_{Ly} \\ a_{Ky} \end{bmatrix}, \quad \text{and} \quad E \equiv \begin{bmatrix} L \\ K \end{bmatrix}. \tag{2-83c}$$

In Figure 2-5, if $L_x' = a_{Lx}$, then point C represents the value a_{Kx}, and the isoquant passing through B represents a unit output. Given the factor endowment E and the factor price ratio (thus the values of k_x and k_y), we can now determine the output of each good along the k_x and k_y rays (Figure 2-6). In other words, points A and B are obtained by drawing lines from E parallel to the k_y and k_x rays. Point C represents the vector a_x which corresponds to the unit output of X. The output of X at A will be OA/OC. It can immediately be seen that the above construction of points is due to equation (2-83c).

Now, suppose that the factor endowment moves from E to E'. Corresponding to this movement, points A and B move to A' and B' respectively (Figure 2-7).

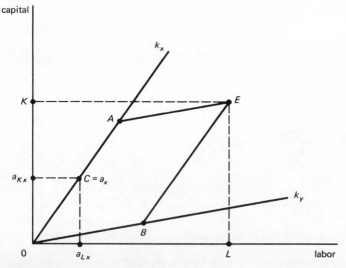

Figure 2-6   Jones' Diagram

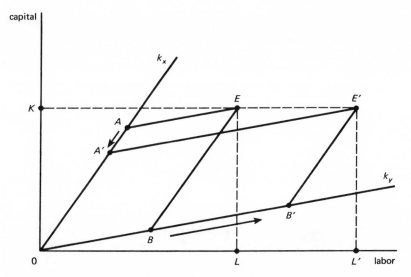

Figure 2-7   Jones' Proof of Rybczynski's Theorem

In the movement from E to E', the total labor supply increases while the stock of capital is kept constant. The output of the capital intensive good, that is, X, decreases ($A \rightarrow A'$) and the output of the labor intensive good, that is, Y, increases ($B \rightarrow B'$). This is simply the statement of Rybczynski's theorem.

A Two-Sector Model of Economic Growth[22]

An easy application of our lemmas to problems outside international trade can be found in growth theory. Consider an economy producing two goods, a capital good (X) and a consumption good (Y), with two factors, capital and labor. The model is then exactly the same as the one developed in the section, "The Basis of the Model and Various Relations," except that we need three more equations to close the model. One is the equation which dynamizes the model. Another is the equation which specifies the demand condition, and the third is the labor supply function.

The first equation can be obtained by assuming the saving investment equilibrium relation along the growth path. Suppose that the capitalists are the only savers and that their propensity to save is constant and equal to s. Hence, the total saving of the economy at each instant of time is equal to srK. Assume that a constant proportion of the stock of the capital goods built in the past falls to bits and needs to be replaced. Let η be the rate of depreciation at each instant of time. Thus, the value of gross investment at each instant of time is

---

[22] The Two-Sector Model of Economic Growth was hotly debated in the early 1960s, especially in the *Review of Economic Studies*. Since Uzawa's paper [A16] comes first in this debate, the model is often linked with his name. The present exposition is based on Takayama [A13], which was written independently of Uzawa [A16] and contains it as a special case. The paper [A13] was completed in the spring of 1961 at the University of Rochester which initiated the author's study of international trade theory [A15].

equal to $p_x(\dot{K} + \eta K)$ where $\dot{K} \equiv dK/dt$. Hence the saving investment equilibrium relation will give

$$srK = p_x(\dot{K} + \eta K) . \tag{2-84}$$

Note that (2-84) can equivalently be written as

$$\frac{\dot{K}}{K} = s\frac{r}{p_x} - \eta . \tag{2-85}$$

Hence,

$$d\left(\frac{\dot{K}}{K}\right) = sd\left(\frac{r}{p_x}\right) . \tag{2-86}$$

Therefore, an increase (decrease) in the real rent (that is, $d(r/p_x) > 0$) will increase (decrease) the rate of capital accumulation (that is, $d(\dot{K}/K) > 0$). Since $d(r/p_x) \gtreqless 0$ according to whether $d(1/q) \gtreqless 0$ by the corollary of lemma 4, we have:

$$d(\dot{K}/K) \gtreqless 0 , \quad \text{according to whether } dq \gtreqless 0 . \tag{2-87}$$

The demand specification of the model is already implied in the above. That is, we assumed that the capitalists are the only savers or that the workers consume all their income and the capitalists save a part of their income. Thus we have

$$p_x X = srK . \tag{2-88}$$

Note that (2-88) can be expressed equivalently as $p_y Y = wL + (1 - s)rK.$[23]

Finally we suppose that the supply of labor, which is assumed to be proportional to population, is determined exogenously as some known function of time. For example,

$$L = L_0 e^{nt}, \quad \text{where } n \text{ is the rate of population growth.} \tag{2-89}$$

Then we have $\hat{L} = n$.

Thus we have 11 equations [equations (2-84), (2-88), and (2-89), together with (2-1), (2-2), (2-5), (2-6), (2-13), and (2-14)]. There are 11 variables in the model, which can be solved as functions of time, that is, L_x, L_y, K_x, K_y, X, Y, w/p_x, r/p_x, p_x/p_y, L, and K.

From equation (2-88), we obtain

$$\hat{X} - \hat{K} = \hat{r} - \hat{p}_x = \hat{v}_x , \quad \text{where the hat (\^{}) signifies } \hat{K} \equiv \dot{K}/K , \quad \text{and so on.} \tag{2-90}$$

Substituting (2-43) (of lemma 5) and (2-38a) (of lemma 3) into (2-90), we obtain

$$\frac{L}{L_x} k_y(\hat{K} - \hat{L}) = \tau\hat{q} , \quad \text{where } \tau \text{ is defined by} \tag{2-91}$$

$$\tau \equiv \{\Gamma_x k_x + (1 - \Gamma_x)k_y\} \sigma_x - (k_x - k_y) + K_y\sigma_y/L_x . \tag{2-92}$$

[23] Recall Walras' law (or the "exhaustion equation") which says $p_x X + p_y Y = wL + rK$.

In view of (2-87), capital and labor grow at the same rate as time extends without limit (assuming $\tau \neq 0$ for all $\hat{K}$ and $\hat{L}$) *if and only if*

$$\tau > 0 . \tag{2-93}$$

In other words, if $\tau > 0$, $\hat{q} \gtreqless 0$ according to whether $\hat{K} \gtreqless \hat{L}(= n)$. And due to (2-87), $d\hat{K} \lesseqgtr 0$ according to whether $\hat{K} \gtreqless \hat{L}$. Thus, if capital grows faster (slower) than labor then there is a decrease (increase) in the rate of capital accumulation. As time extends without limit, $\hat{K}$ approaches $\hat{L}$. On the other hand, if $\tau < 0$, the difference between $\hat{K}$ and $\hat{L}$ gets larger as time elapses. If $\tau = 0$, the initial difference between $\hat{K}$ and $\hat{L}$ remains the same. The above argument can be illustrated by Figure 2-8.

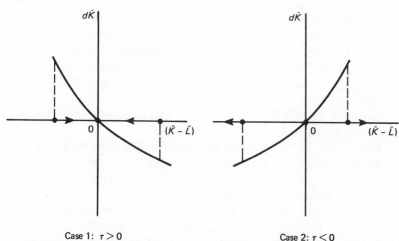

Case 1: $\tau > 0$ Case 2: $\tau < 0$

Figure 2-8   Stable or Unstable Balanced Growth Path

Hence, $\tau > 0$ gives a necessary and sufficient condition for the asymptotic stability to a balanced growth path (that is, the path with $\hat{K} = \hat{L}$). Several sufficient conditions can be given by checking the conditions for τ to be positive.

1. (Uzawa [A16]): The consumption good industry is more capital intensive than the capital good industry (that is, $k_y > k_x$).
2. (Shinkai [A11]): $k_y > k_x$ and $\sigma_x \to 0$, $\sigma_y \to 0$.
3. The elasticity of factor substitution of the capital good industry is equal to or greater than unity (that is, $\sigma_x \geqq 1$).[24]

To see 3, rewrite τ as

$$\tau = k_y[\Gamma_x + \sigma_x(1 - \Gamma_x)] + (\sigma_x - 1)\Gamma_x k_x + K_y \sigma_y/L_x .$$

The reader can attempt to obtain other sufficient conditions.

---

[24] It should be clear that in the entire analysis of this appendix, we are *not* assuming that the elasticities of factor substitution are constant.

REFERENCES

A1.   Amano, A., "Factor Endowments and Relative Prices: A Generalization of Rybczynski's Theorem," *Economica*, XXX, November 1963.

A2.   ———, "A Further Note on Professor Uzawa's Two-Sector Model of Economic Growth," *Review of Economic Studies*, XXXI, April 1964.

A3.   Drandakis, E. M., "Factor Substitution in the Two-Sector Growth Model," *Review of Economic Studies*, XXX, October 1963.

A4.   Guha, A., "Factor and Commodity Prices in an Expanding Economy," *Quarterly Journal of Economics*, LXXVII, February 1963.

A5.   Hahn, F. H., "On Two-Sector Growth Models," *Review of Economic Studies*, XXXII, October 1965.

A6.   Hahn, F. H. and Matthews, R. C. O., "The Theory of Economic Growth: A Survey," *Economic Journal*, LXXIV, December 1964.

A7.   Inada, K., "On a Two-Sector Model of Economic Growth: Comments and a Generalization," *Review of Economic Studies*, XXX, June 1963.

A8.   Jones, R. W., "Duality in International Trade: A Geometrical Note," *Canadian Journal of Economics and Political Science*, XXXI, August 1965.

A9.   Meade, J. E., *A Neo-Classical Theory of Economic Growth* (London: Oxford University Press), 1961.

A10.   Rybczynski, T. M., "Factor Endowments and Relative Commodity Prices," *Economica*, XXII, November 1955.

A11.   Shinkai, Y., "On Equilibrium Growth of Capital and Labour," *International Economic Review*, 1, May 1960.

A12.   Solow, R. M., "Note on Uzawa's Two-Sector Model of Economic Growth," *Review of Economic Studies*, XXIX, 1961–62.

A13.   Takayama, A., "On a Two-Sector Model of Economic Growth: A Comparative Statics Analysis," *Review of Economic Studies*, XXX, June 1963.

A14.   ———, "On a Two-Sector Model of Economic Growth with Technological Progress," *Review of Economic Studies*, XXXII, July 1965.

A15.   ———, *Economic Growth and International Trade*, Ph.D. Dissertation, University of Rochester, March 1962.

A16.   Uzawa, H., "On a Two-Sector Model of Economic Growth," *Review of Economic Studies*, XXIX, 1961–62.

A17.   ———, "On a Two-Sector Model of Economic Growth: II," *Review of Economic Studies*, XXX, June 1963.

3

THE HECKSCHER-OHLIN THEOREM AND RELATED TOPICS

INTRODUCTION

Consider a world consisting of two countries. Suppose that there are differences in the relative prices of the goods between the countries in the absence of international trade. Then, if we abstract from things such as transport costs and other impediments to trade, trade between the countries will occur. Thus, our attention is shifted to the problem of explaining the differences in the relative prices of goods between the countries. The Ricardian formulation of comparative advantage theory was the first brilliant achievement along these lines.[1]

The question of prices is, however, a rather trivial one in the Ricardian theory, for it assumes, among other things, constant costs with only one factor of production—labor. To the extent that one is primarily concerned with the normative aspects of trade, as was the case with the Ricardian theory,[2] these assumptions are not too bothersome. Redefining cost as "real cost", one may include as labor cost[3] those costs associated with the irksomeness of labor, abstinence for the postponement of consumption, and so on. But, even putting

---

[1] Although the Ricardian theory of comparative advantage suffers from the difficulties described below, it gives an application of activity analysis, one of the most important foundations of modern economic theory. We shall take up the classical theory of comparative advantage from this point of view in Part II of this book.

[2] The Ricardian theory was established from the point of view of the "gains from trade" and it proposed a particular policy called free trade. In this sense, this theory is regarded as one concerned with the normative aspect of the economy. See Viner [42].

[3] As Viner [42] insisted, the fact that Ricardo measured real cost in terms of labor input is probably a mere historical accident (p. 490). However, this convention of measuring real cost by labor input convinced many writers that there is a crucial link between the Ricardian theory of comparative advantage and the classical labor theory of value. One of the stronger motives for Ohlin's work, which we will discuss now, was to "rescue international trade theory from the clutches of a labor theory of value" (Caves [4], p. 23).

aside those ambiguities in the verbal arguments traditionally used in the real cost theory, once the positive aspects of trade are emphasized, this assumption of constant cost appears to be rather restrictive. For one thing, these assumptions, more or less, force us to close our eyes to the demand aspect of the general equilibrium framework, because the relative prices under these circumstances will quite likely be determined independently of the demand conditions. Moreover, no satisfactory explanation is offered as to why such differences in labor costs exist between the countries. Thus, the classical theory amounts to explaining the differences in relative prices of goods between the countries in a somewhat arbitrary fashion by reducing them to differences in labor costs due to "climatic conditions."

Bertil Ohlin, trained in the excellent Swedish tradition of general equilibrium analysis by Wicksell and Cassel and influenced by the outstanding work on this problem by Heckscher [8],[4] shows in his masterly work [26] a full awareness of the importance of general equilibrium analysis. He explains thoroughly, in terms of this analysis, the reasons for the differences in prices and the comparative advantage between countries. Instead of reducing the differences in prices to arbitrary differences in labor cost due to "climatic" conditions, he focuses attention on the differences in the factor endowments by imposing the simplifying assumption that the production functions for a given good are the same in both countries. Under this assumption, he was able to obtain the remarkably simple and intuitively appealing conclusion that a country's exports use the country's abundant factor intensively. He also opened the way for more complicated and more general analyses. Thus, this assumption, although often criticized on grounds of unrealism, really demonstrates Ohlin's excellence as a theoretician. Furthermore, his explicit introduction of the two-factor model instead of the one-factor classical model enabled us to consider important questions such as the distribution of income between factors, the allocation of factors between industries, and so on. It also opened the way for a systematic consideration of such new questions as the effect of capital accumulation and international factor movements on trade.

Thus, Ohlin's treatise turns out to be one of the most important cornerstones in the modern theory of international trade. His model, often called the Heckscher-Ohlin Trade Model, has been followed by many important works and thus has increased in importance. Among the many path breaking contributions following the Heckscher-Ohlin model are: Stolper-Samuelson's application of the model to the effects of a tariff on the distribution of income [34]; Samuelson's treatment of the factor price equalization theorem [30] [31];[5]

---

[4] Heckscher's work, written in Swedish, was originally published in 1919. It was first translated into English in 1949. Metzler pointed out that, "the theory of international trade might have been advanced considerably, in the English-speaking world at any rate, by an earlier translation of Heckscher's pioneering article." (Metzler [21], p. 4.)

[5] There have been developments other than those described in this chapter. Since these developments are beyond the scope of the two-good, two-factor model, we shall take them up later.

Leontief's empirical testing resulting in the Leontief paradox [16]; and Jones' factor intensity argument to explain the Leontief paradox [12].

The purpose of this chapter is not to trace the doctrinal history of these developments,[6] but rather to consider the Heckscher-Ohlin model in its current state systematically by clarifying its logic and the assumptions involved. This chapter is indebted to my work, written in 1962 [35] and published in 1963 [36].

THE HECKSCHER-OHLIN THEOREM

Consider a world consisting of two countries, each being able to produce two goods using the same two factors of production, labor (L) and capital (K), the endowments of which are fixed for each country. We may call these two countries the home country and the foreign country, or the home country and the rest of the world, and so on. Here we will simply call them Country 1 and Country 2. The two goods can be called "linen" and "wine," "food" and "cloth," or the "exportable" and the "importable." Here we will simply call them good X and good Y.

We suppose that the model discussed in Chapter 2 holds for each country. In other words, we assume that the production function for each good is linear homogeneous (that is, constant returns to scale) with the property of diminishing returns, that each factor is fully employed, and that perfect competition prevails in both the goods markets and the factor markets. We then suppose that these two countries engage in international trade. We assume that there is free trade and that goods are mobile internationally as well as domestically with no impediments and with negligible transport costs. We also assume that the factors are mobile domestically with no impediments and with negligible transport costs but are completely immobile internationally either because of prohibitively high transport costs or other impediments, such as immigration laws.

Under these conditions international trade will occur as long as there are differences in the relative domestic goods price ratio, or the ratio of costs of production for the two goods, between the two countries in the absence of trade. Notice that the free trade and no impediments to trade assumptions enable us to compare the pre-trade price ratios of the two countries directly. Thus, if good X is relatively cheaper than good Y in Country 1 compared to Country 2 before trade, then Country 1 will usually export X and import Y after trade. Thus, the production of X increases (decreases) and the production of Y decreases (increases) in Country 1 (Country 2). This will presumably cause an increase in the cost of production of X relative to Y in Country 1 (due to the law of diminishing returns). Thus, the price of X relative to Y will increase in Country 1. Similarly, the price of X relative to Y will decrease in Country 2.

[6] For a doctrinal history, see, for example, Caves [4], Chipman [5], Bhagwati, J., "The Pure Theory of International Trade: A Survey," *Economic Journal*, March 1964, and Corden, W. M., *Recent Developments in the Theory of International Trade*, International Finance Section, Princeton University, 1965. For an easy introduction to the topic, see, Johnson [11].

This process will continue until the goods price ratios are the same in both countries and the equilibrium international price ratio is established.

Notice that the exchange rate for the currencies of the two countries does *not* play an important role in the above consideration. Suppose good X and good Y are traded in the ratio of $1:3$ in Country 1 and the ratio of $1:4$ in Country 2 before the international trade. Then regardless of the exchange rate for the currencies, there exists an incentive for traders in Country 1 (or 2) to bring the output of X from Country 1 to Country 2 and trade it for Y in the ratio of $1:4$, instead of $1:3$. Thus, they could earn a profit by bringing the Y thus acquired in Country 2 to Country 1 and trading it for X at the ratio of $1:3$. The profit will be $(\frac{4}{3} - 1 = \frac{1}{3})$ in terms of good X per unit of X initially brought into Country 2. Similarly, traders can earn a profit by bringing Y from Country 2 to Country 1, trading it for X in Country 1, bringing the X thus acquired to Country 2 and trading it for Y. Obviously, after trade, the pre-trade exchange of the two goods in the two countries will not stay the same, hence the actual profits of these traders will in general be less than the figures based on the pre-trade exchange ratios. However the profit incentive for opening of trade still exists. In fact, international trade can occur *even if* the price ratios are the same in the two countries, for, in the absence of transport costs, and so on, it will make no difference to the producers of either country whether they sell their output to consumers in Country 1 or consumers in Country 2. Notice that money *can* exist in this model as a means of payment and a unit of accounting, as long as we can neglect the macrotheoretic monetary repercussions in the markets.

Now then, what are the factors which cause the differences in the pre-trade goods price ratios? Ohlin [26] correctly recognized that they result from four basic influences: consumer tastes, the distribution of ownership of the factors of production (thus the income distribution), the supplies of these factors, and the physical conditions of production. It should be clear that Ohlin clearly and explicitly recognized the general equilibrium of production and consumption here. Of the four factors, the first two are concerned with demand conditions and Ohlin felt that the last one would exert approximately the same influence in both regions and thus drop out of the picture. In other words, for the physical condition of production, Ohlin assumed that the production function for each good will be the same for both countries. In the recognition of the demand conditions, we see a clear progression from Heckscher to Ohlin. As we shall see later in this chapter, the demand conditions can play a crucial role in the theory to the extent that the conclusions conjectured from the production side of the economy can be reversed depending upon the demand conditions. However, Ohlin himself did not realize their importance and considered them "a mere curiosity" (Caves [4], p. 28).

Thus inquiring into both sides of the economy, demand and production, with the two additional and essential assumptions that the production function for each good is the same in both countries and that the differences in demand conditions are negligible, Ohlin reached the conclusion that the essential factor determining a regional (or international) difference in the price ratio is the difference in the factor endowments of the two regions (countries). This conclusion, known as the Heckscher-Ohlin theorem, can be stated as follows:

THE HECKSCHER-OHLIN THEOREM   Under the above assumptions and the specification of the model, a country exports (imports) that good which is relatively more intensive in the factor which is relatively more (less) abundant in that country.

The above theorem has a strong intuitive appeal. For example, the U.S. which is presumably more capital abundant than the rest of the world, would export those goods which are more capital intensive such as machinery, steel, and so on, and import more labor intensive goods. When we restate the theorem in this way, it looks intuitively quite obvious and was in fact accepted enthusiastically by many economists. After World War II, Leontief thought of testing the above theorem empirically using the input-output technique, a celebrated technique which he originated. His results [16] can be summarized in the following table, where each figure represents the amount of capital or labor necessary to produce one million dollars (in 1947 prices) worth of exported goods or import competing goods.

TABLE 3-1   Leontief's Results

	1947		1951	
	Exported	Imported	Exported	Imported
Capital (1947-$)	2,550,780	3,091,339	2,256,800	2,303,400
Labor (man year)	181.31	170.00	173.91	167.81

The above table, in essence, shows that:

1947: $\dfrac{k_{imp}}{k_{exp}} = 1.3$,

1951: $\dfrac{k_{imp}}{k_{exp}} = 1.1058$,

where k_{exp} denotes the capital:labor ratio in the exporting industries and k_{imp} denotes the capital:labor ratio in the import competing industries. This means that in both 1947 and 1951,

$k_{imp} > k_{exp}$.

In other words, in both 1947 and 1951 the import competing goods are more capital intensive than the goods exported by the United States! Since the U.S. was presumably more capital abundant than the rest of the world, these results by Leontief apparently contradict the Heckscher-Ohlin theorem. This then caused a great deal of concern and excitement among economists. Many attempts were made to explain this result, widely known as the *Leontief paradox*. Leontief [16] himself conjectured that this may be due to the fact that American workers are (three times) more efficient or skillful than the workers in the rest of the world. Thus, if the labor were measured in terms of efficiency units (multiply the U.S. labor force by 3), then the U.S. will, in fact, be more *labor abundant* than the rest of the world.

Although Leontief's explanation reveals a very interesting point, it is still an open question as to how we can conclude that the American workers are three times more efficient or skillful than the workers in the rest of the world. In fact, the meaning of efficient in this context should be clarified too. A more important criticism of such an explanation is that it refutes one of the assumptions underlying the Heckscher-Ohlin theorem—homogeneous labor. In fact, we can also explain the Leontief paradox by refuting any one of several other assumptions of the theorem, and many attempts have been made to explain the paradox in this manner. (For a good summary of these discussions, see Caves [4], pp. 275–281.) For example, the following assumptions have been questioned: [7]

1. the homogeneity of the factors of production domestically (Haberler, Keesing) and internationally (Leontief),
2. the two factors of production (the possibility of multi-factors (Haberler), the neglect of the natural resources (Diab, N. Buchanan, Swerling, and Kravis),
3. the non-existence of the demand bias (R. Robinson, Valvanis-Vail, Brown),
4. that the production functions are identical for the same good in different countries (Ellsworth, Amano, Johnson),[8]
5. the absence of trade restrictions (Travis).

[7] Haberler, G., *A Survey of International Trade Theory*, International Finance Section, Princeton University, 1961 (revised and enlarged ed.); Leontief [16]; Keesing, D., "Labor Skills and International Trade," *Review of Economics and Statistics*, XLVII, August 1965; Diab, M.A., *The United States Capital Position and the Structure of Foreign Trade*, Amsterdam, North-Holland, 1965; Buchanan, N. S., "Lines on the Leontief Paradox," *Economia Internazionale*, 8, November 1955; Sweling, B. C., "Capital Shortage and Labor Surplus," *Review of Economics and Statistics*, XXXVI, August 1954; Kravis, I. B., "Availability and Other Influences on the Commodity Composition of Trade," *Journal of Political Economy*, LXIV, April 1956; Robinson [29]; Valvanis-Vail [40]; Brown [3]; Ellsworth [6]; Johnson, H. G., "Effects of Changes in Comparative Costs as Influenced by Technical Change," in *International Trade Theory in a Developing World*, ed. by Harrod, R. F., and Hague, D. C., London: Macmillan, 1963; Amano, A., "Determinants of Comparative Costs: A Theoretical Approach," *Oxford Economic Papers*, 16, November 1964; Travis, W. P., *The Theory of Trade and Protection* (Cambridge, Mass., Harvard University Press), 1964. Some of these papers are theoretical, while others are empirical. See also the surveys by Caves [4], pp. 273–281 and Chipman [5], 1966, pp. 44–57.

[8] Another interesting comment is due to Valvanis-Vail [40], [41], who argues that the Leontief model with its fixed coefficients of production is incompatible with the continuous factor substitution possible in the neoclassical (Heckscher-) Ohlin model. See also Verdoorn, P. J., "Complementarity and Long Range Projections," *Econometrica*, 24, October 1956.

We shall not discuss the above points any further. After all, any theory is based on a set of assumptions, and a good one depends critically upon those assumptions. Hence, if we were to reject any of the assumptions, it is obvious that we would get different conclusions. Instead of pursuing the explanation of the Leontief paradox by refuting assumptions, we shall attempt to clarify the precise meaning of the Heckscher-Ohlin theorem to see whether or not it is possible to explain the paradox granting *all* the assumptions of the theorem. In other words, here we shall pursue the two lines of analysis: a) one developed in a brilliant paper by Jones, and b) the other explicit recognition of the demand developed by Valvanis-Vail [40], and others. Both will make clear the important assumptions hidden in the Heckscher-Ohlin theorem. Our analysis will be a direct corollary of our discussion in the second section of the previous chapter.

Now if we re-read the statement of the Heckscher-Ohlin theorem carefully, we shall see that the statement of the theorem is not clear. For example, what do we mean when we say that a factor is relatively more "abundant" in a given country? Can we define "labor intensive" or "capital intensive" properly?

The latter, that is, the concept of factor intensity, we simply interpret, for the time being, as the capital:labor ratio, in terms of our notation in Chapter 2, k_x and k_y. Then X is more capital intensive than Y if $k_x > k_y$ and X is more labor intensive if $k_x < k_y$. This definition of factor intensity corresponds to the one adopted by Leontief, and there seems to be no difference on this point between Leontief and Ohlin.

What about the definition that we use to determine whether one factor is more abundant than the other? Leontief defined abundance in terms of the factor endowment ratio. For example, he took Country 1 to be more capital abundant than Country 2 if the capital:labor endowment ratio in Country 1 was higher than that in Country 2. In mathematical notation, Country 1 is more capital abundant than Country 2 if

$$\frac{K_1}{L_1} > \frac{K_2}{L_2}, \quad \text{where the subscripts refer to the country.} \tag{3-1}$$

Similarly, if $K_1/L_1 < K_2/L_2$, Country 1 is said to be more labor abundant than Country 2.

When we read Ohlin again, we find that this definition of abundance does not really coincide with his. Ohlin defined Country 1 as more capital abundant than Country 2, if

$$q_1 > q_2, \quad \text{where } q \equiv w/r \text{ and the subscripts refer to the country.} \tag{3-2}$$

Similarly, Country 1 is said to be more labor abundant if $q_1 < q_2$. In other words, if capital (labor) is relatively cheaper, then the country is said to be capital (labor) abundant country.

If we adopt Ohlin's definition of factor abundance, then the proof of the Heckscher-Ohlin theorem is almost immediate. Let us suppose that X is more capital intensive than $Y(k_x > k_y)$ *for all q*, and recall the corollary of lemma 2 of the previous chapter. Since $k_x > k_y$, $\hat{p} \gtreqless 0$ according to whether $\hat{q} \lesseqgtr 0$. Let us suppose further that Country 1 is more capital abundant than Country 2 (according to Ohlin's definition) so that $q_1 > q_2$. We can illustrate our problem by the following diagram (recall Figure 2-1 and the assumption that the production functions of the same good are identical in the two countries). Since $q_1 > q_2$, $p_2 > p_1$ according to Figure 3-1. In other words, p_x/p_y is smaller

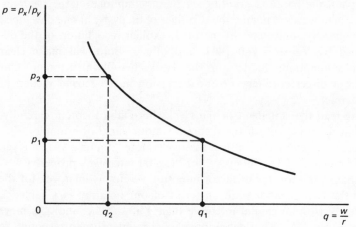

Figure 3-1   The Heckscher-Ohlin Theorem

(X is relatively cheaper than Y) in Country 1, thus Country 1 would export good X and import good Y after trade. But by assumption, X is more capital intensive than Y, and Country 1 is more capital abundant than Country 2. This completes the proof of the Heckscher-Ohlin theorem.

Since the definitions of factor abundance used by Ohlin and Leontief are different, it seems natural that Leontief's empirical observation might not satisfy the Heckscher-Ohlin theorem. A natural question then is whether we can have a situation where Country 1 is more capital abundant (than Country 2) according to Leontief's definition but more labor abundant according to Ohlin's definition ($q_1 < q_2$). If this is the case, then the Leontief paradox can clearly be explained, and the explanation is, in fact, not too difficult to see. Suppose for example that people (in Country 1) have a much stronger preference for good X compared to good Y than people in Country 2. Then, in spite of the fact that Country 1 is more capital abundant than Country 2 (Leontief terminology) so that it has a natural supply bias towards a *lower* opportunity cost for the production of the more capital intensive good X, it is possible that the price of good X relative to Y in Country 1 is in fact higher than that of Country 2. Thus after trade, Country 1 which is more capital abundant as conceived by Leontief exports the more labor intensive good Y and imports the more capital intensive good X. Since p_x/p_y is higher in Country 1 than in Country 2, the factor price ratio $q = w/r$ is lower in Country 1 than in Country 2 ($\therefore$ recall $k_x > k_y$). (Recall Figure 3-1.) That is, $q_1 < q_2$, so that Country 1 is more labor abundant (Ohlin terminology). This is the essence of the *demand bias* argument which is due to R. Robinson [29], Valvanis-Vail [40], and so on.[9]

Can we then conclude that the Heckscher-Ohlin theorem is entirely correct as proved above and that the Leontief paradox is solely due to the demand bias? The answer is "no." In other words, the above proof of the Heckscher-Ohlin theorem is not necessarily correct. The trouble lies in the assumption $k_x > k_y$. There we assumed that the relation $k_x > k_y$ holds for *all* the equilibrium states, or, more precisely, for *all* the equilibrium factor price ratios, q. This statement is not necessarily true. In lemma 4 of the previous chapter we proved that both k_x and k_y are monotone increasing functions of q. But we have not shown that $k_x > k_y$ (or $k_x < k_y$) for all q. It is perfectly possible to conceive of the case illustrated in Figure 3-2. And it is not too difficult to find a situation in which this will occur.

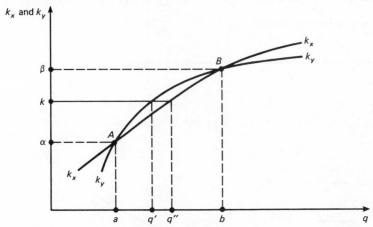

Figure 3-2   Factor Intensity Reversals

In Figure 3-2 notice that $k_x > k_y$ if $q < a$ and $k_x < k_y$ if $(b >) q > a$ and that $k_x > k_y$ again if $q > b$. The points a and b (or the corresponding points A and B) or α and β are called the points of *factor intensity reversal*, because they are the points at which the factor intensity relation (the relative size) is reversed. Note that it is possible to conceive of any number of factor intensity reversals. This phenomenon of the factor intensity reversal was first noticed by Lerner [19] in 1933.[10] It can easily be shown that if the production functions of both goods are of the Cobb-Douglas type, then there will be no such factor intensity reversals. It will be shown in the next section that if the production functions of both goods have constant elasticities of substitution which are

[9] Note that demand bias can exist even if both countries have identical consumers' tastes (the same indifference map). People in Country 1 can have a stronger preference for good X relative to good Y compared with people in Country 2 if they are in different income positions and if the utility function is not linear homogeneous (homothetic). This is the point raised by Robinson [29]. In the next section of this chapter, we shall deal with demand bias again, which should clarify any ambiguities still remaining in the reader's mind.

[10] This was later (independently of Lerner) discovered by Pearce [27], [28].

different, then a factor intensity reversal will always occur and occur only once.

Now, if we admit the possibility of factor intensity reversals, then we can no longer accept the above proof of the Heckscher-Ohlin theorem as it is. This point was pursued by Jones [12] and followed up by Johnson [10]. Their argument can best be illustrated by Figure 3-3, which is known as the Harrod-Johnson diagram.[11]

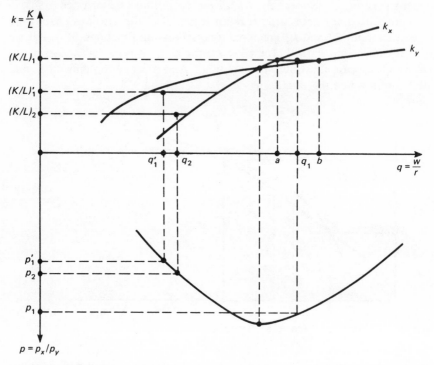

Figure 3-3   Harrod-Johnson Diagram

Notice that in Figure 3-3, Country 1 is more capital abundant than Country 2 according to either the Leontief or the Ohlin definition.[12] Yet $p_1 > p_2$ so that

---

[11] The diagram, in this form, is used by Johnson [10]. He attributes the *original* idea to Harrod, R. F., "Factor-Price Relations Under Free Trade," [7], which was presented at the conference of the British Association of University Teachers of Economics, January 1957. (Johnson [10], p. 18). However, a similar diagram had already been used by Samuelson ([31], p. 188) in 1949. In 1956, Jones also used a similar diagram ([12], p. 9). Incidentally, Harrod's attitude toward the Heckscher-Ohlin Theorem and the factor price equalization theorem is a very suspicious one. His basic approach is to emphasize factors that are *specific* to each country. See also Harrod, R. F., *International Economics*, London, James Nisbet Press, 4th ed., 1957.

[12] Note that the factor endowment ratio of a country determines the range in which its factor price ratio can vary. For example, if Country 1's endowment ratio is given by $(K/L)_1$, then the range of its factor price ratios is given by a and b (Figure 3-3). As long as the factor price ratio (say, of Country 1) lies inside the range (a, b), Country 1 will produce both goods. However, if $q_1 = a$ (respectively $q_1 = b$), then at this factor price ratio, q_1, Country 1 produces only good X (respectively good Y).

Country 1 exports good Y and imports good X. Note that X is more capital intensive in Country 1 and more labor intensive in Country 2.[13] The Leontief paradox holds for Country 1 which is more capital abundant and exports its more labor intensive good, Y.

Now suppose that the factor endowment ratio for Country 1 is given by $(K/L)_1'$ and the factor price ratio of Country 1 is given by q_1' in Figure 3-3. Then Country 1 is more capital abundant in the sense of Leontief and labor abundant in the sense of Ohlin ($\because q_1' < q_2$). Note that X is now more labor intensive than Y for *both* countries. Since $p_1' < p_2$ in the diagram, Country 1 exports the more labor intensive good X. This is a clear and precise account of the above-mentioned explanation of the Leontief paradox in terms of demand bias.

Now we shall briefly discuss the possibility of complete specialization. The discussion can best be illustrated by Figure 3-4. In this figure suppose that the

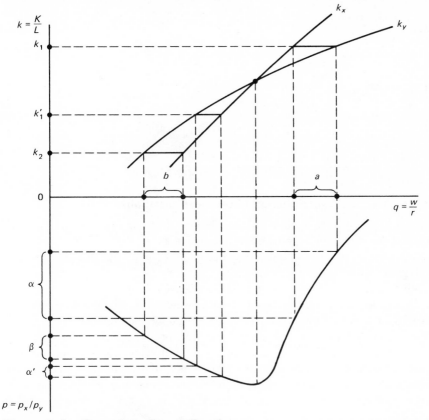

Figure 3-4   Complete Specialization

factor endowment ratio of Country 1 is given by k_1, then the range of Country 1's factor price ratios is given by a. Corresponding to this range a, we have the range in which Country 1's goods price ratios can vary. The range of Country 1's

[13] Note that Jones' diagram, Figure 3-5 (p. 9 [12]), contains an important misprint.

goods price ratios is denoted by α in the diagram. Similarly, we have the range for Country 2's goods price ratios (β), corresponding to her endowment ratio k_2. Note that α and β do *not* overlap. What happens if free trade opens between the countries? Clearly in Figure 3-4 we cannot have a common goods price ratio for the two countries. In other words, this diagram based on the two-good world is inconsistent with international trade. The opening of free trade thus forces at least one of the countries to produce only one good (instead of two). In other words, at least one country must completely specialize in the production of one good.[14] In terms of the production transformation diagram, the international goods price ratio determined after trade comes to the corner of the transformation curve. This is illustrated by Figure 3-5. In Figure 3-5, point A

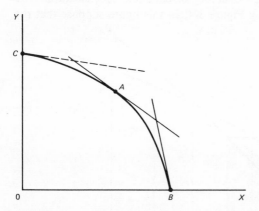

Figure 3-5   Corner Solution (Complete Specialization)

denotes the production point in the absence of trade, and point B (or C) denotes the production point after trade of a particular country. Note that after trade, this country produces only one good X (or Y), but that she produced both good X and good Y before trade.

What then do we know about the Heckscher-Ohlin theorem? In the process of discussing the Leontief paradox, it became clear that the terminology of the theorem was not really explicit. The clear meanings of "relative factor abundance" and "relative factor intensity" are not well recognized. The discussion of demand bias by Valvanis, and others, made it clear that a country can be more capital abundant in Leontief's terminology but more labor abundant in Ohlin's terminology. The consideration of "factor intensity reversals" as conceived by Lerner, Jones, and others, made it clear that a good which is more

[14] Note that the existence of a factor intensity reversal is not crucial for this argument. For example, if the factor endowment ratio of Country 1 is given by k_1' in Figure 3-4, the range of Country 1's good prices is α' and α' and β again do not overlap. If, on the other hand, the ranges of the goods price ratios of the two countries overlap (as in Figure 3-3) and contain an interior point (that is, overlap for a certain interval rather than at a single point), then both countries will keep producing the two goods after trade. For a more detailed discussion of this point, see Johnson [10].

capital intensive in one country can be more labor intensive in the other country. This gives rise to the possibility, as discussed in connection with Figure 3-3, that a country that is *capital* abundant in both the Leontief and Ohlin terminologies can export the more *labor* intensive good and import the more capital intensive good. Hence, we now know that the intuitively appealing Heckscher-Ohlin theorem is not clearly stated unless the demand conditions and factor intensity relations have been specified. That is, the Heckscher-Ohlin theorem holds if, and only if, the demand conditions and factor intensity relations have been correctly specified.

This theorem also sheds some light on the methodological questions in the empirical testing of theories. It illustrates that we cannot be sure that a given empirical test is even relevant unless the theorem has been precisely stated and its logic completely clarified.[15]

Finally, we should comment on the assumption of identical production functions for the same good in the two countries in the Heckscher-Ohlin theorem. As noted previously, this assumption lies at the heart of the Heckscher-Ohlin trade model as compared to the classical trade model. It is certainly possible to generalize the model so that the production functions for the same good can be different in the two countries. But the result of such attempts is already obvious. Since there can be no convincing or a priori way of describing the differences between the production functions of the same good in the two countries, we will not be able to obtain any transparent and definite results. The conclusions will depend, *in a somewhat arbitrary fashion*, on the way that the production functions for the same good differ between the countries. Hence, such attempts could even be considered as making negative progress in the theory. Clearly, Heckscher and Ohlin and the followers of their trade model must have realized that, in reality, the production functions might be different between countries. But they adopted this assumption as a useful approximation for the theory and thus obtained their transparent and definite results.[16] One way to justify this assumption is to say that technological know-how can be transmitted between the countries, that the differences in technological know-how (production functions) amount to items such as patent costs and that these costs are negligible. The assumption of negligible patent costs may be considered as analogous to the assumption of negligible transport cost.

However, this does not imply that the consideration of different production functions is useless.[17] Although we can justify the assumption of identical

[15] We should say, however, that such empirical testing is still better than mere curve-fitting, which is not a test of anything.

[16] We may note, however, that there is one important study that has been left undone. That is a careful empirical study which shows the extent and the nature of differences in production functions between countries and reveals how seriously these differences undermine the validity of the Heckscher-Ohlin theorem. Without such empirical studies, the theorem can hardly make any progress.

[17] A recent revival of discussions about the factor price equalization theorem and the Stolper-Samuelson theorem convinces us that we are on the verge of a breakthrough in the development of a true multi-sector, multi-factor international trade model.

production functions as a reasonable approximation under certain circumstances, this may not be the case under other circumstances. In other words, the conclusions that will explain reality may crucially depend on this assumption, as in the case when we consider trade between the Western countries and the Afro-Asian countries (with the possible exception of Japan). But then we also have to question the validity of the above neoclassical model in the Afro-Asian countries, because it involves the assumptions of perfect competition, marginal productivity theory, free mobility of factors between industries, a two-factor model which does not consider the role of land explicitly, and so on.

CONSIDERATION OF SPECIAL CASES

In the previous section we presented a logical exposition of the Heckscher-Ohlin theorem and showed the process of clarification of this theorem in connection with the Leontief paradox. In this section we shall consider some special cases of the theorem. Although our concern will be with special cases, we shall attempt not to lose too much generality. That is, we shall consider the special cases which are fairly acceptable. This consideration is important because the Heckscher-Ohlin theorem, as we saw in the previous section, depends on specifications of such things as the demand conditions and the factor intensity relations, and because the empirical testing of a theory often requires some special conditions in order to make such a test possible at all.

The Case of CES[18] Production Functions

Here we suppose that the production function for each industry is of the *CES* type, that is, the elasticity of factor substitution in each industry is *constant*. In other words, we suppose that the

$$\sigma_i \equiv \left(\frac{dk_i}{k_i}\right) \bigg/ \left(\frac{dq}{q}\right), \quad i = x, y, \text{ where } q \equiv \frac{w}{r}, \tag{3-3}$$

are constant. This type of production function was first envisioned by Arrow and Solow and has been widely recognized as a very important (especially empirically) type of production function[19] since the publication of Arrow, Chenery, Minhas, and Solow [1]. This type of production function is known to have the following form (taking X as an example):

$$X = L_x\{a[\alpha + (1 - \alpha)k_x{}^\delta]^{1/\delta}\}, \quad \text{where } \alpha, a > 0 \text{ are some constants,}$$

$\delta \equiv (\sigma_x - 1)/\sigma_x$ (σ_x: the elasticity of factor substitution in the X industry) and

$$k_x \equiv K_x/L_x. \tag{3-4}$$

---

[18] "CES" stands for "Constant Elasticity of Substitution." Minhas calls the CES production functions *homohypallagic* production functions.

[19] For a recent survey of studies concerning CES production functions, see Nerlove [25]. Chipman [5] also gives useful surveys of empirical studies of the Heckscher-Ohlin theorem and the Leontief paradox using CES production functions.

It can be shown fairly easily that the above production function becomes the Leontief type (no factor substitution) and the Cobb-Douglas type production function respectively in the limits $\sigma_x \to 0$ and $\sigma_x \to 1$.[20] First we obtain the following lemma.

LEMMA   If the elasticity of factor substitution is constant in the ith industry $(i = x, y)$, we have the following unique relation between the factor intensity and the factor price ratio:

$$k_i = (\lambda_i q)^{\sigma_i}, \quad i = x, y, \text{ where the } \lambda_i \text{s are some constants.} \tag{3-5}$$

PROOF   From the definition of σ_i, we obtain

$$\sigma_i \frac{dq}{q} = \frac{dk_i}{k_i}, \quad i = x, y. \tag{3-6}$$

Integrating both sides of the above equation and taking the constant of integration properly we obtain (3-5).   (Q.E.D.)

REMARK   If we write each production function in the form of equation (3-4), then we can show that $\lambda_i = \beta_i / \alpha_i$, where $\beta_i = 1 - \alpha_i$, $i = x, y$.

Now taking the logarithm of both sides of equation (3-5), we have

$$\tilde{k}_i = \sigma_i \tilde{q} + \sigma_i \tilde{\lambda}_i, \quad i = x, y; \quad \text{where } \tilde{k}_i \equiv \log k_i, \quad \tilde{q} \equiv \log q,$$

and $\tilde{\lambda}_i \equiv \log \lambda_i$. $\tag{3-7}$

Hence the function which relates the factor intensity to the factor price ratio can be drawn in Figure 3-6. In this diagram the k_x and k_y curves are now drawn as straight lines! Therefore the following remarkable theorem is immediately obtained.

THEOREM   If the elasticity of factor substitution for each industry is constant and the same in the two industries, then factor intensity reversals will never occur. On the other hand, if the elasticity of factor substitution for each industry is constant and different for the two industries, then a factor intensity reversal can always occur but occur only once.[21]

---

[20] Hence the CES type of production function constitutes quite a large class of production functions, for α can range from 0 to $+\infty$. Empirically, however, it is generally believed that σ lies somewhere between 0 and 1. See Arrow, Chenery, Minhas, and Solow [1] and Nerlove [25], for example.

[21] This theorem and the above proof are originally due to Takayama [37] (also in [35] and [36]). Minhas [24] was the first article published showing this theorem and a proof. The proof of [37] seems to be much simpler than that of [24]. However [37] was not accepted for publication. [24] is better than [37] in that it contains empirical findings. (Note, however, that some objections have recently been raised against these empirical findings. Apparently, some computational errors are involved.)

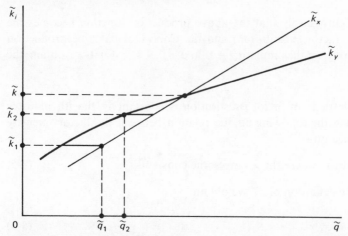

Figure 3-6 The Factor Intensity Relation for the CES Production Functions

REMARK A special example of the theorem is the case in which the production function of each industry is of the Cobb-Douglas type, that is, $\sigma_i = $ constant $= 1, i = x, y$. In this case, as stated in the theorem, a factor intensity reversal will never occur. Note that the conclusion of the above theorem clearly does not depend on the assumption of a two-sector economy. In other words, the theorem holds when there are any number of industries in each country.[22]

When the elasticity of factor substitution is constant and different for the two industries, a factor intensity reversal can, as stated in the theorem, always occur. Whether such a reversal actually occurs or not clearly depends on the factor endowment ratios of the two countries, that is, $k_1 \equiv K_1/L_1$, and $k_2 \equiv K_2/L_2$. As is clear from Figure 3-6, if the difference between k_1 and k_2 is sufficiently large (so that the difference between $\tilde{k}_1 = \log k_1$ and $\tilde{k}_2 = \log k_2$ is sufficiently large), there is a greater probability of a factor intensity reversal. Since the slopes of the $\tilde{k}_x$ and $\tilde{k}_y$ curves depend on σ_x and σ_y respectively, this probability also depends on σ_x and σ_y. If there is not much difference between the factor endowment ratios (which would be the case among European countries), then the factor intensity reversal problem with the Heckscher-Ohlin theorem would probably not occur.

The point of intersection of the $\tilde{k}_x$ and $\tilde{k}_y$ curves in Figure 3-6 can easily be obtained by eliminating $\tilde{q}$ from equation (3-7). Letting the value of the factor endowment ratio at the intersection be k, we get

$$\tilde{k} = \frac{\sigma_x \sigma_y}{\sigma_y - \sigma_x} (\tilde{\lambda}_x - \tilde{\lambda}_y), \quad \text{where } \tilde{k} \equiv \log k . \tag{3-8}$$

[22] In this connection we realize that the two-good assumption of the Heckscher-Ohlin theorem is not crucial. Rather the two-factor assumption is crucial in the sense that we cannot use phrases such as "more labor intensive" or "more capital intensive" otherwise. However, there have been attempts recently to extend the theorem to a multi-factor model. The basic problem there is extending the concept of relative factor intensity to a multi-factor model.

If $\tilde{q}_2 > \tilde{q}_1$, where $\tilde{q}_2$ and $\tilde{q}_1$ are as defined in the diagram, then the ranges of factor price ratios of the two countries will not overlap, and complete specialization will occur at least in one country. The condition of $\tilde{q}_2 > \tilde{q}_1$ can easily be rewritten as

$$(\tilde{k}_2 - \sigma_y\tilde{\lambda}_y)/\sigma_y > (\tilde{k}_1 - \sigma_x\tilde{\lambda}_x)/\sigma_x . \tag{3-9}$$

Condition (3-9) can easily be rewritten as

$$\sigma_x\tilde{k}_2 - \sigma_y\tilde{k}_1 + \sigma_x\sigma_y(\tilde{\lambda}_x - \tilde{\lambda}_y) > 0 . \tag{3-10}$$

The Effect of Demand Conditions—The Case in Which One Good Is the Capital Good

The nature of two goods in the Heckscher-Ohlin Theorem is not usually explicitly specified. A common specification is either that both goods are consumption goods and there is no depreciation of the capital input K, or that one or both goods can be used as capital goods as well as consumption goods and a constant proportion of such goods is devoted to augmenting the depreciating capital stock so that $K = $ constant. Suppose we alter this interpretation slightly so that one good (say, X) is explicitly designated as the capital good and the other good (Y) is the consumption good. A portion of the annual output of X will be devoted to replacing the depreciated capital. Let us now consider implications of this specification of the Heckscher-Ohlin model. In the subsequent analysis, we shall *not* have to assume $K = $ constant, so that the conclusions will hold even for a non-stationary (for example, growing) economy.

Given this specification of the nature of the goods, let us further suppose that demand conditions are such that the workers are the only consumers and the capitalists are the only savers. With these conditions we should be able to obtain a stronger conclusion than before. In order to consider the present problem, we shall make the following suppositions. Suppose first that the two countries are exactly identical (that is, they have the same factor endowment ratio). Suppose further that there is a change in the factor endowment ratio in Country 1. If, after this change, the price of X relative to Y increases in Country 1 vis-à-vis Country 2, we may conclude that Country 1 has a comparative advantage in good Y. (In other words, if trade between the countries starts after such a change, Country 1 will export Y and import X.)

Again writing w: wage rate, r: rent, p_x: the price of X, p_y: the price of Y, L: the labor endowment, and K: the capital endowment, we can write the above conditions on the goods and the demand for the goods as follows:

$$wL = p_yY \quad \text{and} \quad rK = p_xX . \tag{3-11}$$

Initially (that is, before the change in endowments) (3-11) describes the demand conditions for both countries. Now there is a change in L and/or K in Country 1. We can rewrite (3-11) in variational form as

$$\hat{w} + \hat{L} = \hat{p}_y + \hat{Y} \quad \text{and} \quad \hat{r} + \hat{K} = \hat{p}_x + \hat{X} , \quad \text{where } \hat{w} \equiv dw/w ,$$
$$\hat{L} \equiv dL/L , \quad \hat{p}_y = dp_y/p_y , \quad \text{and so on.} \tag{3-12}$$

Combining (3-12) with lemmas 2 and 5 of Chapter 2 (second section), we can immediately obtain

$$\hat{p} = -H(\hat{K} - \hat{L}), \quad \text{where } p \equiv p_x/p_y, \tag{3-13}$$

and $H > 0$ as long as $k_x > k_y$. For the sake of simplicity let us assume that the capital good is *always* more capital intensive than the consumption good in both countries, so that $k_x > k_y$. Then from (3-13), $\hat{K} > \hat{L}$ implies that $\hat{p} < 0$. In other words, we can unambiguously conclude that the relatively more capital abundant country in the sense of Leontief (that is, $\hat{K} > \hat{L}$) will *always* export the capital good X (since $\hat{p} < 0$). In other words, under the present specification the problem of demand bias disappears and the problem of factor intensity reversals is singled out as the most important problem. Recall that the above conclusion holds even for a *non-stationary* economy.

Demand Bias and Supply Bias

Let us come back to the original Heckscher-Ohlin model so that both goods are considered as consumption goods with the assumption of a stationary state. Here we want to obtain conditions necessary for a supply bias and demand bias to exist. In order to sharpen our analysis, we assume that there are *no* factor intensity reversals so that X is always more capital intensive than Y in *both* countries.

We again suppose that both countries are identical in the beginning and then suppose that the factor endowment of Country 1 changes. We can conclude that Country 1 will export Y and import X after this change (and after trade opens) if and only if the price of X relative to Y increases in Country 1 compared to Country 2 after this change in the factor endowments.

If the capital:labor endowment ratio in Country 1 increases after the change, we have $\hat{K} > \hat{L}$. Using lemmas 2 and 5, we obtain

$$\tilde{D}\hat{p} = -C(\hat{K} - \hat{L}) + (\hat{X} - \hat{Y}),$$

where $p = p_x/p_y$ and $\tilde{D} = D/(\Gamma_y - \Gamma_x) > 0$. $\tag{3-14}$

Let us suppose $\hat{X} = \hat{Y}$ so that the proportion of outputs of the two goods is the same in Country 1 before and after the change in the factor endowment. Since $\tilde{D}, C > 0$ by the assumption that $k_x > k_y$ (no factor intensity reversals), $\hat{K} > \hat{L}$ implies unambiguously that $\hat{p} < 0$ due to equation (3-14). This really proves rigorously the situation which was described by Jones as follows: [23]

> If the output of the two commodities is in the same proportion in both countries, the relatively capital abundant country will be able to expand its production of the capital intensive commodity at a lower opportunity cost than the other country ([12], p. 3).

---

[23] Jones did not provide the proof of this statement in his published article [12], although he had an elegant diagrammatical proof in his Ph.D. dissertation at M.I.T. from which [12] was taken. The mathematical proof given here is a simple corollary of our model.

This is called the *bias on the supply side* by Jones. We shall simply call it the *supply bias*.

In other words, the more capital abundant country (in the sense of Leontief) has the above advantage of producing the more capital intensive good (the supply bias). In order for the demand bias to exist, the consumers must have a strong preference for the more labor intensive good, so that this outweighs the supply bias. That is to say, there exists a demand bias when Country 1 has a comparative advantage in the labor intensive good (that is, Y) after an increase in the capital:labor endowment ratio. That is, $p > 0$ gives a necessary and sufficient condition for the demand bias to exist. Hence, due to equation (3-14), a necessary and sufficient condition for the demand bias to exist can be written as [24]

$$-C(\hat{K} - \hat{L}) + (\hat{X} - \hat{Y}) > 0, \quad \text{where } \hat{K} - \hat{L} > 0. \tag{3-15}$$

If $\hat{X} - \hat{Y} < 0$, this condition does not hold and the demand bias does not exist. Hence a necessary condition for the demand bias to exist is $\hat{X} - \hat{Y} > 0$.

A necessary and sufficient condition for the demand bias to exist when Country 1 is more *labor* abundant ($\hat{K} < \hat{L}$) can analogously be obtained as

$$-C(\hat{K} - \hat{L}) + (\hat{X} - \hat{Y}) < 0, \quad \text{where } \hat{K} - \hat{L} < 0. \tag{3-16}$$

Hence a necessary condition for the demand bias to exist in this case is $\hat{X} < \hat{Y}$.

We can illustrate the supply bias and demand bias described above by Figure 3-7, where it is assumed that $k_x > k_y$ and $\hat{K} > \hat{L}$. In this diagram the tangent price line at B is less steep than the tangent price line at A, which illustrates the supply bias. Note also that the tangent line at C is steeper than the tangent line at A, which shows the demand bias.

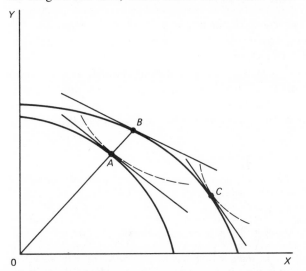

Figure 3-7   Supply Bias and Demand Bias

[24] It is important to note that what we are showing here is that demand bias occurs [and the condition for this can be written as (3-15)] *even if* we assume that every individual in *both* countries has the same tastes and utility function.

THE FACTOR PRICE EQUALIZATION THEOREM AND THE STOLPER-SAMUELSON THEOREM

As mentioned previously, two theorems, in addition to the Leontief paradox, have played important roles in clarifying the structure of the Heckscher-Ohlin trade model. Since these theorems are interesting in themselves and also because they have led to new discussions [25] such as the Gale-Nikaido theorem, we shall discuss them individually here. We shall take up the new developments in a later chapter.

The Factor Price Equalization Theorem

The factor price equalization theorem asserts that the relative and absolute prices of the factors of production [26] will eventually be equalized between the countries.

This theorem had been conceived and proved by Heckscher in 1919 [8]. Ohlin was ambiguous about the theorem, asserting only with many (unnecessary) qualifications that there is a tendency towards equalization. In 1933 Lerner [19] took up this theorem and proved it. But as Caves ([4], p. 76) puts it, neither Heckscher [8] nor Lerner [19] "became generally known to Anglo-American economists until after 1948 [30], when Samuelson advanced the propositions." [27] Then the formal proofs by Samuelson [31] and Tinbergen [39] appeared. As mentioned before, these two papers were followed by many others and played an important role in clarifying the meaning of the Heckscher-Ohlin trade model.

The assumptions and specifications necessary for the factor price equalization theorem are the same as those discussed in the second section. Briefly speaking they are: a two-country, two-good, two-factor world; perfect competition; full employment of the factors; free trade; no transport costs; no international mobility of factors; identical production functions for the same good in both countries; constant returns to scale with diminishing returns; and no joint production. In the factor price equalization theorem, we have to add the new assumption that *both* countries should continue to produce both goods after the opening of trade, that is, the assumption of *incomplete specialization*. The theorem is stated below.

[25] For a survey of these discussions, see Chipman [5], 1966.

[26] It must go without saying by now that "factor price" in the discussions of Chapter 2 and Chapter 3 means the price of a factor *service* and not the price of the factor itself.

[27] The following editorial remark about Lerner [19] by *Economica* may be of interest.

> The following article was prepared by Professor Lerner for a seminar at the London School of Economics in December 1933. It is the paper referred to by Professor Samuelson in his article, "International Factor-Price Equalization Once Again," *Economic Journal*, June 1949, p. 181. It is reproduced here as it was originally written; and it will be of value to students both for its place in the history of ideas and also for the geometric technique employed to demonstrate conditions for the equalization of factor prices (*Economica*, February 1952, p. 1).

THE FACTOR PRICE EQUALIZATION THEOREM   Under the above assumptions and the specifications of the model, the relative and absolute prices of factors will eventually be equalized between the countries.

If the factors of production are freely mobile internationally, then this theorem will be trivially true. In other words, the remarkable feature of this theorem lies in the assertion that even with the complete absence of international factor mobility, the competitive forces through free trade in *goods* will equalize the *factor prices* between the countries.

Since we have obtained a precise understanding of the Heckscher-Ohlin theorem earlier in this chapter, we can prove this theorem immediately and clarify the conditions under which this theorem is true. First, note that the assumption of incomplete specialization requires that there be no factor intensity reversal between the ranges of the factor price ratios of the two countries. In fact, this assumption requires that these two factor price ratio ranges overlap. Now the proof of the theorem can immediately be shown from the Harrod-Johnson diagram (Figure 3-8). As the prices of the goods are equalized between the countries (p_1 and $p_2 \rightarrow p$) by the initiation of free trade, the factor price ratios will be equalized between the countries (q_1 and $q_2 \rightarrow q$) (Figure 3-8).

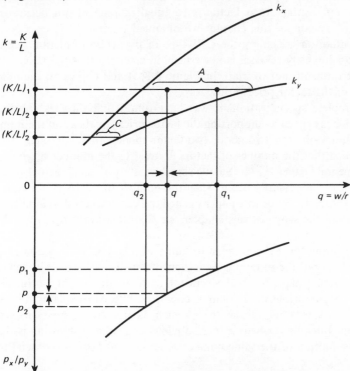

Figure 3-8   The Factor Price Equalization Theorem

In order to see that the absolute factor prices will also be equalized, we recall the factor allocation equation in marginal productivity theory discussed in the previous chapter. That is,

$$w = p_i \mu_i, \quad r = p_i v_i, \quad i = x, y,$$ (3-17)

where μ_i and v_i are the marginal productivities of labor and capital respectively in the ith industry. Due to the assumption of diminishing returns ($f'' < 0$ and $g'' < 0$), μ_i and v_i are single-valued monotone functions with respect to k_i ($i = x, y$). Moreover, lemma 4 of the second section, Chapter 2, asserts that the k_is ($i = x, y$) are single-valued monotone functions of q. Hence, if the relative factor prices q are equalized between the countries, then k_is are also equalized. Thus the values of μ_i and v_i ($i = x, y$) will be the same between the two countries. Hence, since the goods prices p_x and p_y are equalized by trade, w and r must also be equalized between the countries. Moreover, the real factor prices w/p_i and r/p_i ($i = x, y$) must also be equalized between the countries.

It should be clear that the theorem crucially depends on the assumption of incomplete specialization. If, for example, the ranges of the factor price ratios of the two countries are separated by a factor intensity reversal so that these two ranges do not overlap, then factor price equalization will not occur. In fact, in the third section of this chapter we obtained relation (3-9) as a condition for this situation, assuming the *CES* type of production function. Note also that a factor intensity reversal is not crucial in asserting that the ranges of the factor price ratios do not overlap. In Figure 3-8, A and C give an example of such ranges of the factor price ratios.

Besides incomplete specialization, it was later found that there is another assumption which is crucial in supporting the factor price equalization theorem. This is the assumption of a two-good, two-factor model. In this model, it is implicitly assumed that the number of factors is equal to the number of goods. In his monumental paper [33], Samuelson has shown that factor price equalization will not necessarily occur when the number of goods is not equal to the number of factors. Since this paper opened the way for new developments that are not within the scope of this chapter, we shall take them up in a later chapter.

It is always exciting for a theoretician to find that a certain assumption of a theory is indeed crucial for obtaining a particular conclusion, especially when the theory does not explain the real world too well. In the actual world, we know that the factor prices differ among countries. We can explain this by negating certain assumptions of the theory such as free trade, no transport costs, and so on. But this is obvious. Less obvious and more interesting is the fact that the assumption of the same number of goods and factors is crucial to the conclusion.

Should we then discard the factor price equalization theorem at once? The answer seems to be no. First, this theorem contains a very important element of truth and may be appropriate for a certain interesting situation. This is the position that Hicks took. Second, this theorem opened the way for new developments in theory. Hence, even if we do not agree with the above Hicksian contention and want to discard the two-good, two-factor assumption, it is important to understand and appreciate the importance of this theorem as a stepping stone to the later developments in the theory.

Let us now take the first position. In essence, this theorem states that when we *can* aggregate the factors into two factors (labor and capital) and similarly aggregate the goods into two goods, *then* the prices of these aggregated factors will equalize, provided that the above assumptions are all satisfied. Understanding the theorem in this way, Hicks [9] believes that this theorem gives a good approximation of the real world when we consider the situation "in the very long run." The following quotation from Hicks ([9], pp. 266–267) will be useful for understanding this and will also raise certain methodological questions about economic theory.

> As things are in fact, at any particular time, the capital stock of any country is by no means an undifferentiated stock of productive power; it is embodied in a wide variety of useful things of high specificity. Nor is the labour force an undifferentiated mass; the skills and abilities that are possessed are themselves also highly specific. There is nothing surprising, in a world of this sort, in the discovery that there are great international inequalities in factor prices. . . . But is that the whole story? If it were the whole story, we should have to conclude that the theorem we have been examining is a mere curiosity; the sooner we leave it, and go back to something more sensible, the better. I do not believe that this is quite right. There are problems of international economics for which Samuelson's assumptions, or nearer to those assumptions, may be more appropriate. Instead of asking what explains the things which happen now, suppose we ask the more hypothetical, but nevertheless exceedingly interesting, question: suppose that there was a régime of universal free trade, without factor movements, how should we expect that things, in the very long run, would work themselves out? . . . It is not unreasonable to suppose that in this long run, capital stocks . . . could be transformed into whatever form was most appropriate; many specificities in the capital stock can thereafter be taken to disappear. And whatever differences at present exist in the capacities of the labour forces of different nations, may also (I think) be neglected. . . . To the problem thus posed the Samuelson model does seem to be appropriate—not perfectly appropriate, but as appropriate as any simple model is likely to be.

A possible modification of the theorem that Hicks considers important is the possibility of increasing returns to scale, for it is likely to lead to a world of complete specialization.

The above favorable remark on the two-good, two-factor world was written before the full-scale development of the theory by Gale-Nikaido, Kuhn, Chipman, McKenzie, and so on, as surveyed in Chipman [5]. An interesting comment was recently made by Arrow. In his article[28] celebrating the collection of Samuelson's works, he commented on Samuelson's work on the factor price equalization theorem [30], [31], and [33] and the Stolper-Samuelson Theorem [34] as follows:

> Determination of factor prices by commodity prices: . . . In a sense, this research is complementary to that on non-substitution theorems, since it gives more prominence to the multiplicity of factors. But these studies represent the first major effort to go beyond the general Walrasian principle that prices are simultaneously determined to a more specific analysis of the interrelations (p. 732).[29]

The Stolper-Samuelson Theorem: The Effects of a Tariff on the Income Distribution

An important application of the Heckscher-Ohlin trade model appearing immediately after the publication of Ohlin's work was a paper by Stolper and Samuelson [34]. There they considered the effects of the imposition of a tariff on the distribution of income between the factors and concluded that the imposition of an import tariff would increase the reward to the country's relatively scarce factor. This assertion, known as the *Stolper-Samuelson Theorem*, is interesting in itself and prompted the clarification of the Heckscher-Ohlin trade model, together with the factor price equalization theorem and the Leontief paradox, and furthermore became a stepping stone for recent developments in the theory by Chipman, McKenzie, and so on.[30]

The Stolper-Samuelson theorem basically inherits the assumptions of the Heckscher-Ohlin trade model: a two-country, two-good, two-factor world; perfect competition; full employment; no transport costs; complete international immobility of factors; constant returns to scale and diminishing returns; and so on. Now suppose that the two countries in the world are engaged in free trade, each country producing both goods. *Then* suppose that one of the countries decides to impose an import tariff. The problem is to consider the effects of such a tariff on the distribution of income between the factors.[31] In

---

[28] Arrow, K. J., "Samuelson Collected," *Journal of Political Economy*, October 1967.

[29] Such a specific analysis of the interrelations has made the search for a multi-factor, multi-good model more than a mere curiosity, and thus has led to the later significant developments.

[30] For a survey of these developments, again see Chipman [5], 1966.

[31] This kind of problem is not new in the history of economic doctrines. Although the one factor (= labor) assumption prohibited the effective analysis of such problems in the classical theory, there were still some interesting studies with the introduction of concepts such as noncompeting groups and specific factors. See, for example, Bastable, C. R., *The Theory of International Trade*, London: Macmillan 1903 (4th ed.) and Cairnes, J. E., *Some Principles of Political Economy Newly Expounded*, New York: Harper & Brothers, 1874. In such cases the abolition of an import tariff will clearly damage the position of the factors which are specific to the import competing industry, for, by definition, these factors cannot easily be transferred to other industries. This discussion caused much debate among (neo-) classical economists such as Bastable, Sidgwick, Nicholson, and Edgeworth. The first important analysis with an explicit introduction of two factors into the model is due to Wicksell, K.,

order to analyze this problem,[32] Stolper and Samuelson imposed the following three assumptions. These assumptions will be crucially important in their theory.

ASSUMPTION 1   A country imports (exports) a good relatively more intensive in the factor which is relatively scarce (abundant) in that country.

ASSUMPTION 2   The imposition of an import tariff will increase the domestic price of the import competing good relative to that of the export good.

ASSUMPTION 3   The trade pattern will not be altered by the imposition of the tariff. In other words, the exporting good remains the good to be exported and the import competing good remains the good to be imported after the tariff. Also the country produces both goods before and after the tariff.

The reader will immediately recognize that assumption 1 is nothing but the conclusion of the Heckscher-Ohlin theorem, hence we know its precise meaning. Stolper and Samuelson never considered the factor intensity reversal problem as they assume that one good is always more capital intensive than the other in *both* countries. The definition of factor abundance is not too important here. It suffices to suppose that one country (say, Country 1) exports good X and imports good Y and that there is no factor intensity reversal (say, X is always more capital intensive than Y, that is, $k_x > k_y$). It is supposed that capital is relatively more abundant (and labor is relatively scarce) in Country 1 in some sense.

THE STOLPER-SAMUELSON THEOREM   Under the above assumptions and the specifications of the model, the price of the factor which is relatively scarce will increase in terms of the price of the other factor, or in terms of the price of any good, by the imposition of an import tariff.

In other words, suppose that the U.S. is a relatively labor scarce country and that it imports the labor intensive good. Then the real wage of the U.S. workers will be increased in terms of the price of capital or the price of any good by the imposition of an import tariff. This conclusion clearly has important practical significance, especially when we think of the influence of labor in American protectionism.

After the theorem has been precisely stated, its proof is almost trivial by applying the lemmas proved in the second section of Chapter 2. By our supposition and assumption 1, Country 1 is the labor scarce country, and it imports

---

Finaztheoritische Untersuchungen nebst Darstellung und Kritik der Steverwesens Schwedens, Jena, Gustav Fischer Verlag, 1896. Caves [4] thus writes (p. 64), "he (Wicksell) anticipates the result reached forty years later by Stolper and Samuelson, but his proof is not sufficient." Wicksell's argument invited criticism by Ohlin, Manoilesco, etc. A similar problem was also discussed from the mid 1920s to the late 1930s, which later became known as the "Australian Tariff Controversy." The Stolper-Samuelson theorem provided the first clear analysis of such problems.

[32] In this problem, it is important to realize that we are comparing the situation with an import tariff to the tariffless, free trade situation, and *not* to situations with different tariff rates.

the labor intensive good, Y. By assumption 2, we have $\hat{p} < 0$, where $p \equiv p_x/p_y$, and $\hat{p} \equiv dp/p$. Also $k_x > k_y$ implies that $\Gamma_y > \Gamma_x$. Hence, using lemma 2 (in the second section of Chapter 2), we immediately conclude that $\hat{q} > 0$, where $q \equiv w/r$ is wage:rent ratio. In other words, w in terms of r will be increased. Note that, in view of lemma 5 of the second section of Chapter 2, we have

$$\hat{x} = -B\hat{q} \quad \text{and} \quad \hat{y} = \bar{B}\hat{q} , \tag{3-18}$$

where $B > 0$ and $\bar{B} > 0$ by the supposition that $k_x > k_y$. In other words, the imposition of an import tariff will shift the factors of production of that country from the export good industry to the import competing good industry, which is a natural consequence of assumption 2.

In order to see that w/p_x and w/p_y also increase, recall the marginal productivity equation $w = p_x\mu_x = p_y\mu_y$ [equation (3-17)]. Since μ_x and μ_y are monotone increasing functions of k_x and k_y respectively (by the assumption of diminishing returns), and k_x and k_y are monotone increasing functions of q (lemma 4 of Chapter 2), an increase in q will increase μ_x and μ_y. Thus the real wage rate in terms of any goods price will increase. In the above notation, p_x and p_y are the *domestic* prices of X and Y respectively after the tariff. This finishes the proof of the Stolper-Samuelson theorem.

The above simple proof is possible because of our preparation in the second section of Chapter 2, especially lemma 5. We will now illustrate the proof by using the Edgeworth-Bowley box diagram. In fact, Stolper-Samuelson used this diagrammatical technique quite effectively in their proof. It will be useful for the reader to review their proof to familiarize himself with this celebrated technique.

The above diagram (Figure 3-9) represents the production box diagram for Country 1. In the diagram, the labor and capital endowments are measured along the horizontal and the vertical axes respectively. The origin for the X production isoquants is taken to be the southwest corner of the box and the origin for the Y production isoquants is taken to be the northeast corner of the box. By our supposition that $k_x > k_y$, the contract curve (the trace of the tangent points of the X and Y isoquants) will lie above the diagonal line as illustrated by the curve $XBAY$.[33] Let us suppose that point A denotes the point of production of X and Y (in Country 1) before the tariff, and point B denotes the point of production of X and Y after the tariff. By assumption 2, the resources will shift to the Y-industry and point B is below (closer to the X origin than) point A. Then, as is clear from the diagram, the capital:labor ratio of both the X and Y industries will increase by the movement from A to B. An increase in k_x or k_y will increase the factor price ratio q (lemma 4 of the previous chapter). Hence, the price of labor will be increased relative to that of capital by the imposition of the tariff. The proof of the increase of the wage in terms of the

---

[33] This is due to the fact that $k_x > k_y$ implies $k_x > k > k_y$, where $k \equiv K/L$, the endowment ratio. We are assuming away the trivial case in which the contract curve coincides with the diagonal line.

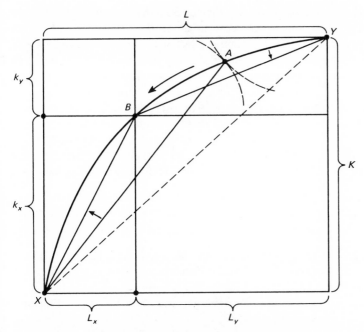

Figure 3-9   The Stolper-Samuelson Theorem

price of any good will be the same as above and hence can be omitted. The above argument is *almost* a proof of the theorem. There is one thing which should be made clear in order to make it a proof of the theorem. We argued above that the movement from A to B will increase the capital:labor ratio of each industry. In the diagram it is clear. But how do we know that this conclusion does not depend on the fact that the contract curve is drawn concave to the diagonal line? In the Appendix to Chapter 3, we shall argue that even though the contract curve is not necessarily concave to the diagonal under the present assumptions on the production function (constant returns to scale and diminishing returns), yet the above diagrammatical technique can provide a proof of the theorem because there is a certain limit to the non-concavity of the contract curve. But in order to say that the above geometric argument is a proof of the theorem, we have to add this argument about the non-concavity of the contract curve.

Let us now examine the assumptions of the theorem. The examination of assumption 1 was finished in the second section of the present chapter. There we showed the importance of the demand condition and the factor intensity reversal. Assumption 3 can be accepted as a necessary simplifying assumption of the theory. What about assumption 2? According to this assumption, the imposition of a tariff on the import competing good will increase the domestic price of this good relative to that of the export good, thus causing a shift of the factors from the export industry to the import competing industry. Surely this will be an immediate effect of the tariff. But the increase in the relative domestic price of the import competing good will then cause a decrease in demand in the import competing good and an increase in demand in the export good (in the tariff imposing country). This demand effect will thus cause a decrease in the relative price of the import competing industry. Furthermore, there will be repercussions from the foreign country. Summing up all these effects, can we still conclude that the relative (domestic) price of the import competing good will increase after the imposition of an import tariff? Metzler [21] showed that this conclusion is *not* necessarily true, and that the condition which guarantees this conclusion depends on the size of the elasticity of import demand of the foreign country (that is, the elasticity of the foreign offer curve) and the marginal propensity to import of the home country. This condition, known as *Metzler's condition*, will be discussed in Chapter 8.[34]

REFERENCES

1. Arrow, K. J., Chenery, H. B., Minhas, B., and Solow, R. M., "Capital-Labor Substitution and Economic Efficiency," *Review of Economics and Statistics*, XLIII, August 1961.

2. Bhagwati, J., "Protection, Real Wages and Real Income," *Economic Journal*, LXIX, December 1959.

3. Brown, A. J., "Professor Leontief and the Pattern of World Trade," *Yorkshire Bulletin of Economic and Social Research*, 9, November 1957.

4. Caves, R. E., *Trade and Economic Structure, Models and Methods* (Cambridge, Mass.: Harvard University Press), 1960.

5. Chipman, J. S., "A Survey of the Theory of International Trade: Part 2 and Part 3," *Econometrica*, 33, October 1965 and 34, January 1966.

6. Ellsworth, P. T., "The Structure of American Foreign Trade: A New View Examined," *Review of Economics and Statistics*, XXXVI, August 1954.

7. Harrod, R. F., "Factor-Price Relations Under Free Trade," *Economic Journal*, LXIII, June 1958.

8. Heckscher, Eli F., "The Effects of Foreign Trade on the Distribution of Income," in *Readings in the Theory of International Trade*, ed. by H. S. Ellis and L. A. Metzler, Philadelphia: Blakiston, 1949, originally published in Swedish in *Economist Tidskrift*, 21, 1919.

9. Hicks, J. R., "The Factor Price Equalization Theorem," in his *Essays in World Economics* (London: Oxford University Press), 1959.

10. Johnson, H. G., "Factor Endowments, International Trade and Factor Prices," Chapter 1 of his *International Trade and Economic Growth*, Cambridge, Mass.: Harvard University Press, 1958, originally published in *Manchester School of Economic and Social Studies*, XXV, September 1957.

[34] There are criticisms, other than those by Metzler. For a survey of such criticisms by Kuh, Lancaster, Kemp, and so on, Caves [4], pp. 72–76 will be useful.

11. ———, "Comparative Costs and Commercial Policy," Chapter II of his *Money, Trade and Economic Growth*, London: George Allen & Unwin, 1962, originally published in *Pakistan Economic Journal*, VIII, June 1958.

12. Jones, R. W., "Factor Proportions and the Heckscher-Ohlin Theorem," *Review of Economic Studies*, XXIV, 1956.

13. Kemp, M. C., *The Pure Theory of International Trade and Investment* (Englewood Cliffs, N.J.: Prentice-Hall), 1969.

14. Lancaster, K., "The Heckscher-Ohlin Trade Model: A Geometric Treatment," *Economica*, N.S., XXIV, February 1957.

15. ———, "Protection and Real Wages: A Restatement," *Economic Journal*, LVII, June 1957.

16. Leontief, W. W., "Domestic Production and Foreign Trade; the American Capital Position Re-examined," *Proceedings of the American Philosophical Society*, 97, September 1953.

17. ———, "Factor Proportions and the Structure of American Trade: Further Theoretical and Empirical Analysis," *Review of Economics and Statistics*, XXXVIII, November 1956, "Reply," *ibid.* (Supplement), XL, February 1958.

18. ———, "An International Comparison of Factor Costs and Factor Use," *American Economic Review*, LIV, June 1964.

19. Lerner, A. P., "Factor Prices and International Trade," in his *Essays in Economic Analysis*, London: Macmillan, 1953, first published in *Economica*, N.S., 19, February 1952. The paper was originally written in 1933 as a seminar paper for Professor L. Robbins in London.

20. Meier, G. M., *International Trade and Development* (New York: Harper & Row), 1963, Chapter 2.

21. Metzler, L. A., "Tariffs, the Terms of Trade, and the Distribution of National Income," *Journal of Political Economy*, LVII, February 1949.

22. Michaely, Michael, "Factor Proportions in International Trade: Current State of Theory," *Kyklos*, 17, Fasc. 4, 1964.

23. Minabe, N., "The Heckscher-Ohlin Theorem, the Leontief Paradox, and Patterns of Economic Growth," *American Economic Review*, LVI, December 1966.

24. Minhas, B. S., "The Homohypallagic Production Function, Factor-Intensity Reversals and the Heckscher-Ohlin Theorem," *Journal of Political Economy*, LX, April 1962.

25. Nerlove, M., "Recent Empirical Studies of the CES and Related Production Functions," in *The Theory and Empirical Analysis of Production, Studies in Income and Wealth* No. 31, ed. by Murray Brown (National Bureau of Economic Research) (New York: Columbia University Press), 1967.

26. Ohlin, B., *Interregional and International Trade* (Cambridge, Mass.: Harvard University Press), 1933.

27. Pearce, I. F., "A Note on Mr. Lerner's Paper," *Economica*, N.S., XIX, February 1952.

28. ———, and James, S. F., "The Factor Price Equalization Myth," *Review of Economic Studies*, XIX, 1951–52.

29. Robinson, R., "Factor Proportions and Comparative Advantage: Part I and Part II," *Quarterly Journal of Economics*, LXX, May 1956 and August 1956.

30. Samuelson, P. A., "International Trade and the Equalization of Factor Prices," *Economic Journal*, LVIII, June 1948.

31. ———, "International Factor Price Equalization Once Again," *Economic Journal*, LIX, June 1949.

32. ———, "A Comment on Factor Price Equalization," *Review of Economic Studies*, XIX, 1951–52.

33. ———, "Prices of Factors and Goods in General Equilibrium," *Review of Economic Studies*, XXI, 1953.

34. Stolper, W. F. and Samuelson, P. A., "Protection and Real Wages," *Review of Economic Studies*, IX, November 1941, reprinted in *Readings in the Theory of International Trade*, 1949.

35. Takayama, A., *Economic Growth and International Trade*, Ph.D. Dissertation, University of Rochester, Rochester, N.Y., March 1962.

36. ———, *International Economics* (Tokyo: Toyo Keizai Shimpo-sha), 1963, Chapter III.

37. ———, "Factor Proportions and Constant Elasticity of Production," Unpublished Manuscript, 1960.

38. ———, "On a Concave Contract Curve," Unpublished Manuscript, 1967.

39. Tinbergen, J., "The Equalization of Factor Prices between Free-Trade Areas," *Metroeconomica*, 1, July 1949, reprinted in his Selected Papers, Amsterdam: North-Holland, 1959.

40. Valvanis-Vail, S., "Leontief's Scarce Factor Paradox," *Journal of Political Economy*, LII, December 1954.

41. ———, "Factor Proportions and the Structure of American Trade: Comment," *Review of Economics and Statistics* (Supplement), XL, February 1958.

42. Viner, J., *Studies in the Theory of International Trade* (New York: Harper & Brothers), 1937, especially Chapter VIII.

Appendix to Chapter 3
On a "Concave" Contract Curve[35]

INTRODUCTION

Traditionally economic theory often uses various diagrams as logical tools. Recently this has been severely criticized for the obvious reason that "the eye is essentially an organ of perception rather than logical reasoning." A simple corollary of this observation is that "assumptions may be concealed in the manner in which the curve is usually drawn, and conclusions may be accepted unconditionally although they actually depend on such unstated assumptions."[36]

One of the most celebrated of such diagrammatical tools in traditional economics is the Edgeworth-Bowley Box Diagram. In the application of this tool, the concept of the contract curve often plays a very important role, and we all know that the contract curve is usually drawn concave to the diagonal line. (See Figure 3-10 in the next section, for example.) (In Chapter 3 we observed such a concave contract curve in connection with the Stolper-Samuelson theorem. There are many other examples in the literature.[37]) The question that now arises is whether the usual practice of drawing a concave contract curve can be justified. If so, on what grounds can we do so? It is often argued that this practice can be justified, for the case of a production box diagram, by assuming that the production functions (of the two goods involved) are differentiable, linear homogeneous, and exhibit the law of diminishing returns. Alternatively, it is conjectured that the practice of drawing a concave contract curve is

---

[35] I am greatly indebted to Maurice McManus for very stimulating discussions. This appendix is taken from the *Australian Economic Papers*, 8, December 1969.

[36] Koopmans [A2], p. 174. We freely admit, however, that a diagram often helps us to think of the essential nature of a given problem before we write it up mathematically.

[37] See, for example: Bator, F. M., "The Simple Analytics of Welfare Maximization," *American Economic Review*, XLVII, March 1957; Black, J., [A1]; Johnson, H. G., "Economic Development and International Trade," *Nationaløkonomisk Tidsskrift*, 97, 1959; Johnson, H.G., "Factor Market Distortions and the Shape of the Transformation Curve," *Econometrica*, 34, July 1966; Mundell, R. A., "International Trade and Factor Mobility," *American Economic Review*, XLVII, June 1957; Rybczynski, T. M., "Factor Endowment and Relative Commodity Prices," *Economica*, XXII, November 1955; Stolper, W. F., and Samuelson, P. A., "Protection and Real Wages," *Review of Economic Studies*, IX, November 1941.

justified if the production functions are concave.[38] Recently Maurice McManus informed me that these conjectures are not necessarily true and that Ivor Pearce had constructed a counter example. The purpose of this appendix is to pursue this problem further and to set out conditions under which the contract curve is really concave.[39] In particular, we shall determine a necessary and sufficient condition for the contract curve to be concave. We shall also establish some sufficient conditions for a concave contract curve. For example, we conclude that if the elasticity of factor substitution for each industry is constant, then the contract curve is always concave. One simple corollary of this is that if both production functions are of the Cobb-Douglas type, then the contract curve is always concave.[40]

In practical applications of the box diagram technique, how often the conclusion crucially hinges on the concavity of the contract curve is still an open question. As far as we have checked, we found no example in which the logical deduction of the conclusion crucially hinges on the concave character of the contract curve. This seems to be due to the fact that there is a certain limit on the degree of non-concavity of the contract curve. We shall consider this limit at the end of the next section.

The fact that the concavity of the contract curve is not crucial in deriving the conclusion is certainly a happy coincidence. However, we may stress the following points:

1. One should be careful in the use of a contract curve as a logical tool of analysis.

2. It is not necessarily easy to re-check the results, which were obtained by a concave contract curve, in terms of a non-concave contract curve. This point undermines the strength of the box diagram as a tool of analysis, for we always have to check any result, obtained by using the contract curve analysis, in terms of a non-concave contract curve.

[38] A real valued function $f(x)$ (where x is an n-vector) is said to be concave if:
$$f[\theta x + (1 - \theta)x^0] \geqq \theta f(x) + (1 - \theta)f(x^0), \qquad 0 \leqq \theta \leqq 1.$$
(That is, the cord joining any two points lies everywhere on or below the function.) It is called *strictly concave* if the strict inequality holds for all $x \neq x^0$ and $0 < \theta < 1$. An ordinary production function $Y = F(L, K)$ is concave if $\partial^2 F/\partial L^2 < 0$, $\partial^2 F/\partial K^2 < 0$, and $(\partial^2 F/\partial L^2)(\partial^2 F/\partial K^2) - [\partial^2 F/(\partial L \partial K)]^2 \geqq 0$. Note that the first two conditions are the law of diminishing returns, and the third condition is satisfied with equality if F is homogeneous of degree one.

[39] Obviously we can carry out a similar analysis for the box diagram for the pure exchange problem in which a contract curve describes the common tangency condition for the indifference curves of two consumers. The actual analysis will be left to the interested reader. The linear homogeneity assumption of the production function will correspond to the homotheticity assumption with regard to the utility function. The concavity of the production function is often much more acceptable than the concavity of the utility function. Very often only the quasi-concavity is considered to be an acceptable assumption with regard to the utility function. In short, a concave contract curve in the pure exchange box diagram will be even harder to accept than a concave contract curve in the production box diagram. In fact, any serious mathematical economist never draws a concave contract curve in this context, even if he only uses it for an illustrative purpose.

[40] McManus told me that this result under the Cobb-Douglas production function is known.

3. The previous point justifies our study of the degree of non-concavity of a contract curve.

4. In any case it will be important to know the conditions under which a contract curve is concave.

ANALYSIS

We consider a two-commodity model with the following production functions:

$$X = F(L_x, K_x) \tag{3-19a}$$

$$Y = G(L_y, K_y), \tag{3-19b}$$

where L_i and K_i are the amount of labor input and capital input in the ith industry ($i = x, y$) respectively. We assume that F and G are differentiable, linear homogeneous, and exhibit the law of diminishing returns.[41] In other words,

$$X = L_x f(k_x), \quad \text{where } k_x = K_x/L_x, \quad f' > 0, \quad \text{and} \quad f'' < 0 \tag{3-20a}$$

$$Y = L_y g(k_y), \quad \text{where } k_y = K_y/L_y, \quad g' > 0, \quad \text{and} \quad g'' < 0. \tag{3-20b}$$

We have the following allocation of the resources equations (or full employment equations):

$$L_x + L_y = L, \tag{3-21a}$$

$$K_x + K_y = K, \tag{3-21b}$$

where L and K respectively denote the total amounts of labor and capital available in the economy.[42]

We suppose that the X-industry is always more capital-intensive than the Y-industry (that is, $k_x > k_y$), so that our contract curve is always on one side of the diagonal line. As is well known, the contract curve never crosses the diagonal line,[43] so that a factor intensity reversal will never occur within the relevant range of factor prices (and endowments) of the country.

[41] In other words, $\partial^2 F/\partial L_x^2$, $\partial^2 G/\partial L_y^2$, $\partial^2 F/\partial K_x^2$, $\partial^2 G/\partial K_y^2$ are all negative. This condition is equivalent to $f'' < 0$ and $g'' < 0$. In the subsequent analysis ($'$) and ($''$) respectively represent the first and the second total derivative with respect to their arguments. For example, $f'' \equiv d^2 f/dk_x^2$. Note also that linear homogeneity and diminishing returns imply the concavity of the production function. See footnote 38.

[42] Note that we are considering a very "nice" case with the assumptions of linear homogeneity and the diminishing returns. In other words, we are interested in finding out if a non-concave contract curve is possible under such a case.

[43] If the contract curve passes the diagonal line, it should coincide with the diagonal line. This is due to the linear homogeneity of the production functions. This is really the entire content of the ordinary proof of the assertion. It, among other things, assumes that the contract curve is unique and continuous. If it is discontinuous, for example, it can cross the diagonal line with a discontinuity ("a hole") at its intersection with the diagonal, and the above argument does not hold. Later in the book we shall provide an alternative proof of the statement that the contract curve does not cross the diagonal line, so that one industry is always more capital intensive than the other industry. The above argument, however, does not preclude the possibility of the contract curve coinciding with the diagonal line. For our consideration in this appendix we shall rule out this trivial case.

We may now illustrate the contract curve in the following diagram (Figure 3-10). Here the contract curve is drawn in such a way that it is concave towards the diagonal line.[44]

The contract curve is the locus of factor combinations for which the production isoquants of both industries are tangent to each other. Noting that $L_y = L - L_x$ and $K_y = K - K_x$ from equations (3-21a) and (3-21b), we may write this tangency condition as follows:

$$-\frac{\partial F/\partial L_x}{\partial F/\partial K_x} = \frac{dK_x}{dL_x} = \frac{d(K - K_x)}{d(L - L_x)} = -\frac{\partial G/\partial L_y}{\partial G/\partial K_y}. \tag{3-22}$$

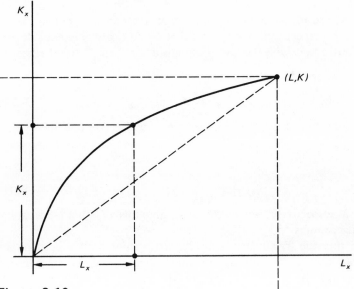

Figure 3-10

Note that equations (3-20a) and (3-20b) with the relations described there imply[45]

$$\varphi(k_x) \equiv \frac{\partial F/\partial L_x}{\partial F/\partial K_x} = \frac{f(k_x) - f'(k_x)k_x}{f'(k_x)} \quad \text{and} \quad \varphi' > 0, \tag{3-23}$$

$$\psi(k_y) \equiv \frac{\partial G/\partial L_y}{\partial G/\partial K_y} = \frac{g(k_y) - g'(k_y)k_y}{g'(k_y)} \quad \text{and} \quad \psi' > 0. \tag{3-24}$$

[44] If $k_y > k_x$, then the contract curve will lie below the diagonal line and the concave contract curve will again be one that is concave to the diagonal line. Since this case is completely analogous to the case illustrated in Figure 3-11, we may omit its consideration without any loss of generality.

[45] Note that $\varphi' = -f''f/(f')^2$ and $\psi' = -g''g/(g')^2$ and thus we have $\varphi' > 0$ and $\psi' > 0$. An intuitive understanding of this condition is simple. As the capital-labor ratio in a given industry increases, the marginal product of labor (MPP_L) increases and the marginal product of capital (MPP_K) decreases. Hence the marginal rate of transformation, MPP_L/MPP_K, must increase.

Using φ and ψ, the contract curve as described in (3-22) can also be written as

$$\varphi\left(\frac{K_x}{L_x}\right) = \psi\left(\frac{K - K_x}{L - L_x}\right). \tag{3-25}$$

In other words, the contract curve is the locus of the values of (L_x, K_x) which satisfy equation (3-25).

We can easily see that the contract curve is concave to the diagonal line if $dK_x/dL_x > 0$ and $d^2K_x/dL_x^2 \leqq 0$.[46] We can easily obtain the expression for dK_x/dL_x from equation (3-25) as

$$\frac{dK_x}{dL_x} = \frac{\varphi'k_xL_y + \psi'k_yL_x}{\varphi'L_y + \psi'L_x}. \tag{3-26}$$

Since $\varphi' > 0$ and $\psi' > 0$, $dK_x/dL_x > 0$, so that our contract curve is upward sloping. After a somewhat tedious (but mechanical) computation, we obtain:

$$\frac{d^2K_x}{dL_x^2} = \frac{k_y - k_x}{\alpha^3}\left[(k_x - k_y)L_xL_y(\varphi''\psi'^2 - \psi''\varphi'^2) + 2L\varphi'\psi'(\varphi'L_y + \psi'L_x)\right], \tag{3-27}$$

where $\alpha \equiv \varphi'L_y + \psi'L_x$.

Although the second term of the *RHS* of equation (3-27) is always negative the first term is not necessarily negative. That is, φ'' and ψ'' can take any sign since they involve f''' and g'''. The explicit expressions for φ'' and ψ'' can easily be obtained as:[47]

$$\varphi'' = \varphi'\left[\frac{f'''}{f''} + \frac{f'}{f} - 2\frac{f''}{f'}\right], \tag{3-28a}$$

$$\psi'' = \psi'\left[\frac{g'''}{g''} + \frac{g'}{g} - 2\frac{g''}{g'}\right]. \tag{3-28b}$$

Therefore d^2K_x/dL_x^2 can be positive. In other words, the contract curve is *not* necessarily concave. A necessary and sufficient condition for a concave contract curve is obtained from (3-27) as

$$(k_x - k_y)L_xL_y(\varphi''\psi'^2 - \psi''\varphi'^2) + 2L\varphi'\psi'(\varphi'L_y + \psi'L_x) \geqq 0. \tag{3-29}$$

A sufficient condition for a concave contract curve is obviously that the first term of the *LHS* of (3-29) be non-negative. In other words

$$\varphi''\psi'^2 - \psi''\varphi'^2 \geqq 0 \quad (\because k_x > k_y \text{ by supposition}). \tag{3-30}$$

---

[46] We may note that these conditions imply that K_x, as a function of L_x, is a concave function. Hence the concavity of the contract curve can also mean the concavity of the relevant function. Note also that if the contract curve is strictly concave to the diagonal line in the sense that it does not contain linear segments, then the relevant function is a strictly concave function.

[47] Note that $\varphi' = -f''f/(f')^2$. Taking a logarithm of both sides of this equation we obtain (3-28a). Similarly, we obtain (3-28b).

Now write equation (3-25) as $Q \equiv \varphi(k_x) = \psi(k_y)$,[48] and define the elasticity of factor substitution for each industry as follows:

$$\sigma_x \equiv \frac{dk_x}{dQ}\frac{Q}{k_x}\left(= \frac{Q}{\varphi' k_x}\right),$$ (3-31a)

$$\sigma_y \equiv \frac{dk_y}{dQ}\frac{Q}{k_y}\left(= \frac{Q}{\psi' k_y}\right).$$ (3-31b)

Suppose now that σ_x and σ_y are *constant*.[49] Then after a little simple but tedious manipulation,[50] we can show that condition (3-29) is always satisfied with strict positivity. In other words, if the elasticities of factor substitution in both industries are constant, the contract curve is always strictly concave to the diagonal line. In particular, if the production function of each industry is of the Cobb-Douglas type, the contract curve is always strictly concave. From condition (3-29), we may also construct a situation in which the contract curve is non-concave. We leave this to the interested reader. Thus we have obtained:

PROPOSITION   A contract curve is not necessarily concave to the diagonal line. A *necessary and sufficient* condition for a contract curve to be concave under the supposition of $k_x > k_y$ is given by (3-29). A sufficient condition is given by $\varphi''\psi'^2 - \psi''\varphi'^2 \geq 0$ if $k_x > k_y$. If the elasticities of factor substitution of both industries are constant, then it is always strictly concave.

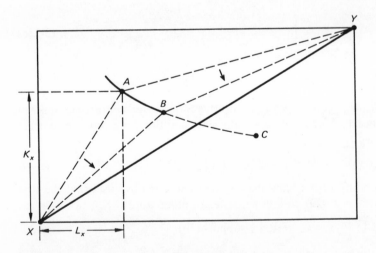

Figure 3-11

[48] In other words, Q is the value of the common marginal rate of transformation.
[49] Such a production function is often known as the CES production function.
[50] Note that $Q \equiv \varphi = \psi$, and first obtain $\varphi'' = (\varphi')^2[1 - \sigma_x]/Q$ and $\psi'' = (\psi')^2[1 - \sigma_y]/Q$ from (3-31a) and (3-31b). Then substitute these expressions into condition (3-29).

Thus we know that a contract curve is not necessarily concave. But there is a limit on the degree of non-concavity of a contract curve. For example, if we draw any lines from the origin of each commodity, these two lines should lie on one side of the contract curve. In other words, the situation illustrated in Figure 3-11 *cannot* happen.

In order to see this, suppose that we move from point A to B (along the contract curve). Then as we move from A to B, the capital-labor ratio of the X-industry decreases while the capital-labor ratio of the Y-industry increases. In other words, as we move from A to B, k_x decreases, hence the value of $\varphi(k_x)$ decreases, while the value of $\psi(k_y)$ increases since k_y increases.[51] Point B therefore cannot satisfy the tangency condition $[\varphi(k_x) = \psi(k_y)]$, and hence it fails to be a point on the contract curve.

It is important to note that the above also reasserts more rigorously the well-known statement that the contract curve never crosses the diagonal line. For if the contract curve crossed the diagonal line there would exist a contract curve connecting points such as B and C, and there must be a point on the contract curve such that lines from the two origins (X and Y) meet each other from opposite sides of the curve.

We should note, however, that this consideration does not preclude the case in which a contract curve contains a portion which is somewhat convex to the diagonal. This is illustrated in Figure 3-12. Note that in Figure 3-12 the ray from each origin has a monotone decreasing (increasing) angle to the horizontal axis as the amount of output for each industry increases.[52]

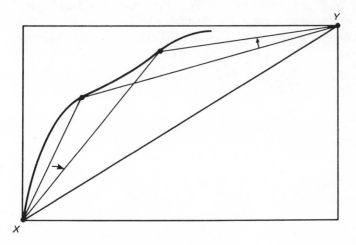

Figure 3-12

[51] Note that $\varphi' > 0$ and $\psi' > 0$.

[52] In order to keep the equality $[\varphi(k_x) = \psi(k_y)]$, either both k_x and k_y increase or both k_x and k_y decrease. This is the background of the monotonicity of the angle of the ray.

In any case our conditions $[\varphi' > 0$ and $\psi' > 0]$ together with $f' > 0$ and $g' > 0$ impose a certain limit on the degree of non-concavity of a contract curve. In the application of a contract curve, this limit plays a somewhat important role so that we can usually get a correct conclusion in spite of the fact that we normally draw a nicely concave contract curve. This is indeed a happy observation. The above analysis tells us that one of the essential parts of a contract curve analysis seems to be the conditions $\varphi' > 0$ and $\psi' > 0$ together with $f' > 0$ and $g' > 0$ rather than the concavity of a contract curve. Or more specifically, $f' > 0$, $g' > 0$ and $f'' < 0$, $g'' < 0$ (diminishing returns) together with the linear homogeneity of the production functions (which justifies the use of f, g instead of F and G). This is not too surprising because these conditions will imply the usual assumption that the production transformation curve is downward sloping and concave to the origin. However, we should recall once again that this does not justify the unconditional use of a concave contract curve as a logical tool of analysis.

REFERENCES

A1. Black, J., "A Formal Proof of the Concavity of the Production Possibility Function," *Economic Journal*, LXVII, March 1957.

A2. Koopmans, T. C., *Three Essays on the State of Economic Science* (New York: McGraw-Hill, Inc.), 1957.

A3. Lerner, A. P., "Factor Prices and International Trade," *Economica*, February 1952. Also in his *Essays in Economic Analysis* (London: Macmillan & Co., Ltd.), 1953.

A4. Stolper, W. F. and Samuelson, P. A., "Protection and Real Wages," *Review of Economic Studies*, IX, November 1941.

A5. Takayama, A., *International Economics* (Tokyo: Toyo Keizaishimposha), 1963.

PART II
THE CLASSICAL THEORY OF COMPARATIVE ADVANTAGE AND ITS MODERN DEVELOPMENTS

4

THE RICARDIAN THEORY OF COMPARATIVE ADVANTAGE AND ITS MODERN IMPLICATIONS

THE RICARDIAN THEORY OF COMPARATIVE ADVANTAGE

In Part I, we considered the question of what determines the pattern of international trade. In other words, given two countries each being able to produce two goods, what are the factors that determine when a certain country exports a particular good and when it imports a particular good? By assuming that there are two factors of production and that the countries have identical production functions, the Heckscher-Ohlin theorem provided an answer to this question, by focusing our attention on the factor endowments of the countries.

However, as we mentioned in Part I, this question is not new in the literature. During the formation of modern economics by the English classical economists in the early nineteenth century, this question was raised and answered in a remarkably satisfactory way for a theory of that time. This theory, widely known as *Ricardo's theory of comparative advantage*, attempted the first rigorous theoretical justification of free trade, a very important cornerstone of Adam Smith's economic theory of "laissez faire."[1] Suppose again that the world consists of two countries each being able to produce two goods; that each good can be produced using only one factor—labor, in both countries; that labor is completely immobile between the countries and completely mobile within each country. The amount of labor required to produce a unit output of each good is supposed to be different in the two countries because of the "climatic conditions." Ricardo considered the two countries, England and Portugal, each being able to produce cloth and wine. The amounts of labor required to produce one unit each of cloth and wine are summarized in the following table.

---

[1] It is known, of course, to every student of economics that Adam Smith attempted the first modern formulation of economics and that his formulation contained a strong attack on a number of institutional bondages grouped under the name of "mercantilism." The term "laissez faire" was the catch phrase of his theory. "Free trade" and "free competition" were the economic content of laissez faire, and they succeeded in dominating the social thought of his age.

TABLE 4-1   Ricardo's Example[2]

	Cloth	Wine
England	100	120
Portugal	90	80

It is important to observe, in the above example, that Portugal can produce both cloth and wine with *less* amounts of labor than England. Thus, Portugal is said to have an *absolute advantage* in the production of both goods. Now suppose that both cloth and wine can move freely with negligible transport cost within each country and between the countries. Under these suppositions, the following two questions were raised:

1. From the point of view of world welfare, which country should export (or import) which good?
2. Is the above pattern of trade desirable from the point of view of each country?

These two questions are obviously strongly normative in nature and show the normative aspect of the Ricardian theory of comparative advantage. The positive question, "Under free trade what will be the actual pattern of trade?" was not particularly emphasized. This question was first raised and answered in a satisfactory way by J. S. Mill with the introduction of the demand conditions. On the whole, the positive aspect of the international division of labor was not a matter of great concern for the classical economists. They were more concerned with its normative aspects (questions such as the gains from trade). On this point, Viner writes, "The classical theory of international trade was formulated primarily with a view to its providing guidance on questions of national policy. . . . It was most conspicuously true in the field which is sometimes called the theory of international value. . . . Recognition of its welfare analysis orientation is essential to the understanding and the appraisal of the classical doctrine" ([10], p. 437). This point clearly distinguishes it from the modern formulation of the theory of comparative advantage—the Heckscher-Ohlin theorem. As long as we assume fixed coefficients of production, real cost

---

[2] This is Ricardo's famous example, which is contained in the following passage ([5], p. 135).

> England may be so circumstanced, that to produce the cloth may require the labour of 100 men for one year; and if she attempted to make the wine, it might require that labour of 120 men for the same time. England would therefore find it in her interest to import wine, and to purchase it by the exportation of cloth. To produce the wine in Portugal, might require only the labour of 80 men for one year, and to produce the cloth in the same country, might require the labour of 90 men for the same time. It could therefore be advantageous for her to export wine in exchange for cloth.

The conclusion that England should export cloth and Portugal should export wine, in the above passage, does not follow from the sentences of the passage alone. Ricardo made a more careful analysis leading to this conclusion in the passage immediately following the above.

can be truly meaningful even in a multi-factor model.[3] In fact, under certain assumptions, real cost can be justified under the multi-factor, non-fixed co-efficient production model. Viner is violently opposed to linking the labor theory of value to the classical theory of comparative advantage. "Except for Ricardo, none of the classical expounders of the doctrine of comparative costs, with the relatively unimportant and partial exception of James Mill, was an exponent of a labor-cost theory of value" (Viner [10], p. 490). Viner also claims that "the association of the comparative-cost doctrine with the labor-cost theory of value is a historical accident" ([10], p. 490). Ohlin apparently mis-understood this point and was severely criticized by Viner. Caves writes "Viner is no doubt correct in saying that Ohlin failed to realize that the classical comparative costs doctrine was a system of welfare and not a 'positive' theory designed to explain national specialization."[4]

Now let us come back to Table 4-1, Ricardo's example. As we noted above, Portugal is more efficient than England in the production of both goods in the sense that she can produce each good with less labor than England. However, we should also note that the extent of Portugal's greater efficiency is not the same in cloth production as in wine production. This can be expressed, for example, as follows: "One Englishman is worth 90/100 of a Portuguese in the production of cloth, and 80/120 of a Portuguese in the production of wine." In other words, although Englishmen are less efficient than Portuguese in the production of both goods, the degree of lower efficiency is smaller in the pro-duction of cloth. Or the degree of greater efficiency of the Portuguese is larger in the production of wine. This is really the meaning of comparative advantage. In other words, although Portugal has an absolute advantage in the production of both goods, she has a comparative advantage in wine production, and England has a comparative advantage in cloth production. This can be sum-marized by the following simple inequalities:

$$\frac{90}{100} > \frac{80}{120} \quad \text{or} \quad \frac{90}{80} > \frac{100}{120}. \tag{4-1}$$

The second inequality is simply a restatement of the first.

This notion of comparative advantage is the central point of the Ricardian theory. Ricardo then supposed that England devoted her entire labor supply to the production of cloth and that Portugal devoted her entire labor supply to the production of wine. In other words, he supposed that each country specialized completely in the production of the good in which she had a comparative advantage.

In order to compute the gains from trade, let us now compute the increase in each output for the world as a whole after complete specialization by each country in the good in which she has a comparative advantage. The amounts of

---

[3] Since all factors are used in fixed proportions by assumption, they might as well be repre-sented by one factor, labor.

[4] Caves, R., Trade and Economic Structure, Harvard University Press, 1960, p. 23.

labor required to produce one unit of each good, the world output of each good before specialization, and each country's output and world output of each commodity with the *same* labor inputs after specialization, are summarized in the following table. In other words, with the same labor inputs, the world output of *both* goods is increased by specialization (cloth, $2 \rightarrow 2.2$; wine, $2 \rightarrow 2.125$). Hence international trade of these goods after specialization *can* increase the consumption of both goods in each country.

TABLE 4-2   World Gains from Specialization

	Before Specialization		
	England	Portugal	World Output
Cloth	100 workers = 1 unit	90 workers = 1 unit	2 units
Wine	120 workers = 1 unit	80 workers = 1 unit	2 units
	After Specialization		
	England	Portugal	World Output
Cloth	220 workers = 220/100 units		2.2 units
Wine		170 workers = 170/80 units	2.125 units

The extent of the increase in consumption each country obtains after trade obviously depends on the exchange ratio of the goods (terms of trade). Ricardo supposed that the terms of trade would lie between the two countries' comparative advantage ratios, 90/80 and 100/120. He then illustrated the gains from trade for each country by adopting the exchange ratio 1:1 (obviously 90/80 > 1 > 100/120). With this exchange ratio, suppose that Portugal exports 1.125 units of wine (out of her total production of 2.125 units of wine) and imports 1.125 units of cloth. Then the pattern of consumption after specialization and trade is given in the following table (the figures inside the parentheses). The

TABLE 4-3   Gains from Trade

	England	Portugal
Cloth	1(1.075)	1(1.125)
Wine	1(1.125)	1(1)

figures outside the parentheses give the consumption *before* specialization and trade. In other words, each country *can* increase its consumption of at least one good without decreasing its consumption of the other good, using the *same* amount of labor after specialization and international trade.[5]

Thus we see that the two questions posed above can be answered affirmatively. Complete specialization is desirable from the world's point of view in the sense that it can increase the output of both goods for the world as a whole with the same labor inputs. Also, free trade makes complete specialization desirable from each country's point of view in the sense described above. Adam Smith stumbled on absolute advantage and concluded that international trade could not occur between the countries if one country was definitely superior to the other in the production of all the goods. Ricardo's genius revealed the mistake in this rather appealing logic by simply comparing the relative efficiency of the countries in the production of each good.

We can reformulate our discussion in such a way as to conclude that specialization will (1) decrease the amount of labor required to produce a given amount of each good, in the world as a whole and (2) make it possible for each country to consume at least as much amount of each good as before specialization. The verification of the above statements is now almost trivial and we shall leave it to the interested reader for now, although we shall return to this topic in the next section with a more mathematical formulation.

The above discussion summarizes Ricardo's work on the subject. There do remain, however, many unsatisfactory points in the discussion. First of all, we did not prove that complete specialization is the most desirable situation from the point of view of the world as a whole, or that it is the most desirable situation from each country's point of view (if free trade prevails). Can we assert these conclusions? The answer is not simple, for we have yet to tackle the problem of defining properly the concept of "most desirable" or "optimum." Moreover, the foregoing analysis and discussion in terms of an arithmetic example would certainly be quite unsatisfactory for modern readers accustomed to mathematical techniques and diagrammatical expositions. Discussions in terms of arithmetic examples often obscure the logic of the analysis, make many assumptions implicitly which blur the essence of the points made, and reduce the generality of the discussion. In spite of this, the Ricardian analysis contains many important points and truths, which we shall consider in the following sections and later chapters of Part II. For example, the analysis can be considered one of the earliest forerunners of the theory of linear programming and activity analysis.

Because of the importance of the theory of comparative advantage in the history of economic doctrines, the question of whether Ricardo can really claim the credit for establishing the theory has been debated in the literature. Ricardo's *Principles* [5] which contains the above theory was published in 1817. However, Colonel Torrens published works containing a similar analysis in 1808 (*The Economists Refuted* [8]) and 1815 (*An Essay on the External Corn*

---

[5] These gains from specialization and trade from the point of view of each individual country and the world as a whole justify the coinage of the phrase *international division of labor.*

Trade [9]). This has especially increased the heat of the debate concerning the priority of Ricardo. For summaries of the discussions of the priority of Ricardo or Torrens, see Viner ([10], pp. 441–444) and Chipman ([1], pp. 479–483), for example. We conclude this section with the following quotations from Viner and Chipman which summarize the present feeling of the profession on this point fairly well. Viner writes,

> Torrens clearly preceded Ricardo in publishing a fairly satisfactory formulation of the doctrine. It is unquestionable, however, that Ricardo is entitled to the credit for first giving due emphasis to the doctrine, for first placing it in an appropriate setting, and for obtaining general acceptance of it by economists ([10], p. 442).

Chipman writes,

> There can be little doubt that Ricardo was influenced by it (Torrens' *External Corn Trade*, 1815), whether he was conscious of the indebtedness or not; nevertheless he added a great deal in his own subsequent treatment. . . . Thus it would seem fair to say that both Torrens and Ricardo contributed in essential ways to the development of the law of comparative advantage; and that credit for the principal discovery should go to Torrens ([1], pp. 481–482).

THE RICARDIAN THEORY REFORMULATED

In this section we shall reformulate the Ricardian theory using mathematical and diagrammatical methods. This will increase our understanding of the theory and prepare the way for generalizations in the remaining chapters of Part II. Here the analysis will be strictly confined to a two-country, two-good, one-factor world.

Consider a world consisting of the two countries, 1 and 2, each being able to produce two goods, X and Y, with only one factor of production—labor. Let L_1 and L_2 be the total amounts of labor available in Country 1 and Country 2 respectively. Let l_{xi} and l_{yi} be the amounts of labor required to produce one unit of X and one unit of Y respectively, in Country i ($i = 1, 2$). See Table 4-4 for a diagrammatic representation.

TABLE 4-4 Reformulation of the Ricardian Example

	Good X	Good Y
Country 1	l_{x1}	l_{y1}
Country 2	l_{x2}	l_{y2}

Let x_i and y_i denote the output of X and Y respectively in Country i $(i = 1, 2)$, and let L_{xi} and L_{yi} be the amount of labor input into the X-industry and Y-industry respectively in Country i $(i = 1, 2)$. Then the production function for each good in Country i is simply

$$x_i = (1/l_{xi})L_{xi}, \tag{4-2a}$$

$$y_i = (1/l_{yi})L_{yi}. \tag{4-2b}$$

Since, in general, $l_{x1} \neq l_{x2}$, and $l_{y1} \neq l_{y2}$, the production functions for the same good are not the same in both countries. This is in contrast to the assumption of the Heckscher-Ohlin model that the production functions for the same good are identical in both countries. Differences in l_{xi} or l_{yi} between the countries reflect the climatic differences. Note that in the above production functions the marginal product of labor in each industry is equal to average product of labor and is a constant (that is, $1/l_{xi}$ or $1/l_{yi}$).

Let us suppose that Country 1 (2) has a comparative advantage in the production of X (Y). In other words,

$$\frac{l_{x1}}{l_{x2}} < \frac{l_{y1}}{l_{y2}}, \quad \text{or equivalently,}^6 \tag{4-3a}$$

$$\frac{l_{x1}}{l_{y1}} < \frac{l_{x2}}{l_{y2}}. \tag{4-3b}$$

The amounts of the goods produced in each country are constrained by the total labor endowment of the country. In other words,

$$l_{x1}x_1 + l_{y1}y_1 \leqq L_1, \quad \text{and} \tag{4-4a}$$

$$l_{x2}x_2 + l_{y2}y_2 \leqq L_2. \tag{4-4b}$$

We may rewrite these inequalities as

$$\frac{x_1}{L_1/l_{x1}} + \frac{y_1}{L_1/l_{y1}} \leqq 1 \quad \text{or} \quad \frac{x_1}{a_1} + \frac{y_1}{b_1} \leqq 1; \tag{4-5a}$$

$$\frac{x_2}{L_2/l_{x2}} + \frac{y_2}{L_2/l_{y2}} \leqq 1 \quad \text{or} \quad \frac{x_2}{a_2} + \frac{y_2}{b_2} \leqq 1, \tag{4-5b}$$

where $a_i \equiv L_i/l_{xi}$ and $b_i \equiv L_i/l_{yi}(i = 1, 2)$. The set of combinations (x_i, y_i) in the non-negative orthant which satisfies the appropriate inequality [(4-5a) or

---

[6] It is assumed, of course, that $l_{xi} > 0$ and $l_{yi} > 0$ $(i = 1, 2)$. The equivalence of (4-3a) and (4-3b) shows what Viner said: "It is unessential whether the cost ratios which are compared are the ratios between the costs of producing different commodities within the same countries or the ratios between the costs of producing the same commodities in different countries" ([10], pp. 438–439).

(4-5b)] describes the *production possibilities set* of the *i*th country ($i = 1, 2$). They can be illustrated by the following diagrams (Figure 4-1).

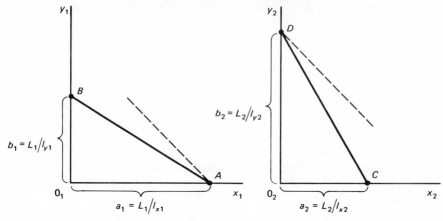

Figure 4-1   The Production Possibilities Set for Each Country

Given the constraint (4-5a) and/or (4-5b), we are now faced with two optimization problems, one from the point of view of the world as a whole and the other from the point of view of each individual country. This immediately leads to the difficult problem of defining "optimal." We can conceive of two concepts of "optimal": (1) minimization of the real cost of obtaining a given amount of real income (say a given bundle of goods), and (2) maximization of real income (each good weighted by a given price ratio) with a given input of labor. In the first section of this chapter, we found that there was an increase in real income, given the same amount of labor input, after specialization. As we pointed out, this could be trivially rephrased as a *decrease* in the real cost (that is, a decrease in the labor input for at least one good and a non-increase in the labor input for the other good) of producing a given bundle of goods. Hence, as long as we are only concerned with an increase or a decrease, the above distinction between the different concepts of optimality does not really matter.[7] However, if we are concerned with maximization or minimization, it is not clear, at least at the outset, that optimization under the two different definitions yields the same result. In other words, maximization of the real income may

---

[7] Although this distinction does not really matter in the above Ricardian formulation, there was a rather confusing discussion between Ricardo and Malthus on this point. Malthus wrote, "Mr. Ricardo always views foreign trade in the light of means of obtaining *cheaper* commodities," and he held that the gain from trade consisted of "the increased value which results from exchanging what is valued less for what is valued more." (Malthus, T. R., *Principles of Political Economy*, 1st ed., 1830, pp. 460–461.) Ricardo, however, did not measure "gains" by changes in "value." In *Notes on Malthus* (1820) Ricardo repeated his position, saying, "The advantage . . . to both places is not (that) they have an increase of value, but with the same amount of value they are both able to consume and enjoy an increased quantity of commodities." For a survey of these discussions, see Viner [10], especially Chapter IX. Chapter VIII of his book is devoted to the saving-in-cost approach and Chapter IX is devoted to the increase-in-income approach.

yield a result different from that obtained by minimizing the real cost. Recently Kuhn [4] showed that these two problems are really equivalent in the sense that good i is produced in some optimal amount for the minimization problem if and only if it is produced in some optimal amount for the maximization problem.

Postponing the discussion of this problem to Chapter 6, let us tentatively adopt the maximization (or increase in income) approach here.[8] We will first consider the problem of maximizing the world's real income given some fixed price ratio p_x/p_y.

PROBLEM 1 (World Welfare) Maximize

$$(p_x/p_y)(x_1 + x_2) + (y_1 + y_2)$$

subject to

$$x_1/a_1 + y_1/b_1 \leqq 1, \quad x_2/a_2 + y_2/b_2 \leqq 1, \quad \text{and} \quad x_1, x_2, y_1, y_2 \geqq 0.$$

Note that in this problem we are maximizing the world's real income measured in terms of good Y. Alternatively, we may maximize the world's real income measured in terms of good X [that is, $(x_1 + x_2) + (p_y/p_x)(y_1 + y_2)$]. Since these two functions differ by a positive constant multiple of each other the solution will be the same under both target functions. In fact, we may replace the target function without altering the solution by the value of the world's output (that is, $p_x(x_1 + x_2) + p_y(y_1 + y_2)$). The essential assumption underlying the above argument is that the world prices, p_x and p_y, are given constants.

Now we can formulate the problem of maximizing each country's real income as follows.

PROBLEM 2 (Country's Welfare)

a) Maximize

$$(p_x/p_y)x_1 + y_1$$

subject to

$$x_1/a_1 + y_1/b_1 \leqq 1 \quad \text{and} \quad x_1, y_1 \geqq 0;$$

b) Maximize

$$(p_x/p_y)x_2 + y_2$$

subject to

$$x_2/a_2 + y_2/b_2 \leqq 1 \quad \text{and} \quad x_2, y_2 \geqq 0.$$

Here the essential assumption is that the price ratio p_x/p_y is a given constant to each country. Again the target functions for the two problems can be replaced

---

[8] This approach is adopted by DOSSO [2], which is apparently based on Samuelson [6]. DOSSO is a widely accepted nickname for Dorfman, Samuelson, and Solow [2].

by $[x_1 + (p_y/p_x)y_1]$ and $[x_2 + (p_y/p_x)y_2]$ respectively, or alternatively by each country's national product, $(p_x x_1 + p_y y_1)$ and $(p_x x_2 + p_y y_2)$ respectively, without altering the solution.

The reader who is familiar with linear programming, will immediately recognize problem 1 and problem 2 as simple linear programming problems. Hence, the problem formulated by Ricardo has an extremely modern character. These problems are simple enough to allow solution with no knowledge of linear programming. We will proceed with the solution on that basis here, postponing further discussion from the point of view of linear programming until later. In order to solve the above problems, it suffices to formalize Ricardo's assumptions as follows:

ASSUMPTION 1

$l_{x1}/l_{y1} < l_{x2}/l_{y2}$ or $b_1/a_1 < b_2/a_2$ (with $l_{xi} > 0$, $l_{yi} > 0$, $i = 1, 2$) .

ASSUMPTION 2

$l_{x1}/l_{y1} < p_x/p_y < l_{x2}/l_{y2}$ or $b_1/a_1 < p_x/p_y < b_2/a_2$ (with $p_x > 0$, $p_y > 0$) .

Note that Ricardo used a numerical example, so that $l_{x1}/l_{y1} = b_1/a_1 = 100/120$, $l_{x2}/l_{y2} = b_2/a_2 = 90/80$ and $p_x/p_y = 1$.

Under these two assumptions, the solution to problem 2 (country's welfare) is almost immediate. By assumption 2, the price line can be superimposed on each country's production transformation triangle (see Figure 4-1). In Figure 4-1, the dashed line is the price line. Now the solution to problem 2 is easily seen from Figure 4-1, that is, $x_1 = a_1, y_1 = 0; x_2 = 0, y_2 = b_2$. In other words, complete specialization (of Country 1 in the production of good X and Country 2 in the production of good Y) will maximize each country's real income.

For those who are still unconvinced, let us explain this further, taking Country 1 as an example. Country 1's production triangle $(0AB)$ and the world price line (AD) are drawn in the following diagram (Figure 4-2). The production point is presumably somewhere on the line AB (any point below AB is inefficient and no point above AB can be achieved), say, C (Country 1 is producing C_x of good X and C_y of good Y). When we measure the real income represented by these outputs, in terms of good Y, at the pre-trade exchange ratio, AB, the total real income will be $0B[= C_y + C_x(0B/0A)]$. Suppose this country specializes completely in the production of X and enters into international trade with the rest of the world (Country 2). Then Country 1's real income measured in terms of good Y is $0D$, given the world price ratio AD (hence the gain is BD). Any point of production other than complete specialization in X is inferior to this point. For example, if the production point is the point C (no specialization), Country 1's real income, after trade, in terms of good Y and the given world price ratio is $0D'$, which is clearly less than $0D$. (Here CD' is parallel to AD.)

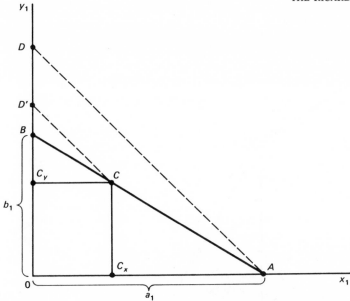

Figure 4-2   Maximization of Country 1's Real Income

Another way to show the gains from complete specialization and trade is to consider the triangle $0AB$ as the pre-trade consumption possibilities set and the triangle $0AD$ as the post-trade consumption possibilities set. The *consumption possibilities set* is defined as the set of amounts of goods X and Y which can possibly be available for consumption. As long as $0AB$ is a proper subset of $0AD$ (that is, the set $0AD$ is strictly larger than the set $0AB$), there is a gain from trade and given the world price ratio, AD, complete specialization will maximize the post-trade consumption possibilities set (if, for example, C is the production point, the post-trade consumption possibilities set is $0ACD'$).

It is important to note that we only showed that *if the relative price is a given constant*, then every country maximizes her real income with respect to this price ratio by specialization. If a country can affect the price ratio by tariffs and so on (through repercussions of demand and supply conditions), then, as is well known, a country may improve her welfare position (see the optimum tariff argument in Chapter 14). In this case the other country may suffer a loss.

Now let us come back to problem 1 (world's welfare). Probably the best way to find the solution to this problem is via the concept of a *world production possibilities set* as depicted by Lerner.[9] The world production possibilities set, for our problem, is represented by the set $0ARB$ in Figure 4-3.

[9] Lerner, A. P., "The Diagrammatical Representation of Cost Conditions in International Trade," *Economica*, XII, August 1932. Such sets have been depicted by Whitin (p. 53), McKenzie (p. 151), DOSSO ([2], p. 35), Takayama ([7], p. 11), Chipman ([1], p. 486), Whitin, T.M., "Classical Theory, Graham's Theory and Linear Programming in International Trade," *Quarterly Journal of Economics*, LXVII, November 1953, McKenzie, L. W., "On Equilibrium in Graham's Model of World Trade and Other Competitive Systems," *Econometrica*, 22, April 1954.

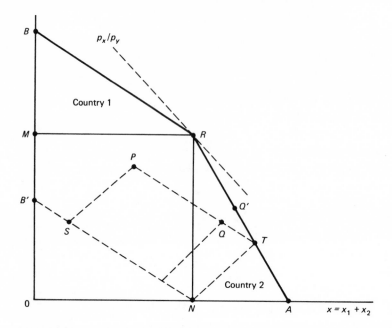

Figure 4-3   World's Production Possibilities Set and World Welfare

In Figure 4-3, MRB or ONB' represents Country 1's production triangle and NAR represents Country 2's production triangle. Geometrically the world production possibilities set may be obtained by sliding NAR along the edge $B'N$ or ONB'. It is the set of possible output combinations of X and Y for the two countries combined. If, for example, both countries specialized in the production of Y, the world output of Y would be given by OB and if both countries specialized in the production of X, the world output of X would be given by OA. If Country 1 specialized in the production of X and Country 2 specialized in the production of Y, then the world output of X and Y is represented by the point R. This point R is called *Ricardo's point* because it corresponds to Ricardo's pattern of specialization.[10]

Suppose now that both countries produced both goods X and Y (incomplete specialization for both countries). Assume that there is full employment of labor in both countries and that each country produces on its production frontier (AB for Country 1 and CD for Country 2, in Figure 4-1). For example, let S be Country 1's production point and let T be Country 2's production point. The world production point under this pattern of incomplete specialization is the point P. Note that the point P is *strictly inside* the world production possibilities set. It is easy to see that incomplete specialization of both countries *always* causes the world production point to lie strictly inside the set $OARB$.

Armed with the concept of a world production possibilities set, the solution to problem 1 (world's welfare) is almost at hand. By assuming 2, the slope

[10] The name "Ricardo's point" is due to DOSSO ([2], p. 35).

of the world price line is between the slopes of the production frontiers of the two countries. The world price line satisfying this assumption is represented by the dotted line passing through R in Figure 4-3. Clearly, under these conditions, the point R gives the solution for problem 1 and also for problem 2 since the pattern of specialization at R (Country 1 in good X and Country 2 in good Y) is the pattern we found as the solution to problem 2. We may now summarize the above analysis as follows.

THEOREM (RICARDO) Under the above specification and assumptions (including assumptions 1 and 2) of the model, given a fixed commodity price ratio, complete specialization by both countries will maximize the real income of the world as a whole and each country individually.[11]

COROLLARY If free (international) trade is started and maintained between the countries, complete specialization on the part of both countries will eventually occur (as long as the world commodity price ratio is strictly between the pre-trade domestic price ratios).

The proof of the above corollary should be obvious since the domestic price ratio of the goods is different in each country in the absence of trade and the post-trade price ratio lies strictly in between the two country's comparative advantage ratios. The theorem states the normative aspect of the classical theory of comparative advantage and the corollary gives its positive aspect.

After reading the foregoing analysis, there must remain at least one big question in the reader's mind. In our analysis we assumed that the world price ratio is a given constant for each country and then discussed the maximization problems (problem 1 and problem 2). Given this assumption, the positive aspect of the theory (the corollary) is really trivial. We have never asked questions such as: "What determines the world price ratio?" "Will the world price ratio always be strictly between the pre-trade domestic price ratios?" and so on.

The reader can immediately see that these questions cannot be answered until the demand conditions have been specified. The task of introducing the demand conditions and hence making the above analysis a full general equilibrium analysis was first completed by J. S. Mill. We shall discuss such an analysis fully (in a modern framework) in the next chapter. Here we will simply point out that as long as we are only interested in the positive aspects of the theory, the analysis will not be too difficult. Suppose that the demand conditions can be represented by a set of community indifference curves. Then the equilibrium production point for each country is the point at which the production frontier is tangent to the community indifference curve. Usually the line which is

---

[11] The alert reader may already have suspected and proved that problem 1 and problem 2 are really equivalent. We shall prove this equivalence in a more general framework. This is relevant to the contention of modern welfare economics that in the absence of externalities maximum total welfare is achieved by decentralization.

tangent to both the production possibilities line and the indifference curve will coincide with the production possibilities line (Case 1 of Figure 4-4), but when the country's preference is heavily biased in favor of one of the goods, this may not be the case (Case 2 of Figure 4-4).

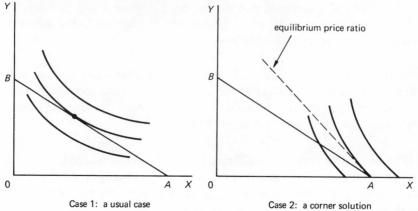

Case 1: a usual case   Case 2: a corner solution

Figure 4-4   Equilibrium Price Ratio for Each Country

Hence, assuming away corner solutions, the equilibrium price ratio for each country before trade is equal to the slope of its production possibilities line. As long as these slopes are different for the two countries, international trade will occur. And if the world price ratio after trade lies strictly between these two slopes, as Ricardo assumed, complete specialization by both countries is inevitable. Hence, the positive aspect of the Ricardian theory holds even after the introduction of the demand conditions.

In the above, we carried out our "welfare analysis", by assuming that the price ratio of the two goods is somehow given. This is unsatisfactory, and we wish to find out the welfare significance of the Ricardian theory without such an assumption. For this purpose, recall our observation in the first section that complete specialization by both countries would increase the world output of both goods. We now pursue the precise meaning of this statement. In the foregoing analysis we noted that incomplete specialization of both countries always caused the world production point to lie strictly inside the world production possibilities set. In terms of Figure 4-3, points such as P always lie strictly inside the set $0ARB$. But the Ricardian statement appears to say more than this—the point R gives more of *each* output. Will this be generally true or is it due to his particular numerical example? The answer is clear from Figure 4-3. If, for example, the world production point is represented by Q (again incomplete specialization by both countries), Ricardo's point R provides the world with a smaller amount of good X (than does point Q). Hence the Ricardian contention that complete specialization according to the pattern indicated by the point R will increase the output of each good looks rather absurd. Is there any way to rescue Ricardo? The answer to this question is in fact "yes." This can be done by replacing the question, "Will the point R increase the world output of each good?" by the question, "Is there any point in the world production possibilities set that will not decrease the outputs of X and Y (in the absence of trade) of the two countries combined?" The answer to the latter question is clearly "yes." For example, in Figure 4-3, the point R gives more output of both goods than point P. For the point Q we can find a point Q' which gives more output of each good. For the point A, we can only find the point A itself which consequently does not give more of each good, but does not give less either. Hence, the question is reduced to one of asking, "Is there any point in the world production possibilities set which will not decrease the output of either X or Y (in the absence of trade) of the two countries combined?" Let us now push this question a little further. Given a point in the world production possibilities set, if we can find another point in this set which will not decrease the output of either of the goods and will increase the output of at least one of the goods, then we call the original point an *inefficient point*. If we cannot find any "better" point, the original point is said to be an *efficient point*. Clearly any point on the kinked line ARB is an efficient point. This reveals another modern feature of the Ricardian theory, that is, its relation to the modern concept of activity analysis. The concept of an efficient point lies at the heart of activity analysis. Moreover, we may also note that any efficient point (that is, any point on the kinked line ARB) can be found as the solution to the linear programming problem, problem 1, when p_x/p_y is allowed to coincide with the pre-trade domestic price ratio of one of the countries (l_{x1}/l_{y1} or l_{x2}/l_{y2}). For example, the point Q' in Figure 4-3 is obtained as a solution to problem 1 if $p_x/p_y = l_{x2}/l_{y2}$. This again is relevant to the modern theory, that is, *parametarization* of a *vector maximum problem*. We shall take up these topics again in later chapters of Part II. We will conclude this section by listing the points of relevance of the Ricardian theory to modern analysis:[12]

1. linear programming (problems 1 and 2),
2. welfare economics (the equivalence of problems 1 and 2),
3. activity analysis (the concept of *efficient point*),
4. parametarization of the vector maximum.

THE LP DUALITY THEOREM AND THE RICARDIAN THEORY

Linear Programming is the problem of maximizing (or minimizing) a linear function subject to a set of linear constraints. Examples are problem 1 and

---

[12] It should be clear that this section is intended to be a reformulation of the Ricardian theory and a clarification of some of its modern implications. It is *not* intended to be a study of the gains from trade. The Ricardian theory is severely impaired as a result of its rather arbitrary introduction of the world price ratio. We shall discuss the gains from trade in a more satisfactory way in later chapters.

problem 2 of the previous section.[13] In general, we can consider the following two types of problem.

(M)   Find $x_1, x_2, \cdots, x_n$ such as to maximize

$$f(x) \equiv p_1 x_1 + p_2 x_2 + \cdots + p_n x_n,$$

subject to

$$a_{11} x_1 + a_{12} x_2 + \cdots + a_{1n} x_n \leqq r_1$$

$$a_{21} x_1 + a_{22} x_2 + \cdots + a_{2n} x_n \leqq r_2$$

$$\cdots$$

$$a_{m1} x_1 + a_{m2} x_2 + \cdots + a_{mn} x_n \leqq r_m,$$

where the p_js, a_{ij}s, and r_is are all given constants.

(m)   Find $w_1, w_2, \cdots, w_m$ such as to minimize

$$g(w) \equiv r_1 w_1 + r_2 w_2 + \cdots + r_m w_m$$

subject to

$$a_{11} w_1 + a_{21} w_2 + \cdots + a_{m1} w_m \geqq p_1$$

$$a_{12} w_1 + a_{22} w_2 + \cdots + a_{m2} w_m \geqq p_2$$

$$\cdots$$

$$a_{1n} w_1 + a_{2n} w_2 + \cdots + a_{mn} w_m \geqq p_n$$

where the r_is, a_{ij}s, and p_js are all given constants.

In ordinary economic problems, the variables are restricted to non-negative values so that we usually have the following non-negativity constraints in addition to the above constraints:

$$x_1 \geqq 0, x_2 \geqq 0, \cdots, x_n \geqq 0 \text{ for (M) and}$$

$$w_1 \geqq 0, w_2 \geqq 0, \cdots, w_m \geqq 0 \text{ for (m)}.$$

---

[13] A systematic way of actually computing the solution for any linear programming problem is known (it is called the simplex method) and has been programmed for electronic computers. This has led to the application of linear programming to problems in many fields. Some of the well-known applications are the gasoline blending problem, the diet problem, the production scheduling problem, and the allocation problem. There are many textbooks available describing the linear programming problems and the simplex method, for example, Hadley, G., *Linear Programming*, Reading, Mass.: Addison-Wesley, 1962. Besides these practical applications, linear programming is very important in the development of modern economic theory. For elementary expositions of similar topics, see, for example, Hicks, J. R., "Linear Theory," *Economic Journal*, December 1960, DOSSO [2], and Samuelson, P. A., "Linear Programming and Economic Theory," in *The Collected Scientific Papers of Paul Samuelson*, Vol. 1, ed. by Stiglitz, M.I.T. Press, 1966. (The article was originally written in 1955.)

Those readers who are familiar with matrix-vector notation can easily rewrite these two types of problems, including the non-negativity constraints, compactly as follows.

(M)   Find x such as to maximize

$$f(x) \equiv p \cdot x$$

subject to

$$Ax \leqq r \text{ and } x \geqq 0,$$

where $A = [a_{ij}]$.

(m)   Find w such as to minimize

$$g(w) = w \cdot r$$

subject to

$$A'w \geqq p \text{ and } w \geqq 0$$

where A' denotes the transpose of the matrix A. Here the dot ($\cdot$) refers to the inner product which is defined as follows: $p \cdot x \equiv \sum\limits_{i=1}^{n} p_i x_i$, and so on. Also, p, x, r, and w denote vectors defined as

$$p = \begin{bmatrix} p_1 \\ p_2 \\ \cdot \\ \cdot \\ \cdot \\ p_n \end{bmatrix}, \quad x = \begin{bmatrix} x_1 \\ x_2 \\ \cdot \\ \cdot \\ \cdot \\ x_n \end{bmatrix}, \quad r = \begin{bmatrix} r_1 \\ r_2 \\ \cdot \\ \cdot \\ \cdot \\ r_m \end{bmatrix}, \quad w = \begin{bmatrix} w_1 \\ w_2 \\ \cdot \\ \cdot \\ \cdot \\ w_m \end{bmatrix}.$$

We shall not distinguish between column vectors and row vectors unless the vector is multiplied by a matrix.

In the problems (M) and (m) the given constants (that is, the p_js, a_{ij}s, and r_is) can be any numbers. However, in terms of our notation, we see that there can be a systematic relationship between the two types of problem. That is,

1. The coefficients of the maximand function of (M) (that is, the p_js) constrain the inequalities of (m).
2. The coefficients of the minimand function of (m) (the r_is) constrain the inequalities of (M).
3. The inequality coefficient matrix of (m) is the transpose of the inequality coefficient matrix of (M).
4. The inequalities of (M) and (m) are reversed.

When the two problems satisfy these four conditions we say that each problem is the *dual* of the other, (M) is the dual of (m) and (m) is the dual of (M). Given one problem we should be able to write out its dual using the four conditions listed above. The most important theorem in the theory of linear programming is the (LP) *duality theorem* which may be stated as follows.

(LP) DUALITY THEOREM [14]   If the maximization problem (M) with the non-negativity constraints has a solution, then the minimization problem (m) with the non-negativity constraints has a solution. The converse of this statement also holds. Moreover, if the solution for (M) (m) is finite, the solution for (m) (M) is also finite. Finally:

1. Max $f(x)$ = min $g(w)$ when a finite solution exists for either (M) or (m).
2. If $x_j^*, j = 1, \cdots, n$ and $w_i^*, i = 1, \cdots, m$ are solutions to (M) and (m) respectively, then

a. $\displaystyle\sum_{j=1}^{n} a_{ij}x_j^* < r_i$ implies $w_i^* = 0$, $i = 1, \cdots, m$,

b. $x_j^* > 0$ implies $\displaystyle\sum_{i=1}^{m} a_{ij}w_i^* = p_j$, $j = 1, \cdots, n$.

c. $\displaystyle\sum_{i=1}^{m} w_i^* a_{ij} > p_j$ implies $x_j^* = 0$, $j = 1, \cdots, n$,

d. $w_i^* > 0$ implies $\displaystyle\sum_{j=1}^{n} a_{ij}x_j^* = r_i$, $i = 1, \cdots, m$.

The purpose of this section is to apply this theorem to the Ricardian theory of comparative advantage as reformulated in the previous section. In particular we shall be concerned with the problem of maximizing each country's national product.

MAXIMIZATION PROBLEM   For each i, $i = 1, 2$, maximize $p_x x_i + p_y y_i$ subject to

$$l_{xi}x_i + l_{yi}y_i \leq L_i, \quad x_i \geq 0, \quad y_i \geq 0.$$

The dual to this maximization problem can be written as:

MINIMIZATION PROBLEM   For each i, $i = 1, 2$, minimize $w_i L_i$ subject to

$$w_i l_{xi} \geq p_x, \quad w_i l_{yi} \geq p_y, \quad w_i \geq 0. \text{ [15]}$$

---

[14] For a proof of the LP duality theorem, see any textbook on linear programming. Two approaches seem to be most common in proving the theorem, one using the separation theorem of convex sets (for example, Nikaido) and the other using the simplex method (for example, Dantzig and Orden).

[15] w_i is the new variable for the (dual) minimization problem. The interpretation of w_i as the shadow price of labor in Country i is very interesting. Such a discussion is well formulated and solved by Samuelson in Samuelson, P. A., "Frank Knight's Theorem in Linear Programming," *Zeitschrift Für Nationalökonomie*, XVIII, 1958.

The *duality theorem* gives the following results: If there exists a finite, optimal solution for one of the problems, there exists a finite, optimal solution for the other and (omitting * which denotes the optimality of the respective variable):

a. $p_x x_i + p_y y_i = w_i L_i$, $i = 1, 2$.
b. If $w_i l_{xi} > p_x$ then $x_i = 0$, and if $w_i l_{yi} > p_y$,
then $y_i = 0$, $i = 1, 2$.
c. If $l_{xi} x_i + l_{yi} y_i < L_i$ then $w_i = 0$, $i = 1, 2$.

Note that relation b is equivalent to the following statement:

b'. $x_i > 0$ implies $w_i l_{xi} = p_x$ and $y_i > 0$ implies $w_i l_{yi} = p_y$.

If we suppose that a competitive equilibrium with international trade prevails in the two-country world, then we can show that the above relations hold with the interpretation that w_i (the shadow price of labor in Country i) is the money wage for Country i. A complete discussion of such a competitive equilibrium can obviously not be complete until we specify the demand conditions. We shall postpone such a competitive equilibrium interpretation of the Ricardian system for a later chapter. Here we will simply interpret the above relations, taking w_i as the money wage rate for labor in Country i.

Relation a says that at the optimal point, the total national product is equal to the total factor income in each country. Relation b says that at the optimal point if the marginal (= average) cost of a good exceeds its price, then the output of that good is zero. Relation c states that if there is an excess supply of labor in Country i in equilibrium, the price of the country's labor (that is, that country's wage rate) is equal to zero. Relation b' states that if a good is produced, then the marginal (= average) cost of that good is equal to its price. Relations b and b' are often called the *profit conditions*.[16]

Now let us pursue the implications of the above relations. Using the Ricardian supposition that $l_{x1}/l_{y1} < l_{x2}/l_{y2}$, we can easily prove the following four propositions from the above relations. Note that the proofs of these propositions do not depend on any interpretation of w_i (although we adopt the nickname "profit conditions" for relations b and b').

1. Under the above assumption it is not possible for Country 1 to produce good Y and Country 2 to produce X at the same time. In other words, it is not possible for both countries to produce the goods in which they have comparative disadvantages, at the same time.

[16] If the price of a good is equal to its average cost, the profit from producing that good must be zero. If the former is greater than the latter the profit from producing that good must be positive. If the former is less than the latter the profit from producing the good must be negative, hence that good will not be produced. In a competitive situation where there is free entry and exit of firms into and out of each industry the profit in each industry will presumably be zero. Note also that the equality of the marginal cost and the price is the condition for profit maximization in a competitive situation.

PROOF   Suppose that Country 1 produces Y. Then by the profit conditions, $p_y = w_1 l_{y1}$ and $p_x \leqq w_1 l_{x1}$. Hence $p_x/p_y \leqq l_{x1}/l_{y1}$. Similarly, if we suppose that Country 2 produces X, $p_x = w_2 l_{x2}$ and $p_y \leqq w_2 l_{y2}$ by the profit condition. Then we get $p_x/p_y \geqq l_{x2}/l_{y2}$ and, consequently, $l_{x1}/l_{y1} \geqq l_{x2}/l_{y2}$ which contradicts the assumption. Hence, Country 1 cannot produce Y at the same time that Country 2 is producing X.   (Q.E.D.)

2. In order for Country 1 to produce X and Country 2 to produce Y, it is necessary that $l_{x1}/l_{y1} \leqq p_x/p_y \leqq l_{x2}/l_{y2}$.

PROOF   From the profit condition we obtain $p_x = w_1 l_{x1}, p_y \leqq w_1 l_{y1}, p_x \leqq w_2 l_{x2}$ and $p_y = w_2 l_{y2}$. From this we can immediately obtain $l_{x1}/l_{y1} \leqq p_x/p_y \leqq l_{x2}/l_{y2}$.   (Q.E.D.)

3. In order for Country 1 to produce both X and Y it is necessary that $p_x/p_y = l_{x1}/l_{y1}$. Similarly, if Country 2 is to produce both X and Y it is necessary that $p_x/p_y = l_{x2}/l_{y2}$.

PROOF   From the profit conditions given the first case, we obtain $p_x = w_1 l_{x1}$ and $p_y = w_1 l_{y1}$. From this the first statement follows immediately. The second statement is proved in a similar manner.   (Q.E.D.)

Combining the above propositions, we obtain:

4. The pattern of trade and specialization can be obtained as follows:
   CASE 1 $l_{x1}/l_{y1} < p_x/p_y < l_{x2}/l_{y2}$ I(X) and II(Y).[17]
   CASE 2 $l_{x1}/l_{y1} = p_x/p_y < l_{x2}/l_{y2}$ I(X, Y) and II(Y).
   CASE 3 $l_{x1}/l_{y1} < p_x/p_y = l_{x2}/l_{y2}$ I(X) and II(X, Y).
   CASE 4 $p_x/p_y < l_{x1}/l_{y1} < l_{x2}/l_{y2}$ No X is produced.
   CASE 5 $l_{x1}/l_{y1} < l_{x2}/l_{y2} < p_x/p_y$ No Y is produced.

5. In order for at least one country to specialize completely in the production of one good (that is, I(X), II(Y), or both) it is necessary that

$$l_{y2}/l_{y1} < w_1/w_2 < l_{x2}/l_{x1}.$$

PROOF   From the profit conditions we obtain $p_x = w_1 l_{x1}$, $p_y \leqq w_1 l_{y1}$, $p_x \leqq w_2 l_{x2}$ and $p_y = w_2 l_{y2}$. From the first and third of these equations we obtain $w_1 l_{x1} \leqq w_2 l_{x2}$ or $w_1/w_2 \leqq l_{x2}/l_{x1}$. Similarly, from the second and fourth equations we obtain $l_{y2}/l_{y1} \leqq w_1/w_2$. Hence, $l_{y2}/l_{y1} \leqq w_1/w_2 \leqq l_{x2}/l_{x1}$. The equalities correspond to cases of incomplete specialization and hence are excluded.   (Q.E.D.)

REMARK   Since the problem under consideration is so simple, the above propositions are really obvious and can be proved diagrammatically (use Figure

---

[17] The Roman numerals I and II refer to the country. I(X) means that Country 1 specializes in the production of X, I(X, Y) means that Country 1 produces both X and Y (incomplete specialization), and so on.

4-1). However, it is important to notice that these propositions and their proofs provide excellent illustrations of the application of the LP duality theorem and will be useful for more complicated analysis. Also note that the classical theory of comparative advantage has penetrated the duality theorem, another relevance of the Ricardian theory to modern analysis.

REFERENCES

1. Chipman, J. S., "A Survey of the Theory of International Trade: Part 1, The Classical Theory," *Econometrica*, 33, July 1965.
2. Dorfman, R., Samuelson, P. A. and Solow, R. M., *Linear Programming and Economic Analysis* (New York: McGraw-Hill, Inc.), 1958.
3. Haberler, G., *The Theory of International Trade, with its Applications to Commercial Policy* (tr. from German, *Die internationale Handel*, Berlin, 1933), (London: William Hodge), 1936.
4. Kuhn, H. W., "Lectures on Mathematical Economics," in *Mathematics of the Decision Sciences*, Part 2, ed. by Danzig, G. B. and Veinott, A. F. (Providence, R.I.: American Mathematical Society), 1968.
5. Ricardo, D., *On the Principles of Political Economy, and Taxation* (London: John Murray), 1817, in *The Works and Correspondence of David Ricardo*, Vol. I, ed. by Piero Sraffa (Cambridge: Cambridge University Press), 1951. (Page reference is to the latter.)
6. Samuelson, P. A., "Market Mechanism and Maximization," in *The Collected Scientific Papers of Paul Samuelson*, Vol. 1, ed. by Stigliz (Cambridge, Mass.: M.I.T. Press), 1966, (the article is originally written in 1949 as two research memoranda of the RAND Corporation).
7. Takayama, A., *International Economics* (Tokyo: Toyo Keizai Shimposha), 1963, Chapter I.
8. Torrens, R., *The Economists Refuted* (London: S. A. and H. Oddy), 1808. Reprinted with separate pagination in the second and third editions of his *The Principles and Practical Operation of Sir Robert Peel's Act of 1844 Explained and Defended* (London: Longmans), 3rd ed. 1858.
9. ———, *An Essay on the External Corn Trade* (London: J. Hatchard), 1815 (1st ed.).
10. Viner, J., *Studies in the Theory of International Trade* (New York: Harper & Row, Publishers), 1937.

5

THE CLASSICAL THEORY
WITH THE
DEMAND CONDITIONS[1]

INTRODUCTION OF THE DEMAND CONDITIONS

As we saw in the previous chapter, the assumption that the world price ratio (terms of trade) of the two goods lies strictly between the cost ratios of the two goods in the two countries[2] plays a very important role in the Ricardian theory of comparative advantage. On this assumption, we were able to calculate the increase in output given a fixed amount of labor input (or the decrease in labor input required to produce a fixed amount of output) when each country specialized according to the pattern prescribed by Ricardo. In the second section (of Chapter 4) we pointed out that this problem could be considered a linear programming problem where each country's real income and the world's real income are maximized subject to the resource constraints. We also showed that if the world terms of trade are given and lie strictly between the two countries' cost ratios then it is (almost trivially) clear that each country specializes in a different good when free trade between the countries is initiated. The first point is a welfare (or "normative") proposition and the second is a "positive" proposition.

But how do we know that the world price ratio will lie strictly between the two countries' cost ratios? What is the mechanism that determines the world price ratio? J. S. Mill [13], following Torrens, argued that the demand conditions as well as the Ricardian consideration of cost conditions are necessary to answer this problem. He then provided a satisfactory answer to the problem using both sets of conditions.

Let us first consider the positive aspect of this problem: What is the mech-

---

[1] For a doctrinal history of the material presented in this chapter, Chipman [2] and Viner [17] are useful.

[2] Recall that in Ricardo's example, England's cloth:wine cost ratio was 100/120, Portugal's cloth:wine cost ratio was 90/80 and the world cloth:wine price ratio was 1/1.

anism that determines the world price ratio *after* international trade between the two countries has started? The answer to this question is easily found using the offer curve diagram.[3] We start this chapter by recalling our discussion of the offer curve in Chapter 1.

The *offer curve* of a country is a curve (drawn in the commodity space determined by two goods, say cloth and food) that traces the locus of excess supply or excess demand of these goods for that country corresponding to different price ratios of the two goods (with the budget condition satisfied and the factor markets equilibriated). Obviously, such equilibrium points can only be described after proper consideration has been given to the demand and supply conditions. Consider a world consisting of two countries (say, E and G).[4] The offer curves for these two countries can then be shown by the e curve and the g curve respectively in Figure 5-1.

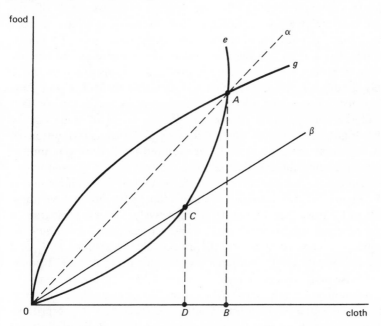

Figure 5-1   The Offer Curve Analysis

[3] The offer curve is also called the *reciprocal demand curve*. The concept of reciprocal demand, as to provide a mechanism for the determination of terms of trade, is a very important contribution by J. S. Mill to economics. Marshall elaborated upon it in geometrical form. It should be noted that the offer curve in the present section is a simple case of the Mill-Marshall offer curve in Chapter 1. Here the production transformation curve is a straight line (that is, the constant cost case). It is expected that the present discussion will enhance the reader's understanding of this important diagrammatical technique as well as clarify some important points in the classical theory of comparative advantage.

[4] Mill, [13] and [14], called the two countries England and Germany. Marshall [9] then called them Country E and Country G. The two goods were called linen and cloth by Mill, and E bales and G bales by Marshall. Marshall's bales are an aggregate concept which gives the theory a more realistic tone than the two goods linen and cloth. Graham attacked this concept sharply ([5], pp. 157–160, 283–284).

Suppose, for example, that the price ratio of the two goods is given by the slope of the line β. The point C is the point at which country E has an excess supply, $0D$, of cloth and an excess demand, CD, for food. (In somewhat sloppy language, Country E is willing to trade $0D$ of cloth for CD of food.) As the slope of the β line varies (that is, as the price ratio of the two goods varies), we obtain the locus of such points—the e curve—which is called *Country E's offer curve*. Similarly, we can draw Country G's offer curve, the g curve. The one point at which both countries are satisfied, is the point at which the two offer curves intersect. In Figure 5-1, the point A is the point of intersection of the two offer curves—the e curve and the g curve. The slope of the α line gives the equilibrium price ratio (or "terms of trade") and at this price ratio Country E (G) exports (imports) an amount $0B$ of cloth and imports (exports) an amount AB of food.

In order to determine the amount of excess demand or excess supply of each good for each country at a given price ratio for the goods, we have to consider the interaction between the demand and supply conditions. To understand this better it is best to use the concepts of the community indifference curves [5] for the demand conditions and the production transformation curve for the supply conditions, neither of which was available to Mill. Using these concepts, the construction of the offer curve for each country (for the constant cost case) and the determination of the equilibrium terms of trade can be illustrated by Figure 5-2. We assume, following the classical tradition of Ricardo and Mill, that the amount of labor required to produce one unit of output of a good is constant and that labor is the only factor of production. Given these assumptions, the production transformation set for each country is a triangle. In Figure 5-2, the triangles E and G denote the production transformation sets of Country E and Country G respectively. Cloth is measured on the horizontal axis and food is measured on the vertical axis. The origins for the two countries are denoted by 0_E and 0_G respectively. The curves, i_1, i_2, and so on, are the community utility indifference curves for Country E. The points of tangency of these indifference curves with the price lines (the lines β, γ, and so on) determine Country E's offer curve (the e curve). For example, if the price ratio is given by the slope of the γ line, Country E specializes in the production of cloth (produces an amount $0_E S$) and trades an amount SB of cloth for an amount AB of food. In other words, with the price line γ, Country E has an excess supply of an amount BS of cloth and an excess demand for an amount AB of food. It should be clear that, given the slope of the transformation curves of the two countries as in Figure 5-2, the slope of the price line cannot be less than that of the SR-line. Point I_E gives the consumption point of Country E under autarky. Note that if the price line coincides with the production transformation line, (SR), Country E will not necessarily specialize completely in

---

[5] As we noted in Chapter 1, a sharp distinction is to be made with regard to the social welfare function, depending on whether it is used to describe the welfare level of the society or it is used to describe the behavior of the society. We are using the concept here for the latter purpose, which is much more acceptable than the former purpose.

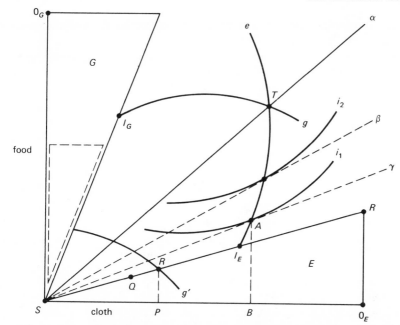

Figure 5-2   The Construction of the Offer Curve and the Determination of the World Terms of Trade

the production of cloth. Usually it will produce both food and cloth (incomplete specialization). It may have to be stressed that the production in this case does *not* have to take place at point I_E, when international trade is allowed.

The world terms of trade (goods price ratio) are determined by the intersection of the two countries' offer curves (the intersection of the e curve and the g curve). Point T is such a point and the slope of the α line gives the equilibrium terms of trade. Notice that if one country is small enough relative to the other, then the equilibrium price line will coincide with the production transformation curve of the larger country. Suppose, for example, that Country G's production transformation set is given by the dotted triangle, and that G's offer curve in this case is given by the curve g', then the point of intersection of the two offer curves is the point R. Here the world goods price ratio is equal to the slope of the line SR. Notice that we have thus obtained a case in which the Ricardian assumption that the world terms of trade lie strictly in between the cost (= price) ratios of the two countries does *not* hold. Note also that, in this case, Country E's consumption takes place at point I_E and her production takes place at point Q where $QI_E = SR$.[6]

Another case in which the world terms of trade do not lie between the cost ratios of the two countries is obtained when the preference relation (that is, the indifference curves) has a strong bias in favor of one good. This case is illustrated by Figure 5-3. In Figure 5-3, the point T is the point of intersection

[6] Obviously Country E exports SP of cloth and imports RP of food.

of the two offer curves (curves e and g), and the equilibrium price line (the α line) coincides with Country E's cost ratio.

If the world terms of trade coincide with one country's pre-trade price ratio, there will be no gains from trade in that country. For example, if, as in Figure 5-3, the world price line (α) coincides with Country E's pre-trade price ratio

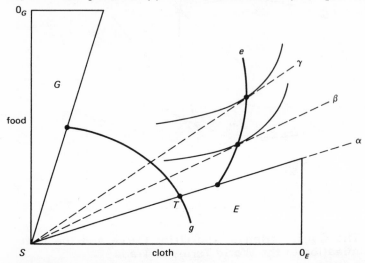

Figure 5-3   Demand Bias

(the ST line), then it does not make any difference to Country E whether or not it enters into international trade. Country G, on the other hand, can now exchange a given amount of food for a larger amount of cloth and thus, by specializing in the production of food, can maximize its real income. In this case Country G's real income after trade will be higher than that in isolation.[7] Hence, in this case Country G reaps all the gains from trade, while Country E gets none. J. S. Mill clearly recognized the possibility of such an extreme case when he wrote:

> It is even possible to conceive an extreme case, in which the whole of the advantage resulting from the interchange would be reaped by one party, the other country gaining nothing at all. There is no absurdity in the hypothesis, that of some given commodity, a certain quantity is all that is wanted at any price; and that when that quantity is obtained, no fall in the exchangeable value would induce other consumers to come forward, or those who are already supplied take more ([13], p. 13, also [14], p. 587).

This is a situation similar to that illustrated in Figure 5-3.

It should be clear that once the equilibrium world price ratio has been determined we can easily compute the gains from trade. For notational simplicity

---

[7] Recall the discussion in the previous chapter. Once the world terms of trade have been established, the rest of the discussion is the same as of that chapter.

let us call the two goods, good X and good Y, and let x and y be the outputs of goods X and Y respectively. Let p be the equilibrium world price ratio of good X and good Y (that is, $p = p_x/p_y$) and let p_E and p_G be the pre-trade domestic price ratios of Countries E and G respectively. Then suppose that $p_E \leqq p \leqq p_G$, as in the above diagrams. If $p_E < p < p_G$, Country E specializes in the production of good X, and Country G specializes in the production of good Y. Let x_E and y_E (x_G and y_G) denote the total amounts of good X and good Y that Country E (Country G) could produce if it specialized completely in the production of X and Y respectively.

Before trade each country may produce both goods or specialize completely in the production of either good. In any case, Country E's real income before trade is x_E in terms of good X or y_E in terms of good Y, as long as p_E coincides with Country E's cost ratio (the slope of Country E's production transformation line which, by assumption, is constant). Similarly, Country G's real income before trade is x_G in terms of good X and y_G in terms of good Y as long as p_G coincides with Country G's cost ratio. Clearly, we have $y_E/x_E = p_E$ and $y_G/x_G = p_G$ on the assumption of the equality of the price ratio and the cost ratio. After trade, the world price ratio, p, is determined, and we observe the above pattern of specialization (Country E in X and Country G in Y) and measure the gains from trade (the increase in real income) in Country E in terms of good Y as $px_E - y_E = (p - p_E)x_E$, or as $(p - p_E)x_E/p$ in terms of good X. Similarly, with this pattern of specialization, the gains from trade in Country G in terms of good X are $(1/p)y_G - x_G = (1/p - 1/p_G)y_G$, or $p(1/p - 1/p_G)y_G$ in terms of good Y. Therefore, as long as $p_E < p$ there is a positive gain from trade for Country E, and as long as $p < p_G$ there is a positive gain from trade for Country G. Moreover, as the difference between p_E and p (p and p_G) increases the gain from trade to Country E (Country G) increases.[8]

Thus the increase in a country's welfare as a result of trade is a function of the difference between that country's cost ratio and the world price ratio. However, this does not necessarily imply that each country increases its consumption of both goods. In fact, it is possible and likely that a country may reduce its consumption of one of the goods after trade. This is illustrated by Figure 5-4 (Case 1). The case in which this is not true is also illustrated in Figure 5-4 (Case 2; Country E).

From the above consideration it is also clear why the world terms of trade have been considered an important criterion in determining the gains from trade. The more the world price ratio diverges from the country's cost ratio, the larger are its gains from trade. This suggests that, if by some policy or other, a country can move the world price ratio away from its cost ratio, then it can increase its gains from trade. This consideration also leads to the following discussion. Suppose that a country is "selfish," that is, she desires that the world

---

[8] This discussion of the gains from trade from the point of view of the terms of trade obviously holds for the previous chapter as well. However, since the terms of trade there were specified by assumption and not determined by the demand conditions, a discussion of the gains from trade in terms of the terms of trade, would have been rather ambiguous.

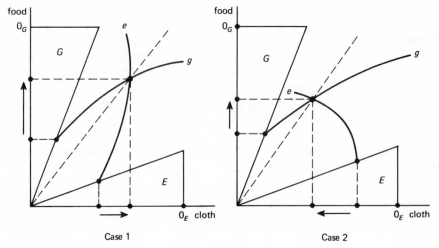

Figure 5-4   Decrease in Consumption After Trade

price ratio equals the other country's cost ratio (whether this is possible or not) and not the price ratio determined by the intersection of the two countries' offer curves (if these two are different). This consideration opens the way for a discussion of the *optimum tariff*, which we shall take up in a later chapter (Chapter 14).

What then is the welfare significance of the equilibrium terms of trade? To answer this question we recall that a country's offer curve is the locus of points of tangency of different price lines and the country's community welfare indifference curves. Suppose we draw the *contract curve* for the two countries, that is, the locus of points at which Country E's indifference curve is tangent to Country G's indifference curve. Then we can easily see that the point of intersection of the two offer curves lies on the contract curve. The meaning of the contract curve is well-known—it is the locus of points at which one party (in this case, one country) cannot increase its welfare without decreasing the welfare of the other party, given a fixed supply of goods (here the total world output of both goods). In other words, the contract curve traces the locus of Pareto optimal points and the equilibrium world terms of trade will bring the world to a Pareto optimal state, since trade under the equilibrium terms of trade will bring both countries to the point at which the two offer curves intersect. Omitting, for the sake of simplicity, the two production transformation triangles from the diagram, we shall illustrate our discussion with Figure 5-5. The situation here is strictly analogous to the one in the second section of Chapter 1, in which the production transformation curve is concave to the origin.

Finally we may point out that our characterization of the *world equilibrium point* (the point of intersection of the two offer curves) as a Pareto optimal point corresponds to our characterization of the Ricardo point as an *efficient point* when the Ricardian theory of comparative advantage is interpreted in terms of activity analysis.

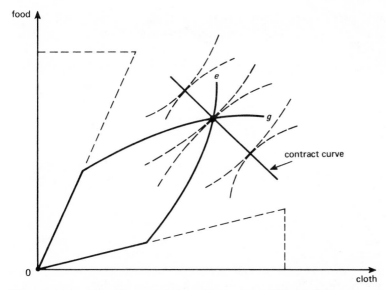

Figure 5-5   The Demand Conditions and World Welfare

MILL'S PROBLEM

In the first section, we first considered the positive aspect of the theory, that is, the mechanism by which the world price ratio is determined. We pointed out that Mill's introduction of the demand conditions is crucial to this mechanism. Then we considered the normative aspect of the theory, the gains from trade.

Here, we shall consider the problem from the point of view of maximizing the world's welfare, assuming that there exists a single utility function (hence, one set of indifference curves) for the world as a whole. For the sake of notational simplicity, we shall abolish the Mill-Marshall convention of calling the countries Country E and Country G and call them Country 1 and Country 2 instead.

Let x_i and y_i denote the production of good X and good Y respectively in Country i ($i = 1, 2$). Let $x \equiv x_1 + x_2$ and $y \equiv y_1 + y_2$ be the world production of goods X and Y respectively. Now suppose that the level of satisfaction of the world as a whole can be represented by a single utility function $u(x, y)$. This can be justified by assuming either that everybody in the world has the same utility function or that the individual utility functions are "aggregatable."[9]

Let l_{xi} and l_{yi} denote the amounts of labor required to produce one unit of X and one unit of Y respectively in Country i ($i = 1, 2$). Let L_i be the total amount of labor available in Country i ($i = 1, 2$). Again it is assumed that l_{x1}, l_{x2}, l_{y1}, and l_{y2} are constants for all levels of output and that labor is the only input. This specification of the production side of the economy has been

---

[9] See Eisenberg [3] for a case of cardinal utility functions. As is well-known, the individual's utility is an ordinal, and not a cardinal, concept. Hence $u(x, y)$ simply measures a utility *index*, the ordering of which must be invariant under any monotone transformation.

essentially inherited from the Ricardian model discussed in the previous chapter. As we noted there, the resource constraint for each country may be written as

$$l_{x1}x_1 + l_{y1}y_1 \leqq L_1 , \quad \text{and} \tag{5-1a}$$

$$l_{x2}x_2 + l_{y2}y_2 \leqq L_2 . \tag{5-1b}$$

Or, equivalently as

$$\frac{x_1}{a_1} + \frac{y_1}{b_1} \leqq 1 , \quad \text{where } a_1 \equiv L_1/l_{x1} \text{ and } b_1 \equiv L_1/l_{y1} , \tag{5-2a}$$

$$\frac{x_2}{a_2} + \frac{y_2}{b_2} \leqq 1 , \quad \text{where } a_2 \equiv L_2/l_{x2} \text{ and } b_2 \equiv L_2/l_{y2} . \tag{5-2b}$$

Thus our problem is to find x_1, x_2, y_1, and y_2 so as to maximize $u(x_1 + x_2, y_1 + y_2)$ subject to (5-2a), (5-2b) and $x_1 \geqq 0$, $x_2 \geqq 0$, $y_1 \geqq 0$, $y_2 \geqq 0$. This, clearly, is a problem in nonlinear programming since the function u is not necessarily linear.

Without loss of generality, we again adopt the Ricardian assumption that:

$$\frac{l_{x1}}{l_{y1}} < \frac{l_{x2}}{l_{y2}} \quad \text{or} \quad \frac{b_1}{a_1} < \frac{b_2}{a_2} . \tag{5-3}$$

That is, Country 1 has a comparative advantage in the production of good X, and Country 2 has a comparative advantage in the production of good Y. Ricardo's doctrine of comparative advantage then specifies the pattern of production and trade, as follows, assuming that the equilibrium world price ratio lies between the two countries' pre-trade cost ratios: Country 1 specializes in the production of good X and Country 2 specializes in the production of good Y [this can be written as I(X) and II(Y)]. Will this still be the pattern of production after the introduction of the demand condition? This question was answered in the previous section. Thus, if the equilibrium world price ratio equals the cost ratio of one of the countries, then this pattern of specialization will, in general, not occur. The country whose cost ratio equals the world price ratio will, in general, produce both goods after trade (that is, be incompletely specialized). Whether or not the world price ratio equals one country's cost ratio depends, among other things, on the demand conditions, and the utility functions for the people of both countries.

Suppose we now ask the following question: Under what conditions will the Ricardian pattern of specialization [I(X) and II(Y)] be the solution to the above nonlinear programming problem? This is Chipman's [2] formulation of Mill's problem. The answer to this question clearly depends on the nature of the utility function, $u(x, y)$. Chipman observed that Mill's specification of the demand conditions[10] was tantamount to specifying the following utility function:

$$u(x, y) = xy .\tag{5-4}$$

The answer to the above question is then easily obtained using the concept of a world production possibilities set, as introduced in the previous chapter.

Due to the specification of the utility function given in equation (5-4), the equation for the indifference curves is simply $xy = $ constant. From this we obtain $ydx + xdy = 0$ or

$$\frac{dy}{dx} = \frac{-y}{x},\tag{5-5}$$

as the slope of the indifference curve.

In the diagram below (Figure 5-6), the point R denotes Ricardo's point signifying the Ricardian pattern of specialization [I(X) and II(Y)]. The co-ordinates of this point are easily found as (a_1, b_2). A necessary and sufficient condition for the solution to the above nonlinear programming problem is that the Ricardian point R is optimal. That is, the slope of the utility indifference curve at the point R must lie between the cost ratios of the two countries as

---

[10] Mill writes, "As the simplest and most convenient, let us suppose that in both countries any given increase of cheapness produces an exactly proportional increase of consumption: or, in other words, that the value expended in the commodity, the cost incurred for the sake of obtaining it, is always the same, whether that cost affords a greater or a smaller quantity of the commodity." ([14], p. 598.) As Chipman points out ([2], p. 484), this means that the own-price-elasticity of demand is unity, that the cross-price-elasticity of demand is zero and that the income elasticity of demand is unity. The utility function that gives rise to such a demand function is known to have the form $u = x^\alpha y^\beta$, $\alpha > 0$, $\beta > 0$. Mill further assumed that one half of the total expenditure is always devoted to each good, so that $u = x^{1/2}y^{1/2}$. Chipman simplified this to $u = xy$. The reader may consider the problem of maximizing $u = x^\alpha y^\beta$ subject to $p_x x + p_y y = M$ and obtain the solution

$$x = \frac{\alpha}{\alpha + \beta} \frac{M}{p_x} \quad \text{and} \quad y = \frac{\beta}{\alpha + \beta} \frac{M}{p_y}$$

(which implies $y = (\beta/\alpha)px$, $p \equiv p_x/p_y$, the equation obtained in Chapter 1, third section). From this it can easily be shown that

$$\frac{\partial x}{\partial p_x} \cdot \frac{p_x}{x} = \frac{\partial y}{\partial p_y} \cdot \frac{p_y}{y} = 1,$$

$$\frac{\partial x}{\partial p_y} \cdot \frac{p_y}{x} = \frac{\partial y}{\partial p_x} \cdot \frac{p_x}{y} = 0,$$

and

$$\frac{\partial x}{\partial M} \cdot \frac{M}{x} = \frac{\partial y}{\partial M} \cdot \frac{M}{y} = 1.$$

The converse problem, that is, the problem of obtaining the utility function from these demand specifications, is a more difficult problem.

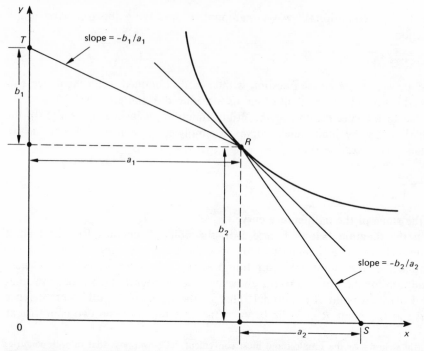

Figure 5-6 Mill's Problem and Mill's Condition

given in equation (5-3). The slope of the utility indifference curve at point R is obtained by differentiating $u(x, y) = $ constant, and evaluating at R,

$$\frac{dy}{dx} = -\frac{u_x}{u_y}, \quad \text{where } u_x \equiv \frac{\partial u}{\partial x} \quad \text{and} \quad u_y \equiv \frac{\partial u}{\partial y}, \tag{5-6}$$

where u_x and u_y are evaluated at point R (that is, $x = a_1, y = b_2$).

   In particular, when $u(x, y) = xy$, we have equation (5-5). Then the necessary and sufficient condition may be expressed as

$$\frac{b_1}{a_1} \leq \frac{u_x}{u_y} \leq \frac{b_2}{a_2} \quad \text{(with at least one strict inequality).} \tag{5-7}$$

That is, if R is optimal, then (5-7) is satisfied, and conversely if (5-7) is satisfied at R, R is optimal. In particular, if $u(x, y) = xy$, then $u_x/u_y = b_2/a_1$, so that equation (5-7) may be rewritten as

$$\frac{b_1}{a_1} \leq \frac{b_2}{a_1} \leq \frac{b_2}{a_2} \quad \text{(with at least one strict inequality).} \tag{5-8}$$

Condition (5-8) is called *Mill's condition*. We should note that this condition does not follow automatically from Ricardo's assumption [equation (5-3)]. Figure 5-7 illustrates a case in which Mill's condition (5-8) is violated at point R. In Figure 5-7, the Ricardian point R can *not* be the solution to the above nonlinear programming problem (with $u(x, y) = xy$).

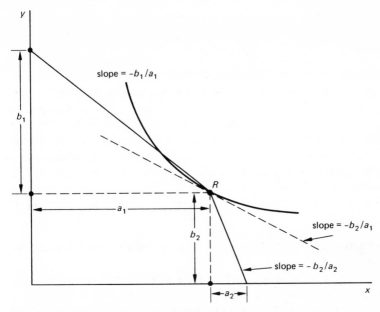

Figure 5-7 Violation of Mill's Condition

Note that Mill's condition (5-8), is equivalent to the following condition:

$$b_1 \leqq b_2 \quad \text{and} \quad a_1 \geqq a_2 \text{ with at least one strict inequality.} \tag{5-9}$$

Or, equivalently,

$$l_{y1}/L_1 \geqq l_{y2}/L_2 \quad \text{and} \quad l_{x1}/L_1 \leqq l_{x2}/L_2 \text{ with at least one strict inequality.} \tag{5-10}$$

If both inequalities of equation (5-10) are strict inequalities and if $L_1 = L_2$, Country 1 must have an absolute advantage in the production of good X and Country 2 must have an absolute advantage in the production of good Y. Recalling that in Ricardo's example Portugal had an absolute advantage in the production of *both* goods, we see that Mill's condition could not be satisfied in that case. Thus, the introduction of the demand condition casts some doubt on the validity of the Ricardian theory of comparative advantage.

As Chipman noted ([2], p. 489), Mill realized that his conclusion, condition (5-8) or (5-9), was crucially dependent on his specification of the demand conditions [equation (5-4)]. By altering the specification of the demand conditions it is possible to obtain different results. Mill attempted to work out more general cases ([14], Book III, Chapter 18, Sections 8 and 9), but his mathematical tools precluded any such generalizations. For a complete discussion of the problem we should use the modern theory of nonlinear programming. We shall return to this topic in the next chapter.

FURTHER REMARKS

Pareto's Problem

Ricardo assumed that, after free trade had been initiated, the world price ratio would lie between the two countries' cost ratios. In the previous chapter, we saw that under this assumption Ricardo's point (point R) was the point at which the world's welfare was maximized. We also obtained this result when we considered the problem from the point of view of linear programming. In the last section, we imposed the demand conditions and obtained the condition under which Ricardo's assumption could be justified—Mill's condition. Pareto [15], without referring to Mill, also asked whether Ricardo's assumption could be justified. He concluded that (see also Chipman [2], p. 488 and Viner [17], pp. 451–453):

1. Specialization could lead to a reduction in the world's output of one of the goods.
2. If the world's output of one of the goods is reduced, it is impossible to say whether specialization has increased or decreased the world's welfare, without taking tastes into account (that is, without specifying demand or utility functions).
3. If the total output of *each* good is increased after specialization, then Ricardo's conclusion that there is an increase in the world's welfare is certainly true.

In the previous chapter we noted the first point. (Compare point Q and point R in Figure 4-3 of Chapter 4). There we noted that the proper way to characterize the welfare implications, without a demand (or utility) specification, is by way of the activity analysis concept of an efficient point. On the other hand, if we introduce the demand conditions, then we can unambiguously conclude whether each country's welfare has been increased or decreased by specialization. In the previous section, we considered this problem from the point of view of the world's welfare, assuming that there existed a single world utility function.

Now, in view of Pareto's interest, let us look at the welfare question from each country's point of view. In order to make our discussion here comparable to that of the previous section, let us assume that each country has a community utility function of the form $u_i(x_i, y_i) = x_i y_i$ where $i = 1, 2$. Both countries' production transformation triangles and equilibrium points are shown in Figure 5-8. As is clear from the diagram, the pre-trade equilibrium values of output (and consumption) are: $x_1 = a_1/2$ and $y_1 = b_1/2$ for Country 1 and $x_2 = a_2/2$ and $y_2 = b_2/2$ for Country 2. Hence, the world output of goods X and Y before trade is

$$X: x_1 + x_2 = (a_1 + a_2)/2,$$

$$Y: y_1 + y_2 = (b_1 + b_2)/2.$$

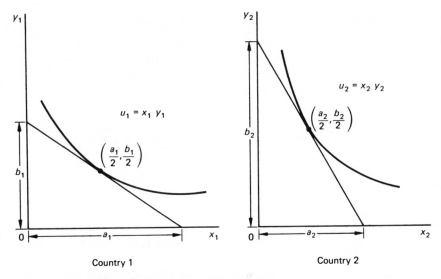

Country 1   Country 2

Figure 5-8   Each Country's Equilibrium

Suppose now that the world adopts the Ricardian pattern of specialization [I(X) and II(Y)] and initiates international trade. Then the output of goods X and Y available to the world as a whole is

$$X: x_1 = a_1, \quad (x_2 = 0),$$

$$Y: y_2 = b_2, \quad (y_1 = 0).$$

Pareto asserted (point 3 above) that if the total output of *each* good is increased after specialization, then the world welfare is increased. If we apply this rather obvious sufficient condition for an increase in the world's welfare to the above we obtain[11]

$$a_1 > (a_1 + a_2)/2 \quad \text{and} \quad b_2 > (b_1 + b_2)/2. \tag{5-11}$$

Or,

$$a_1 > a_2 \quad \text{and} \quad b_2 > b_1. \tag{5-12}$$

If we allow at most one equality in (5-12) we immediately notice that Pareto's sufficient condition for an increase in the world's welfare is equivalent to Mill's condition, (5-9), obtained in the previous section. Thus we find that the approach from the point of view of the world's welfare is related to the approach from the point of view of each country's welfare. We shall pursue this topic further in a later chapter for it goes beyond the scope of diagrammatical analysis.

[11] In general this does not have to be true, as we observed in the first section. The subsequent conclusion that Pareto's criterion coincides with Mill's condition, is crucially dependent on the Millian utility function $u = xy$, that is, half of the total expenditure is always devoted to each good.

Pareto's Paradox

It is possible that the Ricardian pattern of complete specialization is incompatible with the world's tastes. In other words, tastes may be such that the Ricardian pattern of specialization will not occur after the initiation of international trade. This is called *Pareto's paradox* by Chipman ([2], p. 489). At least one country may continue to produce both goods after trading has started. We discussed this in the first section. In the second section, we also noted that the world's welfare may not be maximized at Ricardo's point, R (Figure 5-7). We can also illustrate this by Figure 5-9 where the pattern of production is $I(X, Y)$ and $II(Y)$.

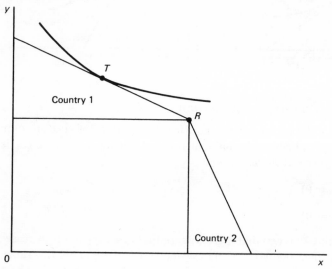

Figure 5-9   Pareto's Paradox

Mill's Paradox

In the first section, we noted that if one country is sufficiently small relative to the other, then the world's price ratio may be equal to the larger country's cost ratio, leaving no gains from trade for this country. From a similar type of analysis, it can easily be conjectured that the world price ratio gets closer to the larger country's cost ratio as this country increases in size, and that as a limiting case the two ratios will be equal when the larger country becomes sufficiently large. Since the gains from trade to a country decrease as the world price ratio approaches that country's cost ratio, we may conjecture that, "As a country gets larger, *ceteris paribus*, the gains from trade to that country decrease." This is called Mill's paradox.[12]

Mill's paradox can also be seen using the world production possibilities set. This was done by Chipman ([2], pp. 489–490). To see the problem in this way,

---

[12] In Mill's own words, "the richest countries, *ceteris paribus*, gain the least by a given amount of foreign commerce." ([14], p. 604.)

let us suppose that one country's production transformation triangle gets bigger and bigger, with no change in the slope of its hypotenuse.[13] In the following diagram (Figure 5-10), the size of Country 1's production transformation triangle increases in such a manner. Notice that, in the diagram, the terms of trade line gets flatter and flatter as Country 1's triangle expands, eventually coinciding with the hypotenuse of Country 1's production transformation triangle (Country 1's cost ratio).

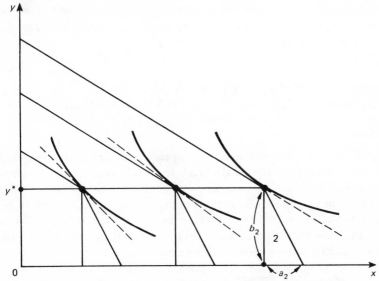

Figure 5-10   Chipman's Exposition of Mill's Paradox

In order to examine the proposition (or conjecture) that the world terms of trade line gets flatter as the size of Country 1's production possibilities triangle increases, recall that the slope of the utility indifference curve is given by $|-u_x/u_y|$. Now increase x, holding y constant at y^*. That is, partially differentiate u_x/u_y with respect to x, thus:

$$\frac{\partial}{\partial x}\left(\frac{u_x}{u_y}\right) = \frac{1}{u_y^2}(u_{xx}u_y - u_{xy}u_x),\tag{5-13}$$

where $u_{xx} \equiv \partial u_x/\partial x$ and $u_{xy} \equiv \partial u_x/\partial y$.

If $u(x, y) = xy$ [equation (5-4)], then $u_{xx}u_y - u_{xy}u_x = -y^* = -b_2 < 0$, which proves the above proposition. But we also notice that, in general, Mill's paradox does *not* necessarily hold since the *RHS* of equation (5-13) is not

---

[13] This question of the effect of growth on the terms of trade has been a hotly debated issue in the theory of international trade, since Hicks' inaugural lecture at Oxford in 1952. This debate will be taken up in a later chapter. It is astonishing that J. S. Mill had already considered this problem ([14], Book III, Chapter XVIII, Section 5). For a short summary of the discussions by Mill, Edgeworth, Bastable, and Nicholson on this subject, see Caves [1], pp. 152–153.

necessarily negative. The conclusion obviously depends on the nature of the demand condition, that is, the shape of the utility function.[14]

Thus, a necessary and sufficient condition for Mill's paradox to hold is that

$$u_{xx}u_y - u_{xy}u_x < 0 .$$ (5-14)

In somewhat loose language, u_x may be considered as the marginal utility of X, so that $u_{xx} \leqq 0$, a non-increasing marginal utility of good X is a condition that can be accepted without difficulty. Hence, given that the marginal utilities of both goods are non-negative ($u_x \geqq 0$ and $u_y \geqq 0$) a sufficient condition for Mill's paradox to hold is that

$$u_{xy} > 0 \quad (\text{and } u_x > 0) .$$ (5-15)

In other words, if the marginal utility of one good increases when the consumption of the other good is increased, then Mill's paradox holds.

Graham's Rebuttal

Graham, using numerical examples, attempted to generalize the classical model to a many-country, many-good model. In the classical theory there are two limiting ratios for the terms of trade ratio. Graham held that one of these two ratios would in fact be the equilibrium terms of trade ratio. Moreover, he argued that this limiting price ratio would be the one that usually prevailed in equilibrium and that the intermediate "limbo" price ratios were exceptions. For example, if there are three goods and two countries, and if one of the goods is produced in both countries, then, he argued, the adjustment would show up as a movement of labor into or out of this industry in the two countries, rather than as a change in the terms of trade. Similarly, if there are three countries and two goods and if the world price ratio coincides with one country's cost ratio, then the shifts in world demand would be reflected in a reallocation of the resources (labor) of this country, rather than in a change in the terms of trade. Graham's proposition can best be illustrated by Figure 5-11 for the three-country, two-good case.

In Figure 5-11, a change in the (world) demand conditions (a shift of the indifference curve from i to j) is absorbed by a shift of labor from the Y industry into the X industry in Country 2, moving the production point of that country from G to G'. The terms of trade line (α) remains unchanged by this change in the demand conditions. Country 2, here, is called the "common country." As the number of countries and goods increases, the probability of there being a common country and/or common good increases. This strengthens the above proposition. In this way, Graham wanted to prove his belief that empirically the terms of trade were stable.

[14] In his consideration of this problem (the effects of growth on the terms of trade), Mill clearly realized that the conclusion depended on the demand condition. Thus he considered three kinds of demand conditions where "the demand would be increased more than the cheapness, as much as the cheapness, or less than the cheapness." He then concluded that the third case was the "most probable" ([14], p. 596).

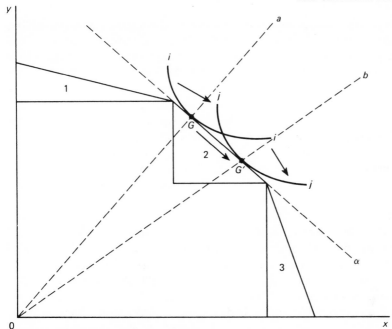

Figure 5-11 Graham's Rebuttal

A weakness in the above argument is fairly clear as is demonstrated in Figure 5-12. The terms of trade line is determined by the tangency of the production transformation curve and the (world) indifference curve. The slope of this line can take any value from 0 to → ∞. We asserted that the terms of

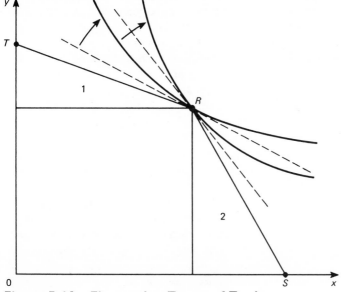

Figure 5-12 Fluctuating Terms of Trade

trade line would coincide with one country's production transformation curve (in terms of Figure 5-12, the terms of trade line would coincide with either RT or SR). But there are only a finite number of these production transformation curves because the number of countries and the number of goods are always finite. The probability of picking any one of a finite number of possibilities out of an infinite number of possibilities is zero, assuming that all of the possibilities are equally likely—and we seem to have no reason to assume otherwise. In any case, we should conclude that the terms of trade line is very likely to be tangent to the world production possibilities set at one of its "vertices." Then, as illustrated in Figure 5-12, any change in demand conditions causes a change in the terms of trade.

In the above we have not made any specific assumptions on the demand conditions. However it is well known that Graham, at least in his earlier work [4], employed a very specific demand assumption—that is, commodities are always consumed in fixed proportions. If this is the case for each country, then the world demand for commodities would also be such that commodities are always consumed in fixed proportions. In terms of Figure 5-11, this means that two commodities are always consumed along a ray from the origin (say the a-ray). It is then certainly more probable that such a ray passes a flat side rather than a vertex of the world transformation curve. A change in tastes can be represented by a rotation of such a ray (for example, from the a-ray to the b-ray in Figure 5-11). In other words, this supports Graham's conclusions that the world terms of trade will be equal to "limbo" country's cost ratio, and that a small change in demand is simply absorbed by a relocation of resources, causing no change in the world terms of trade.

Recently Melvin [11] considered the consequences of the above demand assumption and clarified a possible adjustment mechanism which could create the above conclusion. In particular, he argues that the (global) instability of the equilibrium world terms of trade, when these are not equal to some country's cost ratio, is the major cause of Graham's conclusions. In order to illustrate his point, we have to construct the offer curve of each country under *the demand specification—commodities are always consumed in fixed proportions in each country*. This task is not too difficult. Assuming again the classical two-country, two-commodity model, the determination of equilibrium terms of trade is illustrated in Figure 5-13. The offer curve of Country E, for example, is a ray from the origin 0_E, reflecting the demand assumption. The offer curves of the two countries E and G are denoted by e and g. Note that they are straight lines due to the demand assumption. The equilibrium terms of trade are represented by the α-line, and point U signifies the equilibrium volume of trade.

As Melvin [11] pointed out, these equilibrium terms of trade are not stable. In other words: a slight deviation of the terms of trade from the α-line will cause a further change, such as to widen the gap between them. This is illustrated in Figure 5-14, where e and g respectively denote the offer curves of Countries E and G, and the α-line denotes the equilibrium terms of trade.

Suppose, for example, that the terms of trade move from α to β (that is, the

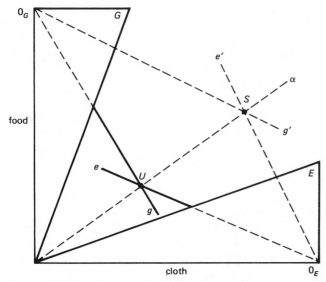

Figure 5-13   Graham's Demand Condition and the Offer Curves

relative price of cloth vis-à-vis food declines). Then Country E's excess supply of cloth increases by AC, while Country G's excess demand for cloth increases by AB. In other words, there is a net increase in the world excess supply for cloth, denoted by BC. Since the world excess supply for cloth is zero at the original terms of trade α, this implies a positive amount of world excess supply of cloth. Hence the cloth:food price decreases further, and this movement of the terms of trade away from its equilibrium value α will continue until it

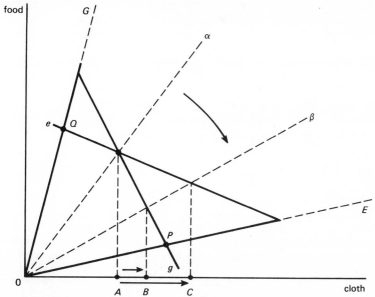

Figure 5-14   An Unstable Graham Equilibrium

becomes equal to Country E's cost ratio (the slope of the $0E$-line). The final equilibrium point then is point P, which is (locally) stable. Clearly the exact opposite would occur, if there were an initial *increase* (instead of decrease) of the cloth:food price ratio. The terms of trade in this case would eventually coincide with Country G's cost ratio (the slope of the $0G$-line), and the equilibrium point would be point Q.

Hence Graham's conclusion that the world terms of trade would coincide with the cost ratio of one of the countries is not particularly surprising. But, this is due to the *instability* implied by his specific assumption on demand and supply. However, it is also to be stressed that even under such an assumption on demand and supply, the instability is not the necessity. In other words, it is perfectly possible and plausible to have a situation in which the intersection of the two offer curves is *stable*, even under the above assumption. Such a stable intersection point is illustrated in Figure 5-13 as point S. Note that even though the demand specification is still such that commodities are always consumed in fixed proportions in each country, yet the equilibrium terms of trade α are stable ones. What Melvin has shown is simply that under the Graham specification of demand and supply there exists a wide range of cases in which the instability exists and that such an instability is the cause of Graham's conclusion.[15] In the second section of Chapter 8, we shall obtain a sufficient condition for stability (known as the *Marshall-Lerner condition*) under a fairly broad class of demand and supply specifications. It is true that under the Graham specification of demand and supply, this condition becomes more difficult to be satisfied compared to other cases in which a price change will cause substitution of goods by consumers and producers. However this is a rather well-known fact, and it may be questionable to argue that the heart of Graham's thesis lies in the instability as much as Melvin advocates.

REFERENCES

1. Caves, R. E., *Trade and Economic Structure, Models and Methods* (Cambridge, Mass.: Harvard University Press), 1960.
2. Chipman, J. S., "A Survey of the Theory of International Trade: Part 1. The Classical Theory," *Econometrica*, 33, July 1965.
3. Eisenberg, E., "Aggregation of Utility Functions," *Management Science*, 7, July 1961.

[15] Thus, Graham's rebuttal, although it makes a very interesting point, contains some weaknesses. But his attempt to extend the classical two-country, two-good model to a multi-country, multi-good model has inspired many economists and could lead to a very important reformulation of the trade model in terms of linear programming or activity analysis (Whitin, McKenzie, and so on). McKenzie's attempt to prove the existence of a solution in Graham's model contained most of the important points of the problem of the existence of a competitive equilibrium and thus made an important contribution to the theory of competitive markets. See, for example, McKenzie, L. W., "On Equilibrium in Graham's Model of World Trade and Other Competitive Systems," *Econometrica*, 22, April 1954.

4. Graham, F. D., "The Theory of International Values Re-examined," *Quarterly Journal of Economics*, XXVIII, November 1923, reprinted in *Readings in the Theory of International Trade*, ed. by Ellis and Metzler (Philadelphia: Blakiston), 1949.

5. ———, "The Theory of International Values," *Quarterly Journal of Economics*, XLVI, August 1932.

6. ———, *The Theory of International Values* (Princeton, N.J.: Princeton University Press), 1948.

7. Haberler, G., *The Theory of International Trade, with Its Applications to Commercial Policy* (tr. from German ed. of 1933) (London: William Hodge), 1936.

8. McKenzie, L. W., "On Equilibrium in Graham's Model of World Trade and Other Competitive Systems," *Econometrica*, 22, April 1954.

9. Marshall, A., *The Pure Theory of Foreign Trade*, published privately, 1879. Reprinted together with *The Pure Theory of Domestic Values* (London: London School of Economics and Political Science), 1930. Also "reproduced with but little change" in *Money, Credit and Commerce* (London: Macmillan & Co., Ltd.), 1923, Appendix J.

10. Meade, J. E., *A Geometry of International Trade* (London: George Allen and Unwin Ltd.), 1952.

11. Melvin, J. R., "On a Demand Assumption Made by Graham," *Southern Economic Journal*, XXXVI, July 1969.

12. Metzler, L. A., "Graham's Theory of International Values," *American Economic Review*, XL, June 1950.

13. Mill, J. S., *Essays on Some Unsettled Questions of Political Economy* (London: John W. Parker, West Strand), 1844, Reprinted by the London School of Economics and Political Science, 1948.

14. ———, *Principles of Political Economy with Some of Their Applications to Social Philosophy* (1st ed. 1848, 3rd ed. 1852, 9th ed. 1885), Ashley edition (London: Longmans, Green & Co., Ltd.), 1929 (page references to the Ashley edition).

15. Pareto, V., *Manuel d'Economie Poltique* (original ed. in Italian, 1906) (Paris: M. Giard et E. Briere), 1909.

16. Takayama, A., *International Economics* (Tokyo: Toyo Keizai Shimpo-Sha), 1963, Chapter I.

17. Viner, J., *Studies in the Theory of International Trade* (New York: Harper & Row, Publishers), 1937.

Appendix to Chapter 5
Nonlinear Programming
and the Classical Theory
of International Trade

DEVELOPMENTS IN THE THEORY OF NONLINEAR PROGRAMMING

In the second section of Chapter 5, we pointed out that there is a very close connection between the classical theory of international trade, as formulated by J. S. Mill, and the modern theory of nonlinear programming. Here we shall summarize some of the most important developments in the theory of nonlinear programming. This will help us improve our understanding of the classical theory of international trade as well as our understanding of many other problems.[16]

Let R^n be an n-dimensional real space, that is, a vector space of which the typical element is represented by an n-tuple of real numbers, such as $x = (x_1, x_2, \cdots, x_n)$. Let R denote the set of real numbers. $X \subset R^n$ indicates that the set X is a subset of R^n, possibly the whole space. That is, $X \subset R^n$ does not mean that X *must* be a *proper* subset of R^n; X can also equal R^n.

DEFINITION $X \subset R^n$ is called a *convex* set if $x, y \in X$ implies

$$\theta x + (1 - \theta)y \in X, \quad \text{for all } \theta \text{ such that } 0 \leqq \theta \leqq 1.[17]$$

DEFINITION   Let f be a real valued function defined on a convex set X in R^n. f is called a *concave function* if

$$f[\theta x + (1 - \theta)y] \geqq \theta f(x) + (1 - \theta)f(y), \quad \text{for all } \theta \text{ such that } 0 \leqq \theta \leqq 1$$

and for all $x, y \in X$.[18]

If the inequalities in the above definition are strict for all $x, y \in X$ with $x \neq y$, that is, if $f[\theta x + (1 - \theta)y] > \theta f(x) + (1 - \theta)f(y)$, where $0 < \theta < 1$ for all

---

[16] For a more systematic treatment of this topic see Takayama [A8].

[17] In other words, X is a convex set if any point on the chord joining any two points in X is in X.

[18] In other words, f is a concave function if the chord joining any two points on the function lies on or below the function. X must be a convex set, otherwise $\theta x + (1 - \theta) y$ may not be in X, so that the *LHS* of the inequality may be meaningless. An ordinary production function $Y = F(L, K)$ is concave if $\partial^2 F/\partial L^2 < 0$, $\partial^2 F/\partial K^2 < 0$, and $(\partial^2 F/\partial L^2)(\partial^2 F/\partial K^2) - (\partial^2 F/\partial L \, \partial K)^2 \geqq 0$. The first two conditions are the law of diminishing returns, and the third condition is satisfied with equality if F is homogeneous of degree one.

$x, y \in X$ with $x \neq y$, then f is called a *strictly concave function*. f is called a *convex (strictly convex) function*, if $-f$ is a concave (respectively strictly concave) function.

REMARK In particular, if f is linear,[19] so that it can be written as

$$\sum_{i=1}^{n} a_i x_i + a_0, \quad \text{where the } a_i, i = 0, 1, \cdots, n, \text{ are constants,}$$

then f is both concave and convex, but neither strictly concave nor strictly convex.

Let $f, g_1, g_2, \cdots, g_m$ be real valued functions defined on R^n. Then the non-linear programming problem can be formulated as follows.

MAXIMIZATION PROBLEM Maximize $f(x)$ subject to

$$g_j(x) \geqq 0, j = 1, 2, \cdots, m,$$

and $x_i \geqq 0, i = 1, 2, \cdots, n$.[20]

Clearly the linear programming problem is a special case of the above problem.[21]

An $x^* \in R^n$ which maximizes $f(x)$ subject to $g_j(x) \geqq 0, j = 1, 2, \cdots, m$ and $x_i \geqq 0, i = 1, 2, \cdots, n$, is called a *solution* to the above maximization problem. We can obtain similar formulation, even if we restrict the domain of $f, g_1, g_2, \cdots, g_m$ to some (open) subset X of R^n (see Takayama [A8], for example). When $g_j(x^*) = 0$, we say that the jth constraint is *effective* (or *active*) at $x = x^*$. [By the vector notation $x \geqq 0$, we mean $x_1 \geqq 0, x_2 \geqq 0, \cdots, x_n \geqq 0$.]

The set C, defined as

$$C = \{x : x \in R^n; g_j(x) \geqq 0, j = 1, \cdots, m; x_i \geqq 0, i = 1, \cdots, n\}$$

is called the *constraint set*. The maximization problem can then be restated as: Maximize $f(x)$ over the set C. If C is empty, then the maximization problem obviously has no solution. If C is non-empty and compact, and if f is a continuous function then there always exists a solution (not necessarily unique) for the above maximization problem due to the Weierstrass Theorem.[22] The problem of minimizing $f(x)$ subject to the above constraints can easily be converted to the above problem of maximizing $-f(x)$ subject to the same constraints. The following two theorems give an important characterization to the above maximization problem.

---

[19] Strictly speaking f should be called *linear affine*.

[20] The constraints $x_i \geqq 0, i = 1, \cdots, n$, are in a sense superfluous, for they may be considered as being included in the constraints $g_j(x) \geqq 0$. That is, we may consider some of the $g_j(x) \geqq 0$ to be of the form $x_i \geqq 0$. However, it is often convenient to write down these conditions $(x_i \geqq 0, i = 1, \cdots, n)$ explicitly because they are explicitly binding in many economic problems.

[21] Hence the term *non*linear programming is rather misleading.

[22] See any textbook of elementary analysis, for example W. Rudin, *Principles of Mathematical Analysis*, 2nd ed., New York, McGraw-Hill, 1964.

THEOREM 1 (NECESSITY)   Suppose that one of the following two conditions is satisfied.

1. The $g_j(x), j = 1, 2, \cdots, m$ are all concave, and there exists an $\bar{x} \in R^n$, $\bar{x} \geqq 0$ such that $g_j(\bar{x}) > 0$ for all $j = 1, 2, \cdots, m$.
2. The $g_j(x), j = 1, 2, \cdots, m$ are linear.

Suppose further that the f and $g_j, j = 1, 2, \cdots, m$ are all differentiable in R^n. Then if there exists a solution, x^*, to the above maximization problem, there exists a $\lambda \in R^m, \lambda^* \geqq 0$ such that

$$f_x^* + \lambda^* \cdot g_x^* \leqq 0 , \tag{5-16a}$$

$$[f_x^* + \lambda^* \cdot g_x^*] \cdot x^* = 0 ; \tag{5-16b}$$

$$\lambda^* \cdot g(x^*) = 0 , \tag{5-17a}$$

$$g(x^*) \geqq 0 . \tag{5-17b}$$

Here f_x^* is a vector whose ith element is $\partial f / \partial x_i$ evaluated at $x = x^*$, g_x is a matrix whose i-j element is $\partial g_j / \partial x_i$ evaluated at $x = x^*$, and $g(x)^*$ is a vector whose jth element is $g_j(x^*)$. The dot ($\cdot$) refers to the inner product, so that

$$\lambda^* \cdot g(x^*) = \sum_{j=1}^{m} \lambda_j^* g_j(x^*), \quad \text{and} \quad \lambda^* \cdot g_{xi}^* = \sum_{j=1}^{m} \lambda_j^* \frac{\partial g_j}{\partial x_i}\bigg|_{x = x^*} \quad i = 1, \cdots, n .$$

REMARK $\lambda_1, \lambda_2, \cdots, \lambda_m$ are called the *Lagrangian multipliers*. $\Phi(x, \lambda) \equiv f(x) + \lambda \cdot g(x)$ is called the *Lagrangian*. Using this notation, (5-16a) and (5-16b) can be written as $\Phi_x^* \leqq 0$ and $\Phi_x^* \cdot x^* = 0$, respectively where Φ_x^* is a vector whose ith element is $\partial \Phi / \partial x_i$ evaluated at (x^*, λ^*).

REMARK   The conditions (5-16a), (5-16b), (5-17a), and (5-17b) are the necessary conditions for x to be a solution to the above maximization problem. Condition 1 is called *Slater's condition*. Both condition 1 and condition 2 can replace a more general and more famous condition, called the *Kuhn-Tucker Constraint Qualification (KTCQ)* under which conditions (5-16a), (5-16b), (5-17a), and (5-17b) are the necessary conditions for x^* to be an optimum [A6]. Condition 2 is due to Arrow-Hurwicz-Uzawa [A2][23] and it provides a link with the linear programming problem.

REMARK   Conditions (5-16a) through (5-17b) are known as the *Quasi-Saddle Point Conditions* or the *Kuhn-Tucker-Lagrange Conditions*.

[23] They give some other sufficient conditions, any of which will replace (*KTCQ*) and hence will guarantee the necessity of conditions (5-16a) through (5-17b) for x^* to be an optimum. According to them [2], *any* of the following conditions also replaces the (*KTCQ*): a) $g_j(x), j = 1, 2, \cdots, m$ are convex; b) the constraint set C is convex and possesses an interior point and $g_j'(x^*) \neq 0$ for all $j \in E$, where E is the set of all effective constraints and $g_j'(x)$ denotes a vector whose ith element is $\partial g_j / \partial x_i$ evaluated at $x = x^*$; c) the rank of $[g_j'(x^*)_{j \in E}]$ equals the number of effective constraints. Note that conditions b and c do not presuppose concavity or convexity of the g_js, and that condition c is famous from classical Lagrangian multiplier theory for the case in which all the constraints are effective.

THEOREM 2 (SUFFICIENCY)[24] Suppose f is concave and the constraint set C is a convex set. Then if there exists an $x^* \geq 0$ that satisfies the conditions (5-16a), (5-16b), (5-17a), and (5-17b), x^* is a solution to the above maximization problem. If f is *strictly* concave, x^* is a unique solution.

REMARK C is a convex set if, in particular, $g_j(x), j = 1, 2, \cdots, m$ are all concave functions. (Try the proof of this statement yourself.) Note that in the above theorem, x^* provides a global maximum in the sense that it is not confined to some neighborhood of x^*.

Combining the above theorems, we immediately obtain:

THEOREM 3   Let $f, g_1, g_2, \cdots, g_m$ be concave functions in R^n. Suppose that either condition 1 or condition 2 of Theorem 1 is satisfied, then x^* is a solution to the above maximization problem *if and only if* it satisfies the conditions (5-16a), (5-16b), (5-17a), and (5-17b) with $x_i^* \geq 0, i = 1, 2, \cdots, n$.

REMARK   The above (Kuhn-Tucker-Lagrange) conditions, conditions (5-16a), (5-16b), (5-17a), and (5-17b), are stated in the form of derivatives, hence the differentiability of the f and $g_j, j = 1, 2, \cdots, m$ is implicitly required.

REMARK   When f and the g_js are all concave functions, the above maximization problem is called the *concave programming* problem.

The following theorem gives a characterization of the problem when the functions f and $g_j, j = 1, 2, \cdots, m$, are not necessarily differentiable.

THEOREM 4   Let $f, g_1, g_2, \cdots, g_m$ be concave functions defined on a convex set X in R^n. Suppose that the g_js satisfy the following *Slater's condition.*

   (S) There exists an $\bar{x} \in X$ such that $g_j(\bar{x}) > 0$ for all $j = 1, 2, \cdots, m$. Then a necessary and sufficient condition for x^* to maximize $f(x)$ subject to $g_j(x) \geq 0, j = 1, 2, \cdots, m$, is that there exists a vector λ^* with $\lambda_j^* \geq 0$, $j = 1, 2, \cdots, m$, such that

(SP) $\Phi(x, \lambda^*) \leq \Phi(x^*, \lambda^*) \leq \Phi(x^*, \lambda)$ for all $x \in X$ and $\lambda \geq 0$, where $\Phi(x, \lambda) \equiv f(x) + \lambda \cdot g(x)$.

REMARK   The above theorem is due to Kuhn-Tucker [A6]. A beautiful proof using the separation theorem of convex sets (hence not requiring differentiability of the functions) has been provided by Uzawa [A9]. The condition (SP) is called the *saddle point condition.* With the differentiability of f and the g_js the (SP) clearly implies the quasi-saddle point condition, that is equations (5-16a), (5-16b), (5-17a), and (5-17b), of the previous theorems, if the non-negativity of

---

[24] The proof of this theorem follows immediately from the following important property of concave functions. In other words if f is concave, then $f(x) - f(x^*) \leq f_x^* \cdot (x - x^*)$ for any $x, x^* \in X$. (The inequality is strict if $x \neq x^*$ and f is strictly concave.) For a generalization of this theorem to Quasi-Concave Programming, see Arrow and Enthoven [A1].

the x_i, $i = 1, 2, \cdots, n$ is properly taken into account. The quasi-saddle point conditions[25] do not imply (SP) without conditions such as the concavity of f and the g_js.

MILL'S PROBLEM AND NONLINEAR PROGRAMMING

In the second section of this chapter, we formulated Mill's problem as the problem of choosing x_1, x_2, y_1, and y_2 so as to maximize the world community utility function $u(x_1 + x_2, y_1 + y_2)$ subject to

$$\frac{x_1}{a_1} + \frac{y_1}{b_1} \leqq 1, \quad \frac{x_2}{a_2} + \frac{y_2}{b_2} \leqq 1, \tag{5-18}$$

and $x_1, x_2, y_1, y_2 \geqq 0$, where $a_1, a_2, b_1, b_2 > 0$, and u is defined on the non-negative orthant of R^2.

We also imposed the following Ricardian condition on the a_is and b_is ($i = 1, 2$):

$$\frac{b_1}{a_1} < \frac{b_2}{a_2}. \tag{5-19}$$

Following Chipman ([A3], p. 485), we convert the inequalities of condition (5-18) to

$$\frac{x}{a_1} + \frac{y}{b_1} \leqq \frac{b}{b_1}; \quad \frac{x}{a_2} + \frac{y}{b_2} \leqq \frac{a}{a_2}; \quad \text{and} \quad x \geqq 0, y \geqq 0, \tag{5-20}$$

where $x \equiv x_1 + x_2$, $y \equiv y_1 + y_2$, $a \equiv a_1 + a_2$

and $b \equiv b_1 + b_2$.

To obtain the inequalities of (5-20) from those of (5-18) we multiply the inequalities of (5-18) by b_1 and b_2 respectively and add them to obtain

$$\frac{b_1}{a_1} x_1 + \frac{b_2}{a_2} x_2 + y \leqq b_1 + b_2 \equiv b. \tag{5-21}$$

Using inequality (5-19), we obtain

$$b \geqq \frac{b_1}{a_1} x_1 + \frac{b_2}{a_2} x_2 + y \geqq \frac{b_1}{a_1} (x_1 + x_2) + y = \frac{b_1}{a_1} x + y, \tag{5-22}$$

which is equivalent to the first inequality of (5-20). The second inequality of (5-20) is obtained in the same way after multiplying the inequalities of (5-18) by a_1 and a_2 respectively.

The inequalities of (5-20) can also be obtained from our diagram of the world production possibilities set (Figure 5-6). Using our knowledge of elementary

---

[25] In this theorem Slater's condition (S) can be replaced by the condition that the constraint functions (the g_js) are linear. Theorems 3 and 4 give the reason why the Kuhn-Tucker Constraint Qualification is not mentioned in linear programming. Two important theorems in the theory of linear programming—the LP duality theorem and the Goldman-Tucker theorem—can be proved easily using Theorem 4 with Slater's condition (S) replaced by the condition that the g_j be linear. See Takayama [A8].

analytical geometry, we obtain $x/a_1 + y/b_1 = b/b_1$ as the equation of the line passing through points R and T and $x/a_2 + y/b_2 = a/a_2$ as the equation of the line passing through the points R and S. Hence the world production possibilities set $(OSRT)$ can be characterized by the inequalities of (5-20).

Thus we have obtained the following nonlinear programming problem:

PROBLEM M   Choose x and y such as to maximize $u(x, y)$ subject to (5-20). Let us now introduce the following assumption.

ASSUMPTION 1 u is a continuous and concave function.[26]

Mill's utility function $u = x^{1/2}y^{1/2}$ is a concave function and, in general, $u = x^\alpha y^{1-\alpha}$, $0 < \alpha < 1$, is a concave function.

The Lagrangian for the above nonlinear programming problem can be written as

$$\Phi \equiv u(x, y) + p\left(\frac{b}{b_1} - \frac{x}{a_1} - \frac{y}{b_1}\right) + q\left(\frac{a}{a_2} - \frac{x}{a_2} - \frac{y}{b_2}\right), \tag{5-23}$$

where p and q are the Lagrangian multipliers. Since u is concave, the following Kuhn-Tucker-Lagrange condition (KTL) gives a *necessary and sufficient* condition for (x^*, y^*) to be an optimum (that is, to be a solution for problem M). (Recall Theorem 3 of the previous section.)

There exist p^*, q^*, x^*, and y^* such that

$$(KTL)\begin{cases} u_x{}^* - \dfrac{p^*}{a_1} - \dfrac{q^*}{a_2} \leqq 0 \quad \text{and} \quad u_y{}^* - \dfrac{p^*}{b_1} - \dfrac{q^*}{b_2} \leqq 0\,, & \text{(5-24a)} \\[2mm] \left(u_x{}^* - \dfrac{p^*}{a_1} - \dfrac{q^*}{a_2}\right) x^* + \left(u_y{}^* - \dfrac{p^*}{b_1} - \dfrac{q^*}{b_2}\right) y^* = 0\,, & \text{(5-24b)} \\[2mm] \dfrac{b}{b_1} - \dfrac{x^*}{a_1} - \dfrac{y^*}{b_1} \geqq 0 \quad \text{and} \quad \dfrac{a}{a_2} - \dfrac{x^*}{a_2} - \dfrac{y^*}{b_2} \geqq 0\,, & \text{(5-25a)} \\[2mm] p^*\left(\dfrac{b}{b_1} - \dfrac{x^*}{a_1} - \dfrac{y^*}{b_1}\right) + q^*\left(\dfrac{a}{a_2} - \dfrac{x^*}{a_2} - \dfrac{y^*}{b_2}\right) = 0\,, & \text{(5-25b)} \end{cases}$$

[26] The condition that u be concave can be relaxed to the condition that it be quasi-concave with some additional (but plausible) assumptions such as: a) $u_x > 0$, $u_y > 0$ for all $x, y > 0$, *or* b) u is twice differentiable and $(u_x{}^*, u_y{}^*) \neq 0$. In fact, both a) and b) can be relaxed further. See Arrow and Enthoven [1]. Under such relaxed assumptions, our (KTL) still offers a necessary and sufficient condition for optimality. Theorem 1 of [A1] is concerned with sufficiency conditions and Theorem 2 of [A1] is concerned with necessary conditions. The latter is really a restatement of the results in Arrow-Hurwicz-Uzawa [A2]. In general, a real-valued function $f(x)$ over a convex set X is defined to be a *quasi-concave function* if, for all $x, y \in X, f(x) \geqq f(y)$ implies $f[\theta x + (1 - \theta)y] \geqq f(y), 0 \leqq \theta \leqq 1$. In the present context, where we are concerned with the non-negative orthant, the quasi-concavity of u simply means (as is ordinarily assumed) that the indifference curves are convex to the origin. It can easily be shown that a concave function is always quasi-concave but not vice versa (for example, $u(x, y) = x^\alpha y^\beta$; $\alpha, \beta > 0$, $\alpha + \beta > 1$ is quasi-concave, but not concave).

$$p^* \geqq 0, \quad q^* \geqq 0, \tag{5-26a}$$

$$x^* \geqq 0, \quad y^* \geqq 0, \tag{5-26b}$$

where $u_x^* = \partial u/\partial x$ and $u_y^* = \partial u/\partial y$, both evaluated at (x^*, y^*).

It is important to note that the above (KTL) is a *necessary and sufficient condition* for (x^*, y^*) to be optimal because this means that these conditions give a *complete* characterization of a solution. Hence, on the basis of these conditions, we will be able to make many observations, some of which are unknown in the literature.

Clearly, condition (5-24b) can be rewritten as follows due to conditions (5-24a) and (5-26b).

$$\left(u_x^* - \frac{p^*}{a_1} - \frac{q^*}{a_2}\right) x^* = 0 \quad \text{and} \quad \left(u_y^* - \frac{p^*}{b_1} - \frac{q^*}{b_2}\right) y^* = 0 . \tag{5-24b'}$$

Similarly, (5-25b) can be rewritten as follows due to conditions (5-25a) and (5-26a).

$$p^* \left(\frac{b}{b_1} - \frac{x^*}{a_1} - \frac{y^*}{b_1}\right) = 0 \quad \text{and} \quad q^* \left(\frac{a}{a_2} - \frac{x^*}{a_2} - \frac{y^*}{b_2}\right) = 0 . \tag{5-25b'}$$

Now let us obtain Mill's condition as discussed in the second section of this chapter. To do this, we make the following assumption.

ASSUMPTION 2 $u(x, 0) = 0$ and $u(0, y) = 0$;

$$u_x \equiv \frac{\partial u}{\partial x} > 0 \quad \text{and} \quad u_y \equiv \frac{\partial u}{\partial y} > 0 \quad \text{for all } x > 0, \quad y > 0 .[27]$$

An example of a utility function that satisfies the above assumption is again one of the Cobb-Douglas type, $u = x^\alpha y^{1-\alpha}$, $0 < \alpha < 1$.[28] The feasible set for our nonlinear programming problem is $M = \{(x, y): (5\text{-}20) \text{ is satisfied}\}$.[29] The set M is non-empty and contains a point $(\bar{x}, \bar{y})$ with $\bar{x} > 0$ and $\bar{y} > 0$ (an interior point). Hence, due to assumption 2, an optimal point (x^*, y^*) must have $x^* > 0$ and $y^* > 0$. Then from (5-24b') we obtain

$$u_x^* = \frac{p^*}{a_1} + \frac{q^*}{a_2}, \quad u_y^* = \frac{p^*}{b_1} + \frac{q^*}{b_2} . \tag{5-27}$$

Notice that there are four equations in (5-25b') and (5-27) in the four variables x^*, y^*, p^*, and q^*. In other words, we have replaced the (KTL) conditions by the four equations (5-25b') and (5-27).

---

[27] As we noted in footnote 26, we can relax the condition that u be concave to the condition that it be quasi-concave as a result of the second statement of assumption 2.

[28] If we replace the concavity of u by the condition that it be quasi-concave, $u(x, y) = x^\alpha y^\beta$; $\alpha, \beta > 0$; can serve as our example. Chipman's version of Mill's utility function, $u = xy$, is a special case of this.

[29] Note that this set is also convex.

Mill's problem, as defined by Chipman [A3], is that of finding the condition under which the Ricardian pattern of specialization [I(X) and II(Y)] is optimal. In other words, Mill sought the condition under which Ricardo's point is an optimal point. The coordinates of Ricardo's point (from the second section of this chapter) are $x = a_1$ and $y = b_2$. Note that this is the solution to the two simultaneous equations:

$$\frac{x}{a_1} + \frac{y}{b_1} = \frac{b}{b_1} \quad \text{and} \quad \frac{x}{a_2} + \frac{y}{b_2} = \frac{a}{a_2}.$$

Hence condition (5-25b′) is satisfied at Ricardo's point and (x^*, y^*) is a solution to the above nonlinear programming problem at Ricardo's point ($x^* = a_1$, $y^* = b_2$) if and only if there exists $p^* \geqq 0, q^* \geqq 0$ (with at least one strict inequality)[30] such that

$$u_x(a_1, b_2) = \frac{p^*}{a_1} + \frac{q^*}{a_2} \quad \text{and} \quad u_y(a_1, b_2) = \frac{p^*}{b_1} + \frac{q^*}{b_2}. \tag{5-27′}$$

Write $u_x(a_1, b_2) \equiv u_x^*$ and $u_y(a_1, b_2) \equiv u_y^*$. Clearly $u_x^* > 0$ and $u_y^* > 0$ by assumption 2. The two equations of (5-27′) can be rewritten in the following equivalent form:

$$\left(1 - \frac{a_2}{a_1}\frac{b_1}{b_2}\right) p^* = \left(u_y^* - \frac{a_2}{b_2} u_x^*\right) b_1, \tag{2-28a}$$

$$\left(1 - \frac{a_1}{a_2}\frac{b_2}{b_1}\right) q^* = \left(u_y^* - \frac{a_1}{b_1} u_x^*\right) b_2. \tag{5-28b}$$

But from the Ricardian condition, (5-19), we have

$$\frac{a_2}{a_1} < \frac{b_2}{b_1} \quad \text{or} \quad \frac{a_2}{a_1}\frac{b_1}{b_2} < 1. \tag{5-29}$$

Therefore if $u_y^* \geqq (a_2/b_2)u_x^*$ and $u_y^* \leqq (a_1/b_1)u_x^*$ (with at least one strict inequality) or if

$$\frac{b_1}{a_1} \leqq \frac{u_x^*}{u_y^*} \leqq \frac{b_2}{a_2} \quad \text{(with at least one strict inequality)}, \tag{5-30}$$

then condition (5-27′) is satisfied. Thus, (a_1, b_2) is a solution to the nonlinear programming problem. Conversely if (5-27′) is satisfied, then (5-30) is implied. Hence if Ricardo's point is a solution to the nonlinear programming problem so that (5-27′) is satisfied, then (5-30) is satisfied. Condition (5-30) is Mill's condition we obtained diagrammatically in the second section. Mill's condition (5-30) thus gives a necessary and sufficient condition for Ricardo's point to be a solution to the nonlinear programming problem (M). Recall that u_x^* and u_y^* in (5-30) are defined as

$$u_x^* = u_x(a_1, b_2) \quad \text{and} \quad u_y^* = u_y(a_1, b_2).$$

[30] Suppose that p^* and q^* vanish simultaneously ($p^* = 0, q^* = 0$), then $u_x(a_1, b_2) = 0$ and $u_y(a_1, b_2) = 0$, which contradict assumption 2.

A REMARK ON EISENBERG'S THEOREM

Chipman remarked that Mill's problem is "a problem in homogeneous programming (Eisenberg, 1961)—a special case of nonlinear programming (Kuhn and Tucker, 1951)," (Chipman [A3], p. 485). In the previous section we considered Mill's problem as an application of a general theorem in nonlinear programming. In other words, we took the position that consideration of a special case is hardly necessary. Our theorem in the previous section has a much broader application than Eisenberg's theorem [A4]. However, there is nothing wrong with becoming familiar with Eisenberg's theorem. The purpose of this section, then, is to familiarize the reader with this theorem and to clarify its relationship to Mill's problem.

First recall that the dual problems in *linear programming* can be stated as follows (see the third section of Chapter 4):

(M)   Maximize $p \cdot x$ subject to $Ax \leqq r, x \geqq 0$.
　　　x

(m)   Minimize $w \cdot r$ subject to $A'w \geqq p, w \geqq 0$.
　　　w

Here $p, x \in R^n$; $w, r \in R^m$; A is an $m \times n$ matrix, and A' is its transpose.[31]

The feasible sets for (M) and (m) are defined as:

$$X \equiv \{x : x \geqq 0, x \in R^n, Ax \leqq r\} \text{ for } (M) \text{ and}$$

$$W \equiv \{w : w \geqq 0, w \in R^m, A'w \geqq p\} \text{ for } (m) .$$

Then the above problems can be restated as:

(M)   Maximize $p \cdot x$ for all $x \in X$ and
　　　x

(m)   Minimize $w \cdot r$ for all $w \in W$.
　　　w

The *LP* Duality Theorem states that:

1.   If x^* maximizes $p \cdot x$ for all $x \in X$, then there exists a $w^* \geqq 0$ such that w^* minimizes $w \cdot r$ for all $w \in W$ and $p \cdot x^* = w^* \cdot r = w^* \cdot (Ax^*)$,
2.   If w^* minimizes $w \cdot r$ for all $w \in W$, then there exists an $x^* \geqq 0$ such that x^* maximizes $p \cdot x$ for all $x \in X$ and $p \cdot x^* = w^* \cdot r = w^* \cdot (Ax^*)$.

Eisenberg's theorem is concerned with generalizing the objective functions of the above problems. Thus, $p \cdot x$ is replaced by $\Phi(x)$ and $w \cdot r$ is replaced by $\psi(w)$, where $\Phi(x)$ and $\psi(w)$ are homogeneous of degree one and continuous,

---

[31] The dot ($\cdot$) refers to the inner product of the two vectors. The distinction between a row vector and a column vector is not essential (except when a vector is multiplied by a matrix).

and Φ is a concave function while ψ is convex. Then Eisenberg considers the following four statements.

(a_1) $A'w \geq 0$, $\psi(w) \leq 0$, $w \geq 0$ implies $w = 0$.

(b_1) $Ax \leq 0$, $\Phi(x) \geq 0$, $x \geq 0$ implies $x = 0$.

(a_2) there exists an $\bar{x} \geq 0$ such that $w \cdot (A\bar{x}) < \psi(w)$ for all $w \geq 0$, $w \neq 0$.

(b_2) there exists a $\bar{w} \geq 0$ such that $\bar{w} \cdot (Ax) > \Phi(x)$ for all $x \geq 0$, $x \neq 0$.

Define the following sets, which are analogous to the feasible sets for the above linear programming problems.

$$X_E \equiv \{x: x \geq 0,\ x \in R^n,\ w \cdot (Ax) \leq \psi(w) \text{ for all } w \geq 0\};$$

$$W_E \equiv \{w: w \geq 0,\ w \in R^m,\ w \cdot (Ax) \geq \Phi(x) \text{ for all } x \geq 0\}.$$

Eisenberg was concerned with the following dual problems:

(M_E) Maximize $\Phi(x)$ for all $x \in X_E$;   and
$\quad\quad x$

(m_E) Minimize $\psi(w)$ for all $w \in W_E$.
$\quad\quad\quad w$

We can now state Eisenberg's theorem as follows:

1. (a_1) holds if and only if (a_2) holds; also (b_1) holds if and only if (b_2) holds.
2. If x^* maximizes Φ over X_E and (a_1) holds, then there exists a $w^* \in W_E$ which minimizes $\psi(w)$ over W_E and $\Phi(x^*) = \psi(w^*) = w^* \cdot (Ax^*)$.
3. If w^* minimizes ψ over W_E and (b_1) holds, then there exists an $x^* \in X_E$ which maximizes $\Phi(x)$ over X_E and $\Phi(x^*) = \psi(w^*) = w^* \cdot (Ax^*)$.

The alert reader will immediately realize that statements (a_2) and (b_2) correspond to Slater's condition for (M_E) and (m_E) respectively. Therefore, it is easily conjectured that Eisenberg's theorem is concerned with a special case of concave programming as discussed in the first section of this appendix. (Recall Theorem 1.)

Mill's problem as formulated in the previous section will now be restated as

Maximize $u(z)$,   subject to $Az \leq r$, $z \geq 0$.
$\quad z$

Here A, z, and r are defined as:

$$A \equiv \begin{bmatrix} \dfrac{1}{a_1} & \dfrac{1}{b_1} \\[2mm] \dfrac{1}{a_2} & \dfrac{1}{b_2} \end{bmatrix}, \quad z \equiv \begin{bmatrix} x \\[2mm] y \end{bmatrix}, \quad \text{and} \quad r \equiv \begin{bmatrix} \dfrac{b}{b_1} \\[2mm] \dfrac{a}{a_2} \end{bmatrix}.$$

Clearly condition (a_2) of Eisenberg's theorem is satisfied, hence condition (a_1) is also satisfied (by statement 1 of Eisenberg's theorem). Hence statement 2 of Eisenberg's theorem can now be applied in our discussion. Thus, if $z^* \geqq 0$ is a solution to the above maximization (Mill's) problem, then there exists a $w^* \equiv (p^*, q^*)$ such that

$$
(E) \begin{cases} w^* \geqq 0, & (5\text{-}31) \\ u(z^*) = w^* \cdot r = w^* \cdot (Az^*), & (5\text{-}32) \\ w^* \cdot (Az) \geqq u(z) \text{ for all } z \geqq 0. & (5\text{-}33) \end{cases}
$$

Let us now compare Eisenberg's conditions (E) with the Kuhn-Tucker-Lagrange (KTL) condition obtained in the previous section. First we will rewrite our (KTL) conditions.

Since u must be homogeneous of degree one to satisfy Eisenberg's assumption, we have $u_x x + u_y y = u$ (from Euler's equation). Hence condition (5-24b) can be rewritten as

$$
u(x^*, y^*) = \left(\frac{p^*}{a_1} x^* + \frac{p^*}{b_1} y^*\right) + \left(\frac{q^*}{a_2} x^* + \frac{q^*}{b_2} y^*\right). \tag{5-34}
$$

Then we find that: Condition (5-31) of (E) corresponds to condition (5-26a) of (KTL); $w^* r = w^* \cdot (Az^*)$ of condition (5-32) of (E) corresponds to condition (5-25b) of (KTL); $u(z^*) = w^* \cdot (Az^*)$ of condition (5-32) of (E) corresponds to (5-34) above, and thus to (5-24b) of (KTL). Finally, conditions (5-25a) and (5-26b) are satisfied if (x^*, y^*) is a solution to Mill's problem.

Using the homogeneity of u, condition (5-33) of (E) can be rewritten as

$$
w^* \cdot (Az) \geqq u_x x + u_y y \quad \text{for all } x \geqq 0, y \geqq 0. \tag{5-35}
$$

Then it is easy to see that (5-35) corresponds to (5-24a) of (KTL). Hence, we have seen that Eisenberg's conditions (E) are *equivalent* to the (KTL) conditions for Mill's problem.

However, we should note the following two major limitations resulting from this approach (via Eisenberg's theorem) to Mill's problem.

1. Eisenberg's conditions (E) only give necessary conditions for (x^*, y^*) to be a solution to Mill's problem. Nothing is said about the sufficiency of these conditions. On the other hand, the (KTL) conditions are both necessary and sufficient (with the concavity of u), for the present case.
2. Eisenberg's theorem requires that u be homogeneous of degree one; the (KTL) conditions do not require such an assumption.

REFERENCES

1. Arrow, K. J. and Enthoven, A. C., "Quasi-Concave Programming," *Ecoonmetrica*, 29, October 1961.
2. Arrow, K. J., Hurwicz, L. and Uzawa, H., "Constraint Qualification in Maximization Problems," *Naval Research Logistics Quarterly*, 8, June 1961.

3. Chipman, J. S., "A Survey of the Theory of International Trade: Part 1, The Classical Theory," *Econometrica*, 33, July 1965.

4. Eisenberg, E., "Duality in Homogeneous Programming," *Proceedings of the American Mathematical Society*, 12, October 1961.

5. ———, "Aggregation of Utility Functions," *Management Science*, 7, July 1961.

6. Kuhn, H. W. and Tucker, A. W., "Non-linear Programming," *Proceedings of the Second Berkeley Symposium on Mathematical Statistics and Probability*, ed. by Neymann (Berkeley: University of California Press), 1951.

7. Mill, J. S., *Principles of Political Economy with Some of their Applications to Social Philosophy* (1st ed. 1848, 3rd ed. 1852, 9th ed. 1885), ed. by Ashley (London: Longmans, Green & Co., Ltd.), 1929.

8. Takayama, A., *Mathematical Economics*, forthcoming.

9. Uzawa, H., "The Kuhn-Tucker Theorem in Concave Programming," in *Studies in Linear and Non-linear Programming*, ed. by Arrow, Hurwicz, and Uzawa (Stanford: Stanford University Press), 1958.

6
COMPARATIVE ADVANTAGE WITH A MULTI-COUNTRY, MULTI-GOOD MODEL

A MULTI-COUNTRY AND MULTI-GOOD FORMULATION

The purpose of this section is to extend the Ricardian theory of comparative advantage to cases with many countries and many goods.[1] We shall inherit all the assumptions of the Ricardian model, except those dealing with the number of countries and the number of goods. Hence, we shall again assume that labor is the only factor of production and that the amount of labor required to produce one unit of a good is constant regardless of the level of output. Labor is completely mobile with negligible transport costs within each country and completely immobile among the countries. Goods are completely mobile within each country and among countries, with negligible transport costs. There are m countries and each country is capable of producing all of the n goods.

Let us write l_{ij} for the amount of labor required to produce one unit of good i in Country j, L_j for the total amount of labor available in Country j, x_{ij} for the output of good i in Country j. Then the resource constraint for the jth country is

$$\sum_{i=1}^{n} l_{ij}x_{ij} \leqq L_j, \quad j = 1, 2, \cdots, m. \tag{6-1}$$

Following Ricardo, let us suppose that the world equilibrium price of each good, p_i, $i = 1, 2, \cdots, n$, is given, and consider the problem of maximizing the value of the world's output subject to the above constraints. In other words, let us consider the following linear programming problem.

MAX. PROBLEM I   Maximize

$$p_1 \left(\sum_{j=1}^{m} x_{1j} \right) + \cdots + p_n \left(\sum_{j=1}^{m} x_{nj} \right)$$

subject to

$$\sum_{i=1}^{n} l_{ij}x_{ij} \leqq L_j, \quad j = 1, 2, \cdots, m,$$

and

$$x_{ij} \geqq 0, \quad i = 1, 2, \cdots, n; \quad j = 1, 2, \cdots, m.$$

---

[1] As we noted previously, the formulation of the classical theory of comparative advantage in terms of linear programming or activity analysis, and hence its extension to a multi-country, multi-good model, is due to Whitin [19], McKenzie [10], [11], [12], and Samuelson [17]. Both

In vector-matrix notation, the first constraint can be written as

$$
\begin{bmatrix}
l_{11} & 0 & \cdots & 0 & | \cdots | & l_{n1} & 0 & \cdots & 0 \\
0 & l_{12} & \cdots & 0 & | \cdots | & 0 & l_{n2} & \cdots & 0 \\
\cdot & & & & | \;\; | & & & & \\
\cdot & & & & | \;\; | & & & & \\
\cdot & & & & | \;\; | & & & & \\
0 & 0 & \cdots & l_{1m} & | \cdots | & 0 & 0 & \cdots & l_{nm}
\end{bmatrix}
\begin{bmatrix}
x_{11} \\ x_{12} \\ \cdot \\ \cdot \\ \cdot \\ x_{1m} \\ x_{21} \\ x_{22} \\ \cdot \\ \cdot \\ \cdot \\ x_{2m} \\ \text{- - -} \\ \cdot \\ \cdot \\ \cdot \\ \text{- - -} \\ x_{n1} \\ \cdot \\ \cdot \\ \cdot \\ x_{nm}
\end{bmatrix}
\leqq
\begin{bmatrix}
L_1 \\ L_2 \\ \cdot \\ \cdot \\ \cdot \\ L_m
\end{bmatrix}
$$

The dual of the above problem is easily seen to be that of minimizing $\displaystyle\sum_{j=1}^{m} w_j L_j$ subject to

$$
\begin{bmatrix}
l_{11} & 0 & \cdots & 0 \\
0 & l_{12} & \cdots & 0 \\
\cdot & & & \\
\cdot & & & \\
\cdot & & & \\
0 & 0 & \cdots & l_{1m} \\
\hline
\cdot & & & \\
\cdot & & & \\
\cdot & & & \\
\hline
l_{n1} & 0 & \cdots & 0 \\
0 & l_{n2} & \cdots & 0 \\
\cdot & & & \\
\cdot & & & \\
\cdot & & & \\
0 & 0 & \cdots & l_{nm}
\end{bmatrix}
\begin{bmatrix}
w_1 \\ w_2 \\ \cdot \\ \cdot \\ \cdot \\ w_m
\end{bmatrix}
\geqq
\begin{bmatrix}
p_1 \\ p_1 \\ \cdot \\ \cdot \\ \cdot \\ p_1 \\ \text{- -} \\ \cdot \\ \cdot \\ \cdot \\ \text{- -} \\ p_n \\ \cdot \\ \cdot \\ \cdot \\ p_n
\end{bmatrix}
\quad \text{or,}
$$

Whitin and McKenzie have been strongly influenced by Graham's work. For a brief survey, see Chipman [2], pp. 495–501. This chapter has been strongly influenced by Chipman ([2], pp. 495–509), Kuhn [8], [9], McKenzie [13], and Jones [6].

MIN. PROBLEM I   Minimize

$$\sum_{j=1}^{m} w_j L_j$$

subject to

$$w_j l_{ij} \geqq p_i, \quad i = 1, 2, \cdots, n; \quad j = 1, 2, \cdots, m \qquad (6\text{-}2)$$

and $w_j \geqq 0$, $j = 1, 2, \cdots, m$.

An alternative linear programming formulation has been provided by Chipman ([2], pp. 495–499). We assume that labor is indispensable in the production of every good (that is, $l_{ij} > 0$ for all i and j) and to write $a_{ij} \equiv L_j / l_{ij}$. Then our constraint of equation (6-1) can be rewritten as

$$\sum_{i=1}^{n} x_{ij}/a_{ij} \leqq 1, \quad j = 1, 2, \cdots, m. \qquad (6\text{-}3)$$

Letting $y_{ij} \equiv x_{ij}/a_{ij}$ equation (6-3) can be rewritten as

$$\sum_{i=1}^{n} y_{ij} + \delta_j = 1, \quad j = 1, 2, \cdots, m; \qquad (6\text{-}4)$$

where $\delta_j \geqq 0$ is a "slack variable" for each j. That is,

$$\delta_j \equiv 1 - \sum_{i=1}^{n} y_{ij}, \quad j = 1, 2, \cdots, m.$$

Let x_i be the total (world) production of the ith good, so that $x_i = \sum_{j=1}^{m} x_{ij}$. Then from the definition of y_{ij} we obtain

$$\sum_{j=1}^{m} a_{ij} y_{ij} = x_i, \quad i = 1, 2, \cdots, n. \qquad (6\text{-}5)$$

Hence, we have the following linear programming problem, as formulated by Chipman.

MAX. PROBLEM II   Maximize

$$\sum_{i=1}^{n} p_i x_i$$

subject to (6-4), (6-5), and $x_i \geqq 0$, $i = 1, 2, \cdots, n$; $\delta_j \geqq 0$, $j = 1, 2, \cdots, m$.
    In vector-matrix notation, these constraints are:

$$\begin{bmatrix} 0 & 0 & \cdots & 0 & \vrule & 1 & 1 & \cdots & 1 \end{bmatrix}$$

$$=$$

$$\begin{array}{cccccccccccc} y_{11} & \cdots & y_{n1} & \vrule & \cdots & y_{1m} & \cdots & y_{nm} & \vrule & x_1 & \cdots & x_n & \vrule & \delta_1 & \cdots & \delta_m \end{array}$$

$$
\left[
\begin{array}{cc|cc|cc|c}
0 & 0 & & 0 & 0 & 0 & 1 \\
\vdots & \vdots & & \vdots & \vdots & \vdots & \vdots \\
0 & 0 & & 0 & 0 & 1 & 0 \\
0 & 0 & \cdots & 0 & 1 & 0 & \cdots & 0 \\
\hline
0 & 0 & & 1 & 0 & 0 & 0 \\
\vdots & \vdots & & \vdots & \vdots & \vdots & \vdots \\
0 & 1 & & 0 & 0 & 0 & 0 \\
1 & 0 & \cdots & 0 & 0 & 0 & \cdots & 0 \\
\hline
0 & 0 & -a_{nm} & 0 & 0 & 1 \\
\vdots & \vdots & \vdots & \vdots & \vdots & \vdots \\
0 & -a_{2m} & 0 & 0 & 0 & 1 \\
-a_{1m} & 0 & \cdots & 0 & 0 & 0 & \cdots & 1 \\
\hline
\vdots & \vdots & \vdots & \vdots & \vdots & \vdots \\
0 & 0 & -a_{n1} & 1 & 0 & 0 \\
\vdots & \vdots & \vdots & \vdots & \vdots & \vdots \\
0 & -a_{21} & 0 & 1 & 0 & 0 \\
-a_{11} & 0 & \cdots & 0 & 1 & 0 & \cdots & 0
\end{array}
\right]
$$

The reader can easily verify that the dual of the above maximization problem is:

MIN. PROBLEM II [2] Minimize

$$\sum_{j=1}^{m} s_j \quad \left(= \sum_{i=1}^{n} \bar{p}_i \cdot 0 + \sum_{j=1}^{m} s_j \cdot 1 \right)$$

subject to

$$-\bar{p}_i a_{ij} + s_j \geq 0 , \quad i = 1, 2, \cdots, n; \quad j = 1, 2, \cdots, m , \tag{6-6}$$

$$\bar{p}_i \geq p_i , \quad i = 1, 2, \cdots, n , \tag{6-7}$$

and $s_j \geq 0$, $j = 1, 2, \cdots, m$.

Here the $\bar{p}_i$ and the s_j are the dual variables. From one of the statements of the duality theorem, we know that if $(x_1, x_2, \cdots, x_n)$ is a solution to Max. Problem II, with $x_i > 0$ for all i, then $\bar{p}_i = p_i$, $i = 1, 2, \cdots, n$. Let us assume that this is the case, so that the world output of every good is positive. Then we may replace $\bar{p}_i$ by p_i. Write $s_j/L_j \equiv w_j$ and recall that $a_{ij} \equiv L_j/l_{ij}$. Then we can rewrite the above minimization problem as:

Minimize

$$\sum_{j=1}^{m} w_j L_j$$

subject to

$$w_j l_{ij} \geq p_i , \quad i = 1, 2, \cdots, n; \quad j = 1, 2, \cdots, m$$

and

$$w_j \geq 0 , \quad j = 1, 2, \cdots, m .$$

This is the same as Min. Problem I, which is not surprising because Max. Problem I and Max. Problem II are really the same problem. However, we note that our formulation, Max. Problem I, is a little simpler and more straightforward than Chipman's.

Now let us proceed with the interpretation of the dual problem. Interpreting the dual variable w_j as the *money wage* rate of the jth country, relation (6-2) says that the cost of producing a unit of a good in Country j cannot be less than the price of the good. Since the l_{ij}s are constant, $w_j l_{ij}$ denotes the average cost, as well as the marginal cost, of the good. Thus, relation (6-2) says that the marginal cost of producing the ith good in the jth country cannot be less than the price of this good. If we rewrite (6-2) as:

$$w_j \geq p_i \frac{1}{l_{ij}} , \quad i = 1, 2, \cdots, n; \quad j = 1, 2, \cdots, m , \tag{6-2'}$$

[2] For an interpretation of Mangoldt [14] in terms of the solution to this dual linear programming problem, see Chipman [2], pp. 501–503. Mangoldt's work is known to the English readers mainly through Viner [18], Chapter VIII, after Edgeworth [3]

and assume that $l_{ij} > 0$ for all i and j, it then says that the value of the marginal product in the ith industry in Country j cannot exceed the wage rate in Country j. Thus relations (6-2) and (6-2′) state a very familiar condition for a competitive economy, namely, the "profit condition." Let $(x_{11}^*, \cdots, x_{nm}^*)$ be a solution vector to Max. Problem I and let $(w_1^*, \cdots, w_m^*)$ be a solution vector to Min. Problem I. Then the LP duality theorem states that:

1. $\displaystyle\sum_{i,j} p_i x_{ij}^* = \sum_j w_j^* L_j$;

2. If $\displaystyle\sum_{i=1}^{n} l_{ij} x_{ij}^* < L_j$, then $w_j^* = 0$, $j = 1, \cdots, m$;

3. If $w_j^* > 0$, then $\displaystyle\sum_{i=1}^{n} l_{ij} x_{ij}^* = L$, $j = 1, \cdots, m$;

4. If $w_j^* l_{ij} > p_i$, then $x_{ij}^* = 0$, $i = 1, \cdots, n$; $j = 1, \cdots, m$;

5. If $x_{ij}^* > 0$, then $w_j^* l_{ij} = p_i$, $i = 1, \cdots, n$; $j = 1, \cdots, m$.

Relation 1 states that the value of the total world output is equal to the total factor income of the world. Relation 2 states that if labor becomes redundant in the jth country, its price must be zero; and relation 3 states that if the wage rate is positive in the jth country, then all of the labor available in Country j will be used in production. Relation 4 states that if the unit cost of production of good i in Country j exceeds the price of good i, this good will not be produced in Country j; and relation 5 states that if the ith good is produced in Country j, then its price is equal to its marginal cost ($=$ average cost) in Country j (or the wage rate in Country j is equal to the value of the marginal product of labor in this industry). We can obtain a similar interpretation of the variables in Max. Problem II and Min. Problem II.

The foregoing interpretation of the duality theorem for the present problem obviously depends on the interpretation of the dual variable w_j as the wage rate in Country j. As noted above, this can be justified if we consider our system as a model of a competitive economy. For example, relation (6-2) can hold only when we interpret w_j as the wage rate in a competitive economy.

Now let w_j^* be the wage rate of the jth country and suppose that the ith good is produced in the jth country under competitive conditions, so that

$$w_j^* l_{ij} = p_i, \quad i = 1, 2, \cdots, n; \quad j = 1, 2, \cdots, m. \tag{6-8}$$

Here $l_{ij} > 0$ for all i and j is assumed. Taking logarithms of both sides of equation (6-8), we get

$$\log w_j^* + \log l_{ij} = \log p_i. \tag{6-9}$$

For the sake of notational clarity we will denote the goods, X_i, $i = 1, 2, \cdots, n$ by $A, B, C, \cdots$. Then equation (6-9) enables us to measure the price of each good as follows (Figure 6-1), where the points A_j, B_j, and so on, represent the prices of the goods A, B, and so on in Country j, when the wage rate in that country is w_j^*. The point 0 denotes the origin.

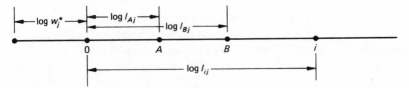

Figure 6-1   Edgeworth Scale

This diagrammatical device was used by Edgeworth [3] to show the comparative advantage relations (hence the name "Edgeworth Scale" for Figure (6-1). Suppose that the world consists of only two countries, Countries I and II. Then the comparative advantage relation can easily be seen when the two Edgeworth scales for these countries are superimposed on each other, as in Figure 6-2. Here the subscripts $_1$, and $_2$ refer to the country.

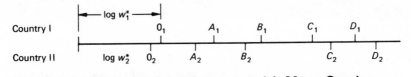

Figure 6-2   Comparative Advantage with Many Goods

In Figure 6-2, Country I would export goods C, D, and so on, and Country II would export goods A, B, and so on. When there are more than two countries, we can carry out a similar analysis by superimposing all the Edgeworth Scales on each other. This extension of the Edgeworth analysis to a multi-country model is due to Viner [18].[3]

The above illustration, using Edgeworth's technique, assumes that the wage rate for each country is given. A natural question now is, how are these wage rates determined? We have already pointed out that they can be obtained as a solution to the dual problem. However, in order to show that these w_j*s of the dual problem are indeed the wage rates in a competitive model, we have to show that they, together with the x_{ij} and the parameters

[3] Viner has an excellent exposition of his technique ([18], pp. 464–467). Chipman was worried because McKenzie's article [10], which is based on a new approach contained a somewhat misleading statement which tended to suggest that "there might be something invalid about Viner's method, or indeed about those of Mangoldt and Edgeworth." (Chipman [2], p. 505.) He then continued to argue that "in fact this is not so and that the two approaches are not at all unrelated as has been supposed." This point looks really obvious for we are essentially dealing with one linear programming problem. See also the next two sections of the present chapter. Chipman seems to believe that McKenzie (and Jones [6]) blamed the classical theorists for arguing that the bilateral comparison of comparative advantage is a sufficient condition for comparative advantage in a multi-country, multi-good framework. This is still a matter of debate. In any case, the following remark by Chipman is illuminating. "Edgeworth (1894, p. 633) and Haberler (1936, p. 137) were careful to point out, and as Ohlin took pains to stress, information on comparative costs alone is not enough to determine where the dividing line (on the Edgeworth scale) will be drawn. Unfortunately, Bastable (1903, p. 36) was not so careful, and appeared to imply that comparative costs would by themselves uniquely determine the pattern of specialization" ([2], p. 506). Bastable's mistake stems from his neglect of the demand conditions.

COMPARATIVE ADVANTAGE WITH A MULTI-GOOD MODEL 171

p_i, are compatible with the *demand conditions*. If we specify the demand conditions and if we can show that there *exists* a solution to the dual problem for some p_is, then we can truly say that the w_j^*s, as solutions to the dual problem, can serve as wage rates given these particular p_is. At the same time we know the mechanism for determining the p_is, w_j^*s, and x_{ij}^*s in a competitive model. This leads to a very difficult question, that of the existence of a competitive equilibrium, which we shall take up in the next chapter.

TWO ADDITIONAL CONSIDERATIONS

World Welfare and Each Country's Welfare

In the previous section we considered the problem of maximizing the total value of the *world's* output, and the duality implications of this problem. Here we wish to show that this problem is equivalent to that of maximizing the value of *each country's* output. First we shall define the following vectors:

$$x_j \equiv (x_{1j}, x_{2j}, \cdots, x_{nj}), \quad l_j \equiv (l_{1j}, l_{2j}, \cdots, l_{nj}),$$

and $p \equiv (p_1, p_2, \cdots, p_n)$. Thus x_j is Country j's output vector, l_j is its labor input coefficient vector, and p is the world price vector. Now we can define the following two problems.

PROBLEM W (World's Welfare)   Maximize

$$\sum_{j=1}^{m} p \cdot x_j$$

subject to

$$l_j \cdot x_j \leq L_j \quad \text{and} \quad x_j \geq 0,^4 \quad j = 1, 2, \cdots, m.$$

Here the dot ($\cdot$) refers to the inner product, so that $l_j \cdot x_j \equiv \sum_{i=1}^{n} l_{ij} x_{ij}$, and so on.

PROBLEM C (Each Country's Welfare)   For each $j = 1, 2, \cdots, m$, Maximize

$$p \cdot x_j$$

subject to

$$l_j \cdot x_j \leq L_j \quad \text{and} \quad x_j \geq 0.$$

Before we consider our problem, we will prove the following lemma, which is of general importance.

LEMMA   Let $f_j(x_j)$, $j = 1, 2, \cdots, m$, be real valued functions defined on R^n. Let $S_j, j = 1, 2, \cdots, m$, be subsets of R^n such that $x_j \in S_j$. Consider $S \equiv \bigotimes_{j=1}^{m} S_j$,

---

[4] By the vector notation $x_j \geq 0$, we mean that $x_{ij} \geq 0$ for all i, that is, all the components of the vector are non-negative.

the Cartesian product of all the S_j. Let $x = (x_1, x_2, \cdots, x_m) \in S \subset R^{mn}$. Define $f(x) \equiv \sum\limits_{j=1}^{m} f_j(x_j)$. Then $f(x)$ achieves its maximum over S at x^* if and only if $f_j(x_j)$ achieves its maximum over S_j at x_j^* for all $j = 1, 2, \cdots, m$, where $x^* = (x_1^*, \cdots, x_m^*)$.

PROOF (*Necessity*) By assumption $f(x^*) \geqq f(x)$ for all $x \in S$, or

$$\sum_{j=1}^{m} f_j(x_j^*) \geqq \sum_{j=1}^{m} f_j(x_j) \quad \text{for all } x_j \in S_j, j = 1, 2, \cdots, m .$$

Let $x_j = x_j^*$ for all j except $j = i$, for some arbitrary i. Then $f_i(x_i^*) \geqq f_i(x_i)$ for all $x_i \in S_i$. Since the choice of i is arbitrary, this proves the necessity.

(*Sufficiency*) By assumption $f_j(x_j^*) \geqq f_j(x_j)$ for all $x_j \in S_j$, $j = 1, 2, \cdots, m$. Hence $\sum\limits_{j=1}^{m} f_j(x_j^*) \geqq \sum\limits_{j=1}^{m} f_j(x_j)$ for all $x_j \in S_j, j = 1, \cdots, m$.   (Q.E.D.)

THEOREM The value of the world's output is maximized if and only if every country maximizes the value of its output.

PROOF Define $S_j \equiv \{x_j : x_j \in R^n, x_j \geqq 0, l_j \cdot x_j \leqq L_j\}$, $j = 1, 2, \cdots, m$, and let $f_j(x_j) = p \cdot x_j$. Note that $f(x) = \sum\limits_{j=1}^{m} p \cdot x_j$. Then by application of the previous lemma, the theorem is proved.   (Q.E.D.)

Note that the above lemma is really very elementary and, indeed, almost trivial. It is possible to prove the above theorem using the saddle point characterization of the optimality (theorem 4, first section of the Appendix to Chapter 5). We shall prove the above theorem again using the saddle point characterization of the optimality in order to enhance the reader's understanding of theorem 4 mentioned above.

Due to theorem 4 of the first section of the Appendix to Chapter 5, a necessary and sufficient condition for $x_j^*, j = 1, 2, \cdots, m$ to be a solution to problem W is that there exists a $w_j^*, j = 1, 2, \cdots, m$ such that

$$\Phi(x, w^*) \leqq \Phi(x^*, w^*) \leqq \Phi(x^*, w) \quad \text{for all } x \geqq 0, \quad w \geqq 0, \tag{6-10}$$

where

$x \equiv (x_1, x_2, \cdots, x_m)$ is an $(n \times m)$ matrix,

$w \equiv (w_1, w_2, \cdots, w_m)$ is an m vector and,

$$\Phi(x, w) \equiv \sum_{j=1}^{m} p \cdot x_j + \sum_{j=1}^{m} w_j(L_j - l_j \cdot x_j) .$$

Also a necessary and sufficient condition for $x_j^0, j = 1, 2, \cdots, m$, to be a solution to problem C is that there exists a $\lambda_j^0, j = 1, 2, \cdots, m$ such that

$$\Phi_j(x_j, \lambda_j^0) \leqq \Phi_j(x_j^0, \lambda_j^0) \leqq \Phi_j(x_j^0, \lambda_j) \quad \text{for all } x_j \geqq 0 \text{ and } \lambda_j \geqq 0 ,$$

$j = 1, 2, \cdots, m$, where $\Phi_j(x_j, \lambda_j) \equiv p \cdot x_j + \lambda_j(L_j - l_j \cdot x_j) .$ \tag{6-11}

Clearly, if (6-11) holds for all $j = 1, 2, \cdots, m$, then (6-10) holds. To show the converse (that is, to show that if (6-10) holds then (6-11) also holds) we put $x_k = x_k^*$ and $w_k = w_k^*$ for all $k = 1, 2, \cdots, m$ except for some j, in relation (6-10). Then if we let $x_j^* = x_j^0$ and $w_j^* = \lambda_j^0$ we obtain relation (6-11). Since the choice of j is arbitrary, relation (6-11) holds for all j.

Thus, we have again proved that the value of the world's output is maximized if and only if every country maximizes the value of its national product.

Maximization of Income and Minimization of Cost

Thus we know that the problem of maximizing the world's welfare is in a sense equivalent to the problem of maximizing each country's welfare. Now recall our discussion in Chapter 4, where we made a distinction between maximizing the (real) national product with the given resources, and minimizing the (real) cost of obtaining a given income. Here real cost can be interpreted as the total amount of labor required to produce a given amount of income. A natural question is whether these two approaches (the minimization approach and the maximization approach) yield the same results. This question was asked and answered by Kuhn [8].[5] To ease notation, we will, in this subsection, omit subscript $_j$ which denotes the jth country.

We are concerned with the following two problems.

(K_M) Maximize $p \cdot x$

subject to

$l \cdot x \leq L$ and $x \geq 0$,

(K_m) Minimize $l \cdot x$

subject to

$p \cdot x \geq I$ and $x \geq 0$,

where I is the value of the given *feasible* output vector $\bar{x}$. That is,

$$I \equiv p \cdot \bar{x} \equiv \sum_{i=1}^{n} p_i \bar{x}_i, \quad \text{with } l \cdot \bar{x} \leq L \text{ and } \bar{x} \geq 0.$$

The following theorem, which asserts that the two approaches are, in a sense, equivalent is due to Kuhn [8].

First we shall introduce three assumptions.

[5] Apparently Kuhn was inspired by Viner's distinction between the two approaches. Following Kuhn, we may quote the following passage from Viner. "The Classical economists followed three different methods of dealing with the question of 'gain' from trade: (1) the doctrine of comparative costs, under which economy in cost of obtaining a given income was the criterion of gain; (2) increase in income as a criterion of gain; and (3) terms of trade as an index of the international division and the trend of gain." (Viner [18], p. 437.)

ASSUMPTION 1 $l_i > 0$ for all i.

This assumption says that labor is indispensable for the production of every good in every country. Since labor is the only factor of production, this also means that there can be no output without some input (that is, "no land of Cockaigne"). We can certainly allow goods for which $l_i = 0$ (for example, air), but assumption 1 says that we simply exclude such goods from our consideration.

ASSUMPTION 2 $p_i > 0$ for all i.

In other words, all n goods are desired. A precise specification of this assumption requires a consideration of the demand conditions (such as "non-satiation").

ASSUMPTION 3 $p_i/l_i, i = 1, 2, \cdots, n$, are all different from each other.

We can now prove the following theorem, due to Kuhn.

THEOREM (KUHN)   Good i is produced in an optimal amount for problem (K_M) *if and only if* it is produced in an optimal amount for problem (K_m).

PROOF   Consider the problems dual to (K_M) and (K_m).

DUAL TO K_M Find $w \geqq 0$ so as to minimize wL subject to $wl_i \geqq p_i$, $i = 1, 2, \cdots, n$. Clearly this problem has an optimal solution $w^0 = \max_i \dfrac{p_i}{l_i} > 0$.
Moreover, if $x_i^0 > 0$ is an optimal output for (K_M), then $w^0 l_i = p_i$. In fact the converse also holds. That is, if $w^0 l_i = p_i$ then $x_i^0 > 0$. For if $x_i^0 = 0$ with $w^0 l_i = p_i$, then $x_i^0 = 0$ for all $i = 1, 2, \cdots, n$,[6] which is impossible. In other words, $x_i^0 > 0$ if and only if $w^0 l_i = p_i$.

DUAL TO K_m Find $\mu \geqq 0$ so as to maximize μI subject to $p_i \mu \leqq l_i$, $i = 1, 2, \cdots, n$. This problem obviously has a solution—$\mu^0 = \min_i \dfrac{l_i}{p_i} > 0$.
Furthermore, $x_i^{00} > 0$ is an optimal output for (K_m) if and only if $\dfrac{l_i}{p_i} = \mu^0$.
Since the indices for which l_i/p_i achieves the minimum μ^0 are the same as those for which p_i/l_i achieves its maximum w^0, this completes the proof of the theorem.   (Q.E.D.)

COROLLARY   If x^0 is a solution to (K_M), then it is a solution to (K_m) with $I = p \cdot x^0$. Conversely x^0 is a solution to (K_M) with $l \cdot x^0 = L$ if it is a solution to (K_m).

---

[6] Suppose not. In other words, suppose that $x_{i_0}^0 > 0$ for some i_0. Then $w^0 l_{i_0} = p_{i_0}$ so that $p_i/l_i = p_{i_0}/l_{i_0} (= w^0)$, which contradicts assumption 3.

PROOF   If x^0 is a solution to (K_M), then $l \cdot x^0 = L$ since $p_i > 0$ for all i. By the duality theorem $p \cdot x^0 = w^0 L$. If μ^0 is a solution to dual of K_m, then $l \cdot x^{00} = \mu^0 I$ where x^{00} is a solution to (K_m). If $\mu^0 = 1/w^0 > 0$, then $I = w^0 l \cdot x^{00}$ or $p \cdot x^0 = w^0 l \cdot x^{00}$.   But $p \cdot x^0 = w^0 L = w^0 l \cdot x^0$,   so $w^0 l (x^0 - x^{00}) = 0$. Since $w^0 > 0$ and $l_i > 0$ for all i, then $x^0 = x^{00}$. But $\mu^0 = 1/w^0 > 0$ from the proof of the above theorem. Hence, the solution x^0 to (K_M) is equal to the solution x^{00} to (K_m) with $I = p \cdot x^0$. The converse can be proved analogously.   (Q.E.D.)

Kuhn's theorem and its corollary[7] can be illustrated by Figure 6-3.

Finally, the following points should be obvious.

1. If x^0 is optimal for (K_M), then it is feasible for (K_m).
2. If x^{00} is optimal for (K_m), then it is feasible for (K_M).

The proof of this is quite simple. If x^0 is optimal for (K_M), then $p \cdot x^0 = p \cdot \bar{x} = I$ since $l \cdot \bar{x} \leq L$, and $\bar{x} \geqq 0$. That is, it is feasible for (K_m). On the other hand, if x^{00} is optimal for (K_m), then $l \cdot x^{00} \leqq l \cdot \bar{x} \leqq L$. That is, it is feasible for (K_M).

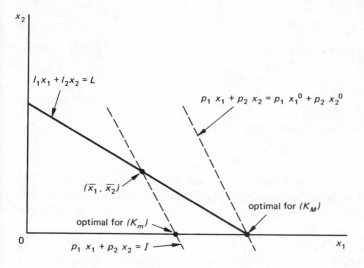

Figure 6-3   Kuhn's Theorem

THE McKENZIE-JONES THEOREM: THE PATTERN OF SPECIALIZATION

In this section we shall consider the characterization of the optimality condition based on the model formulated in the first section. Let p denote the world price vector and let us consider the following maximization problem.

---

[7] The theorem and the corollary can also be proved using Theorem 3 of the Appendix to Chapter 5. The corollary was not mentioned by Kuhn [8].

MAXIMIZATION PROBLEM   For each j, maximize

$$p \cdot x_j$$

subject to

$$l_j \cdot x_j \leqq L_j \text{ and } x_j \geqq 0,$$

where x_j denotes the output vector of Country j and l_j denotes the labor co-efficient vector of Country j. As we discussed in the previous section, this problem is equivalent to the problem of maximizing the value of the total world output. We shall be concerned with the characterization of the solution to the above problem.

First define the Lagrangian $\Phi_j \equiv p \cdot x_j + w_j(L_j - l_j \cdot x_j)$. Due to theorem 3 in the first section of the Appendix to Chapter 5, a necessary and sufficient condition, (KTL), for $x_j{}^0$ to be a solution to the above problem is that there exists a $w_j{}^0$ such that:

$$p_i - w_j{}^0 l_{ij} \leqq 0, \quad 1, 2, \cdots, n; \tag{6-12a}$$

$$(p_i - w_j{}^0 l_{ij})x_{ij}{}^0 = 0, \quad 1 = 1, 2, \cdots, n; \tag{6-12b}[8]$$

$$L_j - l_j \cdot x_j{}^0 \geqq 0; \tag{6-13a}$$

$$(L_j - l_j \cdot x_j{}^0)w_j{}^0 = 0; \quad \text{and} \tag{6-13b}$$

$$w_j{}^0 \geqq 0, \quad x^0 \geqq 0. \tag{6-14}$$

We shall now reintroduce the two assumptions we used in the previous section.

ASSUMPTION 1 $l_{ij} > 0$ for all i and j.

ASSUMPTION 2 $p_i > 0$ for all i.

Note that the condition (6-12a) above requires both assumption 1 and assumption 2. Note that these assumptions then imply that $w_j{}^0 > 0$ for all j. Hence conditions (6-13a) and (6-13b) can be reduced to the following equation:

$$L_j - l_j \cdot x_j{}^0 = 0. \tag{6-15}$$

Following McKenzie [10], Jones [6] considered the following problem.

THE McKENZIE-JONES PROBLEM   Assuming that the number of goods is equal to the number of countries, what is a necessary and sufficient condition for Country j to produce only good j as a solution to the above problem? In other words, what is a necessary and sufficient condition that the "j-j specialization" be optimal?

In order to consider this problem, suppose that good j is produced only in Country j. Then the above necessary and sufficient conditions can be written as:

[8] This may be written as

$\sum\limits_{i=1}^{n} (p_i - w_j{}^0 l_{ij}) x_{ij}{}^0 = 0$, but from (6-12a) and $x_{ij}{}^0 \geqq 0$, this is equivalent to (6-12b).

$$p_j = w_j^0 l_{jj}, \tag{6-16a}$$

$$p_i - w_j^0 l_{ij} \leqq 0, \quad i = 1, 2, \cdots, n, \quad (i \neq j), \tag{6-16b}$$

$$l_{jj} x_j^0 = L_j. \tag{6-17}$$

And of course $w_j^0 > 0$, $x_{jj}^0 > 0$, $x_{ij}^0 = 0$ for $i \neq j$. Hence the necessary and sufficient condition for the j-j specialization (Country j specializes in good j) to be optimal is reduced to (6-16a) and (6-16b), which can be written out as:

$$w_1^0 l_{11} = p_1, \quad w_2^0 l_{12} \geqq p_1, \quad \cdots, \quad w_m^0 l_{1m} \geqq p_1$$

$$w_1^0 l_{21} \geqq p_2, \quad w_2^0 l_{22} = p_2, \quad \cdots, \quad w_m^0 l_{2m} \geqq p_2$$

$$\cdot$$
$$\cdot$$
$$\cdot$$

$$w_1^0 l_{m1} \geqq p_m, \quad w_2^0 l_{m2} \geqq p_m, \quad \cdots, \quad w_m^0 l_{mm} = p_m.$$

(Recall that the number of goods, n, equals the number of countries, m, by assumption.) The above conditions can also be written as

$$\frac{p_1}{l_{11}} \geqq \frac{p_i}{l_{i1}}, \quad \frac{p_2}{l_{22}} \geqq \frac{p_i}{l_{i2}}, \cdots, \frac{p_m}{l_{mm}} \geqq \frac{p_i}{l_{im}}, \quad i = 1, 2, \cdots, m \text{ in each case.}$$

Thus, our necessary and sufficient conditions have been reduced to

$$\frac{p_j}{l_{jj}} \geqq \frac{p_i}{l_{ij}}, \quad i, j = 1, 2, \cdots, m \tag{6-18}$$

(where strict inequality holds if assumption 3 prevails).

This is equivalent to

$$\prod_{j=1}^{m} \frac{p_j}{l_{jj}} \geqq \prod_{j=1}^{m} \frac{p_{\pi(j)}}{l_{\pi(j)j}}, \tag{6-19}$$

(with strict inequality under assumption 3), where $\pi(j)$ is a permutation of the integers of the index set. For example, if the index set is $\{1, 2, 3\}$ then all of the following are permutations of these integers: $\{2, 3, 1\}$, $\{2, 1, 3\}$, $\{3, 1, 2\}$, $\{3, 2, 1\}$, $\{1, 3, 2\}$, and $\{1, 2, 3\}$ itself. If π means the permutation of $\{1, 2, 3\}$ to $\{2, 3, 1\}$, for example, then $\pi(1) = 2$, $\pi(2) = 3$, and $\pi(3) = 1$. It is clear that by considering enough of the possible permutations of the index set, $\pi(j)$, for any j, can be any integer of the index set including j. Then equation (6-19) can be rewritten as

$$\prod_{j=1}^{m} p_j \prod_{j=1}^{m} \frac{1}{l_{jj}} \geqq \prod_{j=1}^{m} p_{\pi(j)} \prod_{j=1}^{m} \frac{1}{l_{\pi(j)j}}. \tag{6-20}$$

Since $\prod_{j=1}^{m} p_j = \prod_{j=1}^{m} p_{\pi(j)}$, this condition is reduced to

$$\prod_{j=1}^{m} l_{jj} \leqq \prod_{j=1}^{m} l_{\pi(j)j} , \quad \text{for any permutation } \pi, \tag{6-21}$$

which we call the *McKenzie-Jones condition*. Thus, we have proved the following theorem. Note that strict inequality holds in (6-21), if assumption 3 prevails.

THEOREM (McKENZIE-JONES)[9] Within the present framework, a necessary and sufficient condition for the pattern of specialization in which Country j specializes in the production of good j to be optimal is in relation (6-18), that is, $l_{jj}/l_{ij} \leqq p_j/p_i$ $i, j = 1, 2, \cdots, m$, which implies that the l_{ij}s must satisfy the McKenzie-Jones condition (6-21)

$$\prod_{j=1}^{m} l_{jj} \leqq \prod_{j=1}^{m} l_{\pi(j)j} .$$

In the Ricardian theory, there are two countries (1 and 2) and two goods (X and Y). Direct application of the above theorem says that a necessary and sufficient condition for Country 1 to specialize in the production of X and Country 2 to specialize in the production of Y is that

$$l_{x1}l_{y2} \leqq l_{x2}l_{y1} ; \quad \text{or} \tag{6-22}$$

$$\frac{l_{x1}}{l_{x2}} \leqq \frac{l_{y1}}{l_{y2}}, \tag{6-23}$$

where strict inequality holds if assumption 3 prevails. In other words, the McKenzie-Jones theorem provides an extension of the Ricardian theory of comparative advantage to a multi-country, multi-good model.

If we set $\pi(j) = j$ except for two arbitrary indices r and s (that is, indices r and s in the index set are interchanged) condition (6-21) becomes:

$$l_{rr}l_{ss} \leqq l_{rs}l_{sr} \quad \text{or} \quad \frac{l_{rr}}{l_{rs}} \leqq \frac{l_{sr}}{l_{ss}}, \tag{6-24}$$

where strict inequality holds if assumption 3 prevails. Since r and s are chosen arbitrarily, this relationship must hold for any pair of indices (r, s). In other words, a necessary condition for the $(j\text{-}j)$ pattern of specialization is that the Ricardian comparative advantage relation holds for any pair of goods. However, as Jones has shown [6], this bilateral condition is not a sufficient condition for the $(j\text{-}j)$ pattern of specialization on a world-wide basis.

---

[9] The first explicit proof of this theorem is due to Jones [6]. He used the Hawkins-Simon theorem for the Leontief matrix and made no explicit use of the (KTL) condition. We provide the proof using the (KTL) condition in order to relate it to other problems in classical comparative advantage theory, which are essentially linear or nonlinear programming problems. Kuhn [8] proved this theorem by using the LP duality theorem.

Finally, we may note that we can extend, by using (6-12), (6-13), and (6-14), our consideration to the case in which the number of goods does not equal the number of countries. Then we can no longer consider the (j-j) pattern of specialization of the Ricardian theory. There may be more than one country specializing in the production of any one good (if, for example, $m > n$) and there may be one country producing more than one good (if, for example, $n > m$).

A GENERALIZATION OF MILL'S PROBLEM[10]

So far we have assumed that the world price vector p is given and fixed and therefore no explicit discussion of the demand conditions has been provided. On the other hand, we have generalized the two-country, two-good model to a model that is maximized under a set of demand conditions. We considered this problem, Mill's problem, from the point of view of nonlinear programming in the Appendix to the previous chapter. Here we shall extend this analysis to a multi-country, multi-good model. This task is not really too difficult after our preparation in the previous sections.

We shall use the notation of the previous sections. Thus there will be n goods and m countries, x_{ij} will denote the amount of the ith good produced in the jth country, and l_{ij} will denote the amount of labor required to produce one unit of the ith good in the jth country. Then the following problem is a generalized version of the nonlinear programming problem considered in connection with Mill's problem in Chapter 5.

THE MILL-CHIPMAN MAXIMIZATION PROBLEM   Maximize

$$u(x_1, x_2, \cdots, x_i, \cdots, x_n)$$

subject to

$$\sum_{i=1}^{n} l_{ij} x_{ij} \leqq L_j, \quad j = 1, 2, \cdots, m, \quad \text{and}$$

$$x_{ij} \geqq 0, \quad i = 1, 2, \cdots, n; \quad j = 1, 2, \cdots, m,$$

where

$$x_i \equiv \sum_{j=1}^{m} x_{ij}.$$

Note the difference between x_i (the world's output of the ith good) and x_j (Country j's output vector).

We again assume:

ASSUMPTION 1 $l_{ij} > 0$ for all i and j,

ASSUMPTION 2 u is concave and $u = 0$ if $x_i = 0$ for any $i = 1, 2, \cdots, n$. Also $u_i > 0$ if $x_i > 0$ for all $i = 1, 2, \cdots, n$ where $u_i \equiv \partial u / \partial x_i$.

[10] This section has been strongly influenced by Kuhn [9].

As we noted in the Appendix to Chapter 5, we can relax the assumption of the concavity of u to the quasi-concavity of u for the (KTL) characterization of the optimality. An example of a u that satisfies the above assumption is

$$u = x_1^{\alpha_1} x_2^{\alpha_2} \cdots x_n^{\alpha_n}, \alpha_i > 0, i = 1, 2, \cdots, n.$$

If $\sum_{i=1}^{n} \alpha_i = 1$, u is concave, and if $\sum_{i=1}^{n} \alpha_i > 1$, u is quasi-concave (but not concave).

First, we shall attempt a generalization of the McKenzie-Jones theorem. Due to assumption 2 and the (quasi-) concavity of the utility function with respect to x_{ij} and the linearity of the constraint functions, we can use theorem 3 of the Appendix to Chapter 5. Thus, a necessary and sufficient condition for x_{ij}^*, $i = 1, 2, \cdots, n; j = 1, 2, \cdots, m$ to be a solution to the above problem is that there exists a $w_j^*, j = 1, 2, \cdots, m$ such that

$$u_{ij}^* - w_j^* l_{ij} \leqq 0, i = 1, 2, \cdots, n; \quad j = 1, 2, \cdots, m, \tag{6-25a}$$

$$(u_{ij}^* - w_j^* l_{ij}) x_{ij}^* = 0, i = 1, 2, \cdots, n; \quad j = 1, 2, \cdots, m. \tag{6-25b}$$

$$\sum_{i=1}^{n} l_{ij} x_{ij}^* \leqq L_j, \quad j = 1, 2, \cdots, m. \tag{6-26a}$$

$$w_j^* \left(L_j - \sum_{i=1}^{n} l_{ij} x_{ij}^* \right) = 0, \quad j = 1, 2, \cdots, m. \tag{6-26b}$$

$$w_j^* \geqq 0, j = 1, 2, \cdots, m; \quad x_{ij}^* \geqq 0, i = 1, 2, \cdots, n \quad \text{and} \quad j = 1, 2, \cdots, m. \tag{6-27}$$

Here $u_{ij}^* \equiv \partial u / \partial x_{ij}$ evaluated at $x_{ij} = x_{ij}^*$, $i = 1, 2, \cdots, n$ and $j = 1, 2, \cdots, m$.

It is clear that there exists some j such that $\bar{x}_{ij} > 0$ for all $i = 1, 2, \cdots, n$, with $\sum_{i=1}^{n} l_{ij} \bar{x}_{ij} \leqq L_j$. In other words, at least one country can produce a positive quantity of every good.[11] Hence, due to the second and third parts of assumption 2, there exists a j such that $x_{ij}^* > 0$ for all $i = 1, 2, \cdots, n$.[12]

Due to (6-25a) and $u_{ij}^* > 0$ (since $x_i^* > 0$),[13] we have $w_j^* > 0$. Thus, (6-26a) and (6-26b) can be reduced to

$$\sum_{i=1}^{n} l_{ij} x_{ij}^* = L_j, \quad j = 1, 2, \cdots, m. \tag{6-28}$$

---

[11] In fact, there exists a $\bar{x}_{ij}$ such that $\sum_{i=1}^{n} l_{ij} \bar{x}_{ij} \leqq L_j$ and $\bar{x}_{ij} > 0$ for all i and j, but this is not relevant to our analysis.

[12] Since there exists a j such that $\bar{x}_{ij} > 0$ for all i, $\bar{x}_i \equiv \sum_{j=1}^{m} \bar{x}_{ij} > 0$ for all i. Hence, due to the monotonicity of u, $x_i^* > 0$ for all i, or there exists j such that $x_{ij}^* > 0$ for all i.

[13] $x_i^* > 0$ implies $u_{ij}^* > 0$ due to the third part of assumption 2.

In order to facilitate a comparison with the McKenzie-Jones theorem, we will now assume that the number of goods is equal to the number of countries, m, and we shall obtain the necessary and sufficient conditions for the pattern of specialization in which Country j specializes in the production of good j (the j-j specialization) to be optimal. This is clearly a generalized version of Mill's problem. These conditions are easily obtained from the above conditions. Note that the necessary and sufficient conditions for Country j to specialize in the production of good j are that there exists $w_j^* > 0, j = 1, 2, \cdots, m$ such that

$$u_{jj}^* - w_j^* l_{jj} = 0, 1, 2, \cdots, m;$$ (6-29)

$$u_{ij}^* - w_j^* l_{ij} \leqq 0, \quad i, j, j = 1, 2, \cdots, m;$$ (6-30)

$$l_{jj} x_{jj}^* = L_j, \quad j = 1, 2, \cdots, m.$$ (6-31)

(The interested reader can check the necessity and sufficiency of the above conditions. Recall the discussion in the previous section.) Hence, the necessary and sufficient conditions for the j-j specialization to be optimal are reduced to equations (6-30) and (6-31), and these can be summarized as

$$\frac{u_{jj}^*}{l_{jj}} \geqq \frac{u_{ij}^*}{l_{ij}} \quad i, j = 1, 2, \cdots, m.$$ (6-32)

This is equivalent to

$$\prod_{j=1}^{m} \frac{u_{jj}^*}{l_{jj}} \geqq \prod_{j=1}^{m} \frac{u_{\pi(j)j}^*}{l_{\pi(j)j}},$$ (6-33)

where $\pi(j)$ is the jth integer in a permutation of the index set.

Equation (6-33) can be rewritten as:

$$\prod_{j=1}^{m} \frac{l_{\pi(j)j}}{l_{jj}} \geqq \prod_{j=1}^{m} \frac{u_{\pi(j)j}^*}{u_{jj}}.$$ (6-34)

Now recall that $u = u(x_1, \cdots, x_i, \cdots, x_m)$ where $x_i \equiv \sum_{j=1}^{m} x_{ij}$. Hence, $\partial u / \partial x_{ij} = \partial u / \partial x_i$ or $u_{ij}^* = u_i^*$. Hence,

$$\prod_{j=1}^{m} \frac{u_{\pi(j)j}^*}{u_{jj}^*} = \prod_{j=1}^{m} \frac{u_{\pi(j)}^*}{u_j^*} = 1.$$ (6-35)

Therefore we obtain

$$\prod_{j=1}^{m} l_{jj} \leqq \prod_{j=1}^{m} l_{\pi(j)j},$$

which is nothing but the McKenzie-Jones condition obtained in the previous section [as (5-21)].

Using the observation that $u_{ij}^* = u_i^*$, we can also rewrite (6-32) as

$$\frac{l_{ij}}{l_{jj}} \geqq \frac{u_i^*}{u_j^*}, \quad i, j = 1, 2, \cdots, m.$$ (6-36)

If there are only two countries (1 and 2) and two goods (1 and 2), we can rewrite (6-36) as

$$\frac{l_{11}}{l_{21}} \leqq \frac{u_1^*}{u_2^*} \leqq \frac{l_{12}}{l_{22}}. \qquad (6\text{-}37)$$

This is Mill's condition, hence we may call (6-36) *Generalized Mill's Condition.* Note that condition (6-36) can be supported by a competitive equilibrium with free trade by choosing the prices such that

$$\frac{u_i^*}{u_j^*} = \frac{p_i}{p_j} \quad i, j = 1, 2, \cdots, m, \qquad (6\text{-}38)$$

where p_i denotes the world price of the ith good.

If we adopt Mill's form of the utility function so that

$$u = (x_{11} + x_{12})(x_{21} + x_{22}) = x_1 x_2, \quad \text{then } u_1^* = x_2^* \quad \text{and} \quad u_2^* = x_1^*.$$

Hence, equation (6-37) can be rewritten as

$$\frac{l_{11}}{l_{21}} \leqq \frac{x_2^*}{x_1^*} \leqq \frac{l_{12}}{l_{22}}. \qquad (6\text{-}39)$$

But due to (6-31) $x_1^* = L_1/l_{11}$ and $x_2^* = L_2/l_{22}$, so that (6-39) can be rewritten again as

$$\frac{L_1}{l_{21}} \leqq \frac{L_2}{l_{22}} \quad \text{and} \quad \frac{L_1}{l_{11}} \geqq \frac{L_2}{l_{12}}. \qquad (6\text{-}40)$$

Then defining $a_{ij} = L_j/l_{ij}$ and letting the subscripts $_x$ and $_y$ be 1 and 2 respectively, we can again rewrite (6-40) as

$$a_{21} \leqq a_{22} \quad \text{and} \quad a_{11} \geqq a_{12}. \qquad (6\text{-}41)$$

These are exactly Mill's conditions as derived by Chipman ([2], p. 487) and Chapter 5.

We can summarize the results of this section by the following theorem:

THEOREM Within the present framework, a necessary and sufficient condition for the pattern of specialization in which Country j specializes in the production of good j to be optimal is

$$\frac{l_{ij}}{l_{jj}} \geqq \frac{u_i^*}{u_j^*}, \quad i, j = 1, 2, \cdots, m,$$

that is, the generalized Mill's condition, which implies that the McKenzie-Jones condition (6-21) must hold for the l_{ij}s. Under these conditions, the (j-j) pattern of specialization can be supported by a competitive equilibrium with free trade.

REFERENCES

1. Caves, R. E., *Trade and Economic Structure, Models and Methods* (Cambridge, Mass.: Harvard University Press), 1960.
2. Chipman, J. S., "A Survey of the Theory of International Trade: Part 1, The Classical Theory," *Econometrica*, 33, July 1965.
3. Edgeworth, F. Y., "The Theory of International Values, I, II, III," *Economic Journal*, IV, March, September, December 1894.
4. Elliot, G. A., "The Theory of International Values," *Journal of Political Economy*, LVIII, February 1950.
5. Haberler, G., *The Theory of International Trade, with its Applications to Commercial Policy* (tr. from German ed. 1933) (London: William Hodge), 1936.
6. Jones, R. W., "Comparative Advantage and the Theory of Tariffs: A Multi-Country Multi-Commodity Model," *Review of Economic Studies*, 28, June 1961.)
7. Koopmans, T. C., *Three Essays on the State of Economic Science* (New York: McGraw-Hill, Inc.), 1957, Essay I.
8. Kuhn, H. W., "Lectures on Mathematical Economics," in *Mathematics of the Decision Sciences*, Part 2, ed. by Dantzig, G. B. and Veinott, A. F. (Providence, R.I.: American Mathematical Society), 1968.
9. ———, "Notes on International Trade, I and II," *Lecture Notes*, Princeton University, Fall Term 1966.
10. McKenzie, L. W., "Specialization and Efficiency in World Production," *Review of Economic Studies*, XXI, June 1954.
11. ———, "On Equilibrium in Graham's Model of World Trade and Other Competitive Systems," *Econometrica*, 22, April 1954.
12. ———, "Specialization in Production and the Production Possibility Locus," *Review of Economic Studies*, XXIII, 1955–56.
13. ———, "The Theory of International Trade: II. Mathematical Theory," forthcoming in the *International Encyclopedia of the Social Sciences*.
14. Mangoldt, H. von., *Grundriss der Volkswirtschaftslehre*, Stuttgart, Verlag von J. Englehorn (1st ed. 1863, 2nd ed. with revision by Kleinwächter, 1871), English tr. of Book III, Chapter 3 of Part I of the 1st ed., "The Exchange Ratio of Goods," *International Economic Papers* (ed. by Peacock, Stolper, Turvey and Liesner), 1962.
15. Mill, J. S., *Principles of Political Economy, with Some Applications to Social Philosophy* (1st ed. 1848), Ashley ed. (London: Longmans, Green & Co., Ltd.), 1929.
16. Ricardo, D., *On the Principles of Political Economy, and Taxation* (London: John Murray), 1817, reprinted in *The Works and Correspondence of David Ricardo*, Vol. I, ed. by Sraffa, (Cambridge: Cambridge University Press), 1951.
17. Samuelson, P. A., "Market Mechanism and Maximization," in the *Collected Scientific Papers of Paul Samuelson*, ed. by Stiglitz (Cambridge,

Mass.: MIT Press), 1966, Vol. 1 (the article was originally written in 1949 as two research memoranda of the RAND Corporation).

18. Viner, J., *Studies in the Theory of International Trade* (New York: Harper & Row, Publishers), 1937.

19. Whitin, T. M., "Classical Theory, Graham's Theory and Linear Programming in International Trade," *Quarterly Journal of Economics*, LXVII, November, 1953.

7

A GENERAL EQUILIBRIUM
OF WORLD TRADE
AND PRODUCTION

The first two sections of this chapter prepare the reader for the remainder of the chapter. These sections provide an introduction to modern economic theory and probably cover more than is required to read the rest of the chapter. Students familiar with modern economic theory can skip these two sections, but others will find this material useful in areas other than international trade theory.

ELEMENTS OF ACTIVITY ANALYSIS

Activity analysis of production is concerned with the *set* of production processes available in a given economy. (Here the word "economy" can mean a firm, a collection of firms, the entire national economy, or the whole world.) This set is called a *production (possibility) set*. An element of this set is an ordered *n*-tuple which describes the technological relation of the input-output combination of one process of production. An element of the production set is called a *process* or an *activity*. We may also call it a *blueprint* to stress its technological nature. Nothing is specified, initially, as to what processes or blueprints in the production set should be adopted or discarded. We assume that there are *n* commodities in the economy and that each commodity is qualitatively homogeneous. In general, a "commodity" is defined by specifying all of its physical characteristics, its availability location, and its availability date. Hence, for example, flows of technically the same commodity in two different locations represent two different commodities. Services and factors of production as well as ordinary goods are commodities, and all commodities appear in every activity (possibly with a zero coefficient). Note that we can always treat different commodities as a single composite commodity, if this facilitates a sharper and deeper analysis of a particular problem.

The production process is described by an ordered *n*-tuple of these commodities. (*n* is usually assumed to be a *finite*, positive integer, but can be infinite.)

The production set is the collection of these n-tuples. The following example is due to Koopmans and Bausch ([19], pp. 99–100). Here we consider an economy with four commodities and two processes:

TABLE 7-1

	Process 1 (Tanning)	Process 2 (Shoemaking)
Commodity 1 (shoes)	0	1
Commodity 2 (leather)	1	$-1/4$
Commodity 3 (hides)	-1	0
Commodity 4 (labor)	$-1/10$	$-1/2$

In each process an input is represented by a negative number and an output is represented by a positive number. Note that there can be any number of processes for tanning or shoemaking. Moreover each process can have more than one positive entry. This is the case of joint production. For example, in a process which produces cowhides, beef may be jointly produced.

Let Y be the set of all the technically possible production processes in a given economy. We assume $Y \subset R^n$ and $y \in Y$ denotes a production process in the economy. We use the convention that the ith component y_i represents an output if $y_i > 0$ and it is an input if $y_i < 0$. $|y_i|$ indicates the amount of the ith commodity involved in this process y. We first impose the following two postulates.

1. ADDITIVITY $\quad y \in Y$ and $y' \in Y$ imply $y + y' \in Y$.
2. PROPORTIONALITY $\quad y \in Y$ implies $\alpha y \in Y$ for all $\alpha \geqq 0$.

Thus Y is a convex cone.[1] Due to the proportionality, the jth process or activity y^j in Y can be written

$$y^j = \begin{pmatrix} a_{1j} \\ \cdot \\ \cdot \\ \cdot \\ a_{nj} \end{pmatrix} \lambda_j \quad \text{where} \quad \lambda_j \in R \quad \text{and} \quad \lambda_j \geqq 0 ,$$

or, in short,

$$y^j = a^j \lambda_j .$$

[1] A set Y in a vector space (say R^n) is called a *convex cone* (with vertex at the origin if (a), $y, y' \in Y$ implies $(y + y') \in Y$ and (b) $y \in Y$ implies $\alpha y \in Y$ for all $\alpha \geqq 0$, $\alpha \in R$ (the set of real numbers). A set Y in a vector space X (say R^n) is said to be a *convex polyhedral cone* spanned by $\{a^1, a^2, \cdots, a^m\}$, where $a^j \in X, j = 1, 2, \cdots, m$, $Y = \{y : y = \sum_{j=1}^{m} a^j \lambda_j, \lambda_j \geqq 0, \lambda_j \in R, j = 1, 2, \cdots, m\}$. Clearly any convex polyhedral cone is a convex cone, but not vice versa.

Here a_{ij} denotes the amount of the ith good involved in one unit level operation of the jth activity and λ_j represents the activity level of the jth activity. Now we impose the third postulate.

3. **FINITE NUMBER OF BASIC ACTIVITIES**   There exists a finite number of a^j such that Y is a convex polyhedral cone spanned by these a^js. These a^js are called *basic activities*.

In other words, a typical element y in Y can be expressed as a non-negative linear combination of $a^1, a^2, \cdots, a^m$, where m is a finite positive integer. Due to the above three postulates, the production set Y in activity analysis can be written as

$$Y = \{y : y = A\lambda, \lambda \geqq 0\}, \quad \text{where } A \text{ is an } n \times m \text{ matrix formed by}$$

$[a^1, \cdots, a^m]$ and λ is an m-vector whose jth element is λ_j.

It should be clear that the proportionality postulate means *complete divisibility of all the commodities and constant returns to scale* and that the additivity postulate means the independent action of each activity (no interaction among activities) or, in Marshallian terminology, there are *no external economies* or *diseconomies*.

That Y is a convex polyhedral cone implicitly entails several other features. The important ones are as follows:

a) $0 \in Y$ (possibility of inaction). That is, it is possible for the producer to do nothing.

b) Y is a closed set. (This is mathematically both a very important and a nice feature.)

Koopmans [7] imposed the following three additional important postulates:

4. **PRODUCTIVENESS**   There exists at least one positive element for some y in Y.

5. **NO LAND OF COCKAIGNE** $y \geq 0$ implies $y \notin Y$. Or $Y \cap \Omega = \{0\}$.[2]

6. **IRREVERSIBILITY** $y \in Y$ implies $-y \notin Y$. Or $Y \cap (-Y) = \{0\}$.

Figure 7-1 illustrates the meaning of the above postulates. In Case A of Figure 7-1, postulate 4 and postulate 5 hold but not postulate 6. In Case B of Figure 7-1, postulate 4, postulate 5, and postulate 6 all hold.

We may note one important consequence of postulate 5, which would illustrate the meaning of the above postulates. For a detailed investigation of the implications of these postulates, see Koopmans [7], Chapter III.

---

[2] The vector notation $y \geq 0$ means $y_i \geqq 0$ for all i and $y \neq 0$, where y_i is the ith component of y. Similarly, $y \geq 0$ means $y_i \geqq 0$ for all i ($y = 0$ is possible) and $y > 0$ means $y_i > 0$ for all i. $\{0\}$ denotes the set which consists only of the element zero, the origin.

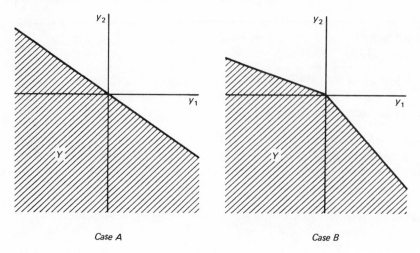

Case A   Case B

Figure 7-1   Illustration of Certain Postulates

THEOREM 1   Let $Y = \{y : y = A\lambda, \lambda \geqq 0\}$. Y satisfies postulate 5 *if and only if* there exists a $p > 0$ such that $p \cdot y \leqq 0$ for all $y \in Y$.

PROOF

  i. (Sufficiency): $y \geqq 0$ implies $p \cdot y > 0$ for any $p > 0$. Hence, by assumption, $y \notin Y$.

  ii. (Necessity): Omitted. It requires the separation theorem for convex sets. The proof is an easy exercise for the reader who is familiar with this theorem.

REMARK   If we interpret p as a *price* vector, then $p \cdot y$ represents the *profit* from the production process y. $p \cdot y \leqq 0$ for all $y \in Y$ implies that the maximum profit is zero.

We stated postulates 4, 5, and 6 in connection with the production set Y which is a convex polyhedral cone. In general, these postulates can be stated even if Y is *not* a convex polyhedral cone. When Y represents the collection of input-output combinations which are technically feasible in a given economy and when we do not restrict Y to a convex polyhedral cone, we call Y a *general production set*. The essential characteristic of activity analysis and modern economic analysis lies in its set theoretic nature. The analysis of production starts with this concept of a *general production set* by imposing certain postulates (axioms) on this set. Some of these postulates have been illustrated above.

The production set Y as described above indicates the technological possibilities of a given economy, hence it is free from resource limitations. In other words, $y \in Y$ indicates how much output can be produced by specifying the amounts of inputs, and we do not ask whether these amounts of inputs are, in fact, available in the economy. (Thus we called $y \in Y$ a "blueprint.") However, we can also consider Y as the production set for which the resource limitations

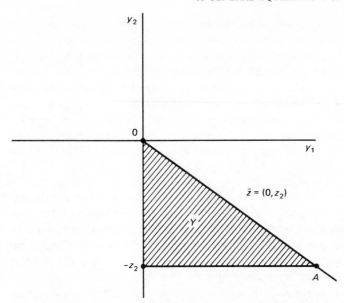

Figure 7-2   A Truncated Production Cone

have been taken into account. For example, Y can indicate a "truncated" convex polyhedral cone, such as $\{y : y = A\lambda,\ \lambda \geqq 0,\ \lambda \in R^m,\ \text{and}\ y + \bar{z} \geqq 0\}$, where $\bar{z} \geqq 0$ denotes the resource limitations of the economy. With the no land of Cockaigne postulate such a set is no longer a convex polyhedral cone, although it is still convex. Note that the set is compact now. This truncation is easily illustrated by Figure 7-2.

REMARK   Strictly speaking, the use of the words "activity analysis" may have to be confined to a study of production processes when the number of basic activities is finite. In other words, Y must be confined to a convex polyhedral cone or a truncated convex polyhedral cone. We shall *not* adopt this narrow definition. The revolutionary character of activity analysis lies not in a particular shape of Y. It lies in the set-theoretic approach which is much more fundamental and powerful than the traditional smooth (differentiable) production function approach.

We will now introduce the most important results of activity analysis.

DEFINITION   Let Y be a general production set. A point y^* in Y is called an *efficient point* of Y, if there does *not* exist $y \in Y$ such that $y \geqq y^*$.

REMARK   An efficient point represents a boundary point, and it corresponds to a point on the classical production function. It is a point where one cannot increase output without increasing input. In terms of the previous diagram, $0A$ is the set of efficient points in the truncated production cone. If the production set is the entire cone, the half line from 0 passing through A is the set of the efficient points.

REMARK An efficient point is often defined with explicit recognition of the resource constraints. As we discussed in the previous remark, a general production set Y can also be regarded as one which takes the resource constraints into account. Thus our concept of an efficient point can include such a case. However, we also note that our interpretation of Y is rather flexible in the sense that it allows the case in which no resource constraints are taken into account. Accordingly, our concept of an efficient point is also flexible. If no resource constraints are taken into account in Y, then some efficient points may not be attainable in the given economy, because they are outside the range of the resource constraints.

REMARK In activity analysis a distinction is often made among primary, intermediate, and desired commodities. The *primary commodities* are the ones which flow into production from outside the productive system; the *intermediate commodities* are the ones which are produced only for use as inputs for further production; and the *desired goods* are the ones that are desired for consumption or other uses outside the production system. However, these distinctions are arbitrary. For example, the same good can often be used for final consumption purposes and as an input for further production. Hence, we shall not emphasize these distinctions.

Now we shall state two fundamental theorems of activity analysis.

THEOREM 2 Let Y be a general production set in R^n. If there exists a y^* in Y and a $p > 0$ such that $p \cdot y^* \geqq p \cdot y$ for all $y \in Y$, then y^* is an efficient point.

PROOF Suppose this is not true. Then there exists a $y \in Y$ such that $y \geqq y^*$. Thus $p \cdot y > p \cdot y^*$, since $p > 0$, which is a contradiction.   (Q.E.D.)

REMARK The above theorem specifies nothing with respect to the postulates on Y.

THEOREM 3 Let Y be a general production set in R^n, which is convex. If y^* is an efficient point of Y, then there exists a $p \geq 0$ such that $p \cdot y^* \geqq p \cdot y$ for all $y \in Y$.

PROOF This is omitted. It requires the separation theorem for convex sets. For the reader who is familiar with this theorem, the proof is an easy exercise.

REMARK If Y, in the above theorem, is a convex polyhedral cone, then it can easily be shown that we can choose $p > 0$.

REMARK Theorem 3 associates the concept of efficient point with *profit maximization*. That is, maximization of $p \cdot y$ with respect to y over Y. The existence of a solution to this maximum problem is guaranteed if, *for example*, Y is a compact set (the Weierstrass theorem), since the inner product is a continuous function.

REMARK   Suppose that Y can be characterized by linear inequalities such as

$$\sum_{j=1}^{m} a_{ij}\lambda_j + \bar{z}_i \geq 0, \quad i = 1, 2, \cdots, n, \quad \lambda_j \geq 0,$$

with

$$y \equiv \sum_{j=1}^{m} a_{ij}\lambda_j, \quad \lambda \equiv (\lambda_1, \cdots, \lambda_m).$$

Then the problem of finding a λ which maximizes $p \cdot y$ subject to the above constraints is a typical linear programming problem, for which a computational method (the simplex method) is well-known. Hence, activity analysis also has practical and computational significance.

It is important to realize some of the differences between the activity analysis of production and the traditional analysis using the production function. The following are the most important differences.

1. The traditional production function, typically supposing a functional relationship between the input vector v and the output x (that is, $x = f(v)$ or $F(x, v) = 0$ if x is a vector), presupposes the existence of an "efficient manager." Given the quantities of factors available, the efficient manager maximizes the amount of output produced. In the joint production case (that is, when x is a vector) this manager supposedly maximizes the production of one arbitrary output with all of the other outputs held constant. Thus, the efficient manager in this case defines a unique surface for any given amount of inputs.

   Activity analysis of production revolutionizes the traditional production analysis by discarding the concepts of a production function and an efficient manager. Instead it postulates the *set* of production processes available in the economy, that is, the "production set." We should point out that the concept of an efficient manager corresponds to the concept of an efficient point in activity analysis.

2. The essential technique in the production function approach is differential calculus, which among other things presupposes the differentiability of the functions.[3]

   The *modus operandi* of activity analysis is the use of set theory and the tools of other branches of modern mathematics. Activity analysis is axiomatic, more fundamental, and often more rigorous than the traditional production function analysis. The separation theorems on convex sets play an important role in activity analysis, just as derivatives play an important role in production function analysis. Differentiability of

---

[3] It is important to realize the basic features of the neoclassical smooth production function approach in terms of activity analysis terminology. Essentially, 1) It deals with a production set which cannot be generated from a finite number of activities (that is, it is *not* a convex polyhedral cone), rather, a continuum of vectors is required to characterize the set. 2) The efficient manager is presupposed, so that production always takes place at an efficient point (the production function). 3) The set of efficient points constitutes a differentiable function.

the functions is not crucial in activity analysis. If we like, however, we can characterize the production set by some functional relations and pursue the analysis using these relations. Then the analysis may look similar to the traditional analysis, except that it is then more general.

3. In activity analysis, computational algorithms are usually available. For example, as mentioned previously, if the production set is a convex polyhedral cone (or its "truncation"), then the simplex method for solving linear programming problems can be used. There is no such systematic method of calculating solutions available for the traditional approach.

CONCEPT OF VECTOR MAXIMUM

The ordinary nonlinear programming problem may be written as follows.

ORDINARY NONLINEAR PROGRAMMING PROBLEM   Find a vector $x \in R^n$ such as to maximize $f(x)$ subject to $g_j(x) \geqq 0, j = 1, 2, \cdots, m$ and $x \geqq 0$. Here f and the g_js are real-valued functions defined on R^n.

We pointed out in the first section of the Appendix to Chapter 5, that the following theorem holds.

THEOREM 4   Let $f(x)$ be a concave function, and suppose that either of the following two conditions holds:

1. $g_j(x), j = 1, 2, \cdots, m$ are all linear;
2. $g_j(x), j = 1, 2, \cdots, m$ are all concave and there exists an $\bar{x} \geqq 0$ such that $g_j(\bar{x}) > 0$ for all $j = 1, 2, \cdots, m$ (Slater's condition).

Then either of the following two conditions is *necessary and sufficient* for x^* to be a solution to the above nonlinear programming problem.

  i.   the (KTL) condition holds,[4] or
 ii.   the (SP) condition holds.[5]

REMARK   Let $\Phi(x, \lambda) \equiv f(x) + \lambda \cdot g(x)$, where $\lambda \in R^m$ and $g(x)$ is an m-vector whose jth component is $g_j(x)$, so that $\lambda \cdot g(x) \equiv \sum_{j=1}^{m} \lambda_j g_j(x)$. Then the (KTL) and (SP) conditions can be spelled out as follows:

KTL   There exists a $\lambda^* \in R^m$ such that

$$\Phi_x^* \leqq 0, \quad \Phi_x^* \cdot x^* = 0, \quad g(x^*) \geqq 0, \quad \lambda^* \cdot g(x^*) = 0$$

and $\lambda^* \geqq 0, x^* \geqq 0$,

where Φ_x^* is an n-vector whose jth element is $\partial\Phi/\partial x_j$ evaluated at (x^*, λ^*).

---

[4] The differentiability of the f and g_js is implicitly assumed, otherwise (KTL) makes no sense.
[5] Clearly for this characterization of the maximality of x^*, we do not need to assume differentiability.

SP   There exists a $\lambda^* \in R^m, \lambda^* \geq 0$, such that $\Phi(x, \lambda^*) \leq \Phi(x^*, \lambda^*) \leq \Phi(x^*, \lambda)$ for all $x \geq 0$ and $\lambda \geq 0$.

REMARK   It can easily be shown that if (SP) holds, then $\lambda^* \cdot g(x^*) = 0$.

REMARK   In the above formulation of the nonlinear programming problem and in the above theorem, we assumed that the f and the g_js are defined on R^n. In general this can be relaxed to the condition that the f and the g_js be defined over some *subset*, say S, of a vector space (say R^n). In order to be able to make the concavity of the f and the g_js meaningful, S has to be a convex set. In order to make the differentiability property meaningful [which is required for the (KTL)], we require S to be an open set. Then consider a convex subset of S, say, X. Our problem can now be restated as: Maximize $f(x)$ subject to $g_j(x) \geq 0, j = 1, \cdots, m, x \in X$. If X is non-empty and compact, the existence of a solution is guaranteed by the Weierstrass theorem (assuming the continuity of f). The (KTL) is then restated as

$$\Phi_x^* \leq 0, \quad \Phi_x^* \cdot x^* = 0, \quad g(x^*) \geq 0, \quad \lambda^* \cdot g(x^*) = 0, \quad \lambda^* \geq 0,$$

and $x^* \in X$.

The (SP) is restated as

$$\Phi(x, \lambda^*) \leq \Phi(x^*, \lambda^*) \leq \Phi(x^*, \lambda) \text{ for all } x \in X \text{ and } \lambda \geq 0.$$

The vector-maximum problem[6] is similar to the general nonlinear programming problem except that $f(x)$ is not a real-valued function, but a vector-valued function. That is, $f(x) = [f_1(x), f_2(x), \cdots, f_k(x)]$. We will start our discussion of the vector-maximum problem with the following definition.

DEFINITION   Let $f_1(x), f_2(x), \cdots, f_k(x)$ and $g_1(x), g_2(x), \cdots, g_m(x)$ be real-valued functions over X in R^n. We say that x^* in X achieves a *vector (global) maximum* of $f(x) = [f_1(x), f_2(x), \cdots, f_k(x)]$ if there does not exist an $\tilde{x}$ in X such that:

$f_i(\tilde{x}) \geq f_i(x^*)$ for all $i = 1, 2, \cdots, k$,

$f_{i_0}(\tilde{x}) > f_{i_0}(x^*)$ for some i_0, and

$\tilde{x}$ and x^* satisfy the constraints:

$g_j(\tilde{x}) \geq 0, \quad j = 1, 2, \cdots, m$,

$g_j(x^*) \geq 0, \quad j = 1, 2, \cdots, m$.

REMARK   The reader may notice that the concept of an efficient point in activity analysis is a special case of the vector maximum, where $f(x) = x$. He may also notice that the vector-maximum problem has immediate relevance to the concept of Pareto optimum, which is an important concept in economic theory.

[6] For the first satisfactory treatment of the vector-maximum problem, see Kuhn and Tucker [11].

REMARK   It follows immediately from the above definition that if $f(x^*)$ is a constrained vector maximum, *then*

x^* maximizes $f_{i_0}(x)$ [that is, $f_{i_0}(x^*) \geq f_{i_0}(x)$]

subject to

$f_i(x) \geq f_i(x^*)$, $i \neq i_0$,

$g_j(x) \geq 0, j = 1, 2, \cdots, m, x \in X$,

where the choice of i_0 is arbitrary.

For if not, then there exists an $\tilde{x}$ and an $\tilde{\imath}$ such that

$f_{\tilde{\imath}}(\tilde{x}) > f_{\tilde{\imath}}(x^*)$ *and*

$f_i(\tilde{x}) \geq f_i(x^*)$, for all $i \neq \tilde{\imath}$,

$g_j(\tilde{x}) \geq 0, j = 1, 2, \cdots, m, \tilde{x} \in X$.

This is a contradiction of the assumption that x^* is a vector maximum.

Utilizing this remark we can easily prove the following theorem, which corresponds to theorem 4 above. The method of proof utilizing the above remark is due to M. El-Hodiri [5], who, in turn, attributes the idea to L. Hurwicz.

THEOREM 5   Let $f_i(x)$, $i = 1, 2, \cdots, k$ and $g_j(x), j = 1, 2, \cdots, m$, be real-valued functions on R^n. Suppose that *either* of the following two conditions holds.

  1.   the $g_j(x), j = 1, 2, \cdots, m$ are all linear;
  2.   the $g_j(x), j = 1, 2, \cdots, m$ are all concave and there exists an $\bar{x} \geq 0$ such that $g_j(\bar{x}) > 0$ for all $j = 1, 2, \cdots, m$ (Slater's condition).

Then if x^* provides a vector maximum of $f(x) = [f_1(x), f_2(x), \cdots, f_k(x)]$ subject to $g_j(x) \geq 0, j = 1, 2, \cdots, m$ and $x \geq 0$ there exist an $\alpha \in R^k$, $\alpha \geq 0$, $\alpha \neq 0$, and a $\lambda^* \in R^m$, $\lambda^* \geq 0$, such that either of the following conditions holds.

  1. (KTL_v): $\psi_x{}^* \leq 0$, $\psi_x{}^* \cdot x^* = 0$, $g(x^*) \geq 0$, $\lambda^* \cdot g(x^*) = 0$, $\lambda^* \geq 0$ and $x^* \geq 0$, where
       $\Psi(x, \lambda) = \alpha \cdot f(x) + \lambda \cdot g(x), g(x) \equiv [g_1(x), g_2(x), \cdots, g_m(x)]$
       and $\psi_x{}^* = \partial \psi / \partial x$ evaluated at (x^*, λ^*).
  2. (SP_v): $\Psi(x, \lambda^*) \leq \Psi(x^*, \lambda^*) \leq \Psi(x^*, \lambda)$, for all $x \geq 0, \lambda \geq 0$.

Conversely if $f_i(x)$, $i = 1, 2, \cdots, k$ and $g_j(x), j = 1, 2, \cdots, m$ are all concave and if there exists an $\alpha \in R^k$ such that $\alpha_i > 0$ for all $i = 1, 2, \cdots, k$, and if either (KTL_v) or (SP_v) holds, then x^* provides a vector maximum of $f(x)$ subject to $g(x) \geq 0$ and $x \geq 0$, and we also have $\lambda^* \cdot g(x^*) = 0$.

PROOF   This is omitted. See Takayama [18] for example. In the light of the previous remark, the reader should be able to prove this theorem using theorem 4.

REMARK   Note that in the latter (converse) part of the theorem we required α to be strictly positive (that is, $\alpha > 0$, or $\alpha_i > 0$ for all i).

REMARK   A remark about the domain of the f and the g_js similar to that made in connection with theorem 4, holds here. In other words, we may suppose that the f_is and the g_js are defined on an open, convex subset, S, of a vector space (say, R^n) and then consider a vector-maximum problem over a convex, compact subset X of S. (That is, (vector) maximize $[f_1(x), f_2(x), \cdots, f_k(x)]$ subject to $g_j(x) \geq 0$, $j = 1, 2, \cdots, m$ and $x \in X$). The (KTL_v) should be rewritten accordingly as

$$\psi_x^* \leq 0, \quad \psi_x^* \cdot x^* = 0, \quad g(x^*) \geq 0, \quad \lambda^* \geq 0 \quad \text{and} \quad x^* \in X.$$

Also, (SP_v) should be rewritten as:

$$\psi(x, \lambda^*) \leq \psi(x^*, \lambda^*) \leq \psi(x^*, \lambda), \quad \text{for all } x \in X \text{ and } \lambda \geq 0.$$

It is important to note that in theorem 5, the vector maximum is really converted to an ordinary nonlinear programming problem, with $\alpha \cdot f(x)$ being maximized subject to $g(x) \geq 0$ and $x \geq 0$. Considering the α_is as parameters, we call this conversion the *parameterization* of the vector-maximum problem.

Theorem 3, one of the fundamental theorems of activity analysis, can be proved easily using theorem 5. To do this, let a_{ij} be the amount of the ith good involved in a unit operation of the jth activity and let a^j be the vector for the jth activity where the ith element is a_{ij}. Assume that there are n goods and m activities. Let x_j be the activity level of the jth activity and let x be the activity vector whose jth element is x_j. Then as we found in the first section of this chapter, the production set Y is:

$$Y = \{y : y = Ax, x \geq 0\}, \quad \text{where } A = [a_{ij}];$$

$$\text{or } Y = \left\{y : y = \sum_{j=1}^{m} a^j x_j, x \geq 0\right\}.$$

An efficient point of Y, y^*, is a point such that there does not exist a $y \in Y$ such that $y \geq y^*$. In other words, this y^* can be obtained as a solution to the following vector-maximum problem.

Maximize y subject to $y \in Y$.

Then due to theorem 5, if y^* is a solution to this problem, there exists a $p \geq 0$ such that

$$p \cdot y^* \geq p \cdot y \quad \text{for all } y \in Y.$$

We can also prove that $p > 0$. This corresponds to theorem 3. Although the converse of the theorem, as discussed in theorem 2, is easy to obtain, we can also obtain this converse by using theorem 5. In other words, if there exists $p > 0$ such that $p \cdot y^* \geq p \cdot y$ for all $y \in Y$, then y^* is an efficient point of Y (or a solution to the above vector maximum problem).

We now suppose that we have a resource constraint which we write as

$$y + \bar{z} \geq 0, \, y \in Y,$$

where $\bar{z}_i$, the ith component of $\bar{z}$, denotes the amount of this ith good (resource) available in the economy. The feasible set Y_F of this economy is then

$$Y_F = \{y : y \in Y, \, y + \bar{z} \geq 0\}.$$

Now we are interested in the problem of finding an efficient point of this feasible set Y_F. y_F^* is an efficient point of Y_F if there does not exist $y \in Y_F$ such that $y \geq y_F^*$. Hence, an efficient point of Y_F can be obtained as a solution to the following *vector maximum* problem.

Maximize y subject to $y + \bar{z} \geq 0$ and $y \in Y$.

Assume Slater's condition so that there exists a $\tilde{y} \in Y_F$ such that $\tilde{y} + \bar{z} > 0$. Then using theorem 5, if y_F^* is a solution to this problem, there exists an $\alpha \geq 0$, $\alpha \neq 0$ and a $\lambda^* \geq 0$ such that

(SP): $\psi(y_F, \lambda^*) \leq \psi(y_F^*, \lambda^*) \leq \psi(y_F^*, \lambda)$ for all $y \in Y$, and $\lambda \geq 0$, where

$$\psi(y, \lambda) \equiv \alpha \cdot y + \lambda \cdot (y + \bar{z}), \text{ and } \lambda^* \cdot (y_F^* + \bar{z}) = 0.$$

The first inequality of the above (SP) condition can be rewritten as

$$\alpha \cdot y + \lambda^* \cdot (y + \bar{z}) \leq \alpha \cdot y_F^* + \lambda^* \cdot (y_F^* + \bar{z}) \text{ for all } y \in Y,$$

or as

$$p \cdot y \leq p \cdot y_F^* \text{ for all } y \in Y, \quad \text{where } p \equiv \alpha + \lambda^*.$$

This again corresponds to theorem 3. Conversely if there exists an $\alpha > 0$, a $\lambda^* \geq 0$, and a y_F^* such that the above (SP) condition holds, then y_F^* is a solution to the above constrained vector-maximum problem. This is a difficult way of obtaining theorem 2, but it illustrates the use of the vector maximum problem.

Now consider the following *linear programming* problem.

Maximize $\alpha \cdot y$, subject to $y + \bar{z} \geq 0$ and $y \in Y$, where $\alpha \in R^n$ and $\alpha \geq 0$
$\quad y$

and $\alpha \neq 0$.

Or, maximize $\alpha \cdot (Ax)$, subject to $Ax + \bar{z} \geq 0$ and $x \geq 0$, where $\alpha \in R^n$ and
$\quad x$

$\alpha \geq 0$ and $\alpha \neq 0$.

Clearly these two problems are equivalent. Hence if x_F^* is a solution to the latter problem, $y_F^* = Ax_F^*$ is a solution to the former problem if and only if there exists a $\lambda^* \geq 0$ such that

(SP): $\psi(y_F, \lambda^*) \leq \psi(y_F^*, \lambda^*) \leq \psi(y_F^*, \lambda)$, for all $y \in Y$ and $\lambda \geq 0$,

$$\text{where } \psi(y, \lambda) \equiv \alpha \cdot y + \lambda \cdot (y + \bar{z}).$$

This (SP) condition means that if y_F^* is a solution to the above constrained vector-maximum problem, then it is a solution to the linear programming problem. Conversely, if we can find a solution x_F^* to the linear programming problem, with $\alpha > 0$, then $y_F^* = Ax_F^*$ is a solution to the above constrained maximum problem, thus providing an efficient point of Y_F. By varying α, we can obtain the complete set of efficient points of Y_F.

THE WORLD PRODUCTION SET AND THE CHARACTERIZATION OF EFFICIENT POINTS

We are now ready to apply the preparation of the previous two sections to the classical model that we discussed in the previous chapters of Part II. First recall that, throughout the entire analysis, we assumed that l_{ij}, the amount of labor required to produce one unit of Good i in Country j, is constant for all i and j regardless of the level of production. This can be illustrated as follows, where each column can be considered as a production process (activity).[7]

TABLE 7-2

	Country 1				Country m		
Good 1	1,	0, $\cdots$,	0	$\cdots\cdots$	1,	0, $\cdots$,	0
Good 2	0,	1, $\cdots$,	0	$\cdots\cdots$	0,	1, $\cdots$,	0
$\cdot$		$\cdot$	$\cdot$	$\cdot$	$\cdot$	$\cdot$	
$\cdot$							$\cdot$
Good n	0,	0, $\cdots$,	1	$\cdots\cdots$	0,	0, $\cdots$,	1
Labor of Country 1	$-l_{11}$,	$-l_{21}, \cdots$,	$-l_{n1}$	$\cdots\cdots$	0,	0, $\cdots$,	0
Labor of Country 2	0,	0, $\cdots$,	0	$\cdots\cdots$	0,	0, $\cdots$,	0
$\cdot$		$\cdot$	$\cdot$	$\cdot$	$\cdot$	$\cdot$	
$\cdot$						$\cdot$	
Labor of Country m	0,	0, $\cdots$,	0	$\cdots\cdots$	$-l_{1m}$,	$-l_{2m}, \cdots$,	$-l_{nm}$

Having written out the classical model in this way, the following assumptions on the production side of the economy become obvious:

a. There is only one activity (process) for producing each good in each country.

b. There is no joint production.

c. Labor is the only factor of production.

d. The intermediate goods are suppressed (or "washed out").

[7] Notice that the unit level of activity is chosen such that one unit of a particular output is produced.

We shall not inherit any of these assumptions. The purpose of this section is to construct a general model which is not constrained by these assumptions, and to characterize this general model. In the previous chapter, we obtained the characterization of the classical model in terms of the pattern of specialization. However, this characterization obviously depended on the assumptions mentioned above. Hence, it is impossible to obtain a characterization of a more general model in terms of the pattern of specialization.

There is another way to characterize the model. As we noted in Chapter 4, the Ricardian theory can be characterized in terms of "efficient points." In the previous section, we saw that the efficient points are related to the vector-maximum problem in the theory of nonlinear programming.

Hence, we shall be concerned with the characterization of a generalized model in terms of activity analysis and nonlinear programming. To do this we first classify the goods into two categories—those that are internationally mobile with negligible transport cost and those which are completely immobile internationally. We shall call the former "goods" and the latter "factors." It is again assumed that both goods and factors are freely mobile, with negligible transport cost, within a given country. This distinction between goods and factors is clearly in accordance with the spirit of the classical theory. In the real world, there are goods which are internationally immobile and factors which are internationally mobile. Moreover, transport costs are not necessarily restricted to the two values 0 and ∞, they can have any intermediate value. These points are obvious and it is not too difficult to construct a more general model which takes them into account. We shall postpone this task to the next section. Here we shall be satisfied with building a more restricted model which bears a closer resemblance to the classical model. This will increase our understanding of the nature of the classical model and of our characterization of the classical theory.

Let b^{jk} be the input-output combination of goods (activity) vector for a one-unit operation of the kth activity in the jth country. Let a^{jk} be the input-output combination of factors vector for a unit operation of the kth activity in the jth country. Negative elements in the vectors a^{jk} and b^{jk} denote inputs. By allowing some elements of a^{jk} to be positive, we allow some of the factors to be produced. The essential distinction between a^{jk} and b^{jk} is the international mobility of the elements of b^{jk}. Let t^{jk} be the activity level (scalar) of the kth activity in the jth country. Let $I_j = \{1, 2, \cdots, k_j\}$ be the index set of production processes available in Country j. Write

$$a^j \equiv [a^{j1}, \cdots, a^{jk_j}], \quad b^j \equiv [b^{j1}, b^{j2}, \cdots, b^{jk_j}], \quad \text{and} \quad t^j \equiv \begin{bmatrix} t_{j1} \\ t_{j2} \\ \cdot \\ \cdot \\ \cdot \\ t_{jk_j} \end{bmatrix}.$$

In other words b^j and a^j are the input-output matrix of goods and the input-output matrix of factors respectively for Country j. t^j denotes the activity level vector for Country j.

Consider now the following equation.

$$
\begin{bmatrix}
b^1, b^2, \cdots, b^m \\
a^1, 0, \cdots, 0 \\
0, a^2, \cdots, 0 \\
\cdot \quad \cdot \qquad \cdot \\
\cdot \quad \cdot \qquad \cdot \\
\cdot \quad \cdot \qquad \cdot \\
0, 0, \cdots, a^m
\end{bmatrix}
\begin{bmatrix}
1 \\
t_2 \\
t \\
\cdot \\
\cdot \\
\cdot \\
t^m
\end{bmatrix}
=
\begin{bmatrix}
z_g \\
z_f{}^1 \\
z_f{}^2 \\
\cdot \\
\cdot \\
\cdot \\
z_f{}^m
\end{bmatrix}
=
\begin{bmatrix}
z_g \\
z_f
\end{bmatrix}.
$$

Or, simply, $\begin{bmatrix} B \\ A \end{bmatrix} t = z$, where $z \equiv \begin{bmatrix} z_g \\ z_f \end{bmatrix}$. Or even more simply, $Dt = z$, where

$D \equiv \begin{bmatrix} B \\ A \end{bmatrix}$.

In the above equation, z_g and the $z_f{}^j$s are defined by the following equations.

$$
z_g \equiv \sum_{j=1}^{m} b^j \cdot t^j, \quad \text{and} \quad z_f{}^j = a^j \cdot t^j.
$$

Let $\bar{z}^j$ denote the vector of resources available in Country j, and assume that $\bar{z}^j$ is a fixed vector. We note that a resource may be either a good or a factor, so that the vector $\bar{z}^j$ can be partitioned into two vectors, $\bar{z}_g{}^j$ and $\bar{z}_f{}^j$, where $\bar{z}_g{}^j$ denotes the vector of goods exogenously available in Country j and $\bar{z}_f{}^j$ denotes the vector of factors (that is, internationally immobile factors) exogenously available in Country j. Then the world resource vector, $\bar{z}$, can be written as

$$
\bar{z} \equiv
\begin{bmatrix}
\sum\limits_{j=1}^{m} \bar{z}_g{}^j \\
\bar{z}_f{}^1 \\
\cdot \\
\cdot \\
\cdot \\
\bar{z}_f{}^m
\end{bmatrix}.
$$

We shall adopt the convention that the elements of $\bar{z}^j$ (and hence also of $\bar{z}$) are non-negative. Since, by convention, inputs are denoted by negative numbers in activity analysis, the world resource constraint can be written as $-z \leq \bar{z}$. Thus the truncated world production (possibilities) set can now be expressed as:

$$
Z \equiv \{z : z = Dt, t \geq 0, -z \leq \bar{z}\}.
$$

We then define an "efficient point" in the usual way. Thus, z^* is an *efficient point* of Z if there does not exist a $z' \in Z$ such that $z' \geq z^*$. Hence if z^* is an efficient point of Z, it means that z^* is a solution to the following vector-maximum problem.

Vector Maximize z for all $z \in Z$.

Hence if $z^* = \begin{bmatrix} z_g^* \\ z_f^* \end{bmatrix}$ is an efficient point of Z, there exists a vector $(p, w) \geq 0$, $(p, w) \neq 0$ such that

$$p \cdot z_g^* + w \cdot z_f^* \geq p \cdot z_g + w \cdot z_f \quad \text{for all} \quad z = \begin{bmatrix} z_g \\ z_f \end{bmatrix} \in Z. \tag{7-1}$$

This is due to theorem 5. Conversely if there exists a $(p, w) > 0$ such that relation (7-1) holds, then by theorem 5, $z^* = \begin{bmatrix} z_g^* \\ z_f^* \end{bmatrix}$ is an efficient point.

Alternatively we can restate the above vector-maximum problem as follows.

Vector-maximize $Dt(= z)$ subject to $Dt + \bar{z} \geq 0$ and $t \geq 0$. Then, again due to theorem 5, if t^* is a solution to this second vector-maximum problem (that is, $z^* \equiv Dt^*$ is an efficient point), then there exist vectors $\alpha \geq 0$, $q^* \geq 0$, and $\alpha \neq 0$ such that:

$$\alpha \cdot (Dt^*) + q^* \cdot (Dt^* + \bar{z}) \geq \alpha \cdot (Dt) + q^* \cdot (Dt + \bar{z}) \quad \text{for all } t \geq 0, \tag{7-2}$$

$$\alpha \cdot (Dt^*) + q^* \cdot (Dt^* + \bar{z}) \leq \alpha \cdot (Dt^*) + q \cdot (Dt^* + \bar{z}) \quad \text{for all } q \geq 0, \tag{7-3}$$

and $\quad q^* \cdot (Dt^* + \bar{z}) = 0. \tag{7-4}$

Conversely, if there exist an $\alpha > 0$ and a $q^* \geq 0$ such that (7-2) and (7-3) hold, then $z^* = Ct^*$ is an efficient point. Letting $\tilde{p} = (\alpha + q^*)$, we can rewrite equation (7-2) in the following equivalent form.

$$\tilde{p} \cdot (Dt^*) \geq \tilde{p} \cdot (Dt) \quad \text{for all } t \geq 0. \tag{7-2'}$$

This is clearly equivalent to equation (7-1) with $\tilde{p} = (p, w)$.

Relation (7-3) can be rewritten as

$$q^* \cdot (Dt^* + \bar{z}) \leq q \cdot (Dt^* + \bar{z}) \quad \text{for all } q \geq 0. \tag{7-3'}$$

Now set $y = y^*$ and $x = x^*$, *except* for the kth activity in Country j, in equation (7-1) [or (7-2')], that is, set $t = t^*$ except for t_{jk}. Then we obtain

$$p \cdot (b^{jk} t_{jk}^*) + w^j \cdot (a^{jk} t_{jk}^*) \geq p \cdot (b^{jk} t_{jk}) + w^j \cdot (a^{jk} t_{jk}), \quad \text{for all } t_{jk} \geq 0. \tag{7-5}$$

Since the choice of j and k is arbitrary, the above inequality holds for all $j = 1, 2, \cdots, m$ and $k = 1, 2, \cdots, k_j$. Conversely, if the above inequality holds for all j and k, then equation (7-2) holds. Thus equation (7-5) provides a complete (that is, necessary and sufficient) characterization of the efficient points of the world production possibilities set. Interpreting p as the world price vector for goods and w as the world price vector for factors, we find that equation (7-5) says that profit is maximized for each activity by operating at an efficient point. Under this interpretation of p and w, equation (7-2) says that the total profit for the world as a whole is also maximized.

Note that an efficient point can also be characterized as a solution to the following linear programming problem.

(M) Maximize $\alpha \cdot (Dt)$
$\quad\quad\quad t$

subject to

$$Dt + \bar{z} \geq 0$$

and

$$t \geq 0 .$$

The dual of the above linear programming problem can be written as:

(m) Minimize $v \cdot \bar{z}$
      v

subject to

$$-D^T v \geq D^T \alpha$$

and

$v \geq 0$, where D^T is the transpose of D.

The LP duality theorem says that a (finite) solution exists for (M) if and only if a (finite) solution exists for (m), and that if t^* is a solution to (M) and v^* is a solution to (m), then

    i. $\alpha \cdot (Dt^*) = v^* \cdot \bar{z}$
    ii. $(Dt^* + \bar{z}) \cdot v^* = 0$, $Dt^* + \bar{z} \geq 0$,   and
    iii. $[D^T(\alpha + v^*)] \cdot t^* = 0$, $D^T(\alpha + v^*) \leq 0$.

Relation iii can be rewritten as

    iii'. $(\alpha + v^*) \cdot (Dt^*) = 0$, $D^T(\alpha + v^*) \leq 0$.

Writing $\alpha + v^* = \tilde{p}$, relation iii can be rewritten further as:

$$\tilde{p} \cdot (Dt^*) = 0 , \quad D^T \cdot \tilde{p} \leq 0 . \tag{7-6}$$

Or,

$$\tilde{p} \cdot (Dt^*) = 0 , \quad \tilde{p} \cdot (Dt) \leq 0 \quad \text{for all } t \geq 0 . \tag{7-7}$$

This equation corresponds to (7-2′) [and hence also to (7-1)]. In fact equation (7-7) also provides some clarification of the earlier equations in that it specifies that the maximum total profit at an efficient point is zero.

    Putting $t = t^*$, except for t_{jk}, we again obtain equation (7-5) [where $\tilde{p} = (p, w)$], *and*

$$p \cdot (a^{jk} t_{jk}{}^*) + w^j \cdot (b^{jk} t_{jk}{}^*) = 0 . \tag{7-8}$$

Relations (7-5) and (7-8) say that no production process can earn a positive profit, and that all processes actually used earn zero profit. This means that efficient points are precisely those points which can appear in a competitive equilibrium. Thus, if we can show that there exists a price vector which is compatible with the demand conditions, then we have demonstrated the existence of a competitive equilibrium in our model of the world economy.

    Under the assumptions of a) one activity for each good, b) no joint production, c) one factor in every country (labor), and d) the equality of the number of goods and the number of countries, it can be shown (exactly as was done in the third section of Chapter 4) that equations (7-5) and (7-8) imply the McKenzie-Jones Theorem.

The Heckscher-Ohlin theorem is concerned with the case in which a) the production set for each country is the same, but the resource constraint $\bar{z}$ differs, that is $I_j = I$ for all j, $a^{jk} = a^k$ and $b^{jk} = b^k$ for all j, such that I is a continuum; b) there is no joint production; c) there are only two factors of production; and d) the intermediate goods are suppressed.

A THEORY OF FREE TRADE EQUILIBRIUM

In Chapter 5, we converted the Ricardian problem of Chapter 4 into a nonlinear programming problem by introducing the demand conditions. In the second section of Chapter 5 we studied this problem after describing the demand conditions in terms of a single aggregate utility function for the world. We extended this discussion to the multi-country, multi-commodity case in the fourth section of Chapter 6. We shall extend the discussion still further by modifying our treatment of the model in the following three ways.

a. Generalize the world production set as much as possible.
b. Allow the possibility that every person in every country has a different utility function, and that there is no aggregate utility function.
c. Do not consider the pattern of specialization as in Mill's problem or the McKenzie-Jones theorem. Instead, consider some other characterization of a free-trade equilibrium.

With regard to the last point, we indicated at the end of the first section of Chapter 5 that a free-trade equilibrium with the demand conditions achieves a Pareto optimum and, hence, this is a possible characterization. In this section we shall construct a general model of world production[8] and show that it is a type of competitive market which has been well discussed in the theory of competitive markets. Then we shall prove the well-known characterization in terms of Pareto optimality and prove the existence of such a free-trade equilibrium.[9]

Consider a world consisting of m countries. There are l primary resources in the world which are supplied exogenously. It is not necessary that every country has some of *each* primary resource before trade and it is not necessary that all of the primary resources be internationally immobile. There are n goods (and services) in the world. It is not necessary that every country be able to

[8] The model of this section is developed in Takayama [16] [17] to prove the existence of a free-trade equilibrium. For the construction of another very general model, see the monumental article by Reiter [15]. He is concerned with the problem of productive efficiency and the factor price equalization theorem. He uses a nonlinear technology model, rather than our linear technology model. The reader can see that our linear model can easily be converted into a nonlinear technology model.

[9] For this reason, we are heavily indebted to Takayama and El-Hodiri [19].

produce each of these goods. We do not distinguish between intermediate goods and final goods since the same commodity may well belong to both categories. International transportation services are not included in this list of goods; instead, we shall list them separately. They are the only commodities whose prices need be the same between countries. There are $\tilde{n}$ international transportation services. We do not assume that every country has the same number of production activities, thus Country j selects from among k_j different production activities. Joint production is allowed. Since we have international transportation services in the model, we do not assume negligible transport costs.

The Graham-McKenzie model [12] is a special case of the above model, where there is only one primary factor—labor. The Heckscher-Ohlin model is a special case, having two countries each with two factors. Each of these countries is able to produce the same two goods using production activities selected from the same set of production activities. That is, the two countries have the same production functions. In both the Graham-McKenzie model and the Heckscher-Ohlin model there is no joint production, no transport costs, and (at least, explicitly) no intermediate goods.

Let a^{jk} be an l-component column vector of the amounts of the primary resources involved in a unit-level operation of the kth activity in Country j. There are k_j activities in Country j, the activities numbered from 1 to $t_j - 1$ deal with regular goods and services, while the activities numbered from t_j to k_j are the international transportation services available to Country j. All the elements of a^{jk}, $k = 1, 2, \cdots, t_j - 1$ are non-positive due to the usual activity analysis convention. We do not assume that the primary resources are completely immobile among the countries, but we do assume that the transportation activity can utilize the primary resources of any country. Then a_{ijk}, the ith element of a^{jk}, $k = t_j, t_j + 1, \cdots, k_j$, is the amount of the ith resource of Country j required for a unit operation of the kth transportation activity if $a_{ijk} < 0$, or the amount of the ith resource transferred to Country j by this transportation activity if $a_{ijk} > 0$.

We now define the matrices:

$$A_G{}^j \equiv \left[a^{j1}, a^{j2}, \cdots, a^{jt_j - 1} \right],$$

$$A_T{}^j \equiv \left[a^{jt_j}, a^{jt_j + 1}, \cdots, a^{jk_j} \right], \quad \text{and}$$

$$A^j \equiv \begin{bmatrix} 0 & A_T{}^1 \\ \cdot & \cdot \\ \cdot & \cdot \\ \cdot & \cdot \\ A_G{}^j & A_T{}^j \\ \cdot & \cdot \\ \cdot & \cdot \\ \cdot & \cdot \\ 0 & A_T{}^m \end{bmatrix}.$$

Let b^{jk} be an n-component column vector, whose ith element, b_{ijk}, denotes the amount of the ith good produced in Country j (or transported to Country j) if $b_{ijk} > 0$, or the amount of the ith good required as an intermediate good in Country j (or transported from Country j) if $b_{ijk} < 0$, for a unit level operation of the kth activity. Now define the following matrices:

$$B_G{}^j \equiv [b^{j1}, b^{j2}, \cdots, b^{jt_j-1}], \quad B_T{}^j \equiv [b^{jt_j}, b^{jt_j+1}, \cdots, b^{jk_j}], \quad \text{and}$$

$$B^j \equiv \begin{bmatrix} 0 & B_T{}^1 \\ \cdot & \cdot \\ \cdot & \cdot \\ \cdot & \cdot \\ B_G{}^j & B_T{}^j \\ \cdot & \cdot \\ \cdot & \cdot \\ \cdot & \cdot \\ 0 & B_T{}^m \end{bmatrix}.$$

We assume that there are $\tilde{n}$ international transportation services. Let $\tilde{b}^{jk}$ be an $\tilde{n}$-component column vector whose ith element, $\tilde{b}_{ijk}$, denotes the ith international transportation service produced ($\tilde{b}_{ijk} > 0$) or required ($\tilde{b}_{ijk} < 0$) for a unit level operation of the kth activity (in Country j).

Consider the following matrix:

$$\tilde{B}^j \equiv \begin{bmatrix} 0 & \cdots & 0 & \tilde{b}_{1jt_j} & \cdots & \tilde{b}_{1jk_j} \\ \cdot & & & & & \\ \cdot & & & & & \\ \cdot & & & & & \\ 0 & \cdots & 0 & \tilde{b}_{\tilde{n}jt_j} & \cdots & \tilde{b}_{\tilde{n}jk_j} \end{bmatrix}$$

$$\equiv [0 \quad \cdots \quad 0 \quad \tilde{b}^{jt_j} \quad \cdots \quad \tilde{b}^{jk_j}] \equiv [0 \quad \tilde{B}_T{}^j].$$

Define $A \equiv [A^1, \cdots, A^m]$, $B \equiv [B^1, \cdots, B^m]$, and $\tilde{B} \equiv [\tilde{B}^1, \cdots, \tilde{B}^m]$.

Let t be the activity level, which is defined as:

$$t \equiv \begin{bmatrix} t^1 \\ \cdot \\ \cdot \\ \cdot \\ t^m \end{bmatrix}, \quad \text{where } t^j \equiv \begin{bmatrix} t_{j1} \\ \cdot \\ \cdot \\ \cdot \\ t_{jk_j} \end{bmatrix}.$$

Let r be the resource supply vector. Thus,

$$r \equiv \begin{bmatrix} r^1 \\ \cdot \\ \cdot \\ \cdot \\ r^m \end{bmatrix}, \quad \text{where } r^j \equiv \begin{bmatrix} r_{j1} \\ \cdot \\ \cdot \\ \cdot \\ r_{jl} \end{bmatrix}.$$

Let x be the vector of commodity outputs, which may be written as:

$$x \equiv \begin{bmatrix} x^1 \\ \cdot \\ \cdot \\ \cdot \\ x^m \end{bmatrix}, \quad \text{where } x^j \equiv \begin{bmatrix} x_{j1} \\ \cdot \\ \cdot \\ \cdot \\ x_{jn} \end{bmatrix}.$$

Let $\tilde{x}$ be the vector of international transportation services supplied. Hence:

$$\tilde{x} \equiv \begin{bmatrix} \tilde{x}^1 \\ \cdot \\ \cdot \\ \cdot \\ \tilde{x}^m \end{bmatrix}, \quad \text{where } \tilde{x}^j \equiv \begin{bmatrix} \tilde{x}_{j1} \\ \cdot \\ \cdot \\ \cdot \\ \tilde{x}_{j\tilde{n}} \end{bmatrix}.$$

Then our world production system can be described as follows:

$$At + r \geqq 0, \quad t \geqq 0, \tag{7-9}$$

$$x = Bt, \quad t \geqq 0, \quad \text{and} \tag{7-10}$$

$$\tilde{x} = \tilde{B}t, \quad t \geqq 0. \tag{7-11}$$

Define the matrix:

$$D \equiv \begin{bmatrix} B \\ \tilde{B} \\ A \end{bmatrix}, \quad \text{and the corresponding vectors,}$$

$$z \equiv \begin{bmatrix} x \\ \tilde{x} \\ At \end{bmatrix} \quad \text{and} \quad \bar{z} \equiv \begin{bmatrix} 0 \\ 0 \\ r \end{bmatrix}.$$

Then equations (7-9), (7-10), and (7-11) can be reduced to:

$$z = Dt, \quad z + \bar{z} \geqq 0, \quad \text{and} \quad t \geqq 0. \tag{7-12}$$

The world production possibilities set is defined to be:

$$Y_w \equiv \{z : z = Dt, t \geqq 0\}, \quad \text{with } z + \bar{z} \geqq 0,$$

Or

$$Y_w \equiv \{z : z = Dt, z + \bar{z} \geqq 0, t \geqq 0\}.$$

Let c_j be the aggregate consumption vector [that is, an $(n + \tilde{n} + l)$-vector] for Country j. Then we have

$$\sum_{j=1}^{m} c_j \leqq z + \bar{z}, \quad z \in Y_w. \tag{7-13}$$

Note that the primary resources can be consumed by the final consumers, and that the international transportation services can also be consumed by the final consumers (for example, tourist travel).

Let c_{sj} denote the consumption vector for individual s of Country j. Clearly, $\sum_s c_{sj} = c_j$. Let $u_{sj}(c_{sj})$ be his utility function. Let C_{sj} denote his consumption possibilities set. In the usual international trade analysis, C_{sj} is taken to be the entire non-negative orthant for all s and j. Here we simply suppose that C_{sj} is a convex subset of the non-negative orthant of the commodity space.

DEFINITION (Feasibility) An array of consumption vectors $\{c_{sj}\}$ is said to be *feasible* if there exist production vectors z such that $z + \bar{z} \geq \sum_{j=1}^{m} c_j$ with $c_{sj} \in C_{sj}$ for all s and j and $z \in Y_w$.

DEFINITION (Pareto Optimality) A feasible array of consumption vectors $\{c_{sj}^{*}\}$ is said to be *Pareto optimal* if there does not exist a feasible array of consumption vectors $\{c_{sj}\}$ such that $u_{sj}(c_{sj}) \geq u_{sj}(c_{sj}^{*})$ for all s and with strict inequality for at least one s.

DEFINITION (Free Trade Equilibrium) $[p^{*}, \{c_{sj}^{*}\}, z^{*}]$ with $p^{*} \geq 0$, $c_{sj} \in C_{sj}$ and $z^{*} \in Y_w$ is called a *free trade equilibrium* if:

1. $u_{sj}(c_{sj}^{*}) \geq u_{sj}(c_{sj})$ for all $.c_{sj} \in C_{sj}$ with $p^{*} \cdot c_{sj} \leq p^{*} \cdot c_{sj}^{*}$ for all s, j.
2. $p^{*} \cdot z^{*} \geq p^{*} \cdot z$ for all $z \in Y_w$.
3. $z + \bar{z} \geq \sum_{j=1}^{m} c_j^{*}$ and $p^{*} \cdot \left(z + \bar{z} - \sum_{j=1}^{m} c_j^{*} \right) = 0$.

REMARK If in statement 2 of the above definition (that is, $p^{*} \cdot z^{*} \geq p^{*} \cdot z$ for all $z \in Y_w$), we put $t_{jk} = t_{jk}^{*}$ (where t_{jk}^{*} corresponds to z^{*}) except for $j = j_0$ and $k = k_0$ then we obtain the profit maximization condition for activity k_0 in Country j_0. Since the choice of j_0 and k_0 is arbitrary, this means that profits are maximized for every production process in every country. Conversely, if profits are maximized for every production process in every country, statement 2 follows immediately.

REMARK From the considerations of the previous section it should be clear that statement 2 means that z^{*} is an efficient point of Y_w. Thus, the existence of a free-trade equilibrium implies that production is taking place at an efficient point.

DEFINITION (Satiation) Individual s of Country j is *satiated at* c'_{sj} if $u_{sj}(c_{sj}') \geq u_{sj}(c_{sj})$ for all $c_{sj} \in C_{sj}$.

REMARK The above definitions are the standard ones in the theory of competitive markets. There free-trade equilibrium corresponds to the concept, *competitive equilibrium*. The following theorems show that a) every Pareto optimal point can be realized as a free-trade equilibrium, b) there exists a free-trade equilibrium, and c) every free-trade equilibrium is Pareto optimal. These are standard results in the theory of competitive markets, which indicates that our extension of the classical trade model now becomes a model of competitive equilibrium. This point of view has been adopted by McKenzie [12], [13] and Reiter [15]. Our model is much more general than McKenzie's [12], [13]. The proofs of the following theorems have been borrowed from Takayama and El-Hodiri [19]. The readers who are not familiar with such concepts as upper semi-continuous mapping may skip the proof of the following theorem.

We shall assume:

ASSUMPTION 1   There exist $c_{sj}^0 \in C_{sj}$ for all s and j and a $z^0 \in Y_w$ such that $\sum_{s,j} c_{sj}^0 < z^0 + \bar{z}$.

ASSUMPTION 2 $u_{sj}(c_{sj})$ is a continuous and concave function for all s and j.

ASSUMPTION 3   Given a point c_{sj}^* and a prevailing price vector p^*, there exists a $c_{sj}^0 \in C_{sj}$ such that $p^* \cdot c_{sj}^* > p^* \cdot c_{sj}^0$ for all s and j.

THEOREM 6   Under assumptions 1 and 2, if $[\{c_{sj}^*\}, z^*]$ is a Pareto optimal point, then there exists a $p^* \geqq 0$ such that $[p^*, \{c_{sj}^*\}, z^*]$ is a free trade equilibrium.

PROOF   Let u be a vector function whose typical element is $u_{sj}(c_{sj})$. Since $[\{c_{sj}^*\}, z^*]$ is a Pareto optimal point, it is a solution to the following vector maximum problem: Maximize u subject to $\sum_{s,j} c_{sj} \leqq z + \bar{z}, c_{sj} \in C_{sj}, z \in Y_w$. Hence, in view of assumptions 1 and 2, there exist vectors $\alpha \geqq 0$, $p^* \geqq 0$, $\alpha \neq 0$ such that

$$\alpha \cdot u^* + p^* \cdot \left(z^* + \bar{z} - \sum_{s,j} c_{sj}^* \right) \geqq \alpha \cdot u + p^* \cdot \left(z + \bar{z} - \sum_{s,j} c_{sj} \right), \quad (7\text{-}14)$$

for all $c_{sj} \in C_{sj}$ (for all s and j) and for all $z \in Y_w$, and

$$p^* \cdot \left(z^* + \bar{z} - \sum_{s,j} c_{sj}^* \right) = 0, \quad z^* + \bar{z} - \sum_{s,j} c_{sj}^* \geqq 0. \quad (7\text{-}15)$$

Condition 3 of the free-trade equilibrium follows directly from equations (7-15). Let $c_{sj} = c_{sj}^*$ for all s and j in relation (7-14), then condition 2 of the free-trade equilibrium follows. Finally, put $c_{sj} = c_{sj}^*$ for all s except $s = s_0$ and $z = z^*$. Then

$$\alpha_{s_0 j} u_{s_0 j}(c_{s_0 j}^*) - \alpha_{s_0 j} u_{s_0 j}(c_{s_0 j}) \geqq p^* \cdot c_{s_0 j}^* - p^* \cdot c_{s_0 j}, \quad \text{for all } c_{s_0 j} \in C_{s_0 j}. \quad (7\text{-}16)$$

If $\alpha > 0$, then condition 1 of the free-trade equilibrium is satisfied for individual s_0 of Country j. If $\alpha_{s_0 j} = 0$, then $p^* \cdot c_{s_0 j}^* \leqq p^* \cdot c_{s_0 j}$ for all $c_{s_0 j} \in C_{s_0 j}$, which contradicts assumption 3. Hence $\alpha_{s_0 j} > 0$. Since the choice of $s_0 j$ is arbitrary, this establishes the theorem.   (Q.E.D.)

COROLLARY If there exists at least one consumer, say individual s_0 of Country j, who is not satiated at $c_{s_0 j}{}^*$, then $p^* \neq 0$.

PROOF From the proof of the above theorem, we know that equation (7-16) holds with $\alpha_{s_0 j} > 0$. Suppose $p^* = 0$, then

$$u_{s_0 j}(c_{s_0 j}{}^*) \geqq u_{s_0 j}(c_{s_0 j}) \quad \text{for all } c_{s_0 j} \in C_{s_0 j} \, .$$

This contradicts the assumption that Mr. s_0 of Country j is not satiated at $c_{s_0 j}{}^*$. (Q.E.D.)

Before we prove the existence of a free-trade equilibrium, we shall add the following to our list of assumptions.

ASSUMPTION 4 C_{sj} is compact for all s and j.

ASSUMPTION 5 (non-satiation) For every $c_{sj} \in C_{sj}$, there is a $c_{sj}{}^0$ which is preferred to c_{sj}.

ASSUMPTION 6 Every consumer can survive in the absence of trade on the basis of the commodities he holds.

Note that free-trade equilibrium, as defined above, can be achieved by allocating the world's total income, $p^* \cdot (z + \bar{z})$, so that consumer s in Country j gets $p^* \cdot c_{sj}{}^*$. In other words, without such a reallocation of income, a Pareto optimum can *not*, in general, be supported by competitive pricing. To prove the existence of a free-trade equilibrium, we have to prove the existence of a price vector which will support the conditions of the free-trade equilibrium without such a reallocation of income. Hence, we have to rephrase condition 1 of the definition of a free-trade equilibrium. First note that the income of consumer s of Country j, denoted by M_{sj}, given the price vector p^* and the output vector z^*, can be written as:

$$M_{sj}(p^*, z^*) \equiv \max \{0, \theta_{sj} p^* \cdot (\bar{z} + z^*)\} \, ,$$

where θ_{sj} is the share of the world's income received by Mr. s of Country j, and $\sum\limits_{s, j} \theta_{sj} = 1$.

THEOREM 7 Under assumptions 1, 2, 4, 5, and 6 there exists a free-trade equilibrium with a non-zero price vector.[10]

PROOF Let $U \equiv \sum\limits_{s, j} \alpha_{sj} u_{sj}(c_{sj})$ and consider the following nonlinear programming problem:

Maximize U subject to
$$\underset{c_{sj}, z}{}$$

$$\sum\limits_{s, j} c_{sj} \leqq z + \bar{z}, \quad c_{sj} \in C_{sj} \quad z \in Y_w \, .$$

[10] For an alternative proof of the existence of a free-trade equilibrium for a similar model, see Takayama [16] [17].

If $[\{c_{sj}'\}, z']$ is a solution to this problem, then there exists a $p' \geqq 0$, such that

$$U' + p' \cdot \left(z' + \bar{z} - \sum_{s,j} c_{sj}'\right) \geqq U + p' \cdot \left(z + \bar{z} - \sum_{s,j} c_{sj}\right), \tag{7-17}$$

for all $c_{sj} \in C_{sj}$ and $z \in Y_w$, where $U' \equiv \sum_{s,j} \alpha_{sj} u_{sj}(c_{sj}')$; and

$$p' \cdot \left(z' + \bar{z} - \sum_{s,j} c_{sj}\right) = 0, \quad z' + \bar{z} - \sum_{s,j} c_{sj} \geqq 0. \tag{7-18}$$

In a manner similar to that used in the proof of theorem 1, we can immediately show that

$$p' \cdot z' \geqq p' \cdot z, \quad \text{for all } z \in Y_w; \tag{7-19}$$

$$u_{sj}(c_{sj}') \geqq u_{sj}(c_{sj}), \quad \text{for all } c_{sj} \in C_{sj} \quad \text{with} \quad p' \cdot c_{sj}' \geqq p' \cdot c_{sj}, \tag{7.20}$$

if $\alpha_{sj} > 0$; and

$$p' \cdot c_{sj} \geqq p' \cdot c_{sj}', \quad \text{for all } c_{sj} \in C_{sj}, \quad \text{if} \quad \alpha_{sj} = 0. \tag{7-21}$$

Since, by assumption, there is no satiation consumption bundle in $C_{sj}, p' \neq 0$. Thus we can normalize p' such that it is in a unit simplex. Let α be a vector whose typical element is α_{sj}. We suppose that in the above maximization problem, α is in a unit simplex.

The remainder of the proof is similar to that of Takayama and El-Hodiri [19] so we shall merely sketch it.[11] Since C_{sj} and Y_w are bounded, there exists a number M such that $\sum_{s,j} |M_{sj}(p, z) - p \cdot c_{sj}| < M$ for all $c_{sj} \in C_{sj}$ and $z \in Y_w$. Define $u_{sj} \equiv \max_{s,j} \{0, \alpha_{sj} + [M_{sj}(p, z) - p \cdot c_{sj}]/M\}$, and $\alpha_{sj}' = u_{sj}/\sum u_{sj}$. Now consider a mapping $[\alpha, \{c_{sj}\}, z] \rightarrow [\alpha'\{c_{sj}'\}, z', p']$. Show that this is an upper-semi-continuous mapping from a convex set into itself, whose image is non-empty and convex. Then due to Kakutani's fixed point theorem,[12] there exists a fixed point $[\alpha^*, \{c_{sj}^*\}, z^*, p^*]$. Show that at this point all of the conditions of a free-trade equilibrium are satisfied. (Q.E.D.)

THEOREM 8   If $[\{c_{sj}^*\}, z^*, p^*]$ is a free-trade equilibrium in theorem 2, then $[\{c_{sj}^*\}, z^*]$ is a Pareto optimum.

PROOF   Note that $[\{c_{sj}^*\}, z^*]$ maximizes $\sum_{s,j} \alpha_{sj}^* u_{sj}(c_{sj})$ (where $\alpha_{sj}^* > 0$ for all s and j), subject to the feasibility condition. Suppose $[\{c_{sj}^*\}, z^*]$ is not a Pareto optimum, then there exist $c_{sj}^0 \in C_{sj}$ for all s and j and a $z^0 \in Y_w$ such that

[11] This part of the proof is originally due to Negishi, T. "Welfare Economics and the Existence of an Equilibrium for a Competitive Economy," *Metroeconomica*, XII, Agosto-Dicembre, 1960.

[12] Kakutani's fixed point theorem can be stated as follows: Let X be a non-empty, convex, and compact subset of R^n. If f is an upper-semi-continuous mapping from X into X, and the set $f(x)$ is nonempty and convex, then there exists an x^* (called the *fixed point*) such that $x^* \in f(x^*)$.

$u_{sj}(c_{sj}^0) \geq u_{sj}(c_{sj})$ holds for all s and j, and holds with strict inequality for at least one s and j, and $\sum_{s,j} c_{sj}^0 \leq z^0 + \bar{z}$. In other words, there exists a feasible $[\{c_{sj}^0\}, z^0]$ such that $\sum_{s,j} \alpha_{sj}{}^* u_{sj}(c_{sj}^0) > \sum_{s,j} \alpha_{sj}{}^* u_{sj}(c_{sj}{}^*)$, which contradicts the condition that $[\{c_{sj}{}^*\}, z^*]$ is a maximum. (Q.E.D.)

REFERENCES

1. Arrow, K. J., "An Extension of the Basic Theorems of Classical Economics," *Proceedings of the Second Berkeley Symposium on Mathematical Statistics and Probability*, ed. by J. Neyman (Berkeley: University of California Press), 1951.

2. Arrow, K. J., and Debreu, G., "Existence of an Equilibrium for a Competitive Economy," *Econometrica*, 22, July 1954.

3. Chipman, J. S., "A Survey of the Theory of International Trade: Part 1, the Classical Theory and Part 2, the Neo-Classical Theory," *Econometrica*, 33, July 1965, and October 1965.

4. Debreu, G., *Theory of Value* (New York: John Wiley & Sons, Inc.), 1959.

5. El-Hodiri, M., *A Note on Constraint Extreme of Functionals*, Purdue University, 1966 (unpublished working paper).

6. Haberler, G., *The Theory of International Trade, with Its Applications to Commercial Policy* (tr. from German ed. 1933) (London: William Hodge), 1936.

7. Koopmans, T. C., ed., *Activity Analysis of Production and Allocation* (New York: John Wiley & Sons), 1951, especially Chapter 3 (by Koopmans).

8. Koopmans, T. C., *Three Essays on the State of Economic Science* (New York: McGraw-Hill, Inc.), 1957, especially the first essay.

9. Koopmans, T. C., and Bausch, A. F., "Selected Topics Involving Mathematical Reasoning," *Journal of SIAM Review*, July 1959, especially topic 3.

10. Kuhn, H. W., "Notes on International Trade III," *Lecture Notes*, Princeton University, Fall Term, 1966.

11. Kuhn, H. W., and Tucker, A. W., "Non-linear Programming," *Proceedings of Second Berkeley Symposium on Mathematical Statistics and Probability*, ed. by J. Neyman (Berkeley: University of California Press), 1951.

12. McKenzie, L. W., "On Equilibrium in Graham's Model of World Trade and Other Competitive Systems," *Econometrica*, 22, April 1954.

13. ———, "The Theory of International Trade: II. Mathematical Theory," in *The International Encyclopedia of the Social Sciences* (New York: The Free Press), 1969.

14. Mosak, J. L., *General Equilibrium Theory in International Trade* (Bloomington, Ind.: Principia Press), 1944.

15. Reiter, S., "Efficient International Trade and Equalization of Factor Prices," *International Economic Review*, 2, January 1961.

16. Takayama, A., *Economic Growth and International Trade*, Ph.D. Dissertation, University of Rochester, March 1962, especially Chapter 1.
17. ———, *International Economics* (Tokyo: Toyo Keizai Shimpo-sha), 1963, Chapter I.
18. ———, *Mathematical Economics*, forthcoming.
19. Takayama, A., and El-Hodiri, M., "Programming, Pareto Optimum and the Existence of Competitive Equilibria," *Metroeconomica*, XX, Gennaio-April 1968 (also chapter 2, section F of [18] as revised).
20. Viner, J., *Studies in the Theory of International Trade* (New York: Harper & Row, Publishers), 1937.

PART III

BALANCE OF PAYMENTS, THE THEORY OF INTERNATIONAL TRADE POLICY AND EXCHANGE DEVALUATION— THE NEOCLASSICAL AND THE KEYNESIAN MODELS

8

THE MARSHALL-LERNER CONDITION AND THE NEOCLASSICAL SYSTEM OF INTERNATIONAL TRADE POLICY[1]

INTRODUCTION

An important aim of the theory of comparative advantage is to clarify the effects of initiating trade. In this sense the theory of comparative advantage is a theory of policy. It was made clear that under a competitive free trade system, international trade will *necessarily* occur between the countries according to each country's comparative advantage as long as the prices are different between the countries. Further, it was made clear that such an analysis is really part of the broader framework of the general equilibrium of world trade and world production: on the extension of a single country general equilibrium analysis to a world general equilibrium analysis. The pattern of trade (that is, which country exports or imports which goods) and the volume of each country's exports and imports are endogenous variables, determined within the system, once the basic premise of this economic system (for example, a competitive free-trade system) has been presupposed.[2]

We now suppose a certain economic system, say a competitive economy, for our world economy. If we like, we can presuppose the existence of things such as tariffs, transfer payments, domestic taxes, and so on. Note that these things may prevent the economy from achieving a Pareto optimal state. The values of the variables such as tariffs, transfer payments, domestic taxes, and so on, are

---

[1] This chapter was originally written as Chapter 7 of [49]. See also Takayama [47].

[2] Under a different economic system, we can obtain different conclusions. There are essentially two questions involved with the premise of a competitive free-trade system. 1) Is such a system a fairly realistic description of the real economy? Here we are more concerned with how well the competitive free-trade model explains the phenomena of the real world rather than how realistic the basic premises of this model are. 2) What is the significance of such a system from the point of view of welfare economics? The answer to this question is simple but very important. We know that such a system will lead to a Pareto optimal state and that a Pareto optimal state can be supported by such a system. Hence this is one system from among many alternative social and economic systems which can achieve a Pareto optimal state.

specified from outside the system.[3] Once they have been specified together with the economic system, we know the magnitudes of the major economic variables such as the volume of exports and the volume of imports for each country, the terms of trade, and so on.

Many problems in the theory of international trade have been connected with the study of actual policy questions. Among them are the transfer problem, the tariff question, and the problem of domestic taxation and subsidies. The classical economists were already concerned with these problems, and their importance has not decreased. It is interesting that, from the analytical point of view, there are similarities among these problems. The most important of these lies in the common analytical technique employed in many of these studies— comparative statics—which was designed for just such questions. This type of analysis examines the effect on important endogenous economic variables, such as the terms of trade when there is a shift in the equilibrium situation due to changes in some policy variables, and exogenous economic variables, such as a unilateral transfer from one country to the other, the imposition of a tariff, or the imposition of a domestic excise tax on the imported good. Actually, there are more than formal similarities among these questions. All of the problems are deeply related to the question of stability, which itself is related to an important policy question, the problem of exchange devaluation (although its importance was not realized until the 1930s). A unilateral transfer from one country to the other will affect the balance of payments, and thus will affect its equilibrium which is attained by movements of the terms of trade.[4] Although there are direct effects such as the increase or decrease of demand for goods resulting from this transfer, we know that the problem is essentially related to the stability problem, for the conclusion will differ depending on whether or not the market mechanism will restore an equilibrium in the goods market. The tariff is similarly related to the stability problem, for imposition of a tariff naturally results in consumer substitution of goods through effects on the domestic price ratio. However, all direct or indirect effects again amount to the balance of payments equilibrium relation and are closely related to the exchange stability problem. The same is true of the effects of a domestic tax. All these considerations naturally suggest the possibility of unified treatment of these problems. One attempt along this line was made by Mundell [37], who clearly recognized that these problems were those of comparative statics and who developed a formal treatment of these problems in clear mathematical terms.

[3] If we wish, we can construct a general equilibrium system in which these policy variables are endogenous variables. We shall not attempt to do this here.

[4] Johnson proposed to treat the problem of exchange stability from the standpoint of the transfer problem. It is true that change in the terms of trade would move real income from one country to the other due to the increased (decreased) price of the imported goods. In fact, such a transfer is inevitable in the tariff problem as well as the problem of domestic taxes. Hence, it is possible to consider all the problems in this chapter from the standpoint of the transfer problem. But such an exercise is a problem of comparative statics, and hence should not be called one of "stability". Johnson's approach, moreover, obscures the importance of the genuine stability analysis.

The purpose of this chapter is to carry out an analysis similar to that of Mundell. In this chapter, we, like Mundell, adopt a neoclassical model in which price plays the crucial role. However, our analysis will be more unified and more transparent than his. For example, we shall not use terms such as "national income" and "inflationary pressures," which obscured the basic neoclassical character of his model. We shall make explicit the role of production activity in our model.

Actually, the recognition of whether our economy is Keynesian or neoclassical is of grave importance to our analysis and conclusions. One of the essential differences is the underemployment of labor, which is, of course, the basic feature of the Keynesian economy, and the only explicit factor of production in the model. In the neoclassical analysis full employment is essential, and price is the key parameter of the system. One consequence of this is that the production side of the economy is sharpened, and attention is focused on the allocation of the productive factors to the industries.

Suppose that our economy is of the neoclassical type, where full employment is the normal and basic assumption to be made. Then we can no longer assume that production takes place *inside* the production transformation schedule; we have to recognize now that production must take place *on* the transformation schedule. General equilibrium analysis becomes complete only when the production side, as well as the demand side, of the economy are fully considered. What are the possible effects from the production side? First, we may want to alter a Keynesian premise by assuming that each country is producing two goods instead of one. In the neoclassical analysis, the complete specialization assumption is generally regarded as too restrictive or uninteresting. To see how the production consideration leads to a more complete equilibrium analysis, suppose there is a change in the terms of trade, say, in favor of the foreign country. This change would shift resources in the home country away from exported goods to imported goods. The domestic production of the imported goods would increase, while the production of the exported goods would decline. This would naturally work as a *stabilizing* factor in the market; thus the stability condition would become less strict than in the case when production is fixed. In fact, the stability condition studied in the literature, known as the *Marshall-Lerner condition*, whose analysis is facilitated by the use of the offer curve, takes account of the production and the demand of the economy. Jones [20], following Mundell [37], made a brilliant study of this and succeeded in separating the "elasticity of the offer curve" into two components, reflecting the production side and the demand side of the economy, respectively. This separation is important because the elasticity of the offer curve is really a mixture of the behavior of two different decision units—producers and consumers. Jones obtained the usual condition that the sum of the elasticities of the offer curves exceeds unity. He then decomposed this into a form in which the behaviors of production and consumption are made explicit. In the next section, after we obtain the condition in a non-decomposed form, we shall obtain this decomposed form of the stability condition directly, *without* bypassing the elasticities of the offer curves. The model which we shall build will also be useful for the analysis of transfer payments, tariffs, domestic taxes, and so on. This analysis will be done in the third section.

In the literature, the Marshall-Lerner condition is often obtained by differentiating the balance of payments equation with respect to the exchange rate or the terms of trade. However, as we shall explain more fully later (the end of the second section of this chapter and the fourth section of Chapter 9), this procedure is not that of stability analysis. Also, it often confuses an exercise in comparative statics with the stability analysis. In the next section, we shall obtain the Marshall-Lerner condition explicitly as a stability condition of the neoclassical trading world. That is, we shall obtain it in the manner which conforms to the general tradition of stability analysis in general economic theory by Walras, Hicks, Samuelson, and Arrow and Hurwicz.

We can view the entire topic in the proper perspective. That is, the policy analyses in the third section are exercises in comparative statics. We should discuss the stability condition before such analysis, since, as we remarked earlier, there is a close relation between the stability condition and the comparative statics analysis, which is a well-established fact in view of Samuelson [45].

In the next section, before we obtain the Marshall-Lerner condition as a sufficient condition for stability, using the model which will be used in later analysis of policy questions, we shall attempt to clarify the meaning of this condition. We shall show that this condition is the condition in which the world market for each good is (dynamically) locally stable, provided that the relative price of the goods is the adjusting parameter of the stability process and that all the other markets (especially the factor markets) are adjusted to an equilibrium instantaneously.

Further remarks on the Marshall-Lerner condition are now in order. First, the conventional term "Marshall" is not particularly appropriate, for Marshall's own stability condition ([27], Appendix J) only partially resembles the condition that the sum of the elasticities of offer curves does not exceed unity. However, this formal similarity embodies an important difference in substance. In other words, Marshall is concerned with the stability analysis in which the quantities, especially those of the outputs rather than the terms of trade (or the relative price of the goods), are the adjusting parameters of the system. In other words, the stability condition which we shall obtain in the next section is not the one that Marshall himself was concerned with. A detailed discussion on Marshall's own treatment is done by Amano [1]. The reason we stick to the elasticity condition, *based on the price-adjusting model*, should be clear. It is due to the fact that the traditional results for the policy questions such as transfer payments, tariffs, and so on (obtained as an application of comparative statics analysis in the later subsections of this chapter), are all linked with the condition on the elasticities in an essential manner as remarked before. Hence, it is important to make the meaning of the elasticity condition explicit. The purpose of the next section is to make the meaning of the elasticity condition clear as a sufficient condition for stability in a Walrasian price-adjusting model, which is essentially in line with analysis by Jones [20].

Negishi [38], in his recent article, attacked Jones [20] on the ground that he neglected the "wealth effect." Essentially speaking, Negishi's analysis is based on the model in which each country spends its income on three commodities— the two physical goods and the home currency. Hence, it is not surprising that he obtained the conclusion in which the "Marshall-Lerner condition is neither the stability condition for a commodity market nor the condition for favorable devaluation." However, in the traditional neoclassical analysis, all the income is supposed to be spent on physical goods, and the currency or money plays only the role of a "veil." In other words, money bears no utility, hence, it is not demanded like physical goods (or services). One consequence of this is that the entire conclusions of the traditional comparative statics analysis on the effect of transfer payments, tariffs, and so on, will be invalidated. It is certainly possible to introduce currency as the third commodity, as in Negishi's analysis, and revise the entire analysis in the literature on the policy questions. But this is not attempted by Negishi.

Suppose, however, that money serves not only as a medium of exchange and as a unit of accounting, but also acts as a store of value. Then we can introduce money in the utility function as a proxy for the consumption of future (real) goods, which can be purchased by the stored money. Then money is introduced as the third commodity in the neoclassical framework. If this is the case, the Marshall-Lerner condition as a stability condition must be greatly revised, as Negishi insists, and the entire policy analysis of the third section should also be rewritten. Is there any way to rescue the neoclassical trade analysis from this difficulty? Or, under what situations is the neoclassical analysis of separating the real system from the monetary system valid? This leads to a well-known "dichotomy controversy" as conceived by Patinkin. Morishima [36] gave an excellent partial answer to the question. Following his point on the separability of the utility function, Sieper [48] and Negishi [39] have pointed out that, under the assumption of the separability of the utility function, the real system and the monetary system in the international trade framework can be "dichotomized," so that the neoclassical tradition of analyzing the two systems separately can be justified. Hence, all the analysis in the present chapter including the Marshall-Lerner condition becomes valid. We shall deal with this problem in the next chapter.

One may observe here that the explicit introduction of money enables us to understand the mechanism which determines the exchange rate (if it is allowed to fluctuate). The exchange rate, being the relative price of two currencies, is determined only with the explicit recognition of money in the model. This point was not fully realized in the literature, especially in earlier discussions on exchange stability. It is therefore rather misleading to call the Marshall-Lerner condition "the condition for exchange stability," although the analysis is centered around the balance of payments equation whether or not money is explicitly introduced into the model. When we introduce money explicitly into the model, the exchange rate, if it is allowed to fluctuate, is determined in the model. Then the exchange stability problem is concerned with the usual stability problem asking the question whether or not the exchange rate, when it is out of equilibrium, will return to equilibrium. If we have a fixed exchange rate system, then the exchange rate is no longer a variable to be determined within the system. Its value is determined a priori. Hence, the analysis of a change in the exchange rate is *not* the problem of stability analysis; it is an exercise in comparative statics. We shall postpone this discussion to the next chapter.

We now summarize the purposes of this chapter. They are: 1) to clarify the meaning of the basic stability problem and the Marshall-Lerner condition under the neoclassical price-adjusting framework, 2) to treat the major policy questions in a neoclassical framework in a consistent and systematic manner using comparative statics with explicit recognition of the stability condition, and 3) to make the assumptions underlying the treatment of these problems explicit.

It is important to notice that our aim really is not to make a further generalization of the existing theories concerning those policy questions,[5] but rather to make the logic in analysis clear and assumptions explicit. Samuelson introduced the transport costs and tariffs in the analysis of the transfer problem and showed the change in the conclusions due to this generalization,[6] but we shall not consider such a generalization. Some economists were concerned with the assumption about the way the transfer or the tariff proceeds are collected and disposed of, for it affects the consumption behavior of the country and people.[7] But we shall avoid all these questions by assuming that they are collected in the form of income tax and distributed in the form of income subsidies so that they do not affect the consumption behavior of the country. Our position is that these generalizations can be done easily and that it is, in fact, a simple mathematical exercise to do these things.[8] We shall, instead, try to make the essential line of analysis in the problem more explicit.

In order to understand the essential points of the problems that we want to consider, we shall adopt a two-country, two-good formulation. Perfect competi-

---

[5] In fact, most of the results presented in this chapter are well-known.

[6] See Samuelson [46] [47]. For an excellent summary of the problem in non-mathematical terms, see Johnson [17]. It is, of course, possible and easy to extend Samuelson's analysis with a thorough recognition of the production side of the economy using the model adopted in the current chapter.

[7] One of the most important considerations in this respect is the introduction of the consumption function by the government. But it is the author's belief that the introduction of the government consumption function is quite arbitrary and that there is no a priori reason for government to behave in a certain way. Of course, the introduction of the government consumption function has an important implication. Analyzing the effect of a certain government consumption behavior upon the analysis, we can see its policy implications immediately. To illustrate this, let us suppose that the government spends its income on goods in a *fixed proportion*. Then it is easy to consider the effect on the conclusions (say, the effect on the terms of trade) when government changes this proportion.

[8] This does not deny the importance of the analysis at all. In fact, it is a great contribution to trade theory to point out the possible ground for generalization. However, once these ideas are presented, the actual computations are easy mathematical exercises, although slight generalizations can be achieved.

tion (except for the possible intervention by the government by means of tariffs, and so on) and full employment of the factors are assumed. In the next section we shall present the basic model for the analysis and consider the problem of stability. In the third section we shall discuss three topics—the transfer problem, the tariff question, and the problem of domestic taxation.

THE MARSHALL-LERNER CONDITION

Consider a world with two countries, 1 and 2, each being able to produce two goods, X and Y. We consider the neoclassical world in which both the production and consumption of each good are determined by the relative prices of the two goods. In other words, we consider the trading world that we considered in Chapter 1. Let (P/Q) be the relative price of Good X vis-à-vis Good Y in the world market. We assume that there are no price distortions such as tariffs, subsidies, and so on, so that P/Q is also the price ratio that each country faces. Suppose that there is a price ratio $(P/Q)^*$ in which world excess demands for X and Y are both zero. Such a price ratio is called an *equilibrium price ratio*. The question that we wish to answer now is whether or not there is a mechanism in the economy which will bring P/Q back to its original equilibrium value. If the answer to this question is "yes," then we say that the equilibrium price ratio $(P/Q)^*$ is *stable*. Such an analysis of stability was already attempted in Chapter 1, third section, using the Oniki-Uzawa type offer curve. The purpose of this section is to define the problem of stability more precisely, obtain the condition for stability (called the Marshall-Lerner condition) and understand its implications.

We start our analysis by illustrating the problem of stability in terms of the Mill-Marshall offer curve. We have seen this for a special case when we discussed Graham's theory of international value (Chapter 5). Here, we do not impose the special assumptions made in Graham's theory such as constant cost and fixed proportions in the consumption of commodities. In Figure 8-1, the α-line represents the initial equilibrium terms of trade and the curves labeled I and II are the offer curves of Countries 1 and 2 respectively. Suppose that the terms of trade move from the α-line to the β-line. Then Country 1's excess supply of X *decreases* by the amount BA and Country 2's excess demand for X *increases* by the amount BC. Hence, in the diagram, there is a net increase in the world excess demand for X by $BA + BC = AC$. Similarly, Country 1's excess demand for Y *decreases* by EF and Country 2's excess supply of Y *increases* by ED, causing a net decrease in the world excess demand for Y by $ED + EF = DF$. By the definition of equilibrium, the world excess demand for X and Y are both zero when the price line α prevails. This consideration implies that the world excess demand for X is positive and that for Y is negative when the new price line β prevails. Assume that the price of X vis-à-vis Y increases (decreases) if the world excess demand for X is positive (negative) and the world excess demand for Y is negative (positive). Then, in the situation described above, the price of X vis-à-vis Y increases at the price

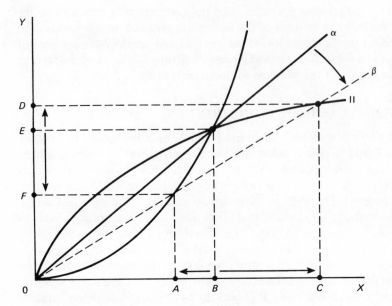

Figure 8-1   Changes in Excess Demands and Excess Supplies

line β. In other words, the price line would move back in the direction of the α-line and this movement will not stop until the price line reaches the original α-line. One can obtain a similar conclusion when the price line originally moves in the opposite direction (the price line gets steeper). Define "stability" by saying that the equilibrium price ratio is (locally) *stable*, if a (small) change in the price ratio from equilibrium causes a movement that brings this deviated price line back to the equilibrium. In the situation described in Figure 8-1, a change in the price ratio from the equilibrium does not have to be small for stability. In this case we say that the equilibrium price is *globally stable*. Note that there is only one equilibrium price ratio (the α-line) in Figure 8-1. When there is more than one equilibrium price ratio, then the concept of local stability becomes important. In general, there is more than one equilibrium price ratio and some of them may be unstable. Figure 8-2 illustrates an unstable equilibrium. In Figure 8-2, when the price ratio moves from α to β, Country 1's excess supply of X increases by AC and Country 2's excess demand for Y decreases by AB, causing a net increase in the world excess supply of X by $AC - AB = BC$. Thus the world excess supply of X becomes positive. This, in turn, causes a further decline in the relative price of X vis-à-vis Y. In other words, point P is not a stable equilibrium point. Note that point P is not a unique equilibrium point. Points Q and R in Figure 8-2 also denote equilibrium points. It can be shown easily that points Q and R are both stable (for sufficiently small changes from Q or R).

The basic premise of the above stability analysis is that a positive (negative) amount of world excess demand for X causes an increase (a decrease) in the

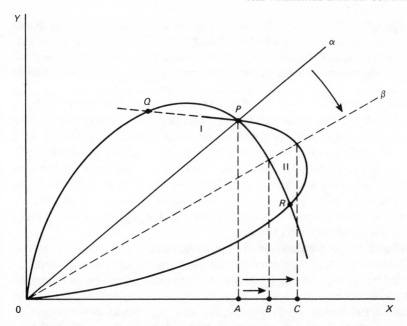

Figure 8-2   Unstable Equilibrium

price of X vis-à-vis Y (that is, P/Q). Hence, if a decrease of P/Q from the equilibrium level makes the world excess demand positive (resp. negative), then the original equilibrium is stable (unstable). Here we can certainly replace the phrase "a positive (negative) world excess demand" by "a negative (positive) world excess supply."

The above premise is the usual assumption made in stability analysis in the literature of economic theory. But there is another assumption hidden in the above analysis, and this assumption is not a particularly common one. It is the assumption that all markets except for the goods markets are held in equilibrium (or brought into equilibrium instantaneously).[9] In particular, we are assuming, in the above analysis, that the factor markets of both countries are held in equilibrium when there is a change in the terms of trade. That is, when the terms of trade move from α to β, we focus our attention on the movement from one point of each country's offer curve to another point on the same offer curve. But if the terms of trade move, then the equilibrium of the factor markets is disrupted in general and it may take a certain period of time before equilibrium is restored in the factor market. The equilibrium in the factor markets will presumably be restored by changes in factor prices, as the equilibrium in the goods markets is restored through changes in the terms of trade or the

[9] Note that the goods market here refers to the market for each good in the world as a whole. This is not really implausible, for we are considering the world in which the goods move between the countries freely without any impediments and transport costs. The factors are not mobile between the countries. Hence, the adjustments in the factor markets and production take place in each country. The role of money markets is abstracted away from the model.

commodity price ratio. Then, in order to analyze the stability of the goods markets, we really have to consider the adjustment process of the factor markets simultaneously. In an extreme case the factor markets may be unstable regardless of the adjustment process of the goods market. Then the above analysis loses its meaning, for the offer curve as drawn above is not relevant.

It is important to make explicit this assumption which underlies the stability analysis leading to the Marshall-Lerner condition. The concept of such a stability, that is, the concept of a stability under the assumption that all other markets are held in equilibrium, is called *imperfect stability* by Hicks [15]. Clearly the above analysis is in terms of imperfect stability. It is sometimes a very useful assumption as it allows us to focus our attention on some particular point of relevance. We shall discuss this topic in the Appendix to Chapter 10. In any case, we shall proceed with our analysis with the explicit caution that our analysis is a kind of imperfect stability.

Let W_x and W_y respectively denote the world excess demand for X and Y. Let P/Q denote the world price of X vis-à-vis Y. In the neoclassical model as represented by the Mill-Marshall offer curve, both production and consumption are considered to be functions of P/Q. Hence, both W_x and W_y, being the differences between the world production and the world consumption of the respective goods, are functions of P/Q. That is, $W_x = W_x(P/Q)$ and $W_y = W_y(P/Q)$ (recall our discussion in Chapter 1, the third section). Moreover, we have

$$(P/Q)W_x + W_y = 0 \,, \tag{8-1}$$

so that $W_x > 0$ (< 0) implies $W_y < 0$ (> 0).

Now, recall the basic premise of the present stability analysis. That is, P/Q increases if $W_x > 0$, and P/Q decreases if $W_x < 0$. Then it can be seen easily that the equilibrium price ratio, say, $(P/Q)^*$, is *locally stable*, if [10]

$$dW_x/d(P/Q) < 0 \,, \tag{8-2}$$

where the derivative is evaluated at $(P/Q)^*$. Since $W_x = 0$ at $(P/Q)^*$, condition (8-2) means that $W_x < 0$ if P/Q increases (from the equilibrium value) and that $W_x > 0$ if P/Q decreases from the equilibrium value. Therefore, due to the basic premise of the stability analysis, (P/Q) will come back to $(P/Q)^*$. Conversely, if

$$dW_x/d(P/Q) > 0 \quad \text{(evaluated at } (P/Q)^*) \,, \tag{8-3}$$

then $(P/Q)^*$ is not stable. In other words, P/Q, if it once deviates from $(P/Q)^*$, will move away from $(P/Q)^*$, however small such a deviation may be. This is due to the fact that if P/Q increases (respectively decreases) then $W_x > 0$ (respectively $W_x < 0$) by (8-3), hence P/Q will increase (respectively decrease) further. $(P/Q)^*$ can be stable or unstable, if $dW_x/d(P/Q) = 0$ at $(P/Q)^*$. Since the derivative $d(P/Q)$ signifies a small change, this stability is *local* stability.

[10] In view of (8-1), condition (8-2) can then equivalently be restated as: $dW_y/d(P/Q) > 0$.

Moreover, the stability condition (8-2) is the condition for imperfect stability, for we assumed away the adjustment process of the other markets. The factor markets of both countries are assumed to be held in equilibrium.

Note that the equilibrium point $(P/Q)^*$ is not necessarily unique. We may illustrate the above concept of local stability by reproducing one of the diagrams from Chapter 1.

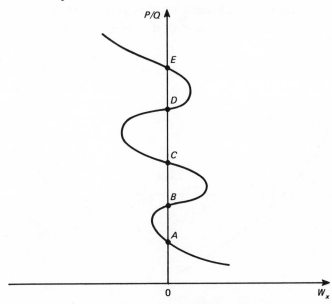

Figure 8-3   The Concept of Local Stability

In Figure 8-3, A, B, C, D, and E are all equilibrium points. That is, at each of these points $W_x = 0$. Points A, C, and E are locally stable and B and D are unstable.

The basic premise of local stability in (8-2) can also be expressed in dynamic terms following Samuelson [45]. First write

$$(P\dot/Q) = k_x W_x, \quad \text{or, equivalently,}^{11}$$

$$(P\dot/Q) = -k_y W_y,$$

where dot ($\cdot$) denotes the total derivative with respect to time. This equation means that P/Q increases (respectively decreases) with time if $W_x > 0$ and $W_y < 0$ (respectively $W_x < 0$ and $W_y > 0$). $k_x > 0$ and $k_y > 0$ are called the *speeds of adjustment* of these markets. Then the equilibrium price ratio $(P/Q)^*$ is said to be (dynamically) *locally stable* if the solution (P/Q) to the above differential equation converges to $(P/Q)^*$ as time extends without limit, when the initial value of (P/Q) is sufficiently close[12] to $(P/Q)^*$. In this formulation

---

[11] The equivalence is due to (8-1).
[12] If (P/Q) approaches $(P/Q)^*$ as $t \to \infty$, regardless of the initial point of (P/Q), then $(P/Q)^*$ is *(dynamically) globally stable*.

we again abstract from the adjustment mechanism in the factor markets. That is, we assume that all the factor markets are stable and their speeds of adjustment are infinite.

A sufficient condition for (dynamic) local stability is again condition (8-2). This is easy to see from Figure 8-4. In other words, if condition (8-2) holds, then (P/Q)-curve is negatively sloped at the point of equilibrium $(P/Q)^*$ as in Figure 8-4. Hence, in a sufficiently small neighborhood of $(P/Q)^*$, $(P/\dot{Q}) > 0$ if $(P/Q) < (P/Q)^*$ and $(P/\dot{Q}) < 0$ if $(P/Q) > (P/Q)^*$, which

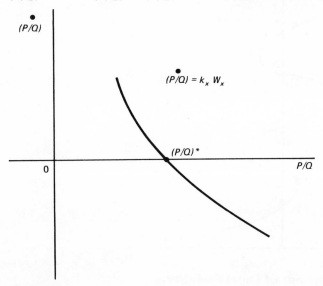

Figure 8-4   Phase Diagram for Dynamic Stability

implies the (local) dynamic stability of $(P/Q)^*$. Conversely, if $dW_x/d(P/Q) > 0$ at $(P/Q)^*$, it is easy to see that the above conclusion is reversed, so that $(P/Q)^*$ is dynamically unstable.[13]

The Marshall-Lerner condition is concerned with obtaining a necessary and sufficient characterization of condition (8-2). We now turn to the task of obtaining such a characterization. Let E_{xi} and E_{yi} respectively be the amounts of excess demand for X and Y in the ith country ($i = 1, 2$). Then $W_x \equiv E_{x1} + E_{x2}$ and $W_y \equiv E_{y1} + E_{y2}$. As we remarked earlier, E_{xi} and E_{yi} are functions of P/Q ($i = 1, 2$). As we discussed in Chapter 3, the exchange rate does not play any essential role here. Formally, let P_i and Q_i respectively be the price of Good X and Good Y in Country i ($i = 1, 2$), and let E be the exchange rate, or the price of Country 2's currency in terms of Country 1's currency. Then, with free trade (that is, with the absence of price distortions such as tariffs, subsidies, and so on) and with negligible transport costs, we have

$$P_1 = EP_2 ; \tag{8-5a}$$

[13] This means that $dW_x/d(P/Q) \leqq 0$ at $(P/Q)^*$ is a necessary condition for the local stability of $(P/Q)^*$.

$$Q_1 = EQ_2 . \tag{8-5b}$$

This implies

$$P_1/Q_1 = P_2/Q_2 , \tag{8-5'}$$

which we write P/Q. (8-5') means the well-known condition that free trade with the absence of transport costs will equalize the exchange ratio of the two goods of the two countries. Note that the exchange rate of the currencies, E, plays no role here. We may call (8-5') the *free-trade condition*.

The budget condition for each country is written as[14]

$$(P/Q)E_{xi} + E_{yi} = 0 , \quad i = 1, 2 . \tag{8-6}$$

We now come back to (8-2), and observe

$$\frac{dW_x}{d(P/Q)} = \frac{d}{d(P/Q)} (E_{x1} + E_{x2}) = \frac{d}{d(P/Q)} \left(-\frac{E_{y1}}{(P/Q)} + E_{x2} \right) . \tag{8-7}$$

Note that E_{xi} and E_{yi} ($i = 1, 2$) are all functions of (P/Q). Here the derivatives of E_{y1} and E_{x2} in (P/Q) are all evaluated at a given equilibrium point, say, $(P/Q)^*$. Define the elasticities η_d and η_f by

$$\eta_d \equiv \frac{dE_{y1}}{d(P/Q)} \frac{(P/Q)^*}{E_{y1}} \quad \text{and} \quad \eta_f \equiv \frac{dE_{x2}}{d(P/Q)} \frac{(P/Q)^*}{E_{x2}} , \tag{8-8}$$

where the derivatives are evaluated at $(P/Q)^*$. $E_{y1}{}^*$ and $E_{x2}{}^*$ also denote that E_{y1} and E_{x2} are evaluated at $(P/Q)^*$. Assuming that Country 1 imports Good Y and Country 2 imports Good X at $(P/Q)^*$, η_d and η_f signify the traditional concept of the *elasticity of the offer curve* of Country 1 and Country 2 respectively. With this concept of elasticity, we may rewrite equation (8-7) as:

$$\frac{dW_x}{d(P/Q)} = -(\eta_d - 1)E_{y1}{}^*/(P/Q)^{*2} - \eta_f E_{x2}{}^*/(P/Q)^* . \tag{8-9}$$

Note that the budget condition (8-6) implies that $E_{x2}/(P/Q) = -E_{y2}/(P/Q)^2$. Since the relation $E_{y1} + E_{y2} \equiv W_y = 0$ holds at equilibrium, $E_{x2}{}^*/(P/Q)^* = E_{y1}{}^*/(P/Q)^{*2}$. Hence we may rewrite (8-9) as

$$\frac{dW_x}{d(P/Q)} = -\frac{E_{y1}{}^*}{(P/Q)^{*2}} (\eta_d + \eta_f - 1) . \tag{8-10}$$

Assuming that Country 1 imports Y and Country 2 imports X at equilibrium (so that $E_{y1}{}^* > 0$), a sufficient condition for local stability, that is, the condition $dW_x/d(P/Q) < 0$, is stated as

$$\eta_d + \eta_f - 1 > 0 . \tag{8-11}$$

This is the well-known *Marshall-Lerner condition*. Notice that, in obtaining this condition, we made no assumptions with regard to the pattern of specialization. The above formula allows the case in which one or both countries

[14] Clearly (8-1) is due to (8-6).

might specialize in the production of one of the goods, although it usually refers to the case in which each country produces both goods (incomplete specialization).

It is also possible to obtain this condition from the Mill-Marshall offer curve diagram. This is illustrated in Figure 8-5. Let P be an equilibrium point (which happens to be unique in Figure 8-5), PT the line tangent to Country 1's offer curve at P, and PQ the line tangent to Country 2's offer curve at Q. It is easy to conclude from our previous consideration in terms of Figures 8-1 and 8-2 that point P is (locally) stable if the PT line is steeper than the PQ line,

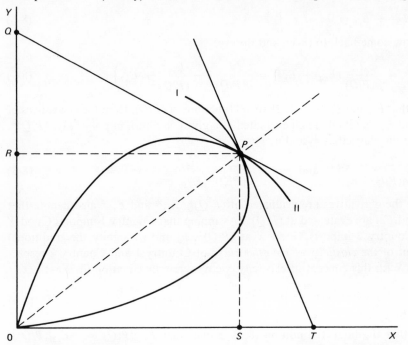

Figure 8-5 A Diagrammatic Derivation of the Marshall-Lerner Condition

which means $SP/ST > RQ/RP$, or $SP/(0T - 0S) > (0Q - 0R)/RP$. Recall now our discussion in Chapter 2, second section (especially Figure 2-10), on the diagrammatical representation of the elasticity of the offer curve. Then η_d and η_f evaluated at point P can be obtained as $\eta_d = 0S/0T$ and $\eta_f = 0R/0Q$. Therefore, using this relation in the above inequality and noting that $0S = RP$ and $SP = 0R$, we obtain $\eta_d + \eta_f - 1 > 0$, which is nothing but the Marshall-Lerner condition obtained in (8-11).

It should be clear that the elasticity of the offer curve, η_d or η_f, is really the result of two different kinds of economic behavior—consumption and production. Hence, it is possible and desirable to rewrite these elasticities in terms of more basic elasticities which are directly pertinent to these two kinds of behavior. This task has been done by Jones [20] and Mundell [37]. Instead of copying their work here, we shall construct the basic two-country, two-commodity trading model and obtain the Marshall-Lerner condition in terms of these basic elasticities. Our model here is essentially a restatement of the one described in Chapter 2, third section, but it is rewritten to fit our comparative statics analysis of trade policies in the later sections of the present chapter. That is, our presentation of the model here has two purposes: 1) to obtain the Marshall-Lerner condition in terms of the basic elasticities, and 2) to state the model in a form which will be more convenient for later analysis.

Let X_i and Y_i respectively denote the output of Good X and Good Y in Country i ($i = 1, 2$). Clearly, all points inside the production transformation curve are producible points, but following the neoclassical tradition we assume that production takes place on the frontier, that is, on the transformation curve. The relative price of the goods determines the point on the transformation curve at which production takes place. In other words, the output of each good in Country i is a function of the relative price of the goods in Country i. We assume that both commodities are produced in both countries (that is, incomplete specialization in both countries). Hence, we have

$$X_i = X_i(P/Q) \quad \text{and} \quad Y_i = Y_i(P/Q), \quad i = 1, 2. \tag{8-12}$$

The cases in which one or both countries specialize in one of the goods can be analyzed analogously, and we shall leave this task to the interested reader. The consumption demand for each good in Country i ($i = 1, 2$) can be expressed as $C_{xi} \equiv X_i + E_{xi}$ and $C_{yi} \equiv Y_i + E_{yi}$. Let U_i be the real income of Country i ($i = 1, 2$), and obtain the following relations:

$$C_{xi} \equiv Y_1 + E_{y1} = \Phi(P/Q, U_1), \tag{8-13}$$

$$C_{yi} \equiv X_2 + E_{x2} = \Psi(P/Q, U_2). \tag{8-14}$$

Φ and Ψ respectively denote the consumption demand function for Good Y in Country 1 and for Good X in Country 2. Using the budget condition (8-6), we can rewrite $E_{x1} + E_{x2} = 0$, the equilibrium condition, as

$$E_{x1} + E_{x2} = -E_{y1}/(P/Q) + E_{x2} = 0.$$

That is,

$$(P/Q)E_{x2} - E_{y1} = 0. \tag{8-15}$$

Equations (8-13), (8-14), and (8-15), together with the production relations $Y_1 = Y_1(P/Q)$ and $X_2 = X_2(P/Q)$, define the equilibrium system which consists of five equations. It is easy to see that under the present neoclassical model U_1 and U_2 are essentially functions of P/Q. Hence, there are five variables to be determined by these five equations—P/Q, Y_1, X_2, E_{y1}, and E_{x2}.[15] It is easy to see that the other variables such as X_1, Y_2, E_{x1}, E_{y2} can be obtained by using the production relations in (8-12) and the budget equations in (8-6).

---

[15] Clearly the determination of these values may not be unique. That is, there can be more than one set of values of these five variables which satisfy the above five equations. This point has already been discussed and illustrated (for example, Figures 8-2 and 8-3).

To sharpen the analysis, we assume that at a given equilibrium, $E_{y1} > 0$ and $E_{x2} > 0$, that is Country 1 exports Good X and imports Good Y, and we write the equilibrium values of E_{y1} and E_{x2} as Y_{21} and X_{12} respectively. Y_{21} and X_{12} then respectively signify the amount of Country 1's import and Country 2's import in equilibrium.

Let B_1 be the excess supply of the foreign currency in Country 1. That is,

$$B_1 \equiv P_2 E_{x2} - Q_2 E_{y1} \,. \tag{8-16}$$

Note that, in view of

$$W_x \equiv E_{x1} + E_{x2} = -E_{y1}/(P_1/Q_1) + E_{x2} = [-E_{y1} + (P_2/Q_2)E_{x2}]/(P_2/Q_2),$$

we have

$$B_1 = W_x P_2 \quad (= -W_y Q_2) \,. \tag{8-17}$$

In other words, the excess demand for the foreign currency is simply a mirror image of the goods market in the present model.

The equilibrium condition (8-15) is obviously a restatement of $W_x = 0$ (or $W_y = 0$), which can be restated as $B_1 = 0$, or

$$B_1/Q_2 \equiv (P/Q)E_{x2} - E_{y1} = 0 \,. \tag{8-15'}$$

This means that our equilibrium condition (8-15) can be equivalently restated as follows: The excess supply of the foreign currency for Country 1 is zero.

Recalling our notations $E_{x2} \equiv X_{12}$ and $E_{y1} \equiv Y_{21}$ in equilibrium, we may rewrite (8-15') as

$$B_1/Q_2 \equiv (P/Q)X_{12} - Y_{21} = 0 \,. \tag{8-18}$$

Or, $B_1 \equiv P_2 X_{12} - Q_2 E_{y1} = 0$, so that B_1 can also be interpreted as the balance of payments of Country 1 expressed in terms of the foreign currency.

Using X_{12} and Y_{21}, we rewrite (8-13) and (8-14) as

$$C_{y1} = Y_1 + Y_{21} = \Phi(P/Q, U_1) \,, \tag{8-19}$$

$$C_{x2} = X_2 + E_{x2} = \Psi(P/Q, U_2) \,. \tag{8-20}$$

Our equilibrium is defined by five equations, (8-18), (8-19), (8-20), $Y_1 = Y_1(P/Q)$, and $X_2 = X_2(P/Q)$, from which the equilibrium values of the five variables (Y_1, X_2, Y_{21}, X_{12}, and P/Q) are to be determined.

In order to facilitate the discussion of the stability of the model, we convert it into "variational form"—the form obtained by differentiating both sides of each equation. Following the convention due to Meade [28], small Latin letters will be used to denote differential changes of the variables. For example, x_1 denotes dX_1. We suppose that each country's currency units are such that $E = 1$, initially, so that $P_1 = P_2 \ (\equiv P)$ and $Q_1 = Q_2 \ (\equiv Q)$, initially, from equation (8-5). Let us also suppose that the unit of measurement of each good is taken so that $P = 1$ and $Q = 1$ initially. Clearly, this arbitrary selection of the units of measurement will not change the conclusions of our analysis.

Since, by supposition, $B_1 = 0$ initially, this convention implies $X_{12} = Y_{21}$ from equation (8-16) and also $p_1 - q_1 = p_2 - q_2 = p - q$.

To convert the model to variational form, we first differentiate our Slutsky-Hicks type demand functions, equations (8-19) and (8-20). To do this we have to consider the (differential) "change in real income." Such a change will be generated in two parts, one part due to price changes and the second attributable to production changes. The change in real income due to price changes is really the difference between the increased (decreased) income from the initial product and the increased (decreased) cost of the initial consumption. In other words, for Country 1, which is importing Y and exporting X, the increased (decreased) income from the initial output due to the price change is equal to

$$\{[(P_1 + p_1)X_1 + (Q_1 + q_1)Y_1] - (P_1 X_1 + Q_1 Y_1)\} = p_1 X_1 + q_1 Y_1 \,,$$

and the increased (decreased) cost of the initial consumption due to the price change is equal to

$$\{[(P_1 + p_1)(X_1 - X_{12}) + (Q_1 + q_1)(Y_1 + Y_{21})]$$
$$- [P_1(X_1 - X_{12}) + Q_1(Y_1 + Y_{21})]\} = p_1(X_1 - X_{12}) + q_1(Y_1 + Y_{21}) \,.$$

Hence, the difference of the two, that is, the change in real income due to the price change, is

$$\{(p_1 X_1 + q_1 Y_1) - [p_1(X_1 - X_{12}) + q_1(Y_1 + Y_{21})]\} = p_1 X_{12} - q_1 Y_{21} \,.$$

The change in real income due to the change in output for Country 1 is simply $(x_1 + y_1)$ (measured in original prices $P_1 = Q_1 = 1$). Hence, the total change in real income for Country 1 is

$$u_1 = (p_1 X_{12} - q_1 Y_{21}) + (x_1 + y_1) \,. \tag{8-21}$$

This relation is very important, for it will also be useful for various topics in comparative statics analysis such as the effects of various trade policies, growth, and so on.

Since our convention of $B_1 = 0$ and $P = Q = 1$ initially implies $X_{12} = Y_{21}$ and $p_1 - q_1 = p - q$, we can simplify (8-21) as

$$u_1 = (p - q)Y_{21} + x_1 + y_1 \,. \tag{8-22}$$

Now recall that equilibrium of the production sector requires that the price line be tangent to the production transformation curve, or $dY_1/dX_1 = -P_1/Q_1$, that is, $y_1/x_1 = -P/Q = -1$. Hence, we have $x_1 + y_1 = 0$, and equation (8-22) is reduced to

$$u_1 = (p - q)Y_{21} \,. \tag{8-23}$$

Similarly, the change in real income in Country 2, u_2, is obtained as $u_2 = (q - p)Y_{21}$. Note that an improvement in the terms of trade of a country (that is, $p - q > 0$ for Country 1 and $q - p > 0$ for Country 2) will, under the present circumstance, increase the real income of that country.

Now we can write the equations derived by differentiating equations (8-19) and (8-20). Writing the change in demand for each country's importable as c_{y1} and c_{x2},

$$c_{y1} = -(Y_1 + Y_{21})(q - p)\eta_1 + \pi_1(p - q)Y_{21}, \tag{8-24}$$

$$c_{x2} = -(X_2 + X_{12})(p - q)\eta_2 + \pi_2(q - p)Y_{21}. \tag{8-25}$$

Here, η_i is the price elasticity of substitution of the imported good in Country i $(i = 1, 2)$ with the real income fixed, and π_i is the marginal propensity to consume of the imported good in Country i $(i = 1, 2)$ with respect to the change in real income. In other words:

$$\eta_1 \equiv \frac{-\partial\Phi}{\partial(Q_1/P_1)} \frac{(Q_1/P_1)}{(Y_1 + Y_{21})} \quad \text{and} \quad \eta_2 \equiv \frac{-\partial\Psi}{\partial(P_2/Q_2)} \frac{(P_2/Q_2)}{(X_1 + X_{12})}, \tag{8-26}$$

$$\pi_1 \equiv \partial\Phi/\partial U_1 \quad \text{and} \quad \pi_2 \equiv \partial\Psi/\partial U_2, \tag{8-27}$$

where the partial derivatives are evaluated at the original equilibrium point. Note that η_1 and η_2 are always positive, but π_1 and π_2 can be negative (the case of an "inferior good").

One important premise in the Marshall-Lerner condition is that the adjustment in the factor markets is instantaneous in both countries. This focuses our attention on the stability of the goods market [as described in (8-2)]. *Under this assumption,* the change in demand for Y in Country 1 and the change in demand for X in Country 2 (that is, c_{y1} and c_{x2}) can respectively be written as

$$c_{y1} = y_1 + y_{21}{}^d \quad \text{and} \quad c_{x2} = x_2 + x_{12}{}^d, \tag{8-28}$$

where $y_{21}{}^d$ and $x_{12}{}^d$ respectively denote the change in the excess demand for Y in Country 1 and for X in Country 2.

In order to simplify our notation, we shall define, following Jones [20], the *elasticity of import demand* for Country i $(i = 1, 2)$, η_i', as

$$\eta_1' \equiv \eta_1(Y_1 + Y_{21})/Y_{21}, \tag{8-29a}$$

$$\eta_2' \equiv \eta_2(X_2 + X_{12})/X_{12}. \tag{8-29b}$$

Then equations (8-24) and (8-25) can be simplified, in view of (8-28), as

$$y_{21}{}^d = -y_1 + (p - q)(\eta_1' + \pi_1)Y_{21}, \tag{8-30}$$

$$x_{12}{}^d = -x_2 + (q - p)(\eta_2' + \pi_2)Y_{21}. \tag{8-31}$$

In order to understand the production side of the economy, it is not necessary to restate the model we used in Chapter 2. The following definition of the *elasticity of production* in Country i $(i = 1, 2)$ will be sufficient. Here we can write $P_i/Q_i = P/Q$ in view of (8-5').

$$\varepsilon_{xi} \equiv \left(\frac{dX_i}{X_i}\right) \Big/ \left[\frac{d(P/Q)}{(P/Q)}\right] = \left(\frac{x_i}{X_i}\right) \cdot \frac{1}{(p - q)}, \tag{8-32a}$$

$$\varepsilon_{yi} \equiv -\left(\frac{dY_i}{Y_i}\right) \Big/ \left[\frac{d(P/Q)}{(P/Q)}\right] = \left(\frac{y_i}{Y_i}\right) \cdot \frac{1}{(q-p)}. \tag{8-32b}$$

Note that in the above equations, $P = Q = 1$ and $d(P/Q) = p - q$ and $d(Q/P) = q - p$.

We may note that the expressions for these elasticities of production in terms of the elasticities of factor substitution, and so on, for a two-factor economy were obtained as equations (2-55) and (2-56) in Chapter 2. Due to the tangency of the price line to the production transformation curve $x_i + y_i = 0$ $(i = 1, 2)$, hence, (8-32a) and (8-32b) imply

$$\varepsilon_{xi} X_i = \varepsilon_{yi} Y_i \quad (i = 1, 2). \tag{8-33}$$

In order to simplify our notation, let us (again following Jones [20]) define the *elasticity of export supply* for Country i $(i = 1, 2)$ as

$$\varepsilon_1' \equiv \varepsilon_{x1} X_1 / X_{12}, \tag{8-34a}$$

$$\varepsilon_2' \equiv \varepsilon_{y2} Y_2 / Y_{21}. \tag{8-34b}$$

Referring to the original definitions of ε_{xi} and ε_{yi} in (8-32a) and (8-32b) and recalling (8-33), equations (8-34a) and (8-34b) can be rewritten as

$$y_1 = \varepsilon_{y1} Y_1 (q - p) = \varepsilon_{x1} X_1 (q - p) = -\varepsilon_1' X_{12}(p - q) = -\varepsilon_1'(p - q) Y_{21}.$$

Similarly,
$$\tag{8-35}$$

$$x_2 = \varepsilon_2'(p - q) Y_{21}. \tag{8-36}$$

It is important to realize that in the derivation of (8-35) and (8-36) changes in output due to the change in the terms of trade (that is, $p - q$) are instantaneous, which means that the adjustment in the factor markets is instantaneous, the basic premise in the Marshall-Lerner condition.

Combining these two equations, (8-35) and (8-36), with equations (8-30) and (8-31) we obtain

$$y_{21}^d = (\eta_1' + \pi_1 + \varepsilon_1')(p - q) Y_{21}, \tag{8-37}$$

$$x_{12}^d = -(\eta_2' + \pi_2 + \varepsilon_2')(p - q) Y_{21}. \tag{8-38}$$

In terms of Figure 8-1, the distance BC measures the magnitude of x_{12}^d and the distance EF measures the magnitude of y_{21}^d. In Figure 8-1, $x_{12}^d > 0$ and $y_{21}^d < 0$. If we denote a change in Country 1's excess supply of X by x_{12}^s and a change in Country 2's excess supply of Y by y_{21}^s, then the distance AB in Figure 8-1 measures the magnitude of x_{12}^s and the distance ED measures the magnitude of y_{21}^s $(x_{12}^s < 0$ and $y_{21}^s > 0$ in Figure 8-1).

Recall (8-15'), and write $b_1^s \equiv dB_1$. Recall also that dE_{x2} and dE_{y1} are denoted by x_{12}^d and y_{21}^d respectively, and that the initial equilibrium values of E_{x2} and E_{y1} are denoted by X_{12} and Y_{21} respectively. Then from the first (definitional) equality of (8-15') we obtain

$$b_1^s = [(p - q) Y_{21} + x_{12}^d - y_{21}^d] Q_2, \tag{8-39}$$

where $B_1 = 0$ initially so that $X_{12} = Y_{21}$.

In view of (8-17), we can rewrite inequality (8-2) in the description of local stability as

$$b_1{}^s/(p - q) < 0. \tag{8-40}$$

To obtain this, simply recall (8-17) and note

$$b_1{}^s/(p - q) = [dW_x/d(P/Q)]P_2, \tag{8-41}$$

where $W_x = 0$ initially.

In other words, the initial equilibrium point is locally stable if $b_1{}^s/(p - q) < 0$. Now using (8-37) and (8-38), we can rewrite (8-39) as

$$b_1{}^s/(p - q) = -\Omega Y_{21}Q_2, \quad \text{where} \tag{8-42}$$

$$\Omega \equiv (\eta_1' + \pi_1 + \varepsilon_1') + (\eta_2' + \pi_2 + \varepsilon_2') - 1. \tag{8-43}$$

Hence the original equilibrium point is locally stable (unstable) if

$$\Omega > 0 \ (\Omega < 0), \tag{8-44}$$

which corresponds to the Marshall-Lerner stability condition obtained in (8-11). Condition (8-44) is a superior statement than (8-11) because it is expressed in terms of more basic elasticities, such as η_i', π_i, and ε_i'. It should also be noted that this decomposition is made in terms of the two basic economic units, consumers (η_i' and π_i) and producers (ε_i'). Comparing (8-11) and (8-44), we can easily note the relations

$$\eta_d = \eta_1' + \pi_1 + \varepsilon_1' \quad \text{and} \quad \eta_f = \eta_2' + \pi_2 + \varepsilon_2', \tag{8-45}$$

which are obtained by Jones [20].

Note that the condition that $b_1{}^s/(p - q) < 0$ means that a decrease (respectively an increase) of the price of the exported good relative to that of the imported good (that is, P/Q) will cause a positive (negative) excess supply of the foreign currency. In informal language this is stated as a decrease (an increase) in P/Q will improve (aggravate) the balance of payments.

In the traditional literature, the Marshall-Lerner condition is often obtained by differentiating the balance of payments equation of one of the countries (say, Country 1), and by defining the "elasticities of import demand" with regard to the derivatives such as x_{12} and y_{21}. In order to see the difficulty of this approach, we summarize its main points. The traditional analysis starts with the following definition of the balance of payments equation:

$$B_1 \equiv P_2 X_{12} - Q_2 Y_{21}. \tag{8-46}$$

Note that the meaning of B_1 is fundamentally different from the one adopted in (8-16). In (8-46) we assume an equilibrium state, while in (8-16) no equilibrium state is assumed. Next, mechanically differentiate both sides in (8-46) and obtain

$$b_1 = (p_2 - q_2)Y_{21} + x_{12} - y_{21}, \tag{8-47}$$

where it is assumed that the unit of measurement is such that $P_2 = Q_2 = 1$ initially.

Impose the following functional relations for the "import demand."

$$Y_{21} = Y_{21}(Q_1/P_1), \tag{8-48a}$$

$$X_{12} = X_{12}(P_2/Q_2). \tag{8-48b}$$

And define the following "elasticities of import demand."

$$\tilde{\eta}_d \equiv -\frac{dY_{21}}{d(Q_1/P_1)}\frac{Q_1/P_1}{Y_{21}}, \tag{8-49a}$$

$$\tilde{\eta}_f \equiv -\frac{dX_{12}}{d(P_2/Q_2)}\frac{P_2/Q_2}{X_{12}}. \tag{8-49b}$$

Assuming that $B_1 = 0$ and the units of measurement are chosen so that $P_1 = Q_1 = P_2 = Q_2 = 1$ initially, we have $X_{12} = Y_{21}$ and $p_1 - q_1 = p_2 - q_2 \equiv p - q$. Hence, we can rewrite (8-49) as

$$y_{21} = -\tilde{\eta}_d(p - q)Y_{21}, \tag{8-50a}$$

$$x_{12} = -\tilde{\eta}_f(p - q)Y_{21}. \tag{8-50b}$$

Then, from (8-47) and (8-50), we obtain

$$b_1 = -(\tilde{\eta}_d + \tilde{\eta}_f - 1)(p - q)Y_{21}. \tag{8-51}$$

Hence, a necessary and sufficient condition for a decline in the price of the exported good vis-à-vis the imported good (that is, $p - q < 0$) to cause an improvement in the balance of payments ($b_1 > 0$) is

$$\tilde{\eta}_d + \tilde{\eta}_f - 1 > 0. \tag{8-52}$$

This is certainly a result similar to that which we obtained in (8-11), and this formula (8-52) is often referred to as the "Marshall-Lerner condition" in the literature. However, we should note the following fundamental difficulties with such a derivation of condition (8-52).

1. Only the balance of payments plays an essential role. There is no explicit recognition of the demand for, and supply of, each good in each country in equations (8-48a) and (8-48b). Also no mention is made of the factor markets. Finally, the equilibrium relations of the general equilibrium system are not clear.

2. The meaning of x_{12} and y_{21} is very unclear. For example, x_{12} can mean a change in the excess demand for X in Country 2 (that is, x_{12}^d) or a change in the excess supply of X in Country 1 (that is, x_{12}^s). See Figure 8-5. Similarly, y_{21} has two interpretations. Equations (8-48a) and (8-48b) suggest that x_{12} and y_{21} correspond to our x_{12}^d and y_{21}^d respectively, but this is not explicitly discussed.

3. The meaning of $\tilde{\eta}_d$ and $\tilde{\eta}_f$ is not clear.

Clearly all these points are related. With proper caution, we may identify condition (8-11) with our condition (8-52) so that we can find the proper answers for the above three points. x_{12} and y_{21} should be interpreted as $x_{12}{}^d$ and $y_{21}{}^d$ respectively, and $\tilde{\eta}_d$ and $\tilde{\eta}_f$ should be interpreted as η_d and η_f respectively. Definitions of $\tilde{\eta}_d$ and $\tilde{\eta}_f$ in (8-49) should be understood in the sense of (8-8). However, the crux of the point is that nothing is clear about the basic meaning of the Marshall-Lerner condition from the above traditional method of differentiating the balance of payment equation (8-46) and obtaining condition (8-52). The proper understanding of the issue requires the consideration of the entire discussion made earlier leading to the condition $b_1{}^s/(p - q) < 0$.

Another way to interpret condition (8-52) is to consider it *not* as a stability condition but as a condition for comparative statics analysis. To illustrate this point, let us suppose that the equilibrium state is moved from one state to another due to a change in the shift parameter. Then the state after the change is an equilibrium state so that the meaning of x_{12} (or y_{21}) is clear. x_{12}, for example, is a change in the excess demand for X in Country 2 *which is equal to a change in the excess supply of X in Country 1*. The part in italics is true only when the new state is an equilibrium state.

Now, following the traditional analysis, let us suppose that the shift parameter is the exchange rate. Differentiating (8-5a) and (8-5b), we obtain

$$p_1 = e + p_2 , \tag{8-53a}$$

$$q_1 = e + q_2 , \quad \text{where } e \equiv dE , \tag{8-53b}$$

where it is assumed that $E = P_1 = P_2 = Q_1 = Q_2 = 1$ initially. Following the traditional analysis assume that the domestic supply elasticity of the export good for each country is infinity, so that $p_1 = 0$ and $q_2 = 0$ (that is, $P_1 = $ constant and $Q_2 = $ constant). Then $p_1 - q_1 = p_2 - q_2 \equiv p - q = -e$. Hence we may rewrite (8-51) as

$$b_1 = (\tilde{\eta}_d + \tilde{\eta}_f - 1)eY_{21} . \tag{8-54}$$

Hence a necessary and sufficient condition for exchange devaluation ($e > 0$) to improve the balance of payments ($b_1 > 0$) is again our condition (8-52). In other words, under this interpretation condition (8-52) is *not* the condition for stability but, rather, a (comparative statics) condition for exchange devaluation although formally they are the same.

However, there is an important difficulty in this approach in addition to the frequent confusion in the literature concerning the sharp conceptual distinction between the stability analysis and the comparative static analysis of devaluation. That is, it is difficult to justify the assumption that $p_1 = 0$ and $q_2 = 0$. This looks justified if a) the output of the export good is a very small fraction of the total national product in each country, *or* if b) there is a Keynesian under-employment situation with a large excess capacity. The first justification is clearly that of partial equilibrium analysis, and the second is not relevant to the neoclassical model. In other words, under this second interpretation our analysis in the present section is irrelevant, and a new interpretation of the elasticities $\tilde{\eta}_d$ and $\tilde{\eta}_f$ together with the construction of a new model is necessary. We shall consider such a Keynesian case in the next chapter.

Confining ourselves to the neoclassical general equilibrium world, the basic difficulty should be clear to the reader from our discussion in the first section. That is, there is no explicit consideration of money in the economy, hence no explicit recognition on the role of exchange rate in the economy. Therefore, it is rather meaningless to consider the effect of a shift of the exchange rate. There is nothing in the model which determines this question. For a further clarification of this point see Chapter 9.

VARIOUS POLICY PROBLEMS

In this section, we treat various policy problems such as transfer payments, tariffs and domestic taxation from the unified analytical viewpoint of comparative statics. The model is that of a usual neoclassical two-country two-commodity trading world, in which money is abstracted away from the analysis. In particular, we shall inherit the model described in the previous section. There are two demand equations, (8-19) and (8-20), and there are two production relations, $Y_1 = Y_1(P_1/Q_1)$ and $X_2(P_2/Q_2)$. The equilibrium relation is denoted by the equilibrium in the balance of payments, or, $B_1 = P_2X_{12} - Q_2Y_{12} = 0$. The prices of the two countries are linked by $P_1 = EQ_1$ and $P_2 = EQ_2$. Our task in this section is to modify this system to accommodate specific policy parameter and analyze the effect of a change in these parameters on the equilibrium values of various variables.

In the previous section we pointed out that the meaning of x_{12} and y_{21} was not clear. For example, x_{12} could be either a change in the excess demand for X in Country 2, or a change in the excess supply of X in Country 1. This ambiguity arises because we supposed that a disequilibrium, that is, a balance of payments disequilibrium, existed after the change in the terms of trade. We shall now suppose that an equilibrium state, a balance of payments equilibrium, exists *before and after* a change in any of the policy variables such as transfer payments. Then x_{12} and y_{21} have a unique meaning since, after the change in the policy variable, the change in the excess demand for X in Country 2 is exactly equal to the change in the excess supply of X in Country 1 ($= x_{12}$) and the change in the excess supply of Y in Country 2 is exactly equal to the change in the excess demand for Y in Country 1 ($= y_{21}$). If they are not equal, the economy is in a state of disequilibrium and the balance of payments cannot be in equilibrium for either country. Thus, in a comparative statics analysis in which we compare two equilibrium states, we can unambiguously use the terms x_{12} and y_{21}.

The Transfer Problem

The first major interest in the transfer problem in this century may be found in Viner's monumental study on capital exports to Canada.[16] The transfer problem

---

[16] See J. Viner, *Canada's Balance of International Indebtedness*, 1900–13, Cambridge, Mass.: Harvard University Press, 1924.

came up again in connection with the German reparations problem. The discussion between Keynes and Ohlin is much too famous [24] [40] to reiterate here. American foreign aid after World War II seems to provide another excellent opportunity to apply these studies. From a purely theoretical point of view, this is extremely important. The pure stability problem, as discussed in the previous section, implicitly contains a transfer problem, for a change in the terms of trade involves a change in the real income of both countries, which is nothing but a transfer. (Recall also footnote 4 of this chapter.) Johnson once remarked ([17], p. 169), "The transfer problem bulks large in the literature of international trade theory."

We now come back to the model we constructed in the previous section. The only major alteration that we have to make here is to include the transfer payments, T, in the balance of payments equation, (8-46). $T > 0 \, (<0)$ means a transfer payment of an amount T by Country 1 to Country 2 (by Country 2 to Country 1). T is measured in terms of Country 2's currency. In other words, we have

$$B_1 = P_2 X_{12} - Q_2 Y_{21} - T. \tag{8-55}$$

Now we shall consider the impact of a change in T on the major economic variables. We assume that the economy is in equilibrium before and after any such change in T. We assume that the Marshall-Lerner stability condition is satisfied. Thus we have $B_1 = 0$ and $b_1 = 0$, a balance of payments equilibrium before and after the change in T. Again we choose the units of measurement such that $P_1 = P_2 = Q_1 = Q_2 = E = 1$ initially. Also $P_i/Q_i = P/Q \, (i = 1, 2)$, so that $d(P/Q) = p - q$ given our selection of the units of measurement. Note also that $p - q = p_2 - q_2 = p_1 - q_1$ regardless of the exchange rate E.

In order to analyze the effect of a change in T, we differentiate our general equilibrium system.[17] For the sake of simplicity we assume that there is no transfer, that is, $T = 0$, initially.[18] First differentiate equation (8-55) bearing in mind that $b_1 = 0$ and $P_1/Q_1 = P_2/Q_2 = E = 1$ initially. We then obtain

$$t = (p - q)Y_{21} + x_{12} - y_{21} \quad \text{or} \quad x_{12} - y_{21} = t - (p - q)Y_{21}. \tag{8-56}$$

In the previous section we noted that a change in the real income of Country 1, in the absence of transfer payments, can be written as $(p - q)Y_{21}$. With transfer payments included, this becomes $(p - q)Y_{21} - t$. A change in the consumption of the two goods in Country 1 evaluated at the initial prices $(= 1)$ is equal to $y_{21} - x_{12}$. In other words, equation (8-56) also tells us that the change in the real income of Country 1 is equal to the change in consumption in Country 2. The change in the real income in Country 2 is $t - (p - q)Y_{21}$ which is equal to the change in consumption, $x_{12} - y_{21}$, in Country 1. This is a reflection of the neoclassical nature of our model, which requires that all the income be spent for consumption.

[17] Differentiate in T, where T is exogenous to the system.
[18] The reader should be able to analyze the case in which $T \neq 0$ initially. Such an analysis will be strictly analogous to the analysis to be presented here, and hence can be omitted.

We assume that the government of the transferee redistributes the amount of the transfer to its citizens in the form of a proportional income subsidy, and that the government of the transferer collects the amount of the transfer in the form of a proportional income tax. This assumption simplifies the problem since it avoids the introduction of a government demand function or possible disturbances in the consumers' demand through a redistribution of their income. Hence, due to this assumption, we can simply differentiate the demand equations (8-19) and (8-20), and obtain

$$y_1 + y_{21} = -(Y_1 + Y_{21})(q - p)\eta_1 + \pi_1[(p - q)Y_{21} - t], \qquad (8\text{-}57)$$

$$x_2 + x_{12} = -(X_2 + X_{12})(p - q)\eta_2 + \pi_2[(q - p)Y_{21} + t]. \qquad (8\text{-}58)$$

Or, using η_i' $(i = 1, 2)$ as defined in equations (8-29a) and (8-29b), we have

$$y_1 + y_{21} = (p - q)(\eta_1' + \pi_1)Y_{21} - \pi_1 t, \qquad (8\text{-}59)$$

$$x_2 + x_{12} = -(p - q)(\eta_2' + \pi_2)Y_{21} + \pi_2 t. \qquad (8\text{-}60)$$

The variational form of the equations representing the production side of the economy is given by equations (8-35) and (8-36). Hence, we have five equations, (8-56), (8-59), (8-60), (8-35), and (8-36), and five endogenous variables, y_1, x_2, y_{21}, x_{12}, and $(p - q)$.[19] The only exogenous variable here is (t). Combining equations (8-35), (8-36), (8-59), and (8-60), we obtain

$$x_{12} - y_{21} = -(p - q)[\eta_1' + \pi_1 + \varepsilon_1' + \eta_2' + \pi_2 + \varepsilon_2']Y_{21} + t(\pi_2 + \pi_1). \qquad (8\text{-}61)$$

Hence, in view of (8-56), we obtain

$$\frac{(p - q)}{t} = \frac{\pi_1 + \pi_2 - 1}{\Omega Y_{21}}, \quad \text{where } \Omega \text{ is defined by equation (8-43).} \qquad (8\text{-}62)$$

A unilateral transfer from Country 1 to Country 2 moves the terms of trade in favor of the recipient country (Country 2) if and only if the right hand side of equation (8-62) is negative. We notice that the stability condition, equation (8-44), requires the denominator to be positive. Hence, *assuming stability* in the goods market and $\Omega > 0$, we obtain the following condition for the transfer problem:

$$\frac{p - q}{t} \gtreqless 0, \quad \text{according to whether } \pi_1 + \pi_2 - 1 \gtreqless 0. \qquad (8\text{-}63)$$

In other words, assuming the Marshall-Lerner condition, a unilateral transfer from Country 1 to Country 2 causes a deterioration in the terms of trade of Country 1 (the paying country) if and only if $\pi_1 + \pi_2 < 1$.

Another important question connected with the transfer problem is the direction of the movement of real income. The classical concern with the movement in the terms of trade is really based upon their concern with the movement

---

[19] The rest of the variables, variables such as x_1 and y_2, are determined from these five variables using each country's budget equation.

of real income. Since the change in real income due to a transfer from Country 1 to Country 2 can be written as $u_1 = (p - q)Y_{21} - t$, we obtain from equation (8-63)

$$\frac{u_1}{t} = -(\eta_1' + \eta_2' + \varepsilon_1' + \varepsilon_2')/\Omega .$$ (8-64)

Since η_i' and ε_i' ($i = 1, 2$) are, in general, positive (unless $\varepsilon_i' < 0$, because the labor supply curve is backward bending, as discussed in Chapter 2), we can conclude that the real income of the paying country always declines regardless of the direction of change of the terms of trade (assume $\Omega > 0$ again).

The Tariff Question

Now let us discuss the age-old problem of tariffs. Many arguments concerning this question have been presented, but two aspects of the problem seem to be somewhat more important than the others. One of these is the effect on the terms of trade of the imposition of a tariff, and the other is the effect of protection on the domestic import-competing industry. The problems of optimum tariffs and maximum revenue tariffs can be obtained as corollaries after we have concluded an analysis of the above problems. Since it is well known by now (especially after a brilliant article by Lerner [26]) that there is a clear symmetry between import tariff and export tariff, we shall confine our analysis to the effect of the import tariff and assume that only one country levies the tariff. The effect of tariff when the other country also levies a tariff can be similarly analyzed, and all other variations or combinations of import or export tax or subsidies can be treated analogously. But none of this is attempted here, since, mathematically at least, they are almost trivial extensions of the case considered in this section.[20]

The imposition of a tariff (or an increase in the level of the tariff) on the imported good would at the outset increase the level of its domestic price. This has impact on two sides—production and demand. For the production side, this would cause a shift of resources from the export industries to the import-competing industries. For the demand side it would generally cause substitution between the imported goods and the exportable goods in favor of the latter. There remains an important question, analogous to the transfer problem, of the disposition of the tariff proceeds. The usual assumption is one of the following: a) The government directly spends the tariff proceeds, in a fixed proportion on import goods and export goods (regardless of the relative price between the goods); or b) The government redistributes all the tariff proceeds to the consumers in the form of the income subsidies. This second assumption

---

[20] Another important problem which is omitted from our analysis is the problem of tariff war. It is the author's current belief that this can be handled more effectively after we have a more satisfactory theory of oligopoly or duopoly. However, we already have an excellent approach to the problem of tariff war. See Johnson, H. G. "Optimum Tariffs and Retaliation," *Review of Economic Studies*, XXI, 1953–54, also reprinted in *International Trade and Economic Growth* (Cambridge, Mass.: Harvard University Press), 1953, Chapter II.

THE MARSHALL-LERNER CONDITION 241

was adopted when we treated the transfer problem in the previous section, and we shall adopt it again in this section. Hence, we do not have demand function for the government and we eliminate one equation. (To consider the effect when the government demand function is introduced is an easy exercise from the mathematical viewpoint.) With this assumption about the manner in which the tariff proceeds are spent, the effect is clear. It would raise the demand for goods through the "income effect" for consumers who received the proceeds as a subsidy, and it would cancel the decline of demand for import goods which resulted from the initial rise in price of the imports for the consumers. The effect of the changes in the domestic price ratio on the production side of the economy—shifting resources from the export industry to the import-competing industry—would again work as the "stabilizing" effect as in the previous two sections. The effect of the foreign repercussion through the balance of payments equation should be considered. As a result, it is not clear, at least offhand, whether the tariff will raise the domestic price of the import commodity relative to that of the export good or whether it will improve the terms of trade for a tariff levying country in the final equilibrium state. Our model again facilitates the analysis by placing the problem in a form analogous to the problem of stability and the transfer problem.

Our analysis here will again be of the comparative statics type. The shift parameter will be the tariff rate. We shall suppose, for the sake of simplicity, that there is only one tariff, Country 1's tariff on its imports of good Y. The cases with other tariffs can be analyzed analogously and hence are not considered here.

Earlier we found that $d(P/Q) = p - q = p_1 - q_1 = p_2 - q_2$. However, with the existence of a tariff, this should be modified. Suppose that Country 1 imposes an import tariff at a rate of $(T - 1)$. Then we have $Q_1 = EQ_2T$, so that $P_2/(Q_2T) = (EP_2)/(EQ_2T) = P_1/Q_1$. Assume that there is no tariff initially, that is, $T = 1$ initially. Then using again the convention of $P_1 = Q_1 = P_2 = Q_2 = E = 1$ *initially*, we obtain

$$p_2 - q_2 = (p_1 - q_1) + t. \tag{8-65}$$

Note that the supposition that there is no tariff initially allows us to suppose that $Q_1 = Q_2 = 1$ initially.[21]

Our problem is to consider the effect of the tariff on terms of trade and on the domestic price ratio of Country 1. The latter question, of course, is really concerned with the conditions under which the import tariff is protective. We shall again suppose the existence of a balance of payments equilibrium before and after the imposition of the tariff (that is, $B_1 = 0$ and $b_1 = 0$).

The basic model will again be that described in the previous section of this chapter. The only basic equations we shall need to change are those linking the prices of the two countries, that is, equations (8-5a) and (8-5b). Then, since

---

[21] If there is an import tariff on Y initially, then $Q_1 \neq Q_2$ and the difference is due to the initial tariff.

Country 2 is the rest of the world, a change in the international price ratio (the terms of trade) is given by $p_2 - q_2$.

The essential point in the tariff question is that after a tariff has been imposed the producers and consumers in the home country base their economic behavior on a price ratio which is different from the international price ratio. Thus, imposition of a tariff causes a change in the price ratio of the home country by $p_1 - q_1$ and it is in response to this change that consumers and producers in this country react. They do not change their behavior in response to the change in the international price ratio, $p_2 - q_2$.

The balance of payments equation, equation (8-46), is not altered by the introduction of a tariff. Differentiation of equation (8-46) with $b_1 = 0$, yields

$$0 = (p_2 - q_2)Y_{21} + x_{12} - y_{21} .\tag{8-66}$$

Note that, as a result of equation (8-65), this can also be written as

$$0 = (p_1 - q_1)Y_{21} + x_{12} - y_{21} + tY_{21} .\tag{8-67}$$

Note that tY_{21} is the tariff revenue received by the government of Country 1. By assumption, it pays this revenue to the people of the country.

With the convention that $P_2 = Q_2 = E = 1$ initially we again obtain $X_{12} = Y_{21}$ from the assumption that $B_1 = 0$. A change in the real income of Country 2 (the rest of the world) is $(q_2 - p_2)Y_{21}$ as before. However, the change in the real income of Country 1 is no longer equal to $(p_1 - q_1)Y_{21}$. We have to include in this change the tariff proceeds, so that the change in Country 1's real income is $(p_1 - q_1)Y_{21} + tY_{21}$, which by equation (8-65) is equal to $(p_2 - q_2)Y_{21}$, the change in Country 2's real income. Note that the balance of payments relation, equation (8-66), also says that a change in consumption (evaluated at the initial prices $= x_{12} - y_{21}$) in Country 2 is equal to the change in its real income. Similarly, equation (8-67) says that a change in the consumption of Country 1 (evaluated at prices P_1 and $Q_1 = 1$), $y_{21} - x_{12}$, is equal to the change in its real income expressed in terms of the domestic currency.[22]

Bearing in mind this remark on the changes in real income and the concept of η_i' ($i = 1, 2$) as defined in equations (8-29a) and (8-29b), differentiation of the demand equations, equations (8-19) and (8-20), yields

$$y_1 + y_{21} = Y_{21}(\eta_1' + \pi_1)(p_1 - q_1) + \pi_1 tY_{21} ,\tag{8-68}$$

$$x_2 + x_{12} = -Y_{21}(\eta_2' + \pi_2)(p_2 - q_2) .\tag{8-69}$$

The equations representing the production side of the economy are, again, essentially equations (8-35) and (8-36). However, we must be careful when we differentiate, because the producers in Country 1 now face a price change $(p_1 - q_1)$ which is different from the price change $(p_2 - q_2)$ faced by Country 2's producers, whereas before they both faced the same price change, $(p - q)$.

---

[22] This again reflects our neoclassical supposition that all the income is spent on consumption.

From (8-35) and (8-36) we obtain

$$y_1 = -\varepsilon_1'(p_1 - q_1)Y_{21} , \tag{8-70}$$

$$x_2 = \varepsilon_2'(p_2 - q_2)Y_{21} . \tag{8-71}$$

Thus we have a system of six equations [equations (8-65) and (8-66), the two demand equations (8-68) and (8-69), and the two supply equations, (8-70) and (8-71)] and six variables to be determined in the system $[y_1, x_2, x_{12}, y_{21}, (p_1 - q_1)$, and $(p_2 - q_2)]$.

Now, combining equations (8-68), (8-69), (8-70), and (8-71), we obtain

$$y_{21} = Y_{21}(\eta_1' + \pi_1 + \varepsilon_1')(p_1 - q_1) + \pi_1 t Y_{21} , \tag{8-72}$$

$$x_{12} = -Y_{21}(\eta_2' + \pi_2 + \varepsilon_2')(p_2 - q_2) . \tag{8-73}$$

Combining these with equations (8-65) and (8-67) we obtain

$$\frac{p_2 - q_2}{t} = \frac{\eta_1' + \varepsilon_1'}{\Omega} , \quad \text{where } \Omega \text{ is defined by equation (8-43).} \tag{8-74}$$

Hence, assuming stability ($\Omega > 0$), an import tariff always improves the terms of trade for the tariff-imposing country (unless there is a phenomenon such as a backward bending labor supply curve which would make ε_1' negative). Condition (8-74) is obtained in this form by Jones [20].

Next we consider the protective effect of the tariff, namely the effect of a tariff on the domestic goods price ratio. Using (8-74) and (8-65) we obtain

$$\frac{p_1 - q_1}{t} = \frac{-1}{\Omega} [\pi_1 + (\eta_2' + \pi_2 + \varepsilon_2') - 1] . \tag{8-75}$$

Assuming $\Omega > 0$ again, the domestic price of the imported good increases relative to that of the exported good *if and only if*

$$\pi_1 + (\eta_2' + \pi_2 + \varepsilon_2') - 1 > 0 . \tag{8-76}$$

This condition corresponds to the famous condition by Metzler [34] which states that the domestic price of the import goods increases relative to that of the export goods if the sum of the domestic marginal propensity to import and the foreign elasticity of its offer curves is greater than 1. We noted this condition in Chapter 3 in connection with the Stolper-Samuelson theorem.

Domestic Taxes and Subsidies on Goods

Finally, let us consider the problem of taxes and subsidies on commodities. The essential feature of this is, as Mundell summarized, that "Taxes on commodities, as distinct from taxes on trade, make it necessary to distinguish between consumers' and producers' price ratios. A consumption tax or subsidy creates a divergence between the price ratio facing consumers in the taxing country and all other ratios, while a production tax causes a discrepancy between the price ratio facing producers and all other price ratios" ([37], p. 92).

Under each category of consumption tax and production tax, there are two kinds of problems according to whether the tax is positive or negative, that is, a tax or a subsidy. Under this there are two sub-categories depending upon which good the tax or subsidy is levied on or given to. Hence, there are eight different taxes or subsidies to be considered (and possibly their combinations). But again we confine our analysis to the problem of tax on imported good as we did in the previous section. We again assume that the tax proceeds are given to the consumers as income subsidies. Since similar analysis is cited in the three previous sections, this section can be brief.

Here again, our analysis is of the comparative statics type, this time with a domestic tax as the shift parameter.

CONSUMPTION TAX   The immediate effect of a consumption tax is to create a discrepancy between the price that producers receive and that consumers have to pay. Let us suppose that Country 1 levies a consumption tax on the imported good, Y, at an *ad valorem* rate of $(T - 1)$, assuming for the sake of simplicity that there is no tax initially. Assume free trade (no tariffs) with no unilateral transfers.

We will denote the prices that the consumer has to pay by a prime $(')$. Then, in variational form, we have

$$q_1' = q_1 + t \quad \text{and} \quad p_1' = p_1 . \tag{8-77}$$

Since Country 2 does not impose such taxes, $p_2 = p_2'$ and $q_2 = q_2'$. Note that a change in the terms of trade (the international price ratio) is $p_2 - q_2$ $(= p_2' - q_2')$ which is equal to $p_1 - q_1$. Equations (8-77) may now be rewritten as

$$p_1' - q_1' = (p_1 - q_1) - t . \tag{8-78}$$

The balance of payments equation, equation (8-46), holds as it is. It is expressed in variational form in equation (8-66). A change in the real income of Country 2 is given by $(q_2 - p_2)Y_{21}$ and this again is equal to the change in consumption, $(x_{12} - y_{21})$. The change in the real income of Country 1 is $-(q_2 - p_2)Y_{21} = (p_1 - q_1)Y_{21} = (p_1' - q_1')Y_{21} + tY_{21}$. By equation (8-66) this is equal to $(y_{21} - x_{12})$, the change in consumption in Country 1.

Bearing in mind that the consumers in Country 1 face a price change of $p_1' - q_1'$ and the above comments about the changes in real income, the variational form of the demand functions can be written as

$$y_1 + y_{21} = Y_{21}(\eta_1' + \pi_1)(p_1' - q_1') + \pi_1 t Y_{21} , \tag{8-79}$$

$$x_2 + x_{12} = -Y_{21}(\eta_2' + \pi_2)(p_2' - q_2') . \tag{8-80}$$

Write $p_1 - q_1 = p_2 - q_2 = p - q$. Then the equations representing the production side of the economy are again equations (8-35) and (8-36). Also, equations (8-79) and (8-80) can then be rewritten as

$$y_1 + y_{21} = Y_{21}(\eta_1' + \pi_1)(p - q) - \eta_1' Y_{21} t , \tag{8-81}$$

$$x_2 + x_{12} = -Y_{21}(\eta_2' + \pi_2)(p - q) . \tag{8-82}$$

Hence, we again have six equations [two for the demand side of the economy, (8-81) and (8-82), two for the production side of the economy, (8-35) and (8-36), and two equations relating the economies and prices of the two countries— equations (8-78) and (8-65)] plus six unknowns to be determined within the system $[y_1, x_2, y_{21}, x_{12}, (p - q),$ and $(p_1' - q_1')]$.

Using equations (8-81), (8-82), (8-35), (8-36), and (8-65), we obtain

$$\frac{p - q}{t} = \frac{\eta_1'}{\Omega}, \quad \text{where } \Omega \text{ is defined by equation (8-43).} \tag{8-83}$$

Hence the terms of trade will normally move in favor of Country 1, assuming again $\Omega > 0$.[23] Since the producers in Country 1 face the same price as the people in Country 2, the above condition also requires that the production of good X be encouraged or increased when Country 1 levies a consumption tax on commodity Y. This will also follow from economic common sense. A subsidy to the consumers who purchase good Y ($t < 0$) will have the exact opposite effect.

What about the effect on the market price ratio, or the price ratio that the consumers of Country 1 have to face? This can easily be obtained from (8-83) and (8-78) bearing $p - q \equiv p_1 - q_1$ in mind.

$$\frac{p_1' - q_1'}{t} = -\frac{1}{\Omega}\left[(\pi_1 + \varepsilon_1') + (\eta_2' + \pi_2 + \varepsilon_2') - 1\right]. \tag{8-84}$$

Assuming $\Omega > 0$, the market price of Y increases relatively more than that of X, if and only if the inside of the bracket on the right-hand side of (8-84) is positive. This condition is stricter than the stability condition (by the amount of η_1'), but less strict than the Metzler condition for the tariff to raise the domestic price of the imports [see condition (8-76)] by the amount of ε_1'.

PRODUCTION TAX   Suppose now that the government levies a production tax instead of a consumption tax. This would work to cancel the stabilizing effect from the production side. Assume that Country 1 levies a production tax on the import good (Y) at an *ad valorem* rate of ($T - 1$). The prices that consumers have to pay will again be denoted by a prime ('). The essence of the problem then, again, is the difference between the prices paid by consumers and those paid to producers. We now have:

$$q_1 = q_1' - t \quad \text{and} \quad p_1 = p_1'. \tag{8-85}$$

Since there are no such taxes in Country 2, we have $p_2 = p_2'$ and $q_2 = q_2'$. Note that a change in the world price ratio is $p_2 - q_2 = p_2' - q_2' = p_1' - q_1' = p - q$. Hence, from equation (8-85), we have

$$p_1 - q_1 = (p - q) + t. \tag{8-86}$$

[23] An explanation of this in terms of simple English might run as follows: The imposition of a consumption tax will *ceteris paribus* lower the demand for this good. Hence, the world demand for this good will be lower than the world supply. Hence, the world price of that good relative to the world price of the other good must decrease. In other words, the terms of trade will move in favor of the country that imports this good.

A change in the real income of Country 2 is $(q - p)Y_{21}$ while in Country 1 it is $(p - q)Y_{21} = [(p_1 - q_1) - t]Y_{21}$. The balance of payments equation, equation (8-65), holds as it is. This equation can also be written as $0 = (p - q)Y_{21} + x_{12} - y_{21}$. In this form, the equation again says that a change in consumption is equal to the change in the real income of the country. The two equations which describe the consumption side of the economy do not change. That is,

$$y_1 + y_{21} = Y_{21}(\eta_1' + \pi_1)(p - q),\tag{8-87}$$

$$x_2 + x_{12} = Y_{21}(\eta_2' + \pi_2)(q - p).\tag{8-88}$$

The equations representing the production side of the economy (equations (8-35) and (8-36)) must be altered slightly in this case. Thus we have

$$y_1 = (q_1 - p_1)Y_{21}\varepsilon_1' = [(q - p) - t]Y_{21}\varepsilon_1',\tag{8-89}$$

$$x_2 = (p - q)Y_{21}\varepsilon_2'.\tag{8-90}$$

Combining equations (8-87), (8-88), (8-89), and (8-90), we obtain

$$y_{21} = Y_{21}(\eta_1' + \pi_1 + \varepsilon_1')(p - q) + \varepsilon_1'tY_{21},\tag{8-91}$$

$$x_{12} = Y_{21}(\eta_2' + \pi_2 + \varepsilon_2')(q - p).\tag{8-92}$$

Hence, using the balance of payments equation, equation (8-66), we obtain

$$\frac{p - q}{t} = \frac{-\varepsilon_1'}{\Omega}.\tag{8-93}$$

Hence, unless $\varepsilon_1' < 0$, as in the case of a backward bending labor supply curve, the terms of trade move against the tax imposing country, provided that the Marshall-Lerner condition holds (that is, $\Omega > 0$).[24] If, on the other hand, Country 1 subsidizes the producers of the imported good (that is, $t < 0$) it will, in general, move the terms of trade in her favor. The effect on the relative price faced by producers can be obtained easily from equations (8-93) and (8-86) as

$$\frac{p_1 - q_1}{t} = \frac{-1}{\Omega}[(\eta_1' + \pi_1) + (\eta_2' + \pi_2 + \varepsilon_2') - 1].\tag{8-94}$$

Hence, with the stability condition ($\Omega > 0$), the imposition of a production tax on the imported good raises the price of that good relative to the price of the other good for the producers in the tax imposing country if and only if $(\eta_1' + \pi_1) + (\eta_2' + \pi_2 + \varepsilon_2') > 1$.

[24] An explanation in terms of simple English might run as follows: The imposition of a production tax will *ceteris paribus* lower the production of that good. Hence, the world supply of that good will be lower than the world demand for it. Hence, the world price of this good relative to the world price of the other good must increase. In other words, the terms of trade move against the country that imports the good.

VARIOUS COMBINATIONS We can also consider various combinations of the production and consumption taxes (or subsidies) and import and export tariffs considered above. Mechanically, conditions for the various conclusions to hold can be obtained simply by putting all of these policy parameters into the model. The analysis then is completely analogous to that carried out above, although it is much more tedious.

However, we can provide some understanding of the basic logic which underlies the more complicated combinations. Suppose a country imposes an import tariff on a certain good. This implies that the producers and consumers of that good in the home country face a new price, which is exactly equal to the old price plus the tariff. Thus, for example, the imposition of an import tariff has an effect similar to the imposition of a domestic consumption tax *and* a domestic production subsidy on the imported good.[25] We can also see that an export tariff on one good has a real effect similar to an import tariff on the other good.[26] Hence, we can summarize all of these relations as follows:

$$\begin{bmatrix} \text{(Import) Tariff} \\ \text{on } Y \\ \\ \text{(Export) Tariff} \\ \text{on } X \end{bmatrix} \Leftrightarrow \begin{cases} \text{(a) Consumption Tax on } Y + \text{Production Subsidy to } Y \\ \text{(b) Consumption Tax on } Y + \text{Production Tax on } X \\ \text{(c) Consumption Subsidy to } X + \text{Production Subsidy to } Y \\ \text{(d) Consumption Subsidy to } X + \text{Production Tax on } X \end{cases}$$

$$\begin{bmatrix} \text{(Import) Subsidy} \\ \text{to } Y \\ \\ \text{(Export) Subsidy} \\ \text{to } X \end{bmatrix} \Leftrightarrow \begin{cases} \text{(a) Consumption Subsidy to } Y + \text{Production Tax on } Y \\ \text{(b) Consumption Subsidy to } Y + \text{Production Subsidy to } X \\ \text{(c) Consumption Tax to } X + \text{Production Tax to } Y \\ \text{(d) Consumption Tax to } X + \text{Production Subsidy to } X \end{cases}$$

In the above summary, the double arrow ($\Leftrightarrow$) is read "has a real effect similar to." The analysis can be extended so as to obtain, for example, a) the optimum tariff formula (which we shall discuss later) as the combination of domestic

[25] Recall that subsidies can be considered as negative taxes, so that production (respectively, consumption) subsidies would have an effect exactly opposite to production (respectively, consumption) taxes.

[26] An export tariff will force the producer of the exported good to accept a price lower than the international price of that good and enables the consumer of that good to enjoy a price lower than the international price of that good. Hence it has an effect similar to that of a production tax *and* a consumption subsidy on the export good. This in turn has an effect similar to that of a production subsidy *and* a consumption tax on the imported good. Hence, an export tariff has a real effect similar to that of an import tariff. The following quotation from Mundell [37] succinctly summarizes this point. "A tax on imports at constant terms of trade raises the relative price of imports in the taxing country and therefore *draws* resources away from export industries into import-competing industries. A tax on exports at constant terms of trade lowers the relative price of exports in the taxing country and thus *pushes* resources into import competing industries. With balanced trade the revenues collected by the two taxes are the same. We may therefore speak of trade restriction or trade promotion without specifying whether the tax or subsidy is on exports or imports" (p. 86). This symmetry was already realized by Marshall, Bastable and Edgeworth. For a brief bibliographical sketch on this, see Lerner [26] p. 306 footnote. Lerner [26] gave a modern treatment on this topic.

taxes and subsidies, b) an expression for the stability condition ($\Omega > 0$) in terms of the effect of domestic taxes and subsidies on the terms of trade, and c) an understanding of international transfer payments as changes in the domestic taxes of both countries.

The above consideration also implies that international agreements for the reduction of tariffs (as in the case of a customs union) are meaningless unless they also include some conditions on the domest taxes and subsidies of the individual countries.

REFERENCES

1. Amano, A., "Stability Conditions in the Pure Theory of International Trade: A Rehabilitation of the Marshallian Approach," *Quarterly Journal of Economics*, LXXXII, May 1968.
2. Baldwin, R. E., "The Effect of Tariffs on International and Domestic Prices," *Quarterly Journal of Economics*, LXXIV, February 1960.
3. Bhagwati, J. and Johnson, H. G., "Notes on Some Controversies in the Theory of International Trade," *Economic Journal*, LXX, March 1960.
4. ———, "A Generalized Theory of the Effects of Tariffs on the Terms of Trade," *Oxford Economic Papers*, 11, October 1961.
5. Bhagwati, J. and Ramaswami, V. K., "Domestic Distortions, Tariffs and the Theory of Optimum Subsidy," *Journal of Political Economy*, 71, February 1963.
6. Bickerdike, C. F., "The Theory of Incipient Taxes," *Economic Journal*, XVI, December 1906.
7. ———, "A Review of A. C. Pigou's Protective and Preferential Duties," *Economic Journal*, XVII, March 1907.
8. Black, J., "Arguments for Tariffs," *Oxford Economic Papers*, n.s. 9, June 1959.
9. Corden, W. M., "Tariffs, Subsidies and the Terms of Trade," *Economica*, n.s. ILIV, August 1957.
10. Elliot, G. A., "Transfer of Means of Payments and the Terms of International Trade," *Canadian Journal of Economics and Political Science*, 2, November 1936.
11. ———, "Protective Duties, Tributes and Terms of Trade," *Journal of Political Economy*, XLV, December 1937.
12. ———, "The Relations of Protective Duties to Domestic Production," *Canadian Journal of Economics and Political Science*, 6, May 1940.
13. Gorman, W. M., "The Effects of Tariffs on the Level and Terms of Trade," *Journal of Political Economy*, June 1959.
14. Haberler, G., *The Theory of International Trade, with Its Application to Commercial Policy* (tr. from German ed. of 1933) (London: William Hodge), 1936.
15. Hicks, J. R., *Value and Capital* (London: Oxford University Press), 2nd ed., 1946.

16. Johnson, H. G., "The Transfer Problem: A Note on Criteria for Changes in the Terms of Trade," *Economica*, n.s. XXII, May 1955.

17. ———, "The Transfer Problem and Exchange Stability," in his *International Trade and Economic Growth* (Cambridge, Mass.: Harvard University Press), 1958 (Chapter VII), an extension of his article of the same title in the *Journal of Political Economy*, LXIV, June 1957.

18. ———, "A General Theory of the Balance of Payments," in his *International Trade and Economic Growth*, Chapter VI.

19. ———, "Income Distribution, the Offer Curve and the Effects of Tariffs," *Manchester School of Economic and Social Studies*, XXVIII, September 1960.

20. Jones, R. W., "Stability Conditions in International Trade: A General Equilibrium Analysis," *International Economic Review*, 2, May 1961.

21. ———, "Algebra of Tariff," (unpublished manuscript), 1959.

22. Kaldor, N., "A Note on Tariffs and the Terms of Trade," *Economica*, n.s., VII, November 1940.

23. Kemp, M. C., *The Pure Theory of International Trade* (Englewood Cliffs, N.J.: Prentice-Hall, Inc.), 1964, especially Chapters five and six.

24. Keynes, J. M., "The German Transfer Problem," *Economic Journal*, XXXIX, March 1929, reprinted in *Readings in the Theory of International Trade* (American Economic Association), ed. by Ellis and Metzler (Homewood, Ill.: Richard D. Irwin, Inc.), 1949.

25. Koo, A. Y. C., "Duty and Non-duty Imports and Income Distribution," *American Economic Review*, XLIII, March 1953.

26. Lerner, A. P., "The Symmetry Between Import and Export Taxes," *Economica*, 3, August 1936, reprinted in his *Essays in Economic Analysis* (London: Macmillan & Co., Ltd.), 1953.

27. Marshall, A., *Money, Credit and Commerce* (London: Macmillan & Co., Ltd.), 1923.

28. Meade, J. E., *The Balance of Payments (The Theory of International Economic Policy Vol. I)* (London: Oxford University Press), 1951.

29. ———, *The Balance of Payments (The Theory of International Economic Policy Vol. I)*, *Mathematical Supplement* (London: Oxford University Press), 1951.

30. ———, *A Geometry of International Trade* (London: George Allen and Unwin), 1952.

31. ———, *Trade and Welfare (The Theory of International Economic Policy Vol. II)* (London: Oxford University Press), 1955.

32. Meade, J. E., *Trade and Welfare (The Theory of International Economic Policy Vol. II)*, *Mathematical Supplement* (London: Oxford University Press), 1955.

33. Metzler, L. A., "The Transfer Problem Reconsidered," *Journal of Political Economy*, L., June 1942, reprinted in *Readings in the Theory of International Trade* (American Economic Association), ed. by Ellis and Metzler, 1949.

34. Metzler, L. A., "Tariffs, the Terms of Trade, and the Distribution of National Income," *Journal of Political Economy*, LVII, February 1949.

35. ———, "Tariffs, International Demand, and Domestic Prices," *Journal of Political Economy*, LVII, August 1949.

36. Morishima, M., "Consumer's Behaviour and Liquidity Preference," *Econometrica*, 20, April 1952.

37. Mundell, R. A., "The Pure Theory of International Trade," *American Economic Review*, L, March 1960.

38. Negishi, T., "Approaches to the Analysis of Devaluation," *International Economic Review*, 9, June 1968.

39. ———, "The Dichotomy of Real and Monetary Analysis in International Trade Theory" (unpublished).

40. Ohlin, B., "The Reparation Problem: A Discussion," *Economic Journal*, XXXIX, June 1929, reprinted in *Readings in the Theory of International Trade* (American Economic Association), ed. by Ellis and Metzler, 1949.

41. Ozga, S. A., "An Essay in the Theory of Tariffs," *Journal of Political Economy*, LXIII, December 1955.

42. Pigou, A. C., "Disturbances of Equilibrium in International Trade," *Economic Journal*, XXXIX, September 1929, reprinted in *Economic Essays and Addresses* (London: P. S. King & Staples, Ltd.), 1931.

43. ———, "The Effects of Reparations on the Rates of International Exchanges, *Economic Journal*, XLII, December 1932.

44. Robertson, D. H., "The Transfer Problem," in his *Essays in Monetary Theory* (London: Staples Press), 1946.

45. Samuelson, P. A., *Foundations of Economic Analysis* (Cambridge, Mass.: Harvard University Press), 1948.

46. ———, "The Transfer Problem and Transport Costs: The Terms Of Trade when Impediments Are Absent," *Economic Journal*, LXII, June 1952.

47. ———, "The Transfer Problem and Transport Costs, II: Analysis of Effects of Trade Impediments," *Economic Journal*, LXIV, June 1954.

48. Sieper, E., "Economic Policy and the Balance of Trade", paper presented at the Christchurch meeting of the Australian and New Zealand Association for the Advancement of Science, Section G, January 1968.

49. Takayama, A., *Economic Growth and International Trade*, Ph.D. Dissertation, March 1962 (University of Rochester).

50. ———, *International Economics* (Tokyo: Toyo Keizai Shimposha), 1963, Chapters IV and V.

51. ———, *Mathematical Economics,* forthcoming.

52. Vanek, J., *International Trade: Theory and Economic Policy* (Homewood, Ill.: Richard D. Irwin, Inc.), 1962.

53. Viner, J., *Studies in the Theory of International Trade* (New York: Harper & Row, Publishers), 1937.

9

THE ROLE OF MONEY IN THE NEOCLASSICAL SYSTEM OF INTERNATIONAL TRADE[1]

INTRODUCTION

In the model that we used in Chapter 8, there is no way to determine the exchange rate of the currencies, E. This is not surprising, for E, being the relative price of the currencies, cannot be determined unless money is explicitly introduced into the model and the absolute prices of the goods are determined. The next question, then, is how to introduce money into the model. As long as the functions of money are limited to the unit of accounting and the media of exchange, then money works only as a "veil" of the real side of the economy, so that there is no reason to introduce money. But if we recognize the store of value function of money, then money is no more a veil. Why, then, should money be stored? Essentially there are two reasons for this. One is the Keynesian speculative demand for money. Money is held instead of bonds in anticipation of a fall in the price of bonds. Here the choice between money and bonds is the essential reason for holding money. The interest rate plays a crucial role in this choice.

The second reason for holding money is in the individual's trust that he can purchase goods in the future with the money stored. Note that the second reason holds even if there are no bonds in the economy. We may consider the function of money in this case as a proxy for future goods. Money enters each individual's utility function just like real goods as the proxy for future goods. Hence, the demand for each good depends on the amount of money held as well as on the prices of goods.[2] If there are bonds in the economy, then bonds

---

[1] I am indebted to Edward Sieper, Takashi Negishi and Akihiro Amano for useful discussions. My indebtedness to important articles such as Sieper [22], Kemp [7], [8], and Negishi [15], [16] is also apparent.

[2] In the literature there is another important reason—that money enters each individual's utility function. That is the convenience in transactions brought about by the introduction of money. For example, see Pesek, B. P. and Saving, T. R., *Money, Wealth and Economic Theory* (New York: Macmillan), 1967, Patinkin [17] also introduced this transaction utility in a different context by emphasizing the lack of synchronization between payments and receipts.

can also act as a store of value for the purchase of real goods in the future, so that the rate of interest also enters in the demand function for each good. But if there are no bonds in the economy, then we may disregard the interest rate in the demand function of each good, including money, assuming, in particular, that money yields no interest.

Following Kemp [7], [8], Negishi [15], [16], and so on, we assume that there are no bonds in the economy, that money is the only means of storing value, and that money yields no interest. In short, we assume that the demands for real goods and for money do not depend on the interest rate. We impose this assumption for the sake of simplicity in order to focus our attention on the role of money. This will sharpen our understanding of the mechanism by which the exchange rate is determined and will illustrate certain important aspects of monetary equilibrium.

In the second section we shall present our model in which money is explicitly introduced and the exchange rate is explicitly determined. The reader will note that the introduction of money essentially increases the number of goods by two—Country 1's money and Country 2's money. Hence, all the conclusions of Chapter 8 should be modified, and the analysis will become much more tedious and messy. One situation in which the conclusions of Chapter 8 hold is known as the case of the "separability between goods and money." The third section is devoted to clarifying the role of this separability. In the fourth section we shall analyze the effect of exchange devaluation after we first clarify some ambiguities left in our model of the second section. The analysis is an exercise in comparative statics. We shall prove that if goods are "gross substitutes" and if none of the goods are inferior goods, then exchange devaluation always improves the balance of payments of the devaluing country, provided that the devaluing country takes a complete sterilization policy.

At the end of this section we shall discuss the case of zero "cross" price effects and point out that the well-known (Bickerdike-) Metzler-Robinson condition is indeed a necessary and sufficient condition for the exchange devaluation problem in such a case. In the last section we shall consider various stability problems, such as the exchange stability problem, the stability problem via the (real) goods market, and the true dynamic stability problem. We shall show that the gross substitutability assumption is sufficient to prove stability in any of these three problems. In the Addendum to Chapter 9, we shall attempt a brief expository account of the concept of separability.

MODEL

We define the following notations for $i = 1, 2$.

E_{xi}, E_{yi}:   The excess demand for X and Y in Country i.
X_i, Y_i: The output of X and Y in Country i.
C_{xi}, C_{yi}:   The consumption demand for X and Y in Country i.
P_i, Q_i: The price of X and Y in Country i.

E: The price of Country 2's currency in terms of Country 1's currency (that is, the exchange rate).

M_i: The demand for money in Country i.

$\overline{M}_i$: The supply of money in Country i.

First we write the budget condition for each country as

$$(P_i C_{xi} + Q_i C_{yi}) + M_i = (P_i X_i + Q_i Y_i) + \overline{M}_i, \quad i = 1, 2, \tag{9-1}$$

or

$$P_i C_{xi} + Q_i C_{yi} + M_i = V_i, \quad \text{where} \tag{9-1'}$$

$$V_i \equiv (P_i X_i + Q_i Y_i) + \overline{M}_i.$$

We can rewrite (9-1) in the following equivalent form:

$$P_i E_{xi} + Q_i E_{yi} + (M_i - \overline{M}_i) = 0, \quad i = 1, 2, \quad \text{where} \tag{9-2}$$

$$E_{xi} \equiv C_{xi} - X_i \quad \text{and} \quad E_{yi} \equiv C_{yi} - Y_i, \quad i = 1, 2.$$

The world equilibrium of each good requires

$$E_{x1} + E_{x2} = 0, \quad \text{and} \tag{9-3}$$

$$E_{y1} + E_{y2} = 0. \tag{9-4}$$

The equilibrium of Country 1's currency requires that

$$M_1 = \overline{M}_1, \tag{9-5}$$

Note that, due to the budget condition (9-2), $M_2 = \overline{M}_2$ is implied by (9-3), (9-4), and (9-5). Equations (9-3), (9-4), and (9-5) define the basic equilibrium relations of the model. Note also that, in view of (9-2), $M_i = \overline{M}_i$, $i = 1, 2$, implies that

$$P_i E_{xi} + Q_i E_{yi} = 0, \quad i = 1, 2, \tag{9-6}$$

holds in equilibrium,[3] or

$$P_2 E_{x2} - Q_2 E_{y1} = 0, \tag{9-6'}$$

signifying the balance of payments equilibrium.[4]

Next we state the well-known free-trade condition

$$P_1/Q_1 = P_2/Q_2. \tag{9-7}$$

Equation (9-8) defines the exchange rate E of the two currencies.

---

[3] The classical "Say's Law" says that $M_i = \overline{M}_i (i = 1, 2)$ holds *always*, whether the economy is in equilibrium or out of equilibrium.

[4] We assume that there is no capital mobility between the countries so that the balance of payments consists solely of the balance of trade.

$$P_1/P_2 \equiv E. \tag{9-8}$$

Note that (9-7) and (9-8) imply $Q_1/Q_2 = E.$[5]

Next we derive the demand functions for each good and for money. To do this we impose the usual aggregation assumption that each country acts as though it were a single consumer. Let u_i be the utility function of Country i. Then $u_i = u_i(C_{xi}, C_{yi}, M_i)$. C_{xi} and C_{yi} are chosen so as to maximize u_i subject to Country i's budget condition as described by (9-2) (for each i). The parameters of this maximization problem are P_i, Q_i, and V_i. Hence, the demand functions are written as:

$$C_{xi} = C_{xi}(P_i, Q_i, V_i), \quad i = 1, 2, \tag{9-9}$$

$$C_{yi} = C_{yi}(P_i, Q_i, V_i), \quad i = 1, 2, \tag{9-10}$$

$$M_i = M_i(P_i, Q_i, V_i), \quad i = 1, 2, \tag{9-11}$$

where C_{xi} and C_{yi} are homogeneous of degree zero and M_i is homogeneous of degree one, assuming the absence of money illusion.

We write the production relations of each country as follows:

(incomplete specialization): $X_i = X_i(P_i/Q_i)$, $Y_i = Y_i(P_i/Q_i)$, $i = 1, 2$; $\tag{9-12a}$

(complete specialization): $X_i = \bar{X}_i$ (constant), $Y_i = 0$; or

$$X_i = 0, \; Y_i = \bar{Y}_i \text{ (constant)};[6] \quad \text{or} \tag{9-12b}$$

a complete specialization for one country and incomplete specialization for the other country.

In all of these three cases we have

$$V_i/Q_i \equiv (P_i X_i + Q_i Y_i + \bar{M}_i)/Q_i = (P_i/Q_i)X_i + Y_i + \bar{M}_i/Q_i, \quad i = 1, 2. \tag{9-13}$$

Recall that $E_{xi} \equiv C_{xi} - X_i$ and $E_{yi} \equiv C_{yi} - Y_i$, $i = 1, 2$, by definition. Then, in view of the homogeneity of functions C_{xi}, C_{yi}, M_i, together with (9-12) and (9-13), we may write

$$E_{xi} = E_{xi}(P_i/Q_i, \bar{M}_i/Q_i), \quad i = 1, 2, \tag{9-14}$$

$$E_{yi} = E_{yi}(P_i/Q_i, \bar{M}_i/Q_i), \quad i = 1, 2, \tag{9-15}$$

$$M_i/Q_i = \tilde{M}_i(P_i/Q_i, \bar{M}_i/Q_i), \quad i = 1, 2. \tag{9-16}$$

---

[5] Or, as we did in Chapter 8, write $P_1/P_2 = Q_1/Q_2 = E$ (or $P_1 = EP_2, Q_1 = EQ_2$) and obtain equation (9-7). In other words, one of the three equations in (9-7), (9-8) and $Q_1/Q_2 = E$ is derived from the other two. Note that (9-2) and (9-8) imply:

$$P_1(E_{x1} + E_{x2}) + Q_1(E_{y1} + E_{y2}) + (M_1 - \bar{M}_1) + (M_2 - \bar{M}_2)E = 0. \tag{9-2'}$$

This signifies Walras' law of the world economy. (9-2) and (9-2') hold whether or not the economy is in equilibrium. Note that if (9-3), (9-4), and (9-5) hold, then (9-2') implies $M_2 = \bar{M}_2$. That is, if the markets for Goods X and Y and Country 1's currency are in equilibrium, Country 2's currency is also in equilibrium.

[6] In order to make international trade meaningful, we may assume that the two countries specialize in different goods if (9-12b) occurs.

We may write (9-16) as

$$M_i = L_i(P_i, Q_i, \overline{M}_i) \quad i = 1, 2.$$ (9-16')

Note that (9-14) and (9-15) differ from the ordinary description of the offer curve due to the term $\overline{M}_i/Q_i$. We assume

$$\partial E_{xi}/\partial(\overline{M}_i/Q_i) > 0 \quad \text{and} \quad \partial E_{yi}/\partial(\overline{M}_i/Q_i) > 0, \quad \text{and}$$

$$\partial \tilde{M}_i/\partial(\overline{M}_i/Q_i) > 0, \quad i = 1, 2.$$ (9-17)

In other words, we assume that the marginal propensity to consume out of the real stock of money is positive for each good including money.[7]

Equations (9-3), (9-4), (9-5) [or (9-6')], (9-7), (9-8), (9-14), (9-15), (9-16) give us 11 equations whereas there are 13 variables to be determined in the system: E_{x1}, E_{y1}, E_{x2}, E_{y2}, P_1, Q_1, P_2, Q_2, M_1, M_2, E, $\overline{M}_1$, and $\overline{M}_2$. Hence, we need to specify two more equations to close the system.

Before we consider these two equations, let us observe that the above 11 equations can be simplified to:

$$E_{x1}\left(\frac{P_1}{Q_1}, \frac{\overline{M}_1}{Q_1}\right) + E_{x2}\left(\frac{P_1}{Q_1}, \frac{E\overline{M}_2}{Q_1}\right) = 0,$$ (9-18)

$$E_{y1}\left(\frac{P_1}{Q_1}, \frac{\overline{M}_1}{Q_1}\right) + E_{y2}\left(\frac{P_1}{Q_1}, \frac{E\overline{M}_2}{Q_1}\right) = 0,$$ (9-19)

$$\tilde{M}_1\left(\frac{P_1}{Q_1}, \frac{\overline{M}_1}{Q_1}\right) Q_1 - \overline{M}_1 = 0.$$ (9-20)

Then we can think of a number of institutional arrangements to specify the two equations necessary for closing the system.

EXAMPLE 1 Consider the case of a flexible exchange rate system where the domestic money supply of each country is fixed. The remaining two equations will be simply

$$\overline{M}_1 = \text{constant} \quad \text{and} \quad \overline{M}_2 = \text{constant}.$$ (9-21)

There are five equations, (9-18) through (9-21), and there are five variables to be determined in the system, P_1, Q_1, E, $\overline{M}_1$, and $\overline{M}_2$.

EXAMPLE 2 Consider the case of a fixed exchange rate system with fiat currencies. Then E drops out of the list of variables. Instead of (9-20) we have

$$W_m \equiv \tilde{M}_1(P_1/Q_1, \overline{M}_1/Q_1)Q_1 - \overline{M}_1, \quad \text{or}$$ (9-22)

$$W_m/Q_1 = \tilde{M}_1(P_1/Q_1, \overline{M}_1/Q_1) - \overline{M}_1/Q_1,$$ (9-22')

and W_m is added to the system. W_m is defined as the excess demand for Country 1's money. As we shall see shortly, W_m also represents the balance of payments

[7] This means that none of the goods, including money, is an inferior good.

(= the balance of trade)[8] for Country 1 measured in terms of Country 1's currency, if the markets of the (two) real goods are in equilibrium. The balance of payments surplus or deficit will, in general, cause a shift in each country's money supply, $\overline{M}_1$ and $\overline{M}_2$. Hence, $\overline{M}_1$ and $\overline{M}_2$ are not constant in general. However, if we consider the case that each country adopts a complete "sterilization policy" in the sense that the link between the money supply and the balance of payments is completely shut off, then we can set both $\overline{M}_1$ and $\overline{M}_2$ constant, that is, we have (9-21). Hence, we have five equations, (9-18), (9-19), (9-21), and (9-22), and there are five variables in the system, P_1, Q_1, W_m, $\overline{M}_1$, and $\overline{M}_2$.

EXAMPLE 3 Consider the case of the classical gold standard system. In this case E is fixed and hence drops out of the list of variables. The international disequilibrium relation (9-22) is changed to the equilibrium relation (9-20) by the "specie flow mechanism," that is, by the free movement of gold. Hence, $\overline{M}_1$ and $\overline{M}_2$ are no longer constant; they move according to international gold inflows or outflows.

$$\overline{M}_1 + E\overline{M}_2 = \text{constant}, \text{ where } E \text{ is fixed.}[9] \tag{9-23}$$

There are four equations, (9-18), (9-19), (9-20), and (9-23), and there are four variables to be determined in the system, P_1, Q_1, $\overline{M}_1$, and $\overline{M}_2$.

In order to understand the significance of W_m, define B_1 by

$$B_1 \equiv P_2 E_{x2} - Q_2 E_{y1}, \tag{9-24}$$

as we did in the previous chapter. If the quantities E_{x2} and E_{y1} are *realized*, then B_1 signifies the actual balance of payments of Country 1 in terms of the foreign currency. Suppose now that the markets for goods X and Y are in equilibrium so that equations (9-18) and (9-19) hold. Then, in view of the budget condition (9-2) and the definition of E, we can rewrite (9-24) as

$$B_1 = (M_1 - \overline{M}_1)/E = -(M_2 - \overline{M}_2). \tag{9-24'}$$

Hence,

$$W_m = EB_1. \tag{9-25}$$

If the economy is under a fixed exchange rate system with a fiat currency, W_m and B_1 are not necessarily zero in equilibrium and W_m thus measures the balance of payments of Country 1 measured in terms of her own currency, provided that the goods markets are in equilibrium. Equation (9-24') states that the balance of payments deficit or surplus itself is essentially a monetary phenomenon. Under a flexible exchange rate system, both B_1 and W_m become zero in equilibrium (presumably through fluctuations in the exchange rate). Hence, B_1 or W_m unequal to zero signifies a disequilibrium state. W_m by definition is the excess demand for Country 1's currency.

---

[8] Recall that we assumed away international capital mobility.
[9] Assume that the total supply of monetary gold is fixed. If this is not the case, $\overline{M}_1 + E\overline{M}_2$ will change.

There are various institutional frameworks to peg the exchange rate (that is, fixed exchange rate) with fiat currencies. One such scheme is to consider an Exchange Stabilization Fund (for example, the I.M.F.),[10] whose function is to buy and sell the two national currencies at a fixed rate of exchange. Each country may have such a Fund, or there can be one international Fund. In any case, the Fund(s) is operated with the cooperation of the two governments so that it takes no risk of exhausting its supply of either currency.

THE ROLE OF THE SEPARABILITY ASSUMPTION

Consider the case in which $\overline{M}_1$ and $\overline{M}_2$ are some fixed constants under the flexible exchange rate system (example 1). Recall the basic equilibrium relations (9-18), (9-19), and (9-20). Observe that in view of (9-24'), (9-20) can be replaced by

$$\frac{P_1}{Q_1} E_{x2}\left(\frac{P_1}{Q_1}, \frac{E\overline{M}_2}{Q_1}\right) - E_{y1}\left(\frac{P_1}{Q_1}, \frac{\overline{M}_1}{Q_1}\right) = 0. \tag{9-26}$$

It is clear that the value of P/Q obtained in the present system is in general different from the value of P/Q obtained in the previous chapter, where there was no explicit consideration of money. Terms such as $E\overline{M}_2/Q_1$ and $\overline{M}_1/Q_1$ in (9-26) illustrate the difference.

To see this more clearly, recall (9-18), (9-19), and (9-22'), and consider the following variables as the endogenous variables of the system of these three equations,

$$\frac{P_1}{Q_1}, \frac{\overline{M}_1}{Q_1}, \frac{E\overline{M}_2}{Q_1}, \tag{9-27}$$

where we note that $P_1/Q_1 = P_2/Q_2$ and $E\overline{M}_2/Q_1 = \overline{M}_2/Q_2$. In other words, the three variables respectively signify the terms of trade, the real stock of Country 1's currency and the real stock of Country 2's currency. Consider W_m as a parameter of the system. Then we have three equations to determine these three *real* variables. In other words, *regardless of the institutional scheme* (such as flexible or fixed exchange rates), the system of equations (9-18), (9-19), and (9-22') comprises a subsystem within a more complete system. It is clear that any change in W_m must in general be accompanied by a change in these three real variables. That is, if W_m signifies the balance of payments, then any change in the balance of payments must in general be accompanied by a change in the real variables including the terms of trade.[11]

With this consideration, all the comparative statics results in Chapter 8, as well as the stability analysis, will in general no longer hold. The question now is, under what circumstances will the results of Chapter 8 hold when money is explicitly introduced into the system. In order to consider this problem, we

[10] See Kemp [7] [8].
[11] I owe this observation to E. Sieper.

introduce an assumption called the *separability between goods and money assumption*.[12]

ASSUMPTION For each i ($i = 1, 2$), the marginal rate of substitution of the two goods is independent of the quantity of money M_i. In other words,

$$\frac{\partial}{\partial M_i} \left(\frac{u_{xi}}{u_{yi}}\right) = 0 \quad \text{for all } (C_{xi}, C_{yi}, M_i), \quad i = 1, 2, \tag{9-28}$$

where $u_{xi} \equiv \partial u_i / \partial C_{xi}$ and $u_{yi} \equiv \partial u_i / \partial C_{yi}$, and u_i denotes i's utility function.

Under this assumption we can show that the demand functions for real goods can be written as[13]

$$C_{xi} = C_{xi}(P_i, Q_i, Z_i), \quad i = 1, 2, \tag{9-29}$$

$$C_{yi} = C_{yi}(P_i, Q_i, Z_i), \quad i = 1, 2, \tag{9-30}$$

in place of (9-9) and (9-10), where Z_i signifies *money expenditures* on real goods in Country i, defined by

$$Z_i \equiv P_i X_i + Q_i Y_i + \overline{M}_i - M_i, \quad i = 1, 2. \tag{9-31}$$

Note that both C_{xi} and C_{yi} are homogeneous functions of degree one in P_i, Q_i, and Z_i in the absence of money illusion. Hence, recalling the production relation (9-12), we obtain

$$E_{xi} = \tilde{E}_{xi}[P_i/Q_i, (\overline{M}_i - M_i)/Q_i], \quad i = 1, 2; \tag{9-32}$$

$$E_{yi} = \tilde{E}_{yi}[P_i/Q_i, (\overline{M}_i - M_i)/Q_i], \quad i = 1, 2, \tag{9-33}$$

where

$$P_1/Q_1 = P_2/Q_2.$$

Hence, if $B_1 = 0$ (or $W_m = 0$) in equilibrium, as in the case of the flexible exchange rate system and of the classical gold standard system, $\overline{M}_i = M_i$, $i = 1, 2$, so that we have, in equilibrium,

$$E_{xi} = \tilde{E}_{xi}(P_i/Q_i, 0), \quad i = 1, 2, \tag{9-34}$$

$$E_{yi} = \tilde{E}_{yi}(P_i/Q_i, 0), \quad i = 1, 2, \tag{9-35}$$

where $P_1/Q_1 = P_2/Q_2$. Therefore, our basic equilibrium relation (9-26) is reduced to

$$\frac{P}{Q} \tilde{E}_{x2}(P/Q, 0) - \tilde{E}_{y1}(P/Q, 0) = 0, \tag{9-36}$$

where we write P/Q, for P_1/Q_1 to ease the notation.

[12] See Morishima [12] and Pearce [18], for example. As Uzawa and Goldman [5] point out, there are three different concepts of separability in the literature. For the relation of these concepts, see [5].

[13] See the last section of this chapter.

This is nothing but the basic equilibrium relation in the neoclassical system noted in the second section of Chapter 8 and the third section of Chapter 1. Equation (9-36) determines the equilibrium value of P/Q. In other words, even if the money is explicitly introduced into the system, the neoclassical equilibrium relation described in Chapters 1 and 8 holds as is, provided that the above-mentioned separability assumption with $B_1 = 0$ holds.[14] The real system and the monetary system can therefore be separated. Separate treatment of the real system can be justified, and all our analyses based solely on the real system holds. That is, the discussions in the previous chapters (for example, Chapters 1, 3, and 8) are justified, even if we introduce the store of value as an explicit function of money (all provided, of course, that the separability assumption holds).

In order to see how the comparative statics results of Chapter 8 hold, let us, for example, take up the case in which Country 2 receives a transfer payment from Country 1 in the amount of T. Assuming that T is measured in terms of Country 2's currency, the budget condition for each country is now written as

$$P_1 E_{x1} + Q_1 E_{y1} + (M_1 - \overline{M}_1) + TE = 0 , \tag{9-37a}$$

$$P_2 E_{x2} + Q_2 E_{y2} + (M_2 - \overline{M}_2) - T = 0 . \tag{9-37b}$$

Hence, the balance of payments $B_1 \equiv P_2 E_{x2} - Q_2 E_{y1}$ is obtained as

$$B_1 = (M_1 - \overline{M}_1)/E + T = -(M_2 - \overline{M}_2) + T, \tag{9-38}$$

assuming that the markets for real goods are in equilibrium ($E_{x1} + E_{x2} = 0$, $E_{y1} + E_{y2} = 0$).

Then assuming $B_1 = 0$ before and after a change in T, (9-38) implies

$$(M_1 - \overline{M}_1) + TE = (M_2 - \overline{M}_2) - T = 0 . \tag{9-39}$$

Now money expenditure for each country, Z_i, is redefined as

$$Z_1 \equiv P_1 X_1 + Q_1 Y_1 + \overline{M}_1 - M_1 - TE , \tag{9-40a}$$

$$Z_2 \equiv P_2 X_2 + Q_2 Y_2 + \overline{M}_2 - M_2 + T . \tag{9-40b}$$

Hence, assuming that the transfer is collected from the public in Country 1 and is given to the public in Country 2, we can rewrite (9-32) and (9-33) as

$$E_{x1} = \tilde{E}_{x1}(P_1/Q_1, \overline{M}_1 - M_1 - TE) , \tag{9-41a}$$

$$E_{y1} = \tilde{E}_{y1}(P_1/Q_1, \overline{M}_1 - M_1 - TE) , \tag{9-41b}$$

$$E_{x2} = \tilde{E}_{x2}(P_2/Q_2, \overline{M}_2 - M_2 + T) , \tag{9-42a}$$

$$E_{y2} = \tilde{E}_{y2}(P_2/Q_2, \overline{M}_2 - M_2 + T) . \tag{9-42b}$$

Therefore (9-39) implies that we again have (9-34) and (9-35), or (9-36). In other words, assuming that the balance of payments is in equilibrium before and after a change in T (as we assumed in Chapter 8), the separability assumption implies that our analysis of transfer payments holds as is.

[14] For a more complete discussion on the role of separability, see Negishi [16].

THE ANALYSIS OF EXCHANGE DEVALUATION

We now come back to our basic relations for monetary equilibrium (9-18), (9-19), and (9-20). We may rewrite these three equations as

$$W_x(P_1, Q_1, E; \overline{M}_1, \overline{M}_2) = 0 , \qquad (9\text{-}43)$$

$$W_y(P_1, Q_1, E; \overline{M}_1, \overline{M}_2) = 0 , \qquad (9\text{-}44)$$

$$W_m(P_1, Q_1; \overline{M}_1) = 0 , \qquad (9\text{-}45)$$

where W_x, W_y, and W_m respectively measure the world excess demand for Good X, the world excess demand for Good Y, and the excess demand for Country 1's money. These three equations determine the equilibrium values of the three variables P_1, Q_1, and E with given amounts of $\overline{M}_1$ and $\overline{M}_2$.

With a fixed exchange rate system, E drops out the list of the variables and equation (9-45) is replaced by

$$W_m = W_m(P_1, Q_1, \overline{M}_1) \equiv \tilde{M}_1(P_1/Q_1, \overline{M}_1/Q_1)Q_1 - \overline{M}_1 . \qquad (9\text{-}46)$$

And *if we can* fix the values of $\overline{M}_1$ and $\overline{M}_2$, then we again have three variables, P_1, Q_1, and W_m, to be determined by the system of three equations (9-43), (9-44), and (9-46). The analysis of exchange devaluation is an exercise of comparative statics, in which E is taken as the shift parameter. As shown earlier [especially in equation (9-24')], W_m then signifies the balance of payments of Country 1 in her own currency.

As we noted earlier, the values of $\overline{M}_1$ and $\overline{M}_2$ are, in general, not constant. Because if W_m is not equal to zero, then this would, in general, change the amount of money supply of each country, hence change the values of $\overline{M}_1$ and $\overline{M}_2$. This is true whether the economy is under a flexible exchange rate system *or* under a fixed exchange rate system. This is easy to see under the fixed exchange rate system, for $W_m \neq 0$, in general. Therefore, unless a complete sterilization policy is taken in each country, the values of $\overline{M}_1$ and $\overline{M}_2$ change according to the value of W_m. Under the flexible exchange rate system, $W_m = 0$ in equilibrium, hence, fixing the values of $\overline{M}_1$ and $\overline{M}_2$ will not usually cause any trouble in equilibrium. But W_m is, in general, *not* equal to zero when the economy is *off equilibrium*. However, in the usual stability analysis with tâtonnement, no actual transactions should be made in disequilibrium (cf. the fourth section of Chapter 10 and also Takayama [24]) so that *no transfers are made in disequilibrium*. This amounts to assuming $\overline{M}_1$ and $\overline{M}_2$ are both constant.

In order to find out the relation between $\overline{M}_i$ and W_m, we have to explore the relations which would precisely define the underlying system in the relation between $\overline{M}_i$ and W_m. To do this, first denote Country i's reserve in terms of Country i's currency by G_i. Then the (accounting) identity between assets and liabilities of the monetary section [assets are distinguished between foreign (G_i) and domestic $(M_i{}^h)$ claims] will yield

$$\overline{M}_1 = M_1{}^h + G_1 , \qquad (9\text{-}47)$$

$$\overline{M}_2 = M_2{}^h + G_2 . \qquad (9\text{-}48)$$

Let $\bar{G}$ be the level of reserves in the world as a whole in terms of Country 2's currency. That is,

$$G_1/E + G_2 \equiv \bar{G}. \tag{9-49}$$

A change in each country's reserve after a change in the exchange rate depends on a change in her balance of payments and a change in the value of her original reserve due to the change in the exchange rate. The latter clearly depends on whether the country keeps her reserve in terms of her own currency, or in terms of the other country's currency, or in terms of something else (say, gold). Let us suppose that each country keeps her reserve in terms of Country 2's currency (say, dollars). We assume, for the sake of simplicity, that the balance of payments is initially in equilibrium in each country.[15] Then we have[16]

$$dG_1 = dW_m + G_1 \, dE \tag{9-50a}$$

$$dG_2 = -dW_m, \tag{9-50b}$$

where, without loss of generality, we set $E = 1$,[17] initially. Since (9-49) implies

$$dG_1 - G_1 dE + dG_2 = d\bar{G}, \tag{9-49'}$$

the above assumption (9-50) amounts to assuming $d\bar{G} = 0$, or, the level of the world reserve in terms of Country 2's currency is fixed.

It is important to notice that a variety of different situations can occur depending on the institutional set-up. For example, each country may wish to hold all her reserve in terms of Country 1's currency, or the international authority (say, I.M.F.) may wish to change the value of the total world reserve $\bar{G}$ (for example, S.D.R.). In the case of the classical gold standard system, the price of each country's currency is pegged to gold, so that $E = $ constant always, or $dE = 0$. Obviously, we cannot then ask such questions as to the effect of exchange devaluation. In any case, we shall leave the analysis of various cases under different institutional frameworks to the interested reader. Here we shall pursue our analysis under (9-50a) and (9-50b). Then total differentiation of (9-47) and (9-48) yields

$$d\bar{M}_1 = dM_1^h + dW_m + G_1 \, dE, \tag{9-51}$$

$$d\bar{M}_2 = dM_2^h - dW_m. \tag{9-52}$$

If we assume that the two countries fix the level of M_1^h and M_2^h, we obtain $dM_1^h = dM_2^h = 0$ so that[18]

[15] As remarked earlier, if the markets for goods X and Y and one of the currencies are in equilibrium, then the market for the other currency is automatically in equilibrium due to (9-2').

[16] The term $G_1 dE$ in the RHS of (9-50a) is obtained by $(G_1/E)(E + dE) - G_1 = G_1 dE$.

[17] In (9-50) it is tacitly assumed that G_1 and G_2 are sufficiently large so that the balance of payments deficit or surplus does not cause negative reserve of each country.

[18] In other words, Country 1's money supply increases due to an improvement of her balance of payments and to an increase in the value of her reserve (which is held in terms of Country 2's currency). Note that our result will be different if Country 1 holds her reserve in terms of her own currency. This point is more or less ignored or forgotten in some literature.

$$d\overline{M}_1 = dW_m + G_1\, dE, \tag{9-53}$$

$$d\overline{M}_2 = -dW_m. \tag{9-54}$$

Instead, we may assume that Country i adjusts the quantity of M_i^h so that

$$d\overline{M}_1 = s_1(dW_m + G_1\, dE) \tag{9-55}$$

$$d\overline{M}_2 = -s_2\, dW_m, \tag{9-56}$$

where we call s_i the *sterilization coefficient* of Country i ($i = 1, 2$). Obviously, we have the following definitional relations:

$$dM_1^h = (s_1 - 1)(dW_m + G_1\, dE) \quad \text{and} \quad dM_2^h = -(s_2 - 1)\, dW_m. \tag{9-57}$$

$s_i = 0$ and $s_i = 1$ respectively signify complete sterilization[19] and no sterilization of Country i. Equations in (9-57) specify the amount of each monetary authority's induced change in money supply which is implied by the sterilization coefficient s_1 or s_2. If we want to allow an autonomous change in money supplies, then (9-54) and (9-55) are generalized as

$$d\overline{M}_1 = d\overline{M}_1^h + s_1(dW_m + G_1\, dE), \tag{9-58}$$

$$d\overline{M}_2 = d\overline{M}_2^h - s_2\, dW_m. \tag{9-59}$$

We may call $\overline{M}_i^h$ the *domestically controlled money supply* (net of sterilization policy) for Country i ($i = 1, 2$). This will be the crucial variable when we discuss the effect of monetary policy (see Chapter 11). Here we simply assume that $\overline{M}_1^h$ and $\overline{M}_2^h$ are fixed.

Using the model developed above we can analyze both the exchange stability problem and the exchange devaluation problem. Here we take up the exchange devaluation problem. In other words, we are concerned with a comparative statics problem of analyzing the effect of a change of E. The variables in the model are P_1, Q_1, W_m, $\overline{M}_1$, and $\overline{M}_2$, where E is a shift parameter. Totally differentiating (9-43), (9-44), and (9-46), we obtain

$$a_{11}\, dP_1 + a_{12}\, dQ_1 + a_{13}\, dE + a_{14}\, d\overline{M}_1 + a_{15}\, d\overline{M}_2 = 0, \tag{9-60}$$

$$a_{21}\, dP_1 + a_{22}\, dQ_1 + a_{23}\, dE + a_{24}\, d\overline{M}_1 + a_{25}\, d\overline{M}_2 = 0, \tag{9-61}$$

$$a_{31}\, dP_1 + a_{32}\, dQ_1 + a_{33}\, d\overline{M}_1 = dW_m, \tag{9-62}$$

where the a_{ij}s are defined by

$$\left. \begin{array}{lll} a_{11} \equiv \partial W_x/\partial P_1, & a_{12} \equiv \partial W_x/\partial Q_1, & a_{13} \equiv \partial W_x/\partial E, \\[4pt] a_{14} \equiv \partial W_x/\partial \overline{M}_1, & a_{15} \equiv \partial W_x/\partial \overline{M}_2, & a_{21} \equiv \partial W_y/\partial P_1, \\[4pt] a_{22} \equiv \partial W_y/\partial Q_1, & a_{23} \equiv \partial W_y/\partial E, & a_{24} \equiv \partial W_y/\partial \overline{M}_1, \\[4pt] a_{25} \equiv \partial W_y/\partial \overline{M}_2, & a_{31} \equiv \partial W_m/\partial P_1, & a_{32} \equiv \partial W_m/\partial Q_1, \\[4pt] a_{33} \equiv \partial W_m/\partial \overline{M}_1, & & \end{array} \right\} \tag{9-63}$$

[19] Kemp [7] and [8] focused his analysis mainly to the case in which $s_1 = s_2 = 1$. He called the result under this case a "short-run" effect or the "impact effect". However, there does not seem any reason to believe that such a case is always short-run. We may instead think the sterilization policy takes some time. Hence Kemp's "short-run" case may in fact be a "long-run" case.

and where all the partial derivatives are evaluated at the original equilibrium point. There are now five equations, (9-60), (9-61), (9-62), (9-50), and (9-51), which determine the five variables dP_1, dQ_1, $d\overline{M}_1$, $d\overline{M}_2$, and dW_m. Our task is to ascertain the values and the signs of dW_m/dE, dP_1/dE, dQ_1/dE, and so on. Concerning the signs of the a_{ij}s we have, in view of (9-17),[20]

$$a_{13} > 0, \quad a_{23} > 0, \quad a_{14} > 0, \quad a_{15} > 0, \quad a_{24} > 0, \quad a_{25} > 0, \quad \text{and}$$

$$a_{33} > 0. \tag{9-64}$$

Using (9-55) and (9-56), we can rewrite (9-60), (9-61), and (9-62) as

$$a_{11}\, dP_1 + a_{12}\, dQ_1 + a_{13}{}'\, dE + a_{14}{}'\, dW_m = 0, \tag{9-65}$$

$$a_{21}\, dP_1 + a_{22}\, dQ_1 + a_{23}{}'\, dE + a_{24}{}'\, dW_m = 0, \tag{9-66}$$

$$a_{31}\, dP_1 + a_{32}\, dQ_1 + a_{33}{}'\, dE + a_{34}\, dW_m = 0, \tag{9-67}$$

where $a_{13}{}'$, $a_{14}{}'$, $a_{23}{}'$, $a_{24}{}'$, $a_{33}{}'$, and a_{34} are defined by

$$a_{13}{}' \equiv a_{13} + s_1 a_{14} G_1, \quad a_{14}{}' \equiv s_1 a_{14} - s_2 a_{15}, \tag{9-68}$$

$$a_{23}{}' \equiv a_{23} + s_1 a_{24} G_1, \quad a_{24}{}' \equiv s_1 a_{24} - s_2 a_{25}, \tag{9-69}$$

$$a_{33}{}' \equiv s_1 a_{33} G_1, \qquad a_{34} \equiv s_1 a_{33} - 1. \tag{9-70}$$

Solving equations (9-65), (9-66), (9-67) with respect to dP_1, dQ_1, dW_m, we obtain

$$\frac{dP_1}{dE} = -\frac{1}{\Delta} \begin{vmatrix} a_{13}{}' & a_{12} & a_{14}{}' \\ a_{23}{}' & a_{22} & a_{24}{}' \\ a_{33}{}' & a_{32} & a_{34} \end{vmatrix}, \tag{9-71}$$

$$\frac{dQ_1}{dE} = -\frac{1}{\Delta} \begin{vmatrix} a_{11} & a_{13}{}' & a_{14}{}' \\ a_{21} & a_{23}{}' & a_{24}{}' \\ a_{31} & a_{33}{}' & a_{34} \end{vmatrix}, \tag{9-72}$$

$$\frac{dW_m}{dE} = -\frac{1}{\Delta} \begin{vmatrix} a_{11} & a_{12} & a_{13}{}' \\ a_{21} & a_{22} & a_{23}{}' \\ a_{31} & a_{32} & a_{33}{}' \end{vmatrix}, \tag{9-73}$$

where

$$\Delta \equiv \begin{vmatrix} a_{11} & a_{12} & a_{14}{}' \\ a_{21} & a_{22} & a_{24}{}' \\ a_{31} & a_{32} & a_{34} \end{vmatrix}. \tag{9-74}$$

Clearly a necessary and sufficient condition for Country 1's devaluation to improve her balance of payments is that the *RHS* of (9-73) is positive. This condition depends, among others, on the relative magnitude of s_1 and s_2. To

[20] Just like (9-17), (9-64) essentially says that none of the goods (including money) are inferior goods.

sharpen our analysis we assume that Country 1 adopts a complete sterilization policy, $s_1 = 0$.[21] Then we have

$$a_{13}' = a_{13}, \quad a_{14}' = -s_2 a_{25}, \quad a_{23}' = a_{23}, \quad a_{24}' = -s_2 a_{25}, \quad a_{33}' = 0) \tag{9-75}$$

Then we can simplify (9-71), (9-72), and (9-73) considerably as

$$\frac{dP_1}{dE} = \frac{-1}{\Delta_1} \left[(a_{13}a_{22} - a_{23}a_{12}) + (a_{14}'a_{22} - a_{24}'a_{12}) \frac{dW_m}{dE} \right], \tag{9-76}$$

$$\frac{dQ_1}{dE} = \frac{-1}{\Delta_1} \left[(a_{11}a_{23} - a_{21}a_{13}) + (a_{11}a_{24}' - a_{21}a_{14}') \frac{dW_m}{dE} \right], \tag{9-77}$$

$$\frac{dW_m}{dE} = \frac{\alpha}{\beta}, \tag{9-78}$$

where Δ_1, α and β are defined by

$$\Delta_1 \equiv a_{11}a_{22} - a_{21}a_{12}, \tag{9-79}$$

$$\alpha \equiv a_{31}(a_{13}a_{22} - a_{23}a_{12}) + a_{32}(a_{11}a_{23} - a_{21}a_{13}), \tag{9-80}$$

$$\beta \equiv a_{34}\Delta_1 - [a_{31}(a_{14}'a_{22} - a_{24}'a_{12}) + a_{32}(a_{11}a_{24}' - a_{21}a_{14}')]. \tag{9-81}$$

Hence, a necessary and sufficient condition that Country 1's devaluation will improve Country 1's balance of payments is

$$\frac{\alpha}{\beta} > 0. \tag{9-82}$$

In order to sharpen this condition, we have to consider the signs of the a_{ij}s further. First we shall see the implication of the homogeneity of excess demand functions. For this purpose, write

$$D_{x1}(P_1, Q_1, \overline{M}_1) \equiv E_{x1}(P_1/Q_1, \overline{M}_1/Q_1), \tag{9-83}$$

$$D_{y1}(P_1, Q_1, \overline{M}_1) \equiv E_{y1}(P_1/Q_1, \overline{M}_1/Q_1), \tag{9-84}$$

$$L_1(P_1, Q_1, \overline{M}_1) \equiv \tilde{M}_1(P_1/Q_1, \overline{M}_1/Q_1)Q_1, \tag{9-85}$$

where D_{x1} and D_{y1} (L_1) are all homogeneous functions of degree zero (one) with respect to P_1, Q_1, and $\overline{M}_1$. Define

$$b_{11} \equiv \partial D_{x1}/\partial P_1, \quad b_{12} \equiv \partial D_{x1}/\partial Q_1, \quad b_{14} \equiv \partial D_{x1}/\partial \overline{M}_1, \tag{9-86}$$

$$b_{21} \equiv \partial D_{y1}/\partial P_1, \quad b_{22} \equiv \partial D_{y1}/\partial Q_1, \quad b_{24} \equiv \partial D_{y1}/\partial \overline{M}_1, \tag{9-87}$$

$$b_{31} \equiv \partial L_1/\partial P_1, \quad b_{32} \equiv \partial L_1/\partial Q_1, \quad b_{33} \equiv \partial L_1/\partial \overline{M}_1, \tag{9-88}$$

[21] Alternatively, we may assume $G_1 = 0$ (Country 1's initial reserve is zero) and carry out a similar analysis.

where the partial derivatives are evaluated at the original equilibrium point. In view of the homogeneity, we have

$$b_{11}P_1 + b_{12}Q_1 + b_{14}\overline{M}_1 = 0, \tag{9-89}$$

$$b_{21}P_1 + b_{22}Q_1 + b_{24}\overline{M}_1 = 0, \tag{9-90}$$

$$b_{31}P_1 + b_{32}Q_1 + b_{33}\overline{M}_1 = L_1, \tag{9-91}$$

where $(P_1, Q_1, \overline{M}_1)$ is the initial equilibrium point. Without loss of generality, we can set $P_1 = Q_1 = E = P_2 = Q_2 = 1$ initially. Since b_{14} and b_{24} are positive by (9-17), (9-89) and (9-90) imply

$$b_{11} + b_{12} < 0 \quad \text{and} \quad b_{21} + b_{22} < 0. \tag{9-92}$$

Also, from (9-91),

$$b_{31} + b_{32} = \overline{M}_1(1 - b_{33}), \tag{9-93}$$

since $L_1 = \overline{M}_1$ is the initial equilibrium.
  Write

$$D_{x2}(P_1, Q_1, E, \overline{M}_2) \equiv E_{x2}(P_1/Q_1, E\overline{M}_2/Q_1), \tag{9-94}$$

$$D_{y2}(P_1, Q_1, E, \overline{M}_2) \equiv E_{y2}(P_1/Q_1, E\overline{M}_2/Q_1). \tag{9-95}$$

Clearly, D_{x2} and D_{y2} are homogeneous of degree zero in P_1, Q_1, and $\overline{M}_2$. Define

$$b_{11}' \equiv \partial D_{x2}/\partial P_1, \quad b_{12}' \equiv \partial D_{x2}/\partial Q_1, \quad b_{15}' \equiv \partial D_{x2}/\partial \overline{M}_2, \tag{9-96}$$

$$b_{21}' \equiv \partial D_{y2}/\partial P_1, \quad b_{22}' \equiv \partial D_{y2}/\partial Q_1, \quad b_{25}' \equiv \partial D_{y2}/\partial \overline{M}_2. \tag{9-97}$$

Noting the Euler equation again as above, we obtain

$$b_{11}' + b_{12}' < 0, \quad b_{21}' + b_{22}' < 0. \tag{9-98}$$

Since $a_{11} = b_{11} + b_{11}'$, $a_{12} = b_{12} + b_{12}'$, $a_{21} = b_{21} + b_{21}'$, and $a_{22} = b_{22} + b_{22}'$,

$$a_{11} + a_{12} < 0 \quad \text{and} \quad a_{21} + a_{22} < 0. \tag{9-99}$$

  Following Hahn [6] and Kemp [7] [8], we may impose the following assumption:[22]

$$a_{11} < 0, \quad a_{12} > 0, \quad a_{21} > 0, \quad a_{22} < 0, \quad b_{31} > 0, \quad b_{32} > 0, \tag{9-100}$$

which we call the *gross substitutability assumption*. Except that this assumption incorporates production, it corresponds to the assumption that all goods

---

[22] Note that $a_{11} < 0$ and $a_{22} < 0$ are implied by $a_{12} > 0$ and $a_{21} > 0$ in view of (9-99). More basically gross substitutability may be defined in terms of b_{ij}s ($b_{11} < 0$, $b_{12} > 0$, $b_{21} > 0$, $b_{22} < 0$, $b_{11}' < 0$, $b_{12}' > 0$, $b_{21}' > 0$, $b_{22}' < 0$, $b_{31} > 0$, $b_{32} > 0$). Then, in view of the homogeneity and the non-inferior goods assumption, we obtain $b_{14} > 0$, $b_{15}' > 0$. $b_{24} > 0$, $b_{25}' > 0$, $b_{33} > 0$.

(Good X, Good Y and money) are "gross substitutes," the definition of which appears in the literature concerning the stability of competitive markets.[23]

Since $W_m \equiv L_1 - \overline{M}_1$, we have

$$a_{31} = b_{31}, \quad a_{32} = b_{32} \quad \text{and} \quad a_{33} = b_{33} - 1. \tag{9-101}$$

Hence, in view of (9-88), we obtain

$$a_{31} + a_{32} = -\overline{M}_1 a_{33}, \tag{9-102}$$

so that the gross substitutability assumption (in particular, $a_{31} > 0$ and $a_{32} > 0$) is consistent with the earlier assumption $a_{33} < 0$ in (9-64). In view of (9-70), $a_{33} < 0$ implies

$$a_{34} < 0. \tag{9-103}$$

Hence, using the sign conditions (9-64) and (9-100), we can assert from (9-80) that

$$\alpha < 0. \tag{9-104}$$

Therefore, condition (9-82) is reduced to $\beta < 0$, or

$$a_{34} \Delta_1 - [a_{31}(a_{14}'a_{22} - a_{24}'a_{12}) + a_{32}(a_{11}a_{24}' - a_{21}a_{14}')] < 0, \tag{9-105}$$

which signifies a necessary and sufficient condition for Country 1's devaluation to improve her balance of payments. We may call (9-105) the *devaluation condition*.

The sign of Δ_1 can be determined, in view of (9-79), (9-99), and (9-100), as

$$\Delta_1 > 0. \tag{9-106}$$

Therefore, a sufficient condition for Country 1's devaluation to improve her balance of payments is:

$$a_{31}(a_{14}'a_{22} - a_{24}'a_{12}) + a_{32}(a_{11}a_{24}' - a_{21}a_{14}') \geqq 0, \tag{9-107}$$

which can be rewritten in the following equivalent form:

$$a_{14}'(a_{31}a_{22} - a_{32}a_{21}) + a_{24}'(a_{32}a_{11} - a_{31}a_{12}) \geqq 0. \tag{9-108}$$

Since $a_{14}' \leqq 0$ and $a_{24}' \leqq 0$, then our sign conditions (9-64) and (9-100) imply that condition (9-108) is always satisfied. In other words, Country 1's devaluation always improves her balance of payments if Country 1 takes a complete sterilization policy ($s_1 = 0$) and if the gross substitutability assumption holds. This is a generalization of Kemp [8], in which he assumes both s_1 and s_2 are zero.

Now let us analyze the effect of devaluation on the price of the goods. Using (9-76) and (9-77) we can easily conclude that

$$dP_1/dE > 0, \quad dQ_1/dE > 0, \tag{9-109}$$

---

[23] See Negishi [14], or Takayama [24], for a survey of the stability of competitive markets.

provided that $dW_m/dE \geq 0$. Hence, if $s_1 = 0$, for example, the prices of both X and Y always increase. That is, under any choice of price index (or any nonnegative combination of the prices of the real goods), Country 1's devaluation always increases her price index, provided that she takes a complete sterilization policy.

Set $P_1 = Q_1 = 1$ initially without loss of generality. Then we can easily obtain the expression for the change in the terms of trade, $d(P_1/Q_1) = dP_1 - dQ_1$, as

$$d(P_1/Q_1)/dE = -\frac{1}{\Delta_1} \left\{ [a_{13}(a_{22} + a_{21}) - a_{23}(a_{12} + a_{11})] \right.$$
$$\left. + [a_{14}'(a_{22} + a_{21}) - a_{24}'(a_{12} + a_{11})] \frac{dW_m}{dE} \right\}, \qquad (9\text{-}110)$$

which can be either positive or negative. In other words, although Country 1's devaluation always improves her balance of payments with $s_1 = 0$, the terms of trade may move in either direction. When $s_1 > 0$, then we cannot even conclude that Country 1's devaluation always improves her balance of payments.

Let us consider the case in which no sterilization policies are taken in both countries, so that (9-53) and (9-54) replace (9-55) and (9-56). Then our system of equations (9-65), (9-66), (9-67) are modified as follows:

$$a_{11}\, dP_1 + a_{12}\, dQ_1 + a_{13}''\, dE + a_{14}''\, dW_m = 0\,, \qquad (9\text{-}111)$$

$$a_{21}\, dP_1 + a_{22}\, dQ_1 + a_{23}''\, dE + a_{24}''\, dW_m = 0\,, \qquad (9\text{-}112)$$

$$a_{31}\, dP_1 + a_{32}\, dQ_1 + a_{33}''\, dE + a_{34}'\, dW_m = 0\,, \qquad (9\text{-}113)$$

where

$$a_{13}'' \equiv a_{13} + a_{14}G_1\,, \quad a_{14}'' \equiv a_{14} - a_{15}\,, \qquad (9\text{-}114)$$

$$a_{23}'' \equiv a_{23} + a_{24}G_1\,, \quad a_{24}'' \equiv a_{24} - a_{25}\,, \qquad (9\text{-}115)$$

$$a_{33}'' \equiv a_{33}G_1\,, \qquad\qquad a_{34}' \equiv a_{33} - 1\,. \qquad (9\text{-}116)$$

Solving (9-111), (9-112), and (9-113) with respect to dW_m (as well as dP_1 and dQ_1), we obtain

$$\frac{dW_m}{dE} = -\frac{1}{\Delta^*} \begin{vmatrix} a_{11} & a_{12} & a_{13}'' \\ a_{21} & a_{22} & a_{23}'' \\ a_{31} & a_{32} & a_{33}'' \end{vmatrix} \qquad (9\text{-}117)$$

where Δ^* is defined by

$$\Delta^* \equiv \begin{vmatrix} a_{11} & a_{12} & a_{14}'' \\ a_{21} & a_{22} & a_{24}'' \\ a_{31} & a_{32} & a_{34}' \end{vmatrix}. \qquad (9\text{-}118)$$

Clearly devaluation improves the balance of payments of the devaluing country if and only if the *RHS* of (9-117) is negative, which clearly depends, among other things, on the relative size of a_{14} and a_{15} and of a_{24} and a_{25}.

In the above we carried out our analysis under the gross substitutability assumption equation (9-100), and the assumption that none of the goods are inferior goods, equation (9-64). Suppose that these assumptions are *not* satisfied, but suppose we have the following case instead:

$$b_{12} = b_{21} = b_{12}' = b_{21}' = 0, \tag{9-119}$$

which may be called the *zero cross price effect assumption*, since (9-119) says that all the "cross" price effects between the real goods are zero. Although gross substitutability is a strong assumption, this assumption is also a strong, perhaps stronger, assumption. However, as Kemp [8] and Negishi [15] discovered, this assumption produces a historically important result, known as the *Robinson-Metzler condition*.

Since $a_{12} = b_{12} + b_{12}'$ and $a_{21} = b_{21} + b_{21}'$, (9-119) says that $a_{12} = 0$ and $a_{21} = 0$. Assume also that both countries take complete sterilization policies ($s_1 = s_2 = 0$), so that $\overline{M}_1 = $ constant and $\overline{M}_2 = $ constant. We can now simplify our results listed as (9-76), (9-77), and (9-78) greatly as:

$$dP_1/dE = -a_{13}/a_{11}, \tag{9-120}$$

$$dQ_1/dE = -a_{23}/a_{22}, \tag{9-121}$$

$$\frac{dW_m}{dE} = -a_{31}\frac{a_{13}}{a_{11}} - a_{32}\frac{a_{23}}{a_{22}}. \tag{9-122}$$

Setting $P_1 = Q_1 = E = P_2 = Q_2 = 1$ initially, observe that (9-119) implies, in view of the homogeneity of the excess demand functions,[24] the following relations:

$$b_{11} = -b_{14}\overline{M}_1, \qquad b_{22} = -b_{24}\overline{M}_1, \tag{9-123}$$

$$b_{11}' = -b_{15}'\overline{M}_2, \qquad b_{22}' = -b_{25}'\overline{M}_2.$$

Since the budget conditions hold whether or not the economy is in equilibrium, we obtain the following relations from (9-2) and (9-119):

$$b_{31} = -E_{x1} - b_{11}, \qquad b_{32} = -E_{y1} - b_{22}. \tag{9-124}$$

Following Robinson [20], we define the following demand (η) and supply (ε) elasticities to be

$$\varepsilon_d \equiv \frac{\partial D_{x1}}{\partial P_1}\frac{P_1}{D_{x1}}, \qquad \eta_d \equiv -\frac{\partial D_{y1}}{\partial Q_1}\frac{Q_1}{D_{y1}}, \tag{9-125a}$$

$$\varepsilon_f \equiv \frac{\partial D_{y2}}{\partial Q_1}\frac{Q_1}{D_{y2}}, \qquad \eta_f \equiv -\frac{\partial D_{x2}}{\partial P_1}\frac{P_1}{D_{x2}}, \tag{9-125b}$$

where the partial derivatives are all evaluated at the original equilibrium point. Obviously, we have

$$\varepsilon_f \equiv \frac{\partial D_{y2}}{\partial Q_2}\frac{Q_2}{D_{y2}}, \qquad \eta_f \equiv -\frac{\partial D_{x2}}{\partial P_2}\frac{P_2}{D_{x2}}, \tag{9-126}$$

[24] Recall (9-89) and (9-90) for Country 1. Similar relations hold for Country 2.

for $P_1 = EP_2$ and $Q_1 = EQ_2$, and

$$\eta_d = \frac{\partial E_{y1}}{\partial(P_1/Q_1)} \frac{P_1/Q_1}{E_{y1}}, \quad \eta_f = \frac{-\partial E_{x2}}{\partial(P_2/Q_2)} \frac{P_2/Q_2}{E_{x2}}. \tag{9-127}$$

In other words, assuming that Country 1 imports Y and Country 2 imports X, η_d and η_f are the usual elasticities of the offer curves of Countries 1 and 2 respectively. In any case, (9-125) implies [25]

$$\varepsilon_d E_{x1} = b_{11}, \quad \eta_d E_{y1} = -b_{22}, \quad \varepsilon_f E_{y2} = b_{22}', \quad \eta_f E_{x2} = -b_{11}'. \tag{9-128}$$

Then we have

$$a_{11} = -E_{x2}(\varepsilon_d + \eta_f) \quad \text{and} \quad a_{22} = E_{y2}(\eta_d + \varepsilon_f), \tag{9-129}$$

for $E_{x1} + E_{x2} = 0$ and $E_{y1} + E_{y2} = 0$ in the initial equilibrium. Note that

$$a_{13} = b_{15}'\bar{M}_2 \quad \text{and} \quad a_{23} = b_{25}'\bar{M}_2 \tag{9-130}$$

by definition of these symbols. Hence, using (9-123) and (9-128), we obtain

$$a_{13} = \eta_f E_{x2} \quad \text{and} \quad a_{23} = -\varepsilon_f E_{y2}. \tag{9-131}$$

Since $a_{31} = b_{31}$ and $a_{32} = b_{32}$, (9-124) and (9-128) imply

$$a_{31} = -E_{x1}(1 + \varepsilon_d), \quad a_{32} = -E_{y1}(1 - \eta_d). \tag{9-132}$$

We now substitute the expressions obtained in (9-129), (9-131), and (9-132) into equations (9-120), (9-121), and (9-122), and obtain

$$\frac{dP_1}{dE} = \frac{\eta_f}{\varepsilon_d + \eta_f}, \quad \frac{dQ_1}{dE} = \frac{\varepsilon_f}{\eta_d + \varepsilon_f}, \tag{9-133}$$

and

$$\frac{dW_m}{dE} = E_{y1} \left[\frac{\eta_f(1 + \varepsilon_d)}{\varepsilon_d + \eta_f} + \frac{\varepsilon_f(\eta_d - 1)}{\eta_d + \varepsilon_f} \right], \tag{9-134}$$

since $E_{x1} + E_{y1} = 0$ in the initial equilibrium ($M_1 = \tilde{M}_1$) by the budget condition (9-2). Therefore, Country 1's devaluation improves her balance of payments if and only if

$$\frac{\eta_f(1 + \varepsilon_d)}{\varepsilon_d + \eta_f} + \frac{\varepsilon_f(\eta_d - 1)}{\eta_d + \varepsilon_f} > 0, \tag{9-135}$$

assuming that Country 1 is the importer of Good Y ($E_{y1} > 0$). This is the Robinson-Metzler condition (Robinson [20] and Metzler [11]), originally obtained by Bickerdike [3],[26] which is well-known in the literature of

[25] If the gross substitutability assumption holds, then $\eta_d > 0, \eta_f > 0, \varepsilon_d > 0, \varepsilon_f > 0$, provided that Country 1 imports Y and Country 2 imports X.

[26] Bickerdike's formula is exactly the same as the one by Robinson, except that he expressed the formula in terms of the inverse of the elasticities. It is rather unfortunate that his paper was either ignored or forgotten until attention was drawn to it by Metzler [11] in 1949.

international trade theory.[27] A change in the terms of trade is easily obtained from (9-133) as

$$d(P_1/Q_1)/dE = \frac{\eta_d\eta_f - \varepsilon_d\varepsilon_f}{(\varepsilon_d + \eta_f)(\eta_d + \varepsilon_f)}, \tag{9-136}$$

since $d(P_1/Q_1)/dE = dP_1/dE - dQ_1/dE$.[28]

STABILITY PROBLEMS

The Exchange Stability Problem

Consider the case of a flexible exchange rate system with the basic equilibrium relations described by (9-18), (9-19), and (9-20)—or, (9-43), (9-44), and (9-45). Consider a particular equilibrium point and suppose that all the markets, including the factor markets, except for Country 1's money market, are held in equilibrium (or brought into equilibrium instantaneously). Let us then ask the question whether or not the original equilibrium will be restored, where the exchange rate E is the adjusting parameter. Since all the markets except for a particular one are held in equilibrium, this is the problem of *imperfect stability* as considered by Hicks. We may recall that the Marshall-Lerner condition was a condition for imperfect stability in which all the markets except for a good market are held in equilibrium.

Here the goods markets are held in equilibrium by supposition. Then we have $W_m = B_1 E$ by (9-25). In other words, for Country 1, W_m measures the excess supply of (or demand for) the foreign exchange in terms of her domestic currency. That is, we are concerned with the stability of the foreign exchange market for Country 1. In view of this, and in view of the fact that the adjusting parameter is the exchange rate, the stability problem posed above is called the *exchange stability problem*.

To consider this problem, assume that if $W_m > 0$, E, being the price of Country 2's currency in terms of Country 1's currency, decreases, and that if $W_m < 0$, E increases. This assumption is the basic premise of the exchange stability problem. Due to this basic premise, a sufficient condition for exchange stability is easily obtained as

$$dW_m/dE > 0, \tag{9-137}$$

where the derivative is evaluated at the original equilibrium. Then $dW_m/dE > 0$

---

[27] However the full significance and the underlying assumptions for the condition are probably not realized by any of these authors.

[28] Bickerdike [2] made a similar consideration in connection with the effect of import duties. ([2] p. 100, footnote). Edgeworth applied this model to the stability problem ("Applications of Mathematical Theories (continued)", *Economic Journal*, XVIII, December 1908, p. 544, footnote). Bickerdike's analysis in [2] also foresees his [3], and hence it constitutes one of the most important works in the history of exchange devaluation.

means that if E increases (decreases) W_m becomes positive (negative), for $W_m = 0$ originally by definition of equilibrium. Hence, by the above basic premise of exchange stability, E will decrease (increase), so that the original equilibrium will be restored. Recalling our discussion of the Marshall-Lerner condition, it should be clear that (9-137) is the condition for local stability and can also be interpreted as a sufficient condition for (local) *dynamic* stability.

Mathematically, the procedure for obtaining the characterization for the above condition is exactly the same as the one for obtaining the devaluation condition described in the previous section, except that the usual tâtonnement assumption prohibits actual transactions in disequilibrium. That is, no transfer should be made in disequilibrium. Mathematically, this amounts to setting $s_1 = s_2 = 0$ (so that both $\overline{M}_1$ and $\overline{M}_2$ are constant) in (9-73). In summary we conclude:

A sufficient condition for (local) exchange stability is that the RHS of (9-73), with $s_1 = s_2 = 0$, is positive. If, in particular, the gross substitutability assumption holds, then the foreign exchange market is always (locally) stable.

This conclusion implies the following important result.

Exchange devaluation under the fixed exchange rate system improves the balance of payments of the devaluing country when both $\overline{M}_1$ and $\overline{M}_2$ are constant only if the foreign exchange market is stable under the flexible exchange rate system.[29]

The Stability Problem via the Goods Markets

Consider again the case of a flexible exchange rate system. Consider again a particular equilibrium point. Now suppose that all the markets (including the money markets, the factor markets, and so on) *except for* the market of Good X are brought into equilibrium instantaneously (or held in equilibrium). Assuming that the price of X, P_1, is the adjusting parameter of the system, let us ask the question whether or not the equilibrium will be restored by the movement of P_1. Note that this is again a problem of imperfect stability. Moreover, the supposition of this imperfect stability problem is exactly in accord with the one used in obtaining the Marshall-Lerner condition. Note that, in view of (9-2'), if the equilibrium of the X-market is disturbed, then the equilibrium of the Y-market should also be disturbed, even if all the other markets are held in equilibrium. Moreover, if the equilibrium of the X-market is restored, then the equilibrium of the Y-market will automatically be restored. We may then call the present stability problem the *stability problem via the goods markets*.

Now let us introduce the basic premise of the present stability problem. Assume that if $W_x > 0$, P_1 increases, and that if $W_x < 0$, P_1 decreases. Under this premise it is immediately concluded that a sufficient condition for the

---

[29] This obviously suggests that there is a close connection between the condition for Hicksian imperfect stability and the comparative statics result. For a general discussion of this problem, see Appendix to Chapter 11.

(dynamic) local stability via the goods markets (or the local stability of the X-market) is[30]

$$dW_x/dP_1 < 0,$$ (9-138)

where the derivative is evaluated at the original equilibrium point. Since $W_x = 0$ initially, $dW_x/dP_1 < 0$ means $W_x \gtreqless 0$ according to whether P_1 decreases or increases. If $W_x > 0\,(<0)$, P_1 increases (decreases) so that the original equilibrium is restored. Note that if $dW_x/dP_1 > 0$ then the equilibrium is unstable. Hence $dW_x/dP_1 \leqq 0$ is a necessary condition for stability.

To consider this problem, first replace (9-43) by

$$W_x \equiv W_x(P_1, Q_1, E; \overline{M}_1, \overline{M}_2),$$ (9-43')

and totally differentiate this with (9-44) and (9-45). Then we obtain

$$a_{11}\,dP_1 + a_{12}\,dQ_1 + a_{13}\,dE + a_{14}\,d\overline{M}_1 + a_{15}\,d\overline{M}_2 = dW_x,$$ (9-139)

$$a_{21}\,dP_1 + a_{22}\,dQ_1 + a_{23}\,dE + a_{24}\,d\overline{M}_1 + a_{25}\,d\overline{M}_2 = 0,$$ (9-140)

$$a_{31}\,dP_1 + a_{32}\,dQ_1 + a_{33}\,d\overline{M}_1 = 0.$$ (9-141)

Since $dW_m = 0$, we have

$$d\overline{M}_1 = s_1 G_1\,dE, \quad d\overline{M}_2 = 0,$$ (9-142)

in view of (9-53) and (9-54). Therefore, equations (9-139), (9-140), and (9-141) can be rewritten as

$$a_{11}\,dP_1 + a_{12}\,dQ_1 + a_{13}'\,dE = dW_x,$$ (9-143)

$$a_{21}\,dP_1 + a_{22}\,dQ_1 + a_{23}'\,dE = 0,$$ (9-144)

$$a_{31}\,dP_1 + a_{32}\,dQ_1 + a_{33}'\,dE = 0,$$ (9-145)

where

$$a_{13}' \equiv a_{13} + s_1 a_{14} G_1, \quad a_{23}' \equiv a_{23} + s_1 a_{24} G_1, \quad a_{33}' \equiv s_1 a_{33} G_1.$$ (9-146)

If complete sterilization policies are taken, then set

$$a_{13}' = a_{13}, \quad a_{23}' = a_{23}, \quad \text{and} \quad a_{33}' = 0.$$ (9-147)

Solving (9-142), (9-144), and (9-145) with respect to dP_1, dQ_1, dE, we obtain, in particular,

$$\frac{dP_1}{dW_x} = \frac{1}{\Delta^0}\begin{vmatrix} a_{22} & a_{23}' \\ a_{32} & a_{33}' \end{vmatrix}$$ (9-148)

where

$$\Delta^0 \equiv \begin{vmatrix} a_{11} & a_{12} & a_{13}' \\ a_{21} & a_{22} & a_{23}' \\ a_{31} & a_{32} & a_{33}' \end{vmatrix}.$$ (9-149)

[30] Equivalently we may state this as $dWy/dQ_1 < 0$, and consider the Y-market instead of the X-market.

Hence, a sufficient condition for the X-market to be locally stable is that the *RHS* of (9-148) be negative. In particular, if the complete sterilization policy is taken so that we have (9-147), then we can obtain

$$\frac{dP_1}{dW_x} = \frac{-1}{\Delta^0} a_{32}a_{23} \,, \tag{9-150}$$

where Δ^0 is simplified as

$$\Delta^0 = a_{31}(a_{12}a_{23} - a_{22}a_{13}) - a_{32}(a_{11}a_{23} - a_{21}a_{13}) \,. \tag{9-151}$$

Assuming the sign conditions (9-64) and gross substitutability (9-100), we can conclude that $\Delta^0 > 0$ always and that $dP_1/dW_x < 0$ always. In other words, the X-market is always locally stable.

True Dynamic Stability

In the last two subsections, we obtained the stability condition assuming that all the markets except for one market are held in equilibrium. We now delete this assumption. Consider the following dynamic adjustment equations:

$$\dot{P}_1 = k_1 W_x(P_1, Q_1, E, \overline{M}_1, \overline{M}_2) \,, \tag{9-152}$$

$$\dot{Q}_1 = k_2 W_y(P_1, Q_1, E, \overline{M}_1, \overline{M}_2) \,, \tag{9-153}$$

$$\dot{E} = -k_3 W_m(P_1, Q_1, \overline{M}_1) \,, \tag{9-154}$$

where $k_1 > 0$, $k_2 > 0$, $k_3 > 0$ respectively denote the speed of adjustment of the X-market, the Y-market, and Country 1's money market. The dot $(\cdot)$ signifies the derivative with respect to time. Again we note that no actual transactions will take place in disequilibrium so that both $\overline{M}_1$ and $\overline{M}_2$ are constant. Expand the *RHS* of (9-152), (9-153), and (9-154) by a Taylor series about an equilibrium point, say, $(P_1{}^*, Q_1{}^*, E^*)$, and, neglecting the second order and the higher order terms, we obtain

$$\dot{S} = H \cdot S \,, \tag{9-155}$$

where S and H are defined by

$$S \equiv \begin{pmatrix} P_1 - P_1{}^* \\ Q_1 - Q_1{}^* \\ E - E^* \end{pmatrix}, \quad H \equiv \begin{vmatrix} k_1 a_{11} & k_1 a_{12} & k_1 a_{13} \\ k_2 a_{21} & k_2 a_{22} & k_2 a_{23} \\ -k_3 a_{31} & -k_3 a_{32} & 0 \end{vmatrix} . \tag{9-156}$$

It is known that this system is stable ($S \to 0$ as time extends without limit) if and only if[31]

$$k_1 a_{11} < 0 \,, \quad \begin{vmatrix} k_1 a_{11} & k_1 a_{12} \\ k_2 a_{21} & k_2 a_{22} \end{vmatrix} > 0 \,, \quad \det H < 0 \,. \tag{9-157}$$

Assume gross substitutability (9-100), then $k_1 a_{11} < 0$. As Arrow-Hurwicz [1] noted, we can choose the unit of measurement properly so that we can set

[31] See Samuelson [21], for example.

$k_1 = k_2 = k_3 = 1$ without loss of generality. Then the second condition of (9-157) also holds in view of (9-106), and the third condition of (9-157) is simplified as

$$-a_{31}(a_{12}a_{23} - a_{22}a_{13}) + a_{32}(a_{11}a_{23} - a_{21}a_{13}) < 0 , \tag{9-158}$$

which always holds in view of (9-64) and (9-100). In other words, the equilibrium point (P_1^*, Q_1^*, E^*) is always locally dynamically stable under gross substitutability. This corresponds to a well-known result in the stability theory of competitive markets.

Addendum: NOTE ON SEPARABILITY[32]

Consider the usual aggregation assumption and drop subscript $_i$ to ease notation. Suppose that a country maximizes

$$u = u(C_x, C_y, M) \tag{9-159}$$

subject to

$$(PC_x + QC_y) + M \leq PX + QY + \overline{M} . \tag{9-160}$$

Demand for X, Y and money are obtained as a solution (C_x^*, C_y^*, M^*) of this maximization problem.

DEFINITION   The real goods and money are said to be *separable*, if

$$\frac{\partial}{\partial M} \left(\frac{u_y}{u_x} \right) = 0 , \quad \text{for all } (C_x, C_y, M) , \tag{9-161}$$

where $u_x \equiv \partial u/\partial C_x$ and $u_y \equiv \partial u/\partial C_y$. We first prove the following lemmas which are due to Sono [23].

LEMMA 1   Suppose u has the separability property (9-161). Then the indifference relation between Good X and Good Y are independent of the quantity of money. In other words, if two bundles (C_x, C_y, M') and (C_x', C_y', M') are indifferent, or if

$$u(C_x, C_y, M') = u(C_x', C_y', M') \tag{9-162}$$

holds, then

$$u(C_x, C_y, M) = u(C_x', C_y', M) , \tag{9-163}$$

for any value of M.

PROOF   From the separability relation (9-161), we obtain

$$\frac{u_{xM}}{u_x} = \frac{u_{yM}}{u_y} , \quad \text{where} \quad u_{xM} \equiv \partial u_x/\partial M, \quad \text{and} \quad u_{yM} \equiv \partial u_y/\partial M . \tag{9-164}$$

---

[32] The discussion here is indebted to Morishima [12].

Hence,

$$\frac{\partial}{\partial M} (u_x dC_x + u_y dC_y) = u_{xM} dC_x + u_{yM} dC_y = \zeta(u_x dC_x + u_y dC_y),$$

where $\zeta \equiv u_{xM}/u_x$.

Therefore, if $u_x dC_x + u_y dC_y = 0$ (if (9-162) holds), then $\partial(u_x dC_x + u_y C_y)/\partial M = 0$ [(9-163) holds].   (Q.E.D.)

LEMMA 2   The utility function u can be written in the form

$$u = U[\varphi(C_x, C_y), M],$$ (9-165)

if and only if the separability relation (9-161) holds.

PROOF   Assume u has the separability property (9-161) and let a be a particular value of M. Write

$$u(C_x, C_y, a) = \varphi(C_x, C_y).$$ (9-166)

In view of lemma 1, if

$$\varphi(C_x, C_y) = \varphi(C_x', C_y'),$$ (9-167)

then

$$u(C_x, C_y, M) = u(C_x', C_y', M)$$ (9-168)

for any M. Hence, once the value of φ and M are determined, the value of u is uniquely determined. That is, relation (9-165) holds. The converse can be proved easily.   (Q.E.D.)

Assume that u is separable so that (9-165) holds, and consider the consumer's maximization problem stated earlier. Write $\varphi_x \equiv \partial\varphi/\partial C_x$, $\varphi_y \equiv \partial\varphi/\partial C_y$, $U_m \equiv \partial U/\partial M$, and $V_\varphi = \partial U/\partial \varphi$. Assume non-satiation, on the partial derivatives of U is always positive, then the first order conditions are, assuming $C_x^* > 0$, $C_y^* > 0$, and $M^* > 0$,

$$PC_x^* + QC_y^* + M^* = PX + QY + \overline{M}$$ (9-169)

and

$$\varphi_x^*/P = \varphi_y^*/Q;$$ (9-170a)

$$\varphi_y^*/Q = U_M^*/U_\varphi^*,$$ (9-170b)

where φ_x^*, φ_y^*, U_M^*, and U_φ^* are evaluated at (C_x^*, C_y^*, M^*).[33] These equations in (9-169) and (9-170) determine the values of C_x^*, C_y^*, and M^* as functions of P, Q, X, Y, and $\overline{M}$, which constitute the demand functions of these three variables.

[33] Under the concavity of U, the first order conditions are sufficient as well as necessary.

Notice now that (9-170a and b) does not contain M^*, for φ (hence, also φ_x and φ_y) is a function of C_x and C_y alone, which, in turn, is due to the separability of u. Therefore, the demand function for C_x and C_y can be written as

$$C_x = C_x(P, Q, Z), \tag{9-171}$$

$$C_y = C_y(P, Q, Z), \tag{9-172}$$

where Z (the *money expenditure on real goods*) is defined by

$$Z \equiv PX + QY + \overline{M} - M. \tag{9-173}$$

In other words, Z can be taken as a parameter of the maximization problem.

We may contrast this form of the demand function to the following form:

$$C_x = C_x(P, Q, V), \tag{9-174}$$

$$C_y = C_y(P, Q, V), \tag{9-175}$$

where

$$V \equiv PX + QY + \overline{M}.$$

In this form the relation between prices (P, Q) and V can be specified by noting the production relation such as $X = X(P/Q)$ and $Y = Y(P/Q)$, while in the previous form the demand functions (9-171) and (9-172), the relation between prices (P, Q) and Z, cannot in general be specified due to the term M in these demand functions. M is to be determined as a result of the entire system (9-169), (9-170a), and (9-170b).

However, the demand functions in the form of (9-171) and (9-172) have important advantages such as:

1. The values of C_x and C_y are determined independently of M, if Z is determined *a priori*. Therefore, the real system X, Y, C_x, C_y, and P/Q are determined without any consideration of the monetary system, once the value of Z is predetermined (say, by the monetary authority). In other words, the real system and the monetary system are *dichotomized*, and they can be treated separately, which justifies the traditional separation of the real system and the monetary system, handing the analysis of the monetary phenomena over to the monetary specialist.

2. Suppose that equilibrium in the money market is achieved. That is, $M = \overline{M}$. Then $V = PX + QY$ (V does not contain any monetary variables such as M or $\overline{M}$. Thus the dichotomy between the real system and the monetary system is achieved *in equilibrium*. Hence, noting the production relations, $X = X(P/Q)$, $Y = Y(P/Q)$, and recalling the linear homogeneity of the demand functions C_x and C_y in the absence of money illusion, we can easily obtain

$$E_x \equiv C_x - X = E_x(P/Q), \tag{9-176}$$

$$E_y \equiv C_y - Y = E_y(P/Q). \tag{9-177}$$

In other words, the excess demand functions contain no term such as $\overline{M}/Q$.

REFERENCES

1. Arrow, K. and Hurwicz, L., "On the Stability of Competitive Markets, I," *Econometrica*, 26, October 1958.
2. Bickerdike, C. F., Book review: *Protective and Preferential Import Duties* by A. C. Pigon (London: Macmillan & Co., Ltd.), *Economic Journal*, XVII, March 1907.
3. ———, "The Instability of Foreign Exchange", *Economic Journal*, XXX, March 1920.
4. Chipman, J. S., "A Survey of the Theory of International Trade: Part 2; The Neoclassical Theory," *Econometrica*, 33, October 1965.
5. Goldman, S. M. and Uzawa, H., "A Note on Separability in Demand Analysis," *Econometrica*, 32, July 1964.
6. Hahn, F. H., "The Balance of Payments in a Monetary Economy," *Review of Economic Studies*, XXVI, February 1959.
7. Kemp, M. C., "The Rate of Exchange, The Terms of Trade and the Balance of Payments in Fully Employed Economies," *International Economic Review*, 3, September 1962.
8. ———, *The Pure Theory of International Trade and Investment* (Englewood Cliffs, N.J.: Prentice-Hall, Inc.), 2nd ed., 1969 (1st ed. 1964), Chapter 14.
9. Krueger, A. O., "Balance of Payments Theory", *Journal of Economic Literature*, VII, March 1969.
10. Meade, J. E., *The Balance of Payments, Mathematical Supplement* (London: Oxford University Press), 1951.
11. Metzler, L. A., "*The Theory of International Trade*," in a Survey of Contemporary Economics (ed. by H. S. Ellis) (Philadelphia: Blakiston), 1949.
12. Morishima, M., "Consumer's Behavior and Liquidity Preference," *Econometrica*, 20, April 1952.
13. Mundell, R. A., *International Economics* (New York: Crowell-Collier and Macmillan, Inc.), 1968.
14. Negishi, T., "The Stability of a Competitive Economy: A Survey Article," *Econometrica*, October 1962.
15. ———, "Approaches to the Analysis of Devaluation," *International Economic Review*, 9, June 1968.
16. ———, "The Dichotomy of Real and Monetary Analyses" (unpublished manuscript).
17. Patinkin, D., *Money, Interest and Prices* (New York: Harper & Row, Publishers), 1965 (1st ed. 1956).
18. Pearce, I. F., "The Problem of the Balance of Payments," *International Economic Review*, 2, January 1961.
19. ———, *A Contribution to Demand Analysis* (Oxford: Clarendon Press), 1964.
20. Robinson, J., "The Foreign Exchange," *Essays in the Theory of Employment*, 1947. Reprinted in *Readings in the Theory of International Trade*, ed. by Ellis and Metzler, 1949.

21. Samuelson, P. A., *Foundation of Economic Analysis* (Cambridge, Mass.: Harvard University Press), 1948.

22. Sieper, E., "Economic Policy and the Balance of Trade," presented at the Christchurch Meeting of the Australian and New Zealand Association for the Advancement of Science, January 1968.

23. Sono, M., "The Effects of Price Changes on the Demand and Supply of Separable Goods," with a historical note by Morishima, *International Economic Review*, 2, 1961.

24. Takayama, A., *Mathematical Economics*—forthcoming.

10

A KEYNESIAN THEORY OF INTERNATIONAL TRADE— SIMPLE MULTIPLIERS, EXCHANGE DEVALUATION, AND THE TRANSFER PROBLEM[1]

THE ELEMENTS OF KEYNESIAN ECONOMICS[2]

One of the most fundamental assumptions of neoclassical economic analysis is that the resources are fully employed. In the neoclassical model the resources are considered scarce, and the unemployment of these scarce resources is not a matter of concern. Rather, the model typically deals with the allocation of these scarce resources. The parameters which are crucial in bringing about full employment of the resources, and which consequently determine their allocation, are the prices of the goods and factors. Each economic unit determines its own behavior, taking these prices as given signals. The result when all economic units have determined their behavior in this way is a (competitive) equilibrium. Thus, the output of each good and the allocation of factors to each good are determined once such an equilibrium has been established.

The primary concern of Keynes' *General Theory of Employment, Interest and Money* [25] was this problem of full employment. Suppose that for some reason full employment of the resources is not achieved. Then the allocation of resources to each industry becomes much less important. If there are unemployed resources, these resources are not really scarce, rather they are redundant. Thus, the primary concern shifts to the problem of creating enough effective total demand for goods which absorbs these redundant resources.

---

[1] This chapter was originally written as Chapters 6 and 7 of [63] and reproduced in [64] and [66].
[2] The purpose of this section is not to carry out a complete discussion of the Keynesian revolution. This would require a much longer treatise since the conclusions have not really been agreed upon by economists. Rather, the purpose of this section is to sketch some of the important points of the Keynesian revolution and to prepare for the discussion of the remaining sections of this chapter.

Aggregate analysis is adopted as an important and useful device for tackling such problems.

A relevant question, then, is why full employment is considered to be a natural state in neoclassical economics, while unemployment is more natural to the Keynesians. The answer, essentially, is that the neoclassical economists rely on the complete flexibility of the prices to attain full employment, while the Keynesians suspect that not all prices are this flexible. In particular, they question the flexibility of the money wage rate and the interest rate. In other words, pressure by labor unions, and so on, leads to some downward rigidity of the money wage rate, and the existence of a "liquidity trap" in the demand for money creates some rigidity in the interest rate. Moreover, there is some conviction that saving and investment are interest inelastic so that even if the interest rate is flexible, an equilibrium in the money market at the full employment level is questionable. Let S be the total real savings ($=$ total income minus total consumption) in the economy, let I be the real investment, and let Y_F be the full employment output. Then, denoting the interest rate by r we have

$$S(r, Y_F) = I(r, Y_F) .$$

If savings or investment is interest elastic so that $\partial S/\partial r$ or $\partial I/\partial r$ is nonzero, then a change in r can bring about an equilibrium, $S = I$, in this market.[3]

The neoclassical conviction is that both saving and investment are interest elastic and that the interest rate is typically flexible (they do not recognize the existence of a liquidity trap).[4] Then an $S = I$ equilibrium at the full employment level of output can be accepted without too much difficulty. The assumption that at full employment the capital accumulation due to saving is equal to the depreciation of the capital stock (the assumption of a stationary state) allows the neoclassical economists to focus their attention on consumption. Moreover, their contention is that the $S = I$ equilibrium in its absence of the real balance effect determines the level of the (natural) interest rate and that the (market) interest rate always follows the natural rate. This enables them to consider the real sector independently of the monetary sector.[5]

---

[3] Even if saving and investment are interest elastic, there is an additional problem: that is the problem of the existence of a positive rate of interest that will satisfy $S(r, Y_F) = I(r, Y_F)$. This point was emphasized by Klein [29] and Patinkin [45]. The neoclassical economists obviously presupposed the existence of such an interest rate; otherwise their entire system becomes meaningless. Note also that this problem can still exist even with the presence of the Pigou effect.

[4] The construction of the demand for money with the recognition of the speculative demand as well as the transactions and precautionary demand is due to Keynes [25]. The speculative demand for money, as is well-known, plays a crucial role in the liquidity trap argument. The neoclassical economists typically neglect the speculative demand for money, although they often admit the possibility of an interest elastic transactions demand for money. (They are not necessarily strict advocates of the naive quantity theory of money which argues the constancy of the velocity of circulation.)

[5] This is often called the *dichotomy* and was one of the central issues of the Patinkin controversy. With the absence of the real balance effect or Pigou effect, the above argument for the dichotomy can be accepted without difficulty. However, if the Pigou effect is significant,

We shall now construct a general Keynesian model based on the work of later Keynesians such as Modigliani [42], Marschak [36], and Brownlee [9]. We shall explicitly introduce international trade into this model. However, we shall assume that capital is internationally immobile and postpone our discussion of internationally mobile capital until the next chapter.

Letting Y be real income; C, real consumption; S, real saving; I, real investment; P, price of output; r, interest rate; A, aggregate net worth (assets) of the private sector; G, government expenditures; and T, the balance of trade in terms of the domestic currency; we can write the equation which denotes the equilibrium in the goods market as follows:[6]

$$I(r, Y, A/P) + G/P + T/P = S(r, Y, A/P),$$ (10-1)

where

$$S(r, Y, A/P) \equiv Y - C(r, Y, A/P).$$

Or we may write

$$V(r, Y, A/P) + G/P + T/P = 0,$$ (10-2)

where $V \equiv I - S$.

From our ordinary knowledge of macroeconomic theory, we may impose the following restrictions on the signs of the partial derivatives of V in the above equation.[7]

$$V_r \leqq 0, \quad V_Y < 0, \quad V_{A/P} \geqq 0.$$ (10-3)

$V_{A/P} = 0$ means the absence of the real balance effect (*Pigou effect*). Clearly, other restrictions like $V_r > 0$, $V_Y > 0$, and so on are possible. Since such cases can be analyzed *mutatis mutandis*, we may omit consideration of these cases.

Letting $\overline{M}$ be the supply of money, we may write the equilibrium condition for the money market as

$$\overline{M}/P = L(r, Y).$$ (10-4)

We may impose the following restrictions:

$$L_r \leqq 0 \quad \text{or} \quad L_r \rightarrow -\infty \text{ (liquidity trap)}; \quad L_Y > 0.$$ (10-5)

---

so that the consumption depends (significantly) on the real value of the assets as well as on the level of output and the interest rate, then the dichotomy holds only under very special conditions (such as no government or central bank money *and* no government debt). See Modigliani [42] and also Patinkin [46].

[6] The real asset effect on investment is often recognized as important. See Patinkin [46], for example.

[7] Throughout this section we denote partial derivatives by putting a subscript, which indicates the differentiating variable, below and to the right of the relevant variable. For example, $\partial S/\partial r = S_r, \partial S/\partial Y = S_Y$, and $\partial S/\partial(A/P) = S_{A/P}$. Similarly, $\partial T/\partial P = T_P, \partial L/\partial r = L_r$, and so on.

The supply side of the economy can be represented by the following equations:[8]

$$Y = f(N) \text{ (production function)} \tag{10-6}$$

where N denotes the level of labor employment.

$$W/P = f'(N), \text{ or } N = n^d(W/P) \text{ (demand for labor)}, \tag{10-7}$$

where W is the money wage rate and $f' \equiv df/dN$.

(downward rigidity of W): $W = \overline{W}$ (constant) if $n^d(\overline{W}/P) < n^s(\overline{W}/P)$;

$$N = n^s(W/P) \text{ if } n^d(\overline{W}/P) \geq n^s(\overline{W}/P). \tag{10-8}$$

One possible case is that there is enough excess capacity in the economy,[9] so that the marginal productivity of labor is constant for a certain range of labor employment. In other words, $f''(N) = 0$ for a certain range of employment, like, $0 \leq N \leq \overline{N}$. Let N_F be the value of N for which the labor demand curve $(n^d(W/P))$ and the labor supply curve $(n^s(W/P))$ intersect. Then as long as $N < N_F$, $W = \overline{W}$ so that equations (10-6), (10-7), and (10-8) are simply reduced to

$$P = \text{constant}, \quad \text{if } N \leq \overline{N}. \tag{10-9}$$

Or, probably more typically, if $f'' < 0$ for $\overline{N} < N < N_F$, equations (10-6), (10-7), and (10-8) yield[10]

$$Y = Y(P), \quad \text{where } dY/dP > 0, \quad \text{if } \overline{N} < N < N_F, \tag{10-10}$$

$$Y = Y_F \text{ (constant)}, \quad \text{if } N = N_F. \tag{10-11}$$

The above argument can be illustrated by Figure 10-1.

If the labor demand curve is the one illustrated by Figure 10-1, equation (10-10) holds for the values of N such that $\overline{N} < N < N_F$, and we obtain values of (W/P) such that $(\overline{W/P}) > (W/P) > (W/P)_F$; equation (10-11) holds for values of N such that $N = N_F$ and gives values of (W/P) such that $(W/P) = (W/P)_F$.

---

[8] The stock of physical capital is assumed to be constant. This is, in a sense, a strange assumption, for investment has been explicitly introduced into the model. See Mundell, R. A., "A Fallacy in the Interpretation of Macroeconomic Equilibrium," *Journal of Political Economy*, LXXIII, February 1965. However, this assumption sharpens the Keynesian analysis considerably.

[9] The concept of excess capacity is not well-defined in the literature. It needs a lot more investigation. Here we will use it more or less as a nickname for the situation in which the marginal product of labor is constant.

[10] If $N < N_F$, $W = \overline{W}$ by equation (10-8). The amount of labor employed (N) is determined by equation (10-7) with $W = \overline{W}$. Hence, if $f'' < 0$, N is an increasing function of P, so that Y is also an increasing function of P due to equation (10-6) and $f' > 0$. If, on the other hand, $N \geq N_F$, $(W/P) = \text{constant} = (W/P)_F$ and $N = \text{constant} = N_F$ due to equations (10-7) and (10-8) (the excess demand for labor is eliminated by an increase in $\overline{W}$). Hence, $Y_F = \text{constant} = f(N_F)$. N_F signifies the full employment of labor.

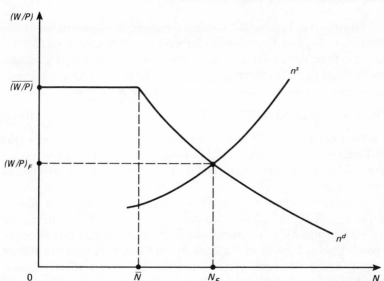

Figure 10-1 Demand and Supply of Labor

Figure 10-2 relates P and Y[11] (where $\overline{Y}$ and Y_F correspond to $\overline{N}$ and N_F respectively).

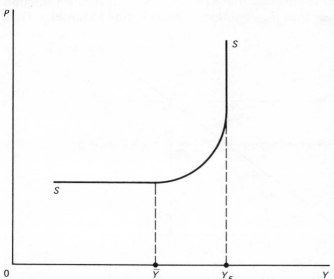

Figure 10-2 Aggregate Supply Curve

---

[11] The assumption that the price level is constant (that is, a flat aggregate supply curve) is often (implicitly) made in simple macroanalyses. This is one of the key assumptions which underlies the simple multiplier analysis. Although it is not quite clear whether Keynes himself adopted this assumption, my contention is that Keynes clearly recognized the importance of the repercussions through the rising supply price (which is, in turn, due to the law of the diminishing marginal productivity). See Keynes [25], Chapter 18. For this reason I would like to call the case with (10-9), the *ultra-Keynesian* case.

The curve illustrated in Figure 10-2 is called the *aggregate supply curve*. It was used by Marschak [36] and Brownlee [9] for macroeconomic analyses.

Assuming that there is no international capital mobility, Country 1's balance of payments is equal to the trade balance. Letting B be the balance of payments of the home country in terms of her currency, we have $B = T$, or:

$$B = PX[P/(P^*E)] - EP^*X^*(P^*E/P, Y),\qquad(10\text{-}12)$$

where P^* is the price level of the rest of the world, E is the exchange rate (the price of the foreign currency in terms of the domestic currency), X is the volume of goods exported by the home country, and X^* is the volume of goods imported by the home country.[12]

One important, simple case of the Keynesian economic model is the case in which the price level of the goods is constant [equation (10-9)] due to the existence of excess capacity and in which the level of the interest rate does not affect the goods market because of the liquidity trap and/or completely interest inelastic saving and investment. Assuming away the Pigou effect ($S_{A/P} = I_{A/P} = 0$) and income induced investment ($I_Y = 0$), and selecting the unit of measurement of the goods so that $P = 1$, we can simplify equation (10-1) to

$$I + G + T = S(Y).$$

If we also neglect international trade ($T = 0$), then this equation describes the famous *Keynesian cross diagram* which is illustrated by Figure 10-3. From

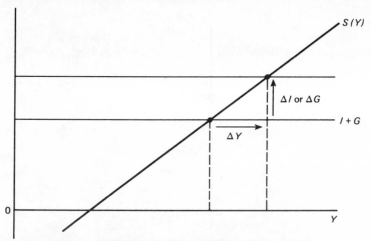

Figure 10-3   The Keynesian Cross Diagram

the diagram it is clear that a change in government expenditure of ΔG changes the level of output by $(1/S_Y)\Delta G = (1/MPS)\Delta G$, where MPS is the marginal propensity to save. This is the famous formula for the government expenditure multiplier.

[12] The use of the asterisk (*) to denote the foreign country is due to Kemp [24].

Such an example of elementary Keynesian analysis should be familiar to the reader from elementary textbooks of economics. However, it is essential that we know the required assumptions before a problem is analyzed in terms of the Keynesian cross diagram, since these assumptions limit the applicability of such an analysis.

In the above exposition of the Keynesian model, we implicitly made several important assumptions for the sake of simplicity. They are as follows:

1. FOREIGN REPERCUSSIONS   The model itself is not complete if we have to reconsider the repercussions from other countries. In other words, a change in the level of economic activity of the home country causes a change in the levels of economic activity in the other countries, which in turn has repercussions in the home countries. In order to analyze such a problem we would have to graft a model similar to that of the home country for the other countries (or "the rest of the world") onto the model discussed above. The above model holds if the home country is so small that the effect of the foreign repercussions is negligible. Due to this reason the assumption of no foreign repercussions is often called the *small country assumption*.

2. TERMS OF TRADE EFFECT   In the consumption function (and also in the investment function and the demand for money equation) the income Y is the output of the home country. However, in the model in which there is international trade, this is not a very precise treatment, for each country consumes at least two goods, the home good and the foreign good. A change in the relative price of the goods will cause a change in the real income of the country. Therefore, the real income, which affects the level of consumption and so on, will be different from the output of the home good. For example, if the imported good becomes relatively more expensive, then it costs more to buy the same bundle of goods as before, which implies a decrease in real income. Such a change in the relative price in the home country can occur either as a result of an exchange devaluation and/or a change in the domestic price of each good due to changes in the levels of production.

    There is, however, one case in which this *terms of trade effect* is unimportant. This is the case in which there is no change in the home price of the home produced good due to changes in the level of output due to excess capacity and so on ("ultra-Keynesian" case), *and* there is no change in the exchange rate of countries' currencies. The model for the simple international trade multipliers, which we will discuss in the next section, will specifically deal with such a problem. However, in the analysis of the exchange devaluation, the terms of trade effect has been one of the crucial issues in the literature, and we have to tackle this problem honestly. In the third section of this chapter, we shall do this with full recognition of the effect of foreign repercussions.

3.   DEMAND FOR MONEY   Equation (10-4) assumes away the asset effect in the demand for money function, which may appear to be a rather strong assumption (especially after our discussions in Chapter 9). The reader, if he wishes, may modify the analysis by changing $L(r, Y)$ to $L(r, Y, A/P)$, where we assume that $L_{A/P} \geqq 0$; that is, money is not an inferior good. Equation (10-4) follows the usual Keynesian assumption that the demand for money consists of transactions, and precautionary and speculative demands. As is well-known, the essence of such a specification of demand for money lies in the choice between money and bonds. Note that both bonds and money function as a means of the store of value, which is a generalization of the model presented in Chapter 9. Regarding equation (10-4) as the equilibrium relation of the bond market has been deleted from consideration. This is due to the fact that the bond market is always in equilibrium if all the other markets are in equilibrium and Walras' law holds. This is a well-known observation in the usual macro-economic theory for a closed economy (see Patinkin [46], pp. 229 and 333). However, the extension of the observation to an open economy is more complicated. Such a complication is mainly due to the fact that we have to specify the degree to which the bonds of each country are internationally tradeable. We shall leave this consideration to the interested reader.

4.   THE TERMS OF TRADE EFFECT IN THE DEMAND FOR MONEY   One of the important components of the demand for money is the transactions demand. The transactions demand for money is an increasing function with respect to money income which, in turn, will depend on the level of the trade balance. In the above model we simplified our treatment by assuming that the transactions demand for real cash balances ("real" in terms of the price of the home goods) is an increasing function in Y (the output of the home goods). When the exchange rate varies, we have to take account of the changes in the country's real income due to variations of the exchange rate, a fact which we explained above. For the sake of simplicity we have completely avoided such discussions in the above, nor has work been done on the subject in the literature.

5.   FLEXIBLE VERSUS FIXED EXCHANGE RATES   Under the flexible exchange rate system, E is a variable to be determined in the system, and B is brought to zero through fluctuations in E. Four equations, (10-2), (10-4), (10-10), and (10-12) (with $B = 0$) determine the equilibrium values of the four variables Y, r, P, and E. Under the fixed exchange rate system, B is not necessarily equal to zero. Assume that this country adopts a complete sterilization policy, so that nonzero B does not affect the country's money supply $\overline{M}$. Then the four equations (10-2), (10-4), (10-10), and (10-12) determine the equilibrium values of the four variables Y, r, P, and B. *Throughout this chapter*, except for the discussion on exchange stability in the subsection entitled "Some Confusions in the Balance of Payments Analyses", *we assume that the*

country adopts a fixed exchange rate system with convertible fiat currencies together with a complete sterilization policy. In the analysis of exchange devaluation, the exchange rate E is the shift parameter of the system.

INTERNATIONAL TRADE MULTIPLIERS

In the decade immediately following World War II, when analyses using the Keynesian cross diagram were fashionable,[13] the study of international trade multipliers received a great deal of attention.[14] These studies, then, were based on the Keynesian model with the assumptions that: 1) the domestic goods price level is constant for all the relevant levels of output, and 2) the impact of the monetary sector, via the interest rate, is negligible because of the existence of a liquidity trap and so on, so that the basic features of the economy are characterized by the Keynesian cross diagram. To study the international trade multipliers, it is necessary to assume that the above conditions hold for the entire world, that is, both for the home country and for the "rest of the world." The analyses can be classified into two categories: first with the small country assumption and second without this assumption. The latter came as a natural extension of the former, and both assume that the exchange rate is fixed.

The Model With the Small Country Assumption

The basic feature of this model is that the home country is assumed to be small enough relative to the rest of the world so that changes in the levels of the economic variables of the home country do not affect the levels of the economic variables of the "rest of the world" (or the "foreign country").[15] Under the additional assumptions that a) the domestic goods price, P, is constant, b) there is no Pigou effect, $S_{A/P} = 0$, and c) there is a liquidity trap ($r = $ constant) and/or savings and investment are completely interest inelastic ($S_r = I_r = 0$), we have the following simplified version of equation (10-1):

$$I(Y) + G + T = S(Y).$$ (10-13)

Now we choose the unit of measurement of the home country's good such that $P = 1$, and under the above assumptions P does not change. Since the exchange rate and the foreign prices are fixed, their units of measurement can also be chosen so that $E = P^* = 1$.[16] Then the balance of payments equation, (10-12), can be rewritten as

$$T = B = X - X^*(Y).$$ (10-14)

Recall that capital is assumed to be internationally immobile so that $B = T$.

---

[13] The publication of the *first edition* of Samuelson's famous introductory textbook on economics, Samuelson, P. A., *Economics: An Introductory Analysis* (New York: McGraw-Hill), 1st ed., 1948, probably best exhibits this fashion.

[14] For an excellent exposition of international trade multipliers, see Kindleberger [27].

[15] Under this assumption, no assumptions about the state of Country 2 (such as an ultra-Keynesian economy) are really necessary.

[16] $P/(P^*E)$ [in equation (10-12)] will always equal to one.

It is assumed that the equality of equation (10-13) can be achieved by an appropriate change in the level of output (Y). However, there is no mechanism which makes the right-hand side of equation (10-14) equal to zero; hence the balance of trade (and balance of payments) can be positive or negative. Equations (10-13) and (10-14) can be reduced to

$$I(Y) + G + [X - X^*(Y)] = S(Y). \tag{10-15}$$

The entire economy is characterized by this equation, where G and X are exogenous to the system.

Now we can consider the effects of a change in government expenditures or a change in the level of exports, or a shift in the investment or savings schedules. For example, an autonomous increase in the level of government expenditures can be analyzed simply by differentiating equation (10-15) with respect to G, to obtain[17]

$$\frac{dY}{dG} = \frac{1}{(S_Y + X_Y^*) - I_Y}. \tag{10-16}$$

If $I_Y = 0$ (no income induced investment), then equation (10-16) can be rewritten as the following well-known formula.

$$\frac{dY}{dG} = \frac{1}{s + \pi}, \quad \text{where} \quad s \equiv S_Y \quad \text{and} \quad \pi \equiv X_Y^*. \tag{10-17}$$

Note that π is the marginal propensity to import (of the home country). If we recall that the present model assumes that each country produces only one good called the national income, then π corresponds to π_1 (the marginal propensity of the home country to consume the imported good) of the previous chapter.

The effect of an autonomous increase in exports or an autonomous shift in the savings or investment schedules can be obtained analogously and will be found to be the same as equation (10-16) or (10-17). For example, the effect of an autonomous increase in exports is given by

$$\frac{dY}{dX} = \frac{1}{s + \pi} \quad \text{if} \quad I_Y = 0. \tag{10-18}$$

This formula [(10-17) or (10-18)] can be illustrated by the following diagram in which $S(Y)$ and $X^*(Y)$ are assumed to be linear.

The change in the balance of payments due to an autonomous change in government expenditures is given by $[dX/dG - dX^*/dG] = -\pi(dY/dG)$, or

$$\frac{dB}{dG} = \frac{-\pi}{s + \pi} \quad (\text{if } I_Y = 0). \tag{10-19}$$

The change in the balance of payments due to an autonomous change in exports

[17] The partial derivatives such as S_Y and so on are evaluated at the equilibrium value of Y.

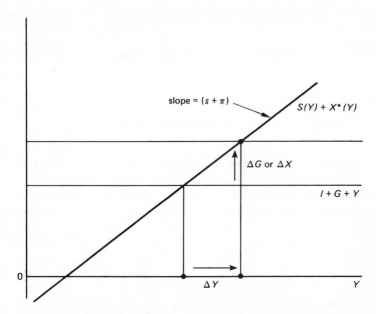

Figure 10-4   Illustration of Simple International Trade Multipliers

is $[dX/dX - dX^*/dX] = 1 - \pi(dY/dX)$. Or:

$$\frac{dB}{dX} = \frac{\pi}{s + \pi} \quad \text{(if } I_Y = 0\text{)}. \tag{10-20}$$

Hence, an autonomous increase in government expenditures aggravates the balance of payments while an autonomous increase in exports improves it. Both will increase the level of output and employment.

Foreign Repercussions

Now we drop the small country assumption made above. Thus, changes in the economic variables of the home country will affect the levels of the economic variables of the rest of the world. These are called the foreign repercussions.[18] We will call the home country Country 1 and the rest of the world Country 2 and suppose that Country 2 is also characterized by the ultra-Keynesian model. The effects of a change in one of the variables on the economic variables of both countries are illustrated schematically by Figure 10–5. Here the changes in the variables are supposed to be due to an initial autonomous increase in the government expenditures in Country 1. The arrow ($\uparrow$) means "an increase," the arrow ($\Rightarrow$) signifies a causal relationship, and ($\|$) reads "is equal to."

[18] A full discussion of such foreign repercussions can be seen in Machlup [33].

[An Increase in G in Country 1]

$$\Downarrow$$

Exports of Country 1 ($\uparrow$) $\Rightarrow$ Output of Country 1 ($\uparrow$) $\Rightarrow$ Imports of Country 1 ($\uparrow$)

$\|$ $\|$

Imports of Country 2 ($\uparrow$) $\Leftarrow$ Output of Country 2 ($\uparrow$) $\Leftarrow$ Exports of Country 2 ($\uparrow$)

Figure 10-5   Illustration of Foreign Repercussions

The analysis of the foreign repercussions is very simple once we have constructed a two-country, general equilibrium system. Since, in the present framework, each country can be characterized by a single equation similar to equation (10-15), the following two equations describe our model.

$$I_1 + G_1 + X_1(Y_2) - X_2(Y_1) + \alpha = S_1(Y_1) ; \tag{10-21}$$

$$I_2 + G_2 + X_2(Y_1) - X_1(Y_2) = S_2(Y_2) . \tag{10-22}$$

Here, for the sake of simplicity, we assume that neither country has income induced investment (that is, $dI_1/dY_1 = 0$, and $dI_2/dY_2 = 0$). The subscripts refer to the country. Note that X_1 denotes Country 1's exports (and Country 2's imports) and that X_2 denotes Country 2's exports (and Country 1's imports). α is the shift parameter so that a change in α signifies an autonomous change in $I_1, G_1, X_1, S_1,$ or X_2.[19] Note that $I_1, I_2, G_1,$ and G_2 are the exogenous variables of the system. Thus, the effect of an autonomous change in any one of these variables can be analyzed simply by differentiating our system [equations (10-21) and (10-22)] with respect to α. Thus, we obtain

$$\pi_2\, dY_2 - \pi_1\, dY_1 + d\alpha = s_1\, dY_1 ; \tag{10-23}$$

$$\pi_1\, dY_1 - \pi_2\, dY_2 = s_2\, dY_2 . \tag{10-24}$$

Here the changes in Y_1 and Y_2 (dY_1 and dY_2) are due to a change in the shift parameter α (that is, $d\alpha$), $\pi_1 \equiv dX_2/dY_1$ and $\pi_2 \equiv dX_1/dY_2$ (the marginal propensity to import of Countries 1 and 2 respectively), $s_1 \equiv dS_1/dY_1$ and $s_2 \equiv dS_2/dY_2$ (the marginal propensity to save of Countries 1 and 2 respectively).
   Solving equations (10-23) and (10-24), we obtain

$$dY_1/d\alpha = \frac{s_2 + \pi_2}{s_1 s_2 + \pi_1 s_2 + \pi_2 s_1} ; \tag{10-25}$$

[19] We are assuming that such a shift occurs in Country 1 only. Clearly the case with a shift initiated in Country 2 can be analyzed analogously and hence is omitted.

$$dY_2/d\alpha = \frac{\pi_1}{s_1 s_2 + \pi_1 s_2 + \pi_2 s_1} \,. \tag{10-26}$$

These are the formulas for the international trade multipliers which include the foreign repercussions. When $d\alpha$ represents an autonomous change in (Country 1's) investment, $(dY_1/d\alpha)$ can be called the *investment multiplier*, and when $d\alpha$ represents an autonomous change in (Country 1's) exports, $(dY_1/d\alpha)$ can be called the *export multiplier*.

The change in Country 1's balance of payments due to an autonomous change in Country 1's investment is obtained as

$$\frac{dB_1}{d\alpha} = \pi_2 \frac{dY_2}{d\alpha} - \pi_1 \frac{dY_1}{d\alpha} = -\frac{\pi_1 s_2}{s_1 s_2 + \pi_1 s_2 + \pi_2 s_1} < 0 \,. \tag{10-27}$$

The change in B_1 due to an autonomous change in Country 1's exports is obtained as

$$\frac{dB_1}{d\alpha} = \pi_2 \frac{dY_2}{d\alpha} + 1 - \pi_1 \frac{dY_1}{d\alpha} = \frac{s_1 s_2 + \pi_2 s_1}{s_1 s_2 + \pi_1 s_2 + \pi_2 s_1} > 0 \,. \tag{10-28}$$

Thus an autonomous increase in Country 1's investment aggravates its balance of payments while an autonomous increase in Country 1's exports helps its balance of payments.

THE ANALYSIS OF EXCHANGE DEVALUATION WITH A CONSTANT INTEREST RATE[20]

The purpose of this section is to analyze the effects of a change in the exchange rate in a systematic manner in a Keynesian framework. We will be especially concerned with the effect of such a change on the balance of payments. Then

[20] This section with some revisions is taken from Chapter 6 of [63]. It is an extension of a lecture delivered at Harvard University in the Fall of 1957 by L. W. McKenzie. Takayama's effort is mainly to rebuild the lecture from its rather sketchy notes, to revise and extend the analysis, and to generalize the conclusions, and hence many formulas are derived from the notes of the lecture. In doing this he is indebted to Professors Ronald Jones and H. G. Johnson for helpful comments. This is rewritten as [64] and [66]. Takayama alone is responsible for any possible errors. Although the contents of this chapter turn out to be very similar to that of Tsiang [67], the work was independently done. The approach used here is simpler and more straightforward than that used by Tsiang.

We have used a comparative statics-type analysis so that the results can be obtained simply by differentiating the model described in the first section with respect to the various parameters. Since there are two countries and since we are not adopting the small country assumption, this approach becomes tedious and complicated. We have tried to avoid these mechanical difficulties as much as possible, but the results obtained are the same as those we would have obtained if we had carried out these tedious differentiations and substitutions.

we will be able to answer the following policy question: "Will an exchange devaluation be helpful in eliminating a balance of payments deficit?" *or* "Starting with a balance of payments equilibrium position, will an exchange devaluation cause a balance of payments surplus?"

The exchange rate is obviously a price variable (the price of one country's currency in terms of the other country's currency). In the preceding analysis of the international trade multipliers we made no use of price variables. But in the analysis of exchange devaluation, the exchange rate shifts. Hence even if each country's good can be produced at a constant cost [that is, the "ultra-Keynesian case", equation (10-9)], the relative price of the domestic good and the foreign good will change by a change in the exchange rate. In this section we shall investigate this problem with full recognition of "foreign repercussions." To sharpen our analysis, we shall later adopt the ultra-Keynesian assumption so that each country's good can be produced at a constant cost. The problem of consumer's substitution between the domestic good and the foreign good due to such a change in the relative price and a consequent change in real income (the terms of trade effect) becomes an important issue in the literature of devaluation.

Suppose that a trading world consists of two countries (Country 1 and Country 2), and each produces one good (its national income). Now consider a devaluation of Country 1's currency. This will, *ceteris paribus*, increase the domestic (Country 1's) price of her imported good and lower the foreign (Country 2's) price of Country 1's export good, which in turn will decrease Country 1's consumption demand for her imported good and increase Country 2's consumption demand for her imported good. In other words, there is a mechanism by which a devaluation of Country 1's currency will improve her balance of payments. This in turn will cause a multiplier effect of the type analyzed in the previous section. Moreover, a devaluation implies that Country 1 must spend more if it is to consume the same bundle of goods (the domestic good and the foreign good) as before because of the increase in the (domestic) price of its imported good. In other words, Country 1's (and Country 2's) real income is affected by the devaluation (the terms of trade effect). A change in a country's real income will affect its savings and imports. The final effect of the devaluation after all of these effects have been considered and the foreign repercussions have been taken into account is not easy to foresee. The discussion of this topic in the literature has become very complicated and diversified, often reflecting a fundamental misunderstanding of the problem.

In this section we shall discuss this problem in a systematic manner with the aid of a mathematical model. This will clarify the fundamental meaning of the analysis. This also provides us with a unified discussion of a topic which is treated in a highly diversified manner in the literature.[21]

Since our problem here is not as simple as that of the previous section, we will have to modify our notation. In order to minimize the possible confusion, our

[21] A short bibliographical discussion concerning consumer's role in the theory is attempted in the last section.

notation will be basically the same as that of Chapter 8. Suppose now that Country 1 produces only Good X (her national income) and Country 2 produces only Good Y. Then the following notation is the same as that used in Chapter 8.

X_1:   the output of Good X in Country 1.

Y_2:   the output of Good Y in Country 2.

X_{12}:   the volume of Good X exported by Country 1 to Country 2.

Y_{21}:   the volume of Good Y exported by Country 2 to Country 1.

P_i: the price of Good X in Country i ($i = 1, 2$).

Q_i: the price of Good Y in Country i ($i = 1, 2$).

E: the exchange rate (the price of Country 2's currency in terms of Country 1's currency) ($P_1 = EP_2$ and $Q_1 = EQ_2$).

B_i: the balance of payments of Country i in terms of Country 2's currency, $i = 1, 2$ (note $B_2 = -B_1$).

The small Latin letters refer to the (differential) changes in the corresponding variables (for example, $x_1 \equiv dX_1$ and so on).

We now construct our model. We first note the equilibrium relation as equation (10-1). This equation, however, should be modified to take account of the "terms of trade effect." In other words the price which is relevant to "real" quantities is not the price of the good produced in that country. The "real" quantities of Country i must be obtained by deflating money quantities (in terms of Country i's currency) by the proper price index of Country i. The proper price index of Country i is obtained as the average of P_i and Q_i weighted by the expenditures to Good X and Good Y. Let $\bar{P}_i$ be such a price index for Country i (see footnote [22]). Adopt the convention of choosing the units of measurement properly so that $P_1 = Q_2 = E = 1$ initially. Assume also that $B_1 = 0$ initially. Note that due to this convention and the assumption, we also have $P_2 = Q_1 = 1$ and $B_2 = 0$ initially. Then we have $\bar{P}_i = 1$ initially for $i = 1, 2$. Now let Z_i be equal to the sum of real consumption, real investment, and real government expenditures of Country i (all deflated by $\bar{P}_i$). Let U_i be the real income of Country i. We now have the following equation which describes the equilibrium relation in the goods market for Country i.

$$Z_1 + B_1 E/\bar{P}_1 = U_1, \quad \text{and} \quad Z_2 + B_2/\bar{P}_2 = U_2 . \tag{10-29}$$

Since $P_i = 1$ and $B_i = 0$ initially ($i = 1, 2$), differentiation of (10-29) yields

$$z_i + b_i = u_i , \quad i = 1, 2 . \tag{10-30}$$

Note that b_is are not necessarily equal to zero under the Keynesian framework with fixed exchange rates due to the lack in the price-adjusting stability mechanism. Let $(1 - \lambda_i)$ be the marginal propensity to spend of Country i and defined by

$$(1 - \lambda_i)u_i = z_i , \quad i = 1, 2 . \tag{10-31}$$

Equation (10-29) [or (10-30) or (10-31)] corresponds to the fundamental equation in Alexander's absorption approach [1]. $(U_1 - B_1 E/\bar{P}_1)$ or

$(U_2 - B_2/\bar{P}_2)$ measures "the difference between the total goods and services produced in that country and the total goods and services taken off the market" [1], and it is called "absorption" by Alexander. We now have to make clear a precise meaning of equation (10-30) or (10-31). As it is defined, Z_i is composed of real consumption, real investment, and real government expenditures. Real consumption and real investment are typically functions of interest rate, real income, and the real value of assets. The third element (real value of assets) can be neglected if we assume the absence of the Pigou effect. Hence, Z_i is typically a function of interest rate, real income, and the domestic price level in Country i. In the above λ_i is interpreted as the one which includes all the effects from these three variables.

This is clearly rather unpleasant. A more transparent way is to define $(1 - \lambda_i)$ as the partial derivative of the expenditures with respect to change in real income. That is, $(1 - \lambda_i) \equiv \partial Z_i/\partial U_i$ ($i = 1, 2$). Then the above equation (10-31) is not necessarily true. It should be rewritten as

$$(1 - \lambda_i)u_i + \delta_i = z_i .$$ (10-32)

Here δ_i denotes the effects on Z_i by changes in the interest rate and the price level. In other words, denoting the level of interest rate in Country i by R_i, $\delta_i \equiv (\partial Z_i/\partial R_i)r_i + (\partial Z_i/\partial \bar{P}_i)\bar{p}_i$. δ_i corresponds to what Alexander called the "direct effect of the devaluation" [1].

Define H_i by $H_i \equiv [U_i - Z_i]$, $i = 1, 2$. Then $H_1 = B_1E/P_1$ and $H_2 = B_2/P_2$ so that we have

$$h_i = b_i , \quad i = 1, 2, \quad \text{and}$$ (10-33a)

$$\partial(U_i - Z_i)/\partial U_i = 1 - (1 - \lambda_i) = \lambda_i , \quad i = 1, 2 .$$ (10–33b)

Note that $H_i > 0$ (respectively $H_i < 0$) signifies Country i's lending (borrowing). H_i is often called Country i's *hoarding*, and λ_i is called Country i's *marginal propensity to hoard*.

When we interpret $(1 - \lambda_i)$ as $\partial Z_i/\partial U_i$, then we have to worry about the direct effects of devaluation, δ_i. The full account of this δ_i with considerations of the foreign repercussions will be extremely complicated. Alexander states, "Such an analysis would be far more complicated than is desirable for the presentation of the main ideas." However, there are certain instances in which we can safely assume that $\delta_i = 0$ so that we can proceed in our analysis with our original equation (10-31) under the definition $(1 - \lambda_i) \equiv \partial Z_i/\partial U_i$. First recall that $\delta_i \equiv (\partial Z_i/\partial R_i)r_i + (\partial Z_i/\partial \bar{P}_i)\bar{p}_i$. Then note that $(\partial Z_i/\partial R_i)r_i = 0$ under any of the following three situations: a) the liquidity trap ($r_i = 0$), b) a completely interest inelastic saving and investment ($\partial Z_i/\partial R_i = 0$), and c) the Keynesian neutral monetary policy—the policy by the monetary authorities which maintains the supply of money and credit infinitely elastic at the existing rate of interest (so that $r_i = 0$). This policy assumption was originally adopted by Meade [38] as a possible case and used by Meade [38] and Tsiang [67]. Note also that this assumption of $\delta_i = 0$ enables us to delete the money market equilibrium relation from our consideration.

What are the situations then under which we can justify $(\partial Z_i/\partial \bar{P}_i)\bar{p}_i = 0$?

The first possible case is the ultra-Keynesian case in which $p_i = 0$ (a constant domestic price level due to an excess capacity and so on) and $\bar{p}_i$ is approximated by $p_i = 0$. This is an assumption underlying the international trade multiplier analysis of the previous section, and it is often (explicitly or implicitly) adopted in the literature. Another way to justify it is by the absence of the Pigou effect combined with the treatment of real government expenditures as an exogenous variable. The latter can be justified if the government always has to consider the real value of her expenditures rather than their monetary value. The assumption of the negligible Pigou effect is a much debated topic in the literature (see, for example, Patinkin [46], Note M). Here we simply assume away the Pigou effect. (The interested reader may investigate a possible justification in terms of the separability of the real goods, and the combined money and bonds.

Whatever the justification for $\delta_i = 0$, we will proceed with our analysis under this assumption [so that (10-31) holds], for it will simplify our analysis considerably and it will, as Tsiang also believed [67], highlight the connection between the elasticity approach and the absorption approach. Alternatively, if we so prefer, we can define $(1 - \lambda_i)$ simply as the proportion of a change in real income of Country i (u_i) to a change in her spending, z_i.

We are now concerned with obtaining the expressions for u_i and z_i. The concept of a change in real income (u_i) of an open economy was already discussed in the previous chapter. There we pointed out the two channels which give rise to this u_i: a change in prices and a change in output. There we obtained the expressions $u_1 = (p_1 - q_1)Y_{21} + x_1 + y_1$ and $u_2 = (q_2 - p_2)Y_{21} + x_2 + y_2$ by using the convention of the initial unit prices and the initial balance ($B_1 = 0$). In the neoclassical analysis of the previous chapter, we noted that $x_i + y_i = 0$, $i = 1, 2$ (the full employment assumption). But in the Keynesian model this kind of relation does not hold. First there is no explicit consideration of the allocation of the resources to various industries, and it is supposed that there is no production of Y in Country 1 and X in Country 2. Thus we have $Y_1 \equiv 0$, $X_2 \equiv 0$ and $y_1 \equiv 0$, $x_2 \equiv 0$. Secondly, we can have an increase in each country's income and output through the use of unemployed resources (especially labor), so that we can have $x_1 > 0$ and $y_2 > 0$. Hence the expression for a change in real income under the Keynesian economy is:[22]

---

[22] If there is no international trade as in the ordinary macroeconomic analyses, $Y_{21} = 0$. Then $u_1 = x_1$ and $u_2 = y_2$. That is, the change in the real income in each country is equal to the change in its (national) output. Note that equation (10-32a), for example, can also be obtained by making the following two equations explicit, taking derivatives, and recalling that $z_1 = (1 - \lambda_1)u_1$. (See Tsiang's derivation of his equation (3-a)—his D_a corresponds to our $Z_1 \bar{P}_1$ [67].)

$$Z_1\bar{P}_1 = (P_1X_1 - X_{12}) + Q_1Y_{21}, \tag{i}$$

$$Z_1 = Z_1(P_1X_1/\bar{P}_1), \tag{ii}$$

where $\bar{P}_1 \equiv \dfrac{Z_1 - Y_{21}}{Z_1} P_1 + \dfrac{Y_{21}}{Z_1} Q_1$. Equation (10-34b) can be obtained similarly. In this way the derivations of equations (10-34a) and (10-34b) are much more cumbersome. It is important to notice that the terms of trade effect were incorporated in equations (10-34a) and (10-34b).

$$u_1 = (p_1 - q_1)Y_{21} + x_1 , \tag{10-34a}$$

$$u_2 = (q_2 - p_2)Y_{21} + y_2 , \tag{10-34b}$$

where u_i ($i = 1, 2$) denotes a change in real income of Country i. Here the convention of $P_i = Q_i = E = 1$ is adopted, together with the initial balance of payments equilibrium ($B_1 = 0$).[23]

A change in real spending of Country i (z_i; $i = 1, 2$) can easily be obtained as:

$$z_1 = (x_1 - x_{12}) + y_{21} \, (= y_{21} - x_{12} + x_1) , \tag{10-35a}$$

$$z_2 = x_{12} + (y_2 - y_{21}) \, (= x_{12} - y_{21} + y_2) . \tag{10-35b}$$

Here we are measuring y_{21}, x_{12}, x_1, and y_2 in terms of their initial prices $P_i = Q_i = 1$ (otherwise, the expressions such as $y_{21} - x_{12}$ are meaningless). Now putting the relations of (10-34) and (10-35) into (10-31), we obtain:[24]

$$(1 - \lambda_1)[(p_1 - q_1)Y_{21} + x_1] = y_{21} - x_{12} + x_1 , \tag{10-36}$$

$$(1 - \lambda_2)[(q_2 - p_2)Y_{21} + y_2] = x_{12} - y_{21} + y_2 . \tag{10-37}$$

Here we have to note that there is a problem which is rather ambiguous in the literature, that is, the problem of interpreting z_i. As we noted, Z_i is composed of real consumption, real investment, and real government expenditures. By assuming that the real government expenditure is exogenous to the model, its change becomes zero. Then z_i is composed of a change in real consumption and real investment. In other words, z_i still has to include a component called a change in real investment. This problem is important, for we have to set up a certain behavior relation to explain z_i. In the literature it is often implicitly or explicitly assumed that the investment expenditures are governed by the same rule as the one which governs consumers' behavior—the Slutsky-Hicks type relation. This is obviously rather absurd, although we can understand the difficulty and the complications involved in explicitly specifying the investment behavior. An alternative way to handle this in the literature is simply to suppose that the (real) investment is exogenous to the income. Hence, it can be treated as a constant for a change in income. If the investment is treated as a constant, then a change in investment would be zero. Under the circumstances, then, we may regard a change in real spending (z_i) as consisting solely of a change in real consumption. Under this interpretation we may also note that λ_i, the marginal propensity to hoard, becomes equal to the marginal propensity to save as defined in the second section (or S_Y in the first section).

[23] Recall that this convention, among others, implies $X_{12} = Y_{21}$. [Note the forthcoming equation (10-41).]

[24] Equation (10-35a), for example, can also be obtained by taking derivative of equation (i) of footnote 22 (keeping the definition of $\overline{P}_1$ in mind). Equation (10-35b) can be obtained similarly. Obviously, we do not need all these computations to derive (10-35a) and (10-35b). These equations are self-evident without going through these computations.

Whatever the interpretation of z_i, we will follow the convention in the literature and suppose that z_i is governed by the Slutsky-Hicks type behavior relation. In other words,

$$y_{21} = -Y_{21}(q_1 - p_1)\eta_1 + \pi_1(y_{21} - x_{12} + x_1), \tag{10-38}$$

$$x_{12} = -X_{12}(p_2 - q_2)\eta_2 + \pi_2(x_{12} - y_{21} + y_2), \tag{10-39}$$

where $\eta_i > 0$ is the elasticity of substitution of the imported good for Country i with respect to a real and fixed consumption (for example, $\eta_1 \equiv \partial\Phi/\partial(P_1/Q_1)$, and so on), and π_i is the marginal propensity to consume the imported good with respect to a change in real spending.[25] The definitions of η_i and π_i exactly correspond to those in Chapter 8. We may note that the distinction between η_i and η_i' disappears due to our supposition that always $Y_1 = X_2 = 0$ (no domestic production of the imported good). Also note that, in the above two equations, we supposed the absence of money illusion. In other words, a change in consumption will be invariant under a proportional change in the prices of the two goods (hence, also money spending). An alternative way to say this is that Y_{21} (respectively X_{12}) is a homogeneous function of degree zero in P_1, Q_1, and $P_1X_1 [= P_1(X_1 - X_{12}) + Q_1Y_{21}]$ (respectively P_2, Q_2, and Q_2Y_2). We can check this simply by checking that Euler's relation holds. For example for Y_{21} we can check that the following (Euler) relation holds:

$$\frac{\partial Y_{21}}{\partial P_1} P_1 + \frac{\partial Y_{21}}{\partial Q_1} Q_1 + \left(\frac{\partial Y_{21}}{\partial(P_1X_1)}\right)(P_1X_1) = 0. \tag{10-40}$$

Tsiang made this use of Euler's equation ([67], footnote 11). Our formulation of (10-38) and (10-39) is simpler than this.

Now we come to the balance of payments equation. Letting B_1 be the balance of payments of Country 1 in terms of Country 2's currency, we have

$$B_1 = P_2X_{12} - Q_2Y_{21}. \tag{10-41}$$

Differentiating this and noting that $X_{12} = Y_{21}$ initially,[26] we have

$$b_1 = (p_2 - q_2)Y_{21} + x_{12} - y_{21}. \tag{10-42}$$

A change in Country 2's balance of payments, b_2, can be obtained simply from $b_2 = -b_1$ $(\because B_2 = -B_1)$.

The price of the same good in the two countries is linked by the exchange rate E. That is,

$$P_1 = EP_2 \quad \text{and} \quad Q_1 = EQ_2. \tag{10-43}$$

Differentiation of (10-43) yields[27]

$$p_1 = e + p_2 \quad \text{and} \quad q_1 = e + q_2. \tag{10-44}$$

[25] This convention is due to Meade [38]. Φ denotes the demand function for Good Y in Country 1 (see equation (8–13) of Chapter 8).
[26] This is due to our convention of $P_1 = Q_2 = E = 1$ and $B_1 = 0$ initially.
[27] Recall again our convention of $P_1 = Q_2 = E = 1$ initially.

This is the same relation that we obtained in the previous chapter. For (10-44) we note again:

$$p_1 - q_1 = p_2 - q_2 . \tag{10-45}$$

We may write this as $p - q \ (\equiv p_i - q_i, i = 1, 2)$. A comparison of (10-42), (10-34), and (10-35) [and noting (10-45)] will give the following relations:

$$u_1 - z_1 = b_1 , \tag{10-46a}$$

$$u_2 - z_2 = b_2 . \tag{10-46b}$$

In other words, the difference between a change in real income and a change in real spending is solely devoted to a change in balance of payments. This means that the equilibrium relation in the goods market, (10-30), is satisfied.

In Chapter 8, we used notation such as $x_{12}{}^d$, $y_{21}{}^d$, and $b_1{}^s$. Here our notation does not have such superscripts. This is not accidental. In the present chapter we are supposing an *equilibrium relation* after the change has occurred, while in the previous chapter we supposed a *disequilibrium relation* after the change. Therefore, in the present chapter we can attach a unique meaning to the notation x_{12}, y_{21}, and b_1. For example, y_{21} denotes a change in excess demand for Y in Country 1 *and* a change in excess supply of Y in Country 2. Recall that these two are not necessarily equal in chapter 8. Since this question involves an important problem, we shall discuss it separately in the next section. We simply note that our analysis here is that of comparative statics which compares the two *equilibrium* situations.

We now proceed to describe the production side of the economy. First write the production function for each country as

$$X_1 = f(N_1) , \tag{10-47}$$

$$Y_2 = g(N_2) , \tag{10-48}$$

where N_i $(i = 1, 2)$ denotes the labor employment of Country i.

Next we write the demand equation for labor which states that the marginal physical product of labor is equal to the real wage rate. In other words, letting W_i be the money wage rate of Country i $(i = 1, 2)$, we have

$$\frac{x_1}{n_1} = \frac{W_1}{P_1} , \tag{10-49}$$

$$\frac{y_2}{n_2} = \frac{W_2}{Q_2} . \tag{10-50}$$

We then assume that the existing money wage is such that there is an excess supply of labor. Then due to the assumption of the downward rigidity of money wage rate under such a circumstance, we have

$$W_i = \text{constant} \ (i = 1, 2) .^{28} \tag{10-51}$$

We now convert equations (10-47), (10-48), (10-49), (10-50), and (10-51) into

---

[28] In the neoclassical economy, this equation is replaced by a labor supply equation such as $N_i = \text{constant}$ $(i = 1, 2)$.

variational form. Before doing this we first properly choose the unit of measurement of each country's labor so that $W_i = 1$ initially. Then (10-49) and (10-50) can be rewritten as

$$x_1 = n_1, \tag{10-52}$$

$$y_2 = n_2. \tag{10-53}$$

Clearly these two equations are also obtained by differentiating (10-47) and (10-48) and noting the relations of (10-49) and (10-50).

Next, differentiation of (10-49) and (10-50) yields

$$w_1 = p_1 + \frac{-1}{\sigma_{x_1}} \frac{n_1}{X_1}, \quad \text{and} \tag{10-54}$$

$$w_2 = q_2 + \frac{-1}{\sigma_{y_2}} \frac{n_2}{Y_2}, \quad \text{where} \tag{10-55}$$

$$\sigma_{x_1} \equiv \frac{\dfrac{x_1}{X_1}}{\dfrac{d(n_1/x_1)}{n_1/x_1}} \quad \text{and} \tag{10-56}$$

$$\sigma_{y_2} \equiv \frac{\dfrac{y_2}{Y_2}}{\dfrac{d(n_2/y_2)}{n_2/y_2}}. \tag{10-57}$$

σ_{x_1} and σ_{y_2} are called the *real elasticity of supply* by Meade [38]. By the above definition, they are usually positive. To understand this concept Figure 10-6 may be useful.

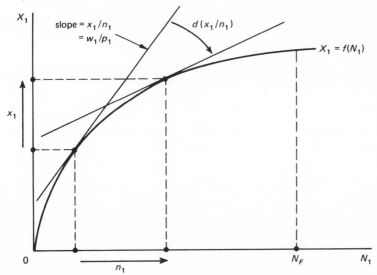

Figure 10-6   Meade's Real Elasticity of Supply

Due to equation (10-49), the marginal physical product of labor must be equal to the real price of labor. Thus the W_1/P_1 line is tangent to the production function curve. A change in W_1/P_1 will cause a change in X_1 which is depicted as x_1 in Figure 10-6. σ_{x_1} is the rate of change of X_1 per unit rate of change of the *inverse* of W_1/P_1, that is, $P_1/W_1 = n_1/x_1$. As is clear from the figure, σ_{x_1} (also σ_{y_2}) is usually positive. If the production function contains a flat portion (a constant marginal physical product of labor due to a large amount of excess capacity, then $d(x_1/n_1)/n_1 = 0$, so that $\sigma_{x_1} \to \infty$ ($\because x_1 = n_1$). In other words, this ultra-Keynesian situation can be characterized by an infinitely elastic real supply. If the economy reaches full employment of labor ($N_1 = N_F$ in the diagram), then $x_1 = 0$ so that $\sigma_{x_1} = 0$. As Meade pointed out, this concept of real elasticity of supply can be useful in characterizing both the Keynesian unemployment situation and the neoclassical full-employment situation. Note that if $w_1 = 0$, $\sigma_{x_1} = x_1/(p_1 X_1)$. Hence σ_{x_1} (also σ_{y_2}) measures the price elasticity of the aggregate supply curve in the Keynesian region (Figure 10-2).

Next we assume that the Keynesian under-employment situation which produces a constant money wage rate (10-51) is still valid *after* devaluation. Then we can differentiate (10-51) and obtain:

$$w_i = 0, \quad i = 1, 2. \tag{10-58}$$

This completes the construction of our model. The equations which describe the model are (10-36), (10-37), (10-38), (10-39), (10-42), (10-44), (10-52), (10-53), (10-54), (10-55), and (10-58), and the total number of equations is 13. The endogenous variables of the model are

$$\{x_1, y_2, x_{12}, y_{21}, n_1, n_2, w_1, w_2, b_1, p_1, q_1, p_2, q_2\},$$

and the total number of these variables is 13. In this model the exchange rate (E) is considered as a shift parameter, and we are concerned with the effect of its change on one of the endogenous variables, the balance of payments of Country 1, b_1/e. In particular, we are concerned with the problem of whether or not the exchange devaluation of Country 1 ($e > 0$) will improve her balance of payments ($b_1 > 0$).

In order to solve this problem, we first solve equations (10-36) and (10-37) with respect to x_1 and y_2. Then using (10-45), we put these expressions for x_1 and y_2 into equations (10-38) and (10-39). Thus we obtain

$$y_{21} = Y_{21}(q_1 - p_1)\left(-\eta_1 - \pi_1 \frac{1 - \lambda_1}{\lambda_1}\right) + \pi_1\left(1 - \frac{1}{\lambda_1}\right)(y_{21} - x_{12}),$$
$$\tag{10-59}$$

$$x_{12} = Y_{21}(p_1 - q_1)\left(-\eta_2 - \pi_2 \frac{1 - \lambda_2}{\lambda_2}\right) + \pi_2\left(1 - \frac{1}{\lambda_2}\right)(x_{12} - y_{21}).$$
$$\tag{10-60}$$

From (10-59) and (10-60) we obtain the expression for $(y_{21} - x_{12})$ and put this into equation (10-42); then we obtain

$$b_1 = \frac{Y_{21}}{A} (1 - \eta_1 - \eta_2)(p_1 - q_1), \quad \text{where} \tag{10-61}$$

$$A \equiv 1 + \pi_1 \frac{1 - \lambda_1}{\lambda_1} + \pi_2 \frac{1 - \lambda_2}{\lambda_2}. \tag{10-62}$$

Now to sharpen our analysis, let us assume the ultra-Keynesian situation for the production side of the economy (both countries). In other words set $\sigma_{x_1} \to \infty$ and $\sigma_{y_2} \to \infty$ (infinitely elastic real supply). Then equations (10-54) and (10-55) are reduced to

$$w_1 = p_1 \quad \text{and} \quad w_2 = q_2. \tag{10-63}$$

Thus, using (10-58), we obtain[29]

$$p_1 = 0 \quad \text{and} \quad q_2 = 0. \tag{10-64}$$

Then, combining (10-64) with (10-44), we obtain

$$p_2 = -e \quad \text{and} \quad q_1 = e, \quad \text{or}, \tag{10-65}$$

$$p_1 - q_1 = p_2 - q_2 = -e. \tag{10-66}$$

Hence, from (10-61) we obtain:[30]

$$\frac{b_1}{e} = \frac{Y_{21}}{A} (\eta_1 + \eta_2 - 1). \tag{10-67}$$

[29] The traditional justifications for an infinite supply elasticity (or constant price) are the assumptions that each country has non-traded goods and that the non-traded goods dominate the budgets of consumers. Although these assumptions are not necessarily unrealistic, they have a marked partial equilibrium flavor. Under our general equilibrium framework we do not adopt these assumptions. In the present context, rather, we interpret it as the assumption which characterizes the ultra-Keynesian economy. Another plausible assumption for making $p_1 = q_2 = 0$ is that the government of each country takes necessary measures, fiscal or monetary, to keep the internal prices of its products constant. This is plausible if we assume that the government regards the changes in internal prices as undesirable and the adjustment through exchange rate variations as more acceptable. This is certainly related to an age-old question of external stability (balance of payments equilibrium at a fixed exchange rate) versus internal stability (stable employment and price levels). See Meade [37]. This assumption, however, seems to cause another difficulty. See Chapter 11. Our purpose here is not to analyze such a problem under the above full-employment assumption but rather to provide the mechanism of price rigidity (or the lack of price mechanism) in the Keynesian under-employment economy. It is important to realize that our concept of the supply elasticity in equations (10-56) and (10-57) can be used for the neoclassical economy as well. We shall consider an application of this concept in such a context in Chapter 12.

[30] In fact, our basic formula (10-67) is not new to the literature. For example Jones [22] obtained a similar formula which can be reduced to our formula if we assume saving is initially equal to zero in his formula. However, our formula has a much simpler expression than his as well as an explicit recognition of Alexander's contribution. Our derivation of the formula is certainly much simpler.

Hence a necessary and sufficient condition that the devaluation improves the balance of payments ($b_1/e > 0$) is

$$\eta_1 + \eta_2 - 1 > 0, \quad \text{provided that} \tag{10-68}$$

$$A > 0. \tag{10-69}$$

It can be shown (see the last section of this chapter) that our condition (10-68) is exactly the same as the one obtained by Laursen and Metzler [31].

Clearly, this condition (10-68) is much more stringent than the Marshall-Lerner condition obtained in Chapter 8.[31] In other words, even if the neoclassical economy is characterized by the Marshall-Lerner condition, we still have a possibility that the Laursen-Metzler condition (10-68) is violated. This is interesting in view of the world-wide depression, and the pessimism and the experience about the exchange devaluation, in the 1930s.

When the economy of each country is not characterized by the ultra-Keynesian model, then we cannot have a simple relation of (10-64). The conclusion will be more complicated. We will leave such a consideration to the interested reader. The extreme case is that in which the economy reaches full employment. Then $x_1 \to 0$, $y_2 \to 0$, $\sigma_{x_1} \to 0$, $\sigma_{y_2} \to 0$, and W_i will go up. This need of the reconsideration of the production side of the economy is the concern of Tsiang [67]. He attempted to consider this problem by explicitly introducing the role of money. We shall discuss this later in the section in this chapter entitled "The Transfer Problem."

The introduction of the term $A \equiv \left(1 + \pi_1 \dfrac{1 - \lambda_1}{\lambda_1} + \pi_2 \dfrac{1 - \lambda_2}{\lambda_2}\right)$, $A > 0$, is an important contribution to the absorption approach whose introduction is facilitated by (10-36) and (10-37). As Alexander [1] pointed out, it is clear that in the case of negative λ_i there is a possibility that the above condition may be reversed. If we admit that in the real world the marginal propensity to hoard is not likely to be negative, then the ordinary elasticity condition can survive. It is, of course, too much to say that the absorption approach is better than the elasticity approach. It is important, however, to notice that some writers feel that the negative propensity to hoard is quite common (see Tsiang [67], for example). In any case, our equation (10-67) can be said to be the equation which weds the traditional elasticity approach to the new absorption approach.

This finishes our main analysis of the exchange devaluation under the ultra-Keynesian economy. We believe that: a) our derivation of condition (10-67) is much more straightforward and simple than ones that have appeared in the literature; b) we have made all the possible assumptions underlying the model and condition (10-67) explicit; and c) condition (10-67) is the one which combines

---

[31] Laursen-Metzler [31] correctly pointed this out by saying that the critical sum should exceed unity by a considerable amount. As we found in the previous chapter, the critical sum of the Marshall-Lerner condition is $(\eta_1' + \pi_1 + \varepsilon_1' + \eta_2' + \pi_2 + \varepsilon_2')$. Recall that η_1' and η_2' there equal η_1 and η_2 respectively in the present context since there is no domestic production of the imported good in this case.

the elasticity condition of Laursen and Metzler and the absorption condition of Alexander.

Finally, we shall reconsider the international trade multiplier analysis of the previous section under the light of the model of the present chapter. This will clarify the limitations of the simple multiplier model and the scope of the present model. In the simple international trade multiplier model, there is no explicit consideration of the production side of the economy. For the demand side it is assumed that an increase in real income (u_1) will be spent for domestic good (X), the imported good (Y), and hoarding $(=$ balance of payments). Hence $\pi_1(1 - \lambda_1)u_1$ is spent on the imported good, $(1 - \pi_1)(1 - \lambda_1)u_1$ is spent on the domestic good, and $\lambda_1 u_1$ is hoarded ($\lambda_1 u_1$ is also equal to the change in the balance of payments). In the analysis of this section, π_1 and λ_1 do not have to be constant as they are in the simple trade multiplier analyses. There is no consumer substitution due to changes in the relative prices; therefore, this has an effect similar to that when there is no price change ($p - q = 0$) as in the previous model. The shift parameter in our present model is the exchange rate; while in the simple trade multiplier analyses, it is α representing autonomous changes in government expenditures, investment, exports, and so on. Now we can write the model for the simple trade multiplier analysis in terms of the present notation as follows:

$$(1 - \lambda_1)x_1 + d\alpha = y_{21} - x_{12} + x_1 , \tag{10-70}$$

$$(1 - \lambda_2)y_2 = x_{12} - y_{21} + y_2 , \tag{10-71}$$

$$(1 - \lambda_1)\pi_1 x_1 = y_{21} , \tag{10-72}$$

$$(1 - \lambda_2)\pi_2 y_2 = x_{12} , \tag{10-73}$$

$$b_1 = x_{12} - y_{21} . \tag{10-74}$$

From equations (10-70) and (10-71) we obtain

$$d\alpha = \lambda_1 x_1 + \lambda_2 y_2 . \tag{10-75}$$

From (10-72) and (10-73) we obtain an expression for $x_{12} - y_{21}$ and then substitute this into equation (10-71) to obtain

$$[\lambda_2 + (1 - \lambda_2)\pi_2]y_2 - (1 - \lambda_1)\pi_1 x_1 = 0 . \tag{10-76}$$

Then combining equations (10-75) and (10-76), we obtain

$$\frac{x_1}{d\alpha} = \frac{\lambda_2 + (1 - \lambda_2)\pi_2}{\lambda_1\lambda_2 + \lambda_2(1 - \lambda_1)\pi_1 + \lambda_1(1 - \lambda_2)\pi_2} , \tag{10-77a}$$

$$\frac{y_2}{d\alpha} = \frac{(1 - \lambda_1)\pi_1}{\lambda_1\lambda_2 + \lambda_2(1 - \lambda_1)\pi_1 + \lambda_1(1 - \lambda_2)\pi_2} . \tag{10-77b}$$

In our treatment of the simple trade multiplier, the marginal propensity to import was defined as the change in imports per unit change in *income*. In the present section, it is defined as the change in imports per unit change in *spending*. Hence π_i in the previous section corresponds to $\pi_i(1 - \lambda_i)$ $(i = 1, 2)$ in this section, and s_i in the previous section corresponds to λ_i $(i = 1, 2)$ in this section. Now it is apparent that equations (10-77a) and (10-77b) are exactly the same as the formulas obtained for the international trade multiplier with foreign repercussions, equations (10-25) and (10-26). Thus we have obtained the formula for the international trade multiplier with foreign repercussions as a special case of the model presented in this section.

TWO REMARKS ON THE DEVALUATION ANALYSIS

Some Confusions in the Balance of Payments Analyses

In the second section of Chapter 8, we pointed out the importance of distinguishing between the comparative statics problem and the stability problem. Although this distinction should be obvious to any economic theoretician, there has been a frequent confusion on this problem in the theory of exchange stability and exchange devaluation. Hence in the literature, until very recently, these two terms—the "exchange stability problem" and the "exchange devaluation problem"—were used almost interchangeably, and there appeared to be no fundamental distinction between them. If these two terms refer to the same problem, then obviously it does not matter what we name such a problem. It is up to the analyst of the problem. However this is not the case. These are two problems which are fundamentally different, in spite of the fact that many writers use the above two terms in an arbitrary way to denote either of the two problems. This confusion was pointed out by Jones [23], who proposed to distinguish between these two problems. The purposes of this section are to make his point clearer and to gain more insight into the problem.

Recall our discussion of stability in Chapter 8. There we used variables which had superscripts such as $x_{12}{}^d$, $y_{21}{}^d$, and $b_1{}^s$. Those superscripts referred to the fact that the new state induced by a change in the terms of trade (P/Q) in the stability analysis was not an equilibrium state in the sense that all the markets were cleared. In Chapter 8, we pointed out that nonzero $b_1{}^s$ signified a *disequilibrium state* in the goods markets. Because the goods market was in a disequilibrium state, we could not assign a unique meaning to x_{12} or y_{21}. As we remarked there, x_{12} could mean either a change in the excess supply of X by Country 1 or a change in the excess demand for X by Country 2. As long as the economy was in a disequilibrium state, these two were not equal. Similarly, y_{21} could mean either a change in the excess demand for Y by Country 1 or a change in the excess supply of Y by Country 2, and these two were not equal if the economy was not in an equilibrium state. Superscript d was attached to x_{12} and y_{21} to make this point unambiguous. Thus $x_{12}{}^d$ meant a change in excess demand for X by Country 2 and $y_{21}{}^d$ meant a change in excess demand for Y by Country 1. $b_1{}^s$ signified a change in excess supply of Country 2's currency in Country 1.

In the previous section of the present chapter we did not put in such superscripts. For example, we used the following equation for a change in the balance of payments of Country 1:

$$b_1 = (p_2 - q_2)Y_{21} + x_{12} - y_{21}.$$

How can we avoid the use of the superscripts in this equation? Can we attach a unique meaning to x_{12}, y_{21}, and b_1? The answer is "yes," and the reason is that the new state after the change (in the exchange rate) is an *equilibrium state.* Hence assuming that the original state is an equilibrium state, a change in the excess demand for X by Country 2 is exactly equal to a change in the excess supply of X by Country 1 and a change in the excess demand for Y by Country 1 is exactly equal to a change in the excess supply of Y by Country 2.[32]

How is such an equilibrium state achieved in the devaluation analysis of the previous section? The answer is simple. It is simply achieved by a transfer payment from Country 1 to Country 2 by the amount of b_1.[33] In the devaluation problem the amount b_1 is *not* a predetermined exogenous variable as in the case of the transfer problem discussed in the previous chapter, but it is an endogenous variable to be determined within the system. The change in the transfer payment is a change in the shift parameter and a change in an exogenous variable, while in the devaluation analysis this transfer b_1 is not a change in the shift parameter. In stability analysis we do not allow such actual payments of transfer. In other words, the amount $b_1{}^s$ is hypothetical. The Marshall-Lerner condition gives a condition which says that this $b_1{}^s$ will be eliminated through changes in the terms of trade if the condition is satisfied. And in this mechanism we do allow the actual transactions and payments of the transfer $b_1{}^s$. This is obviously in accord with the traditional stability analysis in the Walrasian model. In the exchange devaluation analysis such a transfer payment is granted in the model. Although we do not know *a priori* how much the value of b_1 is, we have to grant that a payment in the amount b_1 is made. The very fact that a country

[32] In spite of this important distinction, the literature is full of confusion on this point. For example Johnson writes, "The central theoretical problem concerns the conditions under which a relative reduction in export prices would tend to improve a country's trade balance" ([20], p. 185), and he describes this problem generically as "the exchange stability problem." Meade in his *Geometry* [39] attempts to explore the "relationship(s) between the balance of trade deficit and the rate of exchange or barter terms of trade" (p. 93).

[33] Johnson emphasized this transfer aspect of the devaluation problem (which he called the stability problem) and proposed to formulate the devaluation problem as a transfer problem. He says, "Any actual balance-of-payments disequilibrium involves a transfer in some form, from the surplus to the deficit country (countries) and the problem of rectifying the disequilibrium can be framed as the problem of creating a transfer of equal amount in the opposite direction" ([20], p. 183). We may add that there are two types of transfers: a) a balance of payments deficit or surplus or a change in either (such as b_1), and b) a change in real income due to the change in the terms of trade [$(p - q)Y_{21}$ for Country 1 and $(q - p)Y_{21}$ for Country 2]. In the stability analysis in which there are no actual intermediate transactions until an equilibrium state has been reached, neither transfer is realized, although the second transfer plays an important role in determining the behavior of the consumers in the intermediate process.

actually has a balance of payments deficit implies that the other country allows such a deficit, which implies that the other country is willing to give a credit to the deficit country of an amount exactly equal to the amount of the deficit. Due to this reason the new state created by a devaluation in the analysis of the previous section is an equilibrium state.[34]

Therefore one fundamental difference between the stability analysis in the second section of Chapter 8 and the exchange devaluation analysis in the previous section of the present chapter is whether a new state created is a disequilibrium state or an equilibrium state. Hence we may call the former analysis a *disequilibrium approach* and the latter an *equilibrium approach*. A natural question is which of these two approaches is better. Some readers may have gotten the impression that the disequilibrium approach is better because it involves no implied arbitrary transfer payments. This is not quite correct. The above discussion attempted to clarify the logical difference between the two approaches, and its purpose was not really to judge which is better.

The reader may now recall that the distinction between the disequilibrium approach and the equilibrium approach was clearly recognized in our discussions of Chapter 9. Moreover, we pointed out that unless money is explicitly introduced, we can *not* determine the exchange rate (under the flexible exchange rate system) so that we cannot properly discuss the *exchange* stability problem. We also pointed out that if the exchange rate is flexible, then under a certain stability mechanism the balance of payments is brought into equilibrium so that it is rather meaningless to talk about the exchange devaluation problem under the flexible exchange rate system. Exchange devaluation is a proper subject of analysis under the fixed exchange rate system with fiat currencies, for example. The discussion of exchange devaluation in the previous section of the present chapter is carried out under such a supposition. We may now summarize our discussions in the following table.

TABLE 10-1   Various Approaches in the Balance of Payments Analysis

Chapters	Approach	Disequilibrium (no transfer)	Equilibrium (transfer)
Chapter 8 (second section)	neoclassical	the Marshall-Lerner condition (no explicit role of money)	
Chapter 9	neoclassical	exchange stability (fifth section) flexible exchange rates	exchange devaluation (fourth section) fixed exchange rates
Chapter 10 (third section)	Keynesian		exchange devaluation fixed exchange rates

[34] Hence the devaluation analysis is a comparative statics analysis. We suggest that the name "exchange devaluation analysis" be used for such a comparative statics analysis and that the name "stability analysis" not be used when referring to this problem.

Most of the confusions in the balance of payments analysis seems to originate from the writer's confusion on these points. It may be an interesting exercise for the reader to ask the following questions in reading each article in the literature on the balance of payments analysis:

1. Does it involve money explicitly? If it does, how? If it does not, the exchange rate is, in general, an illegal subject to discuss.
2. Is it a disequilibrium approach or an equilibrium approach? Does the author refer to comparative statics analysis as "stability analysis"?
3. What is the institutional framework of the analysis? In particular ask: Is the exchange rate flexible or fixed? Is the sterilization policy taken? Is money fiat or not? and so on.
4. Is the analysis Keynesian or neoclassical? If it is Keynesian, what is the treatment of the price of the home good, interest rate, and so on? The reader will be surprised to find many confusions on these points.

In passing, we may point out one difficulty in the disequilibrium analysis in the stability analysis. The question is, how can such a disequilibrium actually be possible in the real economy? Walras supposed that all the traders got together in one place and each exchanged a "ticket" which showed the amount of his demand or supply when a price was quoted by the "market manager." The market manager raised the price when there was an excess demand. Until an equilibrium was achieved, no actual transactions were allowed. In other words, there are no actual transactions in disequilibrium states. Only the tickets are exchanged. This process is called *tâtonnement*, and it is still an almost inevitable supposition in the present state of stability analysis. This supposition, although it is very ingenious, is clearly rather arbitrary and unrealistic on at least two points: a) all the traders gather in one place and b) no actual transactions take place until an equilibrium is reached.[35] The author [62] once worried about these points and proposed a model of international trade in which stability analysis is carried out without such a supposition. The basic reason why this is possible in "Stability in the Balance of Payments—A Multi-Country Approach" [62] is simply that we assume that each country holds enough gold so that a disequilibrium in the balance of payments is eliminated through the international movement of gold. It is assumed that such a gold holding has no effect upon the behavior of the spenders of each country. Later, Jones [23] also proposed a stability analysis which does not assume the tâtonnement process. He approached the problem by allowing variations in inventories instead of gold movement. The essence of his argument is essentially similar to the stability argument of the Keynesian cross diagram which appears in elementary textbooks of economics. In any case, there is one basic weakness in my "Stability in the Balance of Payments" [62] and Jones' "Stability Conditions in International Trade: A General Equilibrium Analysis" [23]. That is that there is no explicit behavioral consideration about the holding of stocks of

---

[35] For a more detailed discussion of this problem, see Takayama [62]. The non-tâtonnement analysis was developed after [62] was written. For a short survey of this see Negishi [43].

gold or inventories. In order to overcome this weakness in a truly honest way, we have to develop a general theory of money and capital which involves an explicit behavioral recognition of asset preference or time preference.

In the exchange devaluation analysis we need no such supposition of the tâtonnement process. But since it is a comparative statics analysis, we have to presuppose some sort of stability mechanism. Without some mechanism which brings it to a new equilibrium state, the comparative statics analysis, as is well-known, is rather meaningless. The fact that there is no explicit discussion of such a stability mechanism does not imply that we need no such mechanism. Another question is the problem of the transfer payment (b_1), which was discussed above. Suppose that a country refuses to give such a transfer. Why is each country prepared to give such a transfer? What is the behavioral background for this? These questions again have to be answered. In Chapter 9 we assumed that the currencies of the countries are freely convertible and that a balance of payments disequilibrium accompanies a monetary transfer. The analysis can be extended without too much difficulty by introducing internationally tradeable bonds. In the previous section of the present chapter, the underlying assumption is not explicit. The explicit treatment of this problem by introducing convertible currencies or internationally tradeable bonds is left to the interested reader.

Finally, for the sake of completeness, let us discuss the equilibrium approach in the neoclassical economy with no explicit role of money. This analysis is attempted by Meade in his *Geometry* [39] in which he confused the analysis of the equilibrium approach with that of stability analysis. In other words, he confused his clearly comparative statics analysis with that of the stability analysis.[36] The model is essentially the same as the one used in deriving the Marshall-Lerner condition (Chapter 8). The reader will notice that due to the comparative statics nature of the analysis, the transfer condition sneaks into the final condition. Consider a trading world consisting of two countries. Country 1 exports X and imports Y. The demand function of the imported good for each country was obtained in Chapter 8 as

$$y_1 + y_{21} = Y_{21}(p_1 - q_1)\eta_1' + \pi_1(y_{21} - x_{12}), \qquad (10\text{-}78)$$

$$x_2 + x_{12} = Y_{21}(q_2 - p_2)\eta_2' + \pi_2(x_{12} - y_{21}). \qquad (10\text{-}79)$$

Here again the unit initial prices $P_i = Q_i = E = 1$ and the initial balance $B_1 = 0$ are assumed. η_1' and η_2' are defined in the second section of Chapter 8 [equations (8-29a) and (8-29b)]. $(y_{21} - x_{12})$ measures a change in real consumption in Country 1, and it is now not equal to a change in her real income due to a transfer of b_1. Similarly, $(x_{12} - y_{21})$ measures a change in real consumption in Country 2, and it is not equal to a change in her real income. This gap between a change in real consumption and real income can be seen clearly from the following equation which is obtained by simply differentiating the balance of payments equation $B_1 = P_2 X_{12} - Q_2 Y_{21}$.

$$b_1 = (p_2 - q_2)Y_{21} + x_{12} - y_{21}. \qquad (10\text{-}80)$$

[36] This was first pointed out by Jones [23].

In other words b_1, a change in the balance of payments of Country 1, is sneaked into the system as an endogenous variable signifying a transfer payment from Country 1 to Country 2 (if $b_1 > 0$).

We note again that the exchange rate plays no role in determining the relative price ($P_1/Q_1 = P_2/Q_2$), so that

$$p_1 - q_1 = p_2 - q_2 . \tag{10-81}$$

We write them as $p - q$. The production side of the economy can be described by the following two equations which are the same as equations (8-35) and (8-36) of Chapter 8:

$$y_1 = \varepsilon_1'(q - p)Y_{21} , \tag{10-82}$$

$$x_2 = \varepsilon_2'(p - q)Y_{21} . \tag{10-83}$$

Then (10-78), (10-79), (10-80), (10-81), (10-82), and (10-83) yield

$$\frac{b_1}{p - q} = \frac{\Omega Y_{21}}{\pi_1 + \pi_2 - 1} , \quad \text{where} \tag{10-84}$$

$$\Omega = (\eta_1' + \pi_1 + \varepsilon_1') + (\eta_2' + \pi_2 + \varepsilon_2') - 1 . \tag{10-85}$$

As we recall, the condition $\Omega > 0$ is the Marshall-Lerner stability condition. The condition that the aggravation of the terms of trade to Country 1 ($p - q < 0$) improves the balance of payments ($b_1 > 0$) requires that the denominator of the *RHS* of (10-84) be negative. In other words in assuming the stability condition $\Omega > 0$, a necessary and sufficient condition for $b_1/(p - q) < 0$ is

$$\pi_1 + \pi_2 - 1 < 0 . \tag{10-86}$$

This additional condition (10-86) sneaked into the devaluation analysis because the transfer payment (b_1) was involved. We should note that this condition is identical with the condition that a unilateral transfer will deteriorate the terms of trade of the paying country (condition (8-63) of Chapter 8).

The Role of Money in the Keynesian Devaluation Analysis

In the third section we analyzed the exchange devaluation problem under the Keynesian under-employment framework. There we pointed out that when the economy reaches the full-employment stage from the under-employment state, the σs and x_1, y_2 approach zero[37], and we have to reconsider the model. We also pointed out that Tsiang, in his paper [67], analyzed this problem with an explicit introduction of money. It is the purpose of this section to give a critical review of this work.

---

[37] If a country faces an increase in the demand for its product under the full-employment situation, it cannot provide the additional output by increasing production. "It can only be provided through a reduction in the previous level of real expenditure" (Johnson [21], p. 165). He emphasized this point by saying, "Recognition of this point may be regarded as the fundamental contribution of the absorption approach."

In order to consider the effect of full employment on the problem of exchange devaluation, he distinguishes between the two types of monetary policy: the Keynesian neutral monetary policy and the orthodox neutral monetary policy. The former is the policy which keeps the money supply perfectly elastic by keeping the interest rate constant; while the latter keeps the money supply constant. He concludes that a full employment with the former policy "would imply instability in the balance of trade and exchange rate," while under the latter policy, "full employment at home will cause no difficulty to exchange stability."

The main idea of his paper is to introduce monetary equations similar to Meade's [38].[38] The importance of the role of money has sometimes been emphasized, especially since Alexander's recognition of the fundamental identity of the "absorption approach."[39] Money equations, in differential form, can be written from Meade and Tsiang in terms of our notational system as[40]

$$m_1 = \mu_1(x_1 + p_1 X_1) - v_1 r_1 \,, \tag{10-87}$$

$$m_2 = \mu_2(y_2 + q_2 Y_2) - v_2 r_2 \,, \tag{10-88}$$

where

m_i: the change in the money supply of the ith country ($i = 1, 2$);

μ_i: the partial derivatives of the demand for money with respect to the ith country's income;

v_i: the partial derivatives of the demand for money with respect to the ith country's domestic rate of interest, with sign reversed;[41]

R_i: the rate of interest of the ith country.

Having recognized this basic attitude, it is not too difficult to modify our system in this fashion. Looking back at our system of equations, it is pretty obvious that only the first set of equations (10-36) and (10-37) needs to be modified. This modification can be made more easily than Meade's [38] and Tsiang's [67].

---

[38] Clearly, the monetary equation here is the same as that used in our discussion of the ordinary Keynesian analysis. Recall the first section of the present chapter.

[39] For example, Johnson writes that the absorption approach "directs attention to two important aspects of a deficit—its monetary implication and its relation to the aggregate activity of the economy" ([21], p. 156). He also writes that the basic absorption identity "illuminates the monetary aspects of balance-of-payments disequilibrium, and emphasizes its essentially monetary nature" ([21], p. 158). Incidentally, Johnson's view should be understood in the light of his basic attitude to Keynesian economics, which he regards as an essentially monetary theory. This certainly seems to diverge from Klein's view (Klein [28] [29]). Our view has already been summarized in the first section of the present chapter. The author finds it difficult to understand the precise monetary significance of the absorption approach. It is a bit too intuitive anyway.

[40] Recall that we assumed away the asset effect in the demand for money (first section).

[41] See equations (13) and (14) in Tsiang [67].

The modification can be made as follows. In formulating our first two equations (10-36) and (10-37)), we considered the two channels which affect the changes in the real income: one through the price change and the other through the output change. Now we simply have to add the third channel which represents the change in the interest rate, since the change in the interest rate would certainly change the real expenditure and the real income of a country. Thus we have the following modifications for the first two equations:

$$(1 - \lambda_1)[(p_1 - q_1)Y_{21} + x_1 - \rho_1 r_1] = y_{21} - x_{12} + x_1, \tag{10-89}$$

$$(1 - \lambda_2)[(q_2 - p_2)Y_{21} + y_2 - \rho_2 r_2] = x_{12} - y_{21} + y_2, \tag{10-90}$$

where ρ_i is the partial derivative of Country i's real income with respect to the interest rate of the ith country, with sign reversed. (Tsiang [67] defined the ρs in terms of expenditure rather than income). The ρs represent the effect of the interest rate when prices and outputs are kept unchanged.

The supply side of the economy is described by equations (10-52), (10-53), (10-54), (10-55), and (10-58). They can be reduced to

$$p_1 = \frac{1}{\sigma_{x1}} \frac{x_1}{X_1}, \tag{10-91}$$

$$q_2 = \frac{1}{\sigma_{y2}} \frac{y_2}{Y_2}. \tag{10-92}$$

With an infinite elasticity of real supply ($\sigma_{x1} \to \infty$ and $\sigma_{y2} \to \infty$), $p_1 = 0$ and $q_2 = 0$ as we remarked in equation (10-64).

We now check the consistency of our model. Our model consists of eleven equations: (10-87), (10-88), (10-89), (10-90), (10-91), (10-92), (10-38), (10-39), (10-42), and (10-44). The number of endogenous variables in our model is also eleven: x_1, y_2, x_{12}, y_{21}, p_1, p_2, q_1, q_2, b_1, r_1, and r_2. The shift parameter of the equation is the change in the exchange rate (E), that is (e). Note that the money supply in each country is considered an exogenous variable so that we have m_i = (monetary policy by Country i) with the fixed exchange rate ($e = 0$). The analysis will be analogous, and hence we shall leave this to the interested reader. The exchange devaluation analysis is concerned with obtaining an expression for b_1/e from the above system and deriving the condition for $b_1/e > 0$ (the condition that the devaluing country improves its balance of payments). Our result will be exactly the same as that obtained by Tsiang [67].

Instead of repeating Tsiang's paper, let us consider some of its implications. Tsiang defined Keynesian neutral monetary policy as a particular monetary policy which keeps the monetary supply infinitely interest elastic. Instead of asking whether or not this was proposed by Keynes, let us keep its essence, that is, the constant interest rate. It seems that conclusions similar to Tsiang's under the Keynesian neutral monetary policy can be obtained by either or both of the following assumptions which we already discussed in the first section: a) the economy is in a deep liquidity trap (the demand rather than the supply of money is infinitely interest elastic) so that the interest rate is constant ($r_1 = 0$); b) consumption and investment are completely interest inelastic so that any change in the interest rate would not affect the real expenditure or the real income of a country too much ($\rho_i = 0$).[42]

According to these assumptions, the interpretation seems to be more natural to Keynes and probably more realistic than his Keynesian neutral monetary policy. In any case, if we admit the above, the monetary effect of a devaluation becomes null, and our old result (10-67) can be properly justified. But the two Keynesian assumptions above may break down when the economy has reached full employment. Here Tsiang's analysis becomes important.

Considering this problem Tsiang went to the other extreme. He confined his analysis solely to the orthodox neutral policy, which keeps the money supply constant rather than infinitely elastic with respect to the rate of interest, leaving no clear statement as to why such a monetary policy is desirable in a full-employment economy. Under the Keynesian under-employment situation this is certainly undesirable. A slight generalization of Tsiang's result can be obtained by considering the possible effects of the different levels of m_is upon the exchange devaluation[43]. But, after all, the balance of payments equilibrium is not the sole policy objective of national policy, and the monetary policy is probably not the most powerful policy that a government can adopt.[44]

There is another important contribution by Tsiang, namely his consideration of the danger of negative marginal propensity to hoard as threatening the effect of devaluation. He shows (as it can be shown in our revised model with money equations) that this danger "will be under control if an orthodox monetary policy is adopted." A question may arise whether this negative λ is a common phenomenon. He believes it to be "quite a normal phenomenon." It seems to me that the only way that this may happen is in the cases where the role of investment is explicitly taken into account in our model as a part of spending and where a principle such as the acceleration principle enlarges its effect. The question may then arise whether our equations (10-38) and (10-39) which are the heart of the elasticity approach are really consistent, since they are

---

[42] This point seems to be most emphasized by Klein [29]. It may also be expressed as the impossibility of full employment with an economically meaningful rate of interest. Thus, regarding investment and savings as functions of income only becomes the "heart and soul of the Keynesian system," as noted by Klein before. Although the first assumption was recognized by Tsiang, though not greatly emphasized, it is rather surprising that the second assumption was not even mentioned by him.

[43] It would be possible to set up a duopolistic model, where each country is acting as a duopolist, and the strategy consists of possible monetary policies.

[44] This does not really damage Tsiang's contribution at all, for he made it clear that under a full-employment situation the adoption of the Keynesian monetary policy is very dangerous for exchange stability and that the orthodox neutral monetary policy is far more sound in this respect (Tsiang [67]).

really the Slutsky-Hicks-type consumption functions.[45] The honest way to handle this problem is probably to construct an explicit investment function.[46]

THE TRANSFER PROBLEM

In Chapter 8, we analyzed the transfer problem in the neoclassical framework. In the previous section we pointed out that the exchange devaluation problem is closely related to the transfer problem, and we then treated the devaluation problem under the ultra-Keynesian assumptions. Here we will consider the transfer problem *per se* in the ultra-Keynesian framework.

Consider a unilateral transfer (reparation payments, foreign aid, and so on) from one country to the other. This means that purchasing power is moved from one country to the other. In other words, the purchasing power of the paying country is decreased while the purchasing power of the receiving country is increased. Hence, *ceteris paribus*, imports by the recipient country increase and imports by the paying country decrease. In the neoclassical model, the movement of the terms of trade supposedly clears the goods market so that a balance of payments equilibrium can be achieved. Thus the transfer of purchasing power and the resulting changes in the demand for goods will be reflected in changes in the terms of trade (and accompanying changes in output).[47] However in the Keynesian model with fixed exchange rates the balance of payments is not necessarily brought into equilibrium. Hence the initial impact of the increased imports by the recipient country and the decreased imports by the paying country due to the transfer of purchasing power will not be completely

---

[45] Tsiang's corresponding equations [(7) and (8) in his article] take a slightly different form than ours, for they include the term "expenditure" which may express the role of expenditure on the import functions (although indirectly). But this is somewhat deceptive because his equations (7) and (8) are reduced to exactly the same form as our (10-38) and (10-39) after having taken his "definitional expenditure identities" into account.

[46] In this connection it is to be noted that we neglected important possible roles which may be played by the Pigouvian asset effect. The importance of the Pigou effect was noted by Pearce [47], Alexander [1], and Michaeley [41] for example in the devaluation literature.

[47] Clearly part of the increased purchasing power of the recipient country goes to the demand for the domestically produced good, that is, the exported good (as well as the imported good). Part of the decreased purchasing power of the paying country leads to a decline in the domestic demand for the exported good (as well as its imported good). Hence the direction of the movement of the relative price of the goods can not be ascertained *a priori*. (If a change in the purchasing power of a country never affects the domestic demand for the exported good, then a unilateral transfer will certainly cause a deterioration in the paying country's terms of trade.)

As was argued in the previous chapter, a necessary and sufficient condition for the paying country's terms of trade to deteriorate is that the sum of the marginal propensity to consume the imported good for the two countries is less than $1(\pi_1 + \pi_2 < 1)$. The belief that a transfer will deteriorate the paying country's terms of trade is usually described as the "orthodox" doctrine (see Samuelson [51], p. 278). This view has long been held, often without serious consideration being given to the problem.

absorbed by the change in the relative prices. Moreover the transfer of purchasing power also implies an increase in the effective demand (for goods) in the recipient country and a decrease in the effective demand in the paying country which will induce changes in the consumption of the domestic good and the imported good (and possibly investment). In other words there will be an income-induced increase in imports in the recipient country and an income-induced decrease in imports in the paying country. This would, *ceteris paribus*, improve the balance of payments of the paying country and deteriorate that of the recipient country. This mechanism works even if we assume an infinite elasticity of supply (the ultra-Keynesian case) so that the home price of the domestically produced good is constant in each country. After all the effects including the foreign repercussions have been considered, what will be the final effect? This is the problem we shall concern ourselves with in this section.[48]

Following the Metzler-Machlup-Johnson tradition, assume that all the income of a country is spent on the domestic good, the foreign good, and savings in fixed proportions. In this case, the changes in price have no meaning. The basic mechanism of the system is output (or effective demand) changes. We assume that Country 1 gives a transfer in the amount T to Country 2, and we investigate the effect on the country's balance of payments at the final equilibrium. In the case of the *devaluation* problem the amount of the transfer is a variable to be determined in the system, while in the *proper* transfer problem the transfer is the shifting parameter of the system which moves the system from one equilibrium position to the other. [49] We assume that Country 1 collects the amount of the transfer in the form of income taxes from its people and Country 2 distributes it to its people in the form of an income subsidy so that the transfer does not affect the consumption behavior of either country. Our model is similar to the model considered in the third section, and we will adopt the same notation. Assuming that the amount of transfer is zero initially, we can write our model as follows:[50]

---

[48] Thus the difference in the recognition of the economy, that is whether it can be characterized by the neoclassical model or the Keynesian model, makes a very important difference in the analysis of the transfer problem. In the famous Keynes-Ohlin controversy over the German reparations problem, which occurred several years before the appearance of Keynes' *General Theory*, it was generally believed that Keynes adopted the neoclassical view and Ohlin took what was later called the Keynesian view. See, for example, Ellis, H. S. and Metzler, L. S., *Readings in the Theory of International Trade* (American Economic Association) (Homewood, Ill.: Richard D. Irwin), 1949, pp. x–xi (their introduction). However, a careful reading of these articles [26] [44] reveals that this was not as dramatic as it was often supposed to be. For example, Keynes was very pessimistic about the ability of the paying country to make all the neoclassical adjustments. Metzler's article [40] was probably the first influential analysis of the transfer problem with an explicitly Keynesian (or "modern") point of view.

[49] We may call the type of transfer in the devaluation problem the *endogenous transfer*, and the type of transfer in the *proper* transfer problem *exogenous transfer*.

[50] The parameters such as λ_i and $\pi_i (i = 1, 2)$ mean that $(1 - \lambda_i)$ percent of the change in Country i's income goes to a change in spending, of which π_i percent goes to a change in spending on the imported good. Clearly, it is not necessary to assume that λ_i and π_i are constant. They can be considered as partial derivatives evaluated at the original equilibrium

$$(1 - \lambda_1)(x_1 - \tau) = y_{21} - x_{12} + x_1 , \tag{10-93}$$

$$(1 - \lambda_2)(y_2 + \tau) = x_{12} - y_{21} + y_2 , \tag{10-94}$$

$$y_{21} = \pi_1(y_{21} - x_{12} + x_1) , \tag{10-95}$$

$$x_{12} = \pi_2(x_{12} - y_{21} + y_2) , \tag{10-96}$$

$$b_1 = x_{12} - y_{21} - \tau . \tag{10-97}$$

Here τ measures the change in the transfer payments. The transfer payments are assumed to be zero initially. We again adopt the convention of choosing our units of measurement so that $P_i = Q_i = E = 1$ initially, where P_i, Q_i, and E are defined as in the third section.

There are five equations and the number of unknowns is also five—x_1, y_2, x_{12}, y_{21}, and b_1. The shift parameter is τ. In fact, b_1 is also a transfer in the sense that the amount equal to b_1 should be given by Country 1 to 2 to bring the final state to an equilibrium state. However b_1 is different from τ in the sense that b_1 is endogenous to the system while τ is exogenous to the system. Solving above five equations we obtain

$$\frac{b_1}{\tau} = \frac{-1}{1 + \pi_1 \dfrac{1 - \lambda_1}{\lambda_1} + \pi_2 \dfrac{1 - \lambda_2}{\lambda_2}} . \tag{10-98}$$

The transfer is said to be *undereffected* if $|b_1/\tau| < 1$ and *overeffected* if $|b_1/\tau| > 1$.[51] It is necessary and sufficient, for the transfer to deteriorate her balance of payments, that

$$1 + \pi_1 \frac{1 - \lambda_1}{\lambda_1} + \pi_2 \frac{1 - \lambda_2}{\lambda_2} > 0 . \tag{10-99}$$

This is nothing but our absorption condition, $A > 0$, [condition (10-69)] which is imposed for the devaluation problem. Alexander's concern with the devaluation problems, therefore, ends with the transfer problem.[52]

---

level. In other words, the constant proportions assumption is not crucial in the model. The crucial point here is that we assumed away the consumer's substitution due to relative price changes.

[51] Hence the transfer is *just* effected ($b_1 = \tau$) if and only if $\pi_1 + \pi_2 = 1 + \pi_1/\lambda_1 + \pi_2/\lambda_2$. This corresponds to the condition obtained by Johnson in p. 179 of [20], as a generalization of the Meade-Metzler formulas.

[52] Our condition is slightly less general than Johnson's [20], for he does not assume that the transfer will not be spent on the three items (home good, foreign good, and saving) in the same proportion as the ordinary income. Hence, he allowed the possibility that government may spend it in an arbitrary proportion. But our case has a meaning in connection with the devaluation problem since it does not assume different spending behaviors according to whether the income accrues from endogenous transfer *or* comes from the other sources (changes in output or changes in the relative price). It may be worthwhile to notice the assumptions made by other writers. Metzler and Machlup assumed that the transfer will be spent only for the home good, and Meade assumed that the transfer will be spent for both the domestic good and the foreign good but that it never goes for saving. Compared with these writers, Johnson's contribution is obvious.

We shall now extend the above analysis to the case which incorporates the Hicksian demand substitution between the goods (X and Y). In other words, we shall now introduce equations (10-38) and (10-39) into the analysis. Here we assume that the exchange rate is fixed. Then using equation (10-44) we have $p_1 = p_2$ and $q_1 = q_2$, which we denote by p and q respectively. The model consists of equations (10-91) and (10-92) and the following five equations:

$$(1 - \lambda_1)[(p - q)Y_{21} + x_1 - \tau) = y_{21} - x_{12} + x_1, \tag{10-100}$$

$$(1 - \lambda_2)[(q - p)Y_{21} + y_2 + \tau] = x_{12} - y_{21} + y_2, \tag{10-101}$$

$$y_{21} = -Y_{21}(q - p)\eta_1 + \pi_1(y_{21} - x_{12} + x_1), \tag{10-102}$$

$$x_{12} = -Y_{21}(p - q)\eta_2 + \pi_2(x_{12} - y_{21} + y_2), \tag{10-103}$$

$$b_1 = (p - q)Y_{21} + x_{12} - y_{21} - \tau. \tag{10-104}$$

There are seven variables in the system ($x_1, y_2, x_{12}, y_{21}, p, q$, and b_1), and there are seven equations in the model. In the ultra-Keynesian case, where $\sigma_{x1} \to \infty$, $\sigma_{y2} \to \infty$ so that $p = 0$ and $q = 0$; the above model clearly reduces to the previous one so that we obtain the transfer condition (10-99). Note that if we write $z_1 \equiv y_{21} - x_{12} + x_1$ and $u_1 \equiv (p - q)Y_{21} + x_1 - \tau$, then $b_1 + z_1 = u_1$. A similar relationship holds for Country 2, and these relationships are the same as those noted in the third section.

In order to facilitate our analysis we define the following elasticities, which correspond to the elasticity of export supply as defined in equations (8-34a) and (8-34b) of Chapter 8:

$$\varepsilon_1 \equiv \sigma_{x1}X_1/X_{12}, \tag{10-105a}$$

$$\varepsilon_2 \equiv \sigma_{x2}Y_2/Y_{21}. \tag{10-105b}$$

Given our conventions that $P_i = Q_i = E = 1$, ($i = 1, 2$) initially and that $B_1 = 0$ initially, we can obtain the following equations using equations (10-105a) and (10-105b).

$$x_1 = \varepsilon_1 Y_{21}p, \tag{10-106}$$

$$y_2 = \varepsilon_2 Y_{21}q. \tag{10-107}$$

Hence using these equations and equations (10-100), (10-101), and (10-104) we obtain

$$\lambda_1[(p - q)Y_{21} + \varepsilon_1 pY_{21}] = b_1 + \lambda_1\tau, \tag{10-108}$$

$$\lambda_2[(p - q)Y_{21} - \varepsilon_2 qY_{21}] = b_1 + \lambda_2\tau. \tag{10-109}$$

Solving these two equations for pY_{21} and qY_{21} respectively, we obtain

$$pY_{21} = \frac{b_1[(1 + \varepsilon_2)\lambda_2 - \lambda_1] + \lambda_1\lambda_2\varepsilon_2\tau}{\lambda_1\lambda_2(\varepsilon_1 + \varepsilon_2 + \varepsilon_1\varepsilon_2)}, \tag{10-110}$$

$$qY_{21} = \frac{b_1[\lambda_2 - (1 + \varepsilon_1)\lambda_1] - \lambda_1\lambda_2\varepsilon_1\tau}{\lambda_1\lambda_2(\varepsilon_1 + \varepsilon_2 + \varepsilon_1\varepsilon_2)}. \tag{10-111}$$

From equations (10-102) and (10-103) we obtain

$$(\pi_1 + \pi_2 - 1)(x_{12} - y_{21}) = Y_{21}(p - q)(\eta_1 + \eta_2) + \pi_1 x_1 - \pi_2 y_2 . \quad (10\text{-}112)$$

Hence, using equations (10-110), (10-111), and (10-112) the balance of payments equation can be rewritten as

$$b_1 = Y_{21}(p - q)(1 + \eta/\pi) + (\varepsilon_1 \pi_1 p Y_{21} - \varepsilon_2 \pi_2 q Y_{21})/\pi - \tau , \quad (10\text{-}113)$$

where $\pi \equiv \pi_1 + \pi_2 - 1$ and $\eta \equiv \eta_1 + \eta_2$; or,

$$\pi b_1 = p Y_{21}(\pi + \eta + \varepsilon_1 \pi_1) - q Y_{21}(\pi + \eta + \varepsilon_2 \pi_2) - \pi \tau . \quad (10\text{-}114)$$

Then inserting the expressions for $p Y_{21}$ and $q Y_{21}$ which we obtained in equations (10-110) and (10-111), we obtain after some rather tedious computation

$$\frac{b_1}{\tau} = -\frac{\Delta_1}{\Delta_2} , \quad \text{where} \quad (10\text{-}115)$$

$$\Delta_1 \equiv (\eta_1 + \eta_2)(\varepsilon_1 + \varepsilon_2) + \varepsilon_1 \varepsilon_2 , \quad \text{and} \quad (10\text{-}116)$$

$$\Delta_2 \equiv (\eta_1 + \eta_2 - 1)(\varepsilon_1/\lambda_2 + \varepsilon_2/\lambda_1) + (\varepsilon_1 + \varepsilon_2 + \varepsilon_1 \varepsilon_2)A , \quad (10\text{-}117)$$

where A is the absorption expression $A \equiv 1 + \pi_1(1 - \lambda_1)/\lambda_1 + \pi_2(1 - \lambda_2)/\lambda_2$. It should be clear that when $\varepsilon_1 \to \infty$ and $\varepsilon_2 \to \infty$ (the ultra-Keynesian case), equation (10-115) coincides exactly with equation (10-98) (divide both the numerator and the denominator of (10-115) by $\varepsilon_1 \varepsilon_2$ and then take the limit as $\varepsilon_1 \to \infty$ and $\varepsilon_2 \to \infty$).

In the above expression, $(\eta_1 + \eta_2 - 1) > 0$ is condition (10-68) (the Laursen-Metzler condition) and $A > 0$ is condition (10-69) (the absorption condition). Hence if $(\eta_1 + \eta_2 - 1) > 0$ and $A > 0$ (that is, both conditions are satisfied), b_1/τ is in general negative. In other words under these conditions, a unilateral transfer will cause a deterioration in the balance of payments of the paying country. A necessary and sufficient condition for a unilateral transfer to cause a deterioration in the paying country's balance of payments (with finite ε_1 and ε_2) is given by

$$\Delta_2 \equiv (\eta_1 + \eta_2 - 1)(\varepsilon_1/\lambda_2 + \varepsilon_2/\lambda_1) + (\varepsilon_1 + \varepsilon_2 + \varepsilon_1 \varepsilon_2)A > 0 . \quad (10\text{-}118)$$

This again confirms the statement that the exchange stability is very closely related to the transfer problem.

THE KEYNESIAN DEVALUATION ANALYSIS AND THE THEORY OF CONSUMERS' BEHAVIOR

In the third section we presented a model with which we can analyze the problem of exchange devaluation in the Keynesian framework. One of the most important things we found was that there is a difference between a change in real income and a change in real spending. The purpose of this section is to clarify the doctrinal background of this problem because it involved a rather tedious but important debate, especially in the 1950's. Without understanding this background, our understanding of the model may be rather superficial.

The central issue of the problem is summarized by the name *terms of trade effect* which refers to the effect of a decline (increase) in real income of a devaluing country due to an increase (decrease) in the expenditure required to buy the same bundle of goods as before the devaluation. Let us suppose, as before, that Country 1 is the devaluing country, and let P_i and Q_i respectively be the prices of Good X and Good Y in Country i ($i = 1, 2$). Let D_1 be the total (money) expenditure of Country 1. In other words,

$$D_1 \equiv P_1(X_1 - X_{12}) + Q_1 Y_{21}. \tag{10-119}$$

The terms of trade effect is to ascertain the effect of a change in the exchange rate on D_1. Following the literature, we here assume that $P_1 = $ constant and $Q_2 = $ constant for all the relevant levels of output (the infinite supply elasticity or the ultra-Keynesian assumption). Letting E be the exchange rate and writing the (infinitesimal) change by small letters, we have $p_1 = e + p_2$ and $q_1 = e + q_2$ as was remarked before. Then $p_1 - q_1 = p_2 - q_2 = -e$ since $p_1 = q_2 = 0$. In other words, the devaluation of Country 1 (that is, $e > 0$) means the deterioration of the terms of trade to Country 1. Hence, to ascertain the effect of a change in the exchange rate on D_1 is the same as to ascertain the effect of a change in the terms of trade on D_1. Thus this problem is the so-called terms of trade effect.

The problem of the terms of trade effect thus can be described as that of ascertaining $\partial D_1/\partial E$ or $\partial D_1/\partial Q_1$. ($\because \partial D_1/\partial E = (\partial D_1/\partial Q_1)(\partial Q_1/\partial E) = (\partial D_1/\partial Q_1)Q_2$, since $Q_1 = Q_2 E$ and $Q_2 = $ constant by assumption). We again adopt the convention of choosing the units of measurement properly so that $P_i = Q_i = E = 1$ initially. With this convention, $\partial D_1/\partial Q_1$ can easily be obtained from (10-119) as follows:[53]

$$\frac{\partial D_1}{\partial Q_1} = \frac{\partial X_c}{\partial Q_1} + \frac{\partial Y_{21}}{\partial Q_1} + Y_{21}, \tag{10-120}$$

where $X_c \equiv X_1 - X_{12}$ (the domestic consumption of X in Country 1).

Therefore, our problem is reduced to that of ascertaining $\partial X_c/\partial Q_1$ (the effect of a change in Q_1 or E on the domestic consumption of the exported good) and $\partial Y_{21}/\partial Q_1$ (the effect of a change in Q_1 or E on the consumption of the imported good). Here we assume that investment is exogenous to the system or behaves exactly the same as the consumption. Thus we are now led to the Slutsky-Hicks type of demand theory. As is well-known from this theory, the effect of a price change upon the consumption of the goods can be decomposed into two effects—the income effect and substitution effect. Let α and β respectively denote the income effect and the substitution effect. We put subscripts

[53] Alternatively, we may define the terms of trade effect as $\partial Z_1/\partial Q_1$ instead of $\partial D_1/\partial Q_1$, where Z_1 is the real spending of Country 1 (as defined in the third section), while D_1 is the money spending of Country 1. Here we adopted the definition in terms of $\partial D_1/\partial Q_1$ to ease our survey of the literature.

to refer to the good. For example, α_x refers to the income effect for the consumption of X. In other words,

$$\frac{\partial X_c}{\partial Q_1} = \alpha_x + \beta_x \,, \tag{10-121a}$$

$$\frac{\partial Y_{21}}{\partial Q_1} = \alpha_y + \beta_y \,. \tag{10-121b}$$

Income Effect

The income effect is the loss of real income due to the increased price of the imported good resulting from the devaluation. We measure this by the increase in the expenditure required to buy the same bundle of goods as before the devaluation. In fact, we already ascertained this when we considered a change in real income in Chapter 8. In other words, it is a change in real income through the channel of a price change which we measured as $(p_1 - q_1)Y_{21}$ for Country 1 (with the convention that $P_i = Q_i = E = 1$ initially and $B_1 = 0$ initially). Letting U_1 be the real income of Country 1, we then obtain

$$\frac{\partial U_1}{\partial Q_1} = -Y_{21} \quad (\because P_1 = \text{constant or } p_1 = 0) \,. \tag{10-122}$$

Here we have to point out that there is an implicit assumption involved in this formulation when saving is present in the model. That is, we are tacitly assuming that the effect of a change in Q_1 on saving is negligible. This is pointed out as the existence of money illusion by Spraos [57]. In order to consider this problem, let us suppose that saving is the delay of the present consumption and assume that the proportion of spending to income is constant before and after devaluation. Let S_1 be the amount of real saving (or hoarding) in Country 1. Then Spraos' point can be taken into consideration by modifying equation (10-122) as follows:

$$\frac{\partial U_1}{\partial Q_1} = -Y_{21} \frac{U_1}{U_1 - S_1} \,. \tag{10-123}$$

We may rewrite (10-123) as

$$\frac{\partial U_1}{\partial Q_1} = -\frac{Y_{21}}{1 - (APS)_1} \,, \tag{10-123'}$$

where $(APS)_1$ denotes the average propensity to save (hoard) of Country 1. In any case, the income effects α_x and α_y can now be ascertained. Let λ_1 and π_1 be the marginal propensity to hoard and the marginal propensity to consume the imported good, respectively, for Country 1. Then α_x and α_y can be written as

$$\alpha_x = (1 - \pi_1)(1 - \lambda_1) \left(\frac{\partial U_1}{\partial Q_1} \right), \tag{10-124}$$

$$\alpha_y = \pi_1(1 - \lambda_1) \left(\frac{\partial U_1}{\partial Q_1} \right). \tag{10-125}$$

We may note that

$$\alpha_x + \alpha_y = (1 - \lambda_1)(\partial U_1/\partial Q_1). \tag{10-126}$$

If $(APS)_1 = \lambda_1$, then we obtain the following equations using (10-123′).

$$\alpha_x = -(1 - \pi_1)Y_{21}, \tag{10-124′}$$

$$\alpha_y = -\pi_1 Y_{21}. \tag{10-125′}$$

Substitution Effect

The substitution effect is concerned with the substitution among the various goods when there is a change in income. If we consider saving as a kind of good and if we write β_s for the substitution effect, we have

$$\beta_x + \beta_y + \beta_s = 0, \tag{10-127}$$

which states the fact that the sum of the total substitution effects of all the goods is equal to zero. If we assume $\beta_s = 0$, then the saving is kept at a constant level even after a change in the relative price and after a compensation of income to keep real income constant. In other words, there is no substitution effect between spending and saving.[54]

This finishes the basic consideration of the problem. We shall now attempt a critical review of the arguments in the literature on this problem.

STOLPER [59]   The problem that Stolper was concerned with is not the problem of exchange devaluation, but rather, it is the problem of achieving full employment under flexible exchange rates. However his problem is clearly related to our problem. His basic assumption on consumers' behavior is that a change in the relative price of the goods has no effect on the spending for the domestic good. That is,

$$\frac{\partial X_c}{\partial Q_1} = 0, \quad \text{or} \quad \alpha_x + \beta_x = 0. \tag{10-128}$$

As Spraos [57] pointed out, there is no justification for this assumption. In any case, the terms of trade effect under this assumption can easily be obtained from (10-120) and (10-121) as follows:

$$\frac{\partial D_1}{\partial Q_1} = Y_{21}\left(\frac{\alpha_y}{Y_{21}} + \frac{\beta_y}{Y_{21}} + 1\right). \tag{10-129}$$

HARBERGER [17]   Harberger's introduction of the explicit Keynesian analysis in the exchange devaluation analysis is clearly epoch-making, as is the similar task by Laursen and Metzler [31].

[54] If $(APS)_1 = \lambda_1$, then $\alpha_x + \alpha_y = -Y_{21}$ due to (10-124′) and (10-125′). In addition if $\beta_x + \beta_y = 0$, then (10-120) and (10-121) imply $\partial D_1/\partial Q_1 = 0$. That is, there is no terms of trade effect.

i. *Income Effect:* He implicitly assumed the existence of money illusion and adopted equation (10-122). Hence, the terms of trade effect is obtained from (10-120), (10-121), (10-122), and (10-126) as

$$\frac{\partial D_1}{\partial Q_1} = -(1 - \lambda_1)Y_{21} + \beta_x + \beta_y + Y_{21} = \lambda_1 Y_{21} + \beta_x + \beta_y. \quad (10\text{-}130)$$

ii. *Substitution Effect:* His assumption on the substitution effect can be expressed as

$$\beta_x + \beta_y = 0, \quad \text{or} \quad \beta_s = 0. \quad (10\text{-}131)$$

This is strongly criticized by Day [12], but Spraos [57] accepted this as "a reasonable approximation" (p. 143). Under this assumption, the terms of trade effect is simply reduced to

$$\frac{\partial D_1}{\partial Q_1} = \lambda_1 Y_{21}. \quad (10\text{-}132)$$

DAY [12]   Day criticized Harberger's implicit assumption that $\beta_x + \beta_y = 0$. For the income effect, he implicitly assumed the money illusion as did Harberger. Hence, the terms of trade effect by Day can be written as

$$\frac{\partial D_1}{\partial Q_1} = \lambda_1 Y_{21} - \beta_s. \quad (10\text{-}133)$$

SPRAOS [57]   As remarked before, Spraos accepted the zero substitution effect of saving as a "reasonable approximation." But he strongly criticized the existence of money illusion which underlay the works of Harberger and Day. Hence, the income effect should be expressed like our (10-124). There-fore, the terms of trade effect is

$$\frac{\partial D_1}{\partial Q_1} = -(1 - \lambda_1)Y_{21}\left(\frac{U_1}{U_1 - S_1}\right) + Y_{21}. \quad (10\text{-}134)$$

As we explained before, a change in real income is due to two channels—one part due to a change in the relative price and the other part due to a change in output. Spraos pointed out that the former extends to every member of the society without significant discrimination, but the latter affects more the people newly employed by this output increase who used to be unemployed.

OUR MODEL   We recognize the existence of money illusion as in Harberger's model which was criticized by Spraos, but we assume that the income effect takes the form as represented by (10-122). This can be justified under various reasons such as: a) the existence of money illusion, b) $U_1/(U_1 - S_1) = 1$ (or $APS = 0$) for each country, and c) the initial level of B_1 is equal to zero which implies the initial $S_1 = 0$ so that $U_1/(U_1 - S_1) = 1$ (this is also true for Country 2 since $B_2 = -B_1$). In the third section we adopted assumption c and avoided the problem.

About the substitution effect, we recall that our demand for the imported good depends on real spending instead of real income. In this way we took account of the substitution effect on saving ($\beta_s \neq 0$). In other words when we define the elasticity of substitution η_i, we hold real consumption, rather than real income, constant, and if real consumption is held constant, we obviously have $\beta_x + \beta_y = 0$. Hence, by redefining β_x and β_y as the substitution effect when real consumption is held constant, we obtain $\beta_x + \beta_y = 0$. Therefore, the terms of trade effect will have the same expression as Harberger's:

$$\frac{\partial D_1}{\partial Q_1} = \lambda_1 Y_{21} . \tag{10-135}$$

Finally, we may relate our condition to the condition obtained by Laursen and Metzler [31]. In their notation the Laursen-Metzler condition is written as

$$[(1 - w_1)(1 - w_2)v_1(\eta_1 + \eta_2 - 1) - s_1 m_1(1 - w_2) - s_2 m_2(1 - w_2)] > 0 . \tag{10-136}$$

Here w_i is the marginal propensity to spend of Country i so that $(1 - w_i)$ corresponds to our λ_i. v_1 measures the volume of import of Country 1 before the devaluation, and it corresponds to our Y_{21}. m_i is the marginal propensity to consume the imported good by Country i, and it corresponds to our π_i. s_i measures the terms of trade effect of Country i. Hence, s_1 and s_2 respectively correspond to our $\lambda_1 Y_{21}$ and $\lambda_2 Y_{21}$ due to (10-135). Their η_i corresponds to our $(\eta_i + \pi_i)$. Therefore, in terms of our notation, condition (10-136) can be rewritten as

$$\lambda_1 \lambda_2 Y_{21}(\eta_1 + \eta_2 - 1) > 0 . \tag{10-137}$$

Hence, if $\lambda_1 > 0$ and $\lambda_2 > 0$, condition (10-137) is equivalent to our condition (10-68) obtained in the third section.

REFERENCES

1. Alexander, S. S., "Effects of a Devaluation on a Trade Balance," *International Monetary Fund Staff Papers*, 2, April 1952.
2. ———, "Effects of a Devaluation: A Simplified Synthesis of Elasticities and Absorption Approaches," *American Economic Review*, XLIX, March 1959.
3. Allen, W. R., "Stable and Unstable Equilibria in the Foreign Exchange," *Kyklos*, VII, 1954.
4. ———, "A Note on the Money Income Effect of Devaluation," *Kyklos*, IX, 1956.
5. Beckerman, W., "National Income, Exchange Rates and the Balance of Trade: A Note," *Economica*, n.s., XVIII, August 1951.
6. ———, "Price Changes and the Stability of the Balance of Trade," *Economica*, n.s., XIX, November 1952.

7. Black, J., "A Saving and Investment Approach to Devaluation," *Economic Journal*, LXIX, June 1959.

8. Brems, H., "Devaluation: A Marriage of the Elasticity and Absorption Approaches," *Economic Journal*, LXVII, March 1957.

9. Brownlee, O. H., "The Theory of Employment and Stabilization Policy," *Journal of Political Economy*, LVIII, October 1950.

10. Clement, M. O., Pfister, R. L., and Rothwell, K. J., *Theoretical Issues in International Economics* (Boston: Houghton Mifflin Company), 1967, especially Chapters 7 and 5.

11. Corden, W. M., *Recent Developments in the Theory of International Trade*, International Finance Section, Princeton University, 1965.

12. Day, A. C. L., "Relative Prices, Expenditure and Trade Balance: A Note," *Economica*, n.s., I, February 1954.

13. Diaz, Alejandro, C. F., "A Note on the Impact of Devaluation and the Redistributive Effect," *Journal of Political Economy*, LXXI, December 1963.

14. Ellsworth, P. T., "Exchange Rates and Exchange Stability," *Review of Economics and Statistics*, XXXII, February 1950.

15. Gehrels, F., "Multipliers and Elasticities in Foreign Trade Adjustments," *Journal of Political Economy*, LVIII, February 1950.

16. Haberler, G., *A Survey of International Trade Theory*, rev. ed., Princeton International Finance Section, Princeton University, 1961.

17. Harberger, A. C., "Currency Depreciation, Income, and the Balance of Trade," *Journal of Political Economy*, LVIII, February 1950.

18. ———, "Pitfalls in Mathematical Model Building," *American Economic Review*, XLII, December 1952.

19. Hicks, J. R., *Value and Capital*, 2nd ed. (Oxford: Oxford University Press), 1946.

20. Johnson, H. G., "The Transfer Problem and Exchange Stability," in his International Trade and Economic Growth (Cambridge, Mass.: Harvard University Press), 1958 (Chapter VII), an extension of his article of the same title in the *Journal of Political Economy*, LXIV, June 1957.

21. ———, "Towards a General Theory of the Balance of Payments," in his *International Trade and Economic Growth*, Chapter VI.

22. Jones, R. W., "Depreciation and the Dampening Effect of Income Change," *Review of Economics and Statistics*, XLII, February 1960.

23. ———, "Stability Conditions in International Trade: A General Equilibrium Analysis," *International Economic Review*, 2, May 1961.

24. Kemp, M. C., *The Pure Theory of International Trade and Investment* (Englewood Cliffs, N.J.: Prentice-Hall, Inc.), 1969 (1st ed. 1964).

25. Keynes, J. M., *General Theory of Employment, Interest and Money* (London: Macmillan & Co., Ltd.), 1936.

26. ———, "The German Transfer Problem," *Economic Journal*, XXXIX, March 1929, reprinted in *Readings in the Theory of International Trade*

(American Economic Association), ed. by Ellis and Metzler (Homewood, Ill.: Richard D. Irwin, Inc.), 1949.

27. Kindleberger, C. P., *International Economics*, 4th ed. (Homewood, Ill.: Richard D. Irwin, Inc.), 1968, especially Chapter 16 and Appendix G.

28. Klein, L. R., "Theories of Effective Demand and Employment," *Journal of Political Economy*, LV, April 1947.

29. ———, *The Keynesian Revolution* (New York: Crowell-Collier and Macmillan, Inc.), 1947.

30. Krueger, A. O., "Balance of Payments Theory," *Journal of Economic Literature*, VII, March 1969.

31. Laursen, S. and Metzler, L. A., "Flexible Exchange Rates and the Theory of Employment," *Review of Economics and Statistics*, XXXI, September 1950.

32. Machlup, F., "Transfer und Preisbewegung," *Zeitschrift für Nationalökonomie*, *I*, 1930, pp. 555–560.

33. ———, *International Trade and the National Income Multiplier* (Philadelphia: Blakiston), 1950.

34. ———, "Relative Prices and Aggregate Spending in the Analysis of Devaluation," *American Economic Review*, XLV, June 1955.

35. ———, "The Terms of Trade Effects of Devaluation upon Real Income and the Balance of Trade," *Kyklos*, IX, 1956.

36. Marschak, J., *Income, Employment and the Price Level* (New York: Augustus M. Kelley), 1951.

37. Meade, J. E., *The Balance of Payments* (*The Theory of International Economic Policy Vol. I*) (London: Oxford University Press), 1951.

38. ———, *The Balance of Payments* (*The Theory of International Economic Policy* Vol. I), *Mathematical Supplement* (London: Oxford University Press), 1951.

39. ———, *A Geometry of International Trade* (London: George Allen and Unwin, Ltd.), 1952.

40. Metzler, L. A., "The Transfer Problem Reconsidered," *Journal of Political Economy*, L, June 1942, reprinted in Readings in the *Theory of International Trade* (American Economic Association), ed. by Ellis and Metzler, 1949.

41. Michaeley, M., "Relative Prices and Income Absorption Approaches to Devaluation: A Partial Reconciliation," *American Economic Review*, L, March 1960.

42. Modigliani, F., "Monetary Mechanism and its Interaction with Real Phenomena," *Review of Economics and Statistics*, Supplement, XLV, February 1963.

43. Negishi, T., "The Stability of a Competitive Economy: A Survey Article," *Econometrica*, 30, October 1962.

44. Ohlin, B., "The Reparation Problem: A Discussion," *Economic Journal*, XXXIX, June 1929, reprinted in *Readings in the Theory of International Trade*, ed. by Ellis and Metzler, 1949.

45. Patinkin, D., "Price Flexibility and Full Employment," in *Readings in Monetary Theory* (American Economic Association) (Philadelphia: Blakiston), 1951 (rev. version of the article in *American Economic Review*, September 1948).

46. ———, *Money, Interest, and Price* (New York: Harper & Row, Publishers), 2nd ed. 1965 (1st ed. 1956).

47. Pearce, I. F., "A Note on Mr. Spraos' Paper," *Economica*, XXII, May 1955, 147–151.

48. ———, "The Problem of the Balance of Payments," *International Economic Review*, 2, 1961.

49. Salter, W. E. G., "Internal and External Balances: The Role of Price and Expenditure Effects," *Economic Record*, XXXV, August 1959.

50. Samuelson, P. A., *Foundations of Economic Analysis* (Cambridge, Mass.: Harvard University Press), 1947.

51. ———, "The Transfer Problem and Transport Costs: The Terms of Trade when Impediments are Absent," *Economic Journal*, LXII, June 1952.

52. ———, "The Transfer Problem and Transport Costs, II: Analysis of Effects of Trade Impediments," *Economic Journal*, LXIV, June 1954.

53. Savosnick, K. M., "National Income, Exchange Rates and the Balance of Trade," *Economica*, n.s., XVII, May 1950.

54. Smith, W. L., "Effects of Exchange Rate Adjustments on the Standard of Living," *American Economic Review*, XLIV, December 1954.

55. Sohmen, E., "Demand Elasticities and the Foreign Exchange Market," *Journal of Political Economy*, LXV, October 1957.

56. ———, "The Effects of Devaluation on the Price Level," *Quarterly Journal of Economics*, LXXII, May 1958 ("Reply" November 1958).

57. Spraos, J., "Consumers' Behaviour and the Conditions for Exchange Stability," *Economica*, XXII, May 1955.

58. ———, "Stability in a Closed Economy and in the Foreign Exchange Market, and Redistribution Effect of Price Changes," *Review of Economic Studies*, XXIV, June 1957.

59. Stolper, W. F., "The Multiplier, Flexible Exchanges, and International Equilibrium," *Quarterly Journal of Economics*, LXIV, November 1950.

60. ———, "The Multiplier, Flexible Exchanges and International Equilibrium," *Quarterly Journal of Economics*, LXVII, February 1953.

61. Stuvel, G., *The Exchange Stability Problem* (Oxford: Basil Blackwell & Sons, Ltd.), 1951.

62. Takayama, A., "Stability in the Balance of Payments—A Multi-Country Approach," *Journal of Economic Behaviour*, 1, October 1961.

63. ———, *Economic Growth and International Trade*, Ph.D. Dissertation, March 1962 (University of Rochester).

64. ———, *International Economics* (Tokyo: Toyo Keizai Shimpo-sha), 1963, Chapters IV and V.

65. ———, *Mathematical Economics*, forthcoming.

66. Takayama, A., and McKenzie, L. W., "General Equilibrium Analysis of International Trade" (unpublished manuscript), 1964.
67. Tsiang, S. C., "The Role of Money in Trade-Balance Stability," *American Economic Review*, LI, December 1961.
68. Vanek, J., *International Trade: Theory and Economic Policy* (Homewood, Ill.: Richard D. Irwin, Inc.), 1962.
69. Viner, J., *Studies in the Theory of International Trade* (New York: Harper & Row, Publishers), 1937.
70. White, W. H., "The Multiplier, Flexible Exchanges and International Equilibrium: Comment," *Quarterly Journal of Economics,* LXVII, February 1953.
71. ———, "The Employment-Insulating Advantage of Flexibles: A Comment on Professors Laursen and Metzler," *Review of Economics and Statistics*, XXXVI, May 1954.

11

THE EFFECTS OF FISCAL AND MONETARY POLICIES UNDER FLEXIBLE AND FIXED EXCHANGE RATES[1]

INTRODUCTION

It is often argued that fiscal policy under flexible exchange rates and international capital movements results in a small increase in output and employment, while monetary policy tends to result in a strong increase. Although this conclusion is rather striking, its basic argument is not difficult to understand. It roughly goes as follows. Fiscal policy, for example, will increase the level of the interest rate by shifting the Hicksian *IS*-curve to the right.[2] The increase in the interest rate, in turn, invites an increase in the net inflow of foreign capital.[3] Since the balance of payments is presumably brought into equilibrium by

[1] The content of this chapter was first presented in a lecture given by me at Purdue University in April, 1967, and was published in the *Canadian Journal of Economics*, May 1969. I am grateful to Nancy Baggott, Lee Brown, Marvin Margolis, Yutaka Horiba, of Purdue, and Ajit S. Sabharwal of Rochester, all students in my course, for computational checks and comments. Especially, Miss Baggott carefully checked all the computations. Other students in my course besides the ones cited above also contributed many interesting comments. I should also note that I benefited from the fact that this paper was written parallel to one by Baggott and Flanders [2], which, among others, pointed out computational errors of a recent paper [16] by Johnson.

[2] Hicks [12]. The rightward shift of the *IS*-curve obviously results in an increase in output. An increase in output may generate an increase in the price level due to the law of diminishing marginal productivity of labor. A change in the price level, in general, shifts the *LM*-curve. In the illustration of the problem, we assume that the price level is kept constant so that there are no shifts on the *LM*-curve through changes in the price level. Here we also suppose the trade balance is exogenous to the extent that the original construction of the *IS*-curve can be used as it is.

[3] Obviously we can replace the words "an increase in the net inflow of capital" by "a decrease in the net outflow of capital," depending upon whether the country is a net debtor or a creditor. In this paper, "capital" means a financial capital (primarily with a short term nature) and *not* real capital. Direct (foreign) investment is thus completely assumed away in this paper.

fluctuations in exchange rates under the flexible exchange rate system,[4] this increase in the net inflow (or a decrease in the net outflow) of foreign capital must be accompanied by an offsetting deterioration in the trade balance. The deterioration in the trade balance, then, will shift the *IS*-curve to the left. Thus the increase in the level of output and employment due to the initial rightward shift of the *IS*-curve is somewhat offset by this leftward shift of the curve. If capital mobility is perfect and the country is small enough, then this capital inflow mechanism will continue to operate until the *IS*-curve moves back to its original position so that the level of the interest rate is brought back to its original level.[5] On the other hand, monetary policy (say, through an open market purchase) tends to lower the level of the interest rate by shifting the *LM*-curve to the right. This, in turn, causes a decrease in the net inflow (or an increase in the net outflow) of capital. Hence, a balance of payments equilibrium (through fluctuations in the exchange rate) must mean an improvement of the trade balance which, in turn, means a rightward shift of the *IS*-curve. Thus, the initial increase in the level of output and employment due to the shift of the *LM*-curve will mean a yet further increase because of this shift of the *IS*-curve. The above argument can be illustrated by Figure 11-1.

If the country adapts the fixed exchange rate system instead of the flexible exchange rate system, then we must completely alter the above argument.

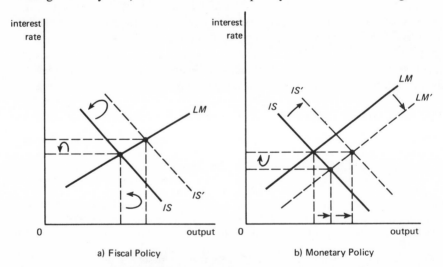

a) Fiscal Policy   b) Monetary Policy

Figure 11-1 The Effects of Fiscal and Monetary Policy under Flexible Exchange Rates

[4] We assume some sort of stability condition here. For a more detailed discussion on this topic, see the Appendix to Chapter 11.

[5] There is a further repercussion through the increase in output. That is, an increase in the level of output (hence of income) may increase the amount of imports thus creating a deterioration in the trade balance. This deterioration, in turn, shifts the *IS*-curve to the left. As long as the marginal propensity to import is less than 1, the *IS*-curve will not move back to its original level.

Under fixed exchange rates, the balance of payments will not be brought automatically into equilibrium. Hence, an increase in the net capital inflow in the case of a fiscal policy will tend to improve the country's balance of payments. Unless a complete sterilization policy is adopted, this increase in the net inflow of capital will increase the country's money supply, which, in turn, causes a rightward shift of the *LM*-curve and an increase in output and employment.[6] On the other hand, if a monetary policy is taken, a decrease in the net capital inflow as described above will tend to deteriorate the balance of payments. Unless a complete sterilization policy is taken, this decrease in the net capital inflow will decrease the country's money supply further, thus causing an offsetting decrease in the level of output and employment.[7] If the country is small enough and capital is perfectly mobile, this capital movement mechanism will not be stopped until the level of the interest rate is brought back to its original position, and hence, monetary policy will have no effect on output and employment. The above argument under fixed exchange rates can be illustrated by Figure 11-2.

The above argument on the relative efficacy of fiscal and monetary policy in an open economy, which was generated by the recent Canadian and American

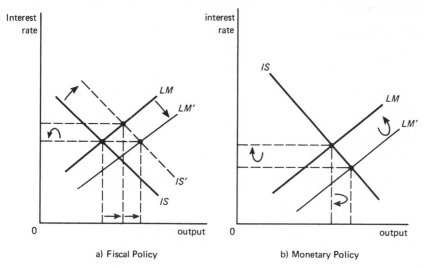

a) Fiscal Policy   b) Monetary Policy

Figure 11-2   The Effects of Fiscal and Monetary Policy under Fixed Exchange Rates

[6] A complete sterilization policy presumably totally separates the link between the country's money supply and its balance of payments. Thus there will be no shift of the *LM*-curve. In any case, if the balance of payments turns to a surplus, gold or some other international means of payments will keep flowing into the country which will eventually be stopped by some sort of policy actions of the foreign country (or even of the home country). Note also that there may be a further repercussion through an increase in imports, which causes a decrease in the level of output. See footnote 5.

[7] If a complete sterilization policy is taken, there is no such further increase in the money supply (see the previous footnote).

experience, reached its climax in the publication of an extremely ingenious and path-breaking article by Mundell [37].[8] By assuming perfect capital mobility, a small country, and an infinite elasticity of supply (a constant price), Mundell both focused and sharpened his argument to produce the above striking conclusions. Moreover, a recent article by Johnson [16] opened the discussion in a new direction. His most important innovation is probably the correct recognition that the international mobility of capital depends upon the level of the country's income, hence profitability of investment. In the case of fixed exchange rates, he focused his attention on the complete sterilization policy case. He also dropped the Mundellian assumption of perfect international mobility of capital, thus drawing us closer to the real world. On the other hand, he kept the constant price assumption.

The essence of the income effect with respect to the international mobility of capital is not hard to see.[9] An increase in the level of output and employment as a result of fiscal or monetary policy will, *ceteris paribus*, increase the net inflow of foreign capital. Under the flexible exchange rate system, this, in turn, implies a deterioration of the trade balance, which shifts the *IS*-curve to the left, causing an offsetting *decrease* in the level of output and employment relative to their initial increases. Under the fixed exchange rate system, the net inflow of capital, in turn, *increases* the country's money supply unless a complete sterilization policy is taken. In other words, there is a further increase in the level of output and employment. If the complete sterilization policy is taken, as is the case in Johnson, there is no such secondary increase.

The Mundellian assumption of perfect international mobility of capital (or, more precisely, of an infinitely interest elastic mobility of international capital) is a very limiting assumption, although it enables Mundell to sharpen his arguments considerably. Under this assumption, the level of the final equilibrium interest rate must be the same as the original level, as long as the world level is constant. This creates a situation similar to that of the Keynesian liquidity trap. In the subsequent analysis we shall see that the Mundellian conclusion as sketched above crucially hinges on this assumption. Johnson's recognition

---

[8] The above arguments are essentially those of Mundell [37]. I believe that we really do not need such complicated diagrams as the ones used by him. A simple use of the *IS*- and *LM*-diagram is quite sufficient for analysis as illustrated in the above. Incidentally, his conclusion may best be summarized by the following quotation from [37].

> Monetary policy has no impact on employment under fixed exchange rates while fiscal policy has no effect on employment under flexible exchange rates. On the other hand, fiscal policy has a strong effect on employment under fixed exchange rates (simple Keynesian conclusions hold) while monetary policy has a strong effect on employment under flexible exchange rates (classical quantity theory conclusion hold) (p. 484).

We note that these conclusions are the result of a series of complicated discussions on the related topics, in which Mundell plays a most important role. See [8], [14], [15], [16], [17], [19], [21], [26], [28], [31], [32], [33], [34], [35], [36], [37], [38], [40], [43], [44], [48], [49], for example. For an introduction of the general discussion of the problem of flexible exchange rates versus fixed exchange rates, see Clement, Pfister and Rothwell [5], for example.

[9] We may call this effect the *Johnson effect*.

of the imperfect mobility of capital has, therefore, great theoretical significance.[10]

The purpose of this chapter is to construct a general equilibrium model which will both include the arguments in the past literature as special cases and point out the special assumptions involved.[11] Although we shall focus our attention mainly on the above cited works by Mundell and Johnson for the sake of the brevity of the paper, we shall always be aware of other works on the topic. As is well-known in any theoretical work, and as is shown in the following analysis in the present context, the conclusions for special cases often crucially hinge on the assumptions made. It is very important to make these assumptions explicit and to point out the relevance of each particular conclusion to its corresponding assumption. We may also note that the generalization of the model will naturally enable us to consider cases which were completely ignored before. Hence, even though we derive some conclusions that are similar to previous analyses, these results will have been, in essence, unknown before and will thus be new. Furthermore, the generalization of the model will bring forth completely unknown results.

In the following analysis, we shall consider both perfect *and* imperfect (and no) international mobility of capital. We shall not assume an infinite supply elasticity. We shall consider both complete sterilization and incomplete (or no) sterilization. Following Johnson, we shall explicitly consider the case in which the international mobility of capital is a function of the country's level of output (as well as the interest rate). Under the assumption of perfect mobility of capital, we can not have a situation like the "Keynesian" liquidity trap, for the level of the interest rate that is held fixed under each assumption may not be the same. (In fact, the two may be thus inconsistent.) When we recognize the imperfect mobility of capital, we can explicitly consider the case of the liquidity trap. After all, this is probably the most important assumption in traditional macro-theory from which we conclude the inadequacy of monetary policy.[12] Finally, our model explicitly recognizes the real balance effect on consumption and

---

[10] This does not mean that Mundell's assumption is altogether unrealistic. It is often pointed out that the international (especially U.S.) capital is quite interest sensitive in the Canadian market. See Poole [42], for example. We may also note the recent discussions between Stein [52] and others [9] with regard to the interest sensitivity of international short-term capital movements. Unfortunately, serious objections to Stein's procedure of empirical estimation were raised in this controversy. Stein's work follows some pioneering works by Bell and Kenen.

[11] Krueger [21] also recognized this. However, both Krueger and Johnson did not make clear under what circumstances the assumption of imperfect capital mobility makes a difference compared to that of perfect capital mobility. One peculiar feature of Krueger's model is that the level of the interest rate is taken as a policy variable. As she herself clearly recognized, the money supply is the variable that the government can control ([21], p. 199), and it is not clear why she switched the monetary policy variable from the money supply to the level of the interest rate. Mundell, in his earlier articles (for example, [35] and [36]) also considered the interest rate as a policy variable. See also footnote 13.

[12] When Mundell [37] emphasized the effectiveness of monetary policy under flexible exchange rates, he assumed there was no liquidity trap. As we show later, under the liquidity trap, monetary policy is quite ineffective even with the flexible exchange rate system. Hence Mundell's conclusion is quite misleading in a sense.

investment. Throughout the chapter, we retain the small country assumption.

It should be pointed out in this context that our model and analysis naturally contain the case of a closed economy (no foreign trade and no international capital movements) as a special case. Since the rigorous mathematical derivations of the conclusions based on the general equilibrium macromodel are not seen in the macroliterature even with the closed economy assumption, our analysis is a step forward even in this respect. For example, one can readily obtain the formula, from the ones in the present paper, for the government expenditure multiplier when the interactions of the goods market with the other markets (the money market and the labor market) are explicitly taken into account under the closed economy assumption.

In some of the past literature, the interest rate level is taken as a policy variable. This analysis is rather inadequate, for the monetary authority does not directly control the interest rate level, but, rather, the supply of money. Just as the government does not directly control the level of output and employment, the monetary authority (or the government) does not directly control the interest rate level.[13] In this context, we may point out the important distinction between the exogenous variables and the endogenous variables of the model. This is certainly an obvious important distinction, but it is often forgotten in the literature.

Under the fixed exchange rate system, the balance of payments of a country is not necessarily in equilibrium. Even if it is in equilibrium in the beginning, the adoption of a monetary or fiscal policy will, in general, disturb this equilibrium. Hence, it may be of some interest to examine an appropriate "mix" of fiscal and monetary policies, that is, the policy mix which will increase the level of output and employment while keeping the balance of payments in equilibrium.[14] One of the conclusions we obtained in this context is that under the fixed exchange rate system, it is usually undesirable to increase both government expenditures and the money supply. And that if the interest elasticity of international capital mobility is sufficiently large, the appropriate policy mix would be to decrease government expenditures and increase the money supply.

As long as we confine our attention to the effect of fiscal and monetary variables on the level of output and employment, we are in the Keynesian under-employment world. For, in the classical world, the full employment of labor is always achieved through the flexibility of the money wage rate (as well

[13] It may be worthwhile to recall the well-known observation that an increase in the money supply may actually increase the level of the interest rate in the final equilibrium even in the context of no trade and no capital mobility. For example, an initial decline in the interest rate due to an increase in the money supply may invite an increase in investment, which then increases the level of output. An increase in the money supply, on the other hand, may mean an increase in the assets held by the public. This, through the real balance effect, tends to push up the level of output also. The increase in the level of output, in turn, will increase the transactions demand for money, and this may increase the level of the interest rate more than the original level.

[14] Using the model in this chapter, we can easily include a wage (or profit) policy in this mix. However, we shall not attempt to do so, for it may blur the more important points of the chapter and the wage policy may be difficult to carry out in practice anyway in some countries.

as the other price variables). However, it may also be of interest to examine the effect of changes in government expenditures, and the money supply on the general price level in the classical full-employment world under alternative assumptions of flexible exchange rates and fixed exchange rates. We shall attempt to do so.

In the second section of this chapter, we shall construct our general equilibrium macromodel for the purpose of our analysis in this chapter. In the third section, we consider the case of flexible exchange rates, and in the fourth section, we consider the case of fixed exchange rates. In the fifth section we consider the problem of an appropriate mix of fiscal and monetary policies under fixed exchange rates. In the sixth section we summarize the limitations of the model. Our analysis is essentially that of comparative statics. Hence, in order to obtain more precise results, the reference to the stability of the system is inevitable. In the Appendix to Chapter 11, we shall consider an analysis along this line.

MODEL

The purpose of this section is to construct a model which will facilitate our analysis in this chapter. Our model is essentially similar to an ordinary macromodel with the possible exception that it explicitly introduces foreign transactions. Letting Y be real income; C, real consumption; S, real saving; I, real investment; P, price of output; r, interest rate; A, aggregate net worth (assets) of the private sector;[15] G, government expenditures; and T, the balance of trade in terms of the domestic currency; we can write the equation which denotes the equilibrium in the goods market as follows:

$$I(r, Y, A/P) + G/P + T/P = S(r, Y, A/P),^{16} \tag{11-1}$$

[15] In the model which includes government and private securities explicitly in the asset A, one has to take account of the effect of the change in the interest rate. Denoting the number of the securities outstanding by H, we may write $A = (kH/r) + M$, where $k(0 < k < 1)$ reflects the degree to which individuals do not discount the future tax liabilities connected with government bonds. See Metzler [29] and Patinkin [41] (especially pp. 288–294), for example. For the sake of simplicity, we omit such a consideration of the Metzler effect from our model.

[16] More precisely, the level of income, Y, which determines the level of saving and investment must be disposable (real) income, which is the difference between earned income and taxes. The taxes, in general, are a function of the earned income. We may explicitly expand the model by explicitly introducing these relations. But the results under such a consideration are well-known in the context of the balanced budget theorem and others. For an excellent exposition of this effect, see Samuelson [46]. In essence, an equal increase in government expenditures and taxes has an expansionary effect. In view of the known results obtained in [46], such a consideration adds nothing to our discussion and simply blurs the analysis. There is another important problem of whether or not we can distinguish fiscal policy and monetary policy. In practice we usually can not. However, to make our argument clear we shall assume away the interaction between these two kinds of policies. The reader can easily extend the analysis to the case in which these policies are mixed together. For example, an increase in government expenditures financed by borrowing from the central bank can be analyzed by simply grafting the analysis of increase in $\bar{M}$ to the effect of an increase in G. Notice also that the terms of trade effect is assumed away here. That is, the "real" income, investment, and so on, means the ones deflated by the price level of the domestic output, P. The effect of the import price is neglected.

where

$$S(r, Y, A/P) \equiv Y - C(r, Y, A/P).$$

Or we may write

$$V(r, Y, A/P) + G/P + T/P = 0, \qquad (11\text{-}2)$$

where

$$V \equiv I - S\, (= I + C - Y).$$

From our ordinary knowledge of macroeconomic theory, we may impose the following restrictions on the signs of the partial derivatives of V in the above equation[17]

$$V_r \leqq 0, \quad V_Y < 0, \quad V_{A/P} \geqq 0. \qquad (11\text{-}3)$$

$V_{A/P} = 0$ means the absence of the real balance effect. Clearly, other restrictions, such as $V_r > 0$, $V_Y > 0$, and so on, are possible. Since such cases can be analyzed *mutatis mutandis*, we may omit consideration of these cases in the present chapter.[18]

The trade balance, T, in equation (11-1) or (11-2) is the difference between exports and imports. We write it as:

$$T = T(P, Y, E), \qquad (11\text{-}4)$$

where E is the exchange rate (the price of foreign currency in terms of the domestic currency). Note that E is defined such that an increase in E means the devaluation of the domestic currency vis-à-vis the foreign currency. We may impose the following restrictions on the partial derivatives of T:

$$T_P \leqq 0, \quad T_E \geqq 0; \quad \text{and} \quad T_Y \leqq 0 \quad (\text{or} > 0).[19] \qquad (11\text{-}5)$$

[17] Throughout this chapter we shall denote partial derivatives by putting a subscript which indicates the differentiating variable below and to the right of the relevant variable. For example $\partial V/\partial r = V_r$, $\partial V/\partial Y = V_Y$, and $\partial V/\partial(A/P) = V_{A/P}$. Similarly, $\partial T/\partial P = T_P$, $\partial L/\partial r = L_r$, and $\partial F/\partial r = F_r$, and so on.

[18] In the ordinary macro text book, it is often (implicitly) assumed that $S_r = 0$ and $V_{A/P} = 0$. These two assumptions are made in the textbooks simply to facilitate the diagramatical exposition of the macro equilibrium mechanism. Since these two assumptions can have very serious implications, we should make them explicit. $V_r = 0$ holds if both investment and saving are completely interest inelastic. $V_r < 0$ is usually justified by the assumption that the investment is a decreasing function of the interest rate *and* that savings are either an increasing function of the interest rate or its dependence on the level of the interest rate is small relative to the sensitivity of investment with respect to the interest rate. $V_Y < 0$ means $I_Y - S_Y < 0$. In the simple Keynesian analysis via the Keynesian cross diagram this is considered as the stability condition for the goods market.

[19] If we assume that exports depend on the level of the home country's income (or output), then T_Y is the difference between the marginal propensity to export and the marginal propensity to import, which can be positive. However, it is usually assumed that the exports do not depend on the home country's income. Then $T_Y \leqq 0$. $T_Y = 0$ is clearly a limiting assumption, but it is sometimes adopted in the literature. Note also that if there is no international trade, $T_P = 0$, $T_E = 0$ and $T_Y = 0$.

These restrictions are closely related to the stability condition, as we shall observe in the Appendix to Chapter 11.

Letting $\overline{M}$ be the supply of money, we may write the equilibrium condition for the money market as

$$\overline{M}/P = L(r, Y).\tag{11-6}$$

We may impose the following restrictions:

$$L_r \leqq 0 \quad \text{or} \quad L_r \to -\infty \quad \text{(liquidity trap)}; \quad L_Y > 0.\tag{11-7}$$

We write the aggregate supply equation as called by Marschak [23], Brownlee [3], and McKenna [24][20] as:

$$Y = Y(P) \quad \text{or} \quad Y(P, \overline{W}).\tag{11-8}$$

We may recall that the above aggregate supply equation is obtained as the locus of (Y, p) values which satisfy the following three equations:[21]

$$Y = f(N) \quad \text{(production function)}\tag{11-9}$$

where N denotes the level of labor employment.[22]

$$W/P = f'(N), \quad \text{or} \quad N = n^d(W/P) \quad \text{(demand for labor)},\tag{11-10}$$

where W is the money wage rate and $f' \equiv df/dN$.

(The classical labor supply): $N = n^s(W/P)$. $\tag{11-11a}$

(The Keynesian case): $W = \overline{W} \text{ (constant)} \quad \text{if} \quad n^d(\overline{W}/P) < n^s(\overline{W}/P),$

$$N = n^s(W/P) \quad \text{if} \quad n^d(\overline{W}/P) \geqq n^s(\overline{W}/P).\tag{11-11b}$$

A little consideration of (11-9), (11-10), and (11-11) would reveal to us the precise information on (11-8).[23] This information can be summarized as follows:

   i. The classical case: $Y = Y_f$ (a constant),

   ii. The ordinary Keynesian case: $dY/dP > 0,$

   iii. The ultra-Keynesian case: $dY/dP \to \infty$ (or $P = $ constant).

---

[20] Their concept of aggregate demand and aggregate supply are very important in macro-analysis.

[21] See Modigliani [30] and our discussion in the first section of Chapter 10.

[22] The stock of physical capital is assumed to be constant.

[23] The process of obtaining (11-8) is essentially that of eliminating two variables, N and W from the three equations (11-9), (11-10), and (11-11), thus reducing the three equations into one. We may assume $f' > 0$ and $f'' < 0$ (the law of diminishing marginal productivity). We may impose further that $f'' = 0$ for a sufficiently small values of N, which can be justified by the existence of a large excess capacity in the low level of employment. It is usually assumed as an increasing function with respect to the real wage rate.

The ultra-Keynesian case will occur if the marginal physical product of labor is constant regardless of the level of labor employment, so that $f' = $ constant or $f'' = 0$.[24]

If we define σ, the *supply coefficient*, as

$$\sigma \equiv dY/dP, \tag{11-12}$$

from equation (11-8), then we may describe the above three cases as:

    i. (The classical case): $\sigma = 0$;
    ii. (The ordinary Keynesian case): $\infty > \sigma > 0$;
    iii. (The ultra-Keynesian case): $\sigma \to \infty$.

Mundell [37] considered the ultra-Keynesian case and Johnson [16], the ordinary Keynesian case.

Letting B be the balance of payments of the home country in terms of the home currency, we may write the balance of payments equation as

$$B = T(P, Y, E) + F(r, Y) \tag{11-13}$$

where F is the net inflow of capital.[25] We assume that an increase in the domestic interest rate will encourage the inflow of foreign capital and discourage its outflow. Also, an increase in the domestic income level may attract capital. Johnson [16] first recognized this income effect. Thus we have

$$F_r \geqq 0 \quad \text{and} \quad F_Y \geqq 0. \tag{11-14}$$

Mundell [37] (implicitly) assumed that $F_Y = 0$.[26] He also assumed that capital

[24] The assumption that the price level is constant is implicitly made in many simple macro-analyses. This is one of the key assumptions which underlies the simple multiplier analysis. Although it is not quite clear whether Keynes himself adopted this assumption, my contention is that Keynes clearly recognized the importance of the repercussions through the rising supply price (which is, in turn, due to the law of the diminishing marginal productivity). See Keynes [20], Chapter 18, for example. This is the reason why I called case iii. as "ultra" Keynesian. Krueger [21] justified equation (11-8) by the Phillips curve analysis (p. 198). Since the Phillips curve analysis can more properly be considered as a dynamic adjustment equation or purely empirical observations, her justification is inappropriate to her comparative statics analysis.

[25] If F is positive, it denotes the net inflow of capital, and if it is negative it denotes the net outflow of capital. This equation (11-13) defines the balance of payments B. If $B = 0$, it describes the equilibrium relation in the foreign exchange market.

[26] For $F_Y > 0$, Johnson wrote, "This assumes that an increase in economic activity attracts international capital and neglects the possibility that an expansion of activity may disturb confidence" ([16], p. 348). If there are no international movements of capital, then $F_r = 0$ and $F_Y = 0$. Closed economy (no trade and no capital movements) means $T_P = 0$, $T_E = 0$, $T_Y = 0$, $F_r = 0$, and $F_Y = 0$. Thus, the case of closed economy comes as a special corollary of the present chapter. As Johnson pointed out, F may depend on the exchange rate, E. This effect is greatly complicated by the possibility of exchange speculation. Following Mundell, Johnson, and so on, we simply assume away this effect in the present chapter for the sake of simplicity. We assume that existing exchange rates are expected to persist indefinitely (static expectation) and that spot and forward exchange rates are identical. Thus, we avoid considering all the complications with regard to exchange speculation. This is again all for the sake of simplicity.

is freely and perfectly mobile internationally and that the country is small enough so that the level of the (domestic) interest rate has no effect on the world interest rate level. (In fact, the former is completely determined by the latter.) In other words, Mundell [37] assumed $F_r \to \infty$ (a constant level of the interest rate equilibrium).[27]

Under the flexible exchange rate system, the balance of payments will be brought into equilibrium through fluctuations of the exchange rate, E, so that $B = 0$ in equilibrium by supposing a proper stability mechanism. With $B = 0$, the equilibrium of our system is completely described by equations (11-1), (11-6), (11-8), and (11-13). The variables to be determined in the system (the endogenous variables) are Y, P, r, and E. The exogenous variables of the system are G, $\overline{M}$, and A (and possibly $\overline{W}$ in the Keynesian case). In the comparative statics analysis, the equilibrium values of Y, P, r, and E will, in general, change when there is a shift in the value(s) of one or more of the exogenous variables such as G and $\overline{M}$. In particular, when the exchange rate E changes, the domestic value of the foreign exchange reserve, if it is held (partially or entirely) in the form of the foreign currency or gold, will change. This, in turn, affects the volume of money supply $\overline{M}$. We assume, for the sake of simplicity, that this effect is completely sterilized so that a change in E will cause no change in $\overline{M}$.

Under the fixed exchange rate system,[28] the exchange rate, E, is held constant by assumption. Hence, we eliminate it from the above list of endogenous variables. But on the other hand, the balance of payments is no longer necessarily in equilibrium so we must include B in the list of endogenous variables. The balance of payments deficit or surplus naturally affects the level of the money supply of the country, the extent of which clearly depends on the degree of the sterilization policy that the country may adopt. Note that the exchange rate does not affect the domestic value of the foreign reserve as long as it is held constant. We may now add the following equation to our model:

$$d\overline{M} = d\overline{M}^h + sdB,\qquad\qquad(11\text{-}15)$$

where d stands for the total derivative; $\overline{M}^h$, the money supply controlled by the home country's monetary authority; and s, the *sterilization coefficient*. In equation (11-15) we assumed for the sake of simplicity, that $B = 0$ initially. If $s = 0$, the home country adopts a complete sterilization policy, so that the balance of payments does not affect the (total) money supply of the country (that is, $d\overline{M} = 0$). In general, we may write

$$s \gimel 0.\qquad\qquad(11\text{-}16)$$

[27] This means that the level of the domestic interest rate is brought to the level of the interest rate in the rest of the world. Under the small country assumption we call this perfectly interest elastic capital mobility *perfect (free) mobility of capital*.

[28] It is important to realize that, in the above model (with either flexible or fixed exchange rates) the variables which denote the level of economic activity of the rest of the world are all assumed to be constant throughout the analysis so that these variables are not explicitly written in the model.

Mundell [37] is concerned with this general case, $s \geq 0$, while Johnson [16] restricted his attention to the case of $s = 0$. Corresponding to the addition of one equation, (11-15), to the system, $\overline{M}$ (the money supply) is dropped from the list of the exogenous variables and $\overline{M}$ is now an endogenous variable. Note that $\overline{M}^h$ is added as an exogenous variable to the system. There are five equations, (11-1), (11-6), (11-8), (11-13), and (11-15), and there are five endogenous variables, Y, P, r, B, and $\overline{M}$.[29]

FLEXIBLE EXCHANGE RATES

Having laid the above groundwork, let us proceed to our analysis of comparative statics. The shift parameters of the system are G (government expenditures) and $\overline{M}$ (the money supply). In this section we shall be mainly concerned with the effects of fiscal and monetary policies[30] under flexible exchange rates.

First we note that we can put $P = E = 1$ initially without loss of generality by choosing the unit of measurement of the respective variable properly. Now totally differentiating equations (11-2), (11-6), (11-8), and (11-13), we obtain

$$V_r \, dr + V_Y \, dY + (dG + dT + V_{A/P} \, dA) - (G + T + V_{A/P} A) \, dP = 0 ,$$
(11-17)

$$d\overline{M} - \overline{M} \, dP = L_r \, dr + L_Y \, dY ,$$
(11-18)

$$dY = \sigma \, dP \quad (\text{or } dP = dY/\sigma) ,$$
(11-19)

$$dB = dT + F_Y \, dY + F_r \, dr .$$
(11-20)

We assume, for simplicity, that there is no autonomous change in A. However, a change in the money supply $\overline{M}$ may certainly induce a change in A. Hence, we write

$$dA = \mu \, d\overline{M} \quad \text{where } \mu \geq 0 .[31]$$
(11-21)

[29] Depending on the type of analysis, the asset variable A can be considered as an exogenous or endogenous variable. In other words, if there is an increase in the money supply this will, in general, increase the level of A. Thus, A is an endogenous variable. In short, we are assuming that there is no autonomous change in A. See footnote 31 also.

[30] By fiscal and monetary policies we mean the policies which alter the level of G and $\overline{M}$ (or $\overline{M}^h$ for the case of fixed exchange rates) respectively. An increase in G can be achieved by an increase in government expenditures. As remarked earlier, an increase in government expenditures often accompanies an increase in the money supply. A most dramatic case is the one where an increase in government expenditures is financed by borrowing from the central bank. If this is financed by borrowing from the non-banking private sector instead, then the accompanying changes in the money supply can be considered negligible, assuming away the further complications of the model such as the Metzler effect and the Gurley-Shaw effect. The latter emphasises the importance of the role of some assets in the public as a close substitute for money. However, it is convenient for our analysis if we separate the effects of changes in G and $\overline{M}$. See Modigliani [30], p. 94.

[31] The following quotation from Warren Smith [51] may be useful for the explanation of μ.

Open market purchases of government securities by the central bank from the non-bank public will leave A unchanged, since the initial purchase transaction will result in a

μ measures the sensitivity of A due to a change in $\overline{M}$. Taking (11-21) into account, we can obtain from (11-17) and (11-18):

$$\alpha' \, dY + dG + dT + \beta' \, d\overline{M} - \gamma \, dP = 0 \tag{11-22}$$

where

$$\alpha' \equiv V_Y - V_r L_Y/L_r \quad \beta' \equiv V_r/L_r + \mu V_{A/P} \quad \gamma \equiv G + T + V_{A/P} A + \overline{M} V_r/L_r \, .$$

From equations (11-18) and (11-20), we have

$$dB = dT + F_Y \, dY + (d\overline{M} - \overline{M} \, dP - L_Y \, dY) F_r/L_r \, . \tag{11-23}$$

Combining (11-22) and (11-23), and keeping (11-19) in mind, we obtain

i. For the Keynesian case ($\infty > \sigma > 0$ or $\sigma \to \infty$),

$$\alpha \, dY + dG + dB + \beta \, d\overline{M} = 0 \, , \tag{11-24}$$

where α and β are defined by:

$$\alpha \equiv \alpha' - F_Y + F_r L_Y/L_r - (\gamma - F_r \overline{M}/L_r)/\sigma = (V_Y - V_r L_Y/L_r)$$
$$- F_Y + F_r L_Y/L_r - (G + T + V_{A/P} A + \overline{M} V_r/L_r - F_r \overline{M}/L_r)/\sigma \tag{11-25}$$

$$\beta \equiv \beta' - F_r/L_r = V_r/L_r + \mu V_{A/P} - F_r/L_r \tag{11-26}$$

ii. For the classical case ($Y = Y_f$, that is, $\sigma = 0$):

$$dG + dB + \beta \, d\overline{M} - (\gamma - F_r \overline{M}/L_r) \, dP = 0 \, . \tag{11-27}$$

Now we introduce the basic premise of the flexible exchange rate system, $dB = 0$. In other words, we assume that in the final equilibrium the balance of payments is brought into equilibrium. We shall first confine our analysis to the Keynesian case. From equation (11-24) with $dB = 0$, we obtain

$$\alpha \, dY + dG + \beta \, d\overline{M} = 0 \, . \tag{11-28}$$

The effects of fiscal and monetary policies can be examined by obtaining the expressions for dY/dG (with $d\overline{M} = 0$) and $dY/d\overline{M}$ (with $dG = 0$) from (11-28).

$$\frac{dY}{dG} = -\frac{1}{\alpha} = \frac{1}{-\alpha' + F_Y - F_r L_Y/L_r + (\gamma - F_r \overline{M}/L_r)/\sigma} \tag{11-29}$$

where α is given by equation (11-25).

---

decline in the public's security holdings and an equal increase in M, while any induced expansion of loans and investment by the banks will result in an increase in M offset by an equal increase in the public's indebtedness to the banks. On the other hand if the Treasury prints currency and gives it to the public, A will be increased by the same absolute amount as M but the increase in A will be proportionately smaller than the increase in M (provided the public's holdings of government securities exceed its indebtedness to the banks so that $A > M$)" ([51], footnote 9).

Note that in the above explanation, the interest induced real balance effect (Metzler effect) is assumed away. Here it is also assumed that the public holding of the foreign bonds is negligible.

$$\frac{dY}{d\overline{M}} = -\frac{\beta}{\alpha} = \frac{(V_r/L_r + \mu V_{A/P}) - F_r/L_r}{-\alpha' + F_Y - F_r L_Y/L_r + (\gamma - F_r \overline{M}/L_r)/\sigma} \tag{11-30}$$

where α' and γ are given by equation (11-22). Hence a *necessary and sufficient* condition for fiscal or monetary policies to be at all effective ($dY/dG > 0$ or $dY/d\overline{M} > 0$) is $\alpha < 0$ (since $\beta \geqq 0$).

Since $V_r \leqq 0$; $V_Y < 0$; $L_r < 0$; $L_Y > 0$; $F_Y \geqq 0$; and $F_r \geqq 0$, we can say that $\alpha < 0$ provided that $G + T \geqq 0$. In other words, so long as $G + T \geqq 0$, an increase in government expenditure or in the money supply will always increase output and employment. There is certainly no *a priori* reason to believe that $G + T \geqq 0$ at all times, or even at any particular time, in the real world. But the literature habitually assumes that we start with an initial balance in which $G > 0$ and $T = 0$. Note that both the Marshall-Lerner condition and the Laursen-Metzler condition assume $T = 0$, and that they assume there is no capital mobility. Finally, it is important to recognize that *when* this condition is satisfied both fiscal policy and monetary policy will be effective weapons against unemployment.[32]

There are other ways of ensuring that the more basic condition—that $\alpha < 0$ —will be satisfied. This condition is closely related to a stability condition for the system. But again we have no *a priori* knowledge of the sign of α. The magnitude of the fiscal multiplier[33] dY/dG or the monetary multiplier $dY/d\overline{M}$ (which reflect the efficacy of fiscal or monetary policy) is determined by the magnitudes of α or α and β, which in turn depend on structural coefficients such as σ, L_r, F_r, V_r, and so on. It is not possible, of course, to single out the effect of the size of these coefficients on the multipliers, for they are interrelated. However, if we are willing to assume that these interactions are negligible, we can obtain the following summary table on the condition that $G + T \geqq 0$ or $\alpha < 0$.

TABLE 11-1

	σ	F_r	F_Y	L_Y	$|L_r|$	$|V_Y|$	$|V_r|$	$V_{A/P}$
dY/dG	↑	↓	↓	↓	↑	↓	↓	↓
$dY/d\overline{M}$	↑	?	↓	↓	↓ if $V_{A/P} = 0$ or $\mu = 0$	↓	?	↓ if $\mu = 0$

Here each arrow indicates the direction of change of dY/dG or $dY/d\overline{M}$ (↑: increase; ↓: decrease; ?: can't be specified) when the size of the corresponding

---

[32] The importance of such a condition is never made clear in the literature. This condition is as important as the Laursen-Metzler condition (Chapter 10) and the Marshall-Lerner condition (Chapter 8).

[33] We may call this the government expenditure multiplier. However we call dY/dG the *fiscal multiplier*. We call $dY/d\overline{M}$ the *monetary multiplier*.

coefficient in the first row *increases*. For example, we can read from the table that both dY/dG and $dY/d\overline{M}$ increase, the larger the size of σ (*assuming* that an increase in σ does not significantly affect the size of all the other partial derivatives in the first row).

If we impose a certain condition we can convert "?" in the table into "↑" or "↓". For example, we can show that $dY/d\overline{M}$ is larger when F_r is larger if and only if the following condition holds:

$$-(1/L_r)(-\alpha' + F_r + \gamma/\sigma) + (V_r/L_r + \mu V_{A/P})(L_Y + \overline{M}/\sigma)/L_r > 0 . \qquad (11\text{-}31)$$

This condition can be obtained by (partially) differentiating (11-30) with respect to F_r.

If $V_{A/P} = 0$, and $\sigma \to \infty$, this can be reduced to $F_Y - V_Y > 0$, which is always satisfied under our assumptions. That is, an increase in F_r always increases the efficacy of monetary policy in this case.

Interesting conclusions can be obtained for some limiting cases *without* the above assumption of lack of interaction between the structural coefficients. For example, if $F_r \to \infty$ (perfect capital mobility), we can easily show from (11-29) that dY/dG goes to zero *regardless* of the level of σ, L_r, F_Y, and so on. This conclusion corresponds to Mundell's result [37], but note that it does *not* depend on the assumption that $\sigma \to \infty$, which Mundell used.

The expression for $dY/d\overline{M}$ when $F_r \to \infty$ is obtained from (11-30) as

$$\frac{dY}{d\overline{M}} = \frac{1}{L_Y + \overline{M}/\sigma} . \qquad (11\text{-}32)$$

When $L_r \to -\infty$ (with a finite F_r) and $V_{A/P} = 0$ (or $\mu = 0$), we can show easily that $dY/d\overline{M}$ goes to zero. This extends the well-known conclusion, that under the liquidity trap monetary policy has no effect on output and employment in the open economy. This well-known conviction is completely disregarded in Mundell [37] because of his assumption that $F_r \to \infty$, which is inconsistent with $L_r \to -\infty$.

The case in which there is no capital mobility ($F_r = 0$, $F_Y = 0$) has some practical importance. In this case, much simpler formulas than (11-29) and (11-30) can easily be obtained for the fiscal and monetary multipliers from (11-29) and (11-30). We shall leave this to the interested reader. If we further assume that $T \equiv 0$ (no trade), $V_r = 0$, completely interest inelastic investment and saving, (or $L_r \to -\infty$, liquidity trap), and $L_Y = 0$ (no income-induced investment), then we can obtain the very familiar formula for the simple government multiplier for a closed economy $dY/dG = 1/S_Y = 1/$(marginal propensity to save).

This finishes our examination of the efficacy of fiscal and monetary policies for the Keynesian case under flexible exchange rates. For the classical case,[34]

---

[34] Following the custom of the macro theory the word "classical" is used to contrast the "Keynesian" case. It should not be taken to mean the classical gold standard system. Incidentally, the gold standard system is a typical case of fixed exchange rates with no sterilization policy.

full employment of labor is always achieved, and it is rather meaningless to examine the effects of fiscal and monetary policy on output and employment. However, as noted before in the first section, we may be interested in the extent of the effect of changes in G and $\overline{M}$ on the general price level in an open economy. In this section we shall consider this question under flexible exchange rates.

Setting $dB = 0$ *and* $d\overline{M} = 0$ or $dG = 0$ in (11-27), we obtain

$$\frac{dP}{dG} = \frac{1}{G + T + V_{A/P}A + \overline{M}(V_r - F_r)/L_r},\tag{11-33}$$

$$\frac{dP}{d\overline{M}} = \frac{(V_r - F_r)/L_r + \mu V_{A/P}}{G + T + V_{A/P}A + \overline{M}(V_r - F_r)/L_r}.\tag{11-34}$$

Hence, under our specifications of the signs of the partial derivatives together with the assumption of $(G + T \geqq 0)$, dP/dG and $dP/d\overline{M}$ are, in general, positive. Their magnitudes depend on the structural coefficients, F_r, L_r, and so on. An analysis similar to the above study of the fiscal and monetary multipliers is possible and left to the interested reader.

Interesting limiting cases are as follows.

    i.   If $F_r \to \infty$, then $dP/dG \to 0$.

    ii. If $L_r \to -\infty$ (with $V_{A/P} = 0$ or $\mu = 0$), then $dP/d\overline{M} \to 0$.

    iii. If $F_r \to \infty$, then $dP/d\overline{M} \to 1/\overline{M}$.

To put it verbally: (i) A change in government expenditures or taxes has no effect on the price level if capital is perfectly mobile. (ii) A change in the money supply has no effect on the price level under the liquidity trap with no Pigou effect. (iii) A change in the money supply causes a proportional change in the price level if capital is perfectly mobile.

Finally we may note again that the positivity of the denominator of the *RHS* of (11-33) or (11-34) can be obtained from the stability condition of the present system (see Appendix to Chapter 11). If we assume the stability condition, then the assumption of $G + T \geqq 0$ in the above statements becomes altogether superfluous.

FIXED EXCHANGE RATES

Now we turn to the case of the fixed exchange rate system.[35] The relevant equations for the model in this case are equations (11-1), [or (11-2)], (11-6), (11-8), (11-13), and (11-15). Here dB is no longer zero, a new parameter (s)— the sterilization coefficient—is added in (11-15), and additional information from equation (11-4) and relation (11-5) will be used. Note also $E = $ constant in the present case by assumption. Again we are mostly concerned with the Keynesian case.

[35] The two most important cases are the current *IMF* pegged exchange rate system and the classical gold standard system.

In order to analyze the case of fixed exchange rates, it is necessary to carry our analysis of the beginning of the previous section a little further. First using equations (11-15) and (11-23) we obtain [36]

$$[1 - sF_r/L_r] \, dB = \delta \, dY + (F_r/L_r) \, d\overline{M}^h, \quad \text{where} \tag{11-35}$$

$$\delta \equiv (T_P/\sigma + T_Y + F_Y) - (\overline{M}/\sigma + L_Y)F_r/L_r. \tag{11-36}$$

Using equations (11-15), (11-22), and the above two equations, we obtain

$$[-\alpha' + \gamma/\sigma - T_P/\sigma - T_Y - s\beta' \, \delta/(1 - sF_r/L_r)] \, dY =$$

$$dG + \{\beta' + (s\beta'F_r)/[(1 - sF_r/L_r)L_r]\} \, d\overline{M}^h. \tag{11-37}$$

We may recall that the expression for β' is given in (11-22). In the case of complete sterilization, $s = 0$, and we can simplify (11-37) as

$$[-\alpha' + (\gamma - T_P)/\sigma - T_Y] \, dY = dG + \beta' \, d\overline{M}^h. \tag{11-38}$$

The magnitude of s reflects the country's policy on the degree of sterilization. The country can affect the level of output and employment by changing the magnitude of s. Here we omit such an analysis simply by assuming $s = $ constant.[37] Comparing (11-37) with (11-38), we see immediately that the analysis of the efficacy of fiscal and monetary policy would be much simpler if $s = 0$ (Johnson's case). However, here we go to (11-37) and consequently obtain much more general formulas (that is, $s \geqq 0$) for these multipliers. In other words,

$$\frac{dY}{dG} = \frac{1}{\Omega_0}, \tag{11-39}$$

where,

$$\Omega_0 \equiv -\alpha' + (\gamma - T_P)/\sigma - T_Y - s\beta' \, \delta/(1 - sF_r/L_r)$$

$$= (-V_Y + V_r L_Y/L_r) + (G + T + V_{A/P}A + \overline{M}V_r/L_r - T_P)/\sigma - T_Y$$

$$- s(V_r/L_r + \mu V_{A/P})$$

$$\times [(T_P/\sigma + T_Y + F_Y) - (\overline{M}/\sigma + L_Y)F_r/L_r]/(1 - sF_r/L_r),$$

$$\frac{dY}{d\overline{M}^h} = \frac{V_r/L_r + \mu V_{A/P}}{\Omega_0(1 - sF_r/L_r)}. \tag{11-40}$$

In the subsequent analysis we assume $\Omega_0 > 0$. In the literature, this condition is not realized, despite the fact that it clearly plays a crucial role in the analysis.

---

[36] Note that $dT = T_P \, dP + T_E \, dE + T_Y \, dY = (T_P/\sigma + T_Y) \, dY$.

[37] This does not mean, of course, that we cannot consider the effect of alternative levels of s on the magnitudes of (dY/dG) and $(dY/d\overline{M})$. Just as we considered the effect of alternative levels of L_r, F_r, and so on, on the magnitude of these multipliers, we can perform a similar analysis with respect to s also. Thus, the government can control the level of these multipliers by setting different levels of s. What we are assuming here is that s will not be changed during the course of the disturbances of the system initiated by a shift of G or $\overline{M}^h$.

As discussed in the Appendix to Chapter 11 this condition is closely related to the stability condition of the model. If, in particular, the policy is complete sterilization ($s = 0$), then we can say that from our specification of the signs of partial derivatives $\Omega_0 > 0$ if $G + T \geqq 0$ and $T_Y \leqq 0$. That is, the condition $G + T \geqq 0$ again plays an important role. If we further assume an infinite supply coefficient ($\sigma \to \infty$), even these conditions ($G + T \geqq 0$, $T_Y \leqq 0$) are unnecessary.

Note that if $s = 0$, F_r and F_Y have no effect on dY/dG and $dY/d\overline{M}^h$. In other words, capital mobility has no effect on the multipliers under fixed exchange rates.

Assuming again that the interactions among the structural coefficients are negligible and that $\Omega_0 > 0$, we can obtain conclusions about the efficacy of fiscal and monetary policies vis-à-vis different magnitudes of the structural coefficients. The following table will summarize the results.

TABLE 11-2

	σ	F_r	F_Y	L_Y	$|L_r|$	$|V_Y|$	$|V_r|$	$V_{A/P}$	$|T_P|$	$|T_Y|$
$\dfrac{dY}{dG}$	$\uparrow$	? (= 0, if $s = 0$)	$\uparrow$	? ($\downarrow$, if $s = 0$)	? ($\uparrow$, if $s = 0$)	$\downarrow$	? ($\downarrow$, if $s = 0$)	? ($\downarrow$, if $s = 0$)	$\downarrow$ (0, if $\sigma = \infty$)	$\downarrow$
$\dfrac{dY}{d\overline{M}^h}$	$\uparrow$	? (0, if $s = 0$)	$\uparrow$	? ($\downarrow$, if $s = 0$)	?	$\downarrow$	?	?	$\downarrow$ (0, if $\sigma = \infty$)	$\downarrow$

The interpretation of this table is the same as for Table 11-1. The effect of an increase in capital mobility (or, more specifically, an increase in F_r) on the magnitudes of dY/dG or $dY/d\overline{M}^h$ cannot, in general, be specified. However, by partial differentiation of these expressions with respect to F, we can obtain some definite conclusions. Thus we can show that a necessary and sufficient condition for an increase in F_r to *increase* dY/dG (with $s > 0$) is

$$(\overline{M}/\sigma + L_Y) - s(T_P/\sigma + T_Y + F_Y) > 0 . \tag{11-41}$$

Clearly, if $F_Y = 0$ (*no* Johnson effect), then this condition is satisfied under the ordinal assumption of $T_Y < 0$. A recognition of the Johnson effect ($F_Y > 0$) is important because it may cause the *LHS* of (11-41) to become negative, so that an increase in F_r may decrease the absolute magnitude of the fiscal multiplier dY/dG.

A necessary and sufficient condition for an increase in F_r to *decrease* $dY/d\overline{M}^h$ (with $s > 0$) is similarly obtained as

$$(V_r/L_r + \mu V_{A/P})(\overline{M}/\sigma + L_Y) - [-\alpha' + (\gamma - T_P)/\sigma - T_Y] < 0 . \tag{11-42}$$

If $\sigma \to \infty$, then we can simplify (11-42) as

$$V_Y + T_Y + \mu V_{A/P} < 0. \tag{11-43}$$

If $V_{A/P} = 0$ (no real balance effect), then condition (11-43) is satisfied under the ordinary conditions $V_Y < 0, T_Y < 0$. In other words, if $\sigma \to \infty$, and $V_{A/P} = 0$, an increase in F_r will, in general, decrease the magnitude of the monetary multiplier.

Very simplified expressions for these fiscal and monetary multipliers can be obtained for some limiting cases. The following ones may be of interest.

    i. $F_r \to \infty$ (with $L_r > -\infty$), $\sigma \to \infty$ and $V_{A/P} = 0$ (the Mundellian case):

$$\frac{dY}{dG} = \frac{-1}{V_Y + T_Y}. \tag{11-44}$$

    ii-a. $F_r \to \infty$ (with $L_r > -\infty$), or
    ii-b. $L_r \to -\infty$ (with $F_r < \infty$):

$$\frac{dY}{d\overline{M}^h} = 0. \tag{11-45}$$

    iii. $F_r = 0, F_Y = 0$ (no capital mobility), $\sigma \to \infty$, and $V_{A/P} = 0$:

$$\frac{dY}{dG} = \frac{1}{V_r(L_Y - sT_Y)/L_r - (V_Y + T_Y)}. \tag{11-46}$$

In the above limiting cases note that we do not need the assumption of $\Omega_0 > 0$ to obtain the conclusions with regard to the direction of changes of these multipliers. Note also that for case ii-a. the additional Mundellian assumptions of $\sigma \to \infty$ and $V_{A/P} = 0$ are not needed. Case ii-b asserts the usual conviction, that under the liquidity trap monetary policy has no effect on output and employment for the fixed exchange rate case.

Now we should recall that under fixed exchange rates there is no guarantee that the balance of payments is brought into equilibrium. Whether the balance of payments will improve or deteriorate due to fiscal or monetary policy can be seen easily by inserting the values of (dY/dG) or $(dY/d\overline{M}^h)$, as obtained in (11-39) or (11-40), into equation (11-35). That is, we find the value of (dB/dG) or $(dB/d\overline{M}^h)$ in this way. Obviously, when we obtain (dB/dG), we set $d\overline{M}^h = 0$ in (11-35). It is clear that whether $dB > 0$ or $dB < 0$ crucially depends on the signs of δ.

This finishes our examination of the efficacy of fiscal and monetary policy for the Keynesian case under fixed exchange rates. We now turn to the *classical case*. In other words, we are now concerned with the effect of changes in G and $\overline{M}$ on the general price level in a full employment, open economy under fixed exchange rates. In order to carry out our analysis for this case, we should proceed further with our result of the third section. Using equations (11-15), (11-22), and (11-23) and noting that $dY = 0$, we obtain

$$dG + \beta' \, d\overline{M}^h/(1 - sF_r/L_r)$$
$$+ [T_P + s\beta'(T_P - \overline{M}F_r/L_r)/(1 - sF_r/L_r) - \gamma] \, dP = 0, \qquad (11\text{-}47)$$

where β' and γ are defined in (11-22).

In the case of complete sterilization ($s = 0$), this is simplified as

$$dG + \beta' \, d\overline{M}^h + (T_P - \gamma) \, dP = 0. \qquad (11\text{-}48)$$

We can analyze the case of non-perfect sterilization or no sterilization ($s > 0$) *mutatis mutandis* and we shall leave this to the reader.

In order to analyze the effects of a change in G, set $d\overline{M}^h = 0$ in (11-48) and obtain

$$\frac{dP}{dG} = \frac{1}{\gamma - T_P} = \frac{1}{G + T + V_{A/P}A + \overline{M}V_r/L_r - T_P}. \qquad (11\text{-}49)$$

Assuming $G + T \geqq 0$, the sign of dP/dG is unambiguously positive, and its magnitude is given by (11-49).

Next we set $dG = 0$ in (11-48) and obtain

$$\frac{dP}{d\overline{M}^h} = \frac{\beta'}{\gamma - T_P} = \frac{(V_r/L_r + \mu V_{A/P})}{G + T + V_{A/P}A + \overline{M}V_r/L_r - T_P}. \qquad (11\text{-}50)$$

Assuming $G + T \geqq 0$, $dp/d\overline{M}^h$ is in general positive (unless $L_r \rightarrow -\infty$ and $V_{A/P} = 0$ for example). If $L_r \rightarrow -\infty$ and $V_{A/P} = 0$, then $dp/d\overline{M}^h = 0$. The analysis of magnitudes of dP/dG or $dP/d\overline{M}^h$ vis-à-vis the magnitude of the structural coefficients is left to the interested reader.

Note again that capital mobility plays no explicit role in the above conclusion. This is due to the complete sterilization assumption. We may note again that the positivity of the denominator of the *RHS* of (11-49) is the outcome of the stability condition (see the Appendix to Chapter 11). That is, if we assume the stability condition, the assumption of ($G + T \geqq 0$) in the above statement becomes superfluous.

APPROPRIATE MIX OF FISCAL AND MONETARY POLICIES

Under the fixed exchange rate system the balance of payments is not necessarily in equilibrium. Obviously, a country cannot maintain either deficits or surpluses in the balance of payments forever. Hence it may be of interest to ask what is the appropriate mix of fiscal and monetary policies which will increase the level of output and employment while keeping the balance of payment in equilibrium under the Keynesian model with fixed exchange rates. We shall pursue this in this section.

Setting $dB = 0$ in equation (11-35), we obtain

$$\frac{dY}{d\overline{M}^h} = \tau, \quad \text{where} \tag{11-51}$$

$$\tau = \frac{-F_r/L_r}{\delta} = \frac{-F_r}{(T_P/\sigma + T_Y + F_Y)L_r - (\overline{M}/\sigma + L_Y)F_r}. \tag{11-52}$$

Combining (11-15) with (11-22) and putting $dB = 0$, we obtain

$$\hat{\alpha}\, dY + dG + \beta'\, d\overline{M}^h = 0, \tag{11-53}$$

where

$$\hat{\alpha} \equiv \alpha' + (T_P/\sigma + T_Y) - \gamma/\sigma$$

$$= (V_Y - V_r L_Y/L_r) - (G + T + V_{A/P}A + \overline{M}V_r/L_r - T_P)/\sigma + T_Y.$$

We may recall that $-\hat{\alpha}$ is the denominator of the *RHS* of equation (11-37) when $s = 0$, which is, in general, positive. About the signs for τ, we have (assuming F_r is finite):

$$\tau \gtreqless 0 \text{ according to whether } (T_P/\sigma + T_Y)L_r + [F_Y L_r - F_r(\overline{M}/\sigma + L_Y)] \gtreqless 0. \tag{11-54}$$

If $F_r \to \infty$ (perfect mobility of capital), τ becomes

$$\tau = \frac{1}{\overline{M}/\sigma + L_Y}. \tag{11-55}$$

Hence, τ is always positive in this case. If $L_r \to -\infty$ (liquidity trap) or $F_r = 0$ (no capital mobility), then $\tau = 0$. In this case of $\tau = 0$, we cannot have a monetary policy which will *increase* the level of output and employment while keeping the balance of payments in equilibrium. Hence, we may omit this case from our consideration. Combining equation (11-53) with (11-51), we obtain

$$dG = -(\hat{\alpha}\tau + \beta')\, d\overline{M}^h. \tag{11-56}$$

Hence, depending on the signs of τ and $(\hat{\alpha}\tau + \beta')$ we have various mixes of fiscal and monetary policy. We summarize this in the following table.

TABLE 11-3 Appropriate Mixes of Fiscal and Monetary Policies

	$\tau > 0$	$\tau < 0$
$(\hat{\alpha}\tau + \beta') < 0$	$dG > 0$ $d\overline{M}^h > 0$	$dG < 0$ $d\overline{M}^h < 0$
$(\hat{\alpha}\tau + \beta') > 0$	$dG < 0$ $d\overline{M}^h > 0$	$dG > 0$ $d\overline{M}^h < 0$

For example, if $F_r \to \infty$ (so that $\tau > 0$) and if $(\hat{a}\tau + \beta') > 0$, then the appropriate mix is to increase the money supply but to decrease government expenditures (or to increase taxes). We may also note that under the ordinary assumption of $\hat{a} < 0$, $\tau < 0$ will, in general, imply $(\hat{a}\tau + \beta') > 0$. In this case again the appropriate mix is not that of increasing both government expenditures and the money supply.

MAJOR LIMITATIONS OF THE MODEL

Without recognizing its limitations, no study makes any progress. Hence, in this section, we shall briefly summarize the major limitations of the model that we discussed in this paper. Although our model is a very general one, we still must point out the following assumptions, which we hope to waive sometime in the future.

1. SMALL COUNTRY   We assumed that the country is small enough so that its level of economic activity does not affect the level of economic activity for the rest of the world. In other words, changes in variables such as Y, r, and P do not have any significant repercussions on the world level of these variables. This assumption can be waived by imposing a similar model for "the rest of the world." For a simple model such as the one discussed by Mundell with all the limiting assumptions, this is not too difficult.[38] Mundell attempted such a generalization himself [38]. Although we can certainly carry out a similar analysis with respect to our generalized model, such a task will involve very tedious computational work.[39]

2. NO TERMS OF TRADE EFFECT   Under the flexible exchange rate system, a change in the exchange rate will change the domestic price of the foreign products. For example, a devaluation of the home currency will increase the domestic price of the foreign goods. In order to buy the same bundle of domestic goods after this devaluation as before, we have to have an increase in income. With the same amount of income, the country can only buy a lesser amount in its commodity bundle. In other words, exchange devaluation will, *ceteris paribus*, reduce the real income of the country. Assuming that the marginal propensity to hoard (the marginal propensity to save minus the marginal propensity to invest) is positive, this will have a positive multiplier effect. That is, the initial favorable impact on the balance of trade is, to a certain extent, offset by this effect. This is called the "terms of trade effect" and was a heated issue in the discussion of exchange devaluation in the 1950s (Spraos, Pearce, Day, Jones, Tsiang, and so on),[40] which followed the path-breaking works in

[38] The procedure is essentially similar to the one adopted in the discussion of foreign repercussions in the simple international trade multiplier theory.

[39] For certain countries, the small country assumption is rather plausible anyway.

[40] See for example Jones [17], Tsiang [60], Takayama and McKenzie [56], and Chapter 10. For a summary of the major points of the debates, see the last section of Chapter 10.

1950 by Laursen and Metzler [22], Harberger [11], and Stolper [53]. In the present study we completely neglect this terms of trade effect. (In fact, our income variable Y is equal to the amount of the domestic output.) Obviously, under the fixed exchange rate system we do not have to consider this effect, but our discussions under flexible exchange rates should be modified by this effect. Since the *explicit* introduction of this effect complicates the model greatly, no such attempt has been made in the literature even for the simplest Mundellian model.

3. DEMAND FOR MONEY   One of the important components of the demand for money is the transactions demand. The transactions demand for money is an increasing function with respect to money income, which, in turn, will depend on the level of the trade balance. In the present paper, we simplified our treatment by assuming that the transactions demand for real cash balances ("real" in terms of the price of the home goods) is an increasing function in Y (the output of the home goods). Under flexible exchange rates, we really have to take account of the changes in the country's real income due to variations of the exchange rate, a fact which we explained above.[41] For the sake of simplicity we completely avoid such discussions in the present paper, nor has work been done on the subject in the literature.

4. INTERNATIONAL CAPITAL MOVEMENTS   We assumed that international capital movements as a flow variable do not affect the level of the total demand for goods. This is certainly a restriction on the model. Again an explicit recognition of this will complicate the model greatly, and, following the custom in the past literature and for the sake of simplicity, we omit this consideration from the present paper. Note also that "capital" in the words, "capital movements," is solely used to mean the financial capital in this paper. In other words, we assumed away direct international investment in the form of capital goods. This again follows the custom in the past literature.

REFERENCES

1. Aliber, R. Z., *The Future of the Dollar as an International Currency* (New York: Frederick A. Praeger, Inc.), 1966.
2. Baggott, N. and Flanders, M. J., "Economic Policy in an Open Economy: A Reader's Guide," *Economia Internazionale*, XXII, November 1969.
3. Brownlee, O. H., "The Theory of Employment and Stabilization Policy," *Journal of Political Economy*, LVIII, October 1950.
4. Caves, R. E., "Flexible Exchange Rates," *American Economic Review*, LIII, May 1963.

[41] The speculative demand for money also plays an important role in this context as long as it constitutes a demand for money. The introduction of the speculative demand, moreover, will be complicated by the possibility of speculation with regard to the foreign securities.

5. Clement, M. O., Pfister, R. L., and Rothwell, K. J., *Theoretical Issues in International Economics* (Boston: Houghton Mifflin Company), 1967, especially Chapter 6.

6. Corden, W. M., *Recent Developments in the Theory of International Trade* (Princeton: Princeton University Press) (International Finance Section), 1965.

7. Fellner, W., Machlup, F., Triffin, R. and eleven others, *Maintaining and Restoring Balance in International Payments* (Princeton: Princeton University Press), 1966.

8. Fleming, J. M., "Domestic Financial Policies under Fixed and under Floating Exchange Rates," *IMF Staff Papers*, IX, November 1962.

9. Gray, H. P., Heckerman, D. G., Laffer, A. F., Hendershott, P. H., and Willett, T. D., "International Short Term Capital Movements: Comments," *American Economic Review*, LVII, June 1967.

10. Haberler, G., *A Survey of International Trade Theory* (Princeton: Princeton University Press) (International Finance Section), revised ed. July 1961.

11. Harberger, A. C., "Currency Depreciation, Income and the Balance of Trade," *Journal of Political Economy*, LVIII, February 1950.

12. Hicks, J. R., "Mr. Keynes and the 'Classics', A Suggested Interpretation," *Econometrica*, 5, April 1937.

13. Hicks, J. R., *Value and Capital* (Oxford: Oxford University Press), 2nd ed. 1946 (1st ed. 1939).

14. Johnson, H. G., "Equilibrium under Fixed Exchanges," *American Economic Review*, LIII, May 1963.

15. ———, "Major Issues in Monetary and Fiscal Policies," *Federal Reserve Bulletin*, L, November 1964.

16. ———, "Some Aspects of the Theory of Economic Policy in a World of Capital Mobility," *Essays in Honour of Marco Fanno*, ed. by Gabiotti, Antonio Milani, Padova, 1966.

17. Jones, R. W., "Monetary and Fiscal Policy for an Economy with Fixed Exchange Rates," *Journal of Political Economy*, 76, July/August 1968, Part II.

18. ———, "Stability Conditions in International Trade: A General Equilibrium Analysis," *International Economic Review*, 2, May 1961.

19. Kemp, M. C., "Monetary and Fiscal Policy under Alternative Assumptions about International Capital Mobility," *Economic Record*, 42, December 1966.

20. Keynes, J. M., *General Theory of Employment, Interest and Money* (London: Macmillan & Co. Ltd.), 1936.

21. Krueger, A. O., "The Impact of Alternative Government Policies Under Varying Exchange Systems," *Quarterly Journal of Economics*, LXXIX, May 1965.

22. Laursen, S. and Metzler, L. A., "Flexible Exchange Rates and the Theory of Employment," *Review of Economic and Statistics*, XXXI, September 1950.

23. Marschak, J., *Income, Employment and the Price Level* (New York: Augustus M. Kelley), 1951.

24. McKenna, J. P., *Aggregate Economic Analysis* (New York: Holt, Rinehart and Winston, Inc.), rev. ed. 1965 (1st ed. 1955).

25. McKinnon, R. I., "Optimum Currency Areas," *American Economic Review*, LIII, September 1963.

26. McLeod, A. N., "Capital Mobility and Stabilization Under Fixed and Flexible Exchange Rates: A Comment," *Canadian Journal of Economics and Political Science*, XXX, August 1964.

27. Meade, J. E., *The Balance of Payments*, The Theory of International Economic Policy, Vol. I (London: Oxford University Press), 1951. Also its *Mathematical Appendix*, 1951.

28. Melvin, J. R., "Capital Flows and Employment Under Flexible Exchange Rates," *Canadian Journal of Economics*, I, May 1968.

29. Metzler, L. A., "Wealth, Saving, and the Rate of Interest," *Journal of Political Economy*, LIX, April 1951.

30. Modigliani, F., "Monetary Mechanism and its Interaction with Real Phenomena," *Review of Economics and Statistics*, Supplement, XLV, February 1963.

31. Modigliani, F. and La Malfa, Giorgia, "Inflation, Balance of Payments Deficit and Their Cure Through Monetary Policy: the Italian Example," *Banca Nazionale Del Lavoro, Quarterly Review*, 80, March 1967.

32. Mundell, R. A., "The Monetary Dynamics of International Adjustment Under Fixed and Flexible Exchange Rates," *Quarterly Journal of Economics*, LXXIV, May 1960.

33. ———, "The International Disequilibrium System," *Kyklos*, XIV, Fasc. 2, 1961.

34. ———, "A Theory of Optimum Currency Areas," *American Economic Review*, LI, September 1961.

35. ———, "Flexible Exchange Rates and Employment Policy," *Canadian Journal of Economics and Political Science*, XXVII, November 1961.

36. ———, "The Appropriate Use of Monetary and Fiscal Policy for Internal and External Stability," *IMF Staff Papers*, IX, March 1962.

37. ———, "Capital Mobility and Stabilization Policy Under Fixed and Flexible Exchange Rates," *Canadian Journal of Economics and Political Science*, XXIX, November 1963.

38. ———, "A Reply: Capital Mobility and Size," *Canadian Journal of Economics and Political Science*, XXX, August 1964.

39. ———, "Hicksian Stability, Currency Markets and the Theory of Economic Policy," in *Value, Capital and Growth* (Essays in Honour of J. R. Hicks), ed. by J. N. Wolfe (Edinburgh: University of Edinburgh Press), 1968.

40. Niehans, J., "Monetary and Fiscal Policies in Open Economies under Fixed Exchange Rates: An Optimizing Approach," *Journal of Political Economy*, 76, July/August 1968, Part II.

41. Patinkin, D., *Money, Interest, and Price* (New York: Harper & Row, Publishers), 2nd ed. 1965 (1st ed. 1956).
42. Poole, W., "The Stability of the Canadian Flexible Exchange Rate, 1950–1962," *Canadian Journal of Economics and Political Science*, XXXIII, May 1967.
43. Quirk, J. P. and Zarley, A. M., "Policies to Attain External and Internal Balance: A Reappraisal," in *Papers in Quantitative Economics*, ed. by Quirk, J. P. and Zarley, A. M. (Lawrence, Kansas, University of Kansas Press), 1968.
44. Rhomberg, R. R., "A Model of the Canadian Economy under Fixed and Fluctuating Exchange Rates," *Journal of Political Economy*, LXXII, February 1964.
45. Samuelson, P. A., *Foundations of Economic Analysis* (Cambridge, Mass.: Harvard University Press), 1947.
46. ———, "The Simple Mathematics of Income Determination," in L. A. Metzler et. al., *Income, Employment and Public Policy: Essays in Honor of Alvin Hansen* (New York: W. W. Norton and Company, Inc.), 1948.
47. Sohmen, E., *Flexible Exchange Rates: Theory and Controversy* (Chicago: University of Chicago Press), 1961.
48. ———, *International Monetary Problems and the Foreign Exchanges* (Princeton: Princeton University Press), 1963.
49. ———, "Preisniveau und Preiserwartungen in der Makroökonomischen Theorie," *Zeitschrift des Instituts für Weltwirtschaft*, 98–1, 1967.
50. ———, "Fiscal and Monetary Policies under Alternative Exchange Rate Systems," *Quarterly Journal of Economics*, LXXXI, August 1967.
51. Smith, W. L., "A Graphical Exposition of the Complete Keynesian System," *Southern Economic Journal*, XXIII, October 1956.
52. Stein, J. L., "International Short-term Capital Movements," *American Economic Review*, March 1965.
53. Stolper, W. F., "The Multiplier, Flexible Exchanges and International Equilibrium," *Quarterly Journal of Economics*, LXIV, November 1950.
54. Takayama, A., "Stability in the Balance of Payments: A Multi-Country Approach," *Journal of Economic Behavior*, I, October 1961 (resume in *Econometrica*, July 1960).
55. ———, *International Economics* (Kokusai Keizai-gaku) (Tokyo: Toyo Keizai Shimpo-sha), 1963.
56. ———, "Aggregate Demand and Aggregate Supply," *Lecture Note*, Purdue University, November 1966.
57. ———, "Stability Conditions, Comparative Statics and the Correspondence Principle in an Open Economy," *Krannert Institute Paper*, Purdue University, No. 207, September 1968, reproduced as the Appendix of the present chapter.
58. Takayama, A. and McKenzie, L. W., "General Equilibrium Analysis of International Trade" (unpublished manuscript), 1964.

59. Tobin, J., "Money Wage Rates and Employment," *The New Economics*, ed. by S. E. Harris (New York: Alfred A. Knopf), 1947.
60. Tsiang, S. C., "The Role of Money in the Stability of Trade Balance and the Synthesis of Elasticity and Absorption Approaches," *American Economic Review*, LII, September 1961.

Appendix to Chapter 11
Stability Conditions, Comparative Statics, and the Correspondence Principle in an Open Economy[42]

INTRODUCTION

In Chapter 11, we developed a comparative statics model to analyze the relative efficacy of fiscal and monetary policies under flexible and fixed exchange rates. Our analysis was quite general in that it included many of the previous studies in the literature (such as Mundell [A9] and Johnson [A4]) as very special cases. There it was noticed that we need certain conditions to determine the signs of the fiscal and monetary multipliers. These conditions were completely overlooked by the other studies through the simplifying assumptions they adopted. In this Appendix to Chapter 11, we shall argue that these conditions reflect some sort of stability condition. We shall point out that the Hicksian notion of imperfect stability plays an important role here. In particular we shall find that the (imperfect) stability condition for the goods market plays a crucial role in determining the results of a comparative statics analysis with regard to the fiscal and monetary multipliers.[43] We shall also discuss the imperfect stability problem of the foreign exchange market, that is, the exchange stability problem.

We shall then in the third section of this appendix turn to the discussion of the exchange devaluation problem. This is an important exercise in comparative statics that we did not discuss in the main text of Chapter 11. We shall obtain a necessary and sufficient condition for an exchange devaluation to improve the balance of payments, when explicit consideration is made of the repercussions of such a devaluation on all markets, namely, the goods market, the money market, and the foreign exchange market. Such a condition is new in the literature.

In our attempt to relate the stability conditions to the comparative statics results we are bound to run into Samuelson's famous Correspondence Principle [A13]. We shall point out that this principle is used in a strange way in the ordinary macroanalysis of a closed or open economy. We shall try to clarify

[42] This Appendix to Chapter 11 is a revised version of [A17]. I am indebted to Ajit S. Sabharwal for comments.
[43] We observed a similar phenomenon in our discussion of exchange stability in Chapter 9, fourth section.

354

the precise meaning of this Principle using the model of this paper as a stepping stone. We shall find a general relation among the Hicksian imperfect stability conditions, the comparative statics results, and the dynamic stability condition, and also point out some difficulties with the way in which the Correspondence Principle has been used in the past.

THE STABILITY CONDITIONS

We are concerned with a full general equilibrium analysis of the Keynesian model, in which the interactions among the goods market, the money market, and the labor market are fully taken into consideration.[44] We also want to introduce the consideration of international capital movements. We shall use the model which is developed in Chapter 11. Defining C, real consumption; I, real investment; P, price of output; r, interest rate; A, aggregate net worth (assets) of the private sector; G, government expenditures; we can write the equation which denotes the equilibrium in the goods market as follows:

$$I(r, Y, A/P) + G/P + T/P = S(r, Y, A/P), \qquad (11\text{-}57)$$

where

$$S(r, Y, A/P) \equiv Y - C(r, Y, A/P).$$

Or we may write

$$V(r, Y, A/P) + G/P + T/P = 0, \qquad (11\text{-}58)$$

where $V \equiv I - S$.

Letting $\overline{M}$ be the supply of money, we may write the equilibrium condition for the money market as

$$\overline{M}/P = L(r, Y). \qquad (11\text{-}59)$$

We write the aggregate supply equation as used by Brownlee [A1] and Marschak [A7] as

$$Y = Y(P) \quad \text{or} \quad Y = Y(P, \overline{W}), \qquad (11\text{-}60)$$

where $\overline{W}$ is the money wage rate. This is obtained from equations denoting the production function, the demand for and supply of labor. (11-60) can be summarized by the following three cases:

   i.   The classical case: $Y = Y_f$ (a constant),
   ii. The ordinary-Keynesian case: $dY/dP > 0$,
   iii. The ultra-Keynesian case: $dY/dP \to \infty$ (or $P = $ constant).
   If we define σ, the *supply coefficient*, as

$$\sigma \equiv dY/dP, \qquad (11\text{-}61)$$

---

[44] The introduction of these interactions will make our analysis very complicated. In order to keep our analysis at a manageable size, we shall keep the small country assumption and neglect the terms of trade effect.

then we may describe the above three cases as:

   i. (The classical case): $\sigma = 0$;
  ii. (The ordinary-Keynesian case): $\infty > \sigma > 0$;
 iii. (The ultra-Keynesian case): $\sigma \to \infty$.

Letting B be the balance of payments of the home country in terms of the home currency, we may write the balance of payments equation as

$$B = T(P, Y, E) + F(r, Y), \tag{11-62}$$

where F is the net inflow of foreign capital. With $B = 0$ the equilibrium of the system with flexible exchange rates is completely described by equations (11-58), (11-59), (11-60), and (11-61). The variables to be determined in the system (the endogenous variables) are Y, P, r, and E. The exogenous variables of the system are G, $\overline{M}$, and A.

In the fixed exchange rate system, the exchange rate, E, is constant by assumption. Hence, we eliminate it from the above list of endogenous variables. But, on the other hand, B is now in the list of endogenous variables. The balance of payments deficit or surplus naturally affects the level of the money supply of the country, depending on the sterilization policy that the country adopts. We may now add the following equation to our model:

$$d\overline{M} = d\overline{M}^h + s\,dB, \tag{11-63}$$

where d stands for the total derivative; $\overline{M}^h$, the money supply controlled by the home country's monetary authority; and s, the sterilization coefficient. Here $B = 0$ initially is assumed. If $s = 0$, the home country adopts a complete sterilization policy. $\overline{M}$ is now dropped from the list of the exogenous variables and is an endogenous variable. Note that $\overline{M}^h$ is added as an exogenous variable to the system. There are five equations, (11-58), (11-59), (11-60), (11-62), and (11-63), and five endogenous variables, Y, P, r, B, and $\overline{M}$.

This completes the summary of the macromodel of a country that we are going to consider. Notice that in the above formulation we adopted the small country assumption (for the home country) so that variables concerning the rest of the world are held constant, while we dropped the assumptions of constant price and interest rate and no income effect with respect to the home country. This will broaden our analysis considerably. We would now like to consider the stability conditions for the above model. Let us begin our analysis by assuming that all the markets except for the goods market are held in equilibrium, and, for the time being, let us define the *stability* of our system as follows. An increase (decrease) in the price of the home goods will reduce (increase) the home excess demand for the goods, *assuming that the rest of the markets are brought into equilibrium*. This is the Hicksian concept of imperfect stability of the goods market, which we call the *stability via the goods market*. Denote the home excess demand for the goods by D. That is,

$$D \equiv C + I + G/P + T/P - Y = V + G/P + T/P. \tag{11-64}$$

Then we have the stability via the goods market if $dD/dP < 0$.

First assume flexible exchange rates so that our system can be described by equations (11-58), (11-59), (11-60), and (11-62) with $B = 0$. A change in the (home) excess demand for goods is obtained by differentiating (11-64).

$$dD = V_r\, dr + V_Y\, dY - (G + T + V_{A/P}A)\, dP + dT\,,\text{[45]} \tag{11-65}$$

where G, $\overline{M}$, and A (exogenous variables) are held constant. Combining this with the equations obtained from the total differentiation of (11-59), (11-60), and (11-62), we obtain [46]

$$dD = \sigma[(V_Y - V_rL_Y/L_r) - F_Y + F_rL_Y/L_r$$
$$- (G + T + V_{A/P}A + \overline{M}V_r/L_r - F_r\overline{M}/L_r)/\sigma]\, dP\,. \tag{11-66}$$

Or, in short,

$$dD = \sigma\alpha\, dP\,, \tag{11-67}$$

where

$$\alpha \equiv (V_Y - V_rL_Y/L_r) - F_Y + F_rL_Y/L_r$$
$$- (G + T + V_{A/P}A + \overline{M}V_r/L_r - F_r\overline{M}/L_r)/\sigma\,.$$

Therefore, a sufficient (a necessary) condition for the stability via the goods market under the flexible exchange rate system is

$$\alpha < 0\ (\alpha \leqq 0)\,. \tag{11-68}$$

In the above consideration, we assumed that the price, P, is the adjusting parameter for the goods market. But in the Keynesian model, output is often taken as the adjustment parameter for the goods market. This is particularly significant for the case of an infinite supply elasticity ($\sigma \to \infty$). For this case the stability condition is $dD/dY < 0$, due to the supposition that an increase (decrease) in the excess demand for goods will cause an increase (reduction) in output. A traditional explanation for this is, of course, the mechanism of unintended inventory decumulation (and accumulation).[47]

We may note immediately that a sufficient condition for the stability via the goods market under this new definition is again condition (11-68). In other

[45] Again we shall denote partial derivatives by putting a subscript which indicates the differentiating variable below and to the right of the relevant variable. For example, $\partial V/\partial r = V_r$, $\partial V/\partial Y = V_Y$, and $\partial V/\partial(A/P) = V_{A/P}$. We choose the units of measurement properly so that $P = 1$ initially. Note for these ordinary restrictions on the signs of these partial derivatives such as $V_r \leqq 0$, $F_r \geqq 0$, $L_r \leqq 0$, $L_r \to \infty$ (liquidity trap), $V_{A/P} \geqq 0$, and so on. Recall Chapter 11.

[46] This is due to the assumption that all the markets except the goods market are brought into equilibrium. The expressions obtained from total differentiation of these three equations are the same as (11-18), (11-19), and (11-21) of Chapter 11.

[47] This convention is adopted in many macro textbooks. The present contention of the author is that this is only plausible under the limiting case of ($\sigma \to \infty$). For the classical case of full employment ($\sigma = 0$), output cannot be the adjusting parameter.

words, condition (11-68) is a sufficient (a necessary) condition for stability in either case. In the discussion of the flexible exchange rate system in Chapter 11, we obtained the following expressions for the fiscal and monetary multipliers $(dY/dG$ and $dY/d\overline{M})$:

$$\frac{dY}{dG} = \frac{-1}{\alpha},$$ (11-69)

$$\frac{dY}{d\overline{M}} = \frac{-1}{\alpha} \left[(V_r - F_r)/L_r + \mu V_{A/P} \right].^{48}$$ (11-70)

Under the ordinary assumptions about the signs of the partial derivatives, the expression inside the bracket of (11-70) is positive. Hence, our stability condition $[\alpha < 0]$ gives as a necessary and sufficient condition that the fiscal multiplier be positive and that the monetary multiplier be positive under the ordinary specifications of the signs of the partial derivatives. We may also note that under the ordinary specifications of the signs of the partial derivatives $\alpha < 0$ if $G + T \geqq 0$. This condition is discussed in the third section of Chapter 11.

For the classical case with $\sigma = 0$, equation (11-67) should be rewritten as

$$dD = -\bar{\alpha} \, dP,$$ (11-71)

where

$$\bar{\alpha} = G + T + V_{A/P}A + \overline{M}V_r/L_r - F_r\overline{M}/L_r.$$ (11-72)

A sufficient condition for the stability via the goods market under the flexible exchange rate system is $dD/dP < 0$, or,

$$\bar{\alpha} > 0,$$ (11-73)

when $\sigma = 0$.

In Chapter 11, the effects of changes in G or $\overline{M}$ on P under the classical case with flexible exchange rates are obtained as

$$\frac{dP}{dG} = \frac{1}{\bar{\alpha}},$$ (11-74)

$$\frac{dP}{d\overline{M}} = \frac{1}{\bar{\alpha}} \left[(V_r - F_r)/L_r + \mu V_{A/P} \right].$$ (11-75)

Again a necessary and sufficient condition for dP/dG or $dP/d\overline{M}$ to be positive is that our stability condition $\bar{\alpha} > 0$ holds. Note again that $G + T \geqq 0$ gives a sufficient condition for $\bar{\alpha} > 0$. Hence, we find that the signs of the fiscal and monetary output (or price) multipliers are crucially related to the stability via the goods market.

Now let us turn to the fixed exchange rate system. Our system is described by equations (11-58), (11-59), (11-60), (11-62), and (11-63). We have the stability

---

[48] μ is the factor which relates the induced change in A to a change in $\overline{M}$. That is, $dA = \mu \, d\overline{M}$. Here we assume that there are no autonomous changes in A. Recall Chapter 11, equation (11-21) and its footnotes.

via the goods market if $dD/dP < 0$ (or $dD/dY < 0$) when all the markets except for the goods market are held in equilibrium. From (11-65) we obtain[49]

$$dD = -\sigma \overline{\Omega}_0 \, dP, \tag{11-76}$$

where

$$\overline{\Omega}_0 = (-V_Y + V_r L_Y/L_r) + (G + T + V_{A/P} A + \overline{M} V_r/L_r - T_P)/\sigma - T_Y. \tag{11-77}$$

Note that the following relation holds:

$$\overline{\Omega}_0 = -\alpha, \tag{11-77'}$$

when $dB = 0$, in view of equations (11-18) and (11-20) of Chapter 11.

Note that $\overline{\Omega}_0$ is equal to Ω_0 in (11-39) of Chapter 11 with $s = 0$. In view of (11-77'), equation (11-76) gives the same expression as equation (11-67), which we will normally expect. Note that $dB = 0$ implies that no transfers are made between this country and the rest of the world.

For the case of the ultra-Keynesian output adjustment model, we have the following equation instead of (11-76):

$$dD = -\overline{\Omega}_0 \, dY. \tag{11-78}$$

We have the stability via the goods market if $(dD/dP < 0)$ for the price adjusting case, and $(dD/dY < 0)$ for the output adjusting case. Hence, a sufficient (a necessary) condition for stability for either case is

$$\overline{\Omega}_0 > 0 \, (\overline{\Omega}_0 \geqq 0), \tag{11-79}$$

which, in view of (11-77') is equivalent to condition (11-68), the condition for the stability via the goods market under the flexible exchange rate system.

In equations (11-39) and (11-40) of Chapter 11, we obtained the comparative statics formulas for the fiscal and the monetary multipliers when $s = 0$ as

$$\frac{dY}{dG} = \frac{1}{\overline{\Omega}_0}, \tag{11-80}$$

$$\frac{dY}{d\overline{M}^h} = \frac{1}{\overline{\Omega}_0} \, (V_r/L_r + \mu V_{A/P}). \tag{11-81}$$

Again the fiscal multiplier is positive if and only if $\overline{\Omega}_0 > 0$, and the monetary multiplier is positive, under the ordinary specifications on the signs of the partial derivatives if and only if $\overline{\Omega}_0 > 0$. Hence, the stability condition via the goods market again plays a crucial role. Note that, in spite of (11-77'), (11-80) is *not* equivalent to (11-69). This is because dB is not, in general, equal to zero under the fixed exchange rate system.

[49] Use equations (11-4), (11-15), (11-18), (11-19), (11-20) of Chapter 11, and note that $dB = 0$ implies $d\overline{M} = d\overline{M}^h = 0$.

For the classical case with $\sigma = 0$, equation (11-76) should be rewritten as

$$dD = -\Omega_1 \, dP, \quad \text{where} \tag{11-82}$$

$$\Omega_1 = (G + T + V_{A/P}A + \overline{M}V_r/L_r) - T_P(= \gamma - T_P). \tag{11-83}$$

A sufficient (a necessary) condition for the stability via the goods market is $dD/dP < 0 \, (\leqq 0)$, or

$$\Omega_1 > 0 \, (\Omega_1 \geqq 0). \tag{11-84}$$

We then recall that in Chapter 11 the effects of changes in G or $\overline{M}^h$ on P when $s = 0$ are obtained as

$$\frac{dP}{dG} = \frac{1}{\Omega_1}, \tag{11-85}$$

$$\frac{dP}{d\overline{M}^h} = \frac{1}{\Omega_1} (V_r/L_r + \mu V_{A/P}). \tag{11-86}$$

Again we see that the stability condition via the goods market plays a crucial role in determining the signs of dP/dG and $dP/d\overline{M}^h$. Note also that the condition $(G + T \geqq 0)$ will guarantee $\Omega_1 > 0$ under the ordinary specification of the signs of the partial derivatives.

In the above analysis we assumed that all the goods markets are brought into equilibrium. Suppose now that all the markets except for the foreign exchange market are held in equilibrium. We consider the flexible exchange rates case. Then this is the problem of exchange stability. In other words, our system is now characterized by equations (11-58), (11-59), (11-60), and (11-62). (dB is not necessarily equal to zero now.) From these equations we obtain (by putting $dG = d\overline{M} = 0$)[50]

$$dB = -\alpha\sigma \, dP, \quad \text{where } \alpha \text{ is defined by equation (11-67).} \tag{11-87}$$

Also we obtain[51]

$$dB = [(T_P/\sigma + T_Y + F_Y) - (\overline{M}/\sigma + L_Y)F_r/L_r]\sigma \, dP + T_E \, dE. \tag{11-88}$$

Combining (11-87) with (11-88), we obtain

$$\frac{dB}{dE} = T_E\alpha/(\alpha + \delta) \tag{11-89}$$

where

$$\delta \equiv (T_P/\sigma + T_Y + F_Y) - (\overline{M}/\sigma + L_Y)F_r/L_r.$$

A sufficient (a necessary) condition for the stability via the foreign exchange market (*exchange stability*) is $dB/dE > 0 \, (\geqq 0)$. Then, assuming $\alpha < 0$ (the

---

[50] Use equations (11-19), (11-24), and (11-25) of Chapter 11. Assume that change in B does not induce a change in $\overline{M}$ so that $d\overline{M} = 0$.

[51] Use equation (11-23) of Chapter 11.

stability condition via the goods market), a sufficient (a necessary) condition for exchange stability is

$$T_E/(\alpha + \delta) < 0 \, (\leqq 0). \tag{11-90}$$

But we can compute

$$\alpha + \delta = (T_Y + T_P/\sigma) + (V_Y - V_r L_Y/L_r) - (G + T + V_{A/P}A + \overline{M}V_r)/\sigma, \tag{11-91}$$

which is negative if either $\sigma \to \infty$ or $G + T \geqq 0$. Assume that $\alpha + \delta < 0$, then (11-90) is reduced to

$$T_E > 0 \quad (\text{that is, } \partial T/\partial E > 0). \tag{11-92}$$

Denote domestic and the foreign exports by X and X^* respectively, and denote the foreign price by P^*, and define the following elasticities.

$$\eta = \frac{\partial X}{\partial (EP^*/P)} \frac{EP^*/P}{X} \quad \text{and} \quad \eta^* = -\frac{\partial X^*}{\partial (EP^*/P)} \frac{EP^*/P}{X^*}. \tag{11-93}$$

Then (11-92) is reduced to the following familiar *elasticity condition*:

$$\eta + \eta^* - 1 > 0, \tag{11-94}$$

by assuming $T = 0$ initially. Note that in the above analysis the stability condition via the goods market ($\alpha < 0$) is used.

THE ANALYSIS OF EXCHANGE DEVALUATION

Let us now discuss the comparative statics condition for exchange devaluation. We assume that a fixed exchange rate prevails. We then consider the effects of a change of E (one of the exogenous variables of the fixed exchange rate model) on the balance of payments, B, assuming all the markets are brought into equilibrium (except the foreign exchange market) after the change of E.

This analysis can be carried out by differentiating each equation of the fixed exchange rate model, (11-58), (11-59), (11-60), and (11-62), with respect to E and combining the information thus obtained with (11-63). Here we suppose $dG = d\overline{M}^h = 0$. Note that $dY = \sigma \, dP$ due to (11-60) and that $dT = T_P \, dP + T_Y \, dY + T_E \, dE$ since $T = T(P, Y, E)$. Then differentiating (11-59) and (11-62), and combining this information with (11-63), we obtain

$$(1 - sF_r/L_r) \, dB = \delta \, dY + T_E \, dE, \tag{11-95}$$

where δ is defined in (11-89).

Next differentiating (11-58) and (11-59), and using (11-63), we obtain

$$[-\alpha' + (\gamma - T_P)/\sigma - T_Y] \, dY = T_E \, dE + s\beta' \, dB, \tag{11-96}$$

where

$$\alpha' \equiv V_Y - V_r L_Y/L_r, \quad \beta' \equiv V_r/L_r + \mu V_{A/P},$$
$$\gamma \equiv G + T + V_{A/P}A + \overline{M}V_r/L_r.$$

Note that these notations α', β', γ, and δ are the same as those used in Chapter 11. Recalling the definition of $\bar{\Omega}_0$ in (11-77), we can immediately notice that $\bar{\Omega}_0 = -\alpha' + (\gamma - T_P)/\sigma - T_Y$. Hence we may rewrite (11-96) as

$$\bar{\Omega}_0 \, dY = T_E \, dE + s\beta' \, dB \,. \tag{11-97}$$

Combining (11-95) and (11-97), we obtain

$$\frac{dB}{dE} = \frac{(\delta + \bar{\Omega}_0)T_E}{\bar{\Omega}_0[1 - s(F_r/L_r + \beta'\delta/\bar{\Omega}_0)]} \,. \tag{11-98}$$

Hence, an exchange devaluation will improve the balance of payments ($dB/dE > 0$) if and only if the *RHS* of (11-98) is positive. That is,

$$\frac{(\delta + \bar{\Omega}_0)T_E}{\bar{\Omega}_0[1 - s(F_r/L_r + \beta'\delta/\bar{\Omega}_0)]} > 0 \,. \tag{11-99}$$

If we assume $T_Y = 0$ (no income effect), $\sigma \to \infty$ (infinite supply elasticity), and $F_r = F_Y = 0$ (no capital mobility), then we can easily see that $\delta = 0$ and $\bar{\Omega}_0 = -\alpha'$, which is usually positive. Hence, the above condition (11-99) is reduced again to $T_E > 0$, which can be restated as (11-94). Note that if $s = 0$ (complete sterilization), then (11-99) can be simplified as

$$(\delta + \bar{\Omega}_0)T_E/\bar{\Omega}_0 > 0 \,. \tag{11-100}$$

We may note that

$$\delta + \bar{\Omega}_0 = (-\alpha' + \gamma/\sigma) + F_Y - (\bar{M}/\sigma + L_Y)F_r/L_r \,, \tag{11-101}$$

which is usually positive if $\gamma > 0$. We can recall here $\gamma > 0$ if $G + T \geqq 0$. Now suppose that this is the case, that is, $\delta + \bar{\Omega}_0 > 0$. Assume that we have the stability via the goods market and $\bar{\Omega}_0 > 0$. Then a necessary and sufficient condition for exchange devaluation to improve the balance of payments is again reduced to the condition $T_E > 0$, or the familiar elasticity condition (11-94).

THE MEANING OF OUR STABILITY CONDITIONS

Now we have to point out the most important feature in the procedure for obtaining the stability condition in the second section of this appendix. The stability conditions above are obtained under the assumption that all the markets except one are brought into equilibrium, and without any explicit reference to the (Samuelsonian) dynamic adjustment process. Thus, our stability conditions precisely correspond to the Hicksian imperfect stability. In other words, what we have shown in the above is that the condition for the Hicksian imperfect stability plays a very important role in obtaining the results of comparative statics.

There is nothing surprising in this conclusion, for the procedure of obtaining the Hicksian stability conditions clearly implies the specific comparative statics results. However, as Samuelson has pointed out, Hicks' notion of either imperfect or perfect stability is not equivalent to Samuelson's own true dynamic stability. This fact, therefore, seriously undermines the logic of the above analysis. This is precisely the question that Mundell raised recently in [A10], where he asked the question, "How does a wrong method yield useful results?" This question is obviously closely related to the question that Samuelson raised under the name of the Correspondence Principle. In [A13], Samuelson, in fact, illustrates the use of this Principle using a simple Keynesian system. Assuming that the reader is familiar with this Principle as stated in [A13], we now summarize Mundell's conclusions which are relevant to the present analysis as follows:

i. Assuming the true stability of the system, the known properties of the comparative statics results must have implications about the properties of dynamic processes. Hicks' analysis of stability, as Mundell pointed out, by its nature contains information about comparative statics and hence about the properties of dynamic processes.

ii. Assuming the true stability of the system, the conditions for the dynamic stability will give information about the nature of the comparative statics results. Even under the Samuelsonian adjustment equation in which the rate of change of each variable is assigned to the excess demand in each market, the Hicksian imperfect stability can be considered as a special case of dynamic stability by taking the speed of adjustment of all the variables except one to be infinity.[52] Furthermore there is no *a priori* reason that the Samuelson adjustment equation is the true kind of adjustment equation in reality. (This is clearly an institutional or empirical question.) Hence, even if we establish the fact that the Hicksian conditions (for imperfect or perfect stability) are neither necessary nor sufficient under one type of adjustment process, it is still possible that the Hicksian conditions can become necessary and sufficient under another type of adjustment process.

In other words, Mundell's consideration probes deeply into the Correspondence Principle. This principle, as proposed by Samuelson, has exactly this relevance to the above two-way relations between the comparative statics and the stability conditions.[53] Here we may show a general formulation of some

[52] Under this assumption our discussion of stability in connection with the present model becomes a true use of the Correspondence Principle.

[53] Not only does the stability condition produce useful information about the comparative statics, but the comparative statics results yield implications on the dynamic properties of the system. As Mundell reminded us, this two-way character of the Correspondence Principle is explicitly stated in Samuelson.

of the points raised above. The reader will easily realize that our conditions such as $\alpha < 0$ correspond to the condition $J_{ii}/|J| < 0$ which is discussed below.

i. Letting $f_i(x_1, x_2, \cdots, x_n; \alpha_1, \cdots, \alpha_m) = 0, x_i \geqq 0, i = 1, 2, \cdots, n$, define the equilibrium relation of a given economic system consisting of n markets. We may consider f_i as an excess demand function for the ith market. x_is are endogenous variables and α_ks are exogenous variables ("parameters" of the system). The Hicksian imperfect stability is defined by $df_i/dx_i < 0$ when $f_j = 0$ for all $j \neq i$ and $\alpha_k = $ constant for all k.

Letting J be the Jacobian matrix of the system (that is, $J = [\partial f_i/\partial x_j]$) and denoting the co-factor of the i-i element of J by J_{ii}, it can be shown easily that the system is Hicks' imperfect stability if and only if $J_{ii}/|J| < 0$, where $|J|$ is the determinant of J.

ii. Comparative statics is concerned with knowing the signs of $dx_i/d\alpha_k$ (with $\alpha_l = $ constant for all $l \neq k$). We can easily obtain $dx_i/d\alpha_k = -(1/|J|) \sum_j J_{ji} f_{j\alpha_k}$, where $f_{j\alpha_k} \equiv \partial f_j/\partial \alpha_k$. Suppose we can assume that $f_{j\alpha_k} = 0$ for all $j \neq i$. Then $dx_i/d\alpha_k = -(J_{ii}/|J|) f_{i\alpha_k}$. Hence, if $f_{i\alpha_k} > 0$, for example, then $dx_i/d\alpha_k > 0$, if and only if $J_{ii}/|J| < 0$. This is nothing but the Hicksian imperfect stability condition.

iii. The Samuelson dynamic adjustment process can be described by $dx_i/dt = \kappa_i f_i, i = 1, 2, \cdots, n$, where $\kappa_i > 0$ (speed of adjustment) and $\alpha_k = $ constant for all κ. Suppose that $\kappa_j = \infty$ for all $j \neq i$ (instantaneous adjustment). In other words, $dx_i/dt = \kappa_i f_i$ and $f_j = 0$ for all $j \neq i$. Then it can be shown easily, that a necessary and sufficient condition for the Samuelsonian dynamic stability for the linear approximation system is again $J_{ii}/|J| < 0$. (See Mundell [A10]).

For the customary use of the Correspondence Principle, we may still add the following criticism. In its customary use, the original nonlinear specifications of the economic equilibrium system are approximated by linearization and the stability conditions of this linearized system are considered in terms of the negative characteristic roots or, equivalently in terms of the Routh-Hurwitz condition. However, as is well-known, the stability of the linear approximation system is *not* a necessary condition for the local (nor global) stability of the original system.[54] Since the Correspondence Principle is directed towards using the implications of the stability of the system (hence its necessary conditions), the extensive or intensive use of the stability properties of the linear approximation system is therefore rather questionable, except that we have the following rather weak relation. The absence of instability in the linear approximation system is a necessary condition for local stability.[55]

[54] For example, the differential equation $\dot{x} = ax - x^3 (x \in R)$ is globally stable about the origin if $a = 0$, but its linear approximation ($\dot{x} = 0$) does not produce the stability about the origin.

[55] Samuelson recognized this in [A13], p. 300, for example. Clearly this statement is equivalent to the statement that the stability for the linear approximation system is sufficient for the local stability of the system.

Finally these dynamic stability discussions are, after all, concerned with the tâtonnement process and we may still question the relevance of tâtonnement stability to the comparative statics results of macro equilibrium.[56]

REFERENCES

A1. Brownlee, O. H., "The Theory of Employment and Stabilization Policy," *Journal of Political Economy*, LVIII, October 1950.

A2. Harberger, A. C., "Currency Depreciation, Income and the Balance of Trade," *Journal of Political Economy*, LVIII, February 1950.

A3. Hicks, J. R., *Value and Capital* (Oxford: Oxford University Press), 2nd ed. 1946 (1st ed. 1939).

A4. Johnson, H. G., "Some Aspects of the Theory of Economic Policy in a World of Capital Mobility," *Essays in Honour of Marco Fanno*, ed. by Gabiotti, Antonio Milani, Padova, 1966.

A5. Jones, R. W., "Stability Conditions in International Trade: A General Equilibrium Analysis," *International Economic Review*, 2, May 1961.

A6. Laursen, S. and Metzler, L. A., "Flexible Exchange Rates and the Theory of Employment," *Review of Economics and Statistics*, XXXI, September 1950.

A7. Marschak, J., *Income, Employment and the Price Level* (New York: Augustus M. Kelley), 1951.

A8. Modigliani, F., "Monetary Mechanism and its Interaction with Real Phenomena," *Review of Economics and Statistics*, Supplement, XLV, February 1963.

A9. Mundell, R. A., "Capital Mobility and Stabilization Policy Under Fixed and Flexible Exchange Rates," *Canadian Journal of Economics and Political Science*, XXIX, November 1963.

A10. ———, "Hicksian Stability, Currency Markets and the Theory of Economic Policy," in *Value, Capital and Growth* (Essays in Honour of J. R. Hicks), ed. by J. N. Wolfe (Edinburgh: Edinburgh University Press), 1968.

A11. Negishi, T., "Stability of a Competitive Economy, A Survey Article," *Econometrica*, 30, October 1962.

A12. Patinkin, D., *Money, Interest, and Price* (New York: Harper & Row, Publishers), 2nd ed. 1965 (1st ed. 1956).

A13. Samuelson, P. A., *Foundations of Economic Analysis* (Cambridge, Mass.: Harvard University Press), 1947.

A14. Takayama, A., "Stability in the Balance of Payments: A Multi-Country Approach," *Journal of Economic Behavior*, I, October 1961 (resume in *Econometrica*, July 1960).

A15. ———, *International Economics* (Kokusai Keizai-gaku) (Tokyo: Toyo Keizai Shimpo-sha), 1963.

---

[56] In this connection, see Takayama [A14].

A16. Takayama, A., "The Effects of Fiscal and Monetary Policies under Flexible and Fixed Exchange Rates," *Canadian Journal of Economics*, XXXV, May 1969.

A17. ———, "Stability Conditions, Comparative Statics and the Correspondence Principle in an Open Economy," *Krannert Institute Paper*, Purdue University, No. 207, September 1968.

A18. Tsiang, S. C., "The Role of Money in the Stability of Trade Balance and the Synthesis of Elasticity and Absorption Approaches," *American Economic Review*, LII, September 1961.

PART IV
ECONOMIC GROWTH, INTERNATIONAL TRADE, AND FACTOR MOBILITY

12

ECONOMIC GROWTH, INTERNATIONAL TRADE, AND THE IMMIGRATION OF LABOR[1]

INTRODUCTION

One of the problems which has attracted a great deal of attention from economists in the field of international trade since World War II is the problem of the dollar shortage. The problem looked particularly important when it appeared to be chronic and structural. Many articles were written in this vein. If the problem is chronic, the explanation for it must be deeply rooted in the basic structure of the economy. One of the most important explanations is given in terms of productivity changes between countries. Thomas Balogh and John H. Williams are important economists who realized this point.[2] But it was J. R. Hicks, in his "Inaugural Lecture" at Oxford [13], who truly legitimized the productivity theory of the dollar shortage and gave a brilliant theoretical analysis of the problem.[3] Many critics have accepted his theory, sharpened his model, and revised and generalized his conclusions.[4] The concern with this topic seemed to have been stimulated by a strong general interest in the theory of growth and development among many economists after the war.

In fact this problem, if it is looked upon as the problem of the impact of technological progress on the terms of trade and the real income of a country, was also of great concern to the classical economists such as J. S. Mill, Edgeworth, Bastable, Nicholson, and so on. In fact we have already noted Mill's

---

[1] This chapter is taken from Takayama [35], Chapter 4, and from [36] and [39]. This chapter like Chapter 9 originated in L. W. McKenzie's lecture at Harvard in 1957.

[2] See Kindleberger, C. P., *The Dollar Shortage*, New York: Wiley, 1956.

[3] Loosely speaking, a rapid productivity increase in the import competing industries in the U.S. is considered as the prime cause of the dollar shortage. There is an empirical study by MacDougall [25] which refutes such a thesis. The question whether or not we should accept such empirical evidence of Hicks' Theory has had a tremendous impact to the international trade theory.

[4] A rather complete bibliography on this topic can be found in Johnson [20].

consideration in Chapter 5 using Chipman's diagram. The critics and followers of the lecture by Hicks mentioned above seem to be inclined to discuss the problem in this way rather than as a balance of payments problem. In fact the postwar dollar shortage problem became much less serious, and instead the dollar surplus became a matter of great concern. It is the purpose of this chapter to consider the problem in a systematic and unambiguous fashion and clarify the essential points made by the various writers on this topic. We shall confine our analysis to the effect of growth on the terms of trade or on the country's real income, and we shall not consider the problem of the balance of payments as such. As a corollary of this analysis, we shall also consider the effect of international labor movements on the terms of trade at the end of this chapter. The neoclassical price mechanism for clearing the goods market and bringing an equilibrium to balance of payments is assumed. Hence, our concern here is more the classical concern with the impact on the terms of trade than the recent concern with the dollar shortage problem. A clear general equilibrium analysis is prepared to facilitate our analysis. The model employed here is basically the same as that developed in Chapter 10 to analyze the Keynesian devaluation problem. Note that basically the same model has application to such completely different problems as devaluation and growth and to such completely different situations of the economy as the neoclassical and the Keynesian situations. This will among other things reveal the strength of our model and the unifying nature of the economic analysis. This chapter is a twin to the next chapter, which was first published in the *Review of Economic Studies* [38].

Consider a two-country world: each country producing two goods, and suppose that a growth occurs. This can mean either technological progress or capital accumulation. This growth can occur in one or both industries of a country, and in one or both countries. Suppose that growth occurs in one industry in one country. This has two initial effects: a) the effect of lowering the cost of production in this industry, and b) the effect of increasing the real income of the country through a productivity increase which in turn increases the demand for goods. These two effects apparently have opposite effects on the relative price of the goods, and the final effect is not easy to foresee. For example, the first effect on the cost, or the supply side, will be different depending on the nature of the productivity increase (that is, technological progress or capital accumulation) and on the nature of the technological progress (neutral, capital saving, labor saving, and so on). The latter demand effect will also depend on how the consumers allocate the increased income to each good, which depends on the income elasticity (or marginal propensity to consume) of each good. After all these effects have been combined the relative price of the goods moves in a certain direction. This then will cause a movement along the new production transformation curve (production substitution and consumers substitution). They will also have secondary repercussions on the supply and demand for each good, thus causing a further change in the relative price of the goods. The final effect is not easy to foresee. In fact, one extreme case is that the terms of trade move against the growing country so much that there is a decline in the real income of the growing country in spite of the growth. This paradoxical case is analyzed by Bhagwati [6] and is called *immiserizing growth*. In any case there are numerous possibilities, and it is not surprising that so much has been written on this topic, mostly discussing special cases.

MODEL

We consider a trading world consisting of two countries, 1 and 2, with each producing two goods, X and Y. Each country is characterized by the neoclassical full employment economy.[5] The notation, defined as follows, is basically the same as that of Chapter 8 and the third section of Chapter 10.

X_1, X_2:	the output of Good X in Countries 1 and 2, respectively,
Y_1, Y_2:	the output of Good Y in Countries 1 and 2, respectively,
X_{12}, Y_{21}:	the exports of Good X from Country 1 to Country 2 and of Good Y from Country 2 to Country 1, respectively,
P_i, Q_i:	the prices of Goods X and Y respectively in Country i $(i = 1, 2)$,
W_1, W_2:	the money wage rates in Countries 1 and 2, respectively,
B_1:	the balance of payments of Country 1 (in terms of Country 2's currency),
L_{xi}:	the quantity of labor devoted to the production of Good X in Country i $(i = 1, 2)$,
L_{yi}:	the quantity of labor devoted to the production of Good Y in Country i $(i = 1, 2)$,
L_i:	the total stock of labor in Country i $(i = 1, 2)$,
A_{x1}, and so on:	the parameter multiplying the production function of Good X in Country 1, and so on.

Again following the convention due to Meade, capital Latin letters are used to refer to the absolute magnitudes of the variables, and small Latin letters designate differential changes in these variables. Let E be the exchange rate of the two currencies so that $P_1 = EP_2$ and $Q_1 = EQ_2$. Note again that $P_1/Q_1 = P_2/Q_2$ regardless of the value of E. We write this as P/Q so that we have $p_1 - q_1 = p_2 - q_2 = p - q$. We choose the units of measurement properly so that $P_1 = P_2 = Q_1 = Q_2 = E = 1$, initially. The balance of payments is assumed to be in equilibrium initially so that $B_1 = 0$. Thus we have $X_{12} = Y_{21}$. Our

---

[5] Hicks' original setting [13] is a little different. Each country consumes three goods—home goods, export goods, and imported goods. The home goods are assumed not to enter international trade by natural immobility or by costs of transport. There is virtually no substitution in consumption between the home goods and the export goods. The home goods are import-competing with the imported goods, but they are not the same goods. This setting facilitates the analysis under constant cost, since otherwise constant cost will usually result in complete specialization. The constant cost assumption is convenient, especially in measuring productivity changes. Later Hicks [14] considers the case of increasing cost also, for he is convinced that the constant cost assumption is "unrealistic."

analysis here is essentially comparative statics analysis, comparing two equilibrium states. And, we also assume a balance of payments equilibrium in the new state, so that $b_1 = 0$. In the moneyless model as the one in the present chapter, the balance of payments equilibrium signifies the equilibrium in the good markets (recall our discussions in Chapter 9). The new equilibrium state is attained by growth, and the adjustment of the goods market to the new equilibrium state is brought about by changes in the relative price of the goods (P/Q). Hence, the spirit of our analysis is very much like that of the neoclassical analysis in Chapter 8.

First, differentiating the balance of payments equation $B_1 = P_2 X_{12} - Q_2 Y_{21}$, we obtain

$$0 = b_1 = (p - q)Y_{21} + x_{12} - y_{21} . \tag{12-1}$$

As discussed in Chapter 8, the change in real income of both countries is derived from two sources—one source being the changes in the prices of the goods (compensating variation) and the second being the change in output of each of the goods. These can be written as follows:

$$u_1 = (p - q)Y_{21} + x_1 + y_1 , \tag{12-2}$$

$$u_2 = (q - p)Y_{21} + x_2 + y_2 , \tag{12-3}$$

where u_i denotes the change in real income of Country i ($i = 1, 2$).

As we noted in Chapter 8, in the static neoclassical economy $x_i + y_i = 0$ ($i = 1, 2$). With growth this is no longer necessarily true. The change in real consumption of Country 1 (respectively 2) is $y_{21} - x_{12} + x_1 + y_2$ (respectively $x_{12} - y_{21} + x_2 + y_2$), and this is equal to u_1 (respectively u_2) due to the balance of payments equation (12-1).

Next we obtain the following equations by differentiating the consumers' demand equations for the imported goods, $Y_1 + Y_{21} = \Phi(Q/P, U_1)$ and $X_2 + X_{12} = \psi(P/Q, U_2)$,

$$y_1 + y_{21} = -(Y_1 + Y_{21})(q - p)\eta_1 + \pi_1[(p - q)Y_{21} + x_1 + y_1] , \tag{12-4}$$

$$x_2 + x_{12} = -(X_2 + X_{12})(p - q)\eta_2 + \pi_2[(q - p)Y_{21} + x_2 + y_2] , \tag{12-5}$$

where $\eta_i > 0$ is the elasticity of substitution of Country i with real income fixed ($\eta_1 \equiv -[\partial\Phi/\partial(Q/P)][(Q/P)/(Y_1 + Y_{21})]$, and so on) and π_i is the marginal propensity to consume of the imported good with respect to the change in real income.

Clearly equations (12-4) and (12-5) are essentially similar to the ones used in Chapter 8, and the definitions of η_i and π_i are exactly the same as those used in Chapter 8. Defining again the *elasticity of import demand* as $\eta_1' \equiv \eta_1 Y_{21}/(Y_1 + Y_{21})$ and $\eta_2' \equiv \eta_2 X_{12}/(X_2 + X_{12})$, we can rewrite equations (12-4) and (12-5) as:

$$y_{21} = (p - q)Y_{21}(\eta_1' + \pi_1) + \pi_1 x_1 + (\pi_1 - 1)y_1 , \tag{12-6}$$

$$x_{12} = (q - p)Y_{21}(\eta_2' + \pi_2) + (\pi_2 - 1)x_2 + \pi_2 y_2 . \tag{12-7}$$

Combining (12-6) and (12-7) with (12-1) we obtain

$$[(\eta_1' + \pi_1) + (\eta_2' + \pi_2) - 1]Y_{21}(p - q)$$
$$+ [\pi_1 x_1 + (\pi_1 - 1)y_1 - (\pi_2 - 1)x_2 - \pi_2 y_2] = 0 . \tag{12-8}$$

Now we shall describe the production side of the economy. The production functions are written as $X_1 = A_{x1}f(L_{x1})$, etc., where A_{x1}, etc., are the multiplying factors set equal to one initially. Note that the only explicit factor of production in the production functions is labor. The other factors, capital, land, or Harrodian "specific factors"; are all implicit, causing diminishing returns with respect to additional labor input. Technological progress and capital accumulation (or if you like, the accumulation of the factors) are all represented by shifts of the production function, and the parameters such as A_{x1} represent these shifts.[6] There are four such production functions, one each for X_1, X_2, Y_1, and Y_2. In differential form, we have the following four equations:

$$x_1 = l_{x1} + a_{x1}X_1 ; \tag{12-9}$$

$$y_1 = l_{y1} + a_{y1}Y_1 ; \tag{12-10}$$

$$x_2 = l_{x2} + a_{x2}X_2 ; \tag{12-11}$$

$$y_2 = l_{y2} + a_{y2}Y_2 . \tag{12-12}$$

Note that the above equations are derived from the production functions by using the equality between the marginal physical product of labor and the real wage rate $(A_{x1}(df/dL_{x1}) = W_1/P_1$, and so on) and adopting the convention of choosing the unit of measurement of labor properly so that $W_1 = W_2 = 1$ initially (so that $f' = 1$, and so on). The explicit recognition of this marginal productivity theory yields the following set of equations, which can be obtained simply by differentiating the equations which equate the marginal product of labor to the real wage rate.

$$w_1 = p_1 + \frac{-1}{\sigma_{x1}} \frac{l_{x1}}{X_1} + a_{x1} ; \tag{12-13}$$

$$w_1 = q_1 + \frac{-1}{\sigma_{y1}} \frac{l_{y1}}{Y_1} + a_{y1} ; \tag{12-14}$$

$$w_2 = p_2 + \frac{-1}{\sigma_{x2}} \frac{l_{x2}}{X_2} + a_{x2} ; \tag{12-15}$$

$$w_2 = q_2 + \frac{-1}{\sigma_{y2}} \frac{l_{y2}}{Y_2} + a_{y2} ; \tag{12-16}$$

[6] This may correspond to what Hicks in his discussion calls the "only alternative" to measuring the improvement in productivity in the case of increasing cost. He says that the only alternative interpretation of the measurement of the improvement in productivity is to measure it by the changes in costs (at unchanged factor prices) which would occur at an unchanged output (Hicks [14], p. 254). This seems naturally to correspond to our A's. But as mentioned in the previous footnote, we must bear in mind that our two-commodity model is different from Hicks' model.

where

$$\sigma_{x1} \equiv \frac{x_1}{X_1} \Big/ \frac{d(l_{x1}/x_1)}{l_{x1}/x_1} \quad (\text{with } a_{x1} = 0), \quad \text{and so on,}$$

signifying the *real elasticity of supply* as in Meade [26]; This concept was discussed in Chapter 10.

Next, assuming full employment with a fixed rate of labor increase in both countries we have the following equations:

$$l_{x1} + l_{y1} = l_1, \tag{12-17}$$

$$l_{x2} + l_{y2} = l_2, \tag{12-18}$$

where l_i/L_i ($i = 1, 2$) are constants or parameters such as α_1 and α_2 respectively. When the total supply of labor of each country is fixed in both countries we have[7]

$$l_1 = 0, \quad l_2 = 0 \quad (\text{or } \alpha_1 = 0, \quad \alpha_2 = 0). \tag{12-19}$$

Alternatively we could assume the downward rigidity of money wage rate. This is the Keynesian case that we discussed in Chapter 10. Here we instead adopt the neoclassical premise of full employment. This premise was also adopted by Hicks [13] when he discussed the barter effect of growth.

Due to these full employment equations (12-17) and (12-18), we obtain from (12-13) and (12-14):

$$p - q + \left(\frac{-1}{\sigma_{x1}X_1} + \frac{-1}{\sigma_{y1}Y_1}\right) l_{x1} + \frac{\alpha_1 L_1}{\sigma_{y1}Y_1} + a_{x1} - a_{y1} = 0. \tag{12-20}$$

Or

$$l_{x1} = \varepsilon_1 \left(p - q + \frac{\alpha_1 L_1}{\sigma_{y1}Y_1} + a_{x1} - a_{y1}\right), \quad \text{where} \tag{12-21}$$

$$\varepsilon_1 \equiv \frac{1}{\dfrac{1}{\sigma_{x1}X_1} + \dfrac{1}{\sigma_{y1}Y_1}} > 0. \tag{12-22}$$

ε_1 is essentially the (weighted) harmonic mean of the supply elasticities of X and Y in Country 1, except that the numerator of the harmonic mean is omitted for simplicity of notation.[8] Using (12-9) and (12-21), we obtain

$$x_1 = \varepsilon_1 \left(p - q + \frac{\alpha_1 L_1}{\sigma_{y1}Y_1} + a_{x1} - a_{y1}\right) + a_{x1}X_1. \tag{12-23}$$

---

[7] Alternatively, we may consider that L_i is a function of real wage rate in Country i. But, as we discussed in Chapter 2, this does not alter the situation, except possibly for the case of a backward-bending labor supply curve.

[8] The true expression for the weighted harmonic mean here should be $(1/X_1 + 1/Y_1)/[(1/(\sigma_{x1}X_1)) + 1/(\sigma_{y1}Y_1)]$. Since the numerator is a given constant in our model, it may be omitted. This concept of ε_1 corresponds to the supply elasticity defined in Chapters 2 and 8. Here an effort is made to relate this concept to Meade's real elasticity of supply (σ_{x1}, and so on). Subsequently, in equation (12-28) we shall relate it to Jones' elasticity of export supply (ε_1', and so on).

Similarly we have

$$y_1 = \varepsilon_1 \left(q - p + \frac{\alpha_1 L_1}{\sigma_{x1} X_1} + a_{y1} - a_{x1} \right) + a_{y1} Y_1 , \tag{12-24}$$

$$x_2 = \varepsilon_2 \left(p - q + \frac{\alpha_2 L_2}{\sigma_{y2} Y_2} + a_{x2} - a_{y2} \right) + a_{x2} X_2 , \tag{12-25}$$

$$y_2 = \varepsilon_2 \left(q - p + \frac{\alpha_2 L_2}{\sigma_{x2} X_2} + a_{y2} - a_{x2} \right) + a_{y2} Y_2 , \tag{12-26}$$

where ε_2 is defined analogously to ε_1. Hence, we have

$$x_1 + y_1 = \alpha_1 L_1 + a_{x1} X_1 + a_{y1} Y_1 , \tag{12-27}$$

$$x_2 + y_2 = \alpha_2 L_2 + a_{x2} X_2 + a_{y2} Y_2 . \tag{12-28}$$

Now let us define the elasticity of Country i's supply of export, as in Jones [21] and as we defined in Chapter 8 in connection with the Marshall-Lerner stability condition. In the following definition we are concerned with the points on the same production transformation curve so that $a_{xi} = a_{yi} = \alpha_i (\equiv l_i / L_i) = 0$ ($i = 1, 2$) are assumed.

$$\varepsilon_1' = \frac{P/Q}{X_{12}} \frac{x_1}{p - q} ; \tag{12-29a}$$

$$\varepsilon_2' = \frac{Q/P}{Y_{21}} \frac{y_2}{q - p} . \tag{12-29b}$$

Then, recalling that $P/Q = 1$ initially, we can obtain the expressions for ε_1' and ε_2' in terms of the production locus before the shift of the production function from equations (12-23) and (12-26). In other words,

$$\varepsilon_1' = \varepsilon_1 / X_{12} , \tag{12-30a}$$

$$\varepsilon_2' = \varepsilon_2 / Y_{21} . \tag{12-30b}$$

Looking at (12-30a) and (12-22), we see that Jones' *elasticity of export supply* is now related to Meade's "real elasticity of supply." Using $P/Q = 1$ and $X_{12} = Y_{21}$, we can rewrite (12-29a) and (12-29b) as follows:

$$x_1 = \varepsilon_1'(p - q)Y_{21} , \tag{12-31a}$$

$$y_2 = \varepsilon_2'(q - p)Y_{21} . \tag{12-31b}$$

Here we have to keep in mind that x_1 and y_2 are on the production transformation curves of Country 1 and Country 2 respectively ($a_{xi} = a_{yi} = l_i = 0$). Noting this, we can also obtain the expression for y_1 and x_2 from (12-24) and (12-25) by putting $a_{xi} = a_{yi} = l_i = 0$.

$$y_1 = \varepsilon_1'(q - p)Y_{21} , \tag{12-32a}$$

$$x_2 = \varepsilon_1'(p - q)Y_{21} . \tag{12-32b}$$

They are exactly the same equations obtained in Chapter 8 (see equations (8-35) and (8-36). Using these concepts of ε_1' and ε_2', we can easily rewrite equations (12-23)—(12-26):

$$x_1 = \varepsilon_1' Y_{21}(p - q) + \varepsilon_1' Y_{21} \left(\frac{\alpha_1 L_1}{\sigma_{y1} Y_1} + a_{x1} - a_{y1} \right) + a_{x1} X_1; \tag{12-33}$$

$$y_1 = \varepsilon_1' Y_{21}(q - p) + \varepsilon_1' Y_{21} \left(\frac{\alpha_1 L_1}{\sigma_{x1} X_1} + a_{y1} - a_{x1} \right) + a_{y1} Y_1; \tag{12-34}$$

$$x_2 = \varepsilon_2' Y_{21}(p - q) + \varepsilon_2' Y_{21} \left(\frac{\alpha_2 L_2}{\sigma_{y2} Y_2} + a_{x2} - a_{y2} \right) + a_{x2} X_2; \tag{12-35}$$

$$y_2 = \varepsilon_2' Y_{21}(q - p) + \varepsilon_2' Y_{21} \left(\frac{\alpha_2 L_2}{\sigma_{x2} X_2} + a_{y2} - a_{x2} \right) + a_{y2} Y_2. \tag{12-36}$$

When the terms of trade are constant so that $(p - q) = 0$, we can rewrite the above equations as:

$$\bar{x}_1 = \varepsilon_1' Y_{21} \left(\frac{\alpha_1 L_1}{\sigma_{y1} Y_1} + a_{x1} - a_{y1} \right) + a_{x1} X_1, \tag{12-37}$$

$$\bar{y}_1 = \varepsilon_1' Y_{21} \left(\frac{\alpha_1 L_1}{\sigma_{x1} X_1} + a_{y1} - a_{x1} \right) + a_{y1} Y_1, \tag{12-38}$$

$$\bar{x}_2 = \varepsilon_2' Y_{21} \left(\frac{\alpha_2 L_2}{\sigma_{y2} Y_2} + a_{x2} - a_{y2} \right) + a_{x2} X_2, \tag{12-39}$$

$$\bar{y}_2 = \varepsilon_2' Y_{21} \left(\frac{\alpha_2 L_2}{\sigma_{x2} X_2} + a_{y2} - a_{x2} \right) + a_{y2} Y_2. \tag{12-40}$$

Here the bar ($^-$) on the variables signifies that the terms of trade are kept constant.

Our system is now composed of five equations: (12-8), (12-33), (12-34), (12-35), and (12-36). Equation (12-8) is the summary of the demand side of the economy; (12-6), (12-7) and the balance of payments equilibrium (12-1). The five variables to be determined in the system are x_1, y_1, x_2, y_2, and $(p - q)$. The shift parameters of the system are $a_{x1}, a_{y1}, a_{x2}, a_{y2}, \alpha_1$, and α_2. The other variables such as $l_{x1}, l_{x2}, l_{y1}, l_{y2}, x_{12}, y_{21}, (w_1 - p_1), (w_2 - p_2), (w_1 - q_1)$, and $(w_2 - q_2)$ can easily be determined after the expressions for the five variables are obtained.[9]

---

[9] For example, l_{x1} is obtained from (12-21) with (12-30a) in mind. $(w_i - p_i)$ is obtained from (12-13) and (12-15) after we determine l_{x1} and l_{y1}. $(w_i - q_i)$ can be similarly determined. y_{21} and x_{12} are determined by (12-6) and (12-7).

ANALYSIS AND THE MAJOR CONCLUSIONS

Using equations (12-37)—(12-40), equations (12-33)—(12-36) are easily rewritten as

$$x_1 = \varepsilon_1' Y_{21}(p - q) + \bar{x}_1 , \tag{12-41}$$

$$y_1 = \varepsilon_1' Y_{21}(q - p) + \bar{y}_1 , \tag{12-42}$$

$$x_2 = \varepsilon_2' Y_{21}(p - q) + \bar{x}_2 , \tag{12-43}$$

$$y_2 = \varepsilon_2' Y_{21}(q - p) + \bar{y}_2 . \tag{12-44}$$

Substituting these into (12-8), we obtain

$$p - q = \frac{-1}{\Omega Y_{21}} \{ [\pi_1 \bar{x}_1 - (1 - \pi_1)\bar{y}_1] + [-\pi_2 \bar{y}_2 + (1 - \pi_2)\bar{x}_2] \} \tag{12-45}$$

where Ω is defined as

$$\Omega \equiv (\eta_1' + \pi_1 + \varepsilon_1' + \eta_2' + \pi_2 + \varepsilon_2') - 1, \tag{12-46}$$

and barred variables such as $\bar{x}_1$ represent the changes of respective variables when $(p - q) = 0$, and their expressions can be obtained from (12-37)–(12-40). Assuming the Marshall-Lerner condition so that $\Omega > 0$, we can conclude that

$$(p - q) \gtreqless 0$$

according to whether

$$[\pi_1 \bar{x}_1 - (1 - \pi_1)\bar{y}_1] + [- \pi_2 \bar{y}_2 + (1 - \pi_2)\bar{x}_2] \gtreqless 0.^{[10]} \tag{12-47}$$

This is a *necessary and sufficient* condition which specifies the movement of the terms of trade, and the condition is general enough so that growth can occur in *both* countries.

To see the change in real income, we have to substitute this into equation (12-2) or (12-3). Here let us assume that economic growth occurs only in the foreign country, Country 2. This was the assumption adopted by Hicks. In other words, we assume that $a_{x1} = a_{y1} = 0$. Then we may say that

$$u_1 \gtreqless 0 \quad \text{according to whether } [-\pi_2 \bar{y}_2 + (1 - \pi_2)\bar{x}_2] \gtreqless 0 . \tag{12-48}$$

Notice that real income for Country 1 (non-growing country) increases if and only if the terms of trade move in favor of Country 1.[11] The condition (12-48) would include various important conclusions of many writers as simple corollaries. To see this we shall first classify the various types of economic growth by the changes in the output when the terms of trade are constant. This was first proposed by Hicks, revised by Johnson, and followed by others.[12]

[10] This condition corresponds to condition (13-49) of Chapter 13.
[11] This is in fact obvious, since Country 1 is not growing and since we are assuming full employment with initial prices 1, $x_1 + y_1 = 0$ (because Country 1 has the same transformation curve as before and the price ratio line should be tangential to the curve). Then the expression for the real income for Country 1 is simply reduced to $(p - q)Y_{21}$.
[12] For example, see Hicks [13], Johnson [18] [20], Black [8], and Seton [34].

We shall define them in terms of Country 2. For Country 2, economic growth is called

UNIFORM $\qquad$ if $\dfrac{\bar{x}_2}{X_2} = \dfrac{\bar{y}_2}{Y_2} > 0$,

EXPORT BIASED $\qquad$ if $\dfrac{\bar{y}_2}{Y_2} > \dfrac{\bar{x}_2}{X_2} > 0$,

ULTRA-EXPORT BIASED $\quad$ if $\bar{y}_2 > 0$ and $\bar{x}_2 \leqq 0$,

IMPORT BIASED $\qquad$ if $\dfrac{\bar{x}_2}{X_2} > \dfrac{\bar{y}_2}{Y_2} > 0$,

ULTRA-IMPORT BIASED $\quad$ if $\bar{x}_2 > 0$ and $\bar{y}_2 \leqq 0$.

Hicks wrote, "if productivity in A is increasing *uniformly*—at the same rate in all of A's industries—the barter effects of the development are most likely to be harmful to B."[13] This point was first taken up by Mishan [30]. In terms of a model similar to ours, he has shown that this statement is true only if the income effect, our π_2, is less than some critical value (or more specifically, the ratio of the domestic production of the importing goods over the total income of the growing country).[14] To see this we transform (12-48) as follows:

$$\pi_2 Y_2 < (1 - \pi_2)X_2 \tag{12-49}$$

due to the definition of "uniform" growth. Hence

$$\pi_2 < X_2/(X_2 + Y_2). \tag{12-50}$$

This is nothing but Mishan's conclusion.

Some of the most important discussions of Hick's original work has been concerned with the problem of biased economic growth. It has been pointed out that it is not right to conclude that *any* import-biased improvement would cause real loss to the other country. It should be associated with a more extreme kind of bias, that is, the ultra-import biased case in the above terminology. It is clear from condition (12-48) and our definition that a simple bias (either export or import) would not result in any clear conclusion with regard to the movement of the real income of the non-growing country (Country 1). But assuming $0 < \pi_2 < 1$ and using (12-48), we can conclude without ambiguity that *the real income of the non-growing country (that is, Country 1) increases (respectively decreases) if the other country's economic growth is ultra-export biased (respectively ultra-import biased).*

The case of ultra-import biased growth (for Country 2) is illustrated in Figure 12-1.

---

[13] Hicks [13], p. 124.
[14] Mishan [30]. He proved this in terms of geometry. Later Asimakopulos offered a simple algebraic proof [3]. See also Chapter 13, especially footnote 12.

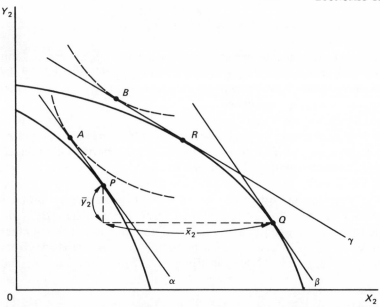

Figure 12-1   Ultra-Import Biased Growth and the Terms of Trade

In Figure 12-1, points P and A respectively signify pre-growth production and consumption points in Country 2, in which the α-line represents the pre-growth terms of trade. After growth occurs in Country 2, the production transformation curve shifts outward. Suppose the terms of trade are kept constant, then the production point moves to point Q where the β-line is parallel to the α-line. Changes in the outputs of X and Y due to a shift in the production transformation curve with *constant terms of trade* are represented by $\bar{x}_2$ and $\bar{y}_2$. However, the post-growth terms of trade would, in general, be different from the pre-trade terms of trade. In Figure 12-1 the post-growth terms of trade are represented by the γ-line. Post-growth production and consumption points are represented by points R and B respectively. In Figure 12-1, the α-line is steeper than the γ-line, which illustrates that the ultra-import biased growth of Country 2 would move the terms of trade against Country 1. A precise specification of the direction of the terms of trade due to various patterns of growth was given in (12-47). We may note that the basic ideas in equations (12-41) to (12-44) are easy to understand in terms of a diagram like Figure 12-1. These equations represent a decomposition of a change in output of each good into two parts—a change in output due to a change in the terms of trade with productivity constant and a change in output due to productivity change with the terms of trade constant. Equations (12-9) to (12-40) give a possible specification which leads to these four intuitively obvious equations: (12-41) to (12-44).

In the above we noted, using (12-48), that ultra-biased growth of one country moves the real income of the non-growing country in a definite direction. These are the situation and results obtained by economists such as Corden [9], Johnson [18], and Findlay and Grubert [11].

Let us now examine them.

CORDEN If one factor remains constant and the other factor increases,[15] this is an ultra-biased growth. The proof is simple. In the above situation by the direct application of the Rybczynski theorem (which was discussed in Chapter 2)[16], the growth has to be ultra-biased.

JOHNSON If a neutral technological progress[17] occurs in one industry and no technological progress occurs in the other, the economic growth is ultra-biased in an industry where technological progress occurs.

PROOF The reduction in cost in one industry due to technological progress should be offset by the inflow of factor input from the other industry if the relative good price is kept constant. Namely, the absolute output of the other industry must diminish. In mathematical terms this can also be shown from our equations (12-39) and (12-40) for Country 2 by putting $\alpha_2 = 0$, and $a_{y2} = 0$.

$$\bar{x}_2 = a_{x2}(\varepsilon_2'Y_{21} + X_2) > 0; \quad \bar{y}_2 = -\varepsilon_2'Y_{21}a_{x2} < 0. \tag{12-51}$$

FINDLAY AND GRUBERT If a labor-saving technological innovation occurs in the relatively labor intensive industry, the technological innovation is ultra-biased to the labor intensive industry (similarly for a capital-saving innovation and the capital intensive industry).

PROOF This can be considered to be equivalent to a situation where a neutral technological innovation occurs in a labor intensive industry *and* there is an increase in labor supply in the economy. Combining the arguments of Corden and Johnson, the above statement follows immediately.[18]

It may seem rather odd to discuss cases with more than one factor in our model where only one factor is explicitly taken account of. But this can easily

[15] It should be pointed out that π_i does not bear the Hicksian meaning any more when the population of the ith country increases. In this case, we have to re-interpret π_i properly. See Hicks [12]. In the last part of the appendix of my [38], a more precise formulation of equations (12-4) and (12-5) is attempted for the reader who wants to adhere to the Hicksian interpretation of π_i.

[16] The Rybczynski theorem states that if one factor increases with the other factor supply constant, the absolute output of the good which uses the increased factor relatively less intensively should diminish in order to keep the relative price of the goods constant. Rybczynski [33]. See also Chapter 2.

[17] The classification of technological progress into neutral, capital-saving, and labor-saving progress is due to Hicks.

[18] The weakness of our one-factor analysis is apparent in the statement of the theorem. As I have shown rigorously in [38] (also Chapter 13), the factor intensity condition should be essential to the conclusion. In other words, the conclusion is different depending upon whether the export industry is more capital (labor) intensive than the import-competing industry or not. See Chapter 13. However, our conclusion here should be valid within the framework and the assumptions of the present model.

be justified, as mentioned before, by supposing that the factors are cooperating with labor resulting in diminishing returns with respect to labor input. The increase in one of the cooperating factors will increase the productivity of labor so that the shifting factor a becomes positive. In this case the situation becomes similar in terms of our mathematical formulation to Johnson's case [18]. But it should be pointed out that we are assuming that these cooperating factors are specific to the industry so that they are not mobile between the industries. A slight generalization is of course possible by constructing a model with more than one mobile factor.[19]

But our treatment has its virtue in its simplicity and in its relevance to Meade's one-factor model which is so important in the literature of international trade.

Most attention has been paid to the case of ultra-biasedness, for it yields some definite results. It is not impossible to consider a more general case. But it will become cumbersome, and conclusions thus derived will not be too revealing and straightforward. To illustrate this it might suffice to just point out that there are at least $3^4 = 81$ different cases in the two-factor model where both factors are perfectly mobile [for example: a) relative growth of two countries—one is faster, slower than, or equal to the other country—three cases; b) relative speed of technological progress between two industries—faster, slower, or equal rate—three cases; c) nature of technological innovation—capital or labor saving, or neutral—three cases; d) relative rate of growth in the supply of two factors—faster, slower or equal rate—three cases; etc.].

Finally we may point out that we can analyze the problem of international labor movement by our model constructed above. For the sake of simplicity, assume that there is no growth in both countries so that $a_{x1} = a_{y1} = a_{x2} = a_{y2} = 0$. Suppose now that there is a labor migration from Country 2 to Country 1 ($l_1 = -l_2 > 0$). Then we can rewrite equations (12-33)—(12-36) as

$$x_1 = \varepsilon_1' Y_{21}[(p - q) + l_1/(\sigma_{y1} Y_1)]; \tag{12-52}$$

$$y_1 = \varepsilon_1' Y_{21}[(q - p) + l_1/(\sigma_{x1} X_1)]; \tag{12-53}$$

$$x_2 = \varepsilon_2' Y_{21}[(p - q) - l_1/(\sigma_{y2} Y_2)]; \tag{12-54}$$

$$y_2 = \varepsilon_2' Y_{21}[(q - p) - l_1/(\sigma_{x2} X_2)]. \tag{12-55}$$

Substituting these four equations into equation (12-18), we obtain

$$\frac{p - q}{l_1} = \frac{1}{\Omega}\left(-\frac{\pi_1 + \pi_2}{Y_{21}} + \frac{\varepsilon_1'}{\sigma_{x1} X_1} + \frac{\varepsilon_2'}{\sigma_{x2} X_2}\right). \tag{12-56}$$

Hence, assuming the Marshall-Lerner condition ($\Omega > 0$), a *necessary and sufficient condition* that the terms of trade move in favor of Country 1 (that is, $(p - q) > 0$) is that

$$\varepsilon_1'/(\sigma_{x1} X_1) + \varepsilon_2'/(\sigma_{x2} X_2) > (\pi_1 + \pi_2)/Y_{21}, \tag{12-57}$$

or

$$\varepsilon_1/(\sigma_{x1} X_1) + \varepsilon_2/(\sigma_{x2} X_2) > \pi_1 + \pi_2. \tag{12-58}$$

[19] An explicit two-factor model will be formalized in the next chapter.

REFERENCES

1. Amano, A., *Theories of International Trade and Economic Growth* (Tokyo: Yuhikaku), 1964 (Japanese), especially chapters 8, 9, 10 and 15.

2. ———, "Determinants of Comparative Costs: A Theoretical Approach," *Oxford Economic Papers*, n.s., 16, November 1964.

3. Asimakopulos, A., "A Note on Productivity Changes and the Terms of Trade," *Oxford Economic Papers*, 9, June 1957, 225–233.

4. Balogh, T., *The Dollar Crisis: Causes and Cure* (Oxford: Basil Blackwell and Sons, Ltd.), 1949.

5. Bhagwati, J., "International Trade and Economic Expansion," *American Economic Review*, LXVIII, December 1958.

6. ———, "Immiserizing Growth: A Geometrical Note," *Review of Economic Studies*, XXV, 1957–1958.

7. ———, "Growth, Terms of Trade and Comparative Advantage," *Economia Internazionale*, 12, August 1959.

8. Black, J., "Economic Expansion and International Trade: A Marshallian Approach," *Review of Economic Studies*, XXIII, June 1956.

9. Corden, W. M., "Economic Expansion and International Trade, A Geometric Approach," *Oxford Economic Papers*, June 1956, 223–228.

10. ———, *Recent Developments in the Theory of International Trade*, International Finance Section, Princeton University, 1965.

11. Findlay, R. E. and Grubert, H., "Factor Intensities, Technological Progress and the Terms of Trade," *Oxford Economic Papers*, February 1959.

12. Hicks, J. R., *Value and Capital*, 2nd ed. (London: Oxford University Press), 1946 (1st ed. 1939).

13. ———, "An Inaugural Lecture," *Oxford Economic Papers*, 5, June 1953, reprinted in his *Essays in World Economics* (London: Oxford University Press), 1959.

14. ———, "A Further Note on Import Bias," in his *Essays in World Economics* (London: Oxford University Press), 1959.

15. ———, "Equilibrium Growth in an International Economy," *Canadian Journal of Economics and Political Science*, XIX, November 1953, reprinted in his *International Trade and Economic Growth* (Cambridge, Mass.: Harvard University Press), 1958 (Chapter V).

16. Johnson, H. G., "Increasing Productivity, Income-Price Trends and the Trade Balance," *Economic Journal*, LXIV, September 1954, reprinted in his *International Trade and Economic Growth* (Cambridge, Mass.: Harvard University Press), 1958 (Chapter V).

17. ———, "Economic Expansion and the Balance of Payments," *Bulletin of the Oxford University Institute of Statistics*, XVII, February 1955.

18. ———, "Economic Expansion and International Trade," *Manchester School of Economic and Social Studies*, XXIII, May 1955, reprinted in his *International Trade and Economic Growth*, 1958, Chapter III.

19. ——, "Economic Development and International Trade," *Pakistan Economic Journal*, IX, December 1959.

20. ——, "Economic Development and International Trade," *National Conomisk Tidsskrift*, 97, 1959, reprinted in his *Money, Trade and Economic Growth* (Cambridge, Mass.: Harvard University Press), 1962, Chapter IV.

21. Jones, R. W., "Stability Conditions in International Trade: A General Equilibrium Analysis," *International Economic Review*, 2, May 1961.

22. ——, "The Structure of Simple General Equilibrium Models," *Journal of Political Economy*, LXXIII, December 1965.

23. Kemp, M. C., "Technological Change, the Terms of Trade and Welfare," *Economic Journal*, LXV, September 1955, 457–473.

24. ——, *The Pure Theory of International Trade and Investment* (Englewood Cliffs, N.J.: Prentice Hall, Inc.), 1969, especially Chapter 4.

25. MacDougall, G. D. A., *The World Dollar Problem* (London: Macmillan), 1957. Machlup, F., "Dollar Shortage and Disparities in the Growth of Productivity," *Scottish Journal of Political Economy*, 1, October 1954.

26. Meade, J. E., *The Balance of Payments: Mathematical Supplement* (London: Oxford University Press), 1951.

27. ——, *Trade and Welfare: Mathematical Supplement* (London: Oxford University Press), 1955.

28. Meier, G. M., *International Trade and Development* (New York: Harper & Row, Publishers), 1963, especially Chapter 3.

29. Minabe, N., "The Heckscher-Ohlin Theorem, the Leontief Paradox, and Patterns of Economic Growth," *American Economic Review*, LVI, December 1966.

30. Mishan, E. J., "The Long-Run Dollar Problem: A Comment," *Oxford Economic Papers*, 7, June 1955, 215–220.

31. Mundell, R. A., "The Pure Theory of International Trade," *American Economic Review*, L, March 1960.

32. Ramaswami, V. K., "The Effects of Accumulation on the Terms of Trade," *Economic Journal*, LXX, September 1960.

33. Rybczynski, T. M., "Factor Endowment and Relative Commodity Prices," *Economica*, XXII, November 1955.

34. Seton, F., "Productivity, Trade Balance, and International Structure," *Economic Journal*, LXVI, December 1956, 676–693.

35. Takayama, A., *Economic Growth and International Trade*, Ph.D. Dissertation, University of Rochester, March 1962.

36. ——, *International Economics* (Tokyo: Toyo Keizai Shimpo-sha), 1963, especially Chapter VII.

37. ——, "On a Two-Sector Model of Economic Growth—A Comparative Statics Analysis," *Review of Economic Studies*, XXX, June 1963.

38. ——, "Economic Growth and International Trade," *Review of Economic Studies*, XXXI, June 1964.

39. ——, and McKenzie, L. W., "General Equilibrium Analysis of International Trade" (unpublished manuscript), 1964.

13

ECONOMIC GROWTH, INTERNATIONAL TRADE, AND INTERNATIONAL MOVEMENTS OF FACTORS[1]

INTRODUCTION

The purpose of this chapter is analogous to the previous chapter. It is to analyze the effects of economic growth and international factor movements on international trade and, in particular, on the trade and the welfare of each country.[2] The method of analysis is again that of comparative statics. The major point of difference is that we now adopt an explicit two-factor model and will analyze the problem more directly, without bypassing concepts such as export-bias, ultra-import-biased growth, and so on. We shall obtain necessary and sufficient conditions, as well as some important sufficient conditions, for the direction of the movement of the terms of trade and real income as a result of growth and factor movements. We shall see that the important results obtained in the literature follow as simple corollaries from our generalizations. The explicit two-factor formulation will make the meaning of economic growth much clearer. For example, we now can talk about capital accumulation explicitly as well as talk about an increase in labor supply. The meaning of technological progress with capital-saving, labor-saving and neutral character-istics can be defined explicitly. Note that the two-factor, two-sector formulation developed in this chapter is similar to the one developed in Chapter 2 of this book in connection with the Heckscher-Ohlin trade model and the two-sector model of economic growth [19] and [22].

Finally note that the problem of factor accumulations and the problem of factor mobility are the same from the analytical viewpoint. For example,

---

[1] The major content of this chapter is taken from [20].

[2] Since we discuss a problem which is similar to the previous chapter, the bibliographical reference is similar. We take up the topics which are discussed by Hicks [6], [7], Mishan [16], Corden [4], Johnson [10], Findlay and Grubert [5], Bhagwati [2], [3], Kemp [13], Seton [18], for example.

$\hat{L}_1 \equiv dL_1/L_1$ can mean either a change in the labor supply due to a natural population change or a change in labor supply due to immigration or emigration of labor.

MODEL

We consider a world consisting of two countries, 1 and 2, each producing the same set of two goods, X and Y, with the use of two factors, capital K and labor L. As is the case in the ordinal analysis of international trade, we shall assume perfect competition in every market, full employment of factors, no transport costs, and immobility of factors between the countries. First we define the following set of notations:

X_1, X_2: the production of X by 1 and 2 respectively.

Y_1, Y_2: the production of Y by 1 and 2 respectively.

X_{12}, Y_{21}: the export of X from 1 to 2 and Y from 2 to 1 respectively.

P_i, Q_i: the prices of X and Y in Country i ($i = 1, 2$) respectively.

B_1, B_2: the balance of payments for 1 and 2 respectively.

W_1, W_2: the rate of money wages in 1 and 2 respectively; W_1 is taken initially as unity.

R_1, R_2: the rent for the use of capital services in 1 and 2 respectively; R_1 is taken initially as unity.

L_{xi}, L_{yi}: the amount of labor used in the production of X and Y respectively in the ith country.

K_{xi}, K_{yi}: the amount of capital used in the production of X and Y respectively in the ith country ($i = 1, 2$).

K_1, K_2: the total capital endowment in 1 and 2 respectively.

L_1, L_2: the total labor endowment in 1 and 2 respectively.

k_{xi}, k_{yi}: the capital-labor ratio (the factor intensity) in the X industry and the Y industry respectively in the ith country ($i = 1, 2$).

The capital Latin letters are used for the absolute magnitude of the variables and the small Latin letters (except for k_{xi} and k_{yi}) are for the differential changes in these variables. The hat (circumflex) for the variable, such as $\hat{X}_1$,[3] refers to the (percentage) rate of change of the variables. We choose the units of measurement properly so that $P_1 = P_2 = Q_1 = Q_2 = 1$ initially. Note $P_1/Q_1 = P_2/Q_2$ always, regardless of the two currencies, so that $p_1 - q_1 = p_2 - q_2$ (which we write $p - q$).

Let us start describing our general equilibrium model by noticing the following two equations which represent the demand side of the economy.

---

[3] We shall take "time" as a shifting parameter of the system. For the sake of convenience, we shall assume that this is responsible for increases in factor supplies as well as technological progress. Hence, we define the hat variable as follows:

$$\hat{X}_1 = \frac{1}{X_1} \left(\frac{dX_1}{d\tau} \right),$$ for example. This may not be an honest notation, for one could argue that

the increase in factor supplies are shifting parameters which are independent of technological progress.

Notice that these two equations are really the reflection of the Slutsky-Hicks demand equation for consumers (Hicks [8]).

$$y_1 + y_{21} = -(Y_1 + Y_{21})(q - p)\eta_1 + \pi_1(y_{21} - x_{12} + x_1 + y_1), \qquad (13\text{-}1)$$

$$x_2 + x_{12} = -(X_2 + X_{12})(p - q)\eta_2 + \pi_2(x_{12} - y_{21} + x_2 + y_2), \qquad (13\text{-}2)$$

where η_i is the elasticity of substitution with real consumption fixed, and π_i is the marginal propensity to consume of the imported commodity with respect to the change in real consumption.[4] Assuming an initial balance, we write the balance of payments equation:

$$b_1 = (p - q)Y_{21} + x_{12} - y_{21}. \qquad (13\text{-}3)$$

Note that the initial balance $B_1 = 0$ together with $P_i = Q_i = 1$ implies $X_{12} = Y_{21}$.

Finally, we have to describe the production side of the economy. Since the details are complicated, I will postpone them until the last section. Here we merely list the basic results. Let us define the following notation, omitting the subscript which designates the country.

σ_x, σ_y: the elasticity of factor substitution for X and Y respectively.

Γ_x, Γ_y: the elasticity of output with respect to labor input for X and Y respectively.[5]

φ_x, φ_y: the rate of growth of the output of X and Y respectively when the factor input in the industry is kept constant.

λ_x, λ_y: the index of technological progress.

In mathematical terms these can be defined as follows:

$$\sigma_i \equiv \left(\frac{W}{R}\bigg/k_i\right)\left(dk_i\bigg/d\,\frac{W}{R}\right), \quad (i = x, y), \qquad (13\text{-}4)$$

$$\Gamma_x \equiv L_x\mu_x/X, \quad \Gamma_y \equiv L_y\mu_y/Y, \qquad (13\text{-}5)$$

where μ_x and μ_y refer to the marginal productivity of labor for X and Y.

$$\varphi_x \equiv \frac{1}{X}\frac{\partial X}{\partial \tau} \quad \varphi_y \equiv \frac{1}{Y}\frac{\partial Y}{\partial \tau}, \qquad (13\text{-}6)$$

where τ refers to time.[6] The partial derivative notations are used here to mean that the factor inputs are kept constant.

$$\lambda_i \equiv \frac{1}{k_i}\frac{\partial k_i}{\partial \tau}, \quad (i = x, y). \qquad (13\text{-}7)$$

---

[4] Notice that π_i does not bear the Hicksian meaning any more when the population of the ith country increases. In this case, we have to reinterpret π_i properly. See Hicks [8]. In the final section, we shall make a more precise formulation of equations (13-1) and (13-2), for the reader who wishes to adhere to the Hicksian interpretation of π_i.

[5] In other words, they are the relative shares of labor.

[6] Technology is assumed to be represented by a real number τ. φs represent the speed of technological progress. If $\varphi_x = \varphi_y$, we say that technological progress occurs in both industries *at the same rate*.

The partial derivative notations mean that the factor price ratio in each industry is kept constant. The exact functional relationships to define the derivatives in (13-4)–(13-7) are given in the last section.

By these definitions it is clear that $\sigma_i \geq 0$, $0 \leq \Gamma_i \leq 1$, and $\varphi_i \geq 0$, $(i = x, y)$. The sign of λ_i specifies the nature of the technological progress. We may say that technological progress in the ith industry is

neutral if $\quad \lambda_i = 0,$

capital-saving if $\quad \lambda_i < 0,$

labor-saving if $\quad \lambda_i > 0.$

This definition, in fact, coincides with the classification of innovations made by Hicks [9].[7]

With these preparations we are now ready to present the relations which describe the production side of the economy. We again omit the subscript which designates the country. The derivation of these relations will be shown in the last section of this chapter.

$$\hat{X} = \frac{1}{k_x - k_y}\left[\frac{K}{L_x}\left(\hat{K} - \frac{k_y}{E}\hat{L}\right) - (\alpha\sigma_x + \beta\sigma_y)(\hat{W} - \hat{R}) - (\alpha\lambda_x + \beta\lambda_y)\right] + \varphi_x,$$

where $\qquad\qquad\qquad\qquad\qquad\qquad\qquad\qquad\qquad\qquad\qquad$ (13-8)

$$\alpha \equiv \Gamma_x k_x + (1 - \Gamma_x)k_y, \quad \beta \equiv K_y/L_x, \quad \text{and} \quad E \equiv K/L.$$

$$\hat{Y} = \frac{-1}{k_x - k_y}\left[\frac{K}{L_y}\left(\hat{K} - \frac{k_x}{E}\hat{L}\right) - (\alpha'\sigma_y + \beta'\sigma_x)(\hat{W} - \hat{R}) - (\alpha'\lambda_y + \beta'\lambda_x)\right]$$
$$+ \varphi_y,$$

where $\qquad\qquad\qquad\qquad\qquad\qquad\qquad\qquad\qquad\qquad\qquad$ (13-9)

$$\alpha' \equiv (1 - \Gamma_y)k_x + \Gamma_y k_y, \quad \text{and} \quad \beta' \equiv K_x/L_y.$$

It is clear that α, α', β, and β' are usually positive.

$$(p - q) + (\varphi_x - \varphi_y) = (\Gamma_x - \Gamma_y)(\hat{W} - \hat{R}). \qquad\qquad (13\text{-}10)$$

$$\Gamma_x \gtreqless \Gamma_y \quad \text{according to whether} \quad k_x \gtreqless k_y. \qquad\qquad (13\text{-}11)$$

Actually, the formal description of the model ends with equation (13-9).

Now let us define the *elasticity of production* (assuming that there is no growth, that is, no increases in factor supplies and no technological innovation).[8]

$$\varepsilon_x \equiv \frac{P/Q}{X}\frac{x}{p - q}, \qquad\qquad\qquad\qquad\qquad (13\text{-}12)$$

$$\varepsilon_y \equiv \frac{Q/P}{Y}\frac{y}{q - p}. \qquad\qquad\qquad\qquad\qquad (13\text{-}13)$$

---

[7] Hick's original classification of innovations is given in terms of the change in the marginal product ratio when the factor intensity is kept constant. It is well-known that this classification is equivalent to the ones adopted here.

[8] Note that ε_x and ε_y can be different between the countries. In other words, we are *not* assuming that the production function of the same good is identical in the countries (unlike the Heckscher-Ohlin trade model).

Or, more specifically, we can write these elasticities, due to (13-8), (13-9), and (13-10) as:

$$\varepsilon_x = \frac{\alpha\sigma_x + \beta\sigma_y}{(k_x - k_y)(\Gamma_y - \Gamma_x)}. \tag{13-14}$$

$$\varepsilon_y = \frac{\alpha'\sigma_y + \beta'\sigma_x}{(k_x - k_y)(\Gamma_y - \Gamma_x)}. \tag{13-15}$$

Due to (13-11), both ε_x and ε_y are positive (unless $\sigma_i = 0$). We define *elasticity of export supply* as follows:

$$\varepsilon_1' \equiv \varepsilon_{x1} X_1/X_{12}, \tag{13-16}$$

$$\varepsilon_2' \equiv \varepsilon_{y2} Y_2/Y_{21}, \tag{13-17}$$

where ε_{x1} is ε_x in Country 1 and ε_{y2} is ε_y in Country 2.

We will now re-define the elasticity of demand substitution of the imported goods as the *elasticity of import demand*:

$$\eta_1' \equiv \eta_1(Y_1 + Y_{21})/Y_{21}, \tag{13-18}$$

$$\eta_2' \equiv \eta_2(X_2 + X_{12})/X_{12}. \tag{13-19}$$

The concepts of ε' and η' are due to Jones [12], as remarked in Chapter 8.

In the case where there is no growth at all, x and y refer to the movements *along* the production transformation schedule due to the change in the relative commodity price; but the price line should be tangential to the production transformation schedule due to the assumption of perfect competition. Recalling $P = Q = 1$ initially, we have $x_i + y_i = 0$ for each $i = 1, 2$. Hence we have

$$\varepsilon_{xi} X_i - \varepsilon_{yi} Y_i = 0 \qquad \text{for } i = 1, 2. \tag{13-20}$$

With the use of the elasticities of production and equation (13-20), we could rewrite our basic formulas, (13-8) and (13-9). Before doing that, however, let us define the following notations:

$$F_x \equiv \frac{K}{L_x}\left(\hat{K} - \frac{k_y}{E}\hat{L}\right), \tag{13-21}$$

$$F_y \equiv \frac{K}{L_y}\left(\hat{K} - \frac{k_x}{E}\hat{L}\right), \tag{13-22}$$

$$\Lambda_x \equiv \alpha\lambda_x + \beta\lambda_y, \tag{13-23}$$

$$\Lambda_y \equiv \alpha'\lambda_y + \beta'\lambda_x, \tag{13-24}$$

where the precise expressions for α, α', β, β' are given in (13-8) and (13-9). Clearly F_x and F_y relate to the factor growth, and Λ_x and Λ_y relate to the technological progress. Subscripts referring to the country are again omitted. Now let us rewrite equations (13-8) and (13-9) as follows [using (13-10)]:

$$\hat{X} = (F_x - \Lambda_x)/(k_x - k_y) + \varepsilon_x(p - q) + \varepsilon_x(\varphi_x - \varphi_y) + \varphi_x, \tag{13-25}$$

$$\hat{Y} = -(F_y - \Lambda_y)/(k_x - k_y) - \varepsilon_y(p - q) + \varepsilon_y(\varphi_y - \varphi_x) + \varphi_y. \tag{13-26}$$

Next we notice the following relationship which is obtained from (13-1), (13-2), and (13-3) with $b_1 = 0$ (which is obtained under the neoclassical stable adjustment process).

$$\pi_1 x_1 - (1 - \pi_1)y_1 + (1 - \pi_2)x_2 - \pi_2 y_2$$

$$= [\pi_1(x_1 + y_1) - y_1] - [\pi_2(x_2 + y_2) - x_2]$$

$$= -(p - q)(\eta_1' + \pi_1 + \eta_2' + \pi_2 - 1)Y_{21}. \tag{13-27}$$

In this case $x_i + y_i$ is not necessarily equal to zero, for the shift does not occur *along* the *same* transformation schedule. Notice that $[\pi_1(x_1 + y_1) - y_1]$ represents the difference between the increase in Country 1's demand for the imported goods when the terms of trade are constant *and* the increase in the domestic production of the import goods are due to growth. A similar interpretation goes for $\pi_2(x_2 + y_2) - y_2$ with respect to Country 2.

Finally, let us obtain some important relations between Λ_x and Λ_y and between F_x and F_y, which will be useful in the future analysis. Postponing the proofs to the last section, we can immediately list the following relations:

$$\Lambda_{xi}X_i - \Lambda_{yi}Y_i = 0, \qquad (i = 1, 2), \tag{13-28}$$

$$X_iF_{xi} - Y_iF_{yi} = (k_{xi} - k_{yi})(v_{xi}k_i + \mu_{xi}l_i), \qquad (i = 1, 2), \tag{13-29}$$

where v_x is the marginal physical productivity of capital for X and μ_x is the marginal physical productivity of labor for X (in Country i). Notice that (13-20), (13-25), (13-26), (13-28), and (13-29) imply

$$x_i + y_i = (F_{xi}X_i - F_{yi}Y_i)/(k_{xi} - k_{yi}) + \varphi_{xi}X_i + \varphi_{yi}Y_i, \qquad (i = 1, 2). \tag{13-30}$$

Here recall that in Country 1, $\mu_{x1} = v_{x1} = 1$ due to our convention that $P = Q = W_1 = R_1 = 1$. We may note that, in view of (13-16) and (13-20), $\varepsilon_{y1}Y_1 = \varepsilon_{x1}X_1 = \varepsilon_1'X_{12} = \varepsilon_1'Y_{21}$. Similarly, we have $\varepsilon_{x2}X_2 = \varepsilon_2'X_{12}$.

FACTOR ACCUMULATIONS

Having laid the groundwork for our analysis, we shall now consider the effect of growth on the terms of trade. The word "growth" can mean either an increase in factor supplies or technological progress (or both of these). In this section we shall confine our analysis to the case when "growth" means only an increase in factor supplies. We shall not ask where these increases come from. We also assume that the growth in factor supplies occurs only in one of the countries, say Country 1. The effect on the terms of trade in such a case is considered by Corden [4]. In terms of our notations, the case that we propose to consider in this section can be expressed as follows:

$$\Lambda_{xi} = \Lambda_{yi} = \varphi_{xi} = \varphi_{yi} = 0, \qquad (i = 1, 2),$$

$$\hat{K}_2 = \hat{L}_2 = 0, \hat{K}_1 \geqq 0, \text{ and } \hat{L}_1 \geqq 0.$$

Using the definitions of the elasticity of export supply and equations (13-25), (13-26), and (13-27), we obtain

$$(p - q)\Omega Y_{21} = \frac{-1}{k_{x1} - k_{y1}} [\pi_1 X_1 F_{x1} + (1 - \pi_1) Y_1 F_{y1}], \qquad (13\text{-}31)$$

where Ω is defined as

$$\Omega \equiv \eta_1' + \pi_1 + \varepsilon_1' + \eta_2' + \pi_2 + \varepsilon_2' - 1. \qquad (13\text{-}32)$$

The Marshall-Lerner stability condition for the commodity markets (recall Chapter 8, second section) requires that Ω be positive.[9] Notice that the stability condition is critically important for the current problem. Assuming stability, a necessary and sufficient condition for the terms of trade to move in favor of the growing country $(p - q > 0)$ is that the inside of the bracket on the right side of (13-31) is negative provided that X (the export good of Country 1) is always more capital intensive than Y (the import-competing good of Country 2). That is, $(k_{x1} > k_{y1})$. It is important that the factor intensity relation may reverse the conclusion. To sharpen the analysis let us assume that $k_{x1} > k_{y1}$ always.[10] We now have

$$p - q \gtreqless 0, \quad \text{according to whether}$$

$$\pi_1 X_1 \frac{K_1}{L_{y1}} \left(\hat{K}_1 - \frac{k_{y1}}{E_1} \hat{L}_1 \right) + (1 - \pi_1) Y_1 \frac{K_1}{L_{x1}} \left(\hat{K}_1 - \frac{k_{x1}}{E_1} \hat{L}_1 \right) \gtreqless 0. \qquad (13\text{-}33)$$

From this necessary and sufficient condition, many results follow. Here we simply note some of the important sufficient conditions. Corden [4] found that the terms of trade would move in a definite direction if one factor increases while the other factor is kept constant. In terms of our notation, this corresponds to the case where $\hat{K}_1 > 0$ and $\hat{L}_1 = 0$, or $\hat{K}_1 = 0$ and $\hat{L}_1 > 0$. Then Corden's result follows immediately from (13-33). The following sufficient conditions are also obvious from (13-33):

$$p - q > 0 \quad \text{if} \quad \hat{K}_1 \leqq k_{y1} \hat{L}_1 / E_1 \quad \text{and} \quad p - q < 0 \quad \text{if} \quad \hat{K}_1 \geqq k_{x1} \hat{L}_1 / E_1. \qquad (13\text{-}34)$$

This is a result obtained in Chapter 2, third section. Now let us recall equations (13-29) and (13-30), with $\mu_{x1} = v_{x1} = 1$, then

$$p - q \gtreqless 0 \quad \text{according to whether} \quad \hat{K} \lesseqgtr \delta \hat{L}/E, \qquad (13\text{-}35)$$

---

[9] See Chapter 8, second section, and also Jones [12].
[10] In other words, we assume factor growth occurs in the country which is exporting the capital intensive goods.

where

$$\delta \equiv \frac{(1 - \Gamma_{x1}) + \pi_1(\Gamma_{y1} - \Gamma_{x1})}{\Gamma_{x1} + \pi_1(\Gamma_{y1} - \Gamma_{x1})}. \tag{13-36}$$

It should be noticed that $0 \leqq \delta$, for we have $0 \leqq \Gamma_{x1} < \Gamma_{y1} \leqq 1$ and we assume $0 \leqq \pi_1 \leqq 1$. Condition (13-35) is a slightly sharper result than (13-33).

Hicks was concerned with the effect on real income of the non-growing country (Country 2). Since the transformation schedule has not moved in Country 2, the change in real income in Country 2 can be measured solely by $(q - p)Y_{21}$. Hence the condition for the change in real income in Country 2 can be given by (13-33) or (13-35). The change in real income in Country 1 is slightly more complicated, for it should be measured by $(p - q)Y_{21} + x_1 + y_1$. But using equations (13-30) and (13-31), we obtain

$$u_1 = \frac{1}{(k_{x1} - k_{y1})\Omega} \left[(\Omega - \pi_1)(F_{x1}X_1 - F_{y1}Y_1) - F_{y1}Y_1 \right], \tag{13-37}$$

where u_1 measures the change in the real income in Country 1.

Next we obtain the formula when there is a growth in both countries, in the sense that the factor supplies of both countries increase. With the use of (13-25), (13-26), and (13-27) we obtain the desired formula which is:

$$p - q = \frac{-1}{(k_{x1} - k_{y1})\Omega Y_{21}} \left[\pi_1 X_1 F_{x1} + (1 - \pi_1)Y_1 F_{y1} \right]$$

$$+ \frac{-1}{(k_{x2} - k_{y2})\Omega Y_{21}} \left[(1 - \pi_2)X_2 F_{x2} + \pi_2 Y_2 F_{y2} \right]. \tag{13-38}$$

Finally, let us mention international factor movements which are analyzed by Johnson in connection with the current topic (Johnson [10]). Let us assume, as he did, that the factors can be moved internationally without any transport costs. Then the capital movement from Country 1 to Country 2 can be simply represented by $k_1 = -k_2 < 0$. Similarly, the movement of labor from Country 1 to 2 can be represented by $l_1 = -l_2 < 0$. The impact of the factor movement upon the terms of trade can be seen simply by inserting these values into equation (13-38), assuming no growth in both countries. The condition which can readily be obtained from (13-38) may be thought of as the mathematical counterpart of Johnson's discussion.[11] We shall take up such an analysis later in this chapter.

TECHNOLOGICAL PROGRESS

Let us now consider the case of technological progress. This time we assume that there are no factor increases and that growth means only technological innovation. First, let us suppose that the growth occurs only in Country 1.

[11] If we make some drastic assumptions such as identical production functions (the Heckscher-Ohlin case) and identical tastes between the countries ($\pi_1 = \pi_2$, and so on), then it is probably possible to draw some more definite conclusions.

This is the case that is considered by Hicks and by many other writers following him. In terms of our notation, we consider the case when $\hat{K}_i = \hat{L}_i = 0$, $\lambda_{x2} = \lambda_{y2} = \varphi_{x2} = \varphi_{y2} = 0$, and $\lambda_{x1} \gtreqless 0$, $\lambda_{y1} \gtreqless 0$, $\varphi_{x1} \gtreqless 0$, $\varphi_{y1} \gtreqless 0$, $(i = 1, 2)$. Using the definition of the elasticity of export supply and equations (13-25), (13-26), (13-27), and (13-28) again, we obtain the following relation:

$$(p - q) = \frac{1}{\Omega Y_{21}} \left[\frac{Y_1 \Lambda_{y1}}{k_{x1} - k_{y1}} \right.$$
$$\left. - [\pi_1 X_1 \varphi_{x1} - (1 - \pi_1) Y_1 \varphi_{y1} + X_1 \varepsilon_{x1}(\varphi_{x1} - \varphi_{y1})] \right]. \tag{13-39}$$

Assume again stability so that $\Omega > 0$. Then we can say

$$(p - q) \gtreqless 0, \quad \text{according to whether} \tag{13-40}$$

$$Y_1 \Lambda_{y1}/(k_{x1} - k_{y1}) - [\pi_1 X_1 \varphi_{x1} - (1 - \pi_1) Y_1 \varphi_{y1} + X_1 \varepsilon_{x1}(\varphi_{x1} - \varphi_{y1})] \gtreqless 0,$$

where

$$\Lambda_{y1} \equiv \alpha' \lambda_{y1} + \beta' \lambda_{x1} \quad \text{and} \quad \alpha', \beta' > 0.$$

This is again a *necessary and sufficient condition*. From looking at (13-40), the following conclusions in the literature are apparent.

1. JOHNSON'S CASE [10] (the case where technological progress is neutral in both industries, or where there is no technological progress in one of the industries ($\lambda_{x1} = \lambda_{y1} = 0$):

   (a) If neutral technological progress occurs only in the import-competing industry (Y) ($\varphi_{x1} = 0$, $\varphi_{y1} > 0$), then the terms of trade would move in favor of the growing country.

   (b) If neutral technological progress occurs only in the export industry (X) ($\varphi_{x1} > 0$, $\varphi_{y1} = 0$), then the terms of trade would move in favor of the non-growing country.

   (c) More generally we have

   $$p - q \gtreqless 0 \quad \text{according to whether} \quad \pi_1 X_1 \varphi_{x1} - (1 - \pi_1) Y_1 \varphi_{y1}$$
   $$+ X_1 \varepsilon_{x1}(\varphi_{x1} - \varphi_{y1}) \gtreqless 0. \tag{13-41}$$

   Hence, if the output of the export good is initially greater than the output of the import good and if technological progress is faster in the export industry than in the import industry, then the terms of trade would always move in favor of the non-growing country. This general condition (13-41) is missing in Johnson [10], and should be new in the literature. It is important to notice that none of the conclusions is invalidated in any of the above three cases, even if we assume that Y is always more capital intensive than X.

2. THE FINDLAY-GRUBERT CASE [5]

   (a) If capital-saving innovation occurs in the capital-intensive industry and there is no technological progress in the other industry, then, from

(13-40), it can easily be seen that the terms of trade would move in favor of the non-growing country, *provided* that the export industry is always more capital intensive than the import-competing industry in the growing country ($k_{x1} > k_{y1}$, $\lambda_{x1} < 0$, $\lambda_{y1} = 0$, $\varphi_{x1} > 0$).

It is important to notice that the above conclusion would be reversed (namely the terms of trade would move against the non-growing country), if the export industry were always more labor intensive than the import-competing industry.

(b) If labor-saving innovation occurs in the labor-intensive industry and there is no technological progress in the other industry, then, from (13-40), it can easily be seen that the terms of trade would move against the non-growing country, *provided* that the export industry is always more capital intensive than the import-competing industry in the growing country ($k_{x1} > k_{y1}$, $\lambda_{x1} = 0$, $\lambda_{y1} > 0$, $\varphi_{x1} = 0$, $\varphi_{y1} > 0$). Notice again that the above conclusion would be reversed (that is, the terms of trade would move in favor of the non-growing country) if the export industry were always more labor intensive than the import-competing industry.

3. MISHAN'S CONDITION [16]

(a) If neutral innovation occurs in both industries at the same rate ($\lambda_{x1} = \lambda_{y1} = 0$, $\varphi_{x1} = \varphi_{y1}$), then the terms of trade would move in favor of the non-growing country if, and only if:

$$\pi_1 X_1 > (1 - \pi_1)Y_1 . \tag{13-42}$$

This correspond's to Mishan's result [16].[12]

If we assume Mishan's condition (13-42) and if we assume that technological progress occurs in both industries at the same rate, the following results, all of which are new in the literature, follow immediately from (13-40).

(b) If capital-saving innovation occurs in both industries, then the terms of trade will move in favor of the non-growing country, provided that the export industry is more capital intensive than the import-competing industry ($k_{x1} > k_{y1}$). (If Mishan's condition does *not* hold and if the export industry is *less* capital intensive than the import-competing industry ($k_{x1} < k_{y1}$), then the terms of trade would move in favor of the growing country.)

[12] Hicks ([6], p. 124) wrote, "If productivity in A is increasing uniformly at the same rate in all of A's industries the barter effects of development are most unlikely to be harmful to B." This point was first taken up by Mishan [16]. In terms of a model similar to ours, he has shown that this statement is true if the "income effect," our π, is greater than some critical value, or, more specifically, the ratio of the domestic production of the importing goods over the total income of the growing country. Or, equivalently, we have (13-42). For this condition to be true, it is sufficient, for example, that the marginal propensity to consume imported goods is equal to the average propensity to consume, for in this case $\pi_1 = (Y_1 + Y_{21})/(X_1 + Y_1)$. Recall also, our discussion in Chapter 12, third section, especially condition (12-50).

(c) If labor-saving innovation occurs in both industries, then the terms of trade will move in favor of the non-growing country, provided that the export industry is less capital intensive than the import-competing industry $(k_{x1} < k_{y1})$. (If Mishan's condition does *not* hold and if the export industry is *more* capital intensive than the import-competing industry $(k_{x1} > k_{y1})$, then the terms of trade would move in favor of the growing country.)

(d) The conclusions of (b) and (c) will not be altered even if we assume that there is neutral technological progress in one of the industries.

THE MAIN THEOREM

We now synthesize the analysis in the previous two sections and obtain the formula where there is growth in both countries in the sense that both technological progress and factor growth occur. Here note also that as we remarked before, our model can analyze the effects of international factor movements simultaneously. $\hat{L}_i$ and $\hat{K}_i$, $(i = 1, 2)$ can be taken to mean either factor growth or international factor movements. If, for example, labor migrates from Country 1 to Country 2 and if there is no natural growth in the labor supplies of both countries, then $-l_1 = l_2 > 0$. There is a slight difficulty when there is an international movement of capital. For example, if capital moves from Country 1 to Country 2 and if there is no factor accumulation due to growth, then $-k_1 = k_2 > 0$. However, we also have to consider the effect of the transfer of the return from capital from Country 2 to Country 1. In other words, the balance of payments equation, (13-3), should be modified to take account of this. In this section we assume away this complication. In other words, we assume that international transfer of the return on capital is in the magnitude of the second order small in the balance of payments equation.

We now define the following notations for the sake of notational convenience.

$$\Lambda_1 \equiv Y_1 \Lambda_{y1}/(k_{x1} - k_{y1}) . \tag{13-43}$$

$$\Lambda_2 \equiv Y_2 \Lambda_{y2}/(k_{x2} - k_{y2}) . \tag{13-44}$$

$$\varphi_1 \equiv \pi_1 X_1 \varphi_{x1} - (1 - \pi_1) Y_1 \varphi_{y1} + X_1 \varepsilon_{x1}(\varphi_{x1} - \varphi_{y1}) . \tag{13-45}$$

$$\varphi_2 \equiv (1 - \pi_2) X_2 \varphi_{x2} - \pi_2 Y_2 \varphi_{y2} + Y_2 \varepsilon_{y2}(\varphi_{x2} - \varphi_{y2}) . \tag{13-46}$$

$$F_1 \equiv [\pi_1 X_1 F_{x1} + (1 - \pi_1) Y_1 F_{y1}]/(k_{x1} - k_{y1}) . \tag{13-47}$$

$$F_2 \equiv [(1 - \pi_2) X_2 F_{x2} + \pi_2 F_{y2}]/(k_{x2} - k_{y2}) . \tag{13-48}$$

Assuming again stability so that $\Omega > 0$, our *necessary and sufficient condition* is no more complicated than:

$p - q \gtreqless 0$ according to

$$\frac{1}{k_{x1} - k_{y1}} (\Lambda_1 - F_1 - \varphi_1) + \frac{1}{k_{x2} - k_{y2}} (\Lambda_2 - F_2 - \varphi_2) \gtreqless 0 . \tag{13-49}$$

If, for example, technological progress is neutral or capital saving in both countries ($\Lambda_1 \leq 0$, $\Lambda_2 \leq 0$), capital grows sufficiently faster than labor in both countries ($\hat{K}_i \geq k_{xi}\hat{L}_i/E_i$ $(i = 1, 2)$ so that $F_1 > 0$ and $F_2 > 0$). If the technological progress of the capital-intensive industry is faster than or equal to that of the labor-intensive industry, and moreover, if Mishan's condition, (13-42) is satisfied ($\varphi_1 > 0$ and $\varphi_2 > 0$), then, assuming $k_{xi} > k_{yi}$, the terms of trade would move in favor of Country 2, which is exporting the labor-intensive good (Y) and importing the capital-intensive good. If the population of Country 2 increases very rapidly (as in many under-developed countries), then F_2 becomes negative, which would result in cancelling the above effect so that the terms of trade may move against Country 2. We can be more certain of this conclusion if there is a migration of labor force from Country 1 to Country 2 such as occurred in the nineteenth century from Europe to America.[13]

INTERNATIONAL FACTOR MOVEMENTS

In order to make out point on international factor movements clear, we shall take up this topic explicitly.[14] To sharpen our analysis, we will say there is no growth and will analyze the effects of labor movements and capital movements separately.

International Movements of Labor

Assume that labor migrates from Country 1 to Country 2 so that $-l_1 = l_2 > 0$. Assume that the immigrants do not send a part (or all) of their income to their home country. Then we can use the balance of payments equation (13-3) as it is. Assume also that for the sake of simplicity the immigrants adopt the taste and consumption behavior of the country that they immigrated to. Hence, the coefficients such as η_2' and π_2 are applicable to the immigrant from Country 1.

The analysis of international movements of labor now can be carried out by putting $\hat{K}_1 = \hat{K}_2 = 0$, and $-l_1 = l_2$, $[(\equiv l) > 0]$, and $\Lambda_{xi} = \Lambda_{yi} = \varphi_{xi} = \varphi_{yi} = 0$, $(i = 1, 2)$ in the model developed in the second section. From (13-21) and (13-22) we obtain

$$F_{x1} = k_{y1}l/L_{x1} \quad \text{and} \quad F_{x2} = -k_{y2}l/L_{x2}; \tag{13-50}$$

$$F_{y1} = k_{x1}l/L_{y1} \quad \text{and} \quad F_{y2} = -k_{y2}l/L_{y2}. \tag{13-51}$$

Thus, $F_{x1} > 0$, $F_{y1} > 0$, $F_{x2} < 0$, and $F_{y2} < 0$.

---

[13] This may explain the Hick's contention that the terms of trade moved in favor of Continental Europe or the U.S. (and against England) during the nineteenth century. However, this requires careful statistical study for verification.

[14] The topic was also analyzed by Meade [14], chapter XXVII, *Mathematical Supplement*, chapter XIX, Johnson [10], chapter III, and most completely by Amano [1]. In Mundell [15], the emphasis is on the substitutibility between international trade and factor movement as in earlier works by Heckscher and Ohlin.

Using (13-25), (13-26) and (13-30) together with (13-27)[15], we obtain

$$[\pi_1 F_{x1} X_1 + (1 - \pi_1) F_{y1} Y_1]/(k_{x1} - k_{y1})$$
$$+ [(1 - \pi_2) F_{x2} X_2 + \pi_2 F_{y2} Y_2]/(k_{x2} - k_{y2}) = -(p - q)\Omega Y_{21}, \qquad (13\text{-}52)$$

where Ω is defined in (13-32). Assuming again the Marshall-Lerner stability condition (so that $\Omega > 0$), a *necessary and sufficient condition* for the terms of trade to move in favor of the labor-exporting country (here Country 1—that is, $p - q > 0$) is that the left-hand side of (13-52) is negative. In view of (13-50) and (13-51) this can be rewritten as

$$[\pi_1 K_{y1} X_1 + (1 - \pi_1) K_{x1} Y_1]/[(k_{x1} - k_{y1}) L_{x1} L_{y1}]$$
$$- [(1 - \pi_2) K_{y2} X_2 + \pi_2 K_{x2} Y_2]/[(k_{x2} - k_{y2}) L_{x2} L_{y2}] < 0. \qquad (13\text{-}53)$$

Note that the left-hand side of (13-53) can be either positive or negative. In other words, the direction of the movements of the terms of trade in general cannot be ascertained. However, if we assume a factor intensity reversal between the countries, so that $(k_{x1} - k_{y1})$ and $(k_{x2} - k_{y2})$ have different signs, then we can ascertain this direction. For example, suppose $k_{x1} - k_{y1} < 0$ and $k_{x2} - k_{y2} > 0$. Then in view of (13-53), we can immediately assert that the terms of trade move in favor of the labor-exporting country (provided that $0 < \pi_1, \pi_2 < 1$). In other words, assuming $0 < \pi_1, \pi_2 < 1$, and the factor intensity reversal between the countries, we can assert that the terms of trade move in favor of or against the labor-exporting country depending on whether it exports the labor-intensive or the capital-intensive commodity. This conclusion corresponds to the one obtained by Amano [1], p. 514.

International Movements of Capital

Here, unlike the previous section, we explicitly introduce the international transfer of investment income in the balance of payments equation and analyze the effect of international capital movement on the terms of trade, assuming there is no growth and no international movements of labor so that $\hat{L}_1 = \hat{L}_2 = 0$, and $\Lambda_{xi} = \Lambda_{yi} = \varphi_{xi} = \varphi_{yi} = 0$, $(i = 1, 2)$.

Let I be the net international indebtedness of Country 2. We assume that I is non-negative. If $I > 0$, then Country 1 is the creditor and Country 2 is the debtor. We may assume that the return on the capital investment I is equal to Country 2's marginal production of capital, C, (which, in money terms, is equal to R_2). Hence, the balance of payments equation is now written as

$$B_1 = P_2 X_{12} - Q_2 Y_{21} + R_2 I. \qquad (13\text{-}54)$$

In order to obtain a sharper result, we assume that international indebtedness does not exist at the initial position so that $I = 0$ initially. Assuming that the balance of payments is in equilibrium initially ($B_1 = 0$), this implies that

[15] Note again that $\varepsilon_{y1} Y_1 = \varepsilon_{x1} X_1 = \varepsilon_1' X_{12} = \varepsilon_1' Y_{21}$ in view of (13-20). Similarly, $\varepsilon_{x2} X_2 = \varepsilon_2' Y_{21}$.

$X_{12} = Y_{21}$ due to our convention that $P_2 = Q_2 = 1$ initially. Differentiating both sides of (13-54), we obtain its variational form

$$b_1 = (p - q)Y_{21} + x_{12} - y_{21} + i, \tag{13-55}$$

where R_2 is initially to be unity. We may recall that this equation appeared in our consideration of transfer payments in Chapter 8, third section. Under the neoclassical stable adjustment process, $b_1 = 0$ is assumed to be achieved. We can now rewrite (13-27) as

$$[\pi_1(x_1 + y_1) - y_1] - [\pi_2(x_2 + y_2) - x_2]$$
$$= -(p - q)(\eta_1' + \pi_1 + \eta_2' + \pi_2 - 1)Y_{21} + [1 - (\pi_1 + \pi_2)]i. \tag{13-56}$$

Substituting $\hat{L}_1 = \hat{L}_2 = 0$ and $-k_1 = k_2$, $[(\equiv k) > 0]$ into (13-21) and (13-22), we obtain

$$F_{x1} = -k/L_{x1} \quad \text{and} \quad F_{x2} = k/L_{x2}; \tag{13-57}$$

$$F_{y1} = -k/L_{y1} \quad \text{and} \quad F_{y2} = k/L_{y2}. \tag{13-58}$$

Thus, $F_{x1} < 0$, $F_{y1} < 0$, $F_{x2} > 0$, $F_{y2} > 0$.

Using (13-25), (13-26), and (13-30) together with (13-56), we obtain

$$[\pi_1 F_{x1} X_1 + (1 - \pi_1)F_{y1} Y_1]/(k_{x1} - k_{y1})$$
$$+ [(1 - \pi_2)F_{x2} X_2 + \pi_2 F_{y2} Y_2]/(k_{x2} - k_{y2})$$
$$= -(p - q)\Omega Y_{21} + [1 - (\pi_1 + \pi_2)]i. \tag{13-59}$$

Under the present supposition of no initial internal indebtedness, $i = k$. Hence, using (13-57) and (13-58), we can obtain the following equation from (13-59):

$$(p - q)\Omega Y_{21}/k = [\pi_1 X_1/L_{x1} + (1 - \pi_1)Y_1/L_{y1}]/(k_{x1} - k_{y1})$$
$$- [(1 - \pi_2)X_2/L_{x2} + \pi_2 Y_2/L_{y2}]/(k_{x2} - k_{y2})$$
$$+ [1 - (\pi_1 + \pi_2)]. \tag{13-60}$$

Therefore, the terms of trade move in favor of the capital-exporting country $(p - q > 0)$ *if and only if* the right-hand side of (13-60) is positive, with the usual assumption of $\Omega > 0$. In general, the sign of the *RHS* of (13-60) cannot be ascertained. However, if the transfer condition (as discussed in Chapter 8, third section) is satisfied so that $\pi_1 + \pi_2 < 1$, and if there is a factor intensity reversal between the countries in the sense that $k_{x1} > k_{y1}$ and $k_{x2} < k_{y2}$, then we can assert that the terms of trade move in favor of the capital-exporting country (provided that $\pi_1 > 0$, $\pi_2 > 0$).

COMPUTATIONAL NOTE

In this section, we shall show briefly how equations (13-6), (13-9), (13-10), (13-28), (13-29), and (13-36) and relationship (13-11) are obtained. The basic feature in these equations is that they describe the production side of the economy. The discussion is analogous to the one developed in Chapter 2. In writing these equations we shall omit the subscripts which refer to the countries, except where it is too confusing to do so. Let us assume linear homogeneity, and write the production functions as follows:

$$X = L_x f(k_x, \tau), \tag{13-61}$$

$$Y = L_y g(k_y, \tau), \tag{13-62}$$

where τ refers to time and represents the shifting parameter of the system. It is important to notice that we are not assuming identical production functions for the two countries as in the Heckscher-Ohlin trade model. Perfect competition implies

$$W = P\mu_x = Q\mu_y, \tag{13-63}$$

$$R = Pv_x = Qv_y, \tag{13-64}$$

where μ_i is the marginal productivity of labor in the ith industry and v_i is that of capital ($i = x, y$). In other words,

$$\mu_x = \frac{\partial X}{\partial L_x}, \quad v_x = \frac{\partial X}{\partial K_x}, \quad \text{and so on.}$$

Due to (13-61) and (13-62), (13-63) and (13-64) may be rewritten as

$$W = P(f - k_x f') = Q(g - k_y g'), \tag{13-63'}$$

$$R = Pf' = Qg'. \tag{13-64'}$$

Full employment of factors means

$$L = L_x + L_y, \tag{13-65}$$

$$K = K_x + K_y. \tag{13-66}$$

This completes the description of the model. Assuming the law of variable proportions (which amounts to saying f'', $g'' < 0$), and taking into account that (13-63') and (13-64') imply $W/R = (f - k_x f')/f' = (g - k_y g')/g'$, we could conclude that k_i is a strictly increasing function with respect to W/R. Or we may write

$$k_x = k_x(W/R, \tau), \tag{13-67}$$

$$k_y = k_y(W/R, \tau), \quad \text{where } \partial k_i/\partial(W/R) > 0 \quad (i = x, y). \tag{13-68}$$

In differential form:

$$\hat{K}_x = \sigma_x(\hat{W} - \hat{R}) + \hat{L}_x + \lambda_x, \tag{13-69}$$

$$\hat{K}_y = \sigma_y(\hat{W} - \hat{R}) + \hat{L}_y + \lambda_y. \tag{13-70}$$

By differentiating our production functions (13-61) and (13-62), we have

$$x = \mu_x l_x + v_x k_x + \varphi_x X, \tag{13-61'}$$

$$y = \mu_y l_y + v_y k_y + \varphi_y Y. \tag{13-62'}$$

Noticing the Euler equation for the linear homogeneous function, we also have from (13-61) and (13-62):

$$X = \mu_x L_x + v_x K_x ,\tag{13-61''}$$

$$Y = \mu_y L_y + v_y K_y .\tag{13-62''}$$

Taking (13-61'') and (13-62'') into account, we may rewrite (13-61') and (13-62'):

$$\hat{X} = \Gamma_x \hat{L}_x + (1 - \Gamma_x)\hat{K}_x + \varphi_x ,\tag{13-71}$$

$$\hat{Y} = \Gamma_y \hat{L}_y + (1 - \Gamma_y)\hat{K}_y + \varphi_y .\tag{13-72}$$

In the differential form, (13-65) and (13-66) are written as

$$L_x \hat{L}_x/L + L_y \hat{L}_y/L = \hat{L},\tag{13-73}$$

$$K_x \hat{K}_x/K + K_y \hat{K}_y/K = \hat{K} .\tag{13-74}$$

Find the expressions for $\hat{L}_x$, $\hat{L}_y$, $\hat{K}_x$, $\hat{K}_y$, from (13-69), (13-70), (13-73), and (13-74), and substitute them in (13-71) and (13-72). We obtain the equations (13-8) and (13-9).

To show equation (13-10) we note that the following equations can be derived from (13-61'') and (13-62''):

$$\hat{X} = \Gamma_x \hat{\mu}_x + \Gamma_x \hat{L}_x + (1 - \Gamma_x)\hat{v}_x + (1 - \Gamma_x)\hat{K}_x ,\tag{13-75}$$

$$\hat{Y} = \Gamma_y \hat{\mu}_y + \Gamma_y \hat{L}_y + (1 - \Gamma_y)\hat{v}_y + (1 - \Gamma_y)\hat{K}_y .\tag{13-76}$$

Taking (13-71) and (13-72) into account,

$$(1 - \Gamma_x)\hat{v}_x + \Gamma_x \hat{\mu}_x = \varphi_x ,\tag{13-77}$$

$$(1 - \Gamma_y)\hat{v}_y + \Gamma_y \hat{\mu}_y = \varphi_y .\tag{13-78}$$

From (13-63) and (13-64) we obtain (recalling $P = Q = 1$ initially so that $\hat{P} = p$, $\hat{Q} = q$):

$$(p - q) + \hat{\mu}_x = \hat{\mu}_y ,\tag{13-79}$$

$$(p - q) + \hat{v}_x = \hat{v}_y ,\tag{13-80}$$

$$(\hat{W} - \hat{R}) = \hat{\mu}_x - \hat{v}_x .\tag{13-81}$$

Combining (13-77), (13-78), (13-79), (13-80), and (13-81), we have equation (13-10). To show relationship (13-11), first we obtain the following equations from (13-61'') and (13-62''):

$$\Gamma_x = (W/R)(k_x + W/R) ,\tag{13-82}$$

$$\Gamma_y = (W/R)/(k_y + W/R) .\tag{13-83}$$

Hence, we have

$$\Gamma_x - \Gamma_y = \frac{(W/R)(k_y - k_x)}{(k_x + W/R)(k_y + W/R)}. \tag{13-84}$$

From this relationship, (13-11) is immediate.

To obtain equations (13-28), (13-29), and (13-36), it is convenient to rewrite αs and βs as follows:

$$\alpha \equiv (1 - \Gamma_x)(W/R + k_y), \tag{13-85}$$

$$\alpha' \equiv (1 - \Gamma_y)(W/R + k_x), \tag{13-86}$$

$$\beta \equiv RK_y(W/R + k_x)/X, \tag{13-87}$$

$$\beta' \equiv RK_x(W/R + k_y)/Y. \tag{13-88}$$

Notice that we use (13-63), (13-64), (13-61''), and (13-62'') in deriving (13-85)–(13-88). From these relations and by definitions of $\Lambda_i (i = x, y)$, equation (13-28) is immediate. Equation (13-29) follows directly from the definitions of F_x and F_y.

To derive (13-36) we should recall our convention that $P = Q = W_1 = R_1 = 1$ initially. Then, from (13-82) and (13-83), we obtain

$$k_{x1} = 1/\Gamma_{x1} - 1, \tag{13-89}$$

$$k_{y1} = 1/\Gamma_{y1} - 1. \tag{13-90}$$

Finally recalling equation (13-29) and using the above relations (13-89), (13-90), and $\mu_{x1} = \mu_{y1} = v_{x1} = v_{y1} = 1$, which is due to our convention for the initial prices, we obtain the desired result, (13-36).

Finally, let us consider how our demand formulation (13-1), (13-2) should be changed when there is a population increase. Or let us make explicit the assumptions which underlie our formulation (13-1), (13-2). First notice that the demand for a commodity generally depends upon the relative price and the per capita real income of the consumers. Hence, for Country 1,

$$\frac{Y_1 + Y_{21}}{L_1} = M_1(Q/P, U_1/L_1), \tag{13-91}$$

where U_1 is the real income of Country 1.

Differentiating both sides of (13-31), we have

$$\frac{L_1(y_1 + y_{21}) - l_1(Y_1 + Y_{21})}{L_1^2} = \eta_1(p - q)\left(\frac{Y_1 + Y_{21}}{L_1}\right) + \pi_1\left(\frac{u_1L_1 - l_1U_1}{L_1^2}\right). \tag{13-92}$$

We can also obtain a similar equation for Country 2.

(13-92) can be rewritten as follows:

$$y_1 + y_{21} = -(Y_1 + Y_{21})(q - p)\eta_1 + \pi_1[(p - q)Y_{21} + x_1 + y_1]$$

$$+ [(1 - \pi_1)(Y_1 + Y_{21}) - \pi_1(X_1 - X_{12})] \frac{l_1}{L_1}. \tag{13-93}$$

Comparing this with (13-1), we can immediately see that the implicit assumption involved in (13-1) is

$$[(1 - \pi_1)(Y_1 + Y_{21}) - \pi_1(X_1 - X_{12})]$$

$$= (Y_1 + Y_{21}) - \pi_1[(X_1 - X_{12}) + (Y_1 + Y_{21})] = 0. \tag{13-94}$$

Or,

$$(Y_1 + Y_{21}) - \pi_1 U_1 = 0. \tag{13-95}$$

If the marginal propensity to consume the import good is equal to its average propensity to consume, and if the terms of trade are kept constant, (13-95) will, in fact, hold true. If these conditions are not satisfied, the left-hand side of (13-95) will also not be too far from zero, and when it is multiplied by l_1/L_1, it may become small enough to be neglected. It goes without saying that the above consideration is completely unnecessary where there is no increase in population or an international movement of labor. Hence, our consideration in the fifth section, for example, would hold true without the above modifications.

REFERENCES

1. Amano, A., "International Factor Movements and the Terms of Trade," *Canadian Journal of Economics and Political Science*, XXXII, November 1966.
2. Bhagwati, J., "International Trade and Economic Expansion," *American Economic Review*, LXVIII, December 1958, 941–953.
3. ———, "Immiserizing Growth: A Geometrical Note," *Review of Economic Studies*, XXV, 1957–1958, 201–205.
4. Corden, W. W., "Economic Expansion and International Trade, A Geometric Approach," *Oxford Economic Papers*, June 1956, 223–228.
5. Findlay, R. E. and Grubert, H., "Factor Intensities, Technological Progress and the Terms of Trade," *Oxford Economic Papers*, February 1959, 111–121.
6. Hicks, J. R., "An Inaugural Lecture," *Oxford Economic Papers*, 5, June 1953, 117–135.
7. ———, "Supplementary Note B," in his *Essays in World Economics* (London: Oxford University Press), 1959, pp. 251–259.
8. ———, *Value and Capital*, 2nd ed. (London: Oxford University Press), 1946.
9. ———, *The Theory of Wages* (London: Macmillan & Co., Ltd.), 1932.

10. Johnson, H. G., *International Trade and Economic Growth* (Cambridge, Mass.: Harvard University Press), 1958, Chapters II, IV, and V.

11. ———, *Money, Trade and Economic Growth* (London: George Allen & Unwin, Ltd.), Chapter IV.

12. Jones, R. W., "Stability Conditions in International Trade: A General Equilibrium Analysis," *International Economic Review*, 2, May 1961, 199–209.

13. Kemp, M. C., "Technological Change, the Terms of Trade and Welfare," *Economic Journal*, LXV, September 1955, 457–473.

14. Meade, J. E., *Trade and Welfare* (London: Oxford University Press), 1955, also its *Mathematical Supplement* (London: Oxford University Press), 1955.

15. Mundell, R. A., "International Trade and Factor Mobility," *American Economic Review*, XLVII, June 1957.

16. Mishan, E. J., "The Long-Run Dollar Problem: A Comment," *Oxford Economic Papers*, 7, June 1955, 215–220.

17. Rybczynski, T. M., "Factor Endowment and Relative Commodity Prices," *Economica* (n.s.), XXII, November 1955, 336–341.

18. Seton, F., "Productivity, Trade Balance and International Structure," *Economic Journal*, LXVI, December 1956, 676–693.

19. Takayama, A., "On a Two-Sector Model of Economic Growth— Comparative Statics Analysis," *Review of Economic Studies*, XXX, June 1963.

20. ———, "Economic Growth and International Trade," *Review of Economic Studies*, XXXI, June 1964.

21. ———, *International Economics* (Tokyo: Toyo Keizai-Shimpo-Sha), 1963, Chapter VII, Section 3.

22. ———, "On a Two-Sector Model of Economic Growth with Technological Progress," *Review of Economic Studies*, XXXII, June 1965.

14

A DYNAMIC ANALYSIS OF THE PATTERNS OF SPECIALIZATION AND FACTOR ACCUMULATION —A FURTHER CONSIDERATION OF THE ONIKI-UZAWA MODEL

INTRODUCTION

In the previous two chapters we considered the effects of economic growth on international trade from the comparative statics viewpoint. Thus we could ascertain the effects fairly well at a given point of time. Suppose now that we are concerned with the time path of these variables. Since such an analysis can be considered as a succession of the comparative statics analysis, the scope of the comparative statics analysis in the previous two chapters in fact includes such a dynamic analysis. This point was illustrated in our exposition of the two-sector growth model in Chapter 2. There, as was illustrated in the phase diagram, the comparative statics analysis is in fact the dynamic analysis.

However, this convention of regarding dynamics as a succession of comparative statics causes two difficulties in terms of the present problem. (These problems did not exist in the two-sector growth model.)

1. When economic growth is defined as the accumulation of the factors, capital and labor, there is a question of where the capital comes from. The only way to answer this is simply to say that a part of the output of at least one of the two goods is also used as a capital good. However, there are some difficulties in this answer. First the Slutsky-Hicks type of consumption behavior as imposed in the previous two chapters is no longer relevant to the portion of the good(s) used for the purpose of capital accumulation. Second, the above answer does not explain the mechanism of capital accumulation. As long as we are only interested in a particular time point, we may not have to answer the above

---

[1] I am indebted to Michihiro Ohyama for helpful comments and discussions.

question, for we can always assume that the amount of capital accumulation is small compared to the total outputs of the two goods so that such a mechanism of capital accumulation is unimportant. However, if we are interested in the dynamics, we cannot keep the mechanism of capital accumulation implicit. We may note that this criticism does not apply when economic growth is taken to be technological progress, since in the previous analysis the technological progress is assumed to be exogenous and free.

2. Even if we do not care about the question of where capital comes from or if we assume economic growth to be exogenous (that is, technological progress), there remains one weakness. It does not make clear questions about the changes in the pattern of trade over time, the pattern of specialization of each country over time, and the behavior of capital accumulation in each country.

To answer the above questions a genuine dynamic analysis should be used. However, the complexity of a genuine dynamic analysis for the present problem can be easily understood. Essentially, we are grafting the capital accumulation mechanism to a complicated set of equations such as those discussed in the previous two chapters. Hence, such a dynamic analysis becomes possible only with certain sacrifices. For example, if we introduce the production of the third good, capital, into the above two-sector model, the analysis becomes too complicated to handle, for it explicitly calls for a genuine three-sector model. So to handle the situation we assume that one of the two goods in the two-sector growth model is the capital good and the other good is the consumption good. Then one sacrifice is obvious—the whole problem of the consumer's choice between the goods (as illustrated in the Hicks-Slutsky analysis) disappears.

But this sacrifice is only the beginning. There are more sacrifices to make. One type of analysis in the literature is based on the assumption that the production function for each good is of the Cobb-Douglas type and technological progress is Hicks-neutral. Although the production function for each good can be different between the countries and the speed of technological progress can be different between the countries, the above assumptions are quite strong. Such an analysis is done by Takayama [10], which was originally written in 1961.

The second type of analysis is to discard technological progress entirely from the analysis. Then without assuming Cobb-Douglas production functions, the analysis becomes manageable, although it turns out to be much more tedious than the first type of analysis and the conclusions become somewhat indeterminate. Such an analysis was attempted by Oniki and Uzawa [7], then followed by Bardhan [1], [2], Ohyama [6], Ethier [4][2], Kemp [5], and so on.

In this chapter we shall follow the line of the Oniki-Uzawa analysis. The reason we take up this line of analysis here, in spite of the indeterminateness

---

[2] Instead of the usual specification that one good is the capital good and the other good is the consumption good, Ethier [4] supposed that either of the goods can be used both as a capital good and as a consumption good. In this way he was able to consider the role of the consumer's choice between the goods explicitly. He then extended the model to incorporate the third good, a non-traded good, into his model.

of its conclusions and the extreme tediousness of its analysis, is that it contains several ingenious points that permit Oniki and Uzawa to carry out their difficult analysis, and due to some of these points their analysis can be used as a model of analysis for other problems of international trade. One important technique developed by them is the construction of their *offer curve*, the curve which relates (per capita) import (or export) to the commodity price ratio. We already discussed this Oniki-Uzawa type offer curve in Chapter 1 in a static context. We now take this up in an explicitly dynamic context.

The model is a traditional trade model of two countries, two commodities, and two factors. The intersection of the offer curves of the two countries determines the international equilibrium commodity price ratio. A change in the factor endowment of a country will, in general, cause a shift of the offer curve of that country. Hence, in the course of economic growth, which is defined in the sense of factor accumulation, the international equilibrium position from time to time causes a change in the pattern of specialization. For example, a country can specialize in the production of one good for one period of time and specialize in the production of the other good for another period of time. It is certainly possible that this country produces both goods for another period of time. The possible changes of the patterns of specialization can first be discussed by considering the mode of the shifts of one country's offer curve due to changes in the factor endowments of this country.

To discuss the dynamic time paths of major economic variables such as the factor endowment ratio of each country and to analyze the changes of the patterns of specialization when the factor endowments of both countries change, Oniki and Uzawa introduced the phase diagram technique in economic dynamics. This chapter will provide the reader with familiarity of this important technique.

We now summarize some important assumptions of the literature which are crucial to their analysis. This will highlight the difference of our analysis from the analysis in the literature.

1. Oniki-Uzawa [7] and Bardhan [2] assumed that the capital good is *less* capital intensive than the consumption good. In addition to its apparent unrealisticness, this condition, (which is often referred to as the *factor intensity condition*), is a serious limitation of the Oniki-Uzawa analysis, for they thus could not ascertain the monotonicity of their A_{min}-curve, which implies that they could not say anything precise about the boundaries of complete specialization in the consumption good.

2. This serious limitation of the factor intensity assumption was partially removed by Bardhan [2]. He argued that if the saving function is such that the workers save nothing *and* if the elasticity of factor substitution of the consumption good industry is sufficiently less than unity then the monotonicity of the A_{min}-curve under the factor intensity condition can be ascertained.[3]

[3] Under the assumption that a constant fraction of total income is saved as in Oniki-Uzawa [7], Ohyama [6] obtained a necessary and sufficient condition for the monotonicity of the A_{min}-curve.

3. We shall not, at least at the outset, assume the factor intensity condition. Later, to illustrate our analysis by ascertaining the dynamic paths of the endowment ratios of the two countries, we shall assume that the capital good is *more* capital intensive than the consumption good. We shall then discover that under this assumption the monotonicity of the A_{min}-curve is established unambiguously if the elasticity of factor substitution in the consumption good industry is greater than labor's relative share in that industry.[4]

4. Oniki and Uzawa [7], assumed that a constant fraction of total income is saved. Bardhan [2] attempted to generalize this to the direction that the workers' propensity to save (s_w) can be different from the capitalists' propensity to save (s_r). (Oniki-Uzawa's case is the one in which $s_r = s_w$.) However, he could not obtain any results about the monotonicity of the A_{min}-curve unless $s_w = 0$. Moreover, he did not pursue his analysis to any important extent under his general circumstance of $s_r \neq s_w > 0$. Hence, his generalization on saving behavior is a failure in the sense that it could not produce anything more than the major conclusions obtained by Oniki and Uzawa. In another article [1], Bardhan assumed that $1 \geqq s_r > 0$ but $s_w = 0$. This article is not a generalization of the Oniki-Uzawa analysis, but is an analysis based on an important alternative assumption on the savings behavior. This stand is similar to the one taken by Takayama [9] in connection with the two-sector model, as contrasted to Uzawa's assumption. In the present chapter, we shall also assume that $1 \geqq s_r > 0$ and $s_w = 0$.

5. Under this assumption, Bardhan [1] discovered that if the elasticity of factor substitution in each industry is *not less* than unity, and if the capital good is *more* capital intensive than the consumption good, then the monotonicity of the offer curve with respect to the commodity price ratio can be ascertained. However, he did not pursue his analysis as much as Oniki-Uzawa did. In particular he *a priori* assumed that either both countries produce both goods (incomplete specialization), or both countries are completely specialized. Then he proved under certain conditions that the endowment ratios of the two countries converge to a certain point as time extends without limit.

6. However, Bardhan's analysis here [1] has a serious limitation. It is wrong to specify the patterns of specialization *a priori*, for as time extends without limit, the combination of the patterns of specialization can move from one combination to another combination. For example, we shall show that it is possible that a country which specializes in the capital good in the beginning can end up in the specialization of the consumption good. *A priori* specification of the combination of the patterns of specialization simply misses the crucial point of dynamic analysis.

---

[4] This condition is satisfied, for example, if the elasticity of factor substitution of the consumption good industry is equal to or greater than one.

7. Moreover, Bardhan's stability theorem is rather empty when both countries produce both goods, for we can show that, except for a knife-edge case, such a case does not exist.

A short summary of the present chapter is now in order. In the next section we shall construct our model and recall some basic relations among the variables, all of which were already developed in Chapter 2. In the third section we shall rigorously construct the offer curve as conceived by Oniki-Uzawa and discuss the shift of the curve. The determination of international equilibrium will also be determined in this section. In the fourth section we first consider the change in the patterns of international specialization when the factor endowment ratio of one of the countries changes. Then we consider the change in the international equilibrium commodity price ratio when the factor endowment ratio of one of the countries changes. With these two preparations we can go to our final analysis which ascertains the change of the patterns of international specialization over time and the factor endowment ratio over time. Global stability of the factor endowment ratio under a certain circumstance will be observed. We shall conclude under a certain circumstance that regardless of the initial pattern of specialization and the initial values of the factor endowment ratios, as time extends without limit, the endowment ratios of each country approach a certain fixed value at which the pattern of international specialization is such that at least one country specializes in the production of one good. We observe that this conclusion always holds, for example, when one country is relatively small in terms of population compared to the other country. Although Oniki-Uzawa [7] did not obtain any specific result on this point, they seem to contend that the eventual equilibrium point is the one in which both countries incompletely specialize (produce both goods). Our analysis contradicts this contention.

MODEL AND BASIC RELATIONS

Consider a two-country world with Country 1 and Country 2 trading with each other. Each country is able to produce two commodities, a capital good (X) and a consumption good (Y), with two factors, capital (K) and labor (L). The basic model of production is similar to the one developed in Chapter 2 of this book. However, unlike the Heckscher-Ohlin model, the production function for each commodity does not have to be identical in both countries. Following the model of Chapter 2, we first develop the two-sector model of the economies. Here, for the sake of notational simplicity, we do not attach subscripts 1 and 2, which refer respectively to Country 1 and Country 2. Letting F and G be the production function of good X and good Y respectively, the total supply of each good (denoted by X and Y) can be written as

$$X = F(L_x, K_x) + M_x,$$ (14-1)

$$Y = G(L_y, K_y) + M_y.$$ (14-2)

Here M_i, $(i = x, y)$, refers to the import of good i if $M_i > 0$ and the export of good i if $M_i < 0$. L_i is the labor input to the ith industry and K_i is the capital input to the ith industry, $(i = x, y)$.

Let p_x = price of good X and p_y = price of good Y. Then writing $p \equiv p_x/p_y$, the balance of payments of this country can be denoted by

$$pM_x + M_y = 0 . \tag{14-3}$$

Now define the following per capita notations:

$$x \equiv X/L, \quad y \equiv Y/L, \quad l_x \equiv L_x/L, \quad l_y \equiv L_y/L, \quad m \equiv M_x/L,$$
$$k_x \equiv K_x/L_x, \quad k_y \equiv K_y/L_y . \tag{14-4}$$

Then, assuming constant returns to scale in both F and G (F and G are linear homogeneous), we obtain the following two equations from equations (14-1), (14-2), and (14-3):

$$x = f(k_x)l_x + m , \tag{14-5}$$

$$y = g(k_y)l_y - pm . \tag{14-6}$$

Let w = wage rate, r = rent of capital. Then assuming the marginal productivity rule of factor allocation, we have the following equations (as we did in Chapter 2):

$$w = p_x(f - k_x f') = p_y(g - k_y g') , \tag{14-7}$$

$$r = p_x f' = p_y g' , \tag{14-8}$$

where $f' \equiv df/dk_x$ and $g' \equiv dg/dk_y$. Equations (14-7) and (14-8) imply

$$q = \frac{f}{f'} - k_x = \frac{g}{g'} - k_y , \quad \text{where } q \equiv \frac{w}{r}; \quad \text{and} \tag{14-9}$$

$$p = \frac{g'}{f'}, \quad \text{where } p \equiv p_x/p_y . \tag{14-10}$$

Clearly (14-9) implies

$$f/f' = q + k_x, \quad \text{and } g/g' = q + k_y . \tag{14-9'}$$

We impose the following usual assumptions about f and g.

$f(k_x) > 0$ for all $k_x > 0$; $g(k_y) > 0$ for all $k_y > 0$;

$$f(0) = 0 \text{ and } g(0) = 0 . \tag{A-1}$$

$f'(k_x) > 0$ for all $k_x > 0$; $g'(k_y) > 0$ for all $k_y > 0$,

$$f'(0) = \infty, g'(0) = \infty, f'(\infty) = g'(\infty) = 0 . \tag{A-2}$$

$f(k_x) - k_x f'(k_x) > 0$ for all $k_x > 0$ and

$$g(k_y) - k_y g'(k_y) > 0 \text{ for all } k_y > 0 . \tag{A-3}$$

$$f''(k_x) < 0 \text{ for all } k_x \geqq 0 \text{ and } g''(k_y) < 0 \text{ for all } k_y \geqq 0 . \tag{A-4}$$

Assuming the full employment of each factor we obtain

$$L = L_x + L_y,$$ (14-11)

$$K = K_x + K_y.$$ (14-12)

We assume that the labor supply grows at a constant rate $n \geq 0$. That is,

$$L = L_0 e^{nt}, \text{ where } t \text{ refers to time } t.$$ (14-13)

The fundamental dynamic equation of the model which describes the capital accumulation, that is,

$$\dot{K} = X - \eta K,$$ (14-14)

where $\eta \geq 0$ is the rate of depreciation of capital. Let k be the endowment ratio, $k \equiv K/L$. Then equations (14-13) and (14-14) imply

$$\dot{k} = x - \lambda k, \quad \text{where } \lambda \equiv n + \eta.$$ (14-15)

In order to close the model, we need an equation which describes the demand side of the country's economy. Oniki and Uzawa [5] assumed that a constant fraction of GNP is saved ($p_x X = \bar{s}(p_x X + p_y Y)$). This assumption is called the *proportional* saving behavior. Here we assume instead that the capitalists are the only savers and that they save a constant fraction of their income (where $0 < s \leq 1$). Workers are assumed to consume all their income. This is called the *classical* saving behavior. Under this assumption we have

$$p_x X = srK.$$ (14-16)

Note that, due to the linear homogeneity of the production function, this is equivalent to the following relation:

$$p_y Y = wL + (1 - s)rK.$$ (14-17)

We are now ready to count the number of equations and the number of the endogenous variables in our model. We have eleven equations for each country [equations (14-1), (14-2), (14-7), (14-8), (14-11), (14-12), (14-13), (14-14), and (14-16)]. Hence, for the two countries there are twenty-two equations. Then, together with equation (14-3) which connects the two countries, we have twenty-three equations in the model. The variables which are to be determined in the model are $L_1, L_2, K_1, K_2, L_{x1}, L_{y1}, L_{x2}, L_{y2}, K_{x1}, K_{y1}, K_{x2}, K_{y2}, X_1, Y_1, X_2, Y_2, M_{x1}, M_{y1}, p, w_1/p_y, w_2/p_y, r_1/p_y, r_2/p_y$, where the subscripts 1 and 2 refer to the respective country. Here the equilibrium relations for the goods markets, $M_{x2} = -M_{x1}$ and $M_{y2} = -M_{y1}$, are used to eliminate M_{x2} and M_{y2} from the list of the variables. Note also that the relations $p_{x1} = p_{x2} \equiv p_x$ and $p_{y1} = p_{y2} \equiv p_y$ are used. This presupposes the assumption of free trade without any impediments of trade and transportation costs, which is an assumption we impose in this chapter.

Note that if p exceeds a certain limit the country will specialize in the production of one good. In other words we have

$$p \geqq p_{max}: \text{complete specialization in } X ; \tag{14-18a}$$

$$p \leqq p_{min}: \text{complete specialization in } Y ; \tag{14-18b}$$

$p_{min} < p < p_{max}:$ incomplete specialization

(production of both goods) . $\tag{14-18c}$

These relations can be understood easily from Figure 14-1. Here the p_{max}-line and the p_{min}-line respectively refer to the line which is tangent to the production transformation curve at point A and B.

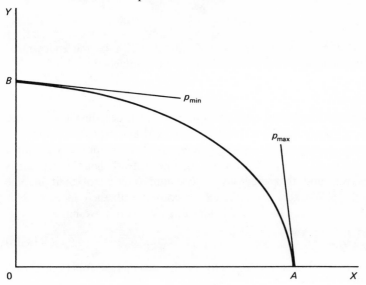

Figure 14-1   The Pattern of Production

When a particular country specializes in the production of good X or good Y, the equations developed above must be modified accordingly. For example, if only good X is produced, then $k_x = k$ and $k_y = 0$. If only good Y is produced, then $k_y = k$ and $k_x = 0$. Equations (14-5), (14-6), (14-7), (14-8), (14-9), (14-11), and (14-12) can be modified easily. Equations (14-13), (14-14), and (14-15) hold as they are. Obviously, equation (14-10) loses its meaning.

With this caution on the possibility of complete specialization, we now rewrite equation (14-16) using (14-8) as follows:

$$x = skf'(k_x), \text{ when good } X \text{ is produced in the country; and} \tag{14-19}$$

$$x = skg'(k_y)/p, \text{ when good } Y \text{ is produced in the country,} \tag{14-20}$$

where p refers to the commodity price ratio which prevails in the international market. If both goods are produced then either (14-19) or (14-20) can be used. Note that in view of (14-17), (14-7), and (14-8), we also have

$$y = [g(k_y) - k_y g'(k_y)] + (1 - s)kg'(k_y) , \tag{14-21}$$

when good Y is produced in the country. When the country specializes in good Y, all the capital good (good X) is imported from the other country ($m = x$). In view of equation (14-6), we then have $x = m = [g(k) - y]/p$ (note $k_y = k$ and $l_y = 1$ due to complete specialization in good Y). If we combine this with equation (14-21), we also obtain (14-20). The reader can also easily check the consistency of (14-20) with (14-21) when the country produces both goods.

We have a model consisting of twenty-three equations. In order to carry out an analysis on such a complex model we have to develop certain basic relations among the variables. A step-by-step advance based on such relations will lead us to the goal. When a country specializes in the production of one good, such relations are almost trivial and we do not have to worry about that too much. However, when a country produces both goods, then there are many complex basic relations among the variables. Fortunately, we have already developed such basic relations in Chapter 2 in connection with the Heckscher-Ohlin theorem. Hence, it suffices to recall some of the relations developed in Chapter 2 which will be useful in the subsequent analysis of this chapter.

Assume both goods are produced in the country. Then due to lemmas 1 and 2 of Chapter 2, we have

$$\frac{dq}{dp} \lessgtr 0, \quad \text{according to whether } k_x \gtrless k_y. \tag{14-22}$$

Or, more precisely (equation (2-23) of Chapter 2)

$$\frac{dq}{dp} = \frac{q}{p} \frac{1}{\Gamma_x - \Gamma_y}, \tag{14-22'}$$

where $\Gamma_i (i = x, y)$ is labor's relative share in the ith industry ($\Gamma_x \equiv \mu_x L_x / X$, and so on), and $\Gamma_x \lessgtr \Gamma_y$ according to whether $k_x \gtrless k_y$. It is assumed that $0 < \Gamma_x < 1$ and $0 < \Gamma_y < 1$. If only good X is produced, then in view of (14-9), we have $q = f(k)/f'(k) - k$ by setting $k_x = k$. Similarly, if only good Y is produced, then $q = g(k)/f'(k) - k$. In either case q is constant as long as k is constant. Hence, even if the commodity price ratio p, which is determined by international equilibrium, changes, q is constant as long as k is constant.

Also from Chapter 2 [(2-20) and (2-21)], we recall the following relations:

$$\Gamma_x = q/(q + k_x), \quad \text{and} \quad \Gamma_y = q/(q + k_y). \tag{14-23}$$

Also recall lemma 4 of Chapter 2 [especially equation (2-41)], which establishes

$$\frac{dq}{dk_x} = -ff''/(f')^2, \quad \text{and} \quad \frac{dq}{dk_y} = -gg''/(g')^2. \tag{14-24}$$

Note that this relation holds even if the country produces only good X (then $k_x = k$) or good Y (then $k_y = k$). From (14-24) we clearly have $dk_x/dq > 0$

and $dk_y/dq > 0$ for $f'' < 0$ and $g'' < 0$ by assumption. In Chapter 2, the elasticity of factor substitution was defined as

$$\sigma_x \equiv (dk_x/dq)(q/k_x), \quad \text{and} \quad \sigma_y \equiv (dk_y/dq)(q/k_y). \tag{14-25}$$

Then in view of (14-24), we have

$$\sigma_x = -\frac{q(f')^2}{k_x ff''} = -\frac{\Gamma_x f'}{k_x f''}, \quad \sigma_y = -\frac{q(g')^2}{k_y gg''} = -\frac{\Gamma_y g'}{k_y g''}. \tag{14-25'}$$

As we did in Chapter 2, we illustrate the relations (14-22) and (14-24) in Figure 14-2 where $k_x > k_y$ is assumed.

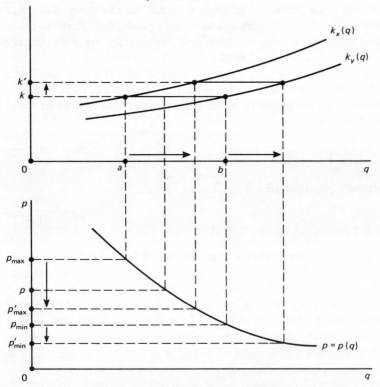

Figure 14-2   Relations among Factor Intensities, Factor Price Ratio, and Commodity Price Ratio

In Figure 14-2, an increase in the capital:labor endowment ratio of the country (say, from k to k') decreases the values of both p_{max} and p_{min}. On the other hand if $k_x < k_y$, it is easy to see that an increase in the endowment ratio increases the value of both p_{max} and p_{min}.[5]

---

[5] Hence, writing $p_{max} = p_{max}(k)$ and $p_{min} = p_{min}(k)$, we obtain $dp_{max}/dk \lessgtr 0$, $dp_{min}/dk \lessgtr 0$ according to whether $k_x \gtrless k_y$. In other words, $dk/dp_{max} \lessgtr 0$, $dk/dp_{min} \lessgtr 0$, according to whether $k_x \gtrless k_y$.

Suppose that $k_x > k_y$ for *all* q. We may now obtain the expression for p_{max} and p_{min}. Observe that $p = g'(k_y)/f'(k_x)$ in view of (14-10), if both goods are produced. Let the values of q which correspond to p_{max} and p_{min} be a and b respectively. That is, $p_{max} = p(a)$ and $p_{min} = p(b)$. Note that $k_x(a) = k_y(b) = k$. (See Figure 14-2.) p_{max} can be characterized by the limit of $g'(k_y)/f'(k_x)$ as $k_x \to k$ and $k_y \to k_y(a)$. Similarly, p_{min} can be characterized by the limit of $g'(k_y)/f'(k_x)$ as $k_x \to k(b)$ and $k_y \to \bar{k}$. Write $k_y(a) = \bar{k}_y$ and $k_x(b) = \bar{k}_x$. Then we have, in view of continuity of (g'/f'),

$$p_{max} = \frac{g'(\bar{k}_y)}{f'(k)} \quad \text{and} \quad p_{min} = \frac{g'(k)}{f'(\bar{k}_x)}, \tag{14-26}$$

provided that $k_x > k_y$.[6]

OFFER CURVE

The Construction of the Offer Curve

Having constructed our model and noted some basic relations, we are now ready to proceed with our analysis. In this section we are concerned with the behavior of the imports and exports of a particular country. The per capita import (or export) or good X for Country i, m, is, in general, a function of the commodity price ratio p and Country i's endowment ratio. Hence, we may write it as $m_i = m_i(p, k_i)$, $i = 1, 2$. We are first concerned with the shape of m_i as a function of p assuming that k_i is held constant. In the third section of Chapter 1, we discussed such a situation in connection with the Oniki-Uzawa-type offer curve. Unlike the Mill-Marshall offer curve, we draw m_i in the plane in which the horizontal axis denotes p. Moreover, m_i can either be positive or negative. That is, good X can be either the import or the export of commodity i. However, since the basic concept of such a curve is the same as that of the Mill-Marshall offer curve, we may call this curve an offer curve. This device will be considered because it is one of the important steps used in later analysis, in addition to being interesting in its own right and constituting one of the important merits of Oniki-Uzawa's paper [7]. When two countries' m-curves are superimposed, we can determine the international equilibrium price when both k_1 and k_2 are constants, as in the Mill-Marshall offer curve analysis. Then the situation is analogous to the static theory of international value such as the Heckscher-Ohlin trade model. The construction of this m-curve and the static theory of international value is the task of this subsection.

As is clear from the construction of the m-curve, this curve will shift when there is a change in k_1 or k_2. In the next subsection we shall consider such a shift, especially the shift of m_1 due to a shift in k_1 (or the shift of m_2 due to a change in k_2). The consideration of a shift due to a change in the endowment ratio of the *other country* will be postponed to the fourth section. In the subsequent analysis, we shall, for the sake of notational simplicity, omit subscripts

---

[6] The expressions for p_{max} and p_{min} when $k_x < k_y$ can be obtained analogously. Relation (14-26) is pointed out by Ohyama [6].

1 and 2 which refer to the country until they become necessary. As was the case in the previous section when subscripts 1 and 2 are omitted, the story holds in either of the two countries. We now turn to the story of this section.

Using equations (14-5) and (14-19), we first obtain

$$m = x - l_x f = skf' - l_x f,\qquad(14\text{-}27)$$

when good X is produced in the country. Note that this equation also holds true when both good X and Y are produced in the country. If only good Y is produced in the country and good X is not produced, then using (14-6) and (14-21) (or (14-5) and (14-20), alternatively), we obtain

$$m = skg'/p .\qquad(14\text{-}28)$$

Note that equations (14-11) and (14-12) imply

$$l_x = \frac{k - k_y}{k_x - k_y} \quad \text{and} \quad l_y = \frac{k_x - k}{k_x - k_y} .\qquad(14\text{-}29)$$

Hence (14-27) can be rewritten as

$$m = \frac{1}{k_x - k_y} \left[sk(k_x - k_y)f' - (k - k_y)f \right].\qquad(14\text{-}30)$$

When only good X is produced, (so that $k_x = k$ and $k_y = 0$), this is simplified to

$$m = skf' - f[= -(f - kf') - (1 - s)kf' < 0]\qquad(14\text{-}31)$$

which can be more easily obtained directly from (14-27) by noting that $l_x = 1$ for this case.

As we remarked before, if $p \geq p_{\max}$, only good X is produced, and if $p \leq p_{\min}$, only good Y is produced. If $p_{\min} < p < p_{\max}$, then both good X and good Y are produced. Thus we may summarize the above expressions for m as follows:

$$p \geq p_{\max}: m = skf' - f < 0;\qquad(14\text{-}32a)$$

$$p \leq p_{\min}: m = skg'(k)/p > 0;\qquad(14\text{-}32b)$$

$$p_{\min} < p < p_{\max}: \text{equation (14-30)} .\qquad(14\text{-}32c)$$

Assuming that k is constant, consider a change in the commodity price ratio p. Suppose that $p_{\min} < p < p_{\max}$. The equilibrium factor price ratio q also changes due to the change in p. Corresponding to this change in q, the equilibrium factor intensity in each industry, k_x and k_y, also moves. Then, in view of relation (14-32), per capita import (or export) m also moves. Therefore, a change in the commodity price ratio p will result in a change in m. Thus, m is reduced to a function of p. Our next task is to ascertain the direction of the change in m due to a change in p. This will give the direction of the slope of m when it is depicted in the $(m - p)$-plane.

From relation (14-32) there are three cases to be considered.[7]

CASE I $p \geqq p_{\max}$: $\dfrac{dm}{dq} = \dfrac{dk}{dq}[skf'' + (s - 1)f'] = 0$ $(\because k = \text{constant})$

then

$$\frac{dm}{dp} = \frac{dm}{dq}\frac{dq}{dp} = 0 .$$ (14-33)

CASE II $p \leqq p_{\min}$: $k_y = k$ so that g' is constant. Hence,

$$\frac{dm}{dp} = \frac{dm}{dq}\frac{dq}{dp} = -\frac{1}{p^2} skg' < 0 .$$ (14-34)

CASE III $p_{\min} < p < p_{\max}$:   write $k_x' \equiv \dfrac{dk_x}{dq}$ and $k_y' \equiv \dfrac{dk_y}{dq}$.

$$\frac{dm}{dq} = skf''k_x' + \frac{\tau}{(k_x - k_y)^2} , \quad \text{where}$$ (14-35)

$$\tau \equiv k_x'(k - k_y)[(f - k_xf') + k_yf'] + k_y'(k_x - k)f .$$ (14-36)

In view of (14-9), τ can further be simplified as

$$\tau = k_x'(k - k_y)f'(q + k_y) + k_y'(k_x - k)f .$$ (14-37)

Note that $k_x' > 0$ and $k_y' > 0$ always, as we remarked in connection with (14-24). We now obtain

$$\frac{dm}{dp} = \frac{dm}{dq} \cdot \frac{dq}{dp} = \left[skf''k_x' + \frac{\tau}{(k_x - k_y)^2} \right] \frac{dq}{dp} .$$ (14-38)

In view of (14-22), if $k_x > k_y$, then $dq/dp < 0$ and if $k_x < k_y$ then $dq/dp > 0$. As we shall see later, the condition that $dm/dp < 0$ will play an important role in the subsequent analysis. To establish this condition, we consider the two cases $k_x < k_y$ and $k_x > k_y$.

If $k_x < k_y$ so that $k_x < k < k_y$ then, in view of (14-37), $\tau < 0$. Hence, $dm/dq < 0$, due to (14-35). Therefore, we always have $dm/dp < 0$. This is the case which is considered by Oniki and Uzawa [7] and Bardhan [2]. On the other hand, if $k_x > k_y$ so that $k_x > k > k_y$, then we cannot necessarily establish the sign of dm/dq. This can be seen easily since $\tau > 0$ for this case. Thus, the sign of dm/dq depends on the relative magnitudes of $skf''k_x'$ and $\tau/(k_x - k_y)^2$. If s is sufficiently close to zero, for example, then we can have $dm/dq > 0$. Then $dm/dp < 0$, since $dq/dp < 0$ when $k_x > k_y$. To sharpen

---

[7] Since $m = m(p, k)$, we may, strictly speaking, have to use $\partial m/\partial p$ for dm/dp, $\partial m/\partial q$ for dm/dq, and so on. However, as long as we understand that k is being held constant, the total derivative notations in this subsection should not confuse the reader. This convention is also used in Oniki-Uzawa [7].

our understanding of the situation when $k_x > k_y$, we further rewrite equation (14-35) using (14-9′), (14-24), and (14-25) as follows:

$$
\begin{aligned}
\frac{dm}{dq} = \frac{f'}{(k_x - k_y)^2(q + k_x)} \\
\times \{-sk(k_x - k_y)^2 + (q + k_x)[\sigma_x k_x(k - k_y)(q + k_y)/q \\
+ \sigma_y k_y(k_x - k)(q + k_x)/q]\}\,.
\end{aligned}
\tag{14-39}
$$

When $\sigma_x = \sigma_y = 1$, this can further be simplified as

$$
\frac{dm}{dq} = \frac{f'}{(k_x - k_y)(q + k_x)q} \{kq[(1 - s)k_x + (q + k_y)] + (q + k_x)k_x k_y\}\,,
\tag{14-40}
$$

which is clearly positive. Hence, in view of (14-39), we can conclude that $dm/dq > 0$, if $\sigma_x \geqq 1$ and $\sigma_y \geqq 1$ with $k_x > k_y$. This is the condition obtained by Bardhan [1].

Using (14-10), (14-22′), (14-23), and (14-29) we may obtain the following equation from (14-39):

$$
\begin{aligned}
\frac{dm}{dp} = \frac{dm}{dq}\frac{dq}{dp} = \frac{qg'}{(k_x - k_y)(\Gamma_y - \Gamma_x)} \\
\times [-sk(k_x - k_y)\Gamma_x + (\sigma_x k_y l_x/\Gamma_y + \sigma_y k_y l_y/\Gamma_x)]\,.
\end{aligned}
\tag{14-41}
$$

Hence a *necessary and sufficient* condition for $dm/dp < 0$ is given by

$$
-sk(k_x - k_y)\Gamma_x + \sigma_x k_x l_x/\Gamma_y + \sigma_y k_y l_y/\Gamma_x > 0\,,
\tag{14-42}
$$

which is new in the literature.

Some of the sufficient conditions for dm/dp are already obtained as

$$
k_y > k_x\,,
\tag{14-43a}
$$

$$
k_x > k_y \quad \text{and a sufficiently small } s\,,
\tag{14-43b}
$$

$$
k_x > k_y \quad \text{and} \quad \sigma_x \geqq 1, \sigma_y \geqq 1\,.
\tag{14-43c}
$$

Henceforth, we shall proceed with our analysis under the assumption of $dm/dp < 0$ when $p_{min} < p < p_{max}$.

Under $dm/dp < 0$ for $p_{min} < p < p_{max}$, we can now illustrate the relation between m and p in Figure 14-3. As we remarked before, $m_i > 0$, $i = 1, 2$ means that good X is the import of Country i, and $m_i < 0$ means that it is the export of Country i. The curve drawn in Figure 14-3 signifies the relation between the commodity price ratio p and m, the per capita import or export of good X, when the capital:labor endowment ratios of the two countries (k_1 and k_2) are held constant. As we remarked before, we call this curve the *offer curve*. Notice that the condition $dm/dp < 0$, for $p_{min} < p < p_{max}$, guarantees that the offer curve intersects with the p-axis only *once* (say, at $\bar{p}$). If $p < \bar{p}$, then

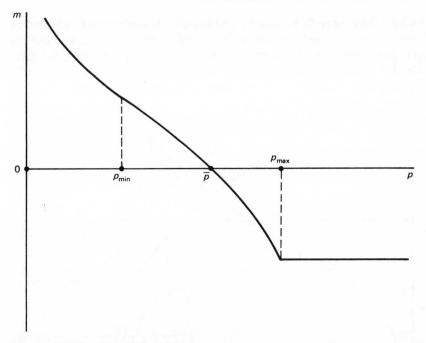

Figure 14-3   The Offer Curve

this country is the importer of good X and the exporter of good Y. On the other hand, if $p > \bar{p}$, then this country is the exporter of good X and the importer of good Y.

In order to determine the equilibrium value of the commodity price ratio p, we consider a similar diagram for the other country and superimpose these two diagrams on one another. We now turn to this task. Note that in equilibrium, the following equations must hold.

$$M_{x1} + M_{x2} = 0, \quad \text{and} \tag{14-44}$$

$$M_{y1} + M_{y2} = 0, \tag{14-45}$$

where the subscripts 1 and 2 refer to the respective country. In view of the balance of payments equilibrium, equation (14-3), one of the the two equations above may be derived from the other equation. Hence, it suffices to consider equation (14-44). We rewrite this equation

$$\alpha_1 m_1 + \alpha_2 m_2 = 0, \tag{14-46}$$

where

$$\alpha_i \equiv L_i/(L_1 + L_2), \quad i = 1, 2; \quad \text{and} \tag{14-47}$$

$$m_i \equiv M_{xi}/L_i, \quad i = 1, 2. \tag{14-48}$$

Here the subscripts 1 and 2 refer to the respective country. Clearly $\alpha_1 + \alpha_2 = 1$. At each instant of time, the total labor supply of each country is fixed. Then, for each t, where we have a short-run equilibrium, α_1 and α_2 can be considered as fixed. Equation (14-46) dictates the international short-run equilibrium relation and determines the international equilibrium commodity price ratio p^*. This is illustrated in Figure 14-4.

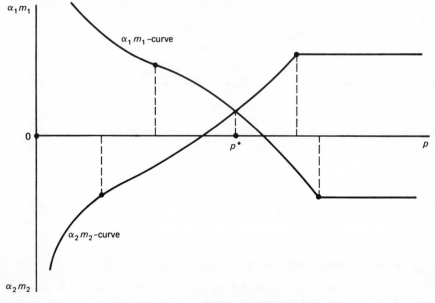

Figure 14-4 The Short-Run International Equilibrium

Note that the assumption of $dm/dp < 0$ for $p_{\min} < p < p_{\max}$ is crucial in establishing the uniqueness of the international equilibrium price p^*. In Figure 14-4, Country 1 exports good Y and imports good X at equilibrium.

The Shift of the Offer Curve

The offer curve above is obtained under the assumption that k_1 or k_2 is constant. When k_1 or k_2 changes, then the above offer curve will shift. We are now interested in finding out the manner of such a shift, especially the shift of $m_i (i = 1, 2)$ when k_i changes. In other words, writing $m_i = m_i(p, k_i)$ we are interested in finding out $\partial m_i / \partial k_i$, $i = 1, 2$. Then, for example, if $\partial m_i / \partial k_i < 0$, at each level of p, an increase in k_i will lower the amount of m_i. In other words, in the region of p in which $\partial m_i / \partial k_i < 0$, the offer curve of Country i shifts downward as its capital-labor endowment ratio (k_i) increases. Since the story for one country holds as it is for the other country, we shall again omit the subscripts which refer to the respective countries.

Referring to (14-32), we consider the three cases again. In other words:

CASE I $p \gtreqqless p_{\max}$: $\dfrac{\partial m}{\partial k} = \dfrac{\partial}{\partial k}\left[skf' - f\right] = skf'' - (1 - s)f' < 0$.

CASE II $\quad p \leqq p_{\min}: \quad \dfrac{\partial m}{\partial k} = \dfrac{\partial}{\partial k}\left[skg'/p\right]$

$$= s[kg'' + g']/p = s[1 - \Gamma_y/\sigma_y]g'/p \quad [\because \text{ equation (14-25')}].$$

CASE III $\quad p_{\min} < p < p_{\max}: \quad \dfrac{\partial m}{\partial k} = \dfrac{-1}{k_x - k_y}\left[f - s(k_x - k_y)f'\right]$

$$= \dfrac{-1}{k_x - k_y}\left[(f - k_xf') + sk_yf'\right.$$

$$\left. + (1 - s)k_xf'\right]$$

$(\because k_x$ and k_y are constants when $q = $ constant).

From this we obtain the following conclusion:

CASE I $\quad p \geqq p_{\max}: \partial m/\partial k < 0$. $\hfill$ (14-49)

CASE II $\quad p \leqq p_{\min}: \partial m/\partial k > 0$, if $\Gamma_y < \sigma_y$

$\qquad$ (which, in turn, is satisfied if $\sigma_y \geq 1$, for example) . $\hfill$ (14-50)

CASE III $\quad p_{\min} < p < p_{\max}: \partial m/\partial k \gtreqless 0$ according to whether $k_x \lesseqgtr k_y$. (14-51)

In other words, if $p \geqq p_{\max}$, for example, then the value of m decreases as k increases for *each* value of p, so that an increase in k will cause a downward shift of the offer curve. In fact, the values of $p_{\max}$ and $p_{\min}$ also move as k changes. If $k_x < k_y$, then both $p_{\max}$ and $p_{\min}$ increase as k increases, while if $k_x > k_y$ then both $p_{\max}$ and $p_{\min}$ decrease as k increases. This is already noted in Figure 14-2. Now we can illustrate the above relations (14-49), (14-50), and (14-51) in the Figures 14-5 and 14-6. We have two diagrams depending on whether $k_x < k_y$ or $k_x > k_y$. The case in which $k_x = k_y$ is assumed away.

Since $p_{\max}$ and $p_{\min}$ move as k changes, the value of m at $p = p_{\max}$ and $p_{\min}$ also moves. The $A_{\max}(k)$-curve in the figures denotes the locus of m at $p = p_{\max}$ as k moves. Similarly the $A_{\min}(k)$-curve denotes the locus of m at $p = p_{\min}$, when k moves. It is easy to see from the diagram that the $A_{\max}(k)$-curve is monotonically decreasing in p when $k_y > k_x$, although the monotonicity of the $A_{\min}$-curve cannot readily be established. Oniki and Uzawa assumed $k_y > k_x$ and could not also establish the monotonicity of the $A_{\min}(k)$-curve, under their assumption of proportional saving behavior (that is, a constant fraction of GNP is saved at each t). This lack of monotonicity causes great difficulty later in their analysis in the sense that they cannot establish certain important specific results concerning the dynamic pattern of specialization.

Under the present assumption of the saving behavior (only the capitalists save), we can unambiguously establish the monotonicity of the $A_{\max}$-curve in either of the two situations, $k_x > k_y$ and $k_x < k_y$. In other words, the $A_{\max}$-curve is monotone increasing if $k_x > k_y$ and monotone decreasing if $k_x < k_y$ (Figure 14-5). The monotonicity of the $A_{\min}$-curve for the $(k_y > k_x)$ case cannot

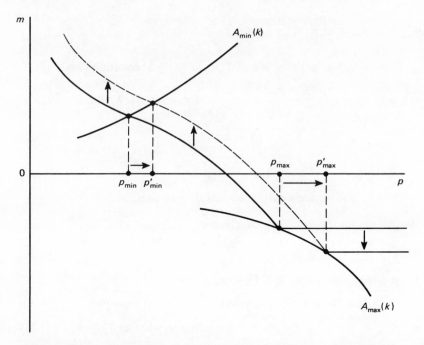

Figure 14-5   The Shift of Offer Curve: The $(k_y > k_x)$-Case

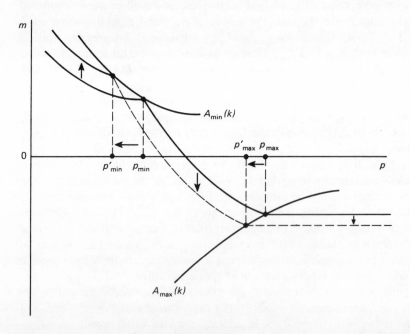

Figure 14-6   The Shift of Offer Curve: The $(k_x > k_y)$-Case

be established under a general situation. In order to see this from computation, first write $m(p, k) \equiv skg'(k)/p$. Let $p = p_{min}$. Then as we remarked in connection with Figure 14-2, we have a functional relation between p_{min} and k, say $k = k(p_{min})$, such that $dk/dp_{min} < 0$ if $k_x > k_y$ and $dk/dp_{min} > 0$ if $k_x < k_y$. Then we can see that the A_{min}-curve is described by the equation $m = m[p_{min}, k(p_{min})]$, or more simply $m = m[p, k(p)]$, where p signifies p_{min}. Or more precisely,[8] $m = sk(p)g'[k(p)]/p = sk(p)f'[\bar{k}_x(p)]$ in view of (14-26), where p again signifies p_{min}.[9]

Now observe:

$$\frac{dm}{dp} = \frac{\partial m}{\partial k}\frac{dk}{dp} + \frac{\partial m}{\partial p} = [s(1 - \Gamma_y/\sigma_y)g'/p]\frac{dk}{dp} - \frac{s}{p^2}kg', \qquad (14\text{-}52)$$

where p signifies p_{min}. Suppose that $k_x > k_y$. Then $dk/dp < 0$ in (14-52) so that as long as $\Gamma_y/\sigma_y \leqq 1$ we have $dm/dp < 0$ unambiguously. On the other hand, if $k_x < k_y$, then $dk/dp > 0$ in (14-52). Note that the sign of dm/dp is, in general, indeterminate. If σ_y is "sufficiently less than unity," or, more precisely, $\sigma_y \leqq \Gamma_y$, in addition to $k_x < k_y$, then we can have $dm/dp < 0$ unambiguously in view of (14-52). This is the situation that Bardhan observed ([2] p. 43). A necessary and sufficient condition for the monotonicity of the A_{min}-curve can be obtained by spelling out the functional relation $k = k(p_{min})$ explicitly and substitute this into (14-52). We leave this to the interested reader.[10]

Bardhan's assumption that σ_y is less than unity (or more precisely $\sigma_y \leqq \Gamma_y$) contradicts our assumption of $\sigma_y > \Gamma_y$. More importantly it negates Bardhan's various conclusions obtained under the assumption of $\sigma_y \geqq 1$. Henceforth, we proceed with our analysis assuming $k_x > k_y$. Then the above difficulty of ascertaining the monotonicity does not arise. Also, it conforms with the author's contention that $k_x > k_y$ (the capital good is more capital intensive than the consumption good) is more realistic than $k_x < k_y$. We assume that $k_x > k_y$ holds for all the relevant range of q for both countries. This also means that we assume away the factor intensity reversal. This assumption is also made by other writers.

---

[8] Note that m is a function of p alone. This is the way the A_{min}-curve is depicted in Figures 14-5 and 14-6. Similarly, the equation which describes the A_{max}-curve is written as $m = sk(p)f'[k(p)] - f[k(p)]$, where $k = k(p)$ and p now signifies p_{max}. Since $dm/dp = (dm/dk) \times (dk/dp) = [skf'' - (1 - s)f'](dk/dp)$, we can unambiguously conclude that $dm/dp > 0$ if $k_x > k_y$ and $dm/dp < 0$ if $k_x < k_y$, as we observed earlier.

[9] Oniki-Uzawa [7] concluded that $A_{min}(k)$ tends to approach infinity as k tends to approach infinity (p. 29). From our expression of A_{min} here, we can see easily that this conclusion is not necessarily true, for $k \to \infty$ implies $k_x \to \infty$ but $f'(\infty) = 0$ (then use L'Hospital's rule).

[10] Write $p = p_{min}$ and assume $k_x > k_y$. Then, using (14-26) and (14-24), we obtain $dk/dp = [f'(\bar{k}_x)(q + \bar{k}_x)]/[g''(k)(\bar{k}_x - k)]$ ($\because k_y = k$ at $p = p_{min}$ since $k_x > k_y$). This expression is obtained by Ohyama [6]. Substituting this expression of dk/dp in (14-52), we can obtain the desired necessary and sufficient condition for the monotonicity of the A_{min}-curve for the case when $k_x > k_y$. The condition taken $k_x < k_y$ can be obtained analogously.

DYNAMICS: FACTOR ACCUMULATION AND PATTERNS OF SPECIALIZATION

Patterns of Specialization

We now introduce the other country (Country 2). To carry out an analysis, with the other country, we impose the following simplifying assumption.

Both α_1 and α_2 are constant . $\qquad$ (14-53)

This is true, for example, if labor supply grows at the same rate in the two countries.

This assumption is due to Oniki and Uzawa [7]. However, this assumption does not hold when the two countries have different rates of growth of their labor supplies. Oniki and Uzawa noted, "The general case of constant but different rates of population growth is handled without much difficulty" ([7], p. 16). Bardhan remarked that this is wrong ([2] p. 39). In his article [1], he showed that, under the assumptions of Oniki and Uzawa, (such as the assumption of proportional saving function, that is, a constant proportion of GNP is saved), growth equilibrium does not exist unless the two countries have the same rate of growth in their labor supplies.

To proceed with our analysis, we fix the value of the capital-endowment ratio of Country 2, k_2. Then Country 2's offer curve will stand still. As the endowment ratio of Country 1 increases Country 1's offer curve moves to the left as remarked before. Thus, the intersection of the offer curves of these two countries, which determines the international equilibrium, moves. Then the international equilibrium price (denoted as p^* in Figure 14-4) also moves to the left. Let $p_{min}{}^i$ and $p_{max}{}^i$ respectively be p_{min} and p_{max} of Country i ($i = 1, 2$). Then, a) if $p^* \geqq p_{max}{}^1$, Country 1 specializes in the production of good X; b) if $p^* \leqq p_{min}{}^1$, Country 1 specializes in the production of good Y; c) if $p_{min}{}^1 < p < p_{max}{}^1$, Country 1 produces both good X and good Y. A similar story goes for Country 2. The changes in the pattern of specialization are now illustrated in Figure 14-7. Here $I(X)$, $I(Y)$, and $I(X, Y)$ respectively denote that Country 1 specializes in good X, good Y, and produces both X and Y. The notations, $II(X)$, $II(Y)$, and $II(X, Y)$, are defined analogously. In Figure 14-7, the dotted curves denote Country 1's offer curves corresponding to various values of her endowment ratio k_1. The arrows indicate the direction of increase in k_1. Note that the $\alpha_1 A_{min}{}^1(k_1)$-curve intersects with the $\alpha_2 m_2$-curve and the intersection is unique. When k_1 increases this intersection point moves, and Country 1 switches from $I(Y)$ to $I(X, Y)$. The corresponding value of k_1 is denoted by $k_1{}^*$. When the $\alpha_1 A_{max}{}^1(k_1)$-curve intersects with the $\alpha_2 m_2$-curve, Country 1 switches from $I(X, Y)$ to $I(X)$. The corresponding value of k_1 is denoted by $k_1{}^{**}$. We are assuming that there exists a unique $k_1{}^{**}$. Now we may summarize the above consideration as

$$k_1 \leqq k_1{}^*: \quad I(Y) \qquad (14\text{-}54a)$$

$$k_1{}^* < k_1 < k_1{}^{**}: \quad I(X, Y) \qquad (14\text{-}54b)$$

$$k_1{}^{**} \leqq k_1: \quad I(X) . \qquad (14\text{-}54c)$$

If the endowment ratio of Country 2, k_2, increases then both p_{max}^2 and p_{min}^2 decrease, assuming good X is more capital intensive than good Y in Country 2. Then Country 2's offer curve moves to the left. Hence, in the case of Figure 14-7, both k_1^* and k_1^{**} increase as k_2 increases. In the following

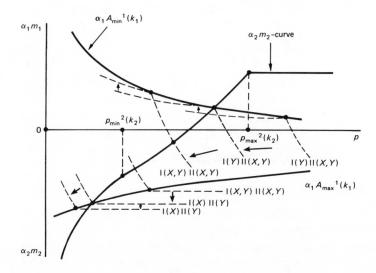

Figure 14-7 Dynamic Patterns of Specialization

diagram, the k_1^{**}-curve and k_2^*-curve respectively denote the locus of these values of k_1^* and k_1^{**} corresponding to different values of k_2. Note that the three regions defined by the k_1^*-curve and the k_1^{**}-curve specify the pattern of specialization in Country 1. Note that for a fixed value of k_2, say, $\bar{k}_2$, the pattern of specialization moves from $I(Y)$ to $I(X, Y)$ and to $I(X)$ as k_1 increases. This is the situation described in Figure 14-8.

Note, however, that the monotonicity of the k_1^*-curve and the k_2^*-curve is not of necessity. For example, in the case in which the $\alpha_1 A_{max}^1(k_1)$-curve intersects with the $\alpha_2 A_{min}^2(k_2)$-curve at a certain p, we can show easily that the k_1^*-curve can either be flat or vertical depending upon the manner of intersection.[11] Although this observation will not change the subsequent discussion in essentials, it is an interesting point to observe. For if the rate of population growth of each country changes from time to time, then the $\alpha_1 A_{min}^1$-, the $\alpha_1 A_{max}^1$-, the $\alpha_2 A_{min}^2$-, and the $\alpha_2 A_{max}^2$-curves all shift from time to time so that such intersections of these curves are likely to occur.

In a very special case in which the $\alpha_1 A_{min}^1$-curve coincides with the $\alpha_2 A_{min}^2$-curve, then not only the monotonicity of the k_1^*- and the k_1^{**}-curve in Figure 14-8 is correct, but also the three regions defined by these curves also describe the patterns of specialization of Country 2 unambiguously. In other words, the I(X)-, the I(X, Y)-, and the I(Y)-regions respectively correspond to the II(Y)-,

[11] This is pointed out to me by M. Ohyama.

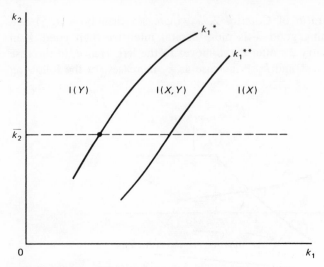

Figure 14-8   Regions of Specialization

the $II(X, Y)$-, and the $II(X)$-regions. The reader can easily examine this by constructing his own diagram.

Although this case will give a very sharp result, it is not so easy to justify on the grounds that it makes certain plausible economic sense. However, there are cases in which we can get as sharp a result as the above case[12] and we can find a certain economic background to justify these cases. As an example, consider the case in which one country is *small* compared to the other, *where the smallness here is defined in terms of population*. In particular assume that Country 1 is *small* compared to Country 2 in the sense that α_1 is sufficiently small compared to α_2 so that the region defined by the $\alpha_1 A_{min}{}^1$- and the $\alpha_1 A_{max}{}^1$-curves is "trapped" by the region defined by the $\alpha_2 A_{max}{}^2$- and the $\alpha_2 A_{min}{}^2$-curves.[13] This is illustrated in Figure 14-9. In view of Figure 14-9, the patterns of specialization of the two countries can easily be obtained, which we illustrate in Figure 14-10. Note that in this case Country 2 will never specialize in the production of the capital good (X).

Factor Accumulation and International Equilibrium Price Ratio

As capital accumulation occurs in one or both countries, or as the capital endowment ratios k_1 and k_2 move, the international equilibrium values of p,

[12] An obvious case is $p_{max} = \infty$ and $p_{min} = 0$ for one of the countries, say, Country 2. In this case Country 2 always produces the two goods (incomplete specialization). The difficulty of this case is that it is not easy to justify this assumption of $p_{max} = \infty$ and $p_{min} = 0$ and still make good economic sense in terms of f and g.

[13] Here we recall that the A_{min}-curve is described by $m = sk(p)f'[k_x(p)]$ while the A_{max}-curve is described by $m = sk(p)f'[k(p)] - f[k(p)]$ (omitting the suffix i for the country's name to ease notation). From this we can show that we can choose α_1 small enough so that the "trapping" situation of Figure 14-9 occurs, if we restrict ourselves to the case in which k is below a certain finite value (which can be very very large). This small country case was also pointed out to me by M. Ohyama.

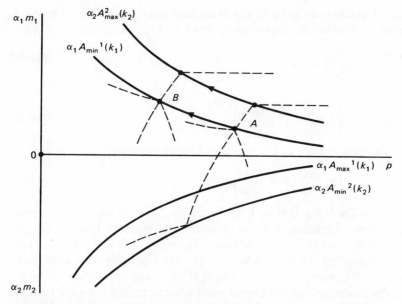

Figure 14-9 The Case of Small Country

m_1 and m_2 also change. We will now consider such changes when the endowment ratio of *one* country changes. To carry out this analysis, we first recall that the international equilibrium condition is described by $\alpha_1 m_1 + \alpha_2 m_2 = 0$ [equation (14-46)]. Note that the equilibrium price ratio p is a function of k_1 and k_2. Hence we may write it as $p = p(k_1, k_2)$, where p now denotes the

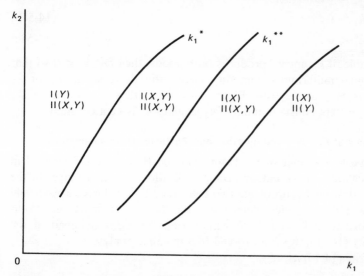

Figure 14-10 The Patterns of Specialization for the Small Country Case

international equilibrium price in the sense that equation (14-46) is satisfied. Differentiating (14-46) with respect to k_1, (with k_2 kept constant),

$$\alpha_1 \left(\frac{\partial m_1}{\partial p} \frac{\partial p}{\partial k_1} + \frac{\partial m_1}{\partial k_1} \right) + \alpha_2 \frac{\partial m_2}{\partial p} \frac{\partial p}{\partial k_1} = 0 . \tag{14-55}$$

Thus we have

$$\frac{\partial p}{\partial k_1} = -\alpha_1 \frac{\partial m_1}{\partial k_1} \bigg/ \left(\alpha_1 \frac{\partial m_1}{\partial p} + \alpha_2 \frac{\partial m_2}{\partial p} \right) . \tag{14-56}$$

Similarly we obtain (when k_2 changes with k_1 kept constant),

$$\frac{\partial p}{\partial k_2} = -\alpha_2 \frac{\partial m_2}{\partial k_2} \bigg/ \left(\alpha_1 \frac{\partial m_1}{\partial p} + \alpha_2 \frac{\partial m_2}{\partial p} \right) . \tag{14-57}$$

We know that $\partial m_i/\partial p \leqq 0$ $(i = 1, 2)$, where $\partial m_i/\partial p = 0$ signifies the region in which Country i specializes in the production of good X. Thus the denominators of (14-56) and (14-57) are negative. The signs of $\partial m_i/\partial k_i$ $(i = 1, 2)$ are already established by (14-49), (14-50), and (14-51). For example, if both goods are produced in Country i, then $\partial m_i/\partial k_i \gtreqless 0$ according to whether $k_{xi} \lesseqgtr k_{yi}$. Since we are assuming that the capital good is more capital intensive than the consumption good in both countries, $(k_{xi} > k_{yi}\ i = 1, 2)$, we have $\partial m_i/\partial k_i < 0$, if both goods are produced in Country i. We assume $\partial m_i/\partial k_i > 0$ if Country i specializes in the production of good X, [the conditions which guarantee this are described in (14-50)]. Then, in view of (14-56) and (14-57) we have the following relations. Here the notations, $i(X)$, $i(Y)$, and $i(X, Y)$ $(i = I, II)$, are defined analogously as $I(X)$, $I(Y)$, and $I(X, Y)$.

$$i(X): \quad \partial p/\partial k_i < 0 ; \tag{14-58a}$$

$$i(Y): \quad \partial p/\partial k_i > 0 ; \tag{14-58b}$$

$$i(X, Y): \quad \partial p/\partial k_i < 0 . \tag{14-58c}$$

Thus, for example, if Country i produces both goods, then $\partial p/\partial k_i < 0$ so that the international equilibrium commodity price ratio decreases as k_1 or k_2 increase. This is easy to see from Figure 14-7. Note that in (14-58), $\partial p/\partial k_1$ signifies that k_2 is kept constant and $\partial p/\partial k_2$ signifies k_1 is kept constant.

Dynamic Analysis of Factor Accumulation and Patterns of Specialization

We now come to the final stage of our analysis. Here we are interested in specifying the changes in the patterns of specialization and the changes in the capital:labor endowment ratio of the two countries. To do this we specifically recall equation (14-15), which determines the factor accumulation. Combining the information from (14-15) with various relations obtained in the above [especially (14-58)], we can proceed to a dynamic analysis.

We first rewrite (14-15) as

$$\frac{\dot{k}_i}{k_i} = \frac{x_i}{k_i} - \lambda_i , \quad i = 1, 2 . \tag{14-59}$$

In view of (14-19) and (14-20), we may rewrite this as

$$\frac{\dot{k_i}}{k_i} = s_i f_i' - \lambda_i, \quad i = 1, 2,$$ (14-60)

if good X is produced in Country i; and

$$\frac{\dot{k_i}}{k_i} = s_i g_i'/p - \lambda_i, \quad i = 1, 2,$$ (14-61)

if good Y is produced in Country i.

Define φ_i by

$$\varphi_i \equiv \frac{\dot{k_i}}{k_i}, \quad i = 1, 2.$$ (14-62)

Since φ_i depends on both k_1 and k_2, we may write it as $\varphi_i = \varphi_i(k_1, k_2)$.

There are various combinations of the patterns of specialization in the two countries. We consider these combinations one by one.

CASE I $\mathrm{I}(X, Y)$ and $\mathrm{II}(X, Y)$

In this case we can use either (14-60) or (14-61). Here we use (14-60). Differentiating both sides of (14-60) with respect to k_i, we obtain

$$\varphi_{ii} \equiv \frac{\partial \varphi_i}{\partial k_i} = s_i f_i'' \frac{\partial k_{xi}}{\partial q_i} \frac{\partial q_i}{\partial p} \frac{\partial p}{\partial k_i}, \quad i = 1, 2.$$ (14-63)

Here the partial derivative notations signify that the capital-labor endowment ratio of the other country is kept constant. Clearly, $\partial k_i/\partial q_i > 0$, and with $k_{xi} > k_{yi}$ we have $\partial q_i/\partial p < 0$ (recall the second section). Moreover, due to (14-58c), $\partial p/\partial k_i < 0$ when Country i produces both goods. Therefore we have $\partial \varphi_i/\partial k_i < 0$. Similarly we can obtain the sign of $\partial \varphi_i/\partial k_j$, $i \neq j$. That is,

$$\varphi_{ij} \equiv \frac{\partial \varphi_i}{\partial k_j} = s_i f_i'' \frac{\partial k_{xi}}{\partial q_i} \frac{\partial q_i}{\partial p} \frac{\partial p}{\partial k_j} < 0, \quad i, j = 1, 2, \quad i \neq j.$$ (14-64)

Next totally differentiate $\varphi_i = 0$, and obtain $\varphi_{i1} dk_1 + \varphi_{i2} dk_2 = 0$. Or, we have

$$\left(\frac{dk_2}{dk_1}\right)_{\varphi_1 = 0} = -\frac{\varphi_{11}}{\varphi_{12}} < 0, \quad \left(\frac{dk_2}{dk_1}\right)_{\varphi_2 = 0} = -\frac{\varphi_{21}}{\varphi_{22}} < 0.$$ (14-65)

Note also

$$-\frac{\varphi_{11}}{\varphi_{12}} = -\frac{\partial p}{\partial k_1} \bigg/ \frac{\partial p}{\partial k_2} = -\frac{\varphi_{21}}{\varphi_{22}}.$$ (14-66)

In view of the negative sign of $(dk_2/dk_1)_{\varphi_i = 0}$, we can conclude that the "$(\varphi_i = 0)$-curve", that is, the locus of (k_1, k_2) combinations which satisfy $\varphi_i(k_1, k_2) = 0$, determines a negatively-sloped curve in the $[\mathrm{I}(X, Y), \mathrm{II}(X, Y)]$-section of the $(k_1 - k_2)$-plane. And also the slope of the $(\varphi_1 = 0)$-curve is equal to the slope of the $(\varphi_2 = 0)$-curve for all the relevant values of (k_1, k_2) for this case in view of (14-65) and (14-66).

CASE II I(X, Y) and II(X)

We can similarly obtain

$$\varphi_{11} < 0 \quad \text{and} \quad \varphi_{12} < 0 . \tag{14-67}$$

Also, in view of $k_{x2} = k_2$, we obtain

$$\varphi_{22} = s_2 f_2'' < 0 \quad \text{and} \quad \varphi_{21} = 0 . \tag{14-68}$$

Thus we obtain

$$\left(\frac{dk_2}{dk_1}\right)_{\varphi_1 = 0} = -\frac{\varphi_{11}}{\varphi_{12}} < 0 , \quad \left(\frac{dk_2}{dk_1}\right)_{\varphi_2 = 0} = -\frac{\varphi_{21}}{\varphi_{22}} = 0 . \tag{14-69}$$

CASE III I(X, Y) and II(Y)

For this case we have to use equation (14-61) for Country 2. Noting $k_{y2} = k_2$, we obtain

$$\varphi_{22} = \frac{s_2}{p^2} \left[g''p - g' \frac{\partial p}{\partial k_2} \right] < 0 , \tag{14-70}$$

since $\partial p / \partial k_2 > 0$ in view of (14-58b). Also we have

$$\varphi_{21} = -\frac{s_2 g_2'}{p^2} \frac{\partial p}{\partial k_1} > 0 . \tag{14-71}$$

The sign of φ_{11} can be ascertained as in Case I, that is, $\varphi_{11} < 0$. For φ_{12} we have

$$\varphi_{12} \equiv \frac{\partial \varphi_1}{\partial k_2} = 0 . \tag{14-72}$$

Hence, we obtain

$$\varphi_{11} < 0 \quad \text{and} \quad \varphi_{12} = 0 . \tag{14-73}$$

Therefore, we have

$$\left(\frac{dk_1}{dk_2}\right)_{\varphi_1 = 0} = -\frac{\varphi_{12}}{\varphi_{11}} = 0 , \quad \left(\frac{dk_2}{dk_1}\right)_{\varphi_2 = 0} = -\frac{\varphi_{21}}{\varphi_{22}} > 0 . \tag{14-74}$$

Here note that, for $\varphi_1 = 0$, (dk_1/dk_2) is used instead of (dk_2/dk_1).

CASE IV I(X) and I(Y)

In a similar manner as above we obtain

$$\varphi_{11} < 0, \quad \varphi_{12} = 0, \quad \varphi_{21} > 0, \quad \varphi_{22} < 0 . \tag{14-75}$$

Hence we have

$$\left(\frac{dk_1}{dk_2}\right)_{\varphi_1=0} = -\frac{\varphi_{12}}{\varphi_{11}} = 0, \quad \left(\frac{dk_2}{dk_1}\right)_{\varphi_2=0} = -\frac{\varphi_{21}}{\varphi_{22}} > 0. \tag{14-76}$$

Since the name of the countries is immaterial to our analysis, the above four cases exhaust all the possible combinations of the pattern of specialization of the two countries.

As we remarked in connection with Case I in the above, the signs of $(dk_2/dk_1)_{\varphi_i=0}$ or $(dk_1/dk_2)_{\varphi_i=0}$ determine the direction of the $(\varphi_i = 0)$-curve in the $(k_1 - k_2)$-plane. We may thus summarize the above considerations as follows:

1. If Country i specializes in the production of good Y, then, *regardless of* the pattern of specialization of the other country (whether the other country specializes in good X or produces both goods), the $(\varphi_i = 0)$-curve is positively sloped.

2. If Country i specializes in good X, then, regardless of the pattern of specialization of the other country, $(dk_i/dk_j)_{\varphi_1=0} = 0$. For example, if Country 1 specializes in good X, then the $(\varphi_1 = 0)$-curve is vertical in the $(k_1 - k_2)$-plane, in which the k_1-axis is taken to be the horizontal axis.

3. If Country i produces both goods (incomplete specialization), then the sign of the $\varphi_i = 0$ curve depends on the pattern of specialization of the other country. That is, if the other country produces only good X or both goods, then the $(\varphi_i = 0)$-curve is negatively sloped, and if the other country specializes in good Y, then $(dk_i/dk_j)_{\varphi_i=0} = 0$. For example, the $(\varphi_1 = 0)$-curve is vertical in the $(k_1 - k_2)$-plane, in which the k_1-axis is taken to be the horizontal axis.

The general shape of the $(\varphi_1 = 0)$-curve is illustrated in Figure 14-11. Here, three regions divided by the dotted curves respectively denote: a) I(Y) and II(X) [or II(X, Y)]; b) I(X, Y) and II(X, Y) [or II(X)]; and c) I(X) and II(Y) [or II(X, Y)]. The $(\varphi_2 = 0)$-curve can be illustrated analogously. Recall $\varphi_i = \dot{k}_i/k_i$ by definition so that the $(\varphi_i = 0)$-curve defines the locus of (k_1, k_2) in which $\dot{k}_i = 0$. Also note the $(\varphi_i = 0)$-curve divides the $(k_1 - k_2)$-plane into two regions, one region in which $\varphi_i > 0$ (so that $\dot{k}_i > 0$) and the other region in which $\varphi_i < 0$ (so that $\dot{k}_i < 0$). To determine the sign of φ_i in a particular region, we simply check the sign of φ_{ij}. For example, if $\varphi_{12} < 0$, then φ_1 is negative in region on the right of the φ_1-curve in Figure 14-11. Recall that the signs of φ_{ii} and φ_{ij} depend on the pattern of specialization. We may summarize the above consideration on this point as follows:

1. If Country i specializes in good Y, then regardless of the pattern of specialization of the other country, $\varphi_{ii} < 0$ and $\varphi_{ij} > 0$, $i \neq j$.

2. If Country i specializes in good X, then regardless of the pattern of specialization of the other country $\varphi_{ii} < 0$ and $\varphi_{ij} = 0$, $i \neq j$.

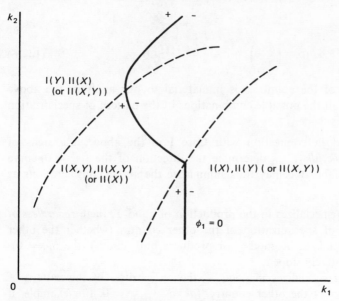

Figure 14-11   The ($\varphi_1 = 0$)-Curve

3. If Country i produces both goods, then the signs of φ_{ii} and φ_{ij} depend on the pattern of specialization of the other country. In other words, if good X is produced in the other country (that is, $j(X, Y)$ or $j(X)$, $j \neq i$), then $\varphi_{ii} < 0$ and $\varphi_{ij} < 0$, $i \neq j$; and if the other country specializes in good Y, then $\varphi_{ii} < 0$ and $\varphi_{ij} = 0$, $i \neq j$.

Hence, the signs of φ_1 depend on the patterns of specialization. In Figure 14-11, the signs of φ_1 in the six regions defined by the patterns of specialization and the ($\varphi_1 = 0$)-curve are illustrated (by $+$ and $-$). It is clear from the diagram that to the left of the ($\varphi_1 = 0$)-curve, φ_1 is always positive, and that to the right of the ($\varphi_1 = 0$)-curve, φ_1 is always negative regardless of the patterns of specialization.

Now we superimpose the ($\varphi_2 = 0$)-curve on the diagram drawn in Figure 14-11, and determine again the signs of φ_2 for each location of (k_1, k_2). Again, in the left (right) of the ($\varphi_2 = 0$)-curve, $\varphi_2 > 0$ ($\varphi_2 < 0$). We now can illustrate the dynamic paths of k_1 and k_2 (Figure 14-12). Here we recall that in the region of $\varphi_i > 0$ ($\varphi_i < 0$), we have $\dot{k}_i > 0$ ($\varphi_i < 0$) so that k_i increases (decreases) over time. The arrows in the diagram show the direction of the movements of (k_1, k_2) over time. In order to superimpose the ($\varphi_2 = 0$)-curve, we have to specify the patterns of specialization of Country 2. In Figure 14-12 we assumed the combinations of the patterns of specialization are $[I(Y), II(X)]$, $[I(X, Y), II(X, Y)]$, and $[I(X), II(Y)]$. It is important to note that regardless of the initial value of (k_1, k_2), the dynamic path of (k_1, k_2) converges to the point of intersection A, of the ($\varphi_1 = 0$)-curve and the ($\varphi_2 = 0$)-curve as time extends without limit. Note that at point A Country 1 specializes in the production of good X and Country 2 specializes in the production of good Y.

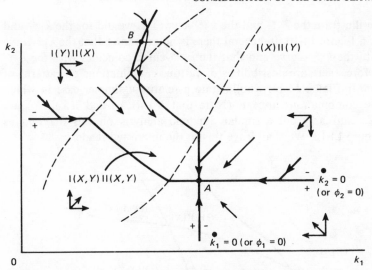

Figure 14-12   Dynamic Paths of k_1 and k_2

Note that the $(\varphi_2 = 0)$-curve can intersect with the $(\varphi_1 = 0)$-curve at a point such as point B. Then we can analogously show that regardless of the initial value of (k_1, k_2) the dynamic path of (k_1, k_2) converges to point B as time extends without limit. Under the present case it is clear from the diagram that the two curves always intersect and the intersection point is unique. Note that at point B, Country 1 specializes in the production of good Y and Country 2 specializes in the production of good X.

The intersection of the two curves, the $(\dot{k}_1 = 0)$-curve and the $(\dot{k}_2 = 0)$-curve, may be called the *dynamic equilibrium point*. It should be noted that, in view of (14-66), the dynamic equilibrium point is never in the region of incomplete specialization in which each country produces both goods, that is, $I(X, Y), II(X, Y)$, unless the knife-edge case occurs in which the two curves coincide. This contradicts Oniki-Uzawa's illustration in which the dynamic equilibrium is the point of incomplete specialization for both countries.

Finally we have to point out one basic assumption involved in the above analysis in terms of Figure 14-12. It was assumed that the patterns of international specialization are such that a) $I(Y)II(X)$, b) $I(X, Y)II(X, Y)$, and c) $I(X)II(Y)$. This is the assumption adopted by Oniki and Uzawa [7]. However, this assumption does *not* necessarily hold. Earlier in this section, we defined the k_1^*- and the k_1^{**}-curve. We can also consider the k_2^*- and k_2^{**}-curves by shifting Country 2's offer curve with Country 1's offer curve fixed. These curves define the patterns of specialization of Country 2, just as the k_1^*- and the k_1^{**}-curves define the patterns of specialization of Country 1 (illustrated in Figure 14-8). We also have the relations similar to (14-54), that is

$$k_2 \leqq k_2^*: \quad II(Y) \tag{14-77a}$$
$$k_2^* < k_2 < k_2^{**}: \quad II(X, Y) \tag{14-77b}$$
$$k_2^{**} \leqq k_2: \quad II(X) \tag{14-77c}$$

Then we can illustrate the $k_2{}^*$- and the $k_2{}^{**}$-curves as we did for the $k_1{}^*$- and $k_1{}^{**}$-curves in Figure 14-10. In general there is no guarantee that the $k_1{}^*$-curve coincides with the $k_2{}^{**}$-curve and that the $k_1{}^{**}$-curve coincides with the $k_2{}^*$-curve. Therefore, there are possibilities of various combinations of patterns of specialization. In Figure 14-13, we illustrate a relatively simpler case in which nine possible combinations appear. (Note that I(Y)II(Y) and I(X)II(X) are possible.) We can carry out a similar dynamic analysis on this diagram as we did in Figure 14-12. We shall leave this to the interested reader.

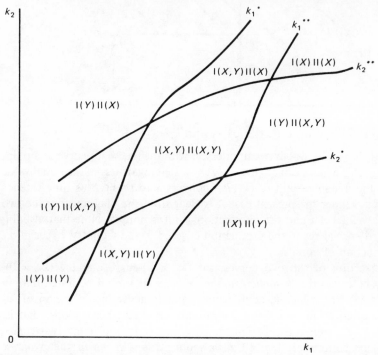

Figure 14-13   Possible Patterns of International Specialization

In Figure 14-13, we assumed that any two curves intersect with each other only once. However, there is no necessity for this to be true, and any two curves can intersect with each other more than once. In other words, even in the case of Figure 14-13, there is a certain ambiguity with regard to dynamic paths.

Now let us recall that we can obtain a specific conclusion with regard to the patterns of specialization for both countries if we assume that one country is small enough compared to the other country. Such patterns of specialization are illustrated in Figure 14-10. Based on such a diagram we can now construct the dynamic paths, as illustrated in Figure 14-14.

In Figure 14-14, the dynamic path of (k_1, k_2) converges to the intersection point, A, of the $(\dot{k}_1 = 0)$-curve and the $(\dot{k}_2 = 0)$-curve as time extends without limit, regardless of the initial value of (k_1, k_2). In Figure 14-14, point A is in the region of I(X) and II(X, Y), so that Country 1 specializes in good X. Note

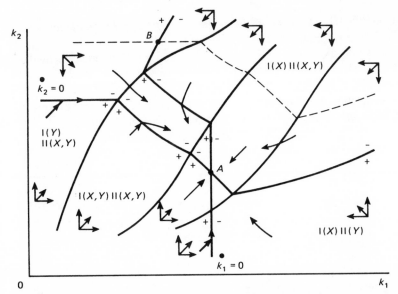

Figure 14-14   Dynamic Paths of k_1 and k_2 when Country 1 is Small

that the point of intersection of the two curves $\dot{k}_1 = 0$ and $\dot{k}_2 = 0$, the dynamic equilibrium point, can also occur in the region of I(Y) and II(X, Y) (for example, point B) or of I(X) and II(Y). It is again accidental in Figure 14-14 that such a point occurs in the region of I(X, Y) and II(X, Y). In other words, except for an accidental case, the dynamic path of (k_1, k_2) converges to a point in which Country 1 specializes in the production of one good as time extends without limit. This again contradicts Oniki-Uzawa's contention that the dynamic equilibrium point is the point in which each country produces both goods (incomplete specialization).

REFERENCES

1. Bardhan, P. K., "Equilibrium Growth in the International Economy," *Quarterly Journal of Economics*, LXXIX, August 1965.
2. ———, "On Factor Accumulation and the Pattern of International Stabilization," *Review of Economic Studies*, XXXIII, January 1966.
3. Inada, K., "International Trade, Capital Accumulation and Factor Price Equalization," *Economic Record*, 44, September 1968.
4. Ethier, W. J., *Models of International Trade and Investment*, Ph.D. dissertation, University of Rochester, January 1970.
5. Kemp, M., *The Pure Theory of International Trade and Investment* (Englewood Cliffs, N.J.: Prentice Hall, Inc.), 1969, especially Chapters 10 and 11.
6. Ohyama, M., "A Note on Endowments and Patterns of Trade," unpublished manuscript, December 1969.
7. Oniki, H. and Uzawa, H., "Patterns of Trade and Investment in a Dynamic Model of International Trade," *Review of Economic Studies*, XXXII, January 1965.

8. Södersten, B., *A Study of Economic Growth and International Trade* (Stockholm: Almqvist & Wiksell), 1964.
9. Takayama, A., "On a Two-Sector Model of Economic Growth—Comparative Statics Approach," *Review of Economic Studies*, XXX, June 1963.
10. ——, "Balanced Growth, Distributed Share and the Terms of Trade," *ICU Social Science Journal*, V, September 1964 (in Japanese).
11. ——, "Economic Growth and International Trade," *Review of Economic Studies*, XXXI, July 1964.

PART V
TRADE AND WELFARE

15

THE THEORY OF OPTIMUM TARIFFS AND INVESTMENT

INTRODUCTION: DETERMINISTIC MODEL VERSUS DECISION MODEL

The purpose of this chapter is to trace the development of the theory of optimal tariffs and investment which has led to the recent works by Kemp [19] and Jones [12]. The theory of optimal tariffs deals with the old problem which led to the famous discussion between Bickerdike [4][5] and Edgeworth [6] early in this century. In a recent article [15], Kemp pointed out a formal similarity between this question and the theory of optimal investment. Kemp, in a more recent article [19], pursued this point to a greater extent and produced a quite comprehensive (and long) argument. This invited careful scrutiny of his argument and produced rebuttals by Jones [12] and further scrutiny by Ohyama [25] and Rakowski [26].

The essential methodology in these arguments, whether or not it is made explicit in the above articles, is not difficult to understand. It is a problem of nonlinear programming. Assuming that there exists a social welfare function for a country, the problem is to choose certain policy parameters such as the rates of tariffs on the goods traded and/or the rate of tax on foreign investment so as to maximize the social welfare function subject to certain constraints. It is true that most papers on this topic have not dealt with the problem in this way, but the basic methodology underlying the discussions is, as Kemp [19] made explicit, this nonlinear programming problem.

There is one very important problem involved in the formulation of such a problem as a nonlinear programming problem. Nonlinear programming is concerned with choosing the values of a certain number of variables, called the choice variables, so as to maximize a nonlinear function subject to nonlinear constraints. The selection of these choice variables is typically listed by the first order conditions. If there are k choice variables and if there are l constraints,

then, assuming an interior solution, there are $(k + l)$ first order conditions.[1]
Suppose that the original economic system consists of n independent equations
and n endogenous variables. Then the values of these n variables are completely determined by the system. This is called a *deterministic model*. There
is no room for choice variables in such a model. But now suppose that we
want to choose k of these n variables so as to maximize (or minimize) a
certain target function. Then we have a nonlinear programming problem and
our original model has to be revised accordingly. First we have to delete k
equations from the n equations of the original model. The rest of the equations,
that is, the remaining $(n-k)$ equations, become the constraints of this nonlinear
programming problem. The solution of the nonlinear programming problem
typically consists of k equations describing optimality (with the assumption
of an interior solution) and of $(n-k)$ equations describing the constraints
(assuming that these constraints are effective at optimum). Thus we again
have n equations to determine n variables. The original deterministic model
has now been converted into a *decision model* (or an *optimization model*).
The k choice variables are also called *control variables, instrumental variables*,
or *policy variables*.

There is another important method for converting a deterministic model into
a decision model. Suppose again that the original deterministic model is composed of n equations and n endogenous variables. Suppose that there are m
exogenous variables and parameters in the system besides the n endogenous
variables. We may choose $r(\leq m)$ of the exogenous variables[2] so as to maximize
(or minimize) a certain target function. The original n equations are now
the constraints of this nonlinear programming problem. Assuming an interior
solution and that these constraints are effective at optimum, the solution of this
problem is characterized by $(n + r)$ equations denoting the first order conditions.[3] These $(n + r)$ equations completely specify the values of $(n + r)$ variables. There is still another way of converting the deterministic model into a
decision model. In this method we choose r of the exogenous variables and k
of the endogenous variables as the choice variables of the nonlinear programming problem. This is clearly a mixture of the above two ways.

The literature in economics is full of conversions of deterministic models into
decision models,[4] although they are very often implicit. In fact, many authors
are not fully aware of the fact that they are making a conversion, thus they are
apt to make mistakes.

[1] The k choice variables and l "Lagrangian multipliers" constitute $(k + l)$ variables to be
determined by the $(k + l)$ first order conditions. The l constraints provide the l of the $(k + l)$
conditions, assuming that these constraints are effective at optimum.

[2] It may so happen that some of the exogenous variables or the parameters (such as marginal
propensity to consume) cannot be chosen or determined by policy authorities.

[3] It may so happen that the number of the choice variables may exceed the number of *independent* conditions for optimum. In the subsequent analysis of optimum tariff, we shall see
that any combination of export and import tariffs will maximize a country's welfare as long
as they satisfy a certain relation.

[4] For more discussion on the topic, see Tinbergen [31], Karlin [14], Mundell [22], and Takayama
[30].

We may also note that the reverse conversion, that is, the conversion from an optimization model to a deterministic model, is also possible. We can consider for example, the classical trade model which was originally conceived of as an optimization model. Free trade with perfect competition gives a means of converting this into a deterministic model. In this chapter we shall study the process of converting a deterministic model into a decision model by choosing certain policy variables such as tariffs and taxes as instrumental variables. Let us take the problem of the optimum tariff. In the analysis of Chapter 8, the rate of tariff was considered as an exogenous variable in a model consisting of a certain number of equations (say, n) and the same number of endogenous variables. The optimal tariff problem is simply one of converting this deterministic model into a decision model by making the tariff rate a choice variable in a nonlinear programming problem, in which the social welfare function of the tariff-imposing country is maximized subject to the constraints consisting of the original n equations. In fact, it will be shown, as was remarked in Chapter 8, that the crucial choice variable here is not the import tariff rate as such, but the gap between the foreign price ratio and the domestic price ratio *or* the ratio of these two price ratios. This gap can certainly also be created by an export tariff. In fact, we can have many combinations of import and export tariffs (and subsidies) to create the desired gap (or the ratio) between the two price ratios. Our problem is simply to choose this ratio so as to maximize a certain target function.

In the next section we shall discuss this optimum tariff problem. First we shall derive a formula for the optimal tariff by way of an elegant geometrical method due to Graaf and Johnson. Then we shall provide a rigorous mathematical formulation and solution of the problem. This optimum tariff problem will serve as a good example of a conversion of a deterministic model into a decision model, and we shall give a complete account of this conversion there.

In the third section we shall discuss the problem of optimal investment. In the fourth section we shall come to the Kemp-Jones synthesis of the optimum tariff and optimum investment problems. Our explanation of the conversion process there is somewhat limited, but the reader should understand that this process of converting a deterministic model to a decision model is the crux of the Kemp-Jones argument.

THE THEORY OF OPTIMAL TARIFF

Introduction: Diagrammatical Analysis

Consider a world consisting of two countries (1 and 2). Suppose that each country produces the same two goods (X and Y). With the absence of any distortions such as domestic taxes and subsidies, free trade will bring the world to a Pareto optimal state, that is, a state in which no country can be made better off without inflicting a loss in welfare on the other country (with a given amount of resources and a given state of technology available to each country.)

But this does not imply that each country cannot increase its welfare by moving from this point. In fact, each country can increase its welfare by inflicting a loss in welfare on the other country. In Part III of this book, we often used a formula which denoted a change in each country's real income. Assuming no growth (no shift of the production transformation curve) and a neoclassical economy, Country 1's (respectively Country 2's) change in real income was represented by a formula such as $(p - q)Y_{21}$ (respectively $(q - p)Y_{21}$). In other words, if a country can improve its terms of trade, it can increase its welfare, given the volume of trade (here it is represented by Y_{21}). We also learned in Chapter 8, that the imposition of an import tariff will always improve a country's terms of trade (assuming the Marshall-Lerner stability condition). Therefore we argued that the imposition of an import tariff improves the welfare of the tariff-imposing country (with a sacrifice in the other country's welfare). Suppose that there is no opposition from the other country. The first question is whether or not the tariff-imposing country can continue to improve its welfare by continuing to increase the rate of import tariff. The answer is clearly no, for the volume of trade will in general decrease as the tariff rate increases, and the gains from trade and the welfare position of the country depend on the volume of trade as well as the terms of trade. In fact, if the tariff rate is too high and the tariff becomes completely protective, no trade will occur, which is clearly a position worse than the free trade position. In the above formula, the volume of the initial import of Country 1 (Y_{21}) is a function of the tariff rate.

Now suppose that the volume of trade is a decreasing function with respect to the tariff rate. Since the terms of trade is an increasing function with respect to the tariff rate as noted above (see equation (8-74) of Chapter 8), this seems to suggest that the gains from trade and the welfare position of the tariff-imposing country will improve monotonically up to a certain point (the first phase), then aggravate monotonically as the tariff rate increases (the second phase). The first phase reflects the situation where the increase in real income due to the improvement in the terms of trade exceeds the decrease in real income due to the decrease in the volume of trade. The second phase corresponds to the situation where the latter exceeds the former.

This implies that there is an optimal rate of tariff which maximizes the real income or welfare of the tariff-imposing country, that is, the tariff rate which lies on the border of the first phase and the second phase. This is the famous argument known as the optimum tariff argument. As remarked before, this argument was originally due to the discussion between Bickerdike [4] [5] and Edgeworth [6]. This argument was revived by Kaldor [13] in 1940, and became well-known (see for example, Graaff [7], Johnson [10]).[5]

---

[5] See also: Amano [1]; Bhagwati and Ramaswami [3]; A. P. Lerner, *The Economics of Control*, New York: Macmillan, 1944, pp. 382–5; I. M. D. Little, "Welfare and Tariffs," *Review of Economic Studies*, XVI, 1948–49; G. D. A. MacDougall, "The Use of Home Resources to Save Imports: A Comment," *Economic Journal*, LX, September 1950; R. F. Kahn, "Tariffs and the Terms of Trade," *Review of Economic Studies*, XV, 1947–48; J. J. Polak, "The Optimum Tariffs and the Cost of Exports," *Review of Economic Studies*, XIX, 1950–51.

The basic argument of the optimal tariff theory can be illustrated by the following offer curve diagram. In Figure 15-1 the I-curve and the II-curve denote the offer curves of Country 1 and of Country 2 respectively when there are no tariffs or domestic distortions. The dotted curves represent the trade indifference curve as it was conceived by Meade (Chapter 1, second section). As Country 1

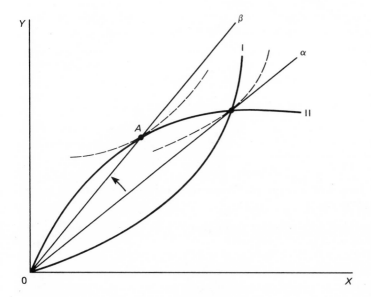

Figure 15-1   The Optimum Tariff Argument

increases the rate of tariff on its import, Country 1's tariff-ridden offer curve will shift, causing a leftward rotation of the terms of trade ray. Clearly Country 1 is in the best position when the terms of trade moves to the β-line in the diagram. The β-line is the ray from the origin, passing through point A, the point at which Country 1's trade indifference curve is tangent to Country 2's offer curve.

The formula for the optimum tariff can easily be obtained from the offer curve diagram. The following argument is due to Johnson [10].[6] In Figure 15-2 the II-curve represents Country 2's offer curve and point A is the point at which the trade indifference curve of Country 1 (the a-curve) is tangent to Country 2's offer curve (the II-curve). The CA-line is tangent to both the a-curve and the II-curve. The $0A$-line corresponds to the β-line of Figure 15-1.

The slope of the $0A$-line measures the exchange ratio of the two goods in the world market (the terms of trade) after the tariff. The slope of the CA-line measures the domestic exchange ratio of the two goods for the producers and the consumers of Country 1 after the tariff. Let P_i and Q_i respectively be the (domestic) price of X and Y in Country i $(i = 1, 2)$. Let $T(\%)$ be the *ad valorem*

---

[6] There he credits the idea to Graaff. See Johnson [10], p. 29, fn 2.

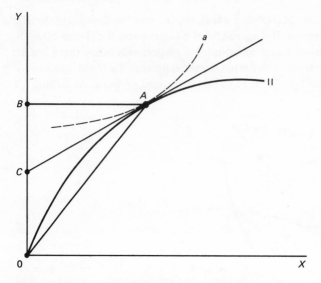

Figure 15-2 The Derivation of Optimum Tariff Formula (Graaff-Johnson)

rate of tariff on Country 1's import at point A of Figure 15-2. Then we have[7]

$$\frac{P_1}{Q_1} = \frac{P_2}{Q_2(1 + T)}. \tag{15-1}$$

Or,

$$1 + T = \frac{P_2}{Q_2} \bigg/ \frac{P_1}{Q_1}. \tag{15-1'}$$

But as remarked above, P_2/Q_2 is represented by the slope of the $0A$-line and P_1/Q_1 is represented by the slope of the CA-line. Hence equation (15-1') can be rewritten as

$$1 + T = \left(\frac{0B}{AB}\right) \bigg/ \left(\frac{BC}{AB}\right). \tag{15-2}$$

Or,

$$1 + T = \frac{0B}{BC}. \tag{15-2'}$$

Let η_f be the elasticity of Country 2's offer curve (at point A). Then, as is well-known (see Chapter 1, second section), η_f can be expressed as

$$\eta_f = \frac{0B}{0C}. \tag{15-3}$$

[7] Note that the exchange rate does not play any role in this argument. If E is the price of Country 2's currency in terms of Country 1's currency, then $P_1 = EP_2$ and $Q_1 = EQ_2(1 + T)$. From this we obtain equation (15-1).

Since $BC = 0B - 0C$, the comparison of (15-2') and (15-3) easily yields

$$T = \frac{1}{\eta_f - 1} . \tag{15-4}$$

This is the well-known formula for the optimal tariff.

The Mathematical Formulation: Deterministic Model versus Decision Model

The above argument is clearly very clever and elegant. However, many things are implicit in the diagram. For example, some of them are hidden because the trade indifference curves and the offer curve are drawn in the usual way as above. Moreover, from the above argument, we cannot easily see the unifying methodology of the above problem and related problems, that is, nonlinear programming and the problem of converting a deterministic model into a decision model. This is somewhat hidden in the tangency between the a-curve and the II-curve. Hence, we shall now turn to a mathematical derivation of the above formula. Since we shall provide a full account of the conversion involved, our exposition will be somewhat lengthy.

Let E_{xi} and E_{yi} be the excess demand (or supply) of Good X and Good Y respectively in Country i ($i = 1, 2$). E_{xi} denotes excess demand if $E_{xi} > 0$ and excess supply if $E_{xi} < 0$. Then $(X_i + E_{xi})$ and $(Y_i + E_{yi})$ denote the total consumption of Good X and Good Y respectively in Country i. In this notation we do not have to presuppose that Country 1 exports Good X and imports Good Y (so that $E_{x1} < 0$ and $E_{y1} > 0$). But in order to make it explicit we assume that Country 1 exports X and imports Y.

Since no tariffs are imposed by Country 2, we can write Country 2's offer curve (in the usual manner) as

$$E_{x2} = E_{x2}(\Pi_2), \quad \text{where } \Pi_2 \equiv P_2/Q_2 , \tag{15-5}$$

and it is assumed that Country 2's economy is organized in a competitive way. The elasticity of Country 2's offer curve is defined (in the usual manner) by

$$\eta_f \equiv \frac{-dE_{x2}}{d(P_2/Q_2)} \frac{(P_2/Q_2)}{E_{x2}} . \tag{15-6}$$

As remarked before, η_f is usually positive.

We *cannot* write Country 1's offer curve simply as $E_{y1} = E_{y1}(P_1/Q_1)$. This is due to the fact that Country 1 levies a tariff and there are proceeds from the tariff. In order to determine Country 1's offer curve, we first must specify Country 1's budget condition. Let E be the exchange rate, that is, the price of Country 2's currency in terms of Country 1's currency. Since Country 1's volume of imports is E_{y1}, (if it is realized), Country 1's government receives tariff revenue in the amount $(Q_1 E_{y1} - E Q_2 E_{y1})$. Since $Q_1 = E Q_2(1 + T)$, Country 1's tariff revenue is equal to $E Q_2 T E_{y1} = Q_1 T E_{y1}/(1 + T)$. Hence Country 1's budget condition can be written as

$$\Pi_1 E_{x1} + E_{y1} = \tau E_{y1} , \tag{15-7}$$

where $\Pi_1 \equiv P_1/Q_1$ and $\tau \equiv T/(1 + T)$. The relation between Π_1 and Π_2 is specified by (15-1), that is, $\Pi_1 = \Pi_2/(1 + T)$. Write the production transformation curve of Country 1 as

$$Y_1 = \varphi(X_1). \tag{15-8}$$

We may prescribe the ordinary neoclassical assumption that the production transformation curve is negatively sloped and strictly concave to the origin. That is,

$$\varphi' < 0 \quad \text{and} \quad \varphi'' < 0. \tag{15-9}$$

If we assume that Country 1's production is organized in a competitive way, we have

$$\varphi' = -\Pi_1. \tag{15-10}$$

Let C_{x1} and C_{y1} be Country 1's consumption of X and Y respectively, and assume that Country 1's preference, under the usual aggregation assumption, is represented by the social welfare function U,

$$U = U(C_{x1}, C_{y1}). \tag{15-11}$$

We assume that U is concave and monotone increasing with respect to each of its arguments. Since $C_{x1} = X_1 + E_{x1}$ and $C_{y1} = Y_1 + E_{y1}$, we may write as

$$U = U(X_1 + E_{x1}, Y_1 + E_{y1}). \tag{15-11'}$$

If we assume that consumption in Country 1 is organized in a competitive way we have

$$v(C_x, C_y) = \Pi_1, \tag{15-12}$$

where

$$v(C_x, C_y) \equiv U_x/U_y, \quad \text{and} \quad U_x \equiv \partial U/\partial C_{x1}, \ U_y \equiv \partial U/\partial C_{y1}. \tag{15-13}$$

Therefore, if Country 1's economy is organized in a competitive way, we can derive Country 1's offer curve from (15-7), (15-10) and (15-12) with $E_{x1} = C_{x1} - X_1$ and $E_{y1} = C_{y1} - Y_1$, assuming that the tariff revenue is given to the public. That is, we can obtain E_{y1} as a function of Π_1 and T (or τ), or

$$E_{y1} = E_{y1}(\Pi_1, T). \tag{15-14}$$

Once Π_1 is given, the amount of production for each good X_1 and Y_1 is determined by (15-7). In other words, $X_1 = X_1(\Pi_1)$ and $Y_1 = Y_1(\Pi_1)$. Noting that $v = v(X_1 + E_{x1}, Y_1 + E_{y1})$, (15-12) together with (15-7) determines the values of E_{x1} and E_{y1} for a given value of T, once X_1 and Y_1 are determined. Thus we obtain (15-14).

The equilibrium relation for each good is described by

$$E_{x1} + E_{x2} = 0, \tag{15-15}$$

$$E_{y1} + E_{y2} = 0. \tag{15-16}$$

Note that the budget condition for Country 2 can be written as

$$\Pi_2 E_{x2} + E_{y2} = 0 . \tag{15-17}$$

Also, in view of the budget conditions (15-7) and (15-17), one of the equilibrium relations (15-15) and (15-16) is redundant. That is, if (15-15) holds then (15-16) holds automatically, and vice versa. Define B_1 by

$$B_1 \equiv P_2 E_{x2} - Q_2 E_{y1} . \tag{15-18}$$

Using the budget conditions (15-7) and (15-17) together with (15-1), we obtain

$$B_1/Q_2 = \Pi_2(E_{x1} + E_{x2}) = -(E_{y1} + E_{y2}) , \tag{15-19}$$

So that the balance of payments equilibrium, $B_1 = 0$, signifies equilibrium in the goods markets, (15-15) and (15-16). This is exactly the same situation that we described in the second section of Chapter 8. Using (15-5) and (15-14), we can express the condition that $B_1 = 0$, by

$$\Pi_2 E_{x2}(\Pi_2) - E_{y1}(\Pi_1, T) = 0 . \tag{15-20}$$

This together with $\Pi_2 = (1 + T)\Pi_1$ [that is, (15-1)] determines the equilibrium values of Π_1 and Π_2 (hence the equilibrium values of $E_{x1}, E_{y1}, E_{x2}, E_{y2}$, and so on) for a given value of T. In other words, (15-20) is the basic relation in the deterministic model.

Let us now turn to the optimum tariff problem. In this problem the value of T is no longer given to the system. Instead the value of T is chosen by Country 1's authority in such a way as to maximize $U = U(C_{x1}, C_{y1})$. T is the control variable of the problem. In order to consider the constraints of this problem, first note that the equilibrium relations (15-15) and (15-16) are now reinterpreted as the feasibility conditions in the sense that the world cannot consume more of each good than is available and that none of the goods should be left for disposal. The budget conditions (15-7) and (15-17) should hold as they are. As remarked in the above, if the budget conditions hold, the feasibility constraints (15-15) and (15-16) are summarized in one equation,

$$\Pi_2 E_{x2} - E_{y1} = 0 , \tag{15-21}$$

where the functional relations of E_{x2} and E_{y1} are not specified. We then assume that Country 2's economy is organized in a competitive fashion so that the functional relation (15-5) holds. We also assume that Country 1's production takes place on her production transformation curve, that is, relation (15-8) holds. Then in view of (15-5), (15-8), and (15-21), we can rewrite our maximand function U [described in (15-11′)] as [8]

$$U = U[X_1 - E_{x2}(\Pi_2), \ \varphi(X_1) + \Pi_2 E_{x2}(\Pi_2)] . \tag{15-22}$$

---

[8] If we presuppose a competitive organization of Country 1's economy so that (15-10) holds, then we can write $X_1 = X_1(\Pi_1) = X_1[\Pi_2/(1 + T)]$. Hence, the problem is reduced to that of choosing only Π_2 (instead of Π_2 and X_1) such as to maximize U in (15-22). The reader can easily check that we shall obtain exactly the same result by this alternative approach as that obtained by the approach taken in the text.

Thus U is considered as a function of X_1 and Π_2 alone. Note that we have not yet assumed that Country 1's economy is organized in a competitive way, so that none of relations (15-10), (15-12), and (15-14) are specified.

The optimum tariff problem is now restated as the problem of choosing X_1 and Π_2 such as to maximize U described in (15-22). Once the values of X_1 and Π_2 are determined, then the values of the rest of the variables may be determined by assuming that Country 1's economy is organized in a competitive fashion so that (15-10), (15-12), and (15-14) hold. In other words, X_1 together with (15-10) yields the value of Π_1, which, in view of (15-1), determines the value of the optimal tariff rate T. Hence the choice of X_1 and Π_2 implies the choice of T, if we assume that production of Country 1 is organized in a competitive way so that (15-10) holds. Assuming further that consumption in Country 1 is organized in a competitive way (so that (15-12) holds), we can determine the values of E_{x1}, E_{y1}, C_{x1}, C_{y1} and Y_1 by Π_1, T and X_1, using (15-14), (15-7), and (15-8). The value of E_{y2} is determined by E_{y1}, using (15-16) [or by $E_{x2}(\Pi_2)$ and Π_2 using (15-17)].

Note that the use of the social welfare function is not essential in maximization. Instead of maximizing $U(C_{x1}, C_{y1})$, we may consider the problem of *vector* maximizing (C_{x1}, C_{y1}). The analysis will be analogous to the subsequent one, and left to the interested reader. (For a general discussion of the vector maximum problem, see the second section of Chapter 7.)

To repeat, our problem is to choose X_1 and Π_2 such as to maximize U described in (15-22). Assuming an interior solution ($X_1 > 0$ and $\Pi_2 > 0$ in the optimal solution), the first order conditions of this maximization problem can be written as:

$$\frac{\partial U}{\partial X_1} = U_x + U_y \varphi' = 0, \quad \text{where } \varphi' \equiv d\varphi/dX_1; \quad \text{and} \tag{15-23}$$

$$\frac{\partial U}{\partial \Pi_2} = -U_x \, dE_{x2}/d\Pi_2 + U_y(E_{x2} + \Pi_2 \, dE_{x2}/d\Pi_2) = 0. \tag{15-24}$$

Rewrite (15-23) in the following equivalent form:

$$\frac{U_x}{U_y} = -\varphi'. \tag{15-25}$$

Using the definition of η_f in (15-6), we can rewrite (15-24) in the following equivalent form:

$$E_{x2}[U_x\eta_f/\Pi_2 + U_y(1 - \eta_f)] = 0. \tag{15-24'}$$

Or,

$$\frac{U_x}{U_y} = \Pi_2 \left(1 - \frac{1}{\eta_f}\right). \tag{15-26}$$

Two equations (15-25) and (15-26) completely determine the optimal values of X_1 and Π_2.

Now assume competitive organization in the production side of Country 1 so that (15-10) holds. Using (15-25), (15-10), and (15-1) in succession, we obtain

$$\frac{U_x}{U_y} = -\varphi' = \Pi_1 = \frac{1}{1 + T} \Pi_2 . \tag{15-27}$$

Hence, comparing this with (15-26), we obtain

$$\frac{1}{1 + T} = \left(1 - \frac{1}{\eta_f}\right); \quad \text{or} \quad T = \frac{1}{\eta_f - 1} . \tag{15-28}$$

This is nothing but the optimum tariff formula already obtained as (15-4). Π_1 can be obtained from this expression for T and Π_2 using (15-27).

Note that (15-27) requires the relation

$$\frac{U_x}{U_y} = \Pi_1 . \tag{15-29}$$

This relation is satisfied if the consumption in Country 1 is organized in a competitive way, which we henceforth assume. In other words, if Country 1's economy is organized in a competitive way (in both production and consumption) and if Country 1 imposes an import tariff with the rate specified by (15-28), then Country 1 can maximize her welfare.

Next we should remind ourselves that the tariff on the imported good is not the only means to create the difference between the domestic price ratio Π_1 and the foreign price ratio Π_2. It can be done, for example, by an export tariff. Let us denote $T_e(\%)$ for the rate of the tariff that Country 1 imposes on her exporting good and $T_m(\%)$ for the rate of the tariff on her imported good. Then we rewrite equation (15-1) as

$$\frac{P_1(1 + T_e)}{Q_1} = \frac{P_2}{Q_2(1 + T_m)} . \tag{15-30}$$

Since $U_x/U_y = -\varphi' = \Pi_1$ due to (15-25) and (15-10), we obtain

$$\frac{U_x}{U_y} = \Pi_2 \frac{1}{(1 + T_m)(1 + T_e)} . \tag{15-31}$$

Hence, in view of (15-26), we obtain,

$$(T_m T_e + T_m + T_e) = \frac{1}{\eta_f - 1} . \tag{15-32}$$

Any combinations of T_m and T_e which satisfy this condition are eligible for an optimum. When $T_e = 0$ (no export tariff), this formula is reduced to (15-4).

Finally we have to note a remark on the first order conditions (15-23) and (15-24) for our maximization problem. Since there are no constraints, these conditions give necessary conditions for an optimum without any qualification. But they do not necessarily give sufficient conditions, *even* if we assume that U is concave with respect to C_{x1} and C_{y1}, that φ is strictly concave [condition

(15-9)] and so on. The second order condition, which assures the sufficiency condition, can be obtained by the condition $d^2 U < 0$. We leave it to the interested reader to carry out this computation. An important thing here is that the second order condition does not necessarily hold *even* if we have the concavity of U and φ, and so on. In other words, the values of Π_2 and X_1 which satisfy the first order condition (15-23) and (15-24) may not be an optimal set of values. It is possible to have a case that the Bickerdike-Edgeworth optimum tariff formula, (15-4), may not give an optimal value of the tariff rate.

In this section we assumed that all the constraints hold with equality or that we can turn our problem into an unconstrained maximization problem. It is certainly possible to consider the problem with inequality constraints. Then, for example, constraints such as $Y_1 = \varphi(X_1)$ should be converted to $\varphi(X_1) - Y_1 \geq 0$, allowing inefficient production. We may also add the non-negativity conditions (such as $X_1 \geq 0$) explicitly. Assuming an interior solution, and so on, the conclusion thus obtained will be exactly the same as the one obtained in the above. We shall leave such a reformulation of the problem to the interested reader.

OPTIMAL FOREIGN INVESTMENT

Consider a world consisting of two countries. Suppose that each country produces only one good (say, national income) and that there is no international trade between the countries. This obviously is an unrealistic supposition but it will be helpful in focusing on the main point of the problem. Let Y_1 and Y_2 denote the output of Country 1 and Country 2, respectively. We do not suppose that production functions of the two countries are the same, even if Y_1 and Y_2 describe the same good. But we suppose capital is essential for production in both countries. Assume that the total amount of the other cooperating factors (for example, labor) available in each country is kept constant. These cooperating factors are assumed to be internationally immobile.

We may write the production function of say, Country 1, as:

$$Y_1 = F(K_1), \tag{15-33}$$

where K_1 denotes the amount of capital used for production in Country 1. Since the amount of the other cooperating factors is assumed to be constant, it is natural to suppose diminishing returns with respect to capital. That is, we assume

$$F' > 0, F'' < 0, \quad \text{where} \quad F' \equiv dF/dK_1, \quad \text{and} \quad F'' \equiv d^2F/dK_1^2. \tag{15-34}$$

Suppose that both countries use the same capital good for production, and consider a movement of capital from one country to the other. In other words, we consider an international direct investment. Given a point of time, there is no reason to believe that the marginal product of capital (return to capital) is the same between the countries. Thus, capital moves from one country to the other, being attracted by a higher return.

Country 1's income consists of its output and the return on its investment in Country 2. Let $I > 0$ be the amount of investment by Country 1 in Country 2. Then the total income of Country 1, Z_1, can be written as

$$Z_1 = Y_1 + r_2 I, \tag{15-35}$$

where r_2 is the rate of return on capital in Country 2, in terms of the output of Country 1.

Let $\bar{K}_1$ be the total amount of capital which exists in Country 1 before investment in Country 2. After the investment, the amount of capital which can be put into the production in Country 1 is $\bar{K}_1 - I$. Hence, in view of (15-33) we have

$$Z_1 = F(\bar{K}_1 - I) + r_2 I. \tag{15-36}$$

Suppose Country 1 wants to choose I so as to maximize its total income Z_1. Then the first order condition can simply be written as

$$\frac{dZ_1}{dI} = -F' + r_2 + \frac{dr_2}{dI} I = 0. \tag{15-37}$$

Note that in (15-36) and (15-37) we are tacitly assuming either that there is no change in the relative price of the two countries' products[9] or that both countries produce the same two goods.

The second order condition for the above maximization problem is written as:

$$\frac{d^2 Z_1}{dI^2} = F'' + 2\frac{dr_2}{dI} + \frac{d^2 r_2}{dI^2} I < 0. \tag{15-38}$$

This condition may not be satisfied, for we cannot, in general, specify the sign of $d^2 r_2/dI^2$. Here we simply assume this condition (15-38). Since F' is the marginal physical product of capital (the rate of return on capital) in Country 1, we may write it as r_1. Thus (15-37) yields

$$r_1 = r_2 + I\frac{dr_2}{dI}. \tag{15-39}$$

Since the diminishing returns with respect to capital would also prevail in Country 2, we have

$$\frac{dr_2}{dI} < 0,$$

so that

$$r_1 < r_2. \tag{15-40}$$

---

[9] r_2 must be measured in terms of Country 1's product to make (15-36) meaningful. This assumption of a constant relative price is necessary in order to carry out the differentiation as it is done in equation (15-37). This implicit assumption of a constant relative price, although it is a strange one, seems to be more acceptable for the model in which there is no international trade.

Under a competitive situation, the foreign investment occurs up to the point in which $r_1 = r_2$. Hence, the above relation (15-40) reveals that this competitive determination of the amount of foreign investment is too much from Country 1's viewpoint.[10]

In order to achieve its optimum, Country 1 may impose a tax on its foreign investment. Let $T\%$ be the rate of such a tax. In other words, if r_2 is the return per unit of foreign investment, $(1 - T)r_2$ becomes the income for Country 1's investors. A competitive situation will result in

$$r_1 = (1 - T)r_2 . \tag{15-41}$$

Combining this with (15-39), we obtain a formula for an optimum tax on the foreign investment. First, define the following elasticity of foreign return on capital:

$$\rho_f \equiv - \frac{dr_2}{dI} \frac{I}{r_2} . \tag{15-42}$$

Since $dr_2/dI < 0$, due to diminishing returns, we have $\rho_f > 0$. In view of (15-42), (15-39) can be rewritten as

$$r_1 = r_2(1 - \rho_f) . \tag{15-43}$$

Combining (15-43) with (15-41), we obtain

$$1 - T = 1 - \rho_f , \quad \text{or} \quad T = \rho_f . \tag{15-44}$$

This gives the tax rate which maximizes Country 1's income.

This is the essence of the theory of optimum foreign investment.[11] Immediately we realize a similarity between the above argument and the optimum tariff argument. In the optimum tariff argument, we argued that free trade, that is, trade in a competitive manner, will bring the volume of international trade to more than the optimum level for a country, and that a country can increase its welfare by restricting trade using import tariffs. Similarly, here we argued that foreign investment in a competitive manner will bring the volume of investment to more than the optimum level, and that a country can increase its income (hence, its welfare) by restricting investment using taxes. This consideration suggests that we may consider these topics in a unified way. This is

[10] For the sake of illustration, assume that both countries produce the same commodity, and let $G(\overline{K}_2 + I)$ describe Country 2's production function. Let I^* denote the optimal amount of foreign investment. Then, using (15-39), we can describe I^* by $F'(\overline{K}_1 - I^*) = G'(\overline{K}_2 + I^*) + G''(\overline{K}_2 + I^*)I^*$. Let I^0 denote the amount of foreign investment under the competitive situation. Then $F'(\overline{K}_1 - I^0) = G'(\overline{K}_2 + I^0)$. Since $G'' < 0$ everywhere, we have $\overline{K}_1 - I^* > \overline{K}_1 - I^0$ (or, equivalently, $\overline{K}_2 + I^* < \overline{K}_2 + I^0$), so that $I^* < I^0$.

[11] Clearly, one can think of a different variety of related problems. For example, one can suppose that foreign investment does not occur in a competitive manner, but rather it is handled by a monopoly. In other words, suppose that capital in Country 1 is owned by a monopoly. Will it also cause an excess investment? The answer to this question can be handled by considering the maximization of return on capital, i.e., maximization of $[r_1(\overline{K}_1 - I) + r_2 I]$. As can be shown easily, this case also results in foreign investment above the level desirable for the country (see Amano [1], p. 111). Note, however, that the admittance of a monopoly into the model creates a host of difficult economic problems; we shall not discuss this any further.

probably the motive which underlies Kemp [19]. In the next section we shall turn to this topic.

Before we go to the next section, we may summarize some apparent weaknesses in the above argument.

1. We assume that there is no international trade between the countries, but we also suppose that the return on the foreign investment will be brought back to the home country. This obviously means a balance of payments surplus to an investing country and a deficit to the country that receives the investment. There is no mechanism in the model which will eliminate this deficit. Presumably such a deficit will not continue forever.

2. One way to solve this problem is to introduce international trade explicitly into the model. Suppose then that each country produces the same two goods and that they trade with each other. In other words, consider a model such as we saw in the neoclassical trade model. Then the above deficit (or surplus) in the balance of payments will be eliminated through fluctuations in the terms of trade. As we argued in our treatment of transfer payments in Chapter 8, such a transfer (return on foreign investment) tends to improve the terms of trade of a recipient country (here Country 1). In other words, the relative price of Country 1's exporting good vis-à-vis her imported good will go up. This, assuming the Marshall-Lerner stability condition, will increase its imports and decrease its exports so that an equilibrium in the balance of payments ($=$ an equilibrium in the goods markets) will be achieved.

3. However if we introduce such an adjustment through fluctuations of terms of trade, we also have to consider a change in real income due to a change in the terms of trade. In Chapter 8, we consider this as a change in real income due to a change in the relative price, and in the devaluation analysis of Chapter 10 we called it the terms of trade effect. Then our procedure of simply maximizing Country 1's income Z_1 is no longer sufficient. We should incorporate this change in real income due to a change in the terms of trade explicitly into the model. As we remarked before, the terms of trade will, in general, move in favor of the investing country. This discussion is due to Jasay [9]. We may note that there is a further discussion by Murphy [23] who argues that the terms of trade effect may be negative. But we shall not proceed to such a debate for it requires the construction of a model which is much more detailed than the above model. Murphy's discussion is not due to such a model construction.

4. There is another very strange feature in the model. That is that both countries use the same capital good. The question is where the capital good comes from. Since each country produces only one good, we may say that this good is also used as a capital good. Then we may ask further whether this implies that both countries produce the same good and save

a part of their output for capital, or that the outputs of the two countries are really different so that only one country's output is eligible as a capital good (since there is only one capital good in the model).

5. In any case, once we introduce an explicit question such as where the capital good comes from, it may be natural to consider capital accumulation, for there is no guarantee that each country remains in a stationary state both before and after a movement of the capital good between the countries. Such an explicit treatment of capital accumulation (hence growth) is attempted by Negishi [24]. But there he imposed very restrictive assumptions such as no international trade and the von Neumann type of balanced growth.

6. Another way to solve this problem is to suppose that each country can produce both a capital good and a consumption good and to consider a dynamic model as in Chapter 14. Then we consider the problem of maximizing one country's welfare (such as the discounted sum of her consumption stream). There is an attempt by Ryder in this direction [28]. However, there he somehow arbitrarily assumes that the Marshallian offer curve is growing exponentially (p. 90). This enables him to consider the problem without specifying the organization of the economy or the mechanism for economic growth of the other country. Hence the treatment is simplified enough so that he can handle the problem.

7. Before we are led to such complicated considerations, we may consider again what is the real significance of the above optimal investment argument as conceived by Kemp, and others. Instead of departing and discarding such an analysis as "unrealistic" or "dishonest," suppose we consider it as a problem of allocating the capital good between the two regions. We consider it purely as a welfare question so that we do not have to worry about such questions as where the capital comes from or how the balance of payments is brought into equilibrium. Then we do not have to worry too much about how such a welfare question works in a real economy. In any case it is important to realize that the crux of the problem is the optimal allocation of the capital good between the countries, and the optimality is purely from one country's viewpoint, as was the case in the optimum tariff argument.

OPTIMAL TARIFF AND OPTIMAL INVESTMENT

We now come to the stage of synthesizing the analyses of the previous two sections. We consider a trading world consisting of two countries (1 and 2). We suppose that Country 2 produces two goods X and Y (incomplete specialization).[12] Major notation for this section is as follows:

[12] As it will be clear, we shall solve a maximization problem. It suffices to assume Country 2's incomplete specialization at the solution point of the forthcoming maximization problem. For discussions of different patterns of specialization in the two countries, see Jones [12] and Ohyama [25]. Incidentally, Jones argues that it is "accidental" to have the case in which both countries incompletely specialize at the optimal position ([12], pp. 31–35). This is a still debatable point. See Inada and Kemp [8], for example.

X_i: output of X in Country i ($i = 1, 2$),

Y_i: output of Y in Country i ($i = 1, 2$),

E_{xi}:   excess demand for (or supply of) X in Country i ($i = 1, 2$),

E_{yi}:   excess demand for (or supply of) Y in Country i ($i = 1, 2$),

C_{xi}:   home consumption of X in Country i ($i = 1, 2$),

C_{yi}:   home consumption of Y in Country i ($i = 1, 2$),

P_i: price of X in Country i ($i = 1, 2$),

Q_i: price of Y in Country i ($i = 1, 2$).

E_{xi} denotes excess demand for (supply of) X in Country i if $E_{xi} > 0$ ($E_{xi} < 0$). Similarly for E_{yi}. Note that $E_{xi} > 0$ ($E_{xi} < 0$) means that X is the import (export) of Country i. Similarly for E_{yi}. Note that $C_{xi} \equiv X_i + E_{xi}$ and $C_{yi} \equiv Y_i + E_{yi}$. As remarked in the second section, we, in equilibrium, have

$$E_{x1} = -E_{x2} \quad \text{and} \quad E_{y1} = -E_{y2}. \tag{15-45}$$

We denote Π_i for P_i/Q_i ($i = 1, 2$).

Denote $\tilde{r}_i$ for the real return to capital in terms of good Y in Country i. In other words, if r_i denotes the money return on capital in Country i (in terms of Country i's currency), $\tilde{r}_i \equiv r_i/Q_i$. Then the balance of payment equilibrium relation (in terms of Country 2's currency) can be written as

$$\Pi_2 E_{x2} + \tilde{r}_2 I = E_{y1}, \tag{15-46}$$

where I signifies the international investment. $I > 0$ denotes that Country 1 is a net investor and $I < 0$ denotes that Country 2 is a net investor. In this notation, we do not *a priori* specify the signs of E_{xi} and I. We assume that Country 2 imposes no tariffs and no domestic taxes (and subsidies) so that we have

$$E_{x2} = E_{x2}(\Pi_2, I). \tag{15-47}$$

Note that I means a change in the capital stock in Country 2 ($I > 0$ means its increase and $I < 0$ means its decrease) so that it affects the production of X (hence E_{x2}) in Country 2.

We suppose that the production transformation curve of Country 1 is characterized by

$$Y_1 = \varphi(X_1, I). \tag{15-48}$$

Here I affects Y_1 because it shifts the production transformation curve. We may suppose

$$\frac{\partial \varphi}{\partial X_1} < 0, \quad \frac{\partial^2 \varphi}{\partial X_1^2} < 0, \quad \text{and} \quad \frac{\partial \varphi}{\partial I} < 0. \tag{15-49}$$

Next we have to specify what determines the real return to capital. Assuming a competitive factor market with the marginal productivity theory, $\tilde{r}_i$ must be equal to the marginal physical product of capital in Country i's Y industry. Let us now suppose that in each country each good is produced by means of two factors (say, capital and labor) with a constant returns to scale production function. Now recall the lemmas in Chapter 2, assuming that both goods are produced in Country 2. Due to the corollary of lemma 4, the real return to capital is a function of the relative factor price only. (Real return to capital is constant if and only if the relative factor price is constant.) But lemma 2 says that the relative price factor is constant if and only if the relative good price is constant. Or, the relative factor price is a function of the relative good price. Hence, the real return to capital is a function of the relative good price only.[13] Note that the amount of factor endowment is irrelevant in the above chain of logic. Thus we have, for Country 2,

$$\tilde{r}_2 = \tilde{r}_2(\Pi_2) .$$ (15-50)

Note that $\tilde{r}_2$ does not depend on I. Due to lemma 3 of Chapter 2, $\tilde{r}_2$ is a decreasing function of wage:rent ratio (of Country 2). Assuming that X is more (less) capital intensive than Y in Country 2, the wage:rent ratio in Country 2 is a decreasing (increasing) function of Π_2 due to lemma 2 of Chapter 2. Combining these, the real return to capital is an increasing (decreasing) function of Π_2 if X is more (less) capital intensive than Y in Country 2. In other words,

$$\frac{d\tilde{r}_2}{d\Pi_2} > 0 , \quad \text{if } X \text{ is more capital intensive than } Y \text{ in Country 2,}$$ (15-51a)

$$\frac{d\tilde{r}_2}{d\Pi_2} < 0 , \quad \text{if } X \text{ is less capital intensive than } Y \text{ in Country 2.}$$ (15-51b)

Now assume that Country 1 has a social welfare function $U = U(C_{x1}, C_{y1})$. In other words,

$$U = U(X_1 + E_{x1}, Y_1 + E_{y1}) .$$ (15-52)

In view of (15-45), (15-46), (15-47), (15-48), and (15-50), this can be rewritten as

$$U = U[X_1 - E_{x2}(\Pi_2, I), \varphi(X_1, I) + \Pi_2 E_{x2}(\Pi_2, I) + \tilde{r}_2(\Pi_2)I] .$$ (15-53)

Our problem is now stated as follows.

Choose X_1, Π_2, and I so as to maximize U. Assuming an interior solution and writing $U_x \equiv \partial U/\partial C_{x1}$ and $U_y \equiv \partial U/\partial C_{y1}$ evaluated at an optimal point,[14]

---

[13] For this point, Kemp writes, "With constant-returns technology, a given price ratio, and incomplete specialization, changes in the factor endowment give rise to changes in outputs but not to changes in factor proportions and (therefore) not to changes in marginal products" ([19], p. 793, fn.).

[14] We omit the symbols such as (*) to denote the optimal value (for example, X_1 instead of X_1^*), for the sake of simplicity. The second order condition for the optimum can be obtained by actually computing $d^2U < 0$. Note that even with strict concavity of U, this condition does not necessarily hold. We, however, assume that this second order condition will hold for the values of $\{X_1, \Pi_2, I\}$ which satisfy the first order conditions (15-54), (15-55), and (15-56). Note also that instead of maximizing the social welfare function U, we may consider the problem of *vector*-maximizing $[C_{x1}, C_{y1}]$. The analysis will be analogous to the subsequent one and omitted from our discussion.

the three first order conditions can be written as follows:

$$\frac{\partial U}{\partial X_1} = U_x + U_y \frac{\partial \varphi}{\partial X_1} = 0,$$ (15-54)

$$\frac{\partial U}{\partial \Pi_2} = -U_x \frac{\partial E_{x2}}{\partial \Pi_2} + U_y \left(E_{x2} + \Pi_2 \frac{\partial E_{x2}}{\partial \Pi_2} + I \frac{d\tilde{r}_2}{d\Pi_2} \right) = 0,$$ (15-55)

$$\frac{\partial U}{\partial I} = -U_x \frac{\partial E_{x2}}{\partial I} + U_y \left(\frac{\partial \varphi}{\partial I} + \Pi_2 \frac{\partial E_{x2}}{\partial I} + \tilde{r}_2 \right) = 0.$$ (15-56)

These three equations determine an optimal value of $\{X_1, \Pi_2, I\}$.

Equation (15-54) is rewritten as

$$\frac{U_x}{U_y} = -\frac{\partial \varphi}{\partial X_1}.$$ (15-57)

In order to obtain a simplified expression for (15-55), we obtain the following elasticity of the foreign excess demand for X.[15]

$$\eta_f \equiv -\frac{\partial E_{x2}}{\partial \Pi_2} \frac{\Pi_2}{E_{x2}}.$$ (15-58)

Here the partial derivative is evaluated at an optimal point. Next we note the following reciprocity relation which was originally due to Samuelson [29].

$$\frac{\partial X_2}{\partial I} = \frac{d\tilde{r}_2}{d\Pi_2}.$$ (15-59)

Recall that we gave our proof of this relation in the third section of Chapter 2 [equation (2-76)].

Using (15-58) and (15-59), we are able to simplify (15-55) as

$$\frac{U_x}{U_y} = -\frac{\Pi_2}{\eta_f} \left(1 - \eta_f + \frac{\partial X_2}{\partial I} \frac{I}{E_{x2}} \right).$$ (15-60)

This can be further simplified by defining the following elasticity, called the *foreign elasticity of the production of X with respect to the borrowed capital:*

$$\varepsilon_f \equiv \frac{\partial X_2}{\partial I} \frac{I}{E_{x2}}.$$ (15-61)

Using (15-61), (15-60) is now simplified as

$$\frac{U_x}{U_y} = -\frac{\Pi_2}{\eta_f} (1 - \eta_f + \varepsilon_f).$$ (15-62)

In order to simplify (15-56), we first note that $\partial \varphi / \partial I$ is nothing but a marginal product of capital in the Y industry of Country 1. Under a competitive situation

[15] If $E_{x2} > 0$, Good X is the import of Country 2 and η_f denotes the elasticity of Country 2's offer curve. Then, as we noted before, η_f is usually positive.

with the marginal productivity theory, this is equal to $\tilde{r}_1 \equiv r_1/Q_1$. In other words, we have[16]

$$\frac{\partial \varphi}{\partial I} = -\tilde{r}_1 . \tag{15-63}$$

Next we note the following relation:

$$\frac{\partial E_{x2}}{\partial I} = -\frac{\partial X_2}{\partial I} . \tag{15-64}$$

For this relation (15-64), Kemp states that,[17] "Given Π_2, a change in I has no effect on foreign demand. Changes in I, therefore, affect $E_{x2}(\equiv C_{x2} - X_2)$ solely through X_2. $\partial E_{x2}/\partial I = -\partial X_2/\partial I$" ([19], pp. 793 fn. 10). A more rigorous mathematical proof for (15-64) is provided by Jones [12]. Using (15-63) and (15-64), condition (15-56) is now simplified as

$$\frac{U_x}{U_y} = \left(\Pi_2 \frac{\partial X_2}{\partial I} + \tilde{r}_1 - \tilde{r}_2\right)\Big/\frac{\partial X_2}{\partial I} . \tag{15-65}$$

Now define μ as follows:

$$\mu \equiv \frac{r_2 I}{P_2 E_{x2}} \left(= \frac{\tilde{r}_2 I}{\Pi_2 E_{x2}}\right) . \tag{15-66}$$

μ denotes the ratio of the earning on capital invested abroad to the value of exports. Using (15-61) and (15-66), we further rewrite (15-65) as

$$\frac{U_x}{U_y} = \Pi_2[(\varepsilon_f - \mu)\tilde{r}_2 + \mu\tilde{r}_1]/(\tilde{r}_2\varepsilon_f) . \tag{15-67}$$

Conditions (15-57), (15-62), and (15-67) are equivalent to conditions (15-54), (15-55), and (15-56) and give a set of necessary conditions for $\{X_1, \Pi_2, I\}$ to be optimum. As we did in our optimum tariff argument in the second section, we now consider how to achieve this by a combination of the organization of an economic system by a competitive mechanism *and* a choice of import (export) tariffs and investment taxes. A competitive organization of Country 1's economy provides

$$\frac{U_x}{U_y} = \Pi_1 = \frac{-\partial \varphi}{\partial X_1} . \tag{15-68}$$

In other words, the marginal rate of consumers' substitution between the two goods is equal to the price ratio, which in turn is equal to the marginal rate of producers' transformation between the two goods. Then due to this equation (15-68), condition (15-57) is achieved. We now show that condition (15-62) can be achieved by the imposition of an import tariff. Let us suppose that

[16] Recall that $I > 0$ means a reduction of the stock of capital in Country 1, hence we have to put the minus sign in front of $\tilde{r}_1$.
[17] The symbols in the quotation are ours, not Kemp's.

$E_{y1} > 0$ so that good Y is the imported good for Country 1. Let T_m denote the rate of the import tariff Country 1 imposes. Then we have

$$\frac{P_1}{Q_1} = \frac{P_2}{(1 + T_m)Q_2}, \quad \text{or} \quad \Pi_1 = \frac{\Pi_2}{1 + T_m}. \tag{15-69}$$

Then using (15-68) and (15-69), we obtain the following equation from (15-62):

$$T_m = \frac{1 + \varepsilon_f}{\eta_f - (1 + \varepsilon_f)}. \tag{15-70}$$

If there is no foreign investment ($I = 0$), $\varepsilon_f = 0$. Thus (15-70) is reduced to the familiar Bickerdike-Edgeworth optimum tariff formula [equation (15-4)]. If there is a foreign investment, $I \neq 0$ and $\varepsilon_f \neq 0$. What do we then know about the sign of ε_f? Suppose $E_{x2} > 0$, so that X is the import of Country 2. Then, due to the definition of ε_f in (15-61), the sign of ε_f depends on $\partial X_2/\partial I$, a change in the output of X per unit change in capital with the relative price of the goods and the supply of labor constant. We now recall the well-known Rybczynski's theorem as discussed in the third section of Chapter 2, and we can immediately determine the sign of $\partial X_2/\partial I$. Writing k_{x2} and k_{y2} respectively for the capital: labor ratio in the X and the Y industry in Country 2, we can conclude:[18]

$$\frac{\partial X_2}{\partial I} > 0, \quad \text{if } k_{x2} > k_{y2}; \tag{15-71a}$$

$$\frac{\partial X_2}{\partial I} < 0, \quad \text{if } k_{x2} < k_{y2}. \tag{15-17b}$$

Hence, assuming $E_{x2} > 0$,

$$\varepsilon_f > 0 \quad \text{if } k_{x2} > k_{y2}; \tag{15-72a}$$

$$\varepsilon_f < 0 \quad \text{if } k_{x2} < k_{y2}. \tag{15-72b}$$

In other words, the sign of ε_f depends on whether or not X is more capital intensive than Y.

We may note that condition (15-62) can be achieved by combinations of import *and* export tariffs (together with a competitive organization of Country 1's economy). Let T_e be the rate of export tariff imposed by Country 1. Then we have

$$\frac{P_1(1 + T_e)}{Q_1} = \frac{P_2}{(1 + T_m)Q_2}; \quad \text{or} \quad \Pi_1(1 + T_e)(1 + T_m) = \Pi_2. \tag{15-73}$$

Combining this with (15-68) and (15-69), we can easily obtain the optimum mix of T_e and T_m. We shall leave this to the interested reader.

We now turn to the last condition, condition (15-67). We shall argue that

[18] The same conclusion can also be obtained by using Samuelson's reciprocity relation (15-59) and the above relation (15-51).

this can be achieved by taxing foreign investment. First, using (15-68) and (15-69), we rewrite (15-67) as[19]

$$\tilde{r}_2 \varepsilon_f = (1 + T_m)[(\varepsilon_f - \mu)\tilde{r}_2 + \mu \tilde{r}_1] . \tag{15-74}$$

Or:

$$\tilde{r}_1 = \tilde{r}_2 \left(1 - \frac{T_m}{1 + T_m \mu} \frac{\varepsilon_f}{\mu}\right) . \tag{15-75}$$

Then, substituting (15-70) into this, we obtain

$$\tilde{r}_1 = \tilde{r}_2[1 - \varepsilon_f(1 + \varepsilon_f)/(\mu \eta_f)] . \tag{15-76}$$

Now suppose that the earnings from foreign investment are taxed. Let τ_1 be the rate of such a tax imposed by Country 1. Suppose that $I > 0$ so that Country 1 is the investor.

$$r_1 = r_2(1 - \tau_1) . \tag{15-77}$$

Recall $\tilde{r}_i = r_i/Q_i$. Suppose that the exchange rate between the two currencies is equal to unity (by choosing the unit of currency properly), so that $Q_1 = (1 + T_m)Q_2$, in view of (15-77). Then we have

$$\tilde{r}_1 \equiv \frac{r_1}{Q_1} = \frac{r_2(1 - \tau_1)}{(1 + T_m)Q_2} = \tilde{r}_2 \frac{1 - \tau_1}{1 + T_m} . \tag{15-78}$$

Substitute this relation into (15-76) and we obtain

$$(1 - \tau_1) = (1 + T_m)[1 - \varepsilon_f(1 + \varepsilon_f)/(\mu \eta_f)] . \tag{15-79}$$

Then, using (15-70), we obtain

$$\tau_1 = \frac{(1 + \varepsilon_f)(\varepsilon_f - \mu)}{[\eta_f - (1 + \varepsilon_f)]\mu} . \tag{15-80}$$

Note that τ_1 can be negative or positive.

Suppose that the investment proceeds are brought back to Country 1 *in the form of Good Y*, and the investment tax is imposed on this. Then we have

$$\tilde{r}_1 = \tilde{r}_2(1 - \tau_1) . \tag{15-81}$$

We now have to use (15-81) instead of (15-78). Using (15-81) and (15-76), we obtain

$$\tau_1 = \frac{\varepsilon_f(1 + \varepsilon_f)}{\mu \eta_f} . \tag{15-82}$$

If X is more capital intensive than Y in Country 2, then τ_1 is, in general, positive

---

[19] We assume that Country 1 imposes only an import tariff and does not impose an export tariff. The case that Country 1 imposes both import and export tariffs can be analyzed analogously.

$[\varepsilon_f > 0$ in view of (15-72a)]. This is the formula obtained by Kemp ([19] p. 795). However, the assumption that the investment proceeds are brought back in the form of Y and taxed is a quite arbitrary assumption. Note that Country 1 is imposing an import duty on her import of good Y by $T_m\%$. When the same good Y is brought back to Country 1 as investment proceeds, no import tariff is levied but the investment tax of $\tau_1\%$ is levied. This is certainly a strange supposition. This assumption is explicit in Kemp and he justified it by monetary reasons.[20] Recall an important difference between (15-80) and (15-82). In (15-80), we cannot *a priori* ascertain the sign of τ_1, while in (15-82) we can ascertain the sign of τ_1.

In the above analysis, we supposed that Country 1 could adopt a mix of the import tariff and the investment tax to achieve her optimum. This case is called the case of *full optimization* by Jones [12]. Following Jones, we may analyze the case in which Country 1 can take either import tariff or investment tax. For example, Country 1 cannot impose any import duty, being bound by commercial agreement. The analysis of such cases in terms of our approach needs reformulation of the problem, for it involves essential changes in the instrumental variable. They cannot be obtained by simply setting $T_m = 0$ (no tariff) or $\tau_1 = 0$ (no tax) in the previous analysis. Instead of asking whether or not such a reformulation is possible, we may point out a fresh attack on this problem by Rakowski [26]. There he argued that only certain combinations of tariff and tax are compatible with equilibrium in the international economy. Then we have to recall tedious discussions both by Kemp and by Jones about the plausible range of values which T_m and τ_1 can take (which, in turn, depends on the plausible range of η_f and ε_f, and so on). Rakowski's discussion probes deeply into this problem, for it constitutes a fresh criticism from the viewpoint of the sustenance of an equilibrium. We shall leave the examination of his analysis to the interested reader. In addition to Rakowski's problem, another problem involved in the further research on the present topic of optimal tariffs and investment will be the check of the second order conditions for the optimum, which we simply assumed, therefore omitting the discussion of these conditions.

Finally, we may recall our criticisms of the optimal investment argument at the end of the third section. The first difficulty is how the balance of payments disequilibrium due to the repatriated dividends will be eliminated. This question is solved by explicitly introducing international trade. As argued at the end of that section, the balance of payments disequilibrium will be eliminated by fluctuations in the terms of trade when international trade is introduced. The

---

[20] See Kemp [19], p. 794, fn 13. There Kemp also points out a difficulty in (15-77) [or (15-78)] by saying that, "Conclusions based on it do not carry over to a monetary economy." It is true that monetary repercussions can cause an overall revision of the model. Here, however, we follow the neoclassical tradition in which the dichotomy between the monetary sector and the non-monetary sector holds and that money is a "veil," functioning as a medium of exchange and unit of account. The arbitrariness of Kemp's assumption of no tariff on repatriated dividends is that it can imply that all investors (capitalists) are "smugglers." See Rakowski [26].

essential mechanism will be similar to the one discussed in connection with the transfer problem, Chapter 8.

However, another criticism that we raised at the end of the third section still holds. That is the problem of how we can keep the assumption of the stationary state for both countries when there is a movement of physical capital between the country. Either before *or* after the imposition of investment tax, or before *or* after any international capital movement, at least one country cannot be in a stationary state. Then we have the conversion of our model to which we explicitly incorporate capital accumulation. No such task is attempted yet.

As remarked at the end of the third section, a plausible way to interpret the problem of the fourth section (as in the third) would be to regard it purely as a welfare question which is concerned with the optimal allocation of physical capital from one country's viewpoint, and to assume (or hope) that in such an optimal state both countries are in a stationary state.

REFERENCES

1. Amano, A., *Theories of Trade and Growth* (in Japanese) (Tokyo: Yuhikaku), 1964, Chapters 5 and 7.
2. Balogh, T. and Streeten, P., "Domestic versus Foreign Investment," *Bulletin of the Oxford University Institute of Statistics*, 22, August 1960.
3. Bhagwati, J. and Ramaswami, V. K., "Domestic Distortions, Tariffs, and the Theory of Optimum Subsidy," *Journal of Political Economy*, LXXI, February 1963.
4. Bickerdike, C. F., "The Theory of Incipient Taxes," *Economic Journal*, XVI, December 1906.
5. ———, "Book Review: *Protective and Preferential Duties* by A. C. Pigou," *Economic Journal*, XVII, March 1907.
6. Edgeworth, F. Y., "Appreciations of Mathematical Theories (continued)," *Economic Journal*, XVIII, December 1908.
7. Graaff, J. de V., "On Optimal Tariff Structures," *Review of Economic Studies*, XVII, 1949–1950. Also his *Theoretical Welfare Economics* (London: Cambridge University Press), 1957, especially Chapter IX.
8. Inada, K. and Kemp, M., "International Capital Movements and the Theory of Tariffs and Trade: Comment", *Quarterly Journal of Economics*, LXXXIII, August 1969.
9. Jasay, A. E., "The Social Choice Between Home and Overseas Investment," *Economic Journal*, LXX, March 1960.
10. Johnson, H. G., "Optimum Welfare and Maximum Revenue Tariffs," *Review of Economic Studies*, XIX, 1950–1951; section I of this paper is reproduced as: "Alternative Optimum Tariff Formulas." Appendix to Chapter II, in his *International Trade and Economic Growth* (Cambridge, Mass.: Harvard University Press), 1958.
11. ———, "Optimum Tariffs, and Retaliation," *Review of Economic*

Studies, XXI, 1953–54, reprinted as Chapter II of his *International Trade and Economic Growth*, 1958.

12. Jones, R. W., "International Capital Movements and the Theory of Tariffs and Trade," *Quarterly Journal of Economics*, LXXXI, February 1967.

13. Kaldor, N., "A Note on Tariffs and Terms of Trade," *Economica*, n.s., VII, November 1940.

14. Karlin, S., *Mathematical Methods and Theory in Games, Programming and Economics* (Reading, Mass.: Addison-Wesley Publishing Company), 1959, Vol. I, especially "Introduction."

15. Kemp, M. C., "Foreign Investment and the National Advantage," *Economic Record*, 38, March 1962.

16. ———, "The Benefits and Costs of Private Investment from Abroad: Comment," *Economic Record*, 38, March 1962.

17. ———, *The Pure Theory of International Trade and Investment* (Englewood Cliffs, N.J.: Prentice-Hall), 1969, chapter 13.

18. ———, "A Guide to Negishi," *Economic Record*, 41, December 1965.

19. ———, "Gains from International Trade and Investment," *American Economic Review*, LVI, September 1966.

20. Keynes, J. M., "Foreign Investment and the National Advantage," *The Nation and Athnaeum*, XXXV, August 9, 1924.

21. MacDougall, G. D. A., "The Benefits and Costs of Private Investment from Abroad: A Theoretical Approach," *Economic Record*, 36, March 1960.

22. Mundell, R. A., *International Economics* (New York: Crowell-Collier and Macmillan, Inc.), 1968, especially Chapter 14.

23. Murphy, J. C., "International Investment and National Interest," *Southern Economic Journal*, XXVII, July 1960.

24. Negishi, T., "Foreign Investment and the Long-Run National Advantage," *Economic Record*, 41, December 1965.

25. Ohyama, M., "Capital Mobility and Foreign Policy," also "continued" *Mitagakkai-Zasshi*, 61, April 1968 and May 1968.

26. Rakowski, J. J., "Capital Mobility in a Tariff-Ridden International Economy," *American Economic Review* (forthcoming).

27. Rybczynski, T. N., "Factor Endowment and Relative Commodity Prices," *Economica*, n.s., XXII, November 1955.

28. Ryder, H., "Optimal Accumulation and Trade in an Open Economy of Moderate Size," in *Essays on the Theory of Optimal Economic Growth*, ed. by Shell, K. (Cambridge, Mass.: M.I.T. Press), 1967.

29. Samuelson, P. A., "Prices of Factors and Goods in General Equilibrium," *Review of Economic Studies*, XXI, 1953–54.

30. Takayama, A., "Book review: Mundell, R. A., *International Economics*," *Journal of Finance*, XXVI, March 1971.

31. Tinbergen, J., *On the Theory of Economic Policy* (Amsterdam: North Holland), 1952.

16

CUSTOMS UNIONS AND THE THEORY OF SECOND BEST

DIAGRAMMATICAL ANALYSIS AND THE THEORY OF SECOND BEST[1]

Introduction

The customs union is not a particularly new phenomenon in history, however, it was particularly important in connection with the formation of modern nation states in Europe. The most well-known example is probably the customs union which was formed as a step towards the unification of modern Germany in the nineteenth century, *der Deutsche Zollverein*.[2] This subject of customs unions received fresh attention after the Second World War in connection with the formation of the European Common Market.

Economic integration, in theory, refers to the elimination of all trade barriers which exist among the integrating countries, such as tariffs, subsidies, quotas, exchange controls, and so on. Customs unions, which eliminate all the tariffs among the member countries, essentially deal with the same phenomenon. In fact, if the countries agree to abolish all the tariffs among themselves, then it is natural for them to abolish the other trade barriers. In this sense customs unions are often treated as analogous to general economic integration.[3] Moreover, if the countries are willing to abolish all the trade barriers among

---

[1] I am grateful to Takashi Negishi and Edward Sieper for comments.

[2] For a bibliography and a list of conventions, decrees, and so on, concerning der Deutsche Zollverein, see Viner [41].

[3] In the literature there does not exist precise agreement in the use of the terms, and there are frequent overlaps among various terms. In general, a *free trade area* abolishes or decreases tariffs and other trade barriers within the area, but each member country can impose its own tariff on imports from non-members. When a free trade area agrees to have common tariffs on imports from non-members, then it is a *customs union*. When a customs union reaches agreement on the removal of factor immobility within the union, then it is a *common market*. When a common market reaches agreement on coordination of national economic policies of the members, then it is an *economic union*. See Balassa [1], for example. In our discussions in this chapter we shall discuss customs unions. We assume that 1) tariffs and subsidies are the only

themselves, then it would become natural for them to have some agreement on factor mobility, domestic tax and subsidy policies, domestic fiscal and monetary policies, and so on. When there exists enough "sense of belonging" among the member countries to have agreements such as free mobility of factors, common currency, and so on, then political integration of these countries may not be too far off. In fact, the importance of der Deutsche Zollverein seems to be based on the fact that it was a step towards the unification of Germany. However, here we are not interested in such political aspects of customs unions. We are only interested in economic aspects, especially the welfare implications of economic integration or customs unions.

Clearly, the welfare aspect is not the only economic problem involved in economic integration. There are many other problems, such as its impact on economic growth, balance of payments, price stability, of each member country and outside countries of the customs union. However, we shall not attempt to discuss these problems here. We shall confine ourselves to the (static) welfare implications of the formation of a customs union. In fact, this is the problem which attracted great attention among economic theorists and produced an excellent survey article by Lipsey [20].

Consider a trading world consisting of three countries. Suppose that perfect competition prevails in each country and suppose also that free trade prevails. Then, as it is well-known, a Pareto optimum situation will be realized in the world. Moreover, any Pareto optimum situation can be supported by competitive pricing and free trade. We already discussed this in Chapters 1 and 7 in this book. But suppose that our world is not characterized by free trade. Then the world is not in a Pareto optimum situation. Now suppose some (but not all) of the countries in the world form a customs union or a free trade area and agree to abolish all the trade barriers among themselves. Will this increase world welfare? Since this is often regarded as a movement towards complete free trade in the world, and since complete free trade in the world will achieve a world Pareto optimum, one may conjecture that "yes" is the answer to this question. In his pioneering work on the subject, *The Customs Union Issue* [41], Viner denied this answer. Suppose that two countries, say, 1 and 2, form a customs union and as a consequence, Country 1 switches her import of, say, Good *Y* from Country 3, a non-member country, to Country 2. If Country 2 is the most efficient producer of Good *Y* in the world, then the formation of this union would increase the welfare of the world (*trade creation*). But, on the other hand, if Country 3 is the most efficient producer of Good *Y*, then the formation of the union may be harmful to world welfare (*trade diversion*).

To consider this problem more precisely suppose that the prices of Good *Y* in the three countries (measured in terms of some numeraire good, say, Good *X*)[4] with absence of trade are as follows.

---

means of trade restriction, 2) a *customs union* abolishes all the tariffs within the union with a uniform tariff on imports from outside the union, and 3) there is no factor mobility even within the union. For the treatment with factor mobility, see Kemp [14].

[4] A similar table was used by Lipsey [20].

TABLE 16-1

Country	1	2	3
Price	8	7	5

Assume that the transport costs among the countries are negligible and assume that each country can produce Good Y at a constant cost. That is, assume that the prices indicated in the table are constant regardless of the level of output. If Country 1 levies 100 percent duty on her import of Good Y, then it will be sufficient to protect her Y-industry. If she forms a customs union with either of Countries 2 and 3, then she will import Good Y from a country who is a more efficient producer of Good Y than herself; hence it will be beneficial to the world and to Country 1. This is an example of *trade creation*. If Country 1 had been levying a 50 percent tariff instead of the 100 percent tariff, then she would have been importing Good Y from Country 3. Hence, the formation of a customs union between Countries 1 and 2 results in Country 1 importing Good Y from Country 2 instead of Country 3 which is more efficient in terms of Good Y. This is an example of *trade diversion*. In the above argument an increase in welfare can be interpreted as there being more of every commodity available for consumption. It is also fairly easy to see that such an increase in welfare is larger, the larger the difference between the cost (= price) in the two countries. This was pointed out by Makower and Morton [23].

Viner's analysis of the above was severely criticized on the ground that it implicitly assumed away the possibility of consumer substitution. This point was discovered by various authors such as Meade [28], Gehrels [8], and Lipsey [18]. In order to increase our understanding of the important welfare concepts of customs unions, trade creation, and trade diversion and to facilitate our understanding of the above consumption effect raised by Meade, Gehrels, and Lipsey, we now turn to a diagrammatical analysis of the theory of customs unions.

Diagrammatical Analysis[5]

The purpose of diagrammatical analysis here is not to present the general theory of customs unions, but rather to illustrate some of the major problems involved. In order to sharpen our understanding of these problems, we shall impose several limiting assumptions.

[5] In preparing this subsection three survey articles on the theory of customs unions—Lipsey [20]; Johnson [13]; and Clement, Pfister, and Rothwell [5]—were particularly helpful. As we shall argue later, the arguments surveyed here contain serious weaknesses, especially from the general equilibrium viewpoint, although each of these arguments is correct as it is. Hence, we shall not make any effort to clarify the general equilibrium significance of the arguments and the concepts (such as consumer's surplus) used in this subsection. The purpose of this subsection is simply to increase the reader's familiarity with the topic of customs unions. The emphasis of this chapter is in the second section and does not lie in this subsection.

Assume, first of all,

1. there are only three countries in the world, Countries 1, 2, and 3;
2. Country 1 is small enough compared to either Countries 2 or 3, so that she cannot change the prices of the goods which prevail in the world market;[6]
3. there are only two goods in the world, Good X and Good Y;
4. Country 1 is able to produce both goods with constant cost (that is, the production transformation curve of Country 1 is a straight line).

Suppose that, at the outset, Country 1 imports Good Y from Country 3, the least-cost source of Good Y in the world, and Country 3 imports Good X from Country 1. Suppose also that Country 1 imposes a tariff on her import of Good Y, while Country 3 imposes no tariffs (or subsidies) on her import or export. Suppose now that Country 1 forms a customs union with Country 2 and that Country 1 then imports Good Y from Country 2 instead of Country 3. This switch of import to a less efficient source is an example of a trade-diverting customs union.

In Figure 16-1, the line AB denotes the production transformation line of Country 1, the line AC denotes the price-ratio line that prevails in the world market before the union,[7] and the line AD denotes the price-ratio line that prevails within the union.

Since Country 3 imposes no tariffs (or subsidies), the AC-line signifies the budget constraint for Country 1 before the formation of the union, so that Country 1's consumption point before the union is on this line.[8] Since Country 1 imposes an import tariff before the union, the domestic price ratio that the producers and the consumers of Country 1 face is different from the slope of the AC-line. Let the slope of the FG-line signify this domestic price ratio, and suppose that the consumption point of Country 1 is point P. Let the FG-line be steeper than the production transformation line, AB, so that Country 1 specializes in the production of Good X before the union (as well as after the union).

If Country 1's consumption behavior is such that Good X and Good Y are always consumed in a fixed proportion, then the consumption point after the formation of the union must be on the intersection of the new budget line, AD, with the 0P-line at point Q. Hence, Country 1 is always worse off by forming a trade-diverting customs union which, according to Lipsey [20], is

---

[6] We may, in addition, assume constant cost productions (infinite supply elasticity) in Countries 2 and 3, in order to make the argument more transparent.

[7] When constant costs prevail in Country 3 and both goods can be produced in Country 3, then the AC-line also denotes the production transformation line of Country 3 due to the assumption that Country 1 is small enough. Note that there is no gain from trade in Country 3, and Country 1 cannot increase welfare by imposing a tariff on her import from Country 3 (the terms of trade cannot move any further in favor of Country 1).

[8] If Country 3 imposes a tariff on her import from Country 1, then this is not true. Similarly, due to free trade with Country 2 after the formation of the union, the AD-line signifies the budget constraint for Country 1 after the formation of the union.

Good Y

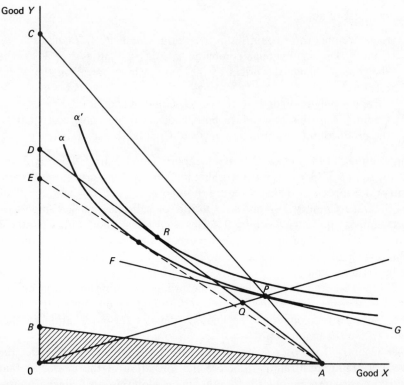

Figure 16-1   An Illustration of a Trade-Diverting Customs Union

a major contention of Viner. Now suppose that we allow consumer substitution and that Country 1's consumption indifference curves are denoted in the usual convex-to-the-origin shape. Let $\alpha, \alpha' \cdots$ be such indifference curves. Note that at point P the FG-line (the domestic price line of Country 1 before the union) must be tangent to one of these indifference curves, say α. With the introduction of this possibility of consumer substitution, Country 1's consumption point after the formation of the union is obtained as the point at which one of the indifference curves is tangent to the budget line (here AD). In Figure 16-1, this is represented by point R. Clearly, point R denotes higher level of satisfaction than point P (for Country 1). This conclusion would be true as long as the new budget line, AD, is steeper than the AE-line, the line which passes point A and is tangent to the α-curve. In any case, trade-diverting customs unions can be beneficial to a union-forming country. Since Country 1 is small enough, this switch of trade by Country 1 presumably does not change the price ratio of the two goods that prevails in the rest of the world. In other words, there is no decrease in welfare in Country 3. Similarly, Country 2's welfare will not be decreased by entering into trade with Country 1.[9] In fact, if Country 2 is not big enough compared to Country 1, she will gain from the move to free trade

[9] A similar conclusion can be obtained by assuming constant costs (infinite elasticity of supply) for all three countries.

with Country 1. In other words, no country loses in the formation of the above customs union. This is an example in which a trade-diverting customs union can increase world welfare as well as the welfare of the union and the union-forming country (Country 1).[10] This is the essence of the consumption substitution effect proposed by Meade [28], Gehrels [8], and Lipsey [18].

We can illustrate the above point more sharply if we are willing to use the partial equilibrium analysis.[11] Let the DD-line in Figure 16-2 denote the demand curve of Good Y in Country 1. The negative slope of the DD-line signifies the consumer substitution in Country 1. The domestic price of Good Y in Countries 2 and 3 is respectively denoted by the P_2Q_2-, and the P_3Q_3-lines in Figure 16-2. These lines are drawn flat to signify that Country 1 is small enough compared to either of Countries 2 and 3.

Suppose that Country 1 initially imposes a tariff on her import of Good Y from Countries 2 and 3. The import price of Good Y (in Country 1) from

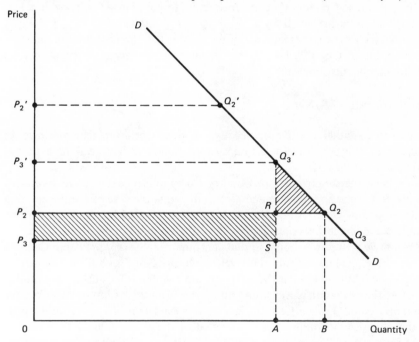

Figure 16-2   Another Illustration of a Trade-Diverting Customs Union

[10] In other words, by the formation of the union, Country 1 is better off and no other countries are worse off. In the literature the phrases such as "the formation of a customs union is beneficial" are often used ambiguously. They can be different depending on various viewpoints, that is, that of a union-forming country, the union as a whole, an outside country, and the world as a whole. Clearly we have to specify the viewpoint when we make the above statement.
[11] The partial equilibrium diagrams, such as Figures 16-2 and 16-3, and the corresponding arguments are used by Humphrey and Ferguson [10] and Johnson [13]. Lipsey [20] in explaining Meade's argument also used such a diagram.

Countries 2 and 3 is respectively denoted by the $P_2'Q_2'$- and the $P_3'Q_3'$-lines in Figure 16-2. We assume that the supply curve of Country 1 is above the $P_2'Q_2'$-line so that Country 1 does not produce Good Y nor does the supply curve location influence the subsequent argument. Clearly, under this situation, all the import of Good Y of Country 1 comes from Country 3 and is sold in Country 1 at the price of $0P_3'$. Now suppose Country 1 forms a customs union with Country 2 so that she abolishes all the tariff for her import from Country 2 but retains the old tariff for the import from Country 3. After the formation of such a customs union, Country 1 now imports Good Y from Country 2 at price $0P_2$ and abolishes her import of Good Y from Country 3. This is again a trade-diverting customs union, for Country 1 switches her import from the least cost source, Country 3, to a less efficient source, Country 2, by the formation of the union. The volume of import increases from $0A$ to $0B$. There is an increase in consumer's surplus, measured by $\triangle P_3'Q_3'Q_2P_2$, due to the decline in the price that Country 1's consumers have to pay. However, there is a loss of tariff revenue measured by $\square P_3'Q_3'SP_3$, out of which $\square P_2RSP_3$ measures the increase in (real) cost of purchasing $0A$, the pre-union quantity of consumption of Good Y. Hence, the net increase (or decrease) of Country 1's welfare can be measured by

$$\triangle Q_3'Q_2R - \square P_2RSP_3 \,,$$

which can be either positive or negative. If this is positive, then we have an example in which a trade-diverting customs union is beneficial to a union-forming country.

In general the supply curve of Country 1 may influence the above argument. To illustrate such an influence and also to illustrate the case of a trade-creating customs union, we consider Figure 16-3. Here the DD-line and the SS-line denote the demand and the supply curve of Country 1 respectively. Here the supply curve is upward sloping so that constant cost does *not* prevail in Country 1. Let the P_2Q_2-line indicate the level of the price of Good Y in Country 2. We assume that Country 2 is the least cost source of Good Y outside of Country 1. Before the formation of a customs union with Country 2, suppose that Country 1 imports Good Y from Country 2, with a certain rate of import tariff on Y, so that its price in Country 1 is represented by the $P_2'Q_2'$-line.

At price $0P_2'$, Country 1 produces Good Y (domestically) in the amount of $P_2'R$ and imports it from Country 2 in the amount of RR'. Now suppose that Country 1 forms a customs union with Country 2 and the price of Good Y in Country 1 now drops from $0P_2'$ to $0P_2$. Since the formation of this union still enables Country 1 to import Good Y from the least cost source, this is an example of a trade-creating customs union. At price $0P_2$, Country 1 produces Good Y in the amount of P_2M and imports it from Country 2 in the amount of MN. The gains in Country 1's consumer's surplus is measured by $\triangle P_2'R'NP_2$ and the loss in producer's surplus is measured by $\diagup P_2'RMP_2$. Furthermore there is a loss of tariff revenue measured by $\square RR'N'M'$.

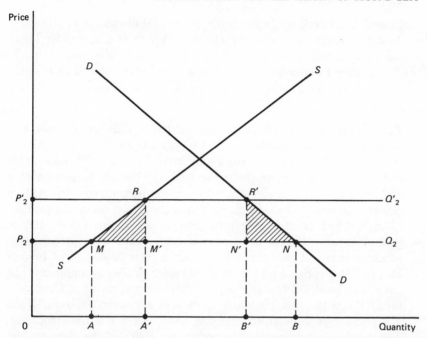

Figure 16-3   An Illustration of a Trade-Creating Customs Union

Hence, the net gain is $\triangle P_2'R'NP_2 - \square P_2'RMP_2 - \square RR'N'M'$, and this is equal to

$$\triangle RM'M + \triangle R'NN',$$

which is clearly positive. In other words, a trade-creating customs union is beneficial to a union-forming country.

There are many obvious criticisms that one can make of the above analysis. We can easily recall the discussions stimulated by the European Common Market in this connection. For example, one can easily question such points as: the possible existence of economies of scale,[12] an increase in effective competition among firms and among industries within the union,[13] a long-term dynamic effect, the effect on technological progress,[14] and so on.

No doubt these points are real and important. However, these criticisms are also outside the scope of the above analysis. Here we shall not go into a detailed exposition of the above criticisms; rather, we proceed with our analysis within

[12] If Country 2 has economies of scale in Good Y, then she may turn out to be the least cost source of Y in the world after the formation of a union, even if she was not before. The importance of economies of scale in the theory of customs unions is emphasized by Balassa ([2], pp. 101–188), Johnson [11], Kindleberger [15], and so on, who are skeptical about this.

[13] This is emphasized by Balassa ([2], pp. 164–165) and Scitovsky ([32], pp. 19–48), for example.

[14] The argument for technological progress is as follows: A customs union enlarges the market which induces an increase in the size of the firms; since larger firms tend to spend proportionately more on research than small firms, a customs union encourages technological progress.

the scope and framework set in the above theoretical discussion of a customs union. In other words, we focus our attention on the (static) welfare implications of resource reallocations caused by the formation of a customs union.

Even if we restrict ourselves to this narrow framework, we still have raised questions about the above diagrammatical analysis of a customs union. We may, for example, point out the following criticisms.

1. There is an inherent difficulty in any partial equilibrium analysis. The analysis which utilizes the demand-supply diagrams such as Figures 16-2 and 16-3 is based on the assumption that these demand-supply curves do not shift throughout the analysis. But the formation of a customs union, if it is significant to a union-forming country, will, in general, cause a shift in the demand and supply curves of the member countries. For example, the formation of a customs union will, in general, cause a change in income of each of the member countries, which in turn will shift the demand curves. Our discussion of Figures 16-2 and 16-3 is based on the standard *ceteris paribus* assumption in the sense that Good Y is "insignificant" for the entire economy of Country 1. But, if this is the case, the whole analysis of a customs union for Good Y is also insignificant. If, on the other hand, Good Y is ever significant, then we have to honestly incorporate the shifts of the demand and supply curves into our analysis. In other words, a true general equilibrium is thus called for.

2. In most of the above analysis, we assumed that the foreign supply price is constant as long as the tariff rates are fixed. Although this assumption sharpens our discussions considerably, it is also a rather silly assumption. Suppose, for example, that this assumption is justified by the small country assumption and the constant cost assumption. Then we may have a situation in which the imposition of an import duty will neither protect the domestic industry of the importing good nor increase the home country's welfare. If we discard the constant cost assumption and adopt the usual increasing cost assumption, and further, if we discard the small country assumption, then the imposition of a tariff will, in general, have the effect of protecting domestic import competing industries and of increasing the welfare of the tariff imposing country, as we discussed in Chapter 8, third section. However, with the increasing cost assumption, Viner's celebrated distinction between trade creation and trade diversion loses its importance. For example, Country 2 may be the least cost source of Good Y before the formation of a customs union, so that a customs union with Country 2 is a trade-creation union. But after the formation of the union, Country 2 may cease to be the least cost source of Good Y due to the expansion of the scale of production in Good Y with an increasing cost.[15] In other words, Viner's concepts of trade creation and trade

[15] If the relevant change due to the formation of a customs union is small enough, then only trade creation occurs. However, if the change is not small enough (which is more likely), then trade diversion follows after the initial trade creation.

diversion are not well-suited for use under the usual increasing cost case (the case in which the production transformation curve is concave to the origin).

3. There is an inherent problem attached to any diagrammatical analysis. That is, a diagrammatical analysis can be useful in illustrating the points of discussion, but it is obscure about the general framework on which a particular analysis is based. This is the crippling limitation of any diagrammatical analysis.

In connection with these remarks on some of the past literature surveyed in the above, we may quote the following passage from Kemp ([14], Preface):

> In reviewing the professional and journalistic literature on preferential trading arrangements I have been struck by the fragmentary and partial equilibrium character of the formal models employed.... The poverty of the theory is more puzzling in that almost all of it has been developed since 1950, a period during which the rest of trade theory has fallen under the powerful unifying influence of the general-equilibrium approach developed by Heckscher, Ohlin, Lerner and Samuelson.... Most of the professional literature on preferential trading arrangements is exceedingly dull. The explanation lies in the multitude of "cases" which must be examined if the treatment is to be complete.

The purpose of this chapter is to present a mathematical theory of customs union based on the general equilibrium analysis without assuming constant foreign supply prices, and so on. In particular we shall present our theory explicitly as an application of nonlinear programming. Needless to say, such a mathematical formulation will enable us to generalize the discussion into a rigorous frame of analysis and will facilitate further extensions.

We now have to mention Vanek [40], an important predecessor to our study and to Kemp [14], who considered the problem of customs union's explicitly under a general equilibrium framework with a possibility of nonconstant foreign supply prices. However, due to the fact that he used diagrams (especially those of offer curves) as the major tool of his analysis, his analysis often became very tedious and his logic was obscured.

In order to rescue Vanek's analysis from this difficulty, Negishi [31] constructed a mathematical model essentially based on Vanek's three-country and two-good model. However, due to the lack of the explicit formulation of the problem from the mathematical programming point of view, his analysis often becomes unclear and seems to contain mistakes. The present chapter aims to remedy this difficuly.[16]

Another important contribution of Negishi [31] is to relate the theory of customs unions to the "piecemeal approach" of the theory of second best. However, he handled this in a rather subtle way so that the real significance of this

---

[16] Negishi [31] also introduced consumption taxes. However, if the basic mathematical formulation of the problem is clear, then such an extension is a trivial exercise. Hence, we shall omit the possibility of consumption taxes from our consideration in the next section. The interested reader could easily extend our analysis to the cases in which various complications such as consumption taxes and production taxes occur.

point is not too clear from his discussion. Since the theory of the second best has been developed in a close relation with the theory of customs unions, it would be worthwhile to review the major discussion of the theory of second best. We shall do so in the next subsection of the present section. This will also facilitate the reader's understanding of our treatment of customs unions in the next section, which is an explicit example of the piecemeal approach in the theory of second best.

The Theory of Second Best

Having realized our problem as a problem of nonlinear programming, we have to discuss the relation of our theory, called the theory of second best, to an important field, which in fact has been developed with a great deal of stimulation from the theory of customs unions.

As remarked before Viner's pioneering work [41], through such concepts as trade creation and trade diversion, pointed out that the formation of a customs union may *decrease* world welfare and the welfare of the union-forming countries, even if it is a movement towards free trade, a situation which achieves a world-welfare maximum.

This observation leads to the following discussion. Consider a problem of optimizing social welfare. Here both "society" and "welfare" can be interpreted quite freely. For example, "society" can mean such things as the world economy, a national economy, a firm, a university, a city, and so on. This problem of maximization will result in a certain set of conditions which will characterize a maximum point. If the problem is formulated as a problem of nonlinear programming, then the first-order conditions with the conditions which describe the constraints of the problem may constitute such a set of conditions. Suppose it is impossible to satisfy *all* of these conditions. Suppose further that more than one of these conditions are violated. Now consider a change in the situation which brings about satisfaction of some of these conditions which were violated before. Will this change increase social welfare? An intuitive answer to this question may be "yes." However, the correct answer is, "No, it is not necessarily the case." Note that a similar question was asked in connection with customs unions. Granting that free trade among all the countries is the condition which achieves a maximum of world welfare, will the formation of a customs union, which is a movement towards overall free trade, increase world welfare? Contrary to an intuitive conviction, Viner [41] answered, "No, it is not necessarily the case."[17]

Given that some of the conditions for optimum are violated, what then can we say about the welfare of such a situation? Lipsey and Lancaster [21] con-

---

[17] Although Viner's argument stimulated the discussion of second best, it is not the first treatment of the theory of second best. Hicks, for example, in his article on consumer's surplus (*Review of Economic Studies*, VIII, 1940–41), had a discussion of the second best problem. That is, the perfect competition of an industry may not be optimal from the point of view of the economy as a whole if other industries are not competitive. The first explicit and extensive treatment of the second best theory is due to Meade [26].

sidered this problem in a general framework, similar to the one which we now present.

Consider the problem of choosing $x = (x_1, x_2, \cdots, x_n)$ to maximize a real valued differentiable function $F(x)$ subject to $\Phi(x) \geqq 0$, $x \geqq 0$, where F and Φ are real-valued differentiable functions.[18] Assuming appropriate conditions such as Slater's condition and concavity and interior solutions, the necessary and sufficient conditions for $x^* = (x_1{}^*, \cdots, x_n{}^*)$ to be a solution of the above problem are that there exists $\lambda \geqq 0$ such that

$$F_i{}^* = \lambda \Phi_i{}^*, i = 1, 2, \cdots, n; \quad \text{and} \quad \Phi(x^*) \geqq 0, \lambda \Phi(x^*) = 0,$$

where $F_i{}^* = \partial F/\partial x_i$ and $\Phi_i{}^* = \partial \Phi/\partial x_i$, each evaluated at x^*. If $\lambda > 0$, then these conditions are reduced to the following $(n + 1)$ conditions

$$F_i{}^* = \lambda \Phi_i{}^*, \quad i = 1, 2, \cdots, n, \quad \Phi(x^*) = 0,$$

from which the values of the $(n + 1)$ variables $(x_i{}^*, i = 1, 2, \cdots, n$, and $\lambda)$ are to be determined. We can eliminate λ from the above conditions by rewriting them as the following n conditions:

$$F_i{}^*/F_1{}^* = \Phi_i{}^*/\Phi_1{}^*, \quad i = 2, \cdots, n; \quad \text{and} \quad \Phi(x^*) = 0,$$

which are now considered as necessary and sufficient conditions for x^* to achieve an optimum. The first $(n - 1)$ of these conditions, $F_i{}^*/F_1{}^* = \Phi_i{}^*/\Phi_1{}^*$, $i = 2, \cdots, n$, may be referred to as the *tangency conditions*. They correspond to the *Paretian (or Lerner) conditions* in welfare economics.

Suppose now that the attainment of at least one of the above conditions is prevented by the following constraint:

$$F_2/F_1 \geqq k\Phi_2/\Phi_1 \quad \text{for all } x,$$

where k is some positive number which is greater than one.

When such a constraint is explicitly present, then the above maximization problem must be reformulated. We now choose x to maximize $F(x)$ subject to $\Phi(x) \geqq 0$, $x \geqq 0$ *and* $F_2/F_1 - k\Phi_2/\Phi_1 \geqq 0$. Let x^0 be a solution of this new maximization problem. It is easy to see that x^0 is in general different from x^*. The tangency (or the Paretian) conditions for x^0 to be a solution are all different from the ones for the previous problem. Thus Lipsey and Lancaster ([21], p. 11) concluded:

> Given that one of the Paretian optimum conditions cannot be fulfilled, then an optimum situation can be achieved only by departing from *all* the other Paretian conditions, ...

which we refer to as the *Lipsey-Lancaster theorem of second best*.

This looks like a rather disastrous conclusion, for it advocates that we can say nothing about welfare when one or more of the Paretian conditions are violated. More specifically even if some other Paretian conditions are satisfied,

---

[18] An example of F is a social welfare function and an example of Φ is a production transformation curve.

we cannot say whether or not it is beneficial to the society. Several attempts have been made to rescue this seemingly disastrous state. The first significant work is due to Kuroiwa [17] which unfortunately did not reach English speaking readers, for it was written in Japanese. He proposed a piecemeal approach, which advocates that even if one or more Paretian conditions are violated some of the other Paretian conditions are still desirable.

The essence of the piecemeal approach is the recognition of different decision units in the society, each of which can make an independent choice. For example, the condition such as $\Phi(x) \geq 0$ is decomposed into different decisions based on different producers, and there are no externalities among these producers. The objective function $F(x)$ may be decomposed into the objective of different consumers. For example, individual i's welfare can be represented by a real-valued function u_i, and it may depend only on his consumption bundle $x^i \in R^n$. (There are no externalities among consumers.) Then instead of maximizing $F(x)$, we may maximize a vector $[u_1(x^1), u_2(x^2), \cdots, u_m(x^m)]$.[19] *As long as interdependence or externalities* do not exist among the consumers and producers, we can obtain an important piecemeal theorem of second best which states that even if the tangency conditions are violated for some decision units (individuals), the tangency conditions *among the rest of the individuals* must still hold.[20] This theorem is proved by Kuroiwa [17] for relatively simpler cases, but his proof can easily be extended to a more general case.

The decomposition of the society or the economy into different decision units and the consideration of the second best problem from a piecemeal approach were carried out in the English language literature in a controversial paper by Davis and Whinston [6].

The essential difference between Kuroiwa [17] and Davis and Whinston [6] is that the latter paper introduced the prices on which various decision units base their decisions. This introduction of the prices no doubt deepened the piecemeal approach in the sense that we can discard rather restrictive and sometimes artificial additional constraints such as $F_2/F_1 - k\Phi_2/\Phi_1 \geq 0$.[21] However, this introduction of the prices created another difficulty in how these prices should be determined. Davis and Whinston [6] simply used the Lagrangian multipliers for a given maximization problem as their prices. This was severely criticized by McManus [25], for there is no *a priori* ground that this is the case.

In spite of such a weakness, the spirit of Davis-Whinston paper [6], that is, the piecemeal approach based on individual's choice according to prices, is very important. To further appreciate this, consider the usual Pareto optimum problem in economics—that of maximizing a vector of individual's utility,

---

[19] It is assumed that there are m such individuals (consumers) in the society.

[20] Although this is a great advance in the theory of second best, this does not necessarily imply that an increase in the number of the tangency conditions fulfilled increases the total social welfare.

[21] Lipsey-Lancaster [21] and their followers used a more restrictive constraint such as $F_2/F_1 - k\Phi_2/\Phi_1 = 0$ for *all* x.

$(u_1, u_2, \cdots, u_m)$ subject to the feasibility conditions of the economy. Under suitable assumptions we can characterize this Pareto optimum by a set of first-order conditions which consist of the tangency conditions and the feasibility conditions. If the economy is organized in a competitive fashion so that there exist prices on which each decision unit makes his choice, then these tangency conditions are all satisfied by equating each ratio to a price. This is the content of the famous theorem in welfare economics, which states that every competitive equilibrium realizes a Pareto optimum and that every Pareto optimum can be supported by competitive pricing.

Now suppose some of the tangency conditions are explicitly violated due to taxes, subsidies, monopolies, and so on. We can incorporate the behavior of the decision units *given such violations* into the maximization problem, assuming there exist certain prices with which each decision unit is concerned. The maximization problem under suitable assumptions yields the first-order conditions. We then interpret these conditions by using a specified organization of the economy (such as perfect competition with taxes) and the given prices. The piecemeal theorem is a consequence of the comparison of these two sets of the first-order conditions.

The above exposition of a new piecemeal approach with prices may sound too abstract to many readers. The proof of the pudding is in the eating. We demonstrate the above piecemeal approach by using the theory of customs unions as an example. In other words, our mathematical formulation of customs unions in the next section has an important purpose—an illustration of the new piecemeal approach in the theory of second best.

We shall start our discussion of the next section by constructing a deterministic model of a three-country, two-commodity world (first subsection). This step is necessary in order to construct an optimization model for the theory of customs unions, although it has its own interest. In the second subsection of the next section we shall convert this deterministic model into an optimization model in which the problem of maximizing a utility vector of the customs union is considered. We shall conclude that in order to maximize the welfare of the union, free trade within the union is required and the union must impose a tariff on the import from the outside country at a certain specified rate. In the third subsection of the next section, we shall consider the problem of maximizing world welfare.

CUSTOMS UNIONS AND THE THEORY OF SECOND BEST

A Deterministic Model of a Three-Country Trading World

Consider a trading world consisting of three countries. The third country is introduced into the traditional two-country model in order to discuss the effect of economic integration of two of the countries among the three. Assume that each country is capable of producing the same two commodities (X and Y). Let X_i and Y_i respectively denote the output of Good X and Good Y in the ith country ($i = 1, 2, 3$). Let us suppose the production transformation curve of Country i can be described by

$$Y_i = F_i(X_i) \quad (\text{with } X_i \geqq 0 \quad \text{and} \quad Y_i \geqq 0), \quad i = 1, 2, 3, \tag{16-1}$$

where

$$F_i'(\equiv dF_i/dX_i) < 0 \quad \text{and} \quad F_i''(\equiv d^2F_i/dX_i^2) < 0, \quad i = 1, 2, 3 .^{22} \tag{16-2}$$

Let C_{xi} and C_{yi}, respectively, denote the consumption of Good X and Good Y in Country i. The excess demand (or supply) of each good for Country i can be defined by

$$E_{xi} \equiv C_{xi} - X_i, \quad i = 1, 2, 3, \tag{16-3a}$$

$$E_{yi} \equiv C_{yi} - Y_i, \quad i = 1, 2, 3 . \tag{16-3b}$$

We assume that each country possesses the social welfare function defined by

$$U_i = U_i(C_{xi}, C_{yi}), \quad i = 1, 2, 3, \tag{16-4}$$

where each U_i is defined over the non-negative orthant of the two-dimensional real space. We assume $\partial U_i/\partial C_{xi} > 0$ and $\partial U_i/\partial C_{yi} > 0$, $i = 1, 2, 3$ for all C_{xi} and C_{yi}. Let $v_i = v_i(C_{xi}, C_{yi})$ be defined by

$$v_i \equiv (\partial U_i/\partial C_{xi})/(\partial U_i/\partial C_{yi}), \quad i = 1, 2, 3 . \tag{16-5}$$

That is, v_i denotes the rate of marginal substitution of Country i at (C_{xi}, C_{yi}). Let Π_i be the commodity price ratio (the price of Good X divided by the price of Good Y) which prevails in Country i. We assume for the sake of simplicity that there are no domestic distortions such as consumption taxes (subsidies) or production taxes (subsidies). The differences among Π_1, Π_2 and Π_3 are due to import and export tariffs (or subsidies). If there are no such tariffs or subsidies, then $\Pi_1 = \Pi_2 = \Pi_3$, which we write as Π.

Suppose that the economy of each country is organized in a competitive fashion so that the commodity price ratio is tangent to both the production transformation curve and the community indifference curve of that country. We can describe these competitive situations by the following set of equations:

$$\Pi_i = -F_i', \quad i = 1, 2, 3; \quad \text{and} \tag{16-6}$$

$$\Pi_i = v_i, \quad i = 1, 2, 3 . \tag{16-7}$$

The budget condition for each country can be described by

$$\Pi_i E_{xi} + E_{yi} = (\text{tariff revenues}) - (\text{expenditures for subsidies}), \quad i = 1, 2, 3 . \tag{16-8}$$

We assume that the tariff revenues are given out to the people of each country in the form of income subsidies, and the expenditures for export or import subsidies are collected in the form of income taxes, so that the consumption behavior of each country is not affected. An alternative approach to this is, of course, that the government of each country could decide the proportion of its

---

[22] Needless to say, by this we assume increasing cost.

tariff revenue to be spent on each good. Then we need another equation which describes an expenditure function of each government. A similar complication would also arise in the case of export and import subsidies.

In equilibrium, we have[23]

$$E_{x1} + E_{x2} + E_{x3} = 0,$$ (16-9a)

$$E_{y1} + E_{y2} + E_{y3} = 0.$$ (16-9b)

Assume that there are no import and export tariffs (or subsidies). Then $\Pi_1 = \Pi_2 = \Pi_3 \equiv \Pi$ and the tariff revenues = the expenditures for export or import subsidies = 0. Therefore there are nineteen variables to be determined in the above model [X_i, Y_i, E_{xi}, E_{yi}, C_{xi}, C_{yi}, ($i = 1, 2, 3$) and Π]. There are altogether twenty equations ((16-1), (16-3), (16-6), (16-7), (16-8), and (16-9)). However, due to Walras' law, one of the equations can be derived from the others. For example, equation (16-9b) can be derived from (16-8) and (16-9a) (assuming $\Pi_i \neq 0$). Therefore, there are nineteen independent equations in the above model which determine the equilibrium values of nineteen variables. Note that if $E_{xi} > 0$ (in equilibrium), Good X is the import of Country i, and that if $E_{xi} < 0$ (in equilibrium), Good Y is the import of Country i. A similar relation holds with E_{yi}.

When there are international distortions of prices due to import and export tariffs (or subsidies), we have essentially the same situation. Instead of Π, we have Π_1, Π_2, and Π_3. Thus we increase the number of variables by two. We then increase the number of equations by two by adding the two equations which describe the relations among Π_1, Π_2, and Π_3 due to the international price distortions.

Suppose now that, in equilibrium, Country 1 exports Good X to the other two countries, the other two countries export Good Y to Country 1 in return, and there is no international trade between Country 2 and Country 3. This means that $E_{x1} < 0, E_{y1} > 0, E_{x2} > 0, E_{y2} < 0, E_{x3} > 0$, and $E_{y3} < 0$. Clearly other specifications are possible, and the analyses for the other cases are left to the interested reader. We also assume that each country imposes tariffs on its imports and there are no export or import subsidies and no export tariffs. Let τ_2 and τ_3 respectively be the rate of import tariff (on Good X) in Countries 2 and 3. Let τ_{12} and τ_{13} be the rate of tariff imposed by Country 1 on her import of Good Y from Countries 2 and 3. Let P_i and Q_i respectively denote the prices of X and Y in Country i ($i = 1, 2, 3$). Let e_i denote the price of the ith currency in terms of Country 1's currency ($i = 2, 3$).[24] Then

$$P_2 = (1 + \tau_2)P_1/e_2, \quad P_3 = (1 + \tau_3)P_1/e_3;$$ (16-10a)

$$Q_1 = (1 + \tau_{12})e_2Q_2, \quad P_3 = (1 + \tau_{13})e_3Q_3.$$ (16-10b)

---

[23] This says that the world demand for each good is equal to its supply. Since this also means that the world consumption of each good is restricted by its supply, this also signifies the feasibility condition of the economy.

[24] Capital letter E was used in our discussion of Part III of this book. Here we use lower-case letter e because E is easily confused with E_{xi} and E_{yi}. Also, here (unlike Part III) the lower case letters do *not* signify small change.

Let Π_i denote P_i/Q_i, $i = 1, 2, 3$. Then from the relations in (16-10), we obtain

$$\Pi_2 = T_2\,\Pi_1, \quad \text{where } T_2 \equiv (1 + \tau_2)(1 + \tau_{12}); \tag{16-11a}$$

$$\Pi_3 = T_3\,\Pi_1, \quad \text{where } T_3 \equiv (1 + \tau_3)(1 + \tau_{13}). \tag{16-11b}$$

Hence by specifying the values of τ_2, τ_3, τ_{12}, and τ_{13}, we again obtain a complete system in which the number of equations, now twenty-one ($=$ nineteen $+$ above two), is equal to the number of variables, after we specify the budget equation (16-8) more explicitly (which we shall do later in equations (16-12a) to (16-12c)).

If there are no tariffs at all so that free trade prevails, then $T_2 = T_3 = 1$. The above relations of imports, exports, and import tariffs are illustrated in Figure 16-4.

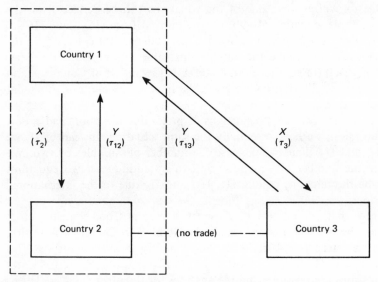

Figure 16-4   An Illustration of the Import-Export Relations

In the above argument we assumed that each country imposes a *tariff* on her import. This means that τ_2, τ_3, τ_{12}, and τ_{13} are all greater than zero. The case of export tariffs and export or import subsidies can be handled analogously by changing the specification of the values of these τs. Suppose Country 2 gives a subsidy to her import of Good X. Then $\tau_2 < 0$ rather than $\tau_2 > 0$. Also τ_2 can be considered to be the rate of export tariff (subsidy) by Country 1 imposed on her export of Good X to Country 2 if $\tau_2 > 0$ ($\tau_2 < 0$). It is not particularly important to the discussion how the discrepancies among Π_1, Π_2, and Π_3 [as in (16-11)] are created. Once these discrepancies (T_2 and T_3) are specified, then the equilibrium values of the variables are to be determined, provided that we make correct specifications of the tariff revenues or subsidy expenditures in equation (16-8). We in fact saw the similar situation in Chapter 8 and Chapter 14. Here, to sharpen the arguments, we assume that all the international price distortions are due to the import tariffs as described by equation (16-10) or (16-11) and leave the other cases to the interested reader.

With this specification in mind, we can determine the right-hand side of (16-8). The right-hand side of (16-8) now solely consists of the revenue from import tariffs. Referring to the import-export relations and tariff situations as illustrated in Figure 16-4, we now obtain the amount of tariff revenue for each country. For Country 2, the volume of import is equal to E_{x2} which comes from Country 1. Country 2's government receives the tariff revenue in the amount of $(P_2 E_{x2} - P_1 E_{x2}/e_2)$. Since $P_2 = (1 + \tau_2)P_1/e_2$, this amount is equal to $\tau_2 P_1 E_{x2}/e_2 = \tau_2 P_2 E_{x2}/(1 + \tau_2)$. Country 3's government receives the tariff revenue in the amount of $(P_3 E_{x3} - P_1 E_{x3}/e_3)$, which, in view of $P_3 = (1 + \tau_3)P_1/e_3$, is equal to $\tau_3 P_1 E_{x3}/e_3 = \tau_3 P_3 E_{x3}/(1 + \tau_3)$. Country 1's government receives the tariff revenue in the amount of

$$- [(Q_1 E_{y2} - e_2 Q_2 E_{y2}) + (Q_1 E_{y3} - e_3 Q_3 E_{y3})], \quad \text{where } E_{y2} < 0 \text{ and } E_{y3} < 0,$$

which in view of (16-10b), is equal to

$$-[\tau_{12} e_2 Q_2 E_{y2} + \tau_{13} e_3 Q_3 E_{y3}] = -[\tau_{12} E_{y2}/(1 + \tau_{12}) + \tau_{13} E_{y3}/(1 + \tau_{13})]Q_1 .$$

Using the above information on the tariff revenue of each country and assuming that each country's government gives the tariff revenue to its public, we can now rewrite equation (16-8) as follows:[25]

$$\Pi_1 E_{x1} + E_{y1} = -(t_{12} E_{y2} + t_{13} E_{y3}) , \tag{16-12a}$$

where

$$t_{12} \equiv \tau_{12}/(1 + \tau_{12}) , \qquad t_{13} \equiv \tau_{13}/(1 + \tau_{13}) ;$$

$$\Pi_2 E_{x2} + E_{y2} = t_2 \Pi_2 E_{x2} , \tag{16-12b}$$

where

$$t_2 \equiv \tau_2/(1 + \tau_2) ;$$

$$\Pi_3 E_{x3} + E_{y3} = t_3 \Pi_3 E_{x3} , \tag{16-12c}$$

where

$$t_3 \equiv \tau_3/(1 + \tau_3) .$$

As we remarked before, with the above specification of the budget condition for each country, we now have a complete system of twenty-one equations which determines the twenty-one variables; X_i, Y_i, E_{xi}, E_{yi}, C_{xi}, C_{yi}, and Π_i, $i = 1, 2, 3$, with the predetermined specification of τ_2, τ_{12}, τ_3, and τ_{13} (or t_2, t_{12}, t_3, and t_{13}). The interested reader can carry out the comparative statics analysis of ascertaining the effect of decreasing the tariff of τ_2 and/or τ_{12} on the

[25] Adding each side of (16-12a) through (16-12c) and using (16-9a), (16-10a), (16-10b), (16-12b), and (16-12c), we can obtain (16-9b). In other words, one of the equations in the present model is not independent of the rest of the equations.

welfare of each country, U_i.[26] The formation of a customs union between Countries 1 and 2 amounts to specifying that the values of τ_2 and τ_{12} both be zero. In the next subsection we shall ascertain the welfare implications of such a union by formulating an explicit maximization problem. Thus, the analysis there is an exercise in nonlinear programming rather than that of comparative statics.

In order to carry out such an analysis, it will be desirable to summarize the production and the consumption relations of Country 3, which we shall do now. The reader should note that the same can be done for the other two countries if we wish to do so.

The production and the consumption relations described in the above model are specified by

$$Y_3 = F_3(X_3),$$

$$\Pi_3 = -F_3'(X_3),$$

$$\Pi_3 = v_3(C_{x3}, C_{y3}),$$

$$E_{x3} = C_{x3} - X_3,$$

$$E_{y3} = C_{y3} - Y_3,$$

$$\Pi_3 E_{x3} + E_{y3} = t_3 \Pi_3 E_{x3}.$$

Now given Π_3, the domestic price ratio for Country 3, the two equations $Y_3 = F_3(X_3)$ and $\Pi_3 = -F_3'$ determine the values of X_3 and Y_3. Then with X_3, Y_3, and Π_3 coming from the remaining four equations, we can determine the values of the remaining four variables C_{x3}, C_{y3}, E_{x3}, and E_{y3} for a given value of t_3. Hence, we may summarize the above relations by

$$X_3 = X_3(\Pi_3),$$

$$Y_3 = Y_3(\Pi_3),$$

$$C_{x3} = C_{x3}(\Pi_3, t_3),$$

$$C_{y3} = C_{y3}(\Pi_3, t_3),$$

$$E_{y3} = E_{y3}(\Pi_3, t_3),$$

and

$$E_{x3} = E_{x3}(\Pi_3, t_3). \tag{16-13}$$

The usual concept of the offer curve under free trade describes equation (16-13) with $t_3 = 0$.

[26] In other words, fix the value of τ_3 (or t_3), compute the values of $dU_i/d\tau_2$ (with τ_{12} fixed) and/or $dU_i/d\tau_{12}$ (with τ_2 fixed), and determine the sign of $dU_i/d\tau_2$ and/or $dU_i/d\tau_{12}$. As an example of the comparative static study on the topic, see Mundell, R.A., "Tariff Preferences and Terms of Trade," *Manchester School of Economic and Social Studies*, 32, January 1964.

Optimal Tariffs for Customs Unions

Assume the three-country, two-commodity world as examined in the last subsection. There by specifying the values of the tariff (or subsidy) rates, τ_{12}, τ_2, τ_{13}, and τ_3, we can determine the equilibrium values of the variables in the system: X_i, Y_i, E_{xi}, E_{yi}, C_{xi}, C_{yi}, and Π_i, $i = 1, 2, 3$. In this section we want to consider the welfare implications of the formation of a customs union between Countries 1 and 2 which abolishes all the tariffs (or subsidies) between Countries 1 and 2.

To consider this problem, we suppose that the rate of tariff (or subsidy) that Country 3 imposes, τ_3 (or t_3), is fixed and consider the problem of maximizing the welfare of the union by choosing the values of the relevant variables properly. In this maximization problem, we do not assume internal free trade within the union, that is, we do not *a priori* specify $\tau_{12} = \tau_2 = 0$. The values of τ_{12} and τ_2 are to be determined by this maximization problem. We obtain a certain set of conditions (the first-order conditions) which characterize the optimum. Assuming that each country is organized in a competitive fashion so that the relation

$$\Pi_i = v_i = -F_i', \quad i = 1, 2, 3,$$

holds at the optimal point, we shall prove in this subsection:

i) The formation of customs unions, that is, free trade within the union, satisfies the conditions for an optimum.

ii) In order to achieve an optimum the union is required to assign a specific rate of tariff on her import from Country 3, and this rate is exactly equal to the one given in the optimal tariff formula for the two-country world that we discussed in the previous chapter.

A complete specification of the optimum conditions is given subsequently in equations (16-16) to (16-20). Our conclusions i) and ii) are important ones, and will be obtained from conditions (16-16) to (16-20).

We now have to discuss the concept of maximizing the welfare of the union. If we can impose (or the member countries of the union can agree on) a certain welfare function such as $V = V(U_1, U_2)$, then this question can be answered easily.[27] The maximization of the welfare of the union means the maximization of the value of V. Here we shall not adopt this concept. Instead we shall define the maximum of the welfare of the union by the vector maximum of $[U_1, U_2]$, which is probably more acceptable to the reader than the maximization of V, the very concept of which is questionable.

We now have to discuss the constraining conditions of the above maximization conditions. There are four major kinds of constraints besides definitional equations such as (16-3a) and (16-3b):

a) The feasibility conditions, (16-9a) and (16-9b).
b) The budget conditions, (16-12a) and (16-12b).

[27] Clearly V is *not* invariant under a monotone transformation of U_1 or U_2. In other words, unless we fix the utility specification of Countries 1 and 2, U_1 and U_2, this function V is meaningless provided that U_1 and U_2 are *not* measurable quantities.

c)   The efficient production, (16-1).

d)   Competitive equilibrium for Country 3, (16-13).

It is important to note that the budget equations, (16-12a) and (16-12b), imply a certain restriction on the trade-tariff relation. Although it is not required to do so, the specification of the trade-tariff relation of the previous subsection (as illustrated in Figure 16-2) certainly satisfies such a restriction. The reader may wish to find some other specification which satisfies (16-12a) and (16-12b), or he may wish to work our problem under different specifications. We shall leave these tasks to the interested reader. Such tasks should be easy, after the fundamental methodology of the present analysis is understood.

We do not assume, at least at the outset, that Countries 1 and 2 are organized in a competitive fashion. In other words, we do *not* impose the conditions $\Pi_i = v_i$ and $\Pi_i = -F_i'$ for $i = 1, 2$ in this maximization problem. We shall see, however, that some of the conditions for the optimum are satisfied *if* the economy of each member country of the union (Countries 1 and 2) is organized in a competitive fashion so that $\Pi_i = v_i = -F_i'$ holds. Moreover, as we remarked above, with this specification we can obtain some important conclusions such as i) and ii) above.

For the concept of vector maximum and the characterization of its solution, we refer the reader to our discussion in the second section of Chapter 7. As we discussed there, the vector maximum problem of maximizing $[U_1, U_2]$ can be converted to that of maximizing a real-valued function $\alpha_1 U_1 + \alpha_2 U_2$ for some $\alpha_i \geq 0, i = 1, 2$ (not vanishing simultaneously) with the same constraints. The characterization of the optimum by the first-order conditions is described by theorem 5 in the second section of Chapter 7. Here, it turns out, we can eliminate all the constraints. That is, we have an unconstrained maximization problem; thus we can disregard all the discussions of the constraints (such as Slater's condition). The procedure of our problem then becomes very similar to the one that we discussed in the previous chapter in connection with the optimum tariff formula.

We start our analysis by noting the following relations which will eliminate all the constraints from our maximization problem. Note that these relations are obtained by taking account of the information provided by the constraints (16-9a), (16-9b), (16-12a), (16-12b), (16-1), (16-3a), (16-3b), and (16-3).

$$C_{x1} = X_1 + E_{x1},\tag{16-14a}$$

$$\begin{aligned} C_{y1} = F_1(X_1) &- (1 - t_2)\Pi_2 E_{x1} \\ &+ [(1 - t_3)\Pi_3 - (1 - t_2)\Pi_2]E_{x3}(\Pi_3, t_3) \end{aligned}\tag{16-14b}$$

$$C_{x2} = X_2 - E_{x1} + E_{x3}(\Pi_3, t_3), \quad \text{and}\tag{16-14c}$$

$$C_{y2} = F_2(X_2) + (1 - t_2)\Pi_2[E_{x1} + E_{x3}(\Pi_3, t_3)].\tag{16-14d}$$

The derivation of (16-14b) may need a little explanation. This is carried out as follows. First using the definition of E_{y1} and (16-9b), we have

$$C_{y1} = Y_1 + E_{y1} = Y_1 - (E_{y2} + E_{y3}),$$

which we transform, using the budget conditions for Countries 2 and 3, (16-12b) and (16-12c), as

$$C_{y1} = Y_1 - [(t_2 - 1)\Pi_2 E_{x2} + (t_3 - 1)\Pi_3 E_{x3}] .$$

Then noting that $E_{x2} = -(E_{x1} + E_{x3})$ and $Y_1 = F_1(X_1)$, (12-14b) follows immediately.

Our problem is now considered to be one of choosing X_1, X_2, E_{x1}, $(1 - t_2)\Pi_2$, and Π_3 to maximize

$$U \equiv \alpha_1 U_1[X_1 + E_{x1}, F_1(X_1) - (1 - t_2)\Pi_2 E_{x1}$$
$$+ \{(1 - t_3)\Pi_3 - (1 - t_2)\Pi_2\}E_{x3}(\Pi_3, t_3)]$$
$$+ \alpha_2 U_2[X_2 - \{E_{x1} + E_{x3}(\Pi_3, t_3)\} ,$$
$$F_2(X_2) + (1 - t_2)\Pi_2\{E_{x1} + E_{x3}(\Pi_3, t_3)\}] \qquad (16\text{-}15)$$

given a fixed value of t_3.

Let $[X_1{}^*, X_2{}^*, E_{x1}{}^*, (1 - t_2{}^*)\Pi_2{}^*, \Pi_3{}^*] \equiv Z^*$ be a solution of this maximization problem. Then we must require (as a set of necessary conditions for the original vector maximum problem) the following conditions to hold for some α_1 and α_2, assuming interior solutions [that is, $X_i{}^* > 0$, $i = 1, 2$, $(1 - t_2{}^*)\Pi_2{}^* > 0$, $\Pi_3{}^* > 0$, and $E_{x1}{}^* < 0$] and $\alpha_1 > 0$ and $\alpha_2 > 0$:

$$\frac{\partial U^*}{\partial X_1} = 0 , \quad \text{or} \quad v_1{}^* = -F_1{}'^*, \qquad (16\text{-}16)$$

$$\frac{\partial U^*}{\partial X_2} = 0 , \quad \text{or} \quad v_2{}^* = -F_2{}'^*, \qquad (16\text{-}17)$$

where $\partial U^*/\partial X_i$ denotes $\partial U/\partial X_i$ evaluated at Z^* and $v_i{}^*$ and $F_i{}'^*$ are evaluated at Z^*, $i = 1, 2$;

$$\frac{\partial U^*}{\partial E_{x1}} = 0 , \quad \text{or} \qquad\qquad\qquad\qquad (16\text{-}18)$$

$$\alpha_1[U_{1x}{}^* - U_{1y}{}^*(1 - t_2{}^*)\Pi_2{}^*] - \alpha_2[U_{2x}{}^* - (1 - t_2{}^*)\Pi_2{}^* U_{2y}{}^*] = 0 ,$$

where $\partial U^*/\partial E_{x1}$ is $\partial U/\partial E_{x1}$ evaluated at Z^*, and $U_{ix}{}^* \equiv \partial U_i/\partial C_{xi}$, and $U_{iy}{}^* \equiv \partial U_i/\partial C_{yi}$, each evaluated at Z^*, $i = 1, 2$;

$$\frac{\partial U^*}{\partial [(1 - t_2)\Pi_2]} = 0 , \quad \text{or} \quad \alpha_1 U_{1y}{}^* = \alpha_2 U_{2y}{}^*, \qquad (16\text{-}19)$$

assuming that $E_{x1}{}^* + E_{x3}(\Pi_3{}^*, t_3) \neq 0$, where $\partial U^*/\partial [(1 - t_2)\Pi_2] = \partial U/\partial [(1 - t_2)\Pi_2]$ evaluated at Z^*;

$$\frac{\partial U^*}{\partial \Pi_3} = 0 , \quad \text{or} \qquad\qquad\qquad\qquad (16\text{-}20)$$

$$\alpha_1 U_{1y}{}^*[(1 - t_3)E_{x3}{}^* + \{(1 - t_3)\Pi_3{}^* - (1 - t_2{}^*)\Pi_2{}^*\}E_{x3}{}'^*]$$
$$- \alpha_2[U_{2x}{}^* - (1 - t_2{}^*)\Pi_2{}^* U_{2y}{}^*]E_{x3}{}'^* = 0 ,$$

where $\partial U^*/\partial \Pi_3$ is $\partial U/\partial \Pi_3$ evaluated at Z^*, $E_{x3}^* \equiv E_{x3}(\Pi_3^*, t_3)$ and $E_{x3}'^* \equiv \partial E_{x3}/\partial \Pi_3$, evaluated at (Π_3^*, t_3).

Conversely, if we can find the value of $[X_1^*, X_2^*, E_{x1}^*, (1 - t_2^*)\Pi_2^*, \Pi_3^*]$ which satisfies the five conditions (16-16) through (16-20) for some strictly positive $\alpha_i > 0$, $i = 1, 2$, then such a Z^* will realize a vector maximum of $[U_1, U_2]$. Note that conditions (16-16) through (16-20) provide five equations to determine the values of the five variables $X_1^*, X_2^*, E_{x1}^*, (1 - t_2^*)\Pi_2^*$, and Π_3^*. The values of the other variables such as Y_1, Y_2, E_{x2}, E_{yi}, Π_1, and so on are all computed by taking account of (16-1), the feasibility conditions (16-9), the budget conditions (16-12), and some definitional equations such as (16-3).[28]

Hence, if we restrict ourselves to the case in which $\alpha_1 > 0$, and $\alpha_2 > 0$, then conditions (16-16) through (16-20) are necessary and sufficient conditions for an optimum. When we take conditions (16-16) through (16-20) as a set of *necessary* conditions, then the α_is are interpreted as the parameters whose variations result in various (Pareto) optimal points for the union. α_i can be interpreted as the weight attached to the ith country ($i = 1, 2$) so that $\alpha_i > 0$ means that the ith country is not disregarded.

Suppose that the union can agree to a common welfare function of the form $V = V(U_1, U_2)$, where U_i is some *fixed* utility indicator for Country i. Then we can carry out the analysis for this case exactly the same as for the previous analysis of the vector maximum by interpreting the α_is as

$$\alpha_i \equiv \frac{\partial V}{\partial U_i}, \quad \text{evaluated at } Z^*, i = 1, 2. \tag{16-21}$$

With these remarks on conditions (16-16) through (16-20) we now turn to the interpretations of these conditions.

Conditions (16-16) and (16-17) state that the rate of marginal production transformation is equal to the rate of marginal consumer substitution for each member country of the union. Conditions (16-16) and (16-17) will be realized if the economy of each member country is organized in a competitive fashion so that there exist price ratios Π_1 and Π_2 such that

$$\Pi_1 = v_1^* = -F_1'^*, \quad \text{and} \quad \Pi_2 = v_2^* = -F_2'^*. \tag{16-22}$$

Now assuming $U_{1y}^* > 0$ and $U_{2y}^* > 0$, we can rewrite condition (16-18) in the following equivalent form:

$$\alpha_1 U_{1y}^*[v_1^* - (1 - t_2^*)\Pi_2^*] = \alpha_2 U_{2y}^*[v_2^* - (1 - t_2^*)\Pi_2^*]. \tag{16-23}$$

[28] It must be assumed, as remarked above, that the budget conditions (16-12a) through (16-12c) hold at Z^*. In particular, this is true if the trade-tariff relation is the one illustrated in Figure 16-4. This assumption should also be retained during the specification of $\tau_2^* = 0$ $\Pi_1^* = \Pi_2^*$, and the value of τ_{13}^* by (16-28) in the subsequent discussion.

Since we assumed the competitive organization of each member country, so that (16-22) holds, (16-23) requires, in view of (16-19), that

$$\Pi_1{}^* - (1 - t_2{}^*)\Pi_2{}^* = \Pi_2{}^* - (1 - t_2{}^*)\Pi_2{}^* , \tag{16-24}$$

or

$$\Pi_1{}^* = \Pi_2{}^* . \tag{16-24'}$$

If no subsidies are allowed within the union so that $\tau_{12} \geqq 0$ and $\tau_2 \geqq 0$, then (16-24') requires $\tau_{12}{}^* = 0$ and $\tau_2{}^* = 0$. In other words, *free trade within the union is after all required for the optimum from the union's point of view.* If negative τ_{12} and/or τ_2 (that is, subsidies) are allowed, (16-24') does not require $\tau_{12}{}^* = \tau_2{}^* = 0$ (internal free trade within the union), for there can be combinations of τ_{12} and τ_2 such that (16-24') is satisfied.

Finally we have to discuss condition (16-20). To do this we define the *elasticity of Country 3's offer curve,* denoted by η_3, (in the usual way) by

$$\eta_3 \equiv - \frac{\partial E_{x3}}{\partial \Pi_3} \frac{\Pi_3}{E_{x3}} . \tag{16-25}$$

Let $\eta_3{}^*$ denote η_3 evaluated at $(\Pi_3{}^*, t_3)$, so that $\eta_3{}^* = -E_{x3}{}'{}^*\Pi_3{}^*/E_{x3}{}^*$. Assume that condition (16-24) is satisfied with free trade within the union so that $t_2{}^* = 0$ and $\Pi_1{}^* = \Pi_2{}^*$. Moreover, a competitive equilibrium of Country 2 requires $\Pi_2{}^* = v_2{}^*$. Hence, the second term of the left-hand side of (16-20) vanishes. Therefore, using the above concept $\eta_3{}^*$, we can rewrite condition (16-20) as

$$(1 - t_3)\Pi_3{}^* - [(1 - t_3)\Pi_3{}^* - \Pi_1{}^*]\eta_3{}^* = 0 , \tag{16-26}$$

where $E_{x3}{}^* \neq 0$ is assumed.

Therefore, using (16-11b), the optimal price distortion between $\Pi_1{}^*$ and $\Pi_3{}^*$, denoted by $T_3{}^*$, is determined by

$$(1 - t_3)T_3{}^* = \frac{\eta_3{}^*}{\eta_3{}^* - 1} , \tag{16-27}$$

where $T_3{}^* = (1 + \tau_3)(1 + \tau_{13}{}^*)$ and $t_3 \equiv \dfrac{\tau_3}{1 + \tau_3}$.

Here $\tau_{13}{}^*$ signifies the optimal rate of tariff that the union imposes on her import of Commodity Y from Country 3. Note that Country 1 is the sole importer of Commodity Y in the union. The explicit expression of τ_{13} can be obtained from (16-27) as,

$$\tau_{13}{}^* = \frac{1}{\eta_3{}^* - 1} \tag{16-28}$$

Note that (16-28) gives an identical expression for the optimum tariff formula for the two-country world.

In the above optimization problem we supposed that τ_{13} is one of the choice variables and obtained the formula (16-28). Suppose now that τ_{13} (as well as τ_3) is fixed *a priori*. For example, we may suppose that τ_{13} and τ_3 are fixed by a tariff agreement between Country 1 and Country 3 and that the union cannot affect these rates. Such a problem is considered by Vanek [40] and Negishi [31]. We shall leave the consideration of this problem to the interested reader. The problem is again reduced to a simple maximization problem.

The Maximization of the World Welfare

In the previous problem we were concerned with the maximization problem from the viewpoint of the union. Now we convert this to the maximization problem from the point of view of the world as a whole. In other words, we want to maximize the vector $[U_1, U_2, U_3]$ (instead of $[U_1, U_2]$) subject to the proper constraints, such as the feasibility conditions, budget conditions, and technological and definitional equations. Actually we know the answer to this problem already from our discussion of Chapters 1 and 7. In other words, we know that free trade among the countries in the world realizes an (Pareto) optimal state of the world and that every such an (Pareto) optimal state can be supported by free trade and competitive pricing.

However, we shall do this maximization problem here to enhance the reader's understanding of the problem involved in this well-known proposition and to provide a reference model for the present problem of the customs union.

If we can prove that free trade is required to achieve an (Pareto) optimal state of the world in the context of the present model, then we can assert that the formation of a free trade area by a customs union satisfies part of the conditions required. This supports the proposition of the piecemeal approach proposed by Kuroiwa [17] and Davis and Whinston [6] in the general theory of second best.

Mathematically our problem is that of a vector maximum problem, and we again refer to our discussion of Chapter 7, second section. The problem of maximizing a vector $[U_1, U_2, U_3]$ subject to a certain set of constraints then can be converted to the problem of maximizing a real-valued function, $\alpha_1 U_1 + \alpha_2 U_2 + \alpha_3 U_3$, subject to the same set of constraints for some $\alpha_1 \geqq 0$, $\alpha_2 \geqq 0$, and $\alpha_3 \geqq 0$ (not vanishing simultaneously).[29]

We start our analysis noting the following relations, which will eliminate all the constraints from our maximization problem. Note that these relations are slight modifications of (16-14a) through (16-14d) with additions for the relations of C_{x3} and C_{y3}:

$$C_{x1} = X_1 + E_{x1}, \tag{16-29}$$

$$C_{y1} = F_1(X_1) - (1 - t_2)\Pi_2 E_{x1} + [(1 - t_3)\Pi_3 - (1 - t_2)\Pi_2]E_{x3}, \tag{16-30}$$

$$C_{x2} = X_2 - (E_{x1} + E_{x3}), \tag{16-31}$$

---

[29] Needless to say, these α_is are in general different from the α_is which appeared in the (vector) maximization of $[U_1, U_2]$ in the previous subsection.

$$C_{y2} = F_2(X_2) + (1 - t_2)\Pi_2(E_{x1} + E_{x3}),$$ (16-32)

$$C_{x3} = X_3 + E_{x3},$$ (16-33)

$$C_{y3} = F_3(X_3) - (1 - t_3)\Pi_3 E_{x3}.$$ (16-34)

Our problem is now considered to be one of choosing X_1, X_2, X_3, E_{x1}, E_{x3}, $(1 - t_2)\Pi_2$, and $(1 - t_3)\Pi_3$ to maximize

$$W \equiv \alpha_1 U_1[X_1 + E_{x1}, F_1(X_1) - (1 - t_2)\Pi_2 E_{x1}$$
$$+ \{(1 - t_3)\Pi_3 - (1 - t_2)\Pi_2\}E_{x3}]$$
$$+ \alpha_2 U_2[X_2 - (E_{x1} + E_{x3}),$$
$$F_2(X_2) + (1 - t_2)\Pi_2(E_{x1} + E_{x3})]$$
$$+ \alpha_3 U_3[X_3 + E_{x3}, F_3(X_3) - (1 - t_3)\Pi_3 E_{x3}].$$ (16-35)

Let $[X_1{}^o, X_2{}^o, X_3{}^o, E_{x1}{}^o, E_{x3}{}^o, (1 - t_2{}^o)\Pi_2{}^o, (1 - t_3{}^o)\Pi_3{}^o] \equiv Z_w{}^o$ be a solution of this maximization problem. Then we must require (as a set of necessary conditions for the original vector maximum problem) the following conditions to hold for some α, $i = 1, 2, 3$ (not vanishing simultaneously), assuming interior solutions $(X_i{}^o > 0$, $(1 - t_i{}^o)\Pi_i{}^o > 0$, $i = 2, 3$, $E_{x1}{}^o < 0$, and $E_{x3}{}^o > 0)$ and $\alpha_i > 0$, $i = 1, 2, 3$:

$$\frac{\partial W^o}{\partial X_1} = 0, \quad \text{or} \quad v_1{}^o = -F_1'{}^o,$$ (16-36)

$$\frac{\partial W^o}{\partial X_2} = 0, \quad \text{or} \quad v_2{}^o = -F_2'{}^o,$$ (16-37)

$$\frac{\partial W^o}{\partial X_3} = 0, \quad \text{or} \quad v_3{}^o = -F_3'{}^o;$$ (16-38)

where $\partial W^o/\partial X_i$ denotes $\partial W/\partial X_i$ evaluated at $Z_w{}^o$. $v_i{}^o$ and $F_i'{}^o$ are also evaluated at $Z_w{}^o$;

$$\frac{\partial W^o}{\partial E_{x1}} = 0, \quad \text{or}$$

$$\alpha_1[U_{1x}{}^o - U_{1y}{}^o(1 - t_2{}^o)\Pi_2{}^o] - \alpha_2[U_{2x}{}^o - (1 - t_2{}^o)\Pi_2{}^o U_{2y}{}^o] = 0,$$ (16-39)

$$\frac{\partial W^o}{\partial E_{x3}} = 0, \quad \text{or}$$

$$\alpha_1 U_{1y}{}^o[(1 - t_3{}^o)\Pi_3{}^o - (1 - t_2{}^o)\Pi_2{}^o] - \alpha_2[U_{2x}{}^o - U_{2y}{}^o(1 - t_2{}^o)\Pi_2{}^o]$$
$$+ \alpha_3[U_{3x}{}^o - U_{3y}{}^o(1 - t_3{}^o)\Pi_3{}^o] = 0,$$ (16-40)

where $\partial W^o/\partial E_{xi}$ is $\partial W/\partial E_{xi}$ evaluated at $Z_w{}^o$, and $U_{ix}{}^o \equiv \partial U_i/\partial C_{xi}$ and $U_{ix}{}^o \equiv \partial U_i/\partial C_{yi}$, each evaluated at $Z_w{}^o$, $i = 1, 2, 3$;

$$\frac{\partial W^o}{\partial[(1 - t_2)\Pi_2]} = 0, \quad \text{or} \quad \alpha_1 U_{1y}{}^o = \alpha_2 U_{2y}{}^o,$$ (16-41)

assuming $E_{x1}^{\,o} + E_{x3}^{\,o} \neq 0$, where $\partial W^o / \partial[(1 - t_2)\Pi_2] = \partial W / \partial[(1 - t_2)\Pi_2]$ evaluated at $Z_w^{\,o}$;

$$\frac{\partial W^o}{\partial[(1 - t_3)\Pi_3]} = 0, \quad \text{or} \quad \alpha_1 U_{1y}^{\,o} = \alpha_3 U_{3y}^{\,o}, \tag{16-42}$$

assuming $E_{x3}^{\,o} \neq 0$, where $\partial W^o / \partial[(1 - t_3)\Pi_3] = \partial W / \partial[(1 - t_3)\Pi_3]$ evaluated at $Z_w^{\,o}$.

Conversely, if we can find the value of $Z_w^{\,o}$ which satisfies the seven equations (16-36) through (16-42) for some strictly positive $\alpha_i > 0$, $i = 1, 2, 3$, then such a $Z_w^{\,o}$ will realize a vector maximum of $[U_1, U_2, U_3]$. Note that conditions (16-36) through (16-42) provide seven equations to determine the values of the seven variables $X_1^{\,o}$, $X_2^{\,o}$, $X_3^{\,o}$, $E_{x1}^{\,o}$, $E_{x3}^{\,o}$, $(1 - t_2^{\,o})\Pi_2^{\,o}$, and $(1 - t_3^{\,o})\Pi_3^{\,o}$. The values of the other variables are computed by taking account of (16-1), (16-3), (16-9), (16-12), and so on.

If we again restrict ourselves to the case in which $\alpha_i > 0$, $i = 1, 2, 3$, then conditions (16-36) through (16-42) are necessary and sufficient conditions for an optimum. α_i can be considered as a weight attached to Country i by the world. As remarked before, these α_is can be different from α_is in our discussion of the last sub-section.[30]

Suppose that the world can agree on a common welfare function of the form $\overline{W} = \overline{W}(U_1, U_2, U_3)$, where U_i is some *fixed* utility indicator for Country i. Then we can carry out the analysis for this case exactly the same as for the previous analysis of the vector maximum by interpreting the α_is as

$$\alpha_i = \frac{\partial \overline{W}}{\partial U_i}, \tag{16-43}$$

evaluated at $Z_w^{\,o}$, $i = 1, 2, 3$.

With these remarks on conditions (16-36) through (16-42), we now turn to the interpretation of these conditions.

Conditions (16-36), (16-37), and (16-38) state that the rate of marginal production transformation is equal to the rate of marginal consumer substitution for each country of the world. Conditions (16-36), (16-37), and (16-38) will be realized if the economy of each country is organized in a competitive fashion so that there exist price ratios Π_1, Π_2, and Π_3 such that

$$\Pi_i = v_i^{\,o} = -F_i^{\prime o}, \quad i = 1, 2, 3. \tag{16-44}$$

Now assuming $U_{ix}^{\,o} > 0$ and $U_{iy}^{\,o} > 0$, $i = 1, 2, 3$, we can rewrite conditions (16-39) and (16-40) in the following equivalent form:

$$\alpha_1 U_{1y}^{\,o}[v_1^{\,o} - (1 - t_2^{\,o})\Pi_2^{\,o}] = \alpha_2 U_{2y}^{\,o}[v_2^{\,o} - (1 - t_2^{\,o})\Pi_2^{\,o}], \tag{16-45}$$

$$\alpha_1 U_{1y}^{\,o}[(1 - t_3^{\,o})\Pi_3^{\,o} - (1 - t_2^{\,o})\Pi_2^{\,o}] - \alpha_2 U_{2y}^{\,o}[v_2^{\,o} - (1 - t_2^{\,o})\Pi_2^{\,o}]$$
$$+ \alpha_3 U_{3y}^{\,o}[v_3^{\,o} - (1 - t_3^{\,o})\Pi_3^{\,o}] = 0. \tag{16-46}$$

---

[30] Needless to say, the budget conditions (16-12a) through (16-12c) hold at $Z_w^{\,o}$. This is true, in particular, if the trade-tariff relation is the one illustrated in Figure 16-4. This assumption should also be retained when we specify $t_2^{\,o} = t_3^{\,o} = 0$ and $\Pi_1^{\,o} = \Pi_2^{\,o} = \Pi_3^{\,o}$ in the subsequent discussion.

Assuming competitive organization so that (16-44) holds, (16-45) and (16-46) respectively require

$$\Pi_1^o = \Pi_2^o, \quad \text{and} \tag{16-47}$$

$$\Pi_2^o = \Pi_3^o. \tag{16-48}$$

In view of (16-41) and (16-42), (16-47) and (16-48) require

$$(1 + \tau_2^o)(1 + \tau_{12}^o) = 1, \quad \text{and} \quad (1 + \tau_3^o)(1 + \tau_{13}^o) = 1. \tag{16-49}$$

Hence, assuming that $\tau_2 \geqq 0$, $\tau_{12} \geqq 0$, $\tau_3 \geqq 0$, $\tau_{13} \geqq 0$, (16-49) implies that

$$\tau_2^o = \tau_{12}^o = \tau_3^o = \tau_{13}^o = 0 \tag{16-50}$$

is required. In other words, free trade among the countries of the world is required after all. This is nothing but a confirmation of our conviction about the Pareto optimum implications of free trade that we discussed in Chapters 1 and 7. Note also that if subsidies are allowed, (16-49) itself does not require (16-50), for there can be tariff-subsidy combinations such that (16-49) holds. However, it is also true that if (16-50) is satisfied, then (16-49) is automatically satisfied.

In the previous subsection, we proved that the maximization of welfare of the union, the vector $[U_1, U_2]$, requires free trade within the union. Now that we have confirmed this, it becomes a part of the conditions for the optimization of world welfare.

Actually, this piecemeal conviction is not particularly surprising. Mathematically speaking, the maximization of the welfare of the union instead of the world as a whole amounts to setting $\alpha_3 = 0$ in the problem of maximizing $\sum_{i=1}^{3} \alpha_i U_i$. Hence, some of the optimization conditions are bound to be the same between the two cases, which is the content of the piecemeal approach.[31] We should also note that the crucial condition, for such a piecemeal approach to be valid, is the lack of any externality among the countries in the sense that U_i depends only on Country i's consumption bundle and F_i depends only on X_i. If, for example, U_1 depended on (C_{x3}, C_{y3}) as well as (C_{x1}, C_{y1}), the piecemeal conclusion would not necessarily be true.

Although we have thus far shown that optimization from the union's point of view satisfies one condition—internal free trade within the union—for the optimization of world welfare, this does not imply that the behavioral formula for the union of her own welfare (obtained in the previous section) achieves a Pareto optimum for the world as a whole. In fact, the new tariff computed by (16-28) would very likely harm Country 3. Hence, it is likely that the formation of such a union does *not* achieve a Pareto optimum for the world as a whole.

---

[31] As remarked before (footnote [20]), the piecemeal approach does not conclude that an increase in the number of the conditions for optimum which are fulfilled will increase the total welfare (here world welfare), even if world welfare can be uniquely defined in terms of $\overline{W} = \overline{W}(U_1, U_2, U_3)$.

Let us now consider the problem of Pareto-optimizing world welfare, assuming that Country 3 does not change her tariff rate. That is, τ_3 is a given datum for the maximization problem.[32]

To consider this problem, first define $\tilde{\Pi}_2$ and k by

$$\tilde{\Pi}_2 \equiv (1 - t_2)\Pi_2 , \tag{16-51}$$

$$k \equiv \Pi_3/\tilde{\Pi}_2 . \tag{16-52}$$

Then from the definition of t_2 and t_3 in (16-12) and also from (16-11), we obtain the following relations:

$$k = T_3/(1 + \tau_{12}) \tag{16-53}$$

$$(1 - t_3)k = (1 + \tau_{13})/(1 + \tau_{12}) . \tag{16-54}$$

The problem of Pareto-optimizing world welfare with a fixed value of τ_3 can be considered as one of choosing X_1, X_2, X_3, E_{x1}, $\tilde{\Pi}_2$, and k to maximize

$$
\begin{aligned}
W_1 = \alpha_1 U_1 [& X_1 + E_{x1}, F_1(X_1) - \tilde{\Pi}_2 E_{x1} \\
& + \{(1 - t_3)k\tilde{\Pi}_2 - \tilde{\Pi}_2\}E_{x3}(k\tilde{\Pi}_2, t_3)] \\
+ \alpha_2 U_2 [& X_2 - \{E_{x1} + E_{x3}(k\tilde{\Pi}_2, t_3)\}, \\
& F_2(X_2) + \tilde{\Pi}_2\{E_{x1} + E_{x3}(k\tilde{\Pi}_2, t_3)\}] \\
+ \alpha_3 U_3 [& X_3 + E_{x3}(k\tilde{\Pi}_2, t_3), F_3(X_3) - (1 - t_3)k\tilde{\Pi}_2 E_{x3}(k\tilde{\Pi}_2, t_3)] ,
\end{aligned}
\tag{16-55}
$$

where τ_3 (or t_3) is a fixed constant.

Partially differentiating with respect to X_1, X_2, X_3, and E_{x1} respectively and setting each equal to zero, we obtain conditions (16-36), (16-37), (16-38), and (16-39). Assume again $U_{ix}{}^o > 0$ and $U_{iy}{}^o > 0$ $(i = 1, 2, 3)$. Then (16-39) can be rewritten as (16-45), or

$$\alpha_1 U_{1y}{}^o\Pi_1{}^o - \tilde{\Pi}_2{}^o = \alpha_2 U_{2y}{}^o\Pi_2{}^o - \tilde{\Pi}_2{}^o , \tag{16-56}$$

provided that the economies of Countries 1 and 2 are organized in a competitive way (so that $v_1{}^o = \Pi_1{}^o$ and $v_2{}^o = \Pi_2{}^o$ hold). Here we again use the superscript $(^o)$ to denote the optimum point for the sake of notational simplicity.[33] Conditions (16-36), (16-37), and (16-38) are again satisfied by assuming a competitive organization of each country's economy. That is, assuming (16-44),

$$v_i{}^o = \Pi_i{}^o = -F_i'{}^o, \quad i = 1, 2, 3 .$$

[32] Similarly, the reader can easily consider the problem of Pareto-optimizing world welfare when the values of τ_{13} as well as τ_3 are fixed *a priori*. For example, the values of τ_{13} and τ_3 are fixed by a tariff agreement between Country 1 and Country 3.

[33] More rigorously, we have to use different notations such as $X_1{}^{oo}$, $X_2{}^{oo}$, and so on, instead of $X_1{}^o$, $X_2{}^o$, and so on, to denote the optimum point, for the optimum point of the present problem is, in general, different from that in the previous problem.

Partially differentiating W_1 with respect to $\tilde{\Pi}_2$ and setting it equal to zero, we obtain

$$\alpha_1 U_{1y}[-E_{x1}{}^o + \{(1 - t_3)k^o - 1\}\{E_{x3}{}^o + k\tilde{\Pi}_2{}^o E_{x3}{}'^o\}]$$

$$+ \alpha_2 U_{2y}{}^o[(E_{x1}{}^o + E_{x3}{}^o) - k^o E_{x3}{}''^o(\Pi_2{}^o - \tilde{\Pi}_2{}^o)]$$

$$+ \alpha_3 U_{3y}{}^o[-(1 - t_3)k^o E_{x3}{}^o + t_3(k\tilde{\Pi}_2^o)E_3{}'^o] = 0, \qquad (16\text{-}57)$$

where $E_{x3}{}'^o = \partial E_{x3}/\partial\Pi_3$ evaluated at $\Pi_3{}^o \equiv k^o\tilde{\Pi}_2{}^o$, and $E_{x3}{}^o \equiv E_{x3}(\Pi_3{}^o, t_3)$, and so on. Here we again used the competitive condition (16-44). Define the elasticity of Country 3's offer curve η_3 as (16-25) and let $\eta_3{}^o$ denote η_3 evaluated at $(\Pi_3{}^o, t_3)$, so that $\eta_3{}^o = -E_{x3}{}'^o\Pi_3{}^o/E_{x3}{}^o$, or $E_{x3}{}'^o/E_{x3}{}^o = -\eta_3{}^o/(k^o\tilde{\Pi}_2{}^o)$. Then recalling (16-53) and (16-54), we can rewrite (16-57) as

$$(1 + \tau_{12}{}^o)(\alpha_1 U_{1y}{}^o - \alpha_2 U_{2y}{}^o)E_{x1}{}^o/E_{x3}{}^o$$

$$= \alpha_1 U_{1y}{}^o[\tau_{13}{}^o(1 - \eta_3{}^o) - \tau_{12}{}^o] - \alpha_3 U_{3y}{}^o(1 + \tau_{13}{}^o)(1 + \tau_3\eta_3{}^o), \qquad (16\text{-}58)$$

where $\tau_{12}{}^o$ and $\tau_{13}{}^o$ are the values of τ_{12} and τ_{13} implied by k^o and $\tilde{\Pi}_2{}^o$. t_3 and τ_3 are given constants by assumption.

Partially differentiating W_1 with respect to k and setting it equal to zero yields

$$\alpha_1 U_{1y}{}^o[1 + \tau_{13}{}^o(1 - \eta_3{}^o)] = \alpha_3 U_{3y}{}^o[(1 + \tau_{13}{}^o)(1 + \tau_3\eta_3{}^o)], \qquad (16\text{-}59)$$

after rearranging terms and keeping (16-53), (16-54), (16-56), (16-44), and the definition of $\eta_3{}^o$ in mind. Six relations, (16-36), (16-37), (16-38), (16-39), (16-58), and (16-59) determine the optimal values of the six choice variables, $X_1{}^o$, $X_2{}^o$, $X_3{}^o$, $E_{x1}{}^o$, $\tilde{\Pi}_2{}^o$, and k^o. The optimal values of the rest of the variables such as $Y_i{}^o$, $\Pi_i{}^o$, $C_{xi}{}^o$, $C_{yi}{}^o$, $E_{yi}{}^o$ $(i = 1, 2, 3)$, $E_{x2}{}^o$, $E_{x3}{}^o$, $\tau_{12}{}^o$, $\tau_2{}^o$, and $\tau_{13}{}^o$ can be computed easily from the production relation (16-1), the competitive condition (16-44), etc.[34]

Combining (16-58) with (16-59), we obtain

$$\alpha_1 U_{1y}{}^o(E_{x1}{}^o + E_{x3}{}^o) = \alpha_2 U_{2y}{}^o E_{x1}{}^o. \qquad (16\text{-}60)$$

This condition is different from condition (16-41). (16-60) can also be written as

$$(\alpha_1 U_{1y}{}^o - \alpha_2 U_{2y}{}^o)E_{x1}{}^o = -\alpha_1 U_{1y}{}^o E_{x3}{}^o. \qquad (16\text{-}61)$$

Assume that Country 1 exports X and Country 3 imports X at the optimum point so that $E_{x1}{}^o < 0$ and $E_{x3}{}^o > 0$. Then (16-61) implies

$$\alpha_1 U_{1y}{}^o > \alpha_2 U_{2y}{}^o. \qquad (16\text{-}62)$$

---

[34] $Y_i{}^o$, $i = 1, 2, 3$ are computed from $X_i{}^o$, $i = 1, 2, 3$ by (16-1). $X_i{}^o$, $i = 1, 2, 3$ also determine $\Pi_i{}^o$, $i = 1, 2, 3$, by (16-54). With a fixed t_3, $E_{x3}{}^o$ is computed by $E_{x3}(\Pi_3{}^o, t_3)$. Also $v_3{}^o = \Pi_3{}^o$ and Country 3's budget condition (16-12c) determines $C_{x3}{}^o$ and $C_{y3}{}^o$ and hence $E_{y3}{}^o$ as well as $E_{x3}{}^o$. (16-48) and $\Pi_2{}^o$ determine $t_2{}^o$ (or $\tau_2{}^o$). $t_2{}^o$, $v_2{}^o = \Pi_2{}^o$, and Country 2's budget condition (16-12b) determine $C_{x2}{}^o$ and $C_{y2}{}^o$; hence $E_{x2}{}^o$ and $E_{y2}{}^o$. Since $\Pi_2{}^o = (1 + \tau_2{}^o)(1 + \tau_{12}{}^o)\Pi_1{}^o$ by (16-11a); $t_2{}^o$, $\Pi_1{}^o$, and $\Pi_2{}^o$ determine $\tau_{12}{}^o$. Also k^o and $\tau_{12}{}^o$ determine $\tau_{13}{}^o$ by use of (16-53). $E_{x1}{}^o$ and $E_{y1}{}^o$ (hence also $C_{x1}{}^o$ and $C_{y1}{}^o$) are computed by (16-9a) and (16-9b).

This means that there are the following three possibilities to satisfy (16-56):

$$\Pi_1{}^o = \tilde{\Pi}_2{}^o = \Pi_2{}^o , \tag{16-63a}$$

$$0 < \Pi_1{}^o - \tilde{\Pi}_2{}^o < \Pi_2{}^o - \tilde{\Pi}_2 , \tag{16-63b}$$

$$0 < \tilde{\Pi}_2{}^o - \Pi_1{}^o < \tilde{\Pi}_2{}^o - \Pi_2{}^o . \tag{16-63c}$$

(16-63b) and (16-63c) can respectively be restated in the following equivalent forms:

$$\Pi_2{}^o > \Pi_1{}^o > \tilde{\Pi}_2{}^o , \tag{16-63b'}$$

$$\tilde{\Pi}_2 > \Pi_1{}^o > \Pi_2{}^o . \tag{16-63c'}$$

Now note that the following relations hold by definition:

$$\Pi_2 = (1 + \tau_{12})(1 + \tau_2)\Pi_1 , \quad \tilde{\Pi}_2 = (1 + \tau_2)\Pi_1 . \tag{16-64}$$

Hence, if we assume $\tau_{12} \geqq 0, \tau_2 \geqq 0$ (no subsidies are allowed within the Union), then (16-64) implies that neither (16-63b') nor (16-63c') can hold.

Hence only (16-64a) is possible, which implies that

$$t_2{}^o = 0 \quad \text{and} \quad t_{12}{}^o = 0 \tag{16-65}$$

are required. In other words, *internal free trade within the union is required for the optimum.* In the first section, we argued that the Lipsey-Lancaster theorem of second best is considerably sharpened by the piecemeal approach proposed by Kuroiwa and Davis-Whinston. We have now obtained a remarkable example of such a piecemeal second best theorem. We have proved the following statement: In order to achieve a Pareto optimum of the world when a distortion τ_3 is given, it is required that all the tariffs between Countries 1 and 2 (τ_{12} and τ_2) be abolished.

Note that our condition (16-59) can be rewritten as

$$\tau_{13}{}^o = [1 - \beta(1 + \tau_3\eta_3{}^o)]/[(\eta_3{}^o - 1) + \beta(1 + \tau_3\eta_3{}^o)] , \tag{16-66}$$

where

$$\beta \equiv \alpha_3 U_{3y}{}^o / \alpha_1 U_{1y}{}^o . \tag{16-67}$$

In particular, if $\alpha_3 = 0$, then $\beta = 0$. Since $\alpha_3 = 0$ means that Country 3 is disregarded in the present maximization problem, the problem is reduced to the maximization of welfare solely from the union's point of view, and condition (16-66) is reduced to condition (16-28). In other words, condition (16-66) is a generalization of condition (16-28).

REFERENCES

1. Balassa, B., "Towards a Theory of Economic Integration," *Kyklos*, XIX (1), 1961.
2. ———, *The Theory of Economic Integration* (Homewood, Ill.: Richard D. Irwin, Inc.), 1961.

3. Bentrick, B. L., "Estimating Trade Creation and Trade Diversion," *Economic Journal*, LXXIII, June 1963.
4. Bohm, P., "On the Theory of 'Second Best'," *Review of Economic Studies*, XXXIV, July 1967.
5. Clement, M. O., Pfister, R. L., and Rothwell, K. J., *Theoretical Issues in International Economics* (Boston: Houghton Mifflin Company), 1967, especially Chapter 4.
6. Davis, O. A. and Whinston, A. B., "Welfare Economics and the Theory of Second Best," *Review of Economic Studies*, XXXII, January 1965.
7. ———, "Piecemeal Policy in the Theory of Second Best," *Review of Economic Studies*, XXXIV, July 1967.
8. Gehrels, F., "Customs Union from a Single Country Viewpoint," *Review of Economic Studies*, (1), XXIV, 1956–57.
9. ———, and Johnson, H. G., "The Economic Gains from European Integration," *Journal of Political Economy*, LXIII, August 1955.
10. Humphrey, D. D. and Ferguson, C. E., "The Domestic and World Benefits of a Customs Union," *Economia Internazionale*, XIII, Maggio, 1960.
11. Johnson, H. G., "The Criteria of Economic Advantage," *Bulletin of the Oxford University Institute of Statistics*, 19, February 1957.
12. ———, "Discriminatory Tariff Reduction: A Marshallian Analysis," *Indian Journal of Economics*, XXVIII, July 1957 and XXXIX, October 1958, reprinted in his *Money, Trade and Economic Growth* (London: George Allen and Unwin, Ltd.), 1962.
13. ———, "The Economic Theory of Customs Union," *Pakistan Economic Journal*, X, March 1960, reprinted in his *Money, Trade and Economic Growth*, 1962.
14. Kemp, M. C., *A Contribution to the General Equilibrium Theory of Preferential Trading* (Amsterdam: North-Holland), 1969.
15. Kindleberger, C. P., "The United States and European Integration," *Social Science*, October 1959.
16. Kreinin, M. E., "European Integration and American Trade," *American Economic Review*, XLIX, September 1959.
17. Kuroiwa, H., "The Theory of Second Best" (Jizenteki Saiteki no Riron), *Journal of Kobe Commercial College*, 42, 1961, also Chapter 5 of his *Theory of Welfare Economics* (Kosei Keizai Riron) (Tokyo: Sobunsha), 1967.
18. Lipsey, R. G., "The Theory of Customs Unions: Trade Diversion and Welfare," *Economica*, XXIV, February 1957.
19. ———, "Mr. Gehrels on Customs Unions," *Review of Economic Studies*, XXIV, (3), 1956–57.
20. ———, "The Theory of Customs Unions: A General Survey," *Economic Journal*, LXX, September 1960.
21. ——— and Lancaster, K., "The General Theory of Second Best," *Review of Economic Studies*, XXIV, (1), 1956–57.

22. —— and ——, "McManus on Second Best," *Review of Economic Studies*, XXVI, June 1959.
23. Makower, H. and Morton, G., "A Contribution Towards a Theory of Customs Unions," *Economic Journal*, LXIII, March 1953.
24. McManus, M., "Comments on the General Theory of Second Best," *Review of Economic Studies*, XXVI, June 1959.
25. ——, "Private and Social Costs in the Theory of Second Best," *Review of Economic Studies*, XXXIV, July 1967.
26. Meade, J. E., *Trade and Welfare (The Theory of International Economic Policy)* Vol. II (London: Oxford University Press), 1955, also its *Mathematical Supplement*, 1955.
27. ——, *Problems of Economic Union* (Chicago: University of Chicago Press), 1953.
28. ——, *The Theory of Customs Unions* (Amsterdam: North Holland), 1955.
29. Mundell, R. A., "Tariff Preferences and the Terms of Trade," *Manchester School of Economic and Social Studies*, 32, January 1964.
30. Negishi, T., "Perceived Demand Curve in the Theory of Second Best, *Review of Economic Studies*, XXXIV, July 1967.
31. ——, "Customs Union and the Theory of the Second Best," *International Economic Review*, 10, October 1969.
32. Scitovsky, T., *Economic Theory and Western European Integration* (London: George Allen and Unwin, Ltd.), 1958.
33. Spraos, J., "The Conditions for a Trade Creating Customs Union," *Economic Journal*, LXXIV, March 1964.
34. Streeten, P., "Common Fallacies about the Common Market," *Weltwirtschaftliches Archiv*, 90, 90(2), 1963.
35. Takayama, A., *Mathematical Economics*, forthcoming.
36. ——, *International Economics* (Kokusai Keizaigaku) (Tokyo: Toyo Keizai Shimpo-sha), 1963, Chapter VI, Section 4.
37. Tinbergen, J., *International Economic Cooperation* (Amsterdam: Elsevier), 1945.
38. ——, *International Economic Integration* (Amsterdam: Elsevier), 1954.
39. Vanek, J., *International Trade: Theory and Economic Policy* (Homewood, Ill.: Richard D. Irwin, Inc.), 1962.
40. ——, *General Equilibrium of International Discrimination* (Cambridge, Mass.: Harvard University Press), 1965.
41. Viner, J., *The Customs Union Issue* (New York: Carnegie Endowment for International Peace), 1950.

17

COMPENSATION PRINCIPLE AND THE THEORY OF INTERNATIONAL TRADE POLICY[1]

COMPENSATION PRINCIPLE—A HISTORICAL BACKGROUND[2]

Introduction

Under the assumption that the country in question is small relative to the rest of the world, Paul Samuelson, in his celebrated article [37], has shown rigorously that the opening of free trade is "better" than the state of no trade. Or in his own words,

> Although it cannot be shown that every individual is made better off by this introduction of trade, it can be shown that through trade every individual *could* be made better off (or in the limiting case, no worse off). In other words, if a unanimous decision were required in order for trade to be permitted, it would always be possible for those who desired trade to buy off those opposed to trade, with the result that all could be made better off ([37], p. 204).

For the meaning of "better off," Samuelson calls attention to the following passage from Viner ([50], pp. 533–534).

> Free trade—given the usual assumptions—necessarily makes *available* to the community *as a whole* a greater physical real income in the form of more of *all* commodities, and that the state, if it chooses, can, by appropriate supplementary legislation, make certain that the removal of duties shall result in more of *every* commodity for *every* class of the community.

[1] I am grateful to James C. Moore for comments.
[2] For summary discussions on the literature of compensation principle, we have, for example, Arrow [2], Chapter IV, Samuelson [39], Bailey [3], Graaff [12], Chapter V, Rothenberg [35], Chapter 3 and 4, Mishan [31], pp. 37–67, Kuroiwa [28], Chapter 6, Tamura [49], and Chipman [8].

As we pointed out in Chapter 1, the above statement of the "gains from trade" can be most succinctly expressed as the expansion of the consumption possibility set which would include the production possibility set (= the consumption possibility set before the opening of trade) as its subset. The original proof by Samuelson [37] is remarkably simple and an excellent example of the applications of his ingenious theory of revealed preference.

In Chapter 7 (fourth section) we constructed a model of international trade which is free from most of the restricting assumptions in the literature and which is characterized by the optimal nature of free-trade equilibrium. There, in the framework of a multi-country, multi-commodity, multi-factor, general equilibrium model in which we discarded such assumptions as no transportation costs, no joint production, no intermediate goods, one activity for producing each good, identical preference ordering on commodity bundles by different people in the world, and so on, we have shown that free-trade equilibrium achieves a Pareto optimum and that every Pareto optimum can be supported as a free-trade equilibrium.

The theorem stated in this way reveals that the theory of free trade and the arguments for the gain from free trade are nothing but a part of general equilibrium theory of competitive markets as explained, for example, in Debreu [10].

However, our problem does not really end here. Although we can prove that the policy action, called the opening of free trade, will bring us to the situation where everybody *could* be better off (or, in the limiting case, no worse off), this does not mean, as Samuelson pointed out, that everybody is made better off by this policy action. There can be "losers" as well as "gainers" in such a policy question. In other words, the theory of gains from free trade as expounded by Samuelson, among others, has a much deeper context than the Pareto optimality criterion. The Pareto optimality criterion only compares the situations such that, in moving from one situation to another, there are no losers. In other words, if nobody is worse off by the movement from situation A to situation B, then the Pareto optimality criterion would assert that "B is not Pareto inferior to A." If, in addition, there is a person who is made better off by this movement, then the Pareto optimality criterion would assert that "B is Pareto superior to A."

Now in the movement from one situation to another caused by free trade, such a Pareto optimality criterion may no longer be applicable due to the possible existence of losers as well as gainers. The theory of the compensation principle is an attempt to find a criterion which would enable us to say that one situation is "better" than another under such a circumstance. Clearly the application of such a theory is neither confined to the question of free trade versus no trade nor to only policy questions of international trade theory. It would have a much broader perspective which would be concerned with the welfare effect of *any economic policy*. The purpose of this chapter is to obtain the basic understanding of this problem and a deeper insight into the welfare effects of economic policy (here, international trade policy).

The motivation of recent research into this problem comes from a famous speech by Harrod in which he said, in connection with the gains from trade,

> Consider the Repeal of the Corn Laws. This tended to reduce the value of a specific factor of production—land. It can no doubt be shown that the gain to the community as a whole exceeded the loss to the landlords— but only if individuals are treated in some sense as equal. Otherwise how can the loss to some—and that there was a loss can hardly be denied— be compared with the general gain? ([15], pp. 396–397).

In other words, there can be losers (landlords) as well as gainers in the movement of the situation before the repeal of the Corn Laws to the situation after the repeal of the Corn Laws. Here we should note that the phrase "if individuals are treated in some sense equal" involves a serious difficulty. On this point, Robbins [33] [34] powerfully advocated that interpersonal comparison of utility is impossible for an individual's utility is not measurable, and it involves ethical value judgments anyway. In fact, even if individuals' utilities were measurable, we could not obtain the social utility by, say, adding individuals' utilities. (If this were possible, we could simply add the losers' losses to the gainers' gains and check the sign of the sum.) It involves ethical value judgments. To understand this, it may suffice to consider the following question. "Is it beneficial, from the social point of view, to bring hardship (such as death, confinement in a concentration camp, and so on) onto a certain minority group (say, the Orientals, the Negroes, the Jews, and so on) if that action will increase the welfare of the whole society—that is, the sum of all the utilities of *all* the members of the society will increase?" Note that the essence of this question would be invariant even if we choose a more general form of "social welfare function" than the mere sum of the individuals' utilities.

This problem of welfare comparison, when there are both losers and gainers, should not be particularly new, for this is the kind of problem that any society must face from its beginning. If there is a "dictator" in the society who can impose his values on the members of the society, the answer to the question is clear. The situation will be the same if the society can generate its "social welfare function". On the other hand, if there is no dictator or if there is no such mechanism in the society which can generate its social welfare function, then the answer to the above question is not easy.

Should economists remain silent on the welfare effect of a certain policy question when there are both gainers and losers on the ground that it involves an ethical value judgment? Clearly, there is something unsatisfactory in such an attitude. Although there are both gainers and losers, we all feel that prosperity is better than depression, technological progress is better than no technological progress, free trade is better than no trade, and so on. What should be the rationale to justify that one situation is better than the other in these examples?

Barone is probably the first economist who considered this problem explicitly. In [5] he was concerned with the welfare effect of departing from a competitive situation. He argued that if conditions depart from the competitive situation,

Some individuals will be benefited, others will suffer loss; the loss to the latter will be decidedly greater than the advantage to the former, in the sense that even taking all their gain from those who have gained in the change (which takes them back to their former condition) and giving it to those who have lost by it, the latter, even with such an addition, remain in a worse situation than originally: or, indeed, what comes to the same thing, some of the latter with such an addition might be brought back to their former situation, but all of them certainly could not ([5], pp. 255–256).

A little later, after the publication of the English edition of Barone's article, Hotelling, in his celebrated article, advocated a similar principle by stating that, "If some distribution of the burden is possible such that every one concerned is better off than without the new investment, then there is a *prima facie* case for making the investment" ([21], p. 267).[3]

In other words, both Barone and Hotelling attempted to avoid the value judgment involved in the welfare comparison of two situations, by considering the possibility of compensation. Thus, in the movement from one situation to the other, if the gainers could compensate all the losses of the losers and if by this everybody could be made better off, then Barone and Hotelling would conclude that the new situation is better than the old situation without implying any sort of intolerable value judgment.

It is important to note that the crucial concept in such a consideration of welfare comparison is that of *compensation*. By introducing the concept, we seem to be able to reach a definite conclusion in the welfare comparison of a certain situation. All the subsequent theories and the controversies which attempt to make a welfare comparison of certain situations by using this concept of compensation are thus known as those of the *compensation principle*. The purpose of this chapter is to obtain the basic understanding of such a comparison of welfare by this compensation principle.

The Kaldor Criterion

Roughly speaking, the criterion that Barone and Hotelling are looking for can be summarized by the question of whether or not the gainers could "bribe" the losers in the movement from one situation to the other. Barone said "no" for the movement deviating from competitive situation. Hotelling found a rationale for new investment if the answer is "yes."

The following version of compensation principle was first stated fully and powerfully by Kaldor in his famous article in 1939, "It is quite sufficient for him to show that even if all those who suffer as a result are fully compensated for their loss, the rest of the community will still be better off than before" ([22], p. 550). In other words, according to Kaldor, the new situation is said to be better if it can be made into a Pareto superior situation in relation to the

---

[3] He then continued to say, "This leaves aside the question whether such a distribution is *practicable*."

old situation by a proper compensation.[4] We shall call this the *Kaldor criterion*. In other words, the new situation is better than the old situation according to the Kaldor criterion if the gainers could compensate for all the losses of the losers and if the gainers are still better off even after this (hypothetical) compensation to the losers.

An alert reader will notice that this concept of compensation creates at least two questions immediately. One is the problem of the cost involved in such a compensation. In other words, the process of such a compensation (if it is actually to be carried out) will necessarily result in a certain cost and damage to the efficient allocation and use of productive resources. The second problem is how one can justify the value judgment attached to the income redistribution due to such a compensation (if it is real). Kaldor and the other advocates of the compensation principle completely avoid these questions by assuming that such a compensation is merely *hypothetical* rather than actual.[5] It is certainly plausible to ask the philosophical question of whether or not an economist can wash his hands of these difficult problems. But we shall not go any further into these problems here. In other words, we shall henceforth be content to consider only *potential* (instead of actual) increases in welfare.[6]

In order to understand the real meaning of the above Kaldor criterion and to further carry out our discussions, it is necessary here to digress a little and obtain familiarity with the concept of *utility possibility frontier*, the "crucial importance" of which was established by Samuelson [39]. Roughly, the utility possibility frontier is defined as the locus of all utility combinations of members of the society for all the possible reallocations of goods and services (= wealth) among the members of the society (assuming the absence of any sort of inefficiency or waste). This is illustrated in Figure 17-1. Here we are concerned with the two-person pure exchange economy. The left-hand diagram is the famous Edgeworth-Bowley box diagram for such an economy and the right-

---

[4] A proper compensation here means a proper (lump-sum) redistribution of goods and services between the gainers and the losers. Kaldor interpreted the compensation in monetary terms which creates an obvious ambiguity of which prices should be used for computing the compensation. Baumol [6] criticizes this ambiguity. However, as Arrow pointed out ([2], p. 39), this is the criticism concerning only the mechanics of the principle and not an objection to the principle itself.

[5] As is clear from the previous quotation, this is also the attitude taken by Samuelson [37] in his argument of the gains from trade. The reader may have noted that in the above we consistently used the subjunctive form such as "the gainers *would* bribe the losers," to emphasize this hypothetical nature of compensation. The critics of the compensation principle largely take the position that the compensation must be actual in order to make the conclusions meaningful. For a summary and evaluation of this position, see Rothenberg [35], chapter 3, for example.

[6] In summary, the advocates of the compensation principle thus avoid both the question of the costs of (actual) compensation and the problem of ethical judgment involved in the redistribution of income through actual compensation. For the latter point, Kaldor writes, for example, "Whether the landlords, in the free-trade case, should in fact be given compensation or not, is a political question on which the economist could hardly pronounce an opinion" ([22], p. 551).

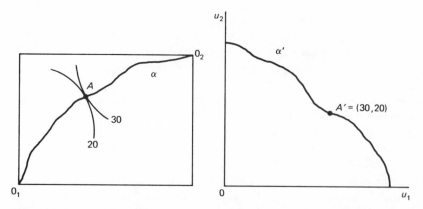

Figure 17-1   An Illustration of the Utility Possibility Frontier

hand diagram illustrates the utility possibility frontier of this economy. In the left-hand diagram of Figure 17-1, the α-curve is the contract curve of the two-person case so that for any point on the curve the indifference curves of the two-person case are tangent. This is illustrated by point A. Numbers 30 and 20 indicate the levels of the utility indicators of Individual 1 and Individual 2 respectively. Point A' in the right-hand diagram corresponds to point A. Here u_1 and u_2 indicate the levels of utility indicators of the two people. Hence, corresponding to the contract curve α, we obtain the utility possibility frontier α' in the right-hand diagram. Notice that if the amount of resources available in the above economy increases and the above box expands accordingly, then the utility possibility frontier will be pushed out in the north-east direction (provided that more of each good is preferred by each member of the society).[7]

In Figure 17-2 points A and B represent the welfare of the two people in the utility space corresponding to the two different situations. If the utility possibility frontier (α) passing through point A is northeast of point B, then, by carrying out a proper compensation (hypothetically) along the frontier α (say, to point A'), everybody in the society could be better off. This should be the interpretation of the statement: situation A is (*potentially*) better than situation B in the movement from B to A according to the *Kaldor criterion*. When we say "the gainers could bribe the losers in such a movement" (from situation B to situation A), we mean precisely the situation illustrated in Figure 17-2. Note the ambiguity in this statement which is due to the fact that the final situation is not A but A'. Moreover, as remarked before, the movement from A to A' is a hypothetical one and not an actual one. It neglects the important question of the cost involved and the possible value judgment implied in the movement from A to A' due to the sacrifice of Individual 2.

---

[7] This may not be true in general if, for example, consumer's satiation occurs or if some goods are undesired goods, such as garbage. However, in the usual argument of the compensation principle, this point is usually assumed away.

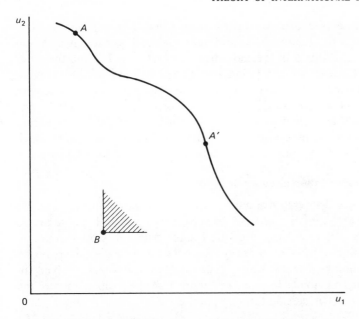

Figure 17-2   An Illustration of the Kaldor Criterion

Scitovsky in his 1941 article [42] pointed out a serious contradiction involved in the above Kaldor criterion. The contradiction can be illustrated by Figure 17-3. In Figure 17-3, the utility possibility frontier passing through point A

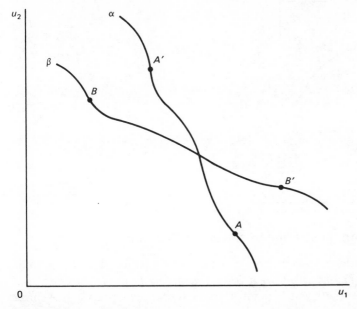

Figure 17-3   An Illustration of the Contradiction of the Kaldor Criterion

(the α-curve) crosses the one passing through point B (the β-curve). Now compare situation A to situation B. According to the Kaldor criterion, situation A is better than situation B in the movement from B to A because the compensation along the α-curve to a point, say A', could bring the economy to a point which dominates situation B in the sense that everybody is better off. However, it is also true that situation B is better than situation A in the movement from A to B according to the Kaldor criterion for the compensation along the β-curve to a point, say, B', could bring the economy to a point which dominates situation A. We may call this contradiction the *Scitovsky paradox*.

The Hicks Criterion and the Scitovsky Criterion

Before we go into Scitovsky's discussion of the compensation principle, we should point out an alternative criterion proposed by Hicks in his 1940 article [17].[8] The contrast of this criterion to the Kaldor criterion is often stated in terms of the question of whether or not the losers could bribe the gainers not to move to a new situation. The best way to state the Hicks criterion is probably in terms of the utility possibility frontier. In Figure 17-4 the β-curve denotes the utility possibility frontier passing through point B.

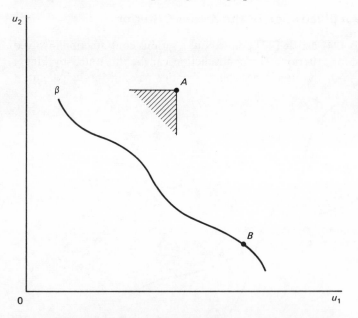

Figure 17-4   An Illustration of the Hicks Criterion

Now consider the movement from situation B to situation A. A is said to be *better than B in the movement from B to A according to the Hicks criterion* if the β-curve passes southwest of point A, or more precisely, if in the movement

[8] In his 1939 article [16] Hicks showed a strong agreement with the Kaldor criterion, and in his 1941 article [18] he again supported the Kaldor criterion.

from B to A there exists no compensation along the β-curve which could make no one worse off with some one better off compared to A.[9]

In order to remove the Scitovsky paradox involved in the Kaldor criterion (and the Hicks criterion), Scitovsky proposed the use of the Hicks criterion *in addition* to the Kaldor criterion. This is called *Scitovsky's double criterion* or simply the *Scitovsky criterion*. In other words, situation A is said to be *better than situation B in the movement from B to A according to the Scitovsky criterion* if A is better than B in the movement from B to A according to both the Kaldor criterion and the Hicks criterion. Scitovsky thus imposes two tests in order to make a welfare comparison in the movement from situation B to situation A by asking two questions: 1) Does there exist a compensation along the utility possibility frontier passing through A such that everybody could be made better off compared to situation B (the Kaldor criterion)? 2) Does there exist a compensation along the utility possibility frontier passing through point B such that no one could be made worse off and some one made better off compared to situation A (the Hicks criterion)? If the answer to the first question is yes and the answer to the second question is no, then situation A is better than situation B in the movement from B to A according to the Scitovsky criterion.[10] It is important to note that this ordering of the two situations is not complete in the sense that there exist cases in which two situations cannot be compared. The concept of the Scitovsky criterion is illustrated in Figure 17-5. Here, $A \bigotimes_s B$ reads that A is better than B in the movement from B to A according to the Scitovsky criterion. Similarly, $A \bigcirc_s B$ reads that we cannot compare the welfare level of the two situations in the movement from B to A according to the Scitovsky criterion.

It is important to note that if situation A is better than situation B in the movement from B to A according to the Scitovsky criterion, then A is also better than B in the movement from A to B, according to the Scitovsky criterion. This is because if A is better than B in the movement from B to A according to the Kaldor criterion (respectively, the Hicks criterion), then B is worse than A in the movement from A to B according to the Hicks criterion (respectively, the Kaldor criterion). In other words, the type of problem involved in the

---

[9] As an alert reader may have realized, this Hicks criterion also contains the Scitovsky paradox. In Figure 17-3, for example, A' is better than B' according to the Hicks criterion in the movement from B' to A', but B' is better than A' according to the Hicks criterion in the movement from A' to B'.

[10] In Scitovsky's own words,

> We must first see whether it is possible in the new situation so to redistribute income as to make everybody better off than he was in the initial situation; secondly, we must see whether starting from the initial situation it is not possible by a mere redistribution of income to reach a position superior to the new situation, again from everybody's point of view. If the first is possible but the second is impossible, we shall say that the new situation is better than the old was. If the first is impossible but the second possible, we shall say that the new situation is worse; whereas if both are possible or both are impossible, we shall refrain from making a welfare proposition ([42], pp. 86–87).

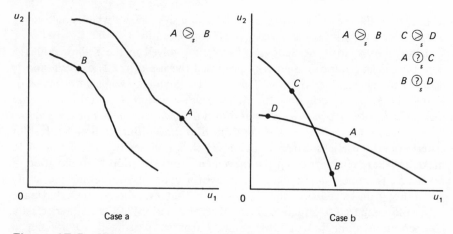

Case a   Case b

Figure 17-5   Illustrations of the Scitovsky Criterion

Scitovsky paradox disappears in the Scitovsky criterion. That is, the direction of the movement is immaterial in the Scitovsky criterion.

Now compare three situations, A, B, and C, and suppose that $A \gtrsim_s B$ and $B \gtrsim_s C$. Can we then conclude $A \gtrsim_s C$? In other words, can we ascertain transitivity in the ordering according to the Scitovsky criterion? Unfortunately the answer to this question turns out to be "no". A counterexample to transitivity was constructed by Gorman [11] in 1955. In Figure 17-6, the curves α, β, γ, and δ denote respectively the utility possibility surface passing through situations A, B, C, and D.

In this figure, note that $A \gtrsim_s B$, $B \gtrsim_s C$, $C \gtrsim_s D$, and $D \gtrsim_s A$. That is, we obtain intransitivity. The reader should be able to construct a similar example of the intransitivity for the comparison of three situations.

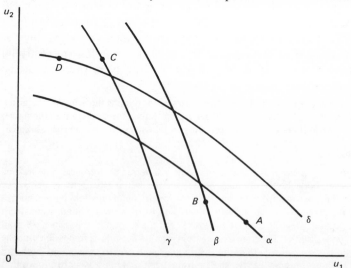

Figure 17-6   The Intransitivity of the Scitovsky Criterion

The Samuelson Criterion

We now have to take up an important criticism by Samuelson [38] [39] to the above stated criterion by Kaldor, Hicks, and Scitovsky. To understand this, we consider the two points A and B in Figure 17-7.

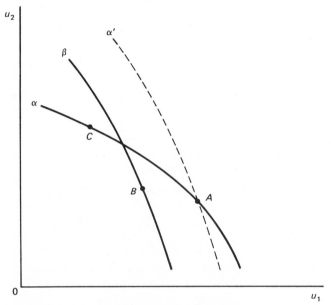

Figure 17-7   The Samuelson Criterion

Suppose that the two curves α and β are the utility possibility curves which correspond to the situations A and B respectively. Consider the movement from situation B to situation A. The Kaldor criterion would say that A is better than B because a compensation along the α-curve would enable everyone to be better off. Note that here any compensation along the β-curve is not considered. In other words, the utility allocation of the *status quo ante* (that of B) is considered to be fixed and given in this consideration of this welfare comparison of the two situations. In fact, this is the source of the contradiction pointed out by Scitovsky (the Scitovsky paradox). To understand this, consider the two situations B and C in Figure 17-7. According to the Kaldor criterion, B is better than C in the movement from C to B and C is better than B in the movement from B to C. Note that in the welfare comparison for the movement from C to B, the utility allocation of C is considered to be fixed, and in the welfare comparison of the movement from B to C, the utility allocation of B is considered to be fixed. In other words, this convention of fixing the utility allocation of the *status quo ante* is the source of the Scitovsky paradox.

This paradox is removed in the Scitovsky criterion. Consider again the movement from B to A in Figure 17-7. In addition to the Kaldor criterion, we now impose the test of the Hicks criterion, and we see that there does not exist any compensation along the β-curve which would make everyone better off compared to A (and thus conclude that A is better than B according to the Scitovsky criterion). Notice that in this application of the Hicks criterion the utility allocation of the *status quo post*, that of situation A, is assumed to be fixed, and only the compensation along the β-curve is considered. The crucial reason that the Scitovsky criterion is successful in removing the Scitovsky paradox is precisely this procedure of considering *both* cases of fixing the utility allocation of A and of fixing that of B. In this way the problems of switching the fixed utility allocation do not appear; hence, the Scitovsky paradox is removed.

However, can we really justify this procedure of fixing the utility allocation of a certain point (that is, that of the *status quo ante* and/or *status quo post*)? This is the question raised by Samuelson. This procedure of fixing the utility allocation of a certain point involves the value judgment that the utility allocation of that point is the right one. The correct comparison of the two situations must be the one which depends on the totality of all possible (compensation) positions in each situation. In other words, the only way to say A is better than B is the case in which the utility possibility frontier passing through A is uniformly outside of the utility possibility frontier passing through B. Such a utility possibility frontier passing through A is illustrated by the dotted curve in Figure 17-7 (the α'-curve). We call this criterion the *Samuelson criterion*. Hence, if the utility possibility frontiers are the ones illustrated by the α- and β-curves, we can not say that A is better than B according to the Samuelson criterion, although we can say this under the Scitovsky criterion.

It should be clear that under the Samuelson criterion there is no Scitovsky paradox. In other words, if A is better than B in the movement from B to A, then A is also better than B in the movement from A to B. This should be obvious because A is better than B according to the Samuelson criterion if there is a uniform outward shift of the utility possibility frontier. It should also be clear that the intransitivity of the Scitovsky criterion pointed out by Gorman does not arise under the Samuelson criterion.

Next, we may be interested in the relation between a uniform outward shift of the utility possibility frontier and a change in the quantity of the commodities available in the society. Assuming the non-satiation of every member of the society in the consumption of every commodity, it is clear that an increase in the quantities available will imply a uniform outward shift of the utility possibility frontier, so that we have an increase in the social welfare according to the Samuelson criterion.[11] This is the major content of Samuelson's proof in his 1939 article [37] that free trade is better than no trade under the small country assumption. Similarly we can conclude that prosperity is better than

---

[11] The converse of this statement is not necessarily true. However, under certain additional conditions we can show that the converse also holds. (See the next section and Chipman and Moore [9].)

depression and that technological progress is better than no technological progress.

Although the above discussion on the various criteria leading to the Samuelson criterion clarifies the meaning of these cases of welfare comparison, its scope is quite limited if its applications are confined only to these cases. After all, statements such as "If the quantities of goods available in the society increases, then the society would be better off" is a rather obvious statement, and it may not be worth having such a lengthy, complicated discussion as this.[12]

However, it should also be realized that without this intellectual meandering we would still be astray in the problem of welfare criteria, and we would probably be embarrassed with the many confused discussions on the topic. We are now clear that the Samuelson criterion is the only appropriate criterion for a welfare comparison of different situations. We are now left with the following tasks.

1. A RIGOROUS (MATHEMATICAL) REFORMULATION OF THE PROBLEM INVOLVED IN THE COMPENSATION PRINCIPLE This will open the way for further research, as well as make our understanding of the problem clear and precise, and generalize some results.

2. THE CHARACTERIZATION OF THE SAMUELSON CRITERION Although it is fairly obvious that the expansion of the consumption possibility set would normally imply a potential improvement of social welfare, the converse of this statement is not necessarily true.

3. CLARIFICATION OF THE UTILITY POSSIBILITY FRONTIER This is the crucially important point in the topic, and we should know more about this as well as its proper definition. A precise relation of this concept with Samuelson's criterion should also be investigated.

4. VALUATION OF REAL NATIONAL INCOME Suppose we can observe a price vector as we do in the real economy. Can we say anything more precise about a welfare change with this additional information? This question has been asked in the literature (for example, Hicks [17], Samuelson [39], and Kennedy [25]) as a natural extension of the problem of the compensation principle. It is known as the problem of *valuation of real national income*.

In the next section we shall consider all these questions and would like to obtain a deeper insight into this difficult problem of the compensation principle.

---

[12] Little [30] proposed to add a third test, the redistribution test, to Scitovsky's double test. This triple test thus produces $2^3 = 8$ cases. However, this Little criterion is criticized on the ground that the redistribution test involves an ethical value judgment as well as containing the difficulty of the Scitovsky test. This was pointed out by Samuelson.

A MATHEMATICAL ANALYSIS[13]

Formulation

Suppose there are n kinds of commodities and m people in a society. Let x_{ij} be the consumption of the jth commodity by the ith individual. Let x_i be the consumption vector of the ith individual. That is,

$$x_i = (x_{i1}, x_{i2}, \cdots, x_{in}), \quad i = 1, 2, \cdots, m. \tag{17-1}$$

Let X_i be the consumption set of the ith individual, which is assumed to be a convex subset of the non-negative orthant of the n-dimensional Euclidian space R^n. Let X be the Cartesian product of the X_i, that is, $X \equiv \overset{m}{\underset{i=1}{\otimes}} X_i$. We now list some important assumptions.

ASSUMPTION 1 X_i is closed and convex for all $i = 1, 2, \cdots, m$.[14]

REMARK   The usual convention is that X_i is taken to be the entire non-negative orthant of R^n (see Chipman and Moore [9], for example). Hence, it obviously satisfies assumption 1. Note also that assumption 1 implies X is closed and convex.[15]

ASSUMPTION 2   The preference ordering of the ith individual can be represented by a continuous real-valued function $u_i(x_i)$ defined on X_i, $i = 1, 2, \cdots, m$.

REMARK   Note that u_i depends only on x_i and not any other x_k, $k \neq i$. This assumption is often called *selfishness* or *individualism*.[16] It means that the ith individual is concerned only with his own consumption bundle.

REMARK   Clearly the representability of a preference ordering by a real-valued function (in assumption 2) is not necessarily unique.[17] The fact that we did not

---

[13] This section is heavily indebted to or at least inspired by Chipman [8] and Chipman and Moore [9]. Nonmathematical readers may wish to skip reading this section. For the proofs of the mathematical theorems used in this section, the reader is referred to any standard textbook on elementary analysis such as Rudin, W., *Principles of Mathematical Analysis*, New York: McGraw-Hill, 2nd ed., 1964, or Simmons, F. G., *Introduction to Topology and Modern Analysis*, New York: McGraw-Hill, 1963.

[14] A set S is called *closed* if x^q is a sequence in S such that $x^q \to x^o$ as $q \to \infty$ implies $x^o \in S$. S is called *convex* if $x, x' \in S$ implies $[\theta x + (1 - \theta)x'] \in S$ for all θ with $0 \leqq \theta \leqq 1$. The assumption that X_i is closed is used for its mathematical convenience rather than for its economic significance and is often adopted in the literature. The convexity prescribes the divisibility of all the commodities. See Takayama [46] and Debreu [10], for example, for these concepts.

[15] This is due to the fact that the Cartesian product of closed sets is closed and that the Cartesian product of convex sets is convex.

[16] Arrow used the term "selfish" in [1], p. 511, and "individualistic" in [2].

[17] For example, any order-preserving (monotone increasing) function of a particular utility function can also be a utility function.

specify the method of representation in assumption 2 implies that the subsequent discussion will hold under *any* such representation. This representability[18] is only for convenience and is not essential in the subsequent discussions. A mathematically trained reader can easily convert our discussion to the case in which each consumer has only some sort of preference ordering (for example, total, individualistic, and reflexive).

Define the vector ordering in the usual fashion. $x_i \geqq x_i'$ means $x_{ij} \geqq x_{ij}'$ for all j, $x_i \geq x_i'$ means $x_{ij} \geqq x_{ij}'$ for all j with strict inequality for at least one j, and $x_i > x_i'$ means $x_{ij} > x_{ij}'$ for all j. We may impose a further assumption on the utility function.

ASSUMPTION 3 (Monotonicity) $x_i \geq x_i'$ and $x_i, x_i' \in X_i$ implies that $u_i(x_i) > u(x_i')$, $i = 1, 2, \cdots, m$, that is, all the commodities are "desired commodities."

REMARK   This assumption holds, for example, if every consumer is not satiated with any commodity.

Consider a vector $x = (x_1, x_2, \cdots, x_m)$, where x_i is defined by (17-1). We call x an *allocation*, if $x_i \in X_i$ for all i. Alternative allocations are denoted by x', x'', and so on. We choose our notation such that x_i, x_i', and x_i'' are the ith components of x, x', and x'' respectively. Define $u(x)$, $u(x')$, $u(x'')$, and so on by $u(x) \equiv [u_1(x_1), \cdots, u_m(x_m)]$, $u(x') \equiv [u_1(x_1'), \cdots, u_m(x_m')]$, $u(x'') \equiv [u_1(x_1''), \cdots, u_m(x_m'')]$, and so on. We now define the *Pareto ordering*.

DEFINITION (Pareto Ordering)   Given two arbitrary allocations x and x', then a social ordering $[I, R, P]$, defined by the following relations is called a *Pareto ordering*.

$$x \, I \, x' \quad \text{if and only if} \quad u(x) = u(x'); \tag{17-2a}$$

$$x \, R \, x' \quad \text{if and only if} \quad u(x) \geqq u(x'); \tag{17-2b}$$

$$x \, P \, x' \quad \text{if and only if} \quad u(x) \geq u(x'). \tag{17-2c}$$

Clearly this ordering is not complete; that is, there can be an allocation which cannot be ordered by I, R, and P. Also note that $u(x) = u(x')$ does not necessarily imply that $x = x'$. If $x \, I \, x'$, we say that the two allocations x and x' are *Pareto equivalent*; if $x \, R \, x'$, we say x is *not Pareto inferior to x'*, and if $x \, P \, x'$, we say x is *Pareto superior to x'* (or x' is *Pareto inferior to x*).

Let z be an n-vector whose jth element is $\sum_{i=1}^{m} x_{ij}$, $(x_i \in X_i, i = 1, 2, \cdots, m)$, the society's total consumption of the jth commodity. In other words, z is an *aggregate consumption bundle* of the society. We assume that z is also equal

---

[18] The representability of preference orderings by a continuous real-valued function is discussed in Debreu [10], for example.

to the aggregate bundle made available for consumption within the society.
Let σ be an $(m \times n) \times n$ matrix such that

$$
\sigma = \begin{bmatrix} I_1 \\ I_2 \\ \cdot \\ \cdot \\ \cdot \\ I_i \\ \cdot \\ \cdot \\ \cdot \\ I_m \end{bmatrix}, \tag{17-3}
$$

where I_i, $i = 1, 2, \cdots, m$, are all $n \times n$ identity matrices. Then $x\sigma$ is an
n-vector whose jth element is $\sum_{i=1}^{m} x_{ij}$. Thus $x\sigma$ is an aggregate consumption
bundle. Moreover, given an aggregate bundle z, $z = x\sigma$ means that z is allocated
according to x. Clearly $z \in R^n$ does not necessarily imply that there exists an
allocation x such that $z = x\sigma$, for x_i may not be in X_i for some i.

DEFINITION (Situation) Let S be a subset of the non-negative orthant of
R^n. S is called a *situation* if it denotes a set of aggregate bundles available for
consumption within the society. A situation S is called *simple* if S consists of
only one element, and is called *composite* if it consists of more than one
element.[19]

Note that $z \in S$, where S is a situation, does not necessarily imply that there
exists an allocation x such that $x\sigma = z$. This is because z may be so small
that, for any allocation, there may exist a person whose consumption does not
belong to his consumption set (for example, he starves to death). The concept
of situation can be illustrated by Figure 17-8. Here the shaded area OPR
represents the production transformation block of a given country. The consumption set of each individual is assumed to be the non-negative orthant of
two-dimensional Euclidian space.

Suppose point Q is the production point before the opening of trade, and
point T is the production point after the opening of trade. The one-point set
$S_1 \equiv \{Q\}$ or $S_2 \equiv \{T\}$ is a simple situation. The compensation principle
discussed in the previous section compares two simple situations such as S_1
and S_2. If the commodities can be thrown away freely (free disposability),
then $\{Q\}$ is a situation that implies that all the points in the box $0Q_1QQ_2$ are
also a situation, which is a composite situation. Suppose that the line MN is
the price ratio of the two commodities which prevails in the world market.
Suppose also that this country is small enough compared to the rest of the
world so that this country's volume of export and import does not affect the

---

[19] These terms are due to Chipman [8]. They are borrowed from statistics (simple hypothesis
and composite hypothesis).

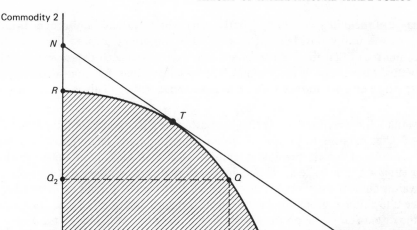

Figure 17-8   An Illustration of Situations

price ratio MN (to any significant extent). Then, under free disposability, all the points in the triangle OMN become a (composite) situation for the country after the opening of free trade. Let S_3 = the set of all the points in the production block $OPQR$ and S_4 = the set of all the points in the triangle OMN. Then the situation of the country moves from S_3 to S_4 by the opening of free trade. The gains from trade can be defined by the expansion of set S_3 to set S_4. Both S_3 and S_4 are composite situations. Clearly, it is possible to define the utility possibility frontier corresponding to a composite situation as well as to a simple situation. Hence, all the discussions of the compensation principle for the comparison of two simple situations (which we did in the first section) can be extended *mutatis mutandis* to the cases of comparing two composite situations, or one composite to one simple situation.

We now introduce an ordering between situations which is of fundamental importance in the discussion of the compensation principle.

DEFINITION (Samuelson Ordering)   The ordering $\geqq$ of situations (say, S and S'), defined as follows, is called the *Samuelson ordering*.

$S \geqq S'$ if and only if, for *any* allocation x' with $x'\sigma \in S'$, there exists

an allocation x (which may depend on x') such that $x\sigma \in S$ and $x \, R \, x'$.   (17-4)

If this is the case, we say that S is *not Samuelson inferior* to S'.

REMARK   Note that the Samuelson ordering is defined in situations while the Pareto ordering need not be. If $S \geqq S'$ but not $S' \geqq S$, then we say that S is *Samuelson superior to S'*. We denote this by $S \gneqq S'$. Roughly, $S \gneqq S'$ means that there exists an allocation of the available commodities in the new situation (S) such that nobody was made worse off and somebody could be made better off compared to any possible allocation in the old situation. In terms of the concept of the utility possibility frontier, this roughly means a uniform outward shift of the utility possibility frontier.[20] It is important to note that $S \geq S'$ does not mean that there exists an allocation x, $x\sigma \in S$ such that $x R x'$ for all x' with $x'\sigma \in S'$. (This is too strong.) Nor does it say that, for *some* x', $x'\sigma \in S'$, there exists an allocation x with $x\sigma \in S$ such that $x R x'$. (This is too weak.)

REMARK   It is one thing to say that the particular allocation x' of the quantities $z' \in S'$ that happens to prevail in the old situation could be bettered by some allocation x of certain possible quantities $z \in S$ that could be obtained in the new situation. It is quite another thing to say that *every* allocation x' that could prevail in the old situation S' (every x' such that $x'\sigma \in S'$) could be bettered by some allocation x which might prevail in the new situation ($x\sigma \in S$). In terms of the discussion in the previous section, the former corresponds to the Kaldor criterion and the latter corresponds to the Samuelson criterion. It is not quite clear which interpretation is adopted in Kaldor's original article [22].[21] In the last section we adopted the former interpretation, which is a common view in the literature, and is the one adopted in [39].

Characterizations of the Samuelson Ordering

As we stated in the first section, the Samuelson ordering plays a crucial role in the discussion of the compensation principle. In fact it gives the only relevant criterion of social ordering between aggregate bundles of commodities. Here we shall argue that under certain conditions a necessary and sufficient characterization of the Samuelson ordering can be obtained in terms of either utility possibility sets or situation sets. In the course of the argument, we shall obtain some other important results.

We first define rigorously the concept of the utility possibility set, which corresponds to the concept of the utility possibility frontier introduced in the first section. First define the *set of all allocations of aggregate bundles in S*, $C(S)$, by

$$C(S) \equiv \{x : x\sigma \in S, x_i \in X_i, i = 1, 2, \cdots, m\} . \tag{17-5}$$

For each given situation, S, we can determine this set. Note that this set may be empty, if the available aggregate bundle in the given S is so small that there exists a person who "starves to death" under any allocation in S. We assume, however, that $C(S)$ is non-empty. Writing $f(x) = x\sigma$ we may write $C(S)$ as

$$C(S) = f^{-1}(S) \cap X , \tag{17-6}$$

where $f^{-1}(S) = \{x \in R^{mn} : f(x) \in S\}$.

---

[20] In the following discussions we develop our analysis in terms of $\geqq$ instead of $>$. But an interested reader can easily modify the discussions and carry out the analysis in terms of $>$.
[21] Chipman [8] called this the Kaldor ordering, and Chipman and Moore [9] called this the Kaldor-Hicks-Samuelson ordering.

It is easy to see that $f^{-1}(S)$ is compact if S is compact.[22] Hence, if X is closed and S is compact, then $f^{-1}(S) \cap X$ is closed as an intersection of two closed sets. $f^{-1}(S)$ is bounded so that $f^{-1}(S) \cap X$ is bounded; hence it is compact. Moreover, we can show that $C(S)$ is convex if S and X are convex. To show this, let $x, x' \in C(S)$. Then there exists $z, z' \in C(S)$ such that $x\sigma = z$ and $x'\sigma = z'$. Consider $x'' \equiv \theta x + (1 - \theta)x'$, $0 \leq \theta \leq 1$. Then $x''\sigma = \theta x\sigma + (1 - \theta)x'\sigma = \theta z + (1 - \theta)z' \in S$ due to the convexity of S. Moreover, $x'' \in S$ due to the convexity of X. Hence, $x'' \in C(S)$, which asserts the convexity of $C(S)$. Hence we obtain the following lemma:

LEMMA 1 If S is compact and X is closed, then $C(S)$ is compact. If S and X are convex, then $C(S)$ is also convex.

COROLLARY Under assumption 1, if S is compact and convex, then $C(S)$ is also compact and convex.

Given an allocation $x = (x_1, \cdots, x_m)$, the utility distribution of the society is represented by $u(x) = [u_1(x_1), \cdots, u_m(x_m)]$. The *utility possibility set* [denoted by $U(S)$] is the set of all such utility distributions for all possible allocations in $C(S)$. In other words,

$$U(S) \equiv \{u(x) : x \in C(S)\} . \tag{17-7}$$

Given this concept, we can easily obtain the following characterization of the Samuelson ordering $\gtreqqless$.

$$S \gtreqqless S' \quad \text{if and only if, for every } u' \in U(S'), \text{ there exists } u \in U(S) \tag{17-8}$$

such that $u \geq u'$.

From (17-8), it should be clear that $U(S) \supset U(S')$ implies $S \gtreqqless S'$. But the converse does not necessarily hold. The converse will be established in theorem 3.

REMARK The concept of the utility possibility set is analogous to the concept of the production possibility curve. For example, if we regard u_i as the production function of the ith commodity and x_i as the resource vector used for the production of the ith commodity, $U(S)$ is nothing but the production possibility set. $C(S)$ here obviously signifies the resource constraint. For example, if the resource constraint is given by a fixed n-vector r and if X_i is the nonnegative orthant of R^n for all i, then $C(S)$ can be written as $\{x : 0 \leq \sum x_i \leq r\}$. Therefore, we may argue that the compensation principle is the formal counterpart of the assumption that the factors are perfectly mobile among industries.

---

[22] In the Euclidian space R^n a set is called *compact* if and only if it is closed and bounded. A set $S \subset R^n$ is *bounded* if there exists a finite $r > 0$ such that $S \subset B$, where $B \equiv \{x \in R^n : |x_i| < r, i = 1, 2, \cdots, n\}$. To prove that the compactness of S implies the compactness of $f^{-1}(S)$, just use the definition of $f^{-1}(S)$. $f^{-1}(S)$ is closed since S is closed, and $f^{-1}(S)$ is bounded since S is bounded.

Since u_i is continuous over X_i, $i = 1, 2, \cdots, m$ (under assumption 2), $u = (u_1, \cdots, u_m)$ is continuous over X. Hence, in particular, u is continuous over $C(S)$. Thus if $C(S)$ is compact, then $U(S)$ is compact, as a continuous image of a compact set is compact. Hence, we obtain theorem 1.

THEOREM 1   Suppose that assumption 2 holds. Then if $C(S)$ is compact, $U(S)$ is also compact.

REMARK   The conditions which guarantee the compactness of $C(S)$ are given in lemma 1.

COROLLARY   Suppose that assumptions 1 and 2 hold. Then if S is compact, $U(S)$ is also compact.

Assume $C(S)$ is compact for a given situation S. Then if u is continuous, we can assert, using the Weierstrass theorem,[23] that there exists an $x^o \in C(S)$ such that

$$u(x^o) \leq u(x) \quad \text{for all} \quad x \in C(S). \tag{17-9}$$

Write $u(x^o) \equiv u^o$. Clearly u^o depends on S. We call u^o the *minimum utility allocation* with respect to S.[24] Now, for a given S, define the set $V(S)$ by

$$V(S) = \{u : u^o \leq u \leq u(x) \quad \text{for some } x \in C(S)\}. \tag{17-10}$$

An immediate conjecture that one thinks of from the definition of $V(S)$ is $U(S) = V(S)$. If $u \in U(S)$, then clearly $u \in V(S)$ also. In other words, $U(S) \subset V(S)$. However, $U(S) \supset V(S)$ does not necessarily hold. In other words, $u \in U(S)$ (so that $u = u(\bar{x})$ for some $\bar{x} \in C(S)$) does not necessarily imply $u' \in U(S)$ for all u' such that $u^o \leq u' \leq u$. That is, there may exist $u' \in V(S)$ such that $u' \notin U(S)$. We are now interested in finding a theorem which guarantees $U(S) \supset V(S)$ so that $U(S) = V(S)$. To do this we have to introduce the following assumption.

ASSUMPTION 4 S is (*free*) *disposal*, meaning that $z \in S$ implies $z' \in S$ for all z' such that $0 \leq z' \leq z$.

THEOREM 2   Suppose that assumptions 2, 3, and 4 hold. Suppose also that $C(S)$ is compact and convex. Then we have

$$U(S) = V(S). \tag{17-11}$$

PROOF   It suffices to show that $U(S) \supset V(S)$, that is, that $u^* \in V(S)$ implies $u^* \in U(S)$. Suppose $u^* \in V(S)$. That is,

$$u^o \leq u^* \leq u(\bar{x}) \quad \text{for some } \bar{x} \in C(S). \tag{17-12}$$

---

[23] The Weierstrass theorem asserts that any continuous function attains its minimum (and maximum) on a compact set.

[24] For a diagrammatical exposition and a mathematical convenience, the reader may wish to choose utility function so that $u^o = 0$, the origin.

Due to the monotonicity of u (assumption 3), $x^o \leqq \bar{x}$. Since u is continuous and monotone and $C(S)$ is convex, there exists a set of scalars $\{\theta_1, \theta_2, \cdots, \theta_m\}$ such that

$$u_i^* = u_i(x_i^*) \quad \text{and} \quad x^o \leqq x^* \leqq \bar{x}, \tag{17-13}$$

where $x_i^* \equiv (1 - \theta_i)x_i^o + \theta_i\bar{x}_i$, $0 \leqq \theta_i \leqq 1$, $i = 1, 2, \cdots, m$, and u_i^*, x_i^o, and $\bar{x}_i$ are the ith components of u^*, x^o, and $\bar{x}$ respectively. Therefore, we obtain

$$x^o\sigma \leqq x^*\sigma \leqq \bar{x}\sigma. \tag{17-14}$$

Then, due to the disposability of S, this last inequality implies that $x^*\sigma \in S$. Hence $x^* \in C(S)$. Consequently, $u^* = u(x^*) \in U(S)$.   (Q.E.D.)

REMARK $C(S)$ is compact and convex if S is compact and convex together with assumption 1 (corollary of lemma 1).

REMARK   If $U(S) = V(S)$, then $u \in U(S)$ implies $u' \in U(S)$ for all u' such that $u^o \leqq u' \leqq u$. We say that $U(S)$ *is disposable* if this property holds. In other words, the above theorem can be considered as one which gives a set of conditions which guarantees the disposability of the utility possibility set $U(S)$ for a given S. Note that the concept of the disposability of $U(S)$ presupposes the existence of the minimum utility point u^o.

Another important consequence of the above theorem is that we can get a very important characterization of the Samuelson ordering, $S(\geqq)S'$ *if and only if* $U(S) \supset U(S')$, provided that $U(S) = V(S)$.

THEOREM 3   If $U(S) \supset U(S')$, then $S(\geqq)S'$. Conversely, if $S(\geqq)S'$, then $U(S) \supset U(S')$, provided that $U(S) = V(S)$.

REMARK   Theorem 2 gives a set of conditions which guarantees $U(S) = V(S)$. Thus combining theorem 2 with theorem 3 and lemma 1, we obtain the following corollary.

COROLLARY   Suppose that assumptions 1, 2, 3, and 4 hold. Suppose also that S is compact and convex. Then we have

$$S(\geqq)S' \quad \textit{if and only if} \quad U(S) \supset U(S'). \tag{17-15}$$

Another possible characterization of the Samuelson ordering is the one in terms of the set inclusion of situation sets. Here we obtain theorem 4.

THEOREM 4 $S \supset S'$ implies $S(\geqq)S'$.

PROOF   We have to show that, for all x' such that $x'\sigma \in S'$, there exists an x such that $x\sigma \in S$ and $x R x'$. But $S \supset S'$ implies that we can choose $x = x'$. Clearly $x R x$.   (Q.E.D.)

REMARK   Note that we do not need any assumptions in this theorem. The converse of this theorem, however, requires additional assumptions. It turns out that such a theorem in fact requires a rather tedious proof with strong assumptions such as the identical utility function of all the consumers and the homogeneity of the utility function. For such a theorem, see Chipman and Moore [9].

REMARK   We noted that under certain conditions the gains due to the opening of free trade are represented by the expansion of the set of commodities available for consumption (the expansion of the situation set). In terms of Figure 17-8, this is illustrated by the expansion of the block $0PQR$ $(= S_3)$ to the triangle $0MN$ $(= S_4)$.

The Convexity of the Utility Possibility Set and the Social Welfare Function

As we remarked before, the concept of the utility possibility set is analogous to that of the production possibility set. Hence, it is easy to see that the convexity of the utility possibility set is of fundamental importance. We shall now prove this convexity.

THEOREM 5   Suppose that $u_i(x_i)$ is a concave function for all $i = 1, 2, \cdots, m.$[25] That is,

$$u_i[\theta x_i + (1 - \theta)x_i'] \geqq \theta u_i(x_i) + (1 - \theta)u_i(x_i') \tag{17-16}$$

for all $x_i,\ x_i' \in X_i$ and $0 \leqq \theta \leqq 1$.

Suppose also that $C(S)$ is convex and $U(S)$ is disposable. Then $U(S)$ is a convex set.[26]

PROOF   Let $u, u' \in U(S)$; $u \equiv u(x)$ and $u' \equiv u(x')$, $x, x' \in C(S)$. Since $C(S)$ is convex, we have

$$x'' \equiv \theta x + (1 - \theta)x' \in C(S),\quad 0 \leqq \theta \leqq 1. \tag{17-17}$$

Hence $u(x'') \in U(S)$. But in view of the concavity of u_i for all i,

$$u[\theta x + (1 - \theta)x'] \geqq \theta u(x) + (1 - \theta)u(x'), \tag{17-18}$$

or

$$u(x'') \geqq \theta u + (1 - \theta)u'. \tag{17-19}$$

Therefore, due to the disposability of $U(S)$, $\theta u + (1 - \theta)u' \in U(S)$.   (Q.E.D.)

REMARK   The conditions which guarantee the convexity of $C(S)$ are described by lemma 1, and the conditions which guarantee the disposability of $U(S)$ are described by theorem 2.

---

[25] This assumption presupposes that X_i is convex for all i.

[26] This theorem is not particularly new in the literature. See, for example, Hurwicz, L., "Programming in Linear Space," in *Studies in Linear and Non-linear Programming*, ed. by Arrow, K. J., Hurwicz, L., and Uzawa, H., Stanford University Press, 1958, p. 91.

REMARK   Analogously we can prove the convexity of the production possibility set under the corresponding assumptions such as concavity of the production functions and the convexity of the resource constraint set.

Given a situation S, we obtain the corresponding utility possibility set. Assume that $U(S)$ is compact so that the boundary of $U(S)$ exists. Roughly speaking the concept of the utility possibility frontier corresponds to this boundary. More rigorously, we say that $u \in U(S)$ is a *frontier point* (or an *efficient point*) of $U(S)$ if there does not exist $u' \in U(S)$ such that $u_i' \geqq u_i$, for all i, with strict inequality for some i (that is, $u' \geq u$). The set of all the frontier points of $U(S)$ is called the *utility possibility frontier* of situation S, or the *efficiency boundary* of $U(S)$. We denote it by $F(S)$.

DEFINITION (Pareto Optimum)   Given a situation S, we say $x \in X$ achieves a *Pareto optimum with respect to S*, if there does not exist $x' \in C(S)$ such that $x' P x$.

COROLLARY   Given a situation S, $x \in X$ achieves a Pareto optimum with respect to S if and only if $x \in C(S)$ and $u(x) \in F(S)$.

Note that $F(S)$, by definition, is the set of u's in the utility space such that each u achieves a vector maximum over the utility possibility set $U(S)$. Then, recalling our discussion of vector maximum in the second section of Chapter 7, we obtain the following theorem.

THEOREM 6   Suppose that $u_i(x_i)$ is concave for all $i = 1, 2, \cdots, m$ and $C(S)$ is convex where S is a given situation.

a) If x^* achieves a Pareto optimum with respect to S, then there exists $\alpha \in R^m$, $\alpha \geq 0$ such that

$$\alpha \cdot u(x^*) \geqq \alpha \cdot u(x) \quad \text{for all} \quad x \in C(S). \tag{17-20}$$

b) If there exists $\alpha \in R^m$, $\alpha > 0$, such that (17-20) holds, then x^* achieves a Pareto optimum with respect to S.

PROOF   Consider the following vector maximum problem:

$$\text{Maximize} \quad u(x) \quad \text{subject to} \quad x \in C(S), \tag{17-21}$$
$$x$$

and apply the relevant theorem of the vector maximum problem (theorem 5, third section of Chapter 7).   (Q.E.D.)

REMARK   To obtain statement a), we cannot dispense with the convexity of $C(S)$. To obtain statement b), the concavity of the u_i's can be dispensed with. For a detailed discussion of the vector maximum problem in which such conclusions are obtained, see Takayama [46], for example.

REMARK α in the above theorem can be considered as a "weight" attached to each individual by the society.

Clearly the Pareto optimum point is not necessarily unique. Any point in $F(S)$ achieves a Pareto optimum with respect to S. One way to sharpen this is to impose the following form on the social welfare function.[27]

$$W = U(u), \quad \text{where} \quad u = (u_1, \cdots, u_m). \tag{17-22}$$

We then obtain the social optimum point as a solution of the following non-linear programming problem.

Maximize $\quad U(u) \quad$ subject to $\quad u \in U(S)$. $\tag{17-23}$

If $U(S)$ is convex and $U(u)$ is strictly quasi-concave, then the solution u^* is unique. This is illustrated in Figure 17-9.[28]

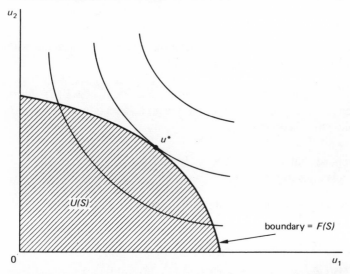

Figure 17-9   A Social Welfare Function and a Social Optimum

If we impose the following type of social welfare function

$$W = W(x), \tag{17-24}$$

---

[27] As we remarked in Chapter 1, the mechanism which generates such a social welfare function in a non-dictatorial society is not yet known. Arrow in [2] has shown that such a mechanism, satisfying a certain set of axioms, does not exist (now known as *Arrow's Impossibility Theorem*). This theorem does not state that the social welfare function does not exist, but it rather states that a *mechanism* which generates such a function does not exist under a certain set of axioms. We do not consider this theorem as a denial of the social welfare function, but rather consider it as an important *warning* which we should keep in mind when we use such a function. See also footnote 30.

[28] In this diagram $u(x)$ is taken so that $u^o = 0$. Thus the shaded area in Figure 17-9 shows $U(S)$.

where x is an allocation vector, then the social optimum point can be obtained as a solution of the following nonlinear programming problem.

Maximize $W(x)$ subject to $x \in C(S)$. (17-23')
x

Again, if W is strictly quasi-concave and $C(S)$ is convex, the solution of this problem is unique. The reader is referred to the fifth subsection for the various forms of the social welfare function and the quasi-concavity of these functions.

Semi-Competitive Equilibrium and the Compensation Principle

Suppose S is a given situation of the economy. Let x be an allocation of S so that $x\sigma \in S$. Suppose further that the economy is organized in a competitive manner such that each consumer cannot affect the market prices of the commodities and each consumer maximizes his satisfaction. Let p be a price vector which prevails in such an economy, and suppose allocation x is chosen under this p. $p(\sigma x)$, then, denotes the national income of the economy. We now investigate possible welfare characterizations of the economy, especially in terms of the national income under this competitive restriction of the economy. We now rigorously define this concept of competitiveness as follows:

DEFINITION (Semi-Competitive Equilibrium) Given a situation S, $[p, x, S]$ is called a *semi-competitive equilibrium*, if $p \in R^n$, $p \geqq 0$, and $x_i \in X_i$, $i = 1, 2, \cdots, m$ such that

1. $u_i(x_i) \geqq u_i(x_i')$ for all $x_i' \in X_i$ with $p \cdot x_i \geqq p \cdot x_i'$, $i = 1, 2, \cdots, m$;
2. $x\sigma \in S$.

REMARK Condition 1 is the familiar rule that each consumer maximizes his satisfaction. Condition 2 is the "feasibility condition," which states that the allocation x is feasible in the given situation S. Note that in the definition above, the profit maximization condition of each producer is not specified. By adding such a specification and modifying Condition 2 accordingly, we obtain the usual definition of competitive equilibrium. (See Takayama and El-Hodiri [47], Debreu [10], and Takayama [46], for example.) Obviously, if the economy is in a competitive equilibrium, it is in a semi-competitive equilibrium.

Assuming that the economy is in a semi-competitive equilibrium, we now investigate the welfare implication of different levels of national income.

DEFINITION (Chosen Point) Let $p \in R^n$, $p \geqq 0$, be a price vector which prevails in the economy. Then $x_i \in X_i$ is said to be a *chosen point* of the ith individual with respect to p if

$$u_i(x_i) \geqq u_i(x_i') \quad \text{for all} \quad x_i' \in X_i \quad \text{such that} \quad p \cdot x_i \geqq p \cdot x_i'. \quad (17\text{-}25)$$

REMARK Hence, that $[p, x, S]$ is a semi-competitive equilibrium means that x_i is a chosen point with respect to p for all i and $x \in C(S)$.

DEFINITION (Non-Satiation) $x_i \in X_i$ is called a *non-satiating* (consumption) point of the ith individual if there exists $x_i' \in X_i$ such that $u_i(x_i') > u_i(x_i)$.

LEMMA 2

1. If x_i is a non-satiating chosen point with respect to p for some i, then $p \geq 0 \ (p \neq 0)$.
2. Suppose that x_i is a chosen point with respect to p and that u_i is monotonic at x_i for *some* individual i; in other words
   for any $j_0 \in \{1, 2, \cdots, n\}$, there exists $x_i' \in X_i$ such that

$$x_{ij}' = x_{ij} \text{ for } j \neq j_0 \text{ and } x_{ij_0}' > x_{ij_0} \text{ with } u_i(x_i') > u_i(x_i),$$

(17-26)

then $p > 0$.

PROOF

1. Since x_i is a chosen point with respect to p, we have $u_i(x_i) \geq u_i(x_i')$ for all $x_i \in X_i$ with $p \cdot x_i \geq p \cdot x_i'$. Suppose $p = 0$. Then $u_i(x_i) \geq u_i(x_i')$ for all $x_i \in X_i$. This contradicts the assumption that x_i is non-satiating.
2. Suppose $p_{j_0} = 0$ for some $j_0 \in \{1, 2, \cdots, n\}$. Let $x_{ij}' = x_{ij}$ for $j \neq j_0$, and choose x_{ij_0}' so that $x_{ij_0}' > x_{ij_0}$ and $x_i' \in X_i$. Then $p \cdot x_i = p \cdot x_i'$ with $u_i(x_i') > u_i(x_i)$, which contradicts the assumption that x_i is a chosen point. Since the choice of j_0 is arbitrary, the proof is complete. (Q.E.D.)

REMARK Condition (17-26) says that there exists a consumer who is not satiated with any commodity at his chosen point. In a semi-competitive equilibrium we can obtain $p > 0$ under a weaker condition: for each commodity j, there exists a consumer who is not satiated at his chosen point.

LEMMA 3 Let x_i be a non-satiating chosen point of the ith individual with respect to a given price vector p. Then, under assumption 2, we have

1. $u_i(x_i') > u_i(x_i)$ implies $p \cdot x_i' > p \cdot x_i$.
2. $u_i(x_i') = u_i(x_i)$ implies $p \cdot x_i' \geq p \cdot x_i$, provided that u_i is quasi-concave.

PROOF

1. Suppose the conclusion does not hold: $p \cdot x_i' \leq p \cdot x_i$. Then $u_i(x_i) \geq u_i(x_i')$ in view of the fact that x_i is a chosen point. This contradicts $u_i(x_i') > u_i(x_i)$.
2. Let $u_i(x_i') = u_i(x_i)$ and suppose that $p \cdot x_i' < p \cdot x_i$. Since x_i is a non-satiating point, there exists $x_i'' \in X_i$ such that $u_i(x_i'') > u_i(x_i)$ so that $u_i(x_i'') > u_i(x_i')$. Choose x_i'' close enough to x_i' so that $p \cdot x_i'' < p \cdot x_i$ (which is possible due to the continuity of the inner product function and the quasi-concavity of u_i). Then $u_i(x_i'') \geq u_i(x_i)$ with $p \cdot x_i'' < p \cdot x_i$; this contradicts the assumption that x_i is a chosen point. (Q.E.D.)

REMARK   For a similar lemma, see Takayama [46], for example. The above proof is illustrated in Figure 17-10.

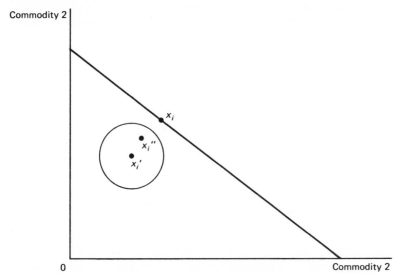

Figure 17-10   An Illustration of the Proof of Lemma 3

We now prove the following theorem, which was originally due to Hicks [17] and Samuelson [39] (see also Kennedy [25]).

THEOREM 7   Let $[p, x, S]$ be a semi-competitive equilibrium with $p \geqq 0$ such that every individual is non-satiated at x_i. Let $z \equiv x\sigma \in S$. Suppose that there exists $z' \in S$ such that

$$p \cdot z \geqq p \cdot z'. \tag{17-27}$$

Then there does not exist any allocation x' in $C(z')$ such that $x' \, P \, x$, that is,

$$u_i(x_i') \geqq u_i(x_i) \quad \text{for all} \quad i = 1, 2, \cdots, m, \tag{17-28}$$

with strict inequality for some i.

PROOF   Suppose there exists $x' \in C(z')$ such that $x' \, P \, x$. (That is, (17-28) holds.) Then, due to the previous lemma, we obtain

$$\sum_{i=1}^{m} p \cdot x_i' > \sum_{i=1}^{m} p \cdot x_i, \quad \text{or} \quad p \cdot z' > p \cdot z, \tag{17-29}$$

which contradicts (17-27).   (Q.E.D.)

REMARK   This theorem roughly says that if there is no decrease in national income (evaluated at the price vector of the new situation, p), then any allocation of the old situation cannot be Pareto superior to the equilibrium allocation of the new situation.

The following theorem says that when there is an increase in national income (evaluated at the price vector of the new situation, p), then the equilibrium allocation of the new situation cannot be Pareto inferior to any allocation of the old situation. The proof of this theorem is analogous to the previous theorem.

THEOREM 8 Suppose condition (17-27) is replaced by

$$p \cdot z > p \cdot z', \tag{17-30}$$

and the other assumptions of theorem 7 hold as they are. Then there does not exist any $x' \in C(z')$ such that $x' \, R \, x$.

PROOF Suppose the conclusion does not hold, so that there exists $x' \in C(z')$ such that $u(x') \geqq u(x)$. Then, due to lemma 3, $p \cdot z' \geqq p \cdot z$, which contradicts (17-30).   (Q.E.D.)

Suppose that national income does not decrease when moving from the old situation to the new situation: $p \cdot z \geqq p \cdot z'$. Can we then conclude that there exists an allocation (say, x') of the old situation (z') such that, under *any* allocation of the new situation, everyone's consumption expenditure does not decrease $[p \cdot x_i \geqq p \cdot x_i'$ for all $x_i \in C(z)]$? In this consideration, the economy does not have to be in a (semi-)competitive situation. Only the price vector is relevant.

To consider this problem, we need a little preparation. Let u_i^o be the minimum utility for individual i, $u_i(x_i) \geqq u_i^o$ for all $x_i \in X_i$.

ASSUMPTION 5 There exists $x_i^o \in X_i$ such that $x_i^o \leqq \tilde{x}_i$ for all $\tilde{x}_i$ with $u(\tilde{x}_i) = u_i^o$, $i = 1, 2, \cdots, m$. Furthermore, $x_i \in X_i$ implies $x_i' \in X_i$ for all x_i' such that $x_i^o \leqq x_i' \leqq x_i$, $i = 1, 2, \cdots, m$. We may call this assumption the *free disposability of X_i* for all i. An obvious example is the usual convention of setting X_i to be the non-negative orthant of R^n (and x_i^o is the origin of R^n). We now prove the following theorem which is a development of the line of thought by Barone, Hicks, Samuelson, Chipman, and so on.

THEOREM 9 Suppose that assumption 5 holds. Suppose also that price vector $p > 0$ prevails in the economy and that we have

$$p \cdot z \geqq p \cdot z', \quad z \geqq 0, \quad z' \geqq 0 \tag{17-31}$$

such that $C(z)$ and $C(z')$ are both non-empty and that $C(z)$ is compact. Then there exists $x' \in C(z')$ such that

$$p \cdot x_i \geqq p \cdot x_i' \quad \text{for all } i = 1, 2, \cdots, m \quad \text{and for all } x \in C(z). \tag{17-32}$$

PROOF Since $p \cdot x_i$ is a continuous function in x_i, its Cartesian product $[p \cdot x_1, \cdots, p \cdot x_m]$ is a continuous function in x. Since $C(z)$ is compact, due to the Weierstrass theorem, there exists $x^* \in C(z)$ such that $p \cdot x_i^* \leqq p \cdot x_i$ for all $x \in C(z)$. In other words, x^* achieves a vector minimum of $[p \cdot x_1, \cdots, p \cdot x_m]$. Clearly $x^*\sigma = z$, since $x^* \in C(z)$. By condition (17-31) we have

$$p \cdot z' \leq p \cdot (x^*\sigma) . \qquad (17\text{-}33)$$

Let x_i^o be the point defined in assumption 5, and let $x^o = (x_1^o, \cdots, x_m^o)$. Clearly $x^* \geq x^o$. Choose x' such that $x_i^o \leq x_i' \leq x_i^*$, $i = 1, 2, \cdots, m$, and $x'\sigma = z'$. Note that this choice is possible because $C(z')$ is non-empty and X_i is disposable for all i. Then, using $p > 0$, we obtain

$$p \cdot x_i' \leq p \cdot x_i^* \leq p \cdot x_i \quad \text{for all } x \in C(z), \quad \text{where } x' \in C(z') . \qquad \text{(Q.E.D.)}$$
$$(17\text{-}34)$$

Various Forms of a Social Welfare Function and (Quasi-) Concavity[29]

We may start with a social welfare function in the following form.

$$W = W(x), \qquad (17\text{-}35)$$

where

$$x = (x_{11}, x_{12}, \cdots, x_{ij}, \cdots, x_{mn}) = (x_1, \cdots, x_i, \cdots, x_m) \in X . \qquad (17\text{-}36)$$

Just as in each individual's utility, no measurability of W—social welfare—is assumed. In the above formulation of a social welfare function $W(x)$, it is assumed W depends only on an individual's consumption and not on any other variables such as environmental variables (climate, customs, working conditions, and so on) and monetary variables (prices of the commodities, money income of each individual, and so on).[30]

In the tradition of the western civilization, the individual's preference is considered crucial in determining the social welfare. Then we may specify the social welfare function as follows:

$$W = U(u_1, u_2, \cdots, u_m) \quad \text{or} \quad U(u), \quad \text{where} \quad u = (u_1, \cdots, u_m), \qquad (17\text{-}37)$$

where u_i represents the level of satisfaction for the ith individual ($i = 1, 2, \cdots, m$). u_i, in general, depends on x. That is, each individual is concerned with the consumption vector of the people in the society as well as that of himself. In the literature (and in the second section), such an externality is often assumed

[29] For the discussion in this subsection, we are indebted to Negishi [32], Bergson [7], Samuelson [38], chapter 8, and Graaff [12]. This subsection is intended to be an appendix to the present section.

[30] The concept of a social welfare function is introduced explicitly into economics by Bergson [7] and Samuelson [38]. It intends to be a real-valued representation of society's *ordering* of all the possible economic states of the society. Clearly the choice of a particular social welfare function involves ethical value judgments to which Robbins objected so much. But this does not imply that there is no room in economics for a social welfare function. As Samuelson argues ([38], p. 220), "It is a legitimate exercise of economic analysis to examine the consequences of various value judgments." The social welfare function achieves "a notable isolation and clarification of the function of value judgements in welfare economics," and it is useful for "the formalization of any set of value assumptions within a welfare analysis and to the compact tracing out of their implications" (Rothenberg [35], p. 8).

away; that is, u_i depends only on x_i, the individual's own consumption vector. Here we assume instead that u_i depends on x; hence, u_i is now defined on X rather than X_i $(i = 1, 2, \cdots, m)$.

DEFINITION The social welfare function is said to be *individualistic* if it is specified in the form of (17-37).[31] Note that functions U and W depend on the choice of the utility indicator of each individual, the u_is.

Assuming that the social welfare function takes the form of (17-37), we may further specify U such that U increases whenever there is an increase in u_{i_0} for any i_0, and there is no decrease in u_i for all $i \neq i_0$. We may call the social welfare function with this specification *Paretian* or *of the Pareto type*.[32] In other words, the social welfare function is Paretian if it takes the form of (17-37) and if

$$u \geq u' \quad \text{implies} \quad W(u) \geq W(u') . \tag{17-38}$$

This Paretian property is certainly not obvious in every society. For example, in a society in which there exists a strong discrimination (say, racial) against a minority group of the society, the social welfare function may fail to be Paretian even if it is individualistic.

Let z be an n-vector which denotes an aggregate consumption bundle of the society. That is, the jth element of z is $\sum_{i=1}^{m} x_{ij}(\equiv z_j)$. Fix the vector z, and consider the following maximization problem.

Maximize $W(x)$ subject to $x \in X$ and $\sum_{i=1}^{m} x_{ij} = z_j$, $j = 1, 2, \cdots, n$.

Let x^* be a solution of this problem. Then x^* denotes the allocation which maximizes the social welfare [assuming it takes the form of (17-35)] with a given amount of the aggregate commodity bundle, z. Clearly this solution x^* depends on z; hence we may write it as $x^* = x^*(z)$. Define

$$B(z) \equiv W[x^*(z)] . \tag{17-39}$$

We call $B(z)$ the *Bergsonian social welfare function*. Note that this form of the social welfare function B depends only on the aggregate commodity bundle. $B(z)$ denotes the maximum level of social welfare which can be obtained from z, by *assuming* that the specification of allocation x^* of z is possible. The locus of z such that $B(z) = $ constant is called the *Bergsonian social indifference curve*.[33] Note that along such a curve, allocation vector x^* will, in general, vary.

[31] This terminology is due to Graaff [12], p. ix.
[32] *Ibid.*
[33] This term is a modification of Graaff's terminology of the "Bergson frontier" ([12], p. 49). The above term, "Bergsonian social welfare function," was invented to match the "Bergsonian social indifference curve." As remarked before, Bergson's own concept of a social welfare function is a much broader one than this. The concept of the Bergson frontier is obtained as the "inner limit" of the family of Scitovsky curves, and it is described as a solution of the dual

THEOREM 10   Suppose that the social welfare function is individualistic so that

$$W(x) = U[u_1(x), u_2(x), \cdots, u_m(x)], \quad x \in X. \tag{17-40}$$

Suppose also that U is Paretian and u_i, $i = 1, 2, \cdots, m$, are all concave. Then if U is quasi-concave in u, W is quasi-concave in $x \in X$.

PROOF   Since u_i is concave,

$$u_i[\theta x + (1 - \theta)x'] \geqq \theta u_i(x) + (1 - \theta)u_i(x'), \quad i = 1, 2, \cdots, m, \tag{17-41}$$

for all θ, $0 \leqq \theta \leqq 1$, and x, $x' \in X$. Write $x'' \equiv \theta x + (1 - \theta)x'$, and $u \equiv [u_1(x), \cdots, u_m(x)]$, $u' \equiv [u_1(x'), \cdots, u_m(x')]$. Since U is Paretian, we have

$$W(x'') = U[u_1(x''), \cdots, u_m(x'')] \geqq U[\theta u + (1 - \theta)u']. \tag{17-42}$$

Now choose x and x' in X so that $W(x) \geqq a$ and $W(x') \geqq a$ (thus $U(u) \geqq a$ and $U(u') \geqq a$). Then

$$U[\theta u + (1 - \theta)u'] \geqq a. \tag{17-43}$$

Combining this with (17-42), we obtain $W(x'') \geqq a$.   (Q.E.D.)[34]

COROLLARY   Suppose that W is individualistic and Paretian and that u_i, $i = 1, 2, \cdots, m$, are all concave. Then if U is concave in u, W is concave in x.

PROOF   Since U is concave,

$$U[\theta u(x) + (1 - \theta)u(x')] \geqq \theta U[u(x)] + (1 - \theta)U[u(x')], \tag{17-44}$$

for *all* x, $x' \in X$, and $0 \leqq \theta \leqq 1$. Combining this with (17-42), we obtain the concavity of W in x.   (Q.E.D.)

REMARK   If U is twice differentiable, then U is concave if and only if the principal minors of U's Hessian matrix alternate in signs (not excluding the possibility that some vanish).[35] Hence, in particular, we have $\partial^2 U/\partial u_i^2 \leqq 0$, for all i. This means that each individual's marginal importance in the society, $\partial U/\partial u_i$, is nonincreasing with respect to his utility level u_i.

We now prove the quasi-concavity of Bergsonian function $B(z)$.

---

problem of the maximization problem in the text. (That is, it tells us the minimum amount of commodity given the amount of the other commodities needed to achieve a given level of social welfare.) See Graaff [12], p. 49 and pp. 53–54. Graaff assumed that W takes the form of (17-37).

[34] This theorem, in essence, is well-known in the literature of mathematics. See, for example, Berge, C., *Topological Spaces* (translated by Patterson), New York: Macmillan, 1963 (French original, 1959), p. 207, theorem 1.

[35] Let $U_{ij} \equiv \partial^2 U/(\partial u_i \, \partial u_j)$. The $n \times n$ matrix whose i-j element is U_{ij} is called the Hessian matrix of U. See Takayama [46], for example.

THEOREM 11   If W is quasi-concave in x, then B is quasi-concave in z.

PROOF   Let z and z' be aggregate consumption bundles such that $B(z) \geqq B(z')$. Let x and x' be the consumption bundles corresponding to z and z'. That is,

$$B(z) = W(x) \quad \text{and} \quad B(z') = W(x'), \tag{17-45}$$

where $z_j \equiv \sum_{i=1}^{m} x_{ij}$ and $z_j' \equiv \sum_{i=1}^{m} x_{ij}'$. Clearly the choice of x (or x') for a given z (or z') may not be unique. But this will not matter to our proof here. Let

$$z'' \equiv \theta z + (1 - \theta)z', \quad 0 \leqq \theta \leqq 1, \tag{17-46}$$

and

$$x'' \equiv \theta x + (1 - \theta)x', \quad 0 \leqq \theta \leqq 1. \tag{17-47}$$

Since W is quasi-concave by assumption and $W(x) \geqq W(x')$, we have

$$W(x'') \geqq W(x'). \tag{17-48}$$

Then

$$B(z'') \geqq W(x''), \tag{17-49}$$

since $B(z'')$ is the maximum value of W for all $x'' \in X$ such that $z_j'' = \sum_{i=1}^{m} x_{ij}''$,

$j = 1, 2, \cdots, n$. Then, combining (17-45), (17-48), and (17-49), we obtain

$$B(z'') \geqq B(z'). \tag{17-50}$$

This, in view of (17-46), establishes the quasi-concavity of B.   (Q.E.D.)

COROLLARY   If W is concave in x, then B is concave in z..

PROOF   Let z and z' be *any* aggregate consumption bundles, and let x and x' be the consumption bundles corresponding to z and z' (so that (17-45) holds). Define z'' and x'' as (17-46) and (17-47). Due to the concavity of W, we have

$$W(x'') \geqq \theta W(x) + (1 - \theta)W(x') = \theta B(z) + (1 - \theta)B(z'). \tag{17-51}$$

But by definition B, we have $B(z'') \geqq W(x'')$, which, in view of (17-51), establishes the concavity of B.   (Q.E.D.)

REFERENCES

1. Arrow, K. J., "An Extension of the Basic Theorems of Classical Welfare Economics," in *Proceedings of the Second Berkeley Symposium on Mathematical Statistics and Probability* (Berkeley: University of California Press), 1951.
2. ———, *Social Choice and Individual Values* (New York: John Wiley & Sons, Inc.), 2nd ed., 1963 (1st ed. 1951).

3. Bailey, M. J., "The Interpretation and Application of the Compensation Principle," *Economic Journal*, LXIV, March 1954.
4. Baldwin, R. E., "Comparison of Welfare Criteria," *Review of Economic Studies*, XXI, 1953–54.
5. Barone, E., "The Ministry of Production in the Collectivist State," in *Collectivist Economic Planning*, ed. by F. A. Hayek (London: Routledge and Kegan Paul), 1935, originally published in Italian, in *Giornale degle Economisti*, August/October, 1908.
6. Baumol, W. J., "Community Indifference," *Review of Economic Studies*, XIV, 1946–47.
7. Bergson, A., "A Reformulation of Certain Aspects of Welfare Economics," *Quarterly Journal of Economics*, LII, February 1938.
8. Chipman, J. S., "Gains from Trade and Commercial Policy," *Lecture Notes*, University of Minnesota, Winter 1966 (unpublished).
9. ———, and Moore, J. C., "The Compensation Principle in Welfare Economics," forthcoming in *Papers in Quantitative Economics*, Vol. 2 (Lawrence, Kansas: University of Kansas Press) (presented at Colorado meeting of the Kansas-Missouri Seminar on Quantitative Economics, Dec. 1968).
10. Debreu, G., *Theory of Value* (New York: John Wiley & Sons, Inc.), 1959.
11. Gorman, W. M., "The Intransitivity of Certain Criteria Used in Welfare Economics," *Oxford Economic Papers*, 7, February 1955.
12. Graaff, J. de V., *Theoretical Welfare Economics* (London: Cambridge University Press), 1967.
13. Haberler, G., "Some Problems in the Pure Theory of International Trade," *Economic Journal*, LX, June 1950, revised and reprinted in *Readings in International Economics*, ed. by Caves, R. E. and Johnson, H. G. (Homewood, Ill.: Richard D. Irwin, Inc.), 1968.
14. ———, "Welfare and Freer Trade—A Rejoinder," *Economic Journal*, LXI, December 1951.
15. Harrod, R. F., "Scope and Method of Economics," *Economic Journal*, XLVIII, September 1938.
16. Hicks, J. R., "Foundations of Welfare Economics," *Economic Journal*, XLIX, December 1939.
17. ———, "The Valuation of Social Income," *Economica*, 26, May 1940.
18. ———, "The Rehabilitation of Consumers' Surplus," *Review of Economic Studies*, VIII, February 1941.
19. ———, *A Revision of Demand Theory* (Oxford: Clarendon Press), 1956.
20. ———, "The Measurement of Real Income," *Oxford Economic Papers*, 10, June 1958.
21. Hotelling, H., "The General Welfare in Relation to Problems of Taxation and of Railway and Utility Rates," *Econometrica*, 6, July 1938.
22. Kaldor, N., "Welfare Propositions of Economics and Interpersonal Comparisons of Utility," *Economic Journal*, XLIX, September 1939.

23. ———, "A Comment," *Review of Economic Studies*, XIV, 1946–47.
24. Kemp, M. C., "The Gains from International Trade," *Economic Journal*, LXII, December 1962.
25. Kennedy, C., "An Alternative Proof of a Theorem in Welfare Economics," *Oxford Economic Papers*, 6, February 1954.
26. Krueger, A. O. and Sonnenschein, H., "The Terms of Trade, the Gains from Trade and Price Divergence," *International Economic Review*, 8, February 1967.
27. Kumagaya, H., *The Basic Theory of Welfare Economics* (Kosei Keizaigaku no Kiso Riron) (Tokyo: Toyo Keizai Shimpo-sha), 1957.
28. Kuroiwa, H., *Theory of Welfare Economics* (Kosei Keizai Riron) (Tokyo: Sobunsha), 1967 (in Japanese), especially Chapter 6.
29. Kuznetz, S., "On the Valuation of Social Income—Reflections on Professor Hicks' Article," *Economica*, XV, Part I, February 1948, Part II, May 1948.
30. Little, I. M. D., *A Critique of Welfare Economics* (Oxford: Clarendon Press), 2nd ed. 1957 (1st ed. 1950).
31. Mishan, E. J., *Welfare Economics, Five Introductory Essays* (New York: Random House, Inc.), 1964.
32. Negishi, T., "On Social Welfare Function," *Quarterly Journal of Economics*, LXXVII, February 1963.
33. Robbins, L. C., "Interpersonal Comparison of Utility, A Comment," *Economic Journal*, XLVIII, December 1938.
34. ———, *An Essay on the Nature and Significance of Economic Science* (London: Macmillan & Co., Ltd.), 1932.
35. Rothenberg, J., *The Measurement of Social Welfare* (Englewood Cliffs, N.J.: Prentice-Hall, Inc.), 1961.
36. Samuelson, P. A., "Welfare Economics and Foreign Trade," *American Economic Review*, XXVIII, June 1938.
37. ———, "The Gains from International Trade," *Canadian Journal of Economics and Political Science*, V, May 1939.
38. ———, *Foundations of Economic Analysis* (Cambridge, Mass.: Harvard University Press), 1947.
39. ———, "Evaluation of Real National Income," *Oxford Economic Papers*, 2, January 1950.
40. ———, "Social Indifference Curves," *Quarterly Journal of Economics*, LXX, February 1956.
41. ———, "The Gains from International Trade Once Again," *Economic Journal*, LXXII, December 1962.
42. Scitovsky, T., "A Note on Welfare Propositions in Economics," *Review of Economic Studies*, IX, November 1941.
43. ———, "A Reconsideration of the Theory of Tariffs," *Review of Economic Studies*, X, Summer 1942.
44. ———, "The State of Welfare Economics," *American Economic Review*, XLI, June 1951.

45. Stigler, G., "The New Welfare Economics, A Communication," *American Economic Review*, XXXIII, June 1943.
46. Takayama, A., *Mathematical Economics*, forthcoming.
47. ———, and El-Hodiri, M., "Programming, Pareto Optimum and the Existence of Competitive Equilibria," *Metroeconomica*, XX, Gennaio-Aprile, 1968.
48. ———, "Compensation Principle," Lecture Note, Purdue University, Spring 1967 (unpublished).
49. Tamura, Y., *Fundamental Problems of Welfare Economics—Criteria of Welfare Judgment* (Kosei Keizaigaku no Kihon Mondai—Kosei Handan no Kijun), 1961.
50. Viner, J., *Studies in the Theory of International Trade* (New York: Harper & Row, Publishers), 1937.

Appendix to Chapter 17
Welfare Change under a
Competitive Equilibrium[36]

Introduction

The purpose of this appendix is to illustrate some of the concepts developed in Chapter 17. In particular, we shall illustrate the application of theorem 7, which gives a welfare criterion under the compensation principle when the economy is organized in a competitive way. In the trade theory literature there are many discussions of this welfare criterion applied to diversified problems such as the gains from trade, the welfare effect of price divergence, the gains from economic growth, the infant industry argument, domestic distortions, the customs union issue, and other topics.

Recently Ohyama [A13] pointed out that we can give a unified treatment to these discussions; there is no need to prove various theorems independently. He produced some formulas in a straightforward way and obtained many of these theorems as simple corollaries. In this appendix we shall take up his approach.

The central idea here is to introduce into our theorem 7 the assumption that production as well as consumption is organized in a competitive way so that each producer maximizes his profit, taking the price vector as a given datum. In other words, we want to examine the applicability of theorem 7 (which we may term the *Hicks-Samuelson criterion*) in a full-blown competitive equilibrium (rather than in a semi-competitive equilibrium).

In order to make our treatment fairly short, we shall not discuss all the possible applications of our approach, for such a treatment would require rather a lengthy explanation of the literature on each topic. Instead, we shall confine ourselves to a few important applications. For some other important applications, we simply refer to Ohyama [A13]. Our purpose here is simply illustrative. However, it is expected that the reader will realize the application of our approach to other topics as well as appreciate the fruitfulness of the compensation principle.

Model

Let x and y be n-vectors denoting the *aggregate* consumption bundle and the *aggregate* production of a country. A negative (positive) element of y denotes input (output). We denote the aggregate production set of the country by Y,

---

[36] I am grateful to Michihiro Ohyama for his kind permission to draw upon his results in [A13] to which this appendix is heavily indebted.

where $Y \equiv \Sigma Y_j$. Y_j denotes the production set of the jth producer. We assume that the consumption set for each consumer is the non-negative orthant of R^n which is completely preordered by his preferences. By e we denote the aggregate excess demand vector,

$$e \equiv x - y - a,$$ \hfill (17-52)

where $a \geq 0$ is an n-vector denoting the aggregate endowments exogenously available in the country. There are n commodities in the economy, including primary factors, intermediate goods, non-traded goods, and so on. The same commodity can be used as a factor of production and as a good for final consumption (for example, the automobile). Following the usual convention of trade theory, we assume away transport costs whenever commodities are traded. This does not preclude that some commodities are completely immobile within the country and among countries due to institutional factors, intrinsic physical characteristics of the commodities, and so on.

Let q be the price vector that prevails in the world market and let p be the (domestic) price vector that the consumers of the country face. If there are no domestic taxes or subsidies on production and consumption, p is equal to the price vector that the producers of the country face. If, in addition, there are no (international) tariffs and subsidies then p would also be equal to q. Let x_i and y_j respectively be the consumption vector of consumer i and the production vector of producer j in the country.

We adopt the (usual) competitive assumption so that, under a given price vector, each consumer maximizes his satisfaction over his budget set and each producer maximizes his profit over his production set. Hence, for example, under free trade with the absence of domestic distortions and with constant technology and endowment, $[\{x_i^*\}, \{y_j^*\}, q^*]$ is an *equilibrium* for the country if $x_i^* \geq 0$ for all i, $y_j^* \in Y_j$ for all j, $p^* \geq 0$, $q^* \geq 0$ *and* if

i) $x_i^* \gtrsim_i x_i$ for all $x_i \geq 0$ with $p^* \cdot x_i \leq p^* \cdot x_i^*$ (for each i);

ii) $p^* \cdot y_j^* \geq p^* \cdot y_j$ for all $y_j \in Y_j$ (for each j);

iii) $q^* \cdot (x^* - y^* - a) = 0$ (that is, $q^* \cdot e^* = 0$);

iv) $q_i^* = p_i^*$,   if the ith commodity is traded.

Condition iv) signifies free trade. Condition iii) denotes the budget condition for the country. We assume that the consumers are *not* satiated for every commodity in equilibrium, so that $p^* \geq 0$. Needless to say, condition iii) does not imply that $e^* = 0$. Let e_i^* be the ith element of e (the excess demand for the ith commodity in equilibrium). Then $e_i^* > 0$ ($e_i^* < 0$) signifies that the ith commodity is imported (exported) in equilibrium. In order to simplify our exposition, we shall assume the uniqueness, as well as the existence, of competitive equilibrium under all the situations that we shall be concerned with in this appendix. Since we shall only be concerned with the equilibrium situation, we henceforth omit the asterisk (*) which denoted the equilibrium in the above.

We now introduce the central welfare criterion in this appendix.

DEFINITION   Suppose that an array of consumption vectors $\{x_i'\}$ is chosen when the consumers face p' and $\{x_i''\}$ is chosen when the consumers face p''. We say that x'' *is non-inferior to* x' (denoted by $x'' (\geqq) x'$), if $p'' \cdot x'' \geqq p'' \cdot x'$, where $x'' \equiv \Sigma x_i''$ and $x' \equiv \Sigma x_i'$.

REMARK   In view of theorem 7 of Chapter 17, $p'' \cdot x'' \geqq p'' \cdot x'$ implies that any allocation of x' cannot be Pareto superior to the equilibrium allocation of x''. The above criterion is called the *Hicks-Samuelson criterion*, as mentioned before.[37]

Ohyama's Formula

Let t_i'' be the ad valorem rate of tariff (or subsidy) on the import or the export of the ith commodity, or more specifically,

$$p_i'' = (1 + t_i'')q_i'', \quad i = 1, 2, \cdots, n. \tag{17-53}$$

Needless to say, if the ith commodity is an import (export), $t_i'' > 0$ signifies an import tariff (export subsidy) and $t_i'' < 0$ signifies an import subsidy (export tariff). Here we assume that there are no domestic distortions so that the consumers and the producers face the same price vector p''. Let T'' be the diagonal matrix whose ith diagonal element is t_i'' (and off-diagonal elements are all zero). Then we may rewrite (17-53) as

$$p'' = (I + T'')q''. \tag{17-54}$$

The budget equation of the country under q'' is written as

$$q'' \cdot e'' = 0; \quad \text{that is,} \quad q'' \cdot (x'' - y'' - a'') = 0. \tag{17-55}$$

Also recall the definition of e in (17-52) so that

$$e' = x' - y' - a'. \tag{17-56}$$

When the jth producer maximizes his profit over his production set we have

$$p'' \cdot y_j'' \geqq p'' \cdot y_j \quad \text{for all} \quad y_j \in Y_j''. \tag{17-57}$$

Hence, in particular,

$$p'' \cdot y_j'' \geqq p'' \cdot y_j'. \tag{17-58}$$

By aggregation over j, we obtain

$$p'' \cdot y'' \geqq p'' \cdot y'. \tag{17-59}$$

Note that this relation also holds when the production set expands from the single prime (') situation to the double prime ('') situation, that is, $Y' \subset Y''$, due to technological progress, and so on.

[37] This criterion is due to Hicks [A5] and Samuelson [A15]. This criterion really originates with Pigou, A. C., *The Economics of Welfare* (London: Macmillan & Co., Ltd.), 1920 (4th ed.), Part I, Chapters V–VII.

LEMMA (Ohyama)   Suppose that the following condition holds:[38]

$$-q'' \cdot e' + (T''q'') \cdot (e'' - e') + (T''q'') \cdot (a'' - a') + q'' \cdot (a'' - a') \geqq 0 .$$
(17-60)

Then the double prime situation is not inferior to the single prime situation, that is, $x'' \geqq x'$.

PROOF   (17-54) and (17-59) imply

$$q'' \cdot y'' + (T''q'') \cdot y'' \geqq q'' \cdot y' + (T''q'') \cdot y' .$$
(17-61)

Then using (17-55) and (17-56), we obtain

$$q'' \cdot x'' - q'' \cdot x' \geqq -q'' \cdot e' + (T''q'') \cdot (y' - y'') + q'' \cdot (a'' - a') .$$
(17-62)

Recalling (17-54), we rewrite (17-62) as

$$
\begin{aligned}
p'' \cdot x'' - p'' \cdot x' \geqq\ & -q'' \cdot e' + (T''q'') \cdot [(y' - x') - (y'' - x'')] \\
& + q'' \cdot (a'' - a') \\
=\ & -q'' \cdot e' + (T''q'') \cdot [(y' + a' - x') - (y'' + a'' - x'')] \\
& + (T''q'') \cdot (a'' - a') + q'' \cdot (a'' - a') \\
=\ & -q'' \cdot e' + (T''q'') \cdot (e'' - e') + (T''q'') \cdot (a'' - a') \\
& + q'' \cdot (a'' - a') .
\end{aligned}
$$
(17-63)

Hence, if condition (17-60) holds, we have $p'' \cdot x'' - p'' \cdot x' \geqq 0$. Then, applying the Hicks-Samuelson criterion, we obtain the statement of the lemma.
(Q.E.D.)

COROLLARY   If there is no change in the endowment vector,[39] then condition (17-60) is simplified to

$$-q'' \cdot e' + (T''q'') \cdot (e'' - e') \geqq 0 .$$
(17-64)

PROOF   Set $a' = a''$ in (17-60).   (Q.E.D.)

REMARK   As we shall see later, the first term of the *LHS* of (17-64) signifies a "terms of trade change." Clearly, $(e'' - e')$ signifies a change in the volume of trade.

[38] Note that condition (17-60) does *not* presuppose that the country is "small" in the sense that it has no influence on world prices. Furthermore, nowhere is it assumed that there is no factor immobility between countries and that there is no economic growth. Moreover, purely "domestic" goods and intermediate goods are allowed. Note also that, unlike many treatments in the literature, the zero (maximum) profit condition is *not* used in deriving (17-60).

[39] The endowment change takes place typically when there is economic growth. However, this is not the only case. For example, if there is a unilateral transfer of commodities (or purchasing power) or international factor movements, then this can be represented by a change of a' to a''. In other words, condition (17-60) is applicable to the welfare analysis of transfer payments and international factor mobility as well as economic growth.

REMARK   We can analogously obtain the conditions for the case in which domestic taxes (or subsidies) are imposed on the production and/or the consumption of the country. As we observed in Chapter 8, these taxes would create a gap between the prices facing the consumers and the prices received by the producers. In the appendix we proceed with our analysis by assuming that there are no such domestic distortions.[40]

Various Theorems

THEOREM 1 (Samuelson, Kemp)   In the absence of an endowment change,

i)   Free trade is not worse than no trade.[41]
ii)   Trade restricted by tariffs is not worse than no trade.[42]

PROOF   Identify the no trade situation by single prime (′) and the trade situation by double primes (″). No trade means $e' \leqq 0$, which implies $-q'' \cdot e' \geqq 0$.

1.   Free trade means $T'' = 0$. Hence, by condition (17-64) the conclusion of i) immediately follows.
2.   Trade restricted tariffs means that if $e_i'' > 0$, $t_i'' > 0$ (import tariffs) and that if $e_i'' < 0$, $t_i'' < 0$ (export tariffs). Hence, we have $(T''q'') \cdot e'' \geqq 0$. Thus, applying condition (17-64), we obtain the conclusion of ii).

$$(\text{Q.E.D.})$$

REMARK   When subsidies are allowed as well as tariffs, we may have $t_i'' < 0$ when $e_i'' > 0$ (import subsidies) and $t_i'' > 0$ when $e_i'' < 0$ (export subsidies). Then $(T''q'') \cdot e''$ can either be negative or positive. However, consider the scheme in which the expenditures for the subsidies are all financed by revenues from tariffs so that we have $(T''q'') \cdot e'' \geqq 0$. Such a scheme is called the *self-financing tariff-subsidy scheme* by Ohyama [A13]. Then applying condition (17-60), we immediately obtain the following theorem.

THEOREM 2 (Ohyama)   With the absence of an endowment change, trade under a self-financing tariff-subsidy scheme is not worse than no trade.

THEOREM 3   Economic growth is non-harmful to the country if

$$-q'' \cdot e' + (T''q'') \cdot (e'' - e') + (T''q'') \cdot (a'' - a') \geqq 0 . \tag{17-65}$$

[40] For the formulas (and their applications) when domestic distortions are involved, see Ohyama [A13].
[41] See Samuelson [A14]. As it was later realized [A16], there is no need to impose the small country assumption to derive this statement. See also Kemp [A7]. Note also that as a special case of this theorem, there is a rather obvious case of "vent for surplus" as conceived by Mynt [A12]. This is the case in which some commodities are free in the country under autarky, while they are not free in the world market.
[42] See Kemp [A7], [A10] (esp. pp. 267–268), and Samuelson [16]. Here the manner in which trade is restricted does matter. That is, there is a difference between trade restricted by tariffs and trade restricted by domestic taxes and subsidies. See Bhagwati [A3].

PROOF The proof is trivial, since economic growth means $Y' \subset Y''$ and $a'' \geqq a'$.

REMARK Economic growth can be harmful to the country if such a condition is not satisfied. Recall Bhagwati's thesis of immiserizing growth [A2].

COROLLARY Under free trade, economic growth with $a'' \geqq a'$ is non-harmful to the country if [43]

$$-q'' \cdot e' \geqq 0 .$$ (17-66)

DEFINITION q'' is said to represent a *terms of trade improvement* relative to q' if $-q'' \cdot e' > 0$.

THEOREM 4 (Krueger-Sonnenschein, Kemp) Suppose that there is no change in the endowments of the country. Then, if free trade prevails under the new situation, a terms of trade improvement is not harmful to the country.[44]

PROOF By assumption, $T'' = 0$. Hence, the conclusion of the theorem follows immediately.

REMARK To increase the understanding of the condition $-q'' \cdot e' > 0$, observe that this is equivalent to $-\Delta q \cdot e' > 0$ where $\Delta q \equiv q'' - q'$, due to the budget condition $q' \cdot e' = 0$. This, in turn, is equivalent to

$$\Delta q \cdot (y' + a') - \Delta q \cdot x' > 0 .$$

Then note that $\Delta q \cdot x'$ measures the change in the cost of purchasing the initial consumption bundle due to the price change Δq (in terms of the world price), and $\Delta q \cdot (y' + a')$ measures the change in the value of the initial output due to the price change (in terms of the world price).

DEFINITION Let p^o be the price vector which would prevail under autarky. q'' is said to *diverge more than* q' from p^o if

1. $\delta_i'' \geqq \delta_i'$, whenever $\delta_i' > 0$, *and*
2. $\delta_i'' \leqq \delta_i'$, whenever $\delta_i' < 0$,

---

[43] If the country is small so that it cannot influence the world price vector, then we can conclude that condition (17-66) is satisfied so that growth is non-harmful to the country. To see this, observe that $q' \cdot e' = 0$ implies $q'' \cdot e' = (q'' - q') \cdot e'$ and that the small country assumption implies $q'' - q' = 0$. See Kemp [A10], pp. 282–285. If the small country assumption is dropped, then the terms of trade may move in such a way as to result in $-q'' \cdot e' < 0$, which opens the possibility of immiserizing growth.

[44] See Kemp [A8], pp. 164–165, [A10], pp. 262–265, and pp. 268–270, also Krueger-Sonnenschein [A11], pp. 125–126. Needless to say, our formulation here as conceived by Ohyama [A13] is much more general than their formulations.

with strict inequality for at least one i either for $\delta_i'' \geqq \delta_i'$ or for $\delta_i'' \leqq \delta_i'$, where δ_i'' and δ_i' are defined by

$$q_i'' = (1 + \delta_i'')p_i^o \quad \text{and} \quad q_i' = (1 + \delta_i')p_i^o; \quad i = 1, 2, \cdots, n. \tag{17-67}$$

We may write (17-67) in terms of matrix notation as

$$q'' = (I + \delta'')p^o \quad \text{and} \quad q' = (I + \delta')p^o, \tag{17-67'}$$

where δ'' (respectively δ') is the diagonal matrix whose ith diagonal element is δ_i'' (respectively δ_i') and off-diagonal elements are all zero.

REMARK The concept of price divergence is a binary relation of the price vectors which is defined relative to the autarkic price vector. By $q'' \text{ v } q'$ we denote that q'' diverges more than q' from p^o.

REMARK The above definition of price divergence is again due to Ohyama [A13]. Kemp [A7] and Sonnenschein-Krueger [A11] defined price divergence as follows: q'' is said to diverge more than q' from p^o if there exists β, $0 < \beta < 1$, such that

$$q_i' = \beta q_i'' + (1 - \beta)p_i^o, \tag{17-68}$$

for all i. In view of (17-67), this can be rewritten as

$$q_i' = (1 + \beta\delta_i'')p_i^o. \tag{17-68'}$$

Hence, $\beta\delta_i'' = \delta_i'$. Since $0 < \beta < 1$, this implies that the definition of Kemp and Sonnenschein-Krueger satisfies conditions 1) and 2) of Ohyama's definition. Note that Ohyama's definition is more general than the K-S-K definition in the sense that the value of β can be different from commodity to commodity.

We now introduce the following assumption:

(A) $\delta_i' < 0$ for all i with $e_i' > 0$, and

$\quad\quad \delta_i' > 0$ for all i with $e_i' < 0$.

This means that if a commodity is to be imported (respectively exported) after the opening of trade, its price after trade is lower (respectively higher) than the one under autarky.

THEOREM 5[45] Suppose that assumption (A) holds and that there is no change in the endowments of the country. Suppose also that free trade prevails in the double prime situation. Then, if $q'' \text{ v } q'$, the double prime situation is not worse than the single prime situation.

---

[45] This theorem was first conjectured by Samuelson [A14]. Krueger-Sonnenschein [A11], pp. 124–125, proved the theorem by using Kemp's concept of price divergence [A8]. Later, Kemp [A10] contended that the theorem is "false", p. 266.

PROOF   We utilize condition (17-64). Since free trade prevails, $T'' = 0$. Hence, it suffices to show that $q'' \cdot e' \leqq 0$. First observe that $q'' \cdot e' = q'' \cdot e' - q' \cdot e' = [(I + \delta'')p^o] \cdot e' - [(I + \delta')p^o] \cdot e' = [(\delta'' - \delta')p^o] \cdot e'$, or

$$q'' \cdot e' = [(\delta'' - \delta')p^o] \cdot e', \tag{17-69}$$

in view of $q' \cdot e' = 0$ and (17-67). $q''\, \mathrm{v}\, q'$ with assumption (A) implies that

$$\delta_i'' > \delta_i', \quad \text{if } e_i' < 0, \quad \text{and} \quad \delta_i'' \leqq \delta_i', \quad \text{if } e_i' > 0,$$

with strict inequality for at least one i either for $\delta_i'' \geqq \delta_i'$ or for $\delta_i'' \leqq \delta_i'$. Therefore,

$$[(\delta'' - \delta')p^o] \cdot e' < 0, \tag{17-70}$$

so that $q'' \cdot e' < 0$.   (Q.E.D.)

Now consider three situations: double prime ($''$), single prime ($'$), and the "original" ($^-$) situation. Note that the original situation here does not have to be (although it can be) the autarkic situation. Write $\bar{q} = (I + \delta)p^o$.

LEMMA   The price divergence relation (v) is transitive, that is, $q''\, \mathrm{v}\, q'$ and $q'\, \mathrm{v}\, \bar{q}$ imply $q''\, \mathrm{v}\, \bar{q}$.

PROOF   Observe that, in view of $q'\, \mathrm{v}\, \bar{q}$, $\delta_i > 0$ implies $\delta_i' > 0$ and that $\delta_i < 0$ implies $\delta_i' < 0$. Then, by definition of price divergence, the conclusion of the lemma follows easily.   (Q.E.D.)

Suppose that there is no change in the endowments and free trade prevails both in the double-prime and the single-prime situation. Then by theorem 5, $q''\, \mathrm{v}\, q'$ implies $x'' \geqq x'$ and $q'\, \mathrm{v}\, \bar{q}$ implies $x' \geqq \bar{x}$, if assumption (A) holds. But by virtue of the previous lemma, $q''\, \mathrm{v}\, \bar{q}$, so that we have $x'' \geqq \bar{x}$. In other words, the relation $\geqq$ is *transitive*, as long as a change is brought about by price divergence (v). Following Ohyama [A13], define set $Q(\bar{q}, p^o)$ (or simply Q) by

$$Q(\bar{q}, p^o) = \{q : q\, \mathrm{v}\, \bar{q}\},$$

that is, Q is the set of price vectors which diverge more than $\bar{q}$ from p^o. Needless to say, $q''\, \mathrm{v}\, q'$ and $q' \in Q$ imply that $q'' \in Q$ by the previous lemma. Therefore, the conclusion of theorem 5, that $q''\, \mathrm{v}\, q'$ implies $x'' \geqq x'$, also follows when q'' and q' are restricted in the set $Q(\bar{q}, p^o)$, which probably is the original price divergence conjecture in the literature.

Next we investigate the relation between price divergence and terms of trade improvement. Suppose that we have $q'' \cdot \bar{e} < 0$ and $q' \cdot \bar{e} < 0$. Then by definition, q'' and q' both represent terms of trade improvement relative to the "original" ($^-$) situation. Suppose further that we also observe:

$$q'' \cdot \bar{e} < q' \cdot \bar{e} < 0. \tag{17-71}$$

We then say that "*the degree of terms of trade improvement in the double-prime situation is greater than the one in the single-prime situation*," or "*the double-*

prime situation represents a greater improvement in the terms of trade as compared with the single-prime situation." We are now interested in the relation between (17-71) and price divergence. In particular, we shall assert that under certain conditions $q'' \vee q' \vee \bar{q}$ implies (17-71), or more of price divergence implies more of terms of trade improvement.

Assume

(B) $e_i' \gtreqless 0$ according to whether $\bar{e}_i \gtreqless 0$, $i = 1, 2, \cdots, n$.

This means that the trade pattern is unchanged from the original situation to the single-prime situation. We now prove

THEOREM 6 Under assumptions (A) and (B), $q'' \vee q' \vee \bar{q}$ implies (17-71).

PROOF Since $q' \vee \bar{q}$, we have $q' \cdot \bar{e} = [(\delta' - \delta)p^o] \cdot \bar{e}$ by virtue of (17-69). Similarly, $q'' \vee \bar{q}^{46}$ implies that $q' \cdot \bar{e} = [(\delta'' - \delta)p^o] \cdot \bar{e}$. Hence, we obtain $q'' \cdot \bar{e} - q' \cdot \bar{e} = [(\delta'' - \delta')p^o] \cdot \bar{e}$. But assumptions (A) and (B) imply $\delta_i'' \geqq \delta_i'$ if $\bar{e}_i < 0$ *and* $\delta_i'' \leqq \delta_i'$ if $\bar{e}_i > 0$, with strict inequality at least for one i, either for $\delta_i'' \geqq \delta_i'$ or for $\delta_i'' \leqq \delta_i'$. Hence, $[(\delta'' - \delta')p^o] \cdot \bar{e} < 0$, so that $q'' \cdot \bar{e} - q' \cdot \bar{e} < 0$. Similarly, $q' \vee \bar{q}$ implies that $q' \cdot \bar{e} - \bar{q} \cdot \bar{e} < 0$, or $q' \cdot \bar{e} < 0$.

(Q.E.D.)

If the converse of the above theorem holds, then, by virtue of theorem 5, we may associate more of terms of trade improvement with welfare gain. But this is not true in general. A counterexample is provided by Krueger-Sonnenschein ([A11], p. 127). However, as long as the terms of trade improvement is brought about by price divergence such as $q'' \vee q' \vee \bar{q}$, we have $x'' \gtreqless x' \gtreqless \bar{x}$, provided that the assumptions of theorem 5 hold. This is obviously a trivial point. But it shows that we *can* associate more of terms of trade improvement with welfare gain under a certain class of cases.

To explore this point further, consider a subset $\bar{Q}$ of $Q(\bar{q}, p^o)$ in which $q', q'' \in \bar{Q}$ implies either $q'' \vee q'$ *or* $q' \vee q''$. Obviously there can be many such subsets in Q. We choose any one of them and fix our attention to it. Then the following theorem follows trivially.

THEOREM 7 (Ohyama) Suppose that assumptions (A) and (B) hold and that there is no change in the endowments of the country. Suppose also that free trade prevails in both the double-prime and the single-prime situations. Then, if (17-71) holds for $q'', q' \in \bar{Q}$, $x'' \gtreqless x' \gtreqless \bar{x}$.

PROOF Since $q'', q' \in \bar{Q}$, either $q'' \vee q' \vee \bar{q}$ *or* $q' \vee q'' \vee \bar{q}$. But $q' \vee q'' \vee \bar{q}$ contradicts (17-71) by virtue of theorem 6. Hence, $q'' \vee q' \vee \bar{q}$ so that the conclusion of the theorem follows immediately by virtue of theorem 5. (Q.E.D.)

REMARK Theorem 7 says that if we restrict our attention to set $\bar{Q}$, we can associate more of terms of trade improvement with welfare gain. For the practical significance of this theorem, see Ohyama [A13].

[46] In view of the previous lemma, $q'' \vee q'$ and $q' \vee \bar{q}$ imply $q'' \vee \bar{q}$.

In theorem 4, a weaker definition of terms of trade improvement, in which $-q'' \cdot e' > 0$ is replaced by $-q'' \cdot e' \geq 0$, would be sufficient to ensure the theorem. Similarly, by following the proof of theorem 5, we can easily see that the clause "with strict inequality for some i" in the definition of price divergence is not used there.

However, if we do retain the original definitions of terms of trade improvement and of price divergence, then we should be able to obtain stronger conclusions than those in theorems 4, 5, and 7. For this purpose, recall theorem 8 of Chapter 17. We can then think of a stronger version of the above Hicks-Samuelson criterion.

DEFINITION Suppose that an array of consumption vectors $\{x_i'\}$ is chosen when the consumers face p' and $\{x_i''\}$ is chosen when the consumers face p''. We say that x'' *is superior to* x' (denoted by $x'' \ominus x'$), if $p'' \cdot x'' > p'' \cdot x'$, where $x'' \equiv \sum x_i''$ and $x' \equiv \sum x_i'$. In view of theorem 8 of Chapter 17, $p'' \cdot x'' > p'' \cdot x'$ implies that there exists no allocation of x' which is Pareto non-inferior to the equilibrium allocation of x''.

In order to proceed with our analysis under this criterion, it is convenient to assume that all the relevant prices are positive. For example, if $q' > 0$, then $q' \cdot z > 0$ if $z \geq 0$, although $q' \cdot z$ can be zero if we only know $q' \geq 0$.

We now restate Ohyama's lemma and its corollary under the new criterion, which would be basic in obtaining all the previous theorems.

OHYAMA'S LEMMA If condition (17-60) holds with strict inequality, then $x'' \ominus x'$.

COROLLARY If there is no change in endowments, and if (17-64) holds with strict inequality, then $x'' \ominus x'$.

With this corollary and the proofs which are strictly analogous to the corresponding proofs, we can strengthen theorems 4, 5, and 7 as follows.

THEOREM 4' If free trade prevails under the new situation, a terms of trade improvement is beneficial to the country.

THEOREM 5' Suppose that assumption (A) holds and that there is no endowment change in the country. Suppose also that free trade prevails in the new situation. If q'' v q', then the double-prime situation is superior to the single-prime situation—that is, $x'' \ominus x'$.

THEOREM 7' Suppose that assumptions (A) and (B) hold and that there is endowment change in the country. Suppose also that free trade prevails both in the double-prime and the single-prime situations. Then, if (17-71) holds for q'', $q' \in \bar{Q}$, we have $x'' \ominus x' \ominus \bar{x}$.

REFERENCES

A1. Baldwin, R. E., "The New Welfare Economics and Gains in International Trade," *Quarterly Journal of Economics*, LXVI, February 1952.

A2. Bhagwati, J., "Immiserizing Growth: A Geometrical Note," *Review of Economic Studies*, XXV, June 1958.

A3. ———, "Gains from Trade Once Again," *Oxford Economic Papers*, 20, July 1968.

A4. Haberler, G., "Some Problems in the Pure Theory of International Trade," *Economic Journal*, LX, June 1950.

A5. Hicks, J. R., "Valuation of Social Income," *Economica*, 26, May 1940.

A6. Johnson, H. G., "The Possibility of Income Losses from Increased Efficiency or Factor Accumulation in the Presence of Tariffs," *Economic Journal*, LXXVII, March 1967.

A7. Kemp, M. C., "The Gains from International Trade," *Economic Journal*, LXXII, December 1962.

A8. ———, *The Pure Theory of International Trade* (Englewood Cliffs, N.J.: Prentice-Hall, Inc)., 1964.

A9. ———, "Some Issues in the Analysis of Trade Gains," *Oxford Economic Papers*, 20, July 1968.

A10. ———, *The Pure Theory of International Trade and Investment* (Englewood Cliffs, N.J.: Prentice-Hall, Inc.), 1969.

A11. Krueger, A. O., and Sonnenschein, H., "The Terms of Trade, The Gains from Trade and Price Divergence," *International Economic Review*, 8, February 1967.

A12. Mynt, H., "The Classical Theory of International Trade and the Underdeveloped Countries," *Economic Journal*, LXVII, June 1958.

A13. Ohyama, M., "Trade and Welfare in General Equilibrium," University of Rochester (M.A. Thesis), May 1970 (presented at the 1970 Meeting of Econometric Society).

A14. Samuelson, P. A., "The Gains from International Trade," *Canadian Journal of Economics and Political Science*, 5, May 1939.

A15. ———, "Evaluation of Real National Income," *Oxford Economic Papers*, 2, January 1950.

A16. ———, "The Gains from International Trade Once Again," *Economic Journal*, LXXII, December 1962.

PART VI
A TOPIC IN THE MODERN THEORY OF INTERNATIONAL TRADE

18

THE FACTOR PRICE EQUALIZATION THEOREM AND THE STOLPER-SAMUELSON THEOREM REVISITED[1]

INTRODUCTION

In Chapter 3 we discussed two important theorems, the factor price equalization theorem and the Stolper-Samuelson theorem, as corollaries of the Heckscher-Ohlin trade model. There we pointed out that the two-good, two-factor assumption in these theorems turned out to be crucial for the validity of the theorem. In his monumental paper [31], Samuelson first made a comprehensive study of the factor price equalization theorem in a multi-good, multi-factor model. He argued there, as it might easily be suspected, that there is not too much hope for the validity of the theorem when the number of goods is not the same as the number of factors. The theorem is concerned with the relation between factor price vector w and good price vector p. Suppose w is an m-vector and p is an n-vector. Under a certain set of assumptions and with the cost minimization behavior, we can impose a certain functional relationship between p and w, say, $p = v(w)$. If the production function for each good is the same among the countries, the functional relationship will also be the same among the countries. However, due to the differences in the factor endowments and consumers' taste (demand conditions), the values of p or w will be different among the countries as long as there is no international trade and factor mobility among them. The factor price equalization theorem is concerned with the problem of whether the equalization of the p-vector among the countries due to the opening of international trade will equalize the w-vector. The theorem we discussed in Chapter 3 says that if p and w are both two-dimensional vectors and if both countries produce the same two goods after the opening of trade, then the equalization of p implies the equalization of w.

[1] I am grateful to Yasuo Uekawa for valuable comments, and for letting me see his [36] before its publication.

Clearly such a conclusion depends on the dimensions of p and w. Consider the following simple relation:

$$p = v(w) = w_1 + w_2 .$$

This is the case in which there are one good and two factors ($n = 1$, $m = 2$). Even if two countries have the same p, w_i can be different between the countries. In other words, p does not uniquely determine w. The case of $n = 1$ may sound strange for the model of international trade, but it should not be difficult to understand that the basic logic in the above example extends as long as $n < m$ (the number of goods is less than the number of factors). Since p is an n-vector, there are n equations in the relation $p = v(w)$. If w is an m-vector when $m > n$, then the number of variables (w_is) to be determined in the system (m) exceeds the number of equations in the system (n). Therefore we cannot in general completely specify w from p.

Suppose, on the other hand, that $m < n$. Then there are more equations than variables. Hence, the system is in general over-determined. However, if we can somehow restrict p to an m-dimensional subvector, then factor price equalization is possible. Due to an old but deep topological theorem by Brouwer, any continuous function will map an m-dimensional vector to an m-dimensional space. In other words, if v is continuous, then w is mapped to an m-dimensional subspace of the p-space. Hence, by specifying the value of the p_is in this m-dimensional subspace, there is a possibility of specifying the value of w. In other words, if international trade will bring the equalization of these m p_is, then factor price equalization can occur.

From these considerations, the interest in the factor price equalization is shifted to the $n \times n$ case, the case in which the number of goods is the same as the number of factors.

Considerations of such a case may look rather arbitrary, but it is certainly much more general than 2×2, and it may be considered as a good start for the extension to a multi-good, multi-factor international trade model in which n is not necessarily equal to m. The more important thing probably is the fact that such considerations of the ($n \times n$) case will reveal several important relations which will be useful in other branches of economic analysis.

First, the basic implications of the cost minimizing behavior are investigated and utilized. The most important one is probably the theorem which should be called the Shephard-Samuelson theorem. Samuelson, in his 1953 factor price equalization paper, stated this theorem without providing rigorous proof. In a book published in 1953 by Princeton University Press [34] Shephard independently established this theorem with a rigorous proof. Although Shephard was not concerned with the factor price equalization theorem as such, his theorem, together with Samuelson's article, provided one important progress to this theorem.

Secondly, it was asked whether there exists a w with a given p such that $p = v(w)$. In other words, the existence of w, which is compatible with a competitive equilibrium and with given factor endowments and taste, was asked. This was asked and answered by Kuhn [12].

Thirdly, interest is focused on the possibility of unique inversion of $p = v(w)$ where both p and w are n-vectors. Suppose there exists a unique function v^{-1} so that $v^{-1}(p) = w$, then the equalization of p certainly implies the equalization of w. In the above mentioned paper [12], Kuhn also provided a condition under which the uniqueness of w, for a given p, can be proved. Thus he presented one answer to this question of unique inversion. However, there is another chain of thought essentially originating from the inverse function theorem, which asserts the local inversion. This line of thought has been pursued by Pearce and Samuelson and finally culminated in the Gale-Nikaido theorem [8].

What about the Stolper-Samuelson theorem? This theorem is again concerned with the relation $p = v(w)$. In essence it asks about the effect of a change in the p-vector on the w-vector. Hence, it is not surprising that this theorem has a close connection with the factor price equalization theorem. Thus, together with the above further exploration of the factor price equalization theorem, further studies have been done on the Stolper-Samuelson theorem by economists such as Chipman, McKenzie, Kuhn, Inada, Kemp, Uekawa, and Wegge.

In the next section we shall provide two considerations of the implication of the cost minimizing behavior. In particular we provide: a) a relation between the cost minimizing behavior and the profit maximizing behavior, and b) our proof of the Shephard-Samuelson theorem. In the third section we shall pick up the above topics on the factor price equalization theorem and discuss them in more detail. In the section following we shall discuss the Stolper-Samuelson theorem. Our emphasis in this chapter is on clarifying basic economic and mathematical relations which have become known through the studies of the extension of the factor price equalization theorem and the Stolper-Samuelson theorem, and does not lie in extending these two theorems more than those known in the literature. Hence, we shall devote a certain amount of space to topics which are not directly related to the extension of these theorems if these topics are relevant to our consideration and important in economic theory in general. Our discussion of the relation between the cost minimizing behavior and the profit maximizing behavior and the inverse and implicit function theorems are such examples.

TWO REMARKS ON COST MINIMIZING BEHAVIOR

Profit Maximization and Cost Minimization

Consider a production function $y = f(x)$, which relates the amount of single output, y, and the input vector x. x is an m-vector (in the non-negative orthant of the Euclidean m-space) where the ith element x_i denotes the amount of the ith resource input for the production of y. Let p be the price of the output and w be the price vector for the input, where the ith element w_i denotes the price of the ith resource. We consider a competitive situation so that p and w_i, $i =$

1, 2, $\cdots$, m are given constants. We assume that $p > 0$, and $w_i > 0$, $i = 1, 2, \cdots, m$. The price of the output p is applicable only to the profit maximizer. Hence, the cost minimizer does not have to be competitive in the goods market.

PROFIT MAXIMIZER The profit maximizer is concerned with the following nonlinear programming problem:

(M) Maximize $py - w \cdot x$ subject to $f(x) - y \geqq 0$,[2] and $y \geqq 0$,
(x, y)

$$x \geqq 0.$$

Here, dot ($\cdot$) refers to the inner product so that $w \cdot x \equiv \sum_{i=1}^{m} w_i x_i$.

COST MINIMIZER He is concerned with the following nonlinear programming problem:

(m) Minimize $w \cdot x$ subject to $f(x) \geqq \bar{y}$ and $x \geqq 0$,[3] where
(x)

$$\bar{y} > 0 \text{ is a given constant.}$$

Or, equivalently:

Maximize $-w \cdot x$ subject to $f(x) \geqq \bar{y}$ and $x \geqq 0$.
(x)

Comparing the above two problems, there are two important distinctions between the profit maximizer and the cost minimizer which are obvious. One is that the former chooses both the input level (x) *and* the output level (y); the latter chooses only the input level (x). The output level is a predetermined constant for the cost minimizer. Another important distinction is that the cost minimizer does not care about the price of output, p. His choice of input will be independent of p; while the optimal production for the profit maximizer depends on p, as well as w. Let (x^*, y^*) be a solution for (M) and x^o be a solution for (m). Then we may write $x^* = x^*(p, w)$, $y^* = y^*(p, w)$; $x^o = x^o(w, \bar{y})$, emphasizing the functional relations. We are now interested in comparing the solutions of the above two problems (M) and (m).[4] In order to have

---

[2] This allows an inefficient production (production which takes place inside the production frontier $f(x)$ and a free disposal of output and input). Although we shall show that a profit maximizing production, in general, takes place *on* the production frontier (so that $y = f(x)$), there is no reason to believe that this should hold *a priori*. (Recall our discussion on activity analysis in Chapter 7.)

[3] This again allows an inefficient production and free disposal. Although we shall show that a cost minimizing production, in general, does not allow such inefficiency, there is no reason to believe that this should hold *a priori*.

[4] We assume the existence of a solution for each problem.

a necessary and sufficient characterization of each problem, we impose the following assumptions:

1. f is a differentiable single-valued concave function;
2. There exist $\tilde{y} \geq 0$ and $\tilde{x} \geq 0$ such that $f(\tilde{x}) - \tilde{y} > 0$;
3. There exists $\bar{x} \geq 0$ such that $f(\bar{x}) - \bar{y} > 0$.

Assumption 2 provides Slater's condition for problem (M), and assumption 3 provides Slater's condition for problem (m). (Obviously assumption 3 implies assumption 2; assumption 2 is an assumption for (M); and assumption 3 is for (m).) The Lagrangians for (M) and (m) are respectively written as

$$[(py - w \cdot x) + \mu(f(x) - y)] \quad \text{and} \quad [-w \cdot x + v(f(x) - \bar{y})].$$

Due to assumptions 1 and 2, a necessary and sufficient condition for (x^*, y^*) to be a solution of (M) is described by the following Kuhn-Tucker-Lagrange condition (KTL_M) (use theorem 3 of the Appendix to Chapter 5).[5]

(KTL_M) There exists $\mu^* \geq 0$ (and $x^* \geq 0$) such that

$$p - \mu^* \leq 0, \tag{18-1a}$$

$$-w_i + \mu^* f_i^* \leq 0, \quad i = 1, 2, \cdots, m, \quad \text{where } f_i^* \equiv \partial f / \partial x_i$$

evaluated at $x = x^*$; $\tag{18-1b}$

$$(p - \mu^*) y^* = 0, \tag{18-2a}$$

$$(-w_i + \mu^* f_i^*) x_i^* = 0, \quad i = 1, 2, \cdots, m; \tag{18-2b}$$

$$f(x^*) - y^* \geq 0 \quad \text{and} \quad [f(x^*) - y^*] \mu^* = 0. \tag{18-3}$$

Due to assumptions 1 and 3, a necessary and sufficient condition for x^o to be a solution of (m) is similarly written by the following (KTL_m):[6]

(KTL_m) There exists $v^o \geq 0$ (and $x^o \geq 0$) such that

$$-w_i + v^o f_i^o \leq 0, \quad i = 1, 2, \cdots, m, \quad \text{where } f_i^o \equiv \partial f / \partial x_i$$

evaluated at $x = x^o$. $\tag{18-4}$

$$(-w_i + v^o f_i^o) x_i^o = 0, \quad i = 1, 2, \cdots, m. \tag{18-5}$$

$$f(x^o) - \bar{y} \geq 0 \quad \text{and} \quad [f(x^o) - \bar{y}] v^o = 0. \tag{18-6}$$

[5] In view of Arrow-Enthoven [3] the concavity of f and assumption 2 can be relaxed. For the necessity of (KTL_M), the Kuhn-Tucker Constraint Qualification $(KTCQ)$ [15] replaces the concavity of f and assumption 2. For the sufficiency of (KTL_M) we need, for example, the quasi-concavity of $F(x, y) \equiv f(x) - y$, and $f_i^* > 0$ (positive marginal product of factor i) for some "relevant" i. For some important and useful conditions which replace $(KTCQ)$, see Arrow-Hurwicz-Uzawa [4].

[6] A remark similar to footnote 5 also holds here. For the sufficiency of (KTL_M), $(KTCQ)$ can replace the concavity of f and assumption 3. For the necessity of (KTL_M) we need, for example, the quasi-concavity of $f(x)$, which assures that the set $\{x : f(x) \geq \bar{y}, x \geq 0\}$ is convex.

In order to facilitate the comparison of the two problems we may assume $y^* > 0$ (recall $\bar{y} > 0$ by assumption).[7] Note that if (KTL_M) is satisfied then (KTL_m) is satisfied for $\bar{y} = y^*$. To see this, simply put $v^0 = \mu^*$ and $x^0 = x^*$ and note the correspondences: (18-1b) $\Leftrightarrow$ (18-4), (18-2b) $\Leftrightarrow$ (18-5), and (18-3) $\Leftrightarrow$ (18-6). In other words, if (x^*, y^*) is a solution for the profit maximizer's problem (M), then it is also a solution for the cost minimizer's problem (m) at $\bar{y} = y^*$. Or, profit maximization implies cost minimization at $\bar{y} = y^*$.

The converse of the above statement does not necessarily hold. That is, cost minimization does not necessarily imply profit maximization. This is really obvious for $\bar{y}$; a fixed level of output for the cost minimizer is not necessarily equal to y^*, a solution of (M), and also his decision is independent of price p.

Let us now assume that there exists at least one i such that $x_i^* > 0$ and that there exists at least one i such that $x_i^0 > 0$. In other words, we assume that at least one input is indispensable for production. Since we assumed $y^* > 0$ and $\bar{y} > 0$, this assumption can be accepted without too much difficulty. Then, due to (18-2b), $w_i = \mu^* f_i^*$ for some i so that $\mu^* > 0$ ($\because w_i > 0$ for all i by assumption). Similarly, $w_i = v^0 f_i^0$ for some i due to (18-5), so that $v^0 > 0$. Hence, (18-3) and (18-6) are respectively reduced to $(f(x^*) - y^* = 0)$ and $(f(x^0) - \bar{y} = 0)$. Note that for the case of (KTL_M), $\mu^* > 0$ can also be obtained from (18-1a) since $p > 0$ by assumption.

Now note that $p = \mu^*$ by our assumption $y^* > 0$ and (18-2a). Therefore, (18-1a) and (18-2a) are simply reduced to $p = \mu^*$. Therefore (KTL_M) can simply be reduced to:

(KTL$_M'$)   For $p > 0$, there exists $x^* \geq 0$ such that

$$pf_i^* \leq w_i, \quad i = 1, 2, \cdots, m; \tag{18-7}$$

$$(w_i - pf_i^*)x_i^* = 0, \quad i = 1, 2, \cdots, m; \tag{18-8}$$

$$y^* = f(x^*). \tag{18-9}$$

Condition (18-7) says that the value of the marginal product of the ith factor cannot exceed its price. Condition (18-8) says that if the ith factor is used, then the value of its marginal product is equal to its price; and that if the price of the ith factor exceeds the value of its marginal product, then it is not used at an equilibrium $(x_i^* = 0)$. Condition (18-9) says that production takes place on the production function (production frontier). They are all well-known results.

Our optimality condition for (m), that is, (KTL_m), can similarly be rewritten as:

(KTL$_m'$)   There exists $v^0 > 0$ (and $x^0 \geq 0$) such that

$$v^0 f_i^0 \leq w_i, \quad i = 1, 2, \cdots, m; \tag{18-10}$$

[7] Clearly, $y^* = 0$ (or $\bar{y} = 0$) is indeed an uninteresting case.

$$(w_i - v^o f_i^o)x_i^o = 0, \quad i = 1, 2, \cdots, m; \tag{18-11}$$

$$\bar{y} = f(x^o). \tag{18-12}$$

Clearly (KTL_M') and (KTL_m') are much simpler expressions than (KTL_M) and (KTL_m).

If the production function exhibits constant returns to scale so that f is homogeneous of degree one, then $\sum_{i=1}^{m} f_i x_i = y$ for all x where $f_i \equiv \partial f/\partial x_i$. Thus by summing both sides of (18-8) with respect to i and using (18-9), we obtain

$$\sum_{i=1}^{m} w_i x_i^* = p y^*. \tag{18-13}$$

In other words, profit $(py^* - \sum_{i=1}^{m} w_i x_i^*)$ is zero at an optimal input-output combination. Moreover, if f is linear homogeneous in x, then $f_i, i = 1, 2, \cdots, m$, are all homogeneous functions of degree zero with respect to x. Hence, we can conclude that if (x^*, y^*) satisfies (KTL_M'), then $(\alpha x^*, \alpha y^*)$ also satisfies (KTL_M') for all $\alpha > 0$, hence also (KTL_m') with $v^o = p$ and with $\bar{y} = \alpha y^*$ for *some* α. The cost minimizer is also a profit maximizer, where $p = v^o$.

The Shephard-Samuelson Theorem

In the previous section we showed that, under a certain set of plausible assumptions, a cost minimizer chooses an input vector which satisfies (KTL_m'). In this section we shall explore its further implication; in particular, we want to prove the theorem which is due to Shephard [34] and Samuelson [31].[8] Following Shephard and Samuelson, we shall suppose that our producer is a cost minimizer. Moreover, we assume that f, the production function, is homogeneous of degree one so that $f(x) = \sum_{i=1}^{m} f_i(x)x_i$ for all x, where $f_i(x) \equiv \partial f/\partial x_i$. If the price of output (p) is given to him (if he is a competitive producer), then the linear homogeneity of f implies that he is also a profit maximizer. Here we shall exclude the consideration of the price of his output and shall stick to the supposition that he is a cost minimizer (thus he may not be a competitive producer in the goods market).

Since this producer is a cost minimizer, (KTL_m') must be satisfied. Summing up both sides of equation (18-11) in (KTL_m') with respect to i and using the homogeneity of f, we obtain

$$\sum_{i=1}^{m} w_i x_i^o = v^o f(x^o). \tag{18-14}$$

Write $C \equiv \sum_{i=1}^{m} w_i x_i^o$, denoting the total cost of the production of output $\bar{y}$.

---

[8] Samuelson does not really contain a detailed and rigorous proof. See Samuelson [31], p. 15. Our proof will be somewhat simpler than that of Shephard [34]. There is an elegant recent discussion by Afriat [1] on a broad topic which includes our topic.

Thus, using (18-11), we obtain

$$C = v^o f(x^o) = v^o \bar{y} . \tag{18-15}$$

This equation means that $v^o = $ (average cost) $(\equiv C/\bar{y})$.

We should note that x^o and v^o are functions of w and $\bar{y}$, the parameters of cost minimizer's problem (m). Hence, as remarked before, we may write $x^o = x^o(w, \bar{y})$, $v^o = v^o(w, \bar{y})$, and $C = C(w, \bar{y})$, emphasizing the underlying functional relations. Now consider a change of $\bar{y}$ from one fixed level to another fixed level. In other words, we perform

$$\frac{\partial C(w, \bar{y})}{\partial \bar{y}} = \sum_{i=1}^{m} w_i \frac{\partial x_i^o(w, \bar{y})}{\partial \bar{y}} . \tag{18-16}$$

But, due to the homogeneity of f and equation (18-12), we have

$$\frac{\partial \bar{y}}{\partial \bar{y}} = 1 = \sum_{i=1}^{m} f_i^o \frac{\partial x_i^o(w, \bar{y})}{\partial \bar{y}} , \tag{18-17}$$

where partial (∂) signifies that w is fixed in this operation and $f_i^o = \partial f/\partial x_i$ evaluated at $x = x^o$. Assume now that $x_i^o > 0$ for all i (interior solution) so that relation (18-10) holds with equality for all i. In other words,

$$w_i = v^o f_i^o, \quad i = 1, 2, \cdots, m . \tag{18-18}$$

Then, using (18-18) and (18-17), equation (18-16) is rewritten as:

$$\frac{\partial C}{\partial \bar{y}} = \sum_{i=1}^{m} v^o f_i^o \frac{\partial x_i^o}{\partial \bar{y}} = v^o. \tag{18-19}$$

This, among others, means that $v^o = $ (marginal cost) $(\equiv \partial C/\partial \bar{y})$.

We now show that v^o is independent of $\bar{y}$. (That is, v^o is a function of w only.) To do this it suffices to show that $\partial v^o/\partial \bar{y} = 0$. Using (18-15) and (18-19) we can perform

$$\frac{\partial v^o}{\partial \bar{y}} = \frac{\partial}{\partial \bar{y}} \left(\frac{C}{\bar{y}} \right) = \frac{1}{\bar{y}} \frac{\partial C}{\partial \bar{y}} - \frac{1}{\bar{y}^2} C = \frac{1}{\bar{y}} \left(v^o - \frac{C}{\bar{y}} \right) = 0 .$$

Next we shall show that v^o is a homogeneous function of degree one in w. To show this we first show that $x_i^o = \partial C/\partial w_i$, where (∂) denotes that $\bar{y}$ is fixed in this differentiation. Using the definition of C and equation (18-18) we can perform

$$\frac{\partial C}{\partial w_i} = x_i^o + \sum_{j=1}^{m} w_j \frac{\partial x_j^o(w, \bar{y})}{\partial w_i} = x_i^o + v^o \sum_{j=1}^{m} f_j^o \frac{\partial x_j^o}{\partial w_i} . \tag{18-20}$$

But $\bar{y} = f(x^o)$ (equation (18-12)) implies

$$\frac{\partial \bar{y}}{\partial w_i} = 0 = \sum_{j=1}^{m} f_j^o \frac{\partial x_j^o}{\partial w_i} , \tag{18-21}$$

where (∂) signifies that $\bar{y}$ is a fixed constant in this differentiation. Combining (18-20) and (18-21), we obtain

$$\frac{\partial C}{\partial w_i} = x_i^o. \tag{18-22}$$

Hence, we have

$$C \equiv \sum_{i=1}^{m} w_i x_i^o = \sum_{i=1}^{m} \frac{\partial C}{\partial w_i} w_i. \tag{18-23}$$

Thus, Euler's equation for linear homogeneous functions is satisfied. In other words, C is linear homogeneous with respect to w. Since $C = v^o \bar{y}$, v^o is also linear homogeneous in w. We now summarize the main results.

THEOREM (Shephard-Samuelson) Let $f(x)$ be a production function which exhibits constant returns to scale. Let x^o be an input vector which minimizes the cost of production with a given factor-price vector w and a given level of output $\bar{y}$. Assume x_i^o, the ith component of x^o, is positive for all $i = 1, 2, \cdots, m$ (interior solution). Let $C = \sum_{i=1}^{m} w_i x_i^o$, the cost of production for x^o. Then there exists v^o such that:

   i) $C = v^o \bar{y}$;
   ii) $\partial C/\partial \bar{y} = v^o$;
   iii) v^o depends on w alone and is independent of $\bar{y}$, that is, $v^o = v^o(w)$;
   iv) C and v^o are homogeneous of degree one with respect to w;
   v) $\partial C/\partial w_i = x_i^o$, (and $\partial v/\partial w_i = x_i^o/\bar{y}$).

The following corollary is due to Uzawa [37].

COROLLARY (Uzawa) If f is concave in the above theorem, then v is also concave (or $C(w, \bar{y})$ is concave in w).

PROOF Let $C(w, \bar{y})$ be the minimum cost given factor price vector w and output $\bar{y}$. Let $w^t \equiv (1 - t)w^o + tw^1$, $0 \le t \le 1$. Then, by definition of C, we have

$$C(w^o, \bar{y}) \le w^o \cdot x, \quad \text{for all } x \text{ such that } f(x) \ge \bar{y},$$

$$C(w^1, \bar{y}) \le w^1 \cdot x, \quad \text{for all } x \text{ such that } f(x) \ge \bar{y}.$$

Multiplying the above two equations by $(1 - t)$ and t respectively and adding, we have

$$(1 - t)C(w^o, \bar{y}) + tC(w^1, \bar{y}) \le w^t \cdot x \quad \text{for all } x \text{ such that } f(x) \ge \bar{y}.$$

This implies that

$$(1 - t)C(w^o, \bar{y}) + tC(w^1, \bar{y}) \le C(w^t, \bar{y}), \quad \text{for all } 0 \le t \le 1.$$

Hence, $C(w, \bar{y})$ is concave with respect to w.   (Q.E.D.)

THE FACTOR PRICE EQUALIZATION REVISITED[9]

Introduction

In Chapter 3, we discussed the factor price equalization theorem as a simple corollary of the Heckscher-Ohlin trade model. The model there is that of two countries, two goods, and two factors. Each country is supposed to produce both goods after trade is initiated between the countries (incomplete specialization). Both countries have the identical production function for producing the same good, and every production function exhibits constant returns to scale and diminishing returns (thus a concave function). Under these assumptions a unique monotone relation between the factor price ratios and the goods price ratio exists, and it immediately leads one to conclude that the equalization of the goods price ratio (assuming no transport cost) will bring the equalization of the factor price ratio and of absolute factor prices, even if the factors are all completely immobile between the countries. This much was completely clear by the time of the publication of Samuelson's famous article in 1949 [30].

Now suppose that there are more than two goods and two factors in the economy. Should the above theorem still hold true? This question was first asked by Samuelson in his monumental paper of 1953 [30], and the discussion was followed by McKenzie [16], [18], Pearce [24], [25], Reiter [28], Chipman [5], [6], Kuhn [12], and Gale-Nikaido [8].

Let there be n goods and m factors. Let x_{ji} denote the jth factor input in the ith industry. Let x^i be an m-vector whose jth element is x_{ji}. Let $f_i(x^i)$ denote the production function of the ith good. We assume that it exhibits constant returns to scale and diminishing returns for all i. Assume perfect mobility of factors with negligible transport costs within the country, and assume that perfect competition prevails in the factor market so that factor prices are given constants to each firm, and the price of the same factor will be the same for all firms. Let w_j denote the price of the jth factor, which is common to all firms and all industries. Let w be an m-vector whose jth element is w_j. Assume a cost minimizing behavior for each producer, hence for each industry. Thus, for a given positive value of the ith output y_i,[10] the cost of its production is minimized subject to the production function, $f_i(x) - y_i \geqq 0$ and $x^i \geqq 0$. Under a certain set of plausible assumptions we showed that the solution for this nonlinear programming problem can be completely characterized by a set of relatively simple necessary and sufficient conditions ((18-10), (18-11), and (18-12)). Hence, industry's input and output are characterized by the same set of equations. In other words, given the amount of output y_i of the ith industry, the cost minimizing inputs are characterized by the following three sets of equations:

$$v_i \frac{\partial f_i}{\partial x_{ji}} \leqq w_j; \quad j = 1, 2, \cdots, m; \quad i = 1, 2, \cdots, n. \tag{18-24}$$

---

[9] For the discussions of this section and the next section, I am indebted greatly to an excellent survey article on this topic by Chipman [5].

[10] For notational simplicity, we omit the bar ($^-$) for $\bar{y}_i$, which was used in the previous section.

$$\left(w_j - v_i \frac{\partial f_i}{\partial x_{ji}}\right) x_{ji} = 0, \quad j = 1, 2, \cdots, m; \quad i = 1, 2, \cdots, n. \tag{18-25}$$

$$y_i = f_i(x^i); \quad i = 1, 2, \cdots, n. \tag{18-26}$$

Here we omitted the superscript (^{o}) which had been used to denote optimality in conditions (18-10), (18-11), and (18-12). Henceforth we shall only be concerned with the values of x^i and v_i ($i = 1, 2, \cdots, n$) which satisfy the above conditions. Now recall the Shephard-Samuelson theorem. Let C_i be the minimum cost for the ith industry. That is,

$$C_i \equiv \sum_{j=1}^{m} w_j x_{ji} \tag{18-27}$$

where the x_{ji}s satisfy the above three conditions. Due to the Shephard-Samuelson theorem, C_i can be written as:

$$C_i = y_i v_i(w), \tag{18-28}$$

where $v_i(w)$ is a homogeneous function of degree one (and concave). Thus the minimum average cost, $C_i y_i = v_i(w)$, depends only on the factor prices and not on output.

We now suppose that a competitive condition holds in the goods market and that price vector p prevails in the economy. p is an n-vector whose ith component p_i denotes the price of the ith good, which is a given constant for each firm and industry. We assume that $p_i > 0$ for all i. Clearly if $p_i < C_i/y_i$, this good will not be produced; on the other hand, if the good is produced, the profit will be eliminated by competition, so that we must have:

$$p_i = C_i/y_i = v_i(w), \quad i = 1, 2, \cdots, n. \tag{18-29}$$

Or,

$$p = v(w), \tag{18-30}$$

where v is an n-vector whose ith element is v_i. We might recall our argument in the second section that, under a competitive situation, every cost minimizer is a profit maximizer (provided that the production function is linear homogeneous), and as long as output is produced, we must have (18-29), which says profit is zero for all i. The profit of the profit maximizer under a constant returns to scale technology is always zero.

Suppose now that every country has the identical production function for the same good. Assuming negligible transport costs for goods, free trade will equalize the prices of the goods between the countries. The number of countries is not essential in this argument. The factor price equalization theorem states that this will equalize all the prices of all the factors between the countries. The question is thus asking whether the same p between the countries implies the same w between the countries. (We are allowed to assume the identical production function for the same good.) Clearly this is true. That is, factor price equalization will take place if:

1. all n goods are produced after trade so that we have $p = v(w)$;
2. the function v is globally invertible, that is, for any possible value of p, we can uniquely associate a value of w by a single-valued function $w = v^{-1}(p)$.

The first condition is called the *complete diversification condition* by Chipman ([6], p. 21). It rules out specialization in the production of any good by any country or countries. We may recall that, for the two-good model, this condition was called that of *incomplete specialization*. There it was assumed that each country produces both goods after trade occurs.

The second condition is called the *univalence condition*, signifying the univalence of the mapping $v(w)$ defining one-to-one correspondence between p and w.

As Chipman pointed out and stressed, the above two conditions give *sufficient* conditions for factor price equalization but not necessary conditions. Hence, in a sense, they give a weaker characterization of factor price equalization.[11] However, even these sufficient conditions will create a host of problems.

The three most important problems were presented in the first section. The basic points of each are repeated here.

1. Given p, can we assert that there always *exists* w such that $p = v(w)$? This question is asked by Kuhn [12], and the existence is proved under a certain set of assumptions.[12]
2. Under what conditions can we guarantee the univalence of the mapping? For the local univalence, that is, for *some neighborhood* of a point, say w^o, such a condition is well-known under the assumption of $n = m$ as the non-vanishing Jacobian. That is, if the determinant of $[\partial v_i/\partial w_j]$ (where the partial derivatives are evaluated at $w = w^o$) does not vanish, then such a local invertibility is guaranteed. But we have to be able to assert global invertibility in order to conclude factor price equalization. This question was solved by Gale and Nikaido [8], under the proper assumption $n = m$.
3. Suppose that the number of goods (n) is different from m. Consider $p = v(w)$ as a continuous (and even differentiable) mapping from m-space to n-space. There is an old but deep topological theorem which is due to Brouwer. It essentially asserts the invariance of dimensionality under continuous mapping; $v(w)$ must map w to a point in an m-dimensional space. If $n < m$, this is, in general, impossible. If $n > m$, then

---

[11] For the discussion of a necessary condition, see Reiter [28].

[12] Kuhn also showed the uniqueness of w under certain conditions. With this uniqueness, he is essentially concerned with the same problem as the subsequent problem of the uniqueness of mapping.

this is possible. $v(w)$ maps to an m-dimensional subspace of the n-space. Equalization of m-good prices and of n-good prices can result in factor price equalization, assuming that the above-mentioned Gale-Nikaido condition is satisfied.

In the following parts of this section we shall discuss Kuhn's theorem and the Gale-Nikaido theorem.

Kuhn's Theorem

Suppose that the relation between the factor price vector and the good price vector as a result of cost minimizing behavior is given by $p = v(w)$. Assuming that the number of goods is equal to the number of factors (and equal to n), the univalence of mapping implies factor price equalization. But before we jump to this conclusion, Kuhn properly raised the following question.

(QUERY)   Given $p_i > 0$, $i = 1, 2, \cdots, n$, does there exist $w \geqq 0$ such that (18-29) or (18-30) holds?

Kuhn's theorem [12] asserts the affirmative to the above question. To prove this theorem Kuhn imposed the following assumptions.

1. $n = m$.   That is, the number of factors is equal to the number of goods.
2. $v_i(w)$ is defined for $w \geq 0$ (that is, $w \geqq 0$ and $w \neq 0$).
3. $v_i(w) > 0$ for all $w \geq 0$.
4. (*The factor intensity hypothesis.*) If $w_i = 0$, then there exists $k \neq i$ such that $v_k(w)/p_k > v_i(w)/p_i$.

PROOF OF KUHN'S THEOREM   Let $M(w)$ be defined by

$$M(w) \equiv \max_i \{v_1(w)/p_1, \cdots, v_i(w)/p_i, \cdots, v_n/p_n\}. \tag{18-31}$$

By assumption 3, $v_i(w) > 0$ for all i so that $M(w) > 0$. Define the mapping: h_i by the following formula:

$$h_i(w) \equiv w_i + M(w) - v_i(w)/p_i, \quad i = 1, 2, \cdots, n. \tag{18-32}$$

Clearly, $h_i(w) > 0$. Write $\bar{w}_i = h_i(w)$, and let $\bar{w}$ and h respectively be n-vectors whose ith element is $\bar{w}_i$ and h_i. Let w be normalized so that $\sum_{i=1}^n w_i = 1$. Define $\bar{\bar{w}}_i$ by

$$\bar{\bar{w}}_i = \bar{w}_i \bigg/ \sum_{i=1}^n \bar{w}_i. \tag{18-33}$$

Then clearly we have $\sum_{i=1}^n \bar{\bar{w}}_i = 1$. Then the mapping $w \to \bar{\bar{w}}$ is a mapping from the $(n - 1)$-unit-simplex into itself and is continuous. Hence, due to the Brouwer fixed point theorem, there exists a w^* such that:

$$w_i^* = \bar{w}_i^* \equiv [w_i^* + M(w^*) - v_i(w^*)/p_i]\bigg/\bigg(\sum_{i=1}^n \bar{w}_i^*\bigg), \quad i = 1, 2, \cdots, n, \quad (18\text{-}34)$$

where $\bar{w}_i^* = h_i(w^*) = w_i^* + M(w^*) - v_i(w^*)/p_i$.

Write $\alpha \equiv \sum_{i=1}^n \bar{w}_i^*$. Then we can rewrite (18-34) as

$$(\alpha - 1)w_i^* = M(w^*) - v_i(w^*)/p_i, \quad i = 1, 2, \cdots, n. \quad (18\text{-}35)$$

By the definition of M, $v_{i_0}(w^*)/p_{i_0} = M(w^*)$ for some i_0. Then we have

$$(\alpha - 1)w_{i_0}^* = 0. \quad (18\text{-}36)$$

Suppose $w_{i_0}^* = 0$. Then $v_{i_0}(w^*)/p_{i_0}$ could not have been a maximum, since assumption 4, the intensity hypothesis, implies that $v_k(w^*)/p_k > v_{i_0}(w^*)/p_{i_0}$ for some $k \neq i_0$. This contradicts the choice of i_0. Hence, $w_{i_0}^* \neq 0$. Therefore, we must have $(\alpha - 1) = 0$. Or, in view of (18-35), we have

$$M(w^*) = v_i(w^*)/p_i, \quad \text{for all } i = 1, 2, \cdots, n. \quad (18\text{-}37)$$

Write $M(w^*) \equiv M$ and recall that $M > 0$. Since v_i is homogeneous of degree one due to the Shephard-Samuelson theorem, we have

$$v_i(w^*/M) = v_i(w^*)/M, \quad i = 1, 2, \cdots, n. \quad (18\text{-}38)$$

Hence, in view of (18-37), we have

$$v_i(w^*/M) = p_i, \quad i = 1, 2, \cdots, n. \quad (18\text{-}39)$$

Write $w = w^*/M$, then we have

$$v(w) = p, \quad \text{as desired.} \quad \text{(Q.E.D.)}$$

REMARK A diagrammatical illustration of Kuhn's intensity hypothesis (assumption 4) is given by Chipman ([6], p. 267). As is noted there, this is a rather strong assumption. Chipman relaxed it to a certain degree in his modified intensity hypothesis. But Chipman's hypothesis is also still rather strong and is not easy to accept as a plausible assumption either.[13]

In order to prove uniqueness, Kuhn imposes the following assumption:

$$\sum_{i=1}^n (w_i' - w_i'')[v_i(w_i') - v_i(w_i'')]/p_i > 0, \quad (18\text{-}40)$$

for all w' and w'' in a unit simplex W, where $W \equiv \bigg\{w: \sum_{i=1}^n w_i = 1, w \geq 0\bigg\}$.

[13] Partly due to the difficulty of interpretation of this intensity condition, Samuelson is quite skeptical about Kuhn's work. He writes that Kuhn "gives an intensity condition sufficient to prove existence of equilibrium factor prices. . . . However, I do not see that I had need for such a condition in 1953 since economic intuition assured the existence of the maximizing solution . . . and its equivalence with competitive equilibrium" [33] (p. 292, footnote 4).

Kuhn explains this assumption as follows. "The effect of the unit costs that move in the direction of a change in factor costs outweighs the effect of the unit costs moving in the opposite direction" ([12], p. 144). As Samuelson wrote, this condition "resembles the Weak Axiom of the revealed preference" ([33], p. 292, footnote 4). In any case, the proof under this assumption is immediate, as Kuhn remarked.

PROOF OF UNIQUENESS   Choose w' such that $v_i(w')/p_i = M(w')$ and note that $\sum_{i=1}^{n} (w_i' - w_i'') = 0$ for all w''. Then $v_i(w'')/p_i \neq M(w'')$ for at least one i. Hence, if w' defines an equilibrium, then w'' does not.   (Q.E.D.)

REMARK   We may recall that a similar condition was used by Abraham Wald to prove the uniqueness of a competitive equilibrium.[14]

The Inverse Function Theorem and the Gale-Nikaido Theorem

As remarked before, the crux of the factor price equalization theorem is reduced to the question: Under what conditions can we globally invert function $v, p = v(w)$, so that we have $w = v^{-1}(p)$? Assuming that the number of factors is equal to the number of goods, this question has been debated for over a decade.

The first line of thought comes from the classical implicit function theorem or the inverse function theorem. These two theorems are closely related and, in a sense, equivalent. Since they are both very important in economic theory, we may start this section from an expositional account of the two theorems.

IMPLICIT FUNCTION THEOREM   Let $f_i(x, y)$, $i = 1, 2, \cdots, n$ be a real-valued continuously differentiable function defined on an open set S in R^{n+m}. Consider $f = (f_1, f_2, \cdots, f_n)$. Assume that $f(x^o, y^o) = 0$ for some $(x^o, y^o) \in S$, where x^o is an n-vector and y^o is an m-vector. Assume also that the following determinant of f does not vanish at (x^o, y^o).

$$\begin{vmatrix} \dfrac{\partial f_1}{\partial x_1} & \dfrac{\partial f_1}{\partial x_2} & \cdots & \dfrac{\partial f_1}{\partial x_n} \\[2mm] \dfrac{\partial f_2}{\partial x_1} & \dfrac{\partial f_2}{\partial x_2} & \cdots & \dfrac{\partial f_2}{\partial x_n} \\[2mm] & \cdots & & \\ & \cdots & & \\ \dfrac{\partial f_n}{\partial x_1} & \dfrac{\partial f_n}{\partial x_2} & \cdots & \dfrac{\partial f_n}{\partial x_n} \end{vmatrix} .$$

[14] See, for example, Wald, A., "Über einige Gleichungssysteme der mathematischen Ökonomie," Zeitschrift für Nationalökonomie, 7, 1936 (translated in *Econometrica*, 19, 1951); and H. W. Kuhn, "On a Theorem of Wald," in *Linear Inequalities and Related Systems*, ed. by Kuhn and Tucker, Princeton: Princeton University Press, 1956.

Then there exists a neighborhood Y of y^o and a unique function g, with values in R^n and defined on Y, such that

1. $g(y^o) = x^o$,
2. $f[g(y), y] = 0$ for all $y \in Y$,
3. g is differentiable on Y.

PROOF   See any textbook of advanced calculus.

INVERSE FUNCTION THEOREM   Let $f_i(x)$, $i = 1, 2, \cdots, n$ be a real-valued continuously differentiable function defined on an open set S in R^n. Consider $f = (f_1, f_2, \cdots, f_n)$, and let T be the range set of f, that is, $T \equiv f(S)$. Suppose that the Jacobian f does not vanish at some point x^o of S. In other words,

$$
\begin{vmatrix}
\dfrac{\partial f_1}{\partial x_1} & \dfrac{\partial f_1}{\partial x_2} & \cdots & \dfrac{\partial f_1}{\partial x_n} \\[2ex]
\dfrac{\partial f_2}{\partial x_1} & \dfrac{\partial f_2}{\partial x_2} & \cdots & \dfrac{\partial f_2}{\partial x_n} \\[1ex]
& \cdots & & \\
& \cdots & & \\
\dfrac{\partial f_n}{\partial x_1} & \dfrac{\partial f_n}{\partial x_2} & \cdots & \dfrac{\partial f_n}{\partial x_n}
\end{vmatrix} \neq 0,
$$

where all the partial derivatives here are evaluated at $x = x^o$. Then there exist open sets $X \subset S$ and $Y \subset T$, and a uniquely determined function g with values in R^n and defined on Y such that

1. $x^o \in X$ and $f(x^o) \in Y$;
2. $f(X) = Y$;
3. f is one-to-one on X;
4. $g[f(x)] = x$ for every x in X and we may write $g \equiv f^{-1}$;
5. g is differentiable on Y.

PROOF   See any textbook on advanced calculus.

REMARK   It is easy to prove the inverse function theorem from the implicit function theorem, and it is also easy to prove the other way around. The real task of the proofs of the above two theorems is to prove either one of them.

A couple of applications of the above theorems to economic theory will be useful to the reader. In the theory of consumers' choice, each consumer is supposed to choose a consumption n-vector so as to maximize his utility function $u(x)$ subject to his budget condition $p \cdot x \leq M$ and $x \geq 0$ where p_i and M are given positive constants to him. Assuming the interior solution ($x^* > 0$), the first order condition can be written as

$$\frac{u_1^*}{p_1} = \cdots = \frac{u_i^*}{p_i} = \cdots = \frac{u_n^*}{p_n} \;;\quad M = p \cdot x^*,$$

where $u_i^* \equiv \partial u / \partial x_i$ evaluated at $x = x^*$.

In other words, the above n equations are supposed to determine the optimum consumption n-vector x^*. We may think that they define an implicit functional relation

$$f_i(x^*, p, M) = 0 \,, \quad i = 1, 2, \cdots, n \,.$$

The question is whether or not we can write $x_i^* = g_i(p, M)$ (or $x^* = g(p, M)$, that is, the demand function). The answer obviously lies in a direct application of the implicit function theorem.

In the theory of production, suppose that each producer chooses his output level y and input vector x so as to maximize his profit $[py - w \cdot x]$ subject to $y \leq f(x)$, $x \geq 0$, $y \geq 0$, where f denotes the production function, and x is an m-vector and y is a real number. p and w are given positive constants to him. Assuming the interior solution, the first order condition can be written as

$$f_i^* = w_i/p \,, \quad i = 1, 2, \cdots, m \,, \quad \text{and} \quad y^* = f(x^*) \,, \quad \text{where}$$

$$f_i^* = \partial f / \partial x_i, \text{ evaluated at } x = x^*.$$

Clearly the first m equations are supposed to completely specify the value of the m variables $x_1^*, \cdots, x_m^*$ given w and p. However, whether or not we can write

$$x_i^* = g_i(p, w) \,, \quad i = 1, 2, \cdots, m$$

depends on whether or not function $f^* = [f_1^*, f_2^*, \cdots, f_m^*]$ is invertible. This is the question of a direct application of the inverse function theorem.

Now we come back to the factor price equalization theorem. As remarked above, this problem is reduced to the invertibility of function v, where $p = v(w)$ (p and v are both n-vectors). Hence, it is natural to recall the above inverse function theorem. Assuming non-vanishing Jacobian v at a certain point w^o, we can write $v^{-1}(p) = w$ for some neighborhood of w^o and $v(w^o)$. However, this is not sufficient to conclude the factor price equalization theorem, for it requires that v is invertible everywhere and not just in some neighborhood of w^o and $v(w^o)$.

In fact, the localness prescribes a real limit of the inverse function theorem (and the implicit function theorem). These theorems refer only to *some* neighborhoods of certain points, and these neighborhoods may be very small indeed.

Thus, for the factor price equalization theorem, we need a stronger theorem than the above two.

Let J_v be the Jacobian matrix of v. That is, $J_v = [v_{ij}]$, where $v_{ij} \equiv \partial v_i / \partial w_j$, and let $|J_v|$ be its determinant. It was first conjectured that:

1. If J_v is non-singular ($|J_v| \neq 0$) for *every* possible value of w, then v is globally invertible.

This is a natural conjecture from the above inverse function theorem, which essentially asserts the invertibility of v in some neighborhood of $(w^o, v(w^o))$ when J_v is non-singular at one point w^o. This conjecture is certainly true for $n = 1$. Let $p = f(w)$ where p and w are real numbers. Since $f' \equiv df/dw \neq 0$ everywhere by assumption, either $f' > 0$ or $f' < 0$ for all possible values of w. In other words, either f is monotone increasing or monotone decreasing for all possible values of w. Hence, clearly f is globally invertible. However, James and Pearce [8] pointed out that this conjecture is wrong for $n > 1$. Later Pearce [24] argued that the above conjecture is correct after all, to which McKenzie [18] gave a counterexample, even when the concavity and the linear homogeneity of f is assumed.

Therefore, the above conjecture is wrong. In 1953 [30], Samuelson offered the following theorem.

2. If there exists some renumbering of the p_is and w_js so that *all* the successive principal minors of J_v are non-vanishing for *every* possible value of p and w, then v is globally invertible.

Subsequently Nikaido pointed out that Samuelson's proof of the theorem is inconclusive and offered a counterexample. In their joint effort at Osaka, Nikaido and Gale attempted to modify the above Samuelson theorem and finally obtained the following important theorem, the proof of which is not at all easy.

THEOREM (Gale-Nikaido) Let W be an n-dimensional interval such that $v(w)$ is defined for all $w \in W$ and continuously differentiable. Suppose that all the principal minors of J_v are positive for *all* w in W. That is,

$$v_{ii} > 0, \quad \begin{vmatrix} v_{ii} & v_{ij} \\ v_{ji} & v_{jj} \end{vmatrix} > 0, \quad \begin{vmatrix} v_{ii} & v_{ij} & v_{ik} \\ v_{ji} & v_{jj} & v_{jk} \\ v_{ki} & v_{kj} & v_{kk} \end{vmatrix} > 0, \cdots,$$

then v is globally invertible.

PROOF See Gale-Nikaido [8], and also Nikaido [22].

REMARK A real square matrix is called a *P-matrix*, if its principal minors are all positive. The above condition is called the *Gale-Nikaido condition*.

At this point we are forced to recall the uniqueness theorem in Kuhn's condition as discussed in the previous section. It asserts that, under certain conditions, for any p we can find a unique w, which means the existence of a unique inverse function. In other words, Kuhn is led to a theorem which is concerned with the same problem as the Gale-Nikaido theorem, without passing through the above line of thought via the implicit function theorem. Moreover, Kuhn's uniqueness theorem together with his existence theorem guarantees the non-negativity of w. In fact, this problem is almost trivially taken care of. In applying the Gale-Nikaido theorem, we still cannot guarantee the non-negativity of w. However, we may also note that their theorem is mathematical in nature and will have a much wider application than Kuhn's theorem.[15]

Later in 1967 Pearce [25] established the following theorem, which is essentially a modification of the above conjecture 1.

THEOREM (Pearce) Let Ω be the non-negative orthant of R^n. Let $W \equiv \{w : v(w) \in \text{interior } \Omega\}$. Let D be a convex cone with vertex at the origin. Assume that $v(w)$ is defined for all $w \in D$, where closure $W - \{0\} \subset \text{interior } D$, and that v is continuously differentiable everywhere in the interior of D, and J_v is non-singular for all $w \in \text{interior } D$. Then v is globally invertible for all $p \in \Omega$.

Pearce proved this theorem by appealing to the homotopy theory. McKenzie [19] offered a proof of this theorem in analysis, which is due to Favard. Then he proved a more general theorem. With Samuelson's summarized argument on factor prize equalization, the debate between Pearce and McKenzie is printed in the *International Economic Review* (October 1967).[16]

We may now find out the relevance of the above Gale-Nikaido condition to the 2×2 case, which was extensively studied in Chapter 3. This will help to clarify economic meaning of the above mathematical condition. The Gale-Nikaido condition for the 2×2 case is simply written as

$$v_{11} > 0, \quad v_{22} > 0, \quad \text{and} \quad \begin{vmatrix} v_{11} & v_{12} \\ v_{21} & v_{22} \end{vmatrix} > 0.$$

Let us call the first and the second industry the X and the Y industry, respectively, and let us call the first and the second factor, labor and capital. Let L_x and L_y respectively denote the labor input in the X and in the Y industry, and let K_x and K_y respectively denote the capital input in the X and in the Y industry. Let X and Y respectively denote the output of each industry. Due to the Shephard-Samuelson theorem, v_{ij} is equal to the amount of the jth input to

---

[15] There is an interesting study by McKenzie [16] from the viewpoint of activity analysis, in which he obtained another condition for the univalence of mapping.

[16] There are interesting approaches by Reiter [28] and Uzawa [37] from the point of view of nonlinear programming. However, Reiter used the above incorrect theorem by Samuelson. Uzawa's error was pointed out by Samuelson in his "The Fundamental Singularity Theorem for Non-Joint Production," *International Economic Review*, 7, January 1966, p. 35, footnote 2.

produce one unit of the ith good. Hence, the above conditions can be interpreted as

$$v_{11} = L_x/X > 0 , \quad v_{22} = K_y/Y > 0 ,$$

$$v_{11}v_{22} - v_{12}v_{21} = \frac{L_x}{X}\frac{K_y}{Y} - \frac{K_x}{X}\frac{L_y}{Y} > 0 .$$

The first two conditions are obviously satisfied. The last condition can easily be rewritten as

$$L_xK_y - K_xL_y > 0 , \quad \text{or} \quad k_y - k_x > 0 , \quad \text{for all factor prices, where}$$

$$k_x \equiv \frac{K_x}{L_x} \quad \text{and} \quad k_y \equiv \frac{K_y}{L_y} .$$

Thus the Gale-Nikaido condition is reduced to $k_y > k_x$ for all factor prices. Since the naming of the industries (X and Y) can be switched, the condition is reduced to the famous condition of no factor intensity reversals. In the two-good, two-factor case, this condition is implied by the complete diversification assumption, that is, each country produces both goods after the opening of trade (incomplete specialization).

THE STOLPER-SAMUELSON THEOREM ONCE AGAIN

Consider a two-country trading world, each country producing the same two goods in a neoclassical fashion with two factors. Assume free trade initially, then consider that one country imposes a tariff on her imported good. The Stolper-Samuelson theorem [35] asserts that if the domestic price of the imported good rises by the imposition of an import tariff, the price of the factor which is relatively scarce, in terms of the other factor or the price of any good, will rise. This much we already showed in Chapter 3. It was a simple corollary of the Heckscher-Ohlin trade model. As was made clear in our discussion in Chapter 3, there are essentially three assumptions in proving the theorem: 1) the imposition of an import tariff will raise the domestic price of the imported good; 2) (the *intensity hypothesis*) the imported good employs the relatively scarce factor in the country more intensively; 3) a rise in the relative price of the imported good thus will raise the factor price of the relatively scarce factor. Assumption 1 does not necessarily hold, but under a certain condition (Metzler's condition, Chapter 8, third section) it holds true. Assumption 2, the "intensity hypothesis," is the Heckscher-Ohlin theorem. Assumption 3 is the direct result of a constant returns to scale production function with diminishing returns.

Now the question is how we can extend the above theorem to a model in which there are more than two goods and two factors. The first thought of this question may make us feel that this is indeed a difficult problem, because the theorem appears to be so closely tied up with the two-good, two-factor assumption. The concepts such as *relative price of the good, relative factor price, relative factor intensity*, and *relative factor abundance* carry the peculiar flavor of the two-good, two-factor assumption. Is there any way to break through this? If this can be done, the reward for such a task will be great, because then we can have a better perspective, not being bound by the bondage of the two-good, two-factor assumption. Although still incomplete, such a task has already been attempted by economists such as Chipman, McKenzie, and Uekawa.

We now consider an economy with more than two goods and two factors. The basic premise of the theorem can be restated as: "*If the price of the ith good relative to all other goods rises by the imposition of an import tariff.*" The conclusion of the theorem may be restated as, "*the price of the ith factor relative to all other goods increases.*" Then the natural question is how to relate these i's. In the original theorem they were linked in a nice way through the concept of factor intensity. A rise in the price of an ith factor (say, labor) intensive good will raise the price of the ith factor (labor) relative to any good. In order to have such a link between the premise and the conclusion of the theorem, we assume that the number of goods, say, n, is equal to the number of factors. And we state the theorem as: *There exists an association of goods and factors such that if the price of the ith good rises relative to any other good, the price of the ith factor rises relative to any good.* This formulation is due to Chipman [5], [6]. It may be considered unsatisfactory due to the equality of the number of goods and the number of factors. But still ($n \times n$) is much more general than (2×2). As a first step toward a more general model, this is a quite ingenious approach.

Let p_i be the price of the ith good and w_i be the price of the ith factor. We suppose that each producer minimizes cost. Hence we have $p_i = v_i(w)$, or $p = v(w)$, where v_i is homogeneous of degree one due to the Shephard-Samuelson theorem. The existence of such a w with a given p is guaranteed by Kuhn's theorem under a certain set of assumptions. In view of Chipman's reformulation, the Stolper-Samuelson theorem can now be restated as: For each $i = 1, 2, \cdots, n$, we have

$$d\left(\frac{p_i}{p_j}\right) > 0 \quad \text{for all } j \neq i \quad \text{implies } d\left(\frac{w_i}{p_j}\right) > 0 \quad \text{for all } j = 1, 2, \cdots, n .$$

$$(18\text{-}41)$$

Here d refers to the total derivative, which is caused by a shift of the system due to an imposition of the import tariff. In other words, given that the ith price rises relative to the other prices, the real price of the ith factor increases relative to the price of *any* good (including the ith good). We now claim that a necessary and sufficient condition for the conclusion of the theorem to hold is $d(w_i/p_i) > 0$, that is, the ith factor price in terms of the ith *good* increases.

To show this, first note that $(w_i/p_j) = (w_i/p_i)(p_i/p_j)$. Hence we have

$$d\left(\frac{w_i}{p_j}\right) = \left(\frac{p_i}{p_j}\right) d\left(\frac{w_i}{p_i}\right) + \left(\frac{w_i}{p_i}\right) d\left(\frac{p_i}{p_j}\right) \quad \text{for all } i \text{ and } j. \qquad (18\text{-}42)$$

By assumption, $d(p_i/p_j) > 0$ for all $j \neq i$. Hence, if $d(w_i/p_i) > 0$, then $d(w_i/p_j) > 0$ for all $j \neq i$. Thus, in order to have $d(w_i/p_j) > 0$ for all $j \neq i$, it is sufficient to have $d(w_i/p_i) > 0$. $d(w_i/p_i) > 0$ is certainly necessary to have $(dw_i/dp_j) > 0$ for all j (including i). In other words, a necessary and sufficient condition for the conclusion of the theorem to hold is that $d(w_i/p_i) > 0$.

Now we rewrite this condition. Note that $[d(w_i/p_i)]/(w_i/p_i) = [(dw_i/w_i) - (dp_i/p_i)] > 0$. Since $d \log w_i = dw_i/w_i$ and $d \log p_i = dp_i/p_i$, this means that $(d \log w_i - d \log p_i) > 0$ or $(d \log w_i)/(d \log p_i) > 1$. Let $\pi_i \equiv \log p_i$ and $\omega_i \equiv \log w_i$. Then we can rewrite the condition $d(w_i/p_i) > 0$ as

$$\frac{d\omega_i}{d\pi_i} > 1. \tag{18-43}$$

Therefore, the Stolper-Samuelson theorem is now restated as: There exists an association of goods and factors such that a rise in the price of a good will bring about a more than proportionate increase in the price of its corresponding factor.[17] Next we write the original functional relation $p = v(w)$ in terms of π and ω. Note that

$$\pi_i = \log p_i = \log v_i(w_1, w_2, \cdots, w_n) = \log v_i(e^{\omega_1}, e^{\omega_2}, \cdots e^{\omega_n}).$$

We write this relation as

$$\pi_i = g_i(\omega_1, \omega_2, \cdots, \omega_n), \quad i = 1, 2, \cdots, n; \tag{18-44}$$

or $\pi = g(\omega)$ in vector notation. Consider the Jacobian matrix J_g of this transformation g. That is,

$$J_g \equiv [g_{ij}] \equiv \left(\frac{\partial g_i}{\partial \omega_j}\right). \tag{18-45}$$

Observe

$$\frac{\partial g_i}{\partial \omega_j} = \frac{\partial \log v_i}{\partial \omega_j} = \frac{\partial \log v_i}{\partial v_i} \frac{\partial v_i}{\partial w_j} \frac{\partial w_j}{\partial \omega_j} = \frac{1}{v_i} v_{ij} w_j = \frac{1}{p_i} v_{ij} w_j;$$

where $v_{ij} \equiv \dfrac{\partial v_i}{\partial w_j}$.

In other words, we have,

$$g_{ij} = \frac{w_j}{p_i} v_{ij}, \quad i, j = 1, 2, \cdots, n. \tag{18-46}$$

---

[17] Just as the univalence mapping theorem has both the local and the global version, the Stolper-Samuelson theorem can also have such two versions. The local version would say: Assuming that $v(w)$ is locally invertible at w^o, there exists a neighborhood of w^o, $N(w^o)$, such that $d\omega_i/d\pi_i > 1$ (for all i) for all $p \in v[N(w^o)]$. Note that this association between goods and factors depends on w^o. In the global version, the same association between goods and factors must hold for all w (rather than a particular w^o). The global version is the one that would interest us here.

In the matrix form we have

$$J_g = p^{-1} J_v W, \tag{18-47}$$

where J_v is the Jacobian matrix of v, that is, $[v_{ij}]$, and P and W are diagonal matrices such that

$$P \equiv \begin{bmatrix} p_1 & 0 & \cdots & 0 \\ 0 & p_2 & \cdots & \cdots \\ \cdot & \cdot & & \cdot \\ \cdot & \cdot & & \cdot \\ \cdot & \cdot & & \cdot \\ 0 & \cdots & \cdots & p_n \end{bmatrix} \quad \text{and} \quad W \equiv \begin{bmatrix} w_1 & 0 & \cdots & 0 \\ 0 & w_2 & \cdots & \cdots \\ \cdot & \cdot & & \cdot \\ \cdot & \cdot & & \cdot \\ \cdot & \cdot & & \cdot \\ 0 & \cdots & \cdots & w_n \end{bmatrix}. \tag{18-48}$$

We now show that every row sum of J_g is equal to one. In other words, we want to show that

$$\sum_{j=1}^{n} \frac{w_j}{p_i} v_{ij} = 1 ; \quad \text{or} \quad \frac{1}{p_i} \sum_{j=1}^{n} v_{ij} w_j = 1 .$$

To show this, recall $v_i(w)$ is homogeneous of degree one so that (due to Euler's equation):

$$\sum_{j=1}^{n} v_{ij} w_j = v_i . \tag{18-49}$$

Since $p_i = v_i$, this finishes the proof that every row sum of J_g is equal to one. Furthermore, due to the Shephard-Samuelson theorem, $C_i = y_i v_i(w) = \sum_{j=1}^{n} w_j x_{ji}$ for the minimum cost of the jth good, C_i, $i = 1, 2, \cdots, n$, and

$$x_{ji} = \frac{\partial C_i(y_i, w)}{\partial w_j} = \frac{\partial}{\partial w_j} [y_i v_i(w)] = y_i v_{ij} ,$$

where x_{ji} denotes the amount of the jth factor input for the production of y_i at the cost minimizing level. Since $x_{ji} \geqq 0$, $v_{ij} \geqq 0$. Note also that $v_{ij} = x_{ji}/y_i$, the quantity used of factor i in making one unit of good j at minimum cost when factor price vector w prevails. Since $v_{ij} \geqq 0$, we have $g_{ij} \geqq 0$ (for all i and j). Thus we have shown that $\sum_{j=1}^{n} g_{ij} = 1, g_{ij} \geqq 0$ for all i, j. In other words, J_g is a (row) stochastic matrix.

Now come back to the Stolper-Samuelson theorem as conceived by Chipman. Given $\pi = g(\omega)$, we want to show $\dfrac{d\omega_i}{d\pi_i} > 1$. Note that we have $d\pi = J_g\, d\omega$, where $d\pi$ is an n-vector whose ith component is $d\pi_i$, and $d\omega$ is an n-vector whose ith component is $d\omega_i$. Assuming that J_g is non-singular,[18]

$$d\omega = J_g^{-1}\, d\pi . \tag{18-50}$$

[18] Clearly not all stochastic matrices are nonsingular. An example is
$\begin{bmatrix} 1 & 0 \\ 1 & 0 \end{bmatrix}.$

The premise of the Stolper-Samuelson theorem says that $d(p_i/p_j) > 0$ for all $j \neq i$. In particular, $dp_i > 0$ and $dp_j = 0$ for all $j \neq i$. Or, $d\pi_i > 0$ and $d\pi_j = 0$ for all $j \neq i$.[19] Now we put this assumption ($d\pi_i > 0$ and $d\pi_j = 0$ for all $j \neq i$) into the above equation and obtain

$$a_{ki} \, d\pi_i = d\omega_k, \quad k = 1, 2, \cdots, n, \tag{18-51}$$

where a_{ki} is the $(k-i)$ element of J_g^{-1} (that is, $J_g^{-1} \equiv [a_{ki}]$) .

The conclusion of the Stolper-Samuelson theorem as conceived by Chipman says that $(d\omega_i/d\pi_i) > 1$, which, in view of (18-51), is equivalent to saying $a_{ii} > 1$. Since this statement should be true for each i, this means that $[J_g^{-1}]$ must have all its diagonal elements greater than unity. We may now summarize the above results.

THEOREM (Chipman)   Let p and w be non-negative n-vectors such that $p = v(w)$. Let $\pi_i = \log p_i$ and $\omega_i = \log w_i$ so that $\pi = g(\omega)$. Let J_g be the Jacobian matrix of g. Then

1. $J_g = [g_{ij}]$ is a (row) stochastic matrix. That is, all its elements are non-negative and every row sum of J_g is equal to unity.[20]
2. $g_{ij} = w_j\alpha_{ij}/p_i$, where α_{ij} is the quantity used of factor j in making one unit of good i at minimum cost when factor price vector w prevails for the output y_i. That is, $\alpha_{ij} \equiv x_{ji}/y_i$ at the minimum cost combination of the factors.[21]
3.   A necessary and sufficient condition for the Stolper-Samuelson theorem to hold true is that the inverse of J_g (where it exists) has all diagonal elements greater than one.

Clearly the inverse of every stochastic matrix does not necessarily have all its diagonal elements greater than one. The following example is due to Chipman ([5], p. 402, and [6], p. 34).

$$\begin{bmatrix} 0.55 & 0.40 & 0.05 \\ 0.05 & 0.50 & 0.45 \\ 0.25 & 0.35 & 0.40 \end{bmatrix}^{-1} = \begin{bmatrix} 0.77 & -2.59 & 2.82 \\ 1.18 & 3.77 & -4.45 \\ -1.95 & -1.68 & 4.64 \end{bmatrix} .$$

[19] In view of this assumption, we may restate the theorem as: There exists an association of goods and factors such that if the price of the ith goods rises *when the prices of all other goods remain constant*, the real price of the ith factor in terms of all the goods (including the ith good) rises." This is the statement used by Chipman [5].

[20] Note that if J_g is row stochastic, then the inverse J_g^{-1} also has unit row sums. To show this, let σ be the column vector whose elements are all one, and observe: $J_g^{-1}\sigma = J_g^{-1}(J_g\sigma) = (J_g^{-1}J_g)\sigma = \sigma$.

[21] When one unit of the ith good is produced at minimum cost, the payment to the jth factor would be $w_j\alpha_{ij}$. Hence, $g_{ij} = (w_j\alpha_{ij})/p_i = (w_jx_{ji})/(p_iy_i)$ measures the relative share of the jth factor in the ith industry. That is, g_{ij}s correspond to Γ_xs in Chapter 3. The matrix $[g_{ij}]$ may be called the *share matrix* (cf. Uekawa [36], theorem 1).

Our question now turns to the problem of finding the conditions under which this is true. For the case $n = 2$, Chipman wrote:

> For the case $n = 2$, it is always true that the inverse of a stochastic matrix (when it exists) has its diagonal elements either greater than one or less than zero; so by appropriate permutations of rows and columns (that is, by a suitable association of commodities with their "intensive" factor— indeed, this provides us with a definition of "intensity"), these diagonal elements will always exceed unity ([6], p. 38).

As Kuhn [14] remarked, this is wrong. A simple example is the unit matrix

$$\begin{bmatrix} 1 & 0 \\ 0 & 1 \end{bmatrix}.$$

Kuhn [14] restated the above as follows and proved it (pp. 80–81).

THEOREM (Kuhn) Let J_g be a 2×2 (row) stochastic matrix *with positive determinant*, and let A be its inverse. Write

$$J_g = \begin{bmatrix} g_{11} & g_{12} \\ g_{21} & g_{22} \end{bmatrix}, \quad A \equiv J_g^{-1} = \begin{bmatrix} a_{11} & a_{12} \\ a_{21} & a_{22} \end{bmatrix}.$$

Then $a_{11} \geqq 1$ and $a_{22} \geqq 1$. Furthermore, $a_{11} > 1$ if and only if $g_{12} > 0$, and $a_{22} > 1$ if and only if $g_{21} > 0$.

PROOF By direct calculation:

$$a_{11} = \frac{g_{22}}{g_{11}g_{22} - g_{12}g_{21}} \quad \text{and} \quad a_{12} = \frac{-g_{12}}{g_{11}g_{22} - g_{12}g_{21}}. \tag{18-52}$$

Clearly $a_{11} \geqq 0$. Since J_g is row stochastic, $g_{11} = (1 - g_{12})$ and $g_{21} = (1 - g_{22})$, so that $g_{11}g_{22} - g_{12}g_{21} = g_{22}(1 - g_{12}) - g_{12}(1 - g_{22}) = g_{22} - g_{12}$. Thus we have $a_{11} \geqq 1$; and

$$a_{11} + a_{12} = \frac{g_{22} - g_{12}}{g_{22} - g_{12}} = 1. \tag{18-53}$$

Hence, if $g_{12} > 0$, then $a_{12} < 0$ so that $a_{11} > 1$. Conversely, if $a_{11} > 1$, then $a_{12} < 0$ so that $g_{12} > 0$. The proof for a_{22} is exactly analogous. (Q.E.D.)

The following two remarks are due to Kuhn.

REMARK There is no restriction involved in the assumption that the determinant is positive; if the inverse exists, then the determinant is non-zero and any possible permutation of the rows can be assumed to be positive. For example, if $g_{11}g_{22} - g_{12}g_{21} < 0$, then consider

$$\begin{vmatrix} g_{21} & g_{22} \\ g_{11} & g_{12} \end{vmatrix}.$$

The permutation of the rows means renumbering the goods.

REMARK   The assumption that J_g has a positive determinant corresponds to the intensity hypothesis, which was mentioned in the beginning of this section. To see this, recall that $g_{ij} = \dfrac{w_j}{p_i} \alpha_{ij}$, where α_{ij} is the quantity used of factor j in making one unit of good i at minimum cost when w prevails. Assume that $p_i > 0$ for all i and $w_j > 0$ for all j. Then $g_{11}g_{22} - g_{12}g_{21} > 0$ means

$$\alpha_{11}\alpha_{22} - \alpha_{12}\alpha_{21} > 0. \tag{18-54}$$

Due to the above theorem, in order to ensure $a_{11} > 1$ and $a_{22} > 1$, we must have $g_{12} > 0$ and $g_{21} > 0$. Moreover, $a_{11} > 1$, $a_{22} > 1$ also imply $g_{11} > 0$ and $g_{22} > 0$ due to (18-52). Hence, $\alpha_{11}, \alpha_{12}, \alpha_{21}, \alpha_{22} > 0 \ (\neq 0)$, so that:

$$\frac{\alpha_{11}}{\alpha_{12}} > \frac{\alpha_{21}}{\alpha_{22}}. \tag{18-55}$$

This says that relatively more factor 1 is used in making one unit of good 1 than in making one unit of good 2. In other words, good 1 is relatively more factor 1 intensive than good 2. As we noted before, this assumption underlies the original Stolper-Samuelson theorem. (In the original terminology, good 1 is the imported good which uses factor 1, the relative scarce factor in the country, more intensively.) Since α_{ij}s are determined by the minimum cost principle when w prevails, α_{ij}s are functions of w, that is, $\alpha_{ij} = \alpha_{ij}(w)$. The factor intensity non-reversal condition for the 2×2 case (cf. Chapter 3) says that (18-55) should hold for all values of w.

Chipman's study stimulated other economists[22] besides Kuhn, and produced important results. Among these the most important work is probably the one by Uekawa [36]. Here we shall state some of his results.

DEFINITION   Let J_g be non-singular $n \times n$ row stochastic matrix and let $[a_{ij}]$ be its inverse, that is, J_g^{-1}. We say that J_g satisfies the *strong Stolper-Samuelson criterion*[23] if $a_{ii} > 1$ *and* $a_{ij} \leqq 0$ for all $j \neq i$, $i = 1, 2, \cdots, n$.[24]

---

[22] See, for example, Inada [9], Kemp and Wegge [11], Wegge and Kemp [39], and Uekawa [36] (which is based on his Ph.D dissertation at the University of Rochester, 1966). An earlier version of [36] was in circulation at least as early as spring of 1966. Inada [9] gave an alternative version of the univalence mapping theorem: Let $v(w)$ be a continuously differentiable function defined over an n-dimensional interval of R^n. Suppose that the Jacobian matrix J_v is continuous and that everywhere all the principal minors of J_v are negative and J_v has at least one positive element. Then v is globally invertible. See also [22] and Uekawa [36].

[23] Again we can distinguish the local and the global version of this.

[24] In view of footnote 20, J_g^{-1} has unit row sums, if J_g is row stochastic. Hence, $a_{ij} \leqq 0$ for all $j \neq i$ implies that $a_{ii} > 1$ if and only if there exists at least one $j(\neq i)$ such that $a_{ij} < 0$. In other words, the condition $a_{ii} > 1$ for all i can be replaced by "there exists at least one $j(\neq i)$ such that $a_{ij} < 0$ for all i," provided that J_g is row stochastic.

REMARK Compared with the usual Stolper-Samuelson theorem, the above condition imposes the additional restriction $a_{ij} \leq 0$ for all $j \neq i$. In view of (18-51) this means:

$$d\pi_i/d\omega_j \leq 0 \quad \text{for all} \quad j \neq i; \tag{18-56}$$

that is, $(dp_i/p_i)/(dw_j/w_j) \leq 0$, for all $j \neq i$.

This means that an increase in the price p_i of any good will lead to a non-increase of the price of all factors except for the corresponding factor. In the 2×2 case ($n = 2$), this strong Stolper-Samuelson theorem holds, as is clear from our discussion in Chapter 3.

REMARK If $a_{ii} > 1$, then we can show that $g_{ii} < 1$ and $g_{ij} > 0$ for some $j(\neq i)$. Hence, in order that the strong Stolper-Samuelson criterion be meaningful for the stochastic matrix J_g, we must require the following condition (Γ).

CONDITION Γ Given a row stochastic matrix $J_g = [g_{ij}]$, there exists at least one $j(\neq i)$ such that $g_{ij} > 0$ for all i.

Let A be a subset of the index set $\{1, 2, \cdots, n\}$, and consider the following condition.[25]

CONDITION U_1 For any given k and A with $k \notin A$, there exist $\theta_j^{(k)} \geq 0$, $j \in A$ such that

1. $\displaystyle\sum_{j \in A} g_{ij}\theta_j^{(k)} \geq g_{ik}$ for all $i \in A$;

2. $\displaystyle\sum_{j \in A} g_{ij}\theta_j^{(k)} \leq g_{ik}$, for all $i \notin A$;

with strict inequality for $i = k$.

With this condition, we can now state the following remarkable theorem, which is due to Uekawa [36].

THEOREM Suppose that condition Γ holds. Then condition U_1 is *necessary and sufficient* for any row stochastic matrix to satisfy the strong Stolper-Samuelson criterion.

REMARK The economic interpretation of condition U_1 is as follows (cf. Uekawa [36]). Define α_{iA}^* by $\alpha_{iA}^* \equiv \displaystyle\sum_{j \in A} \alpha_{ij}(w_j\theta_j^{(k)})$, and consider α_{iA}^* as the amount of the aggregate factor A used in the ith industry. $(w_j\theta_j^{(k)})$s signify the "weights" used in this aggregation of factors. Then condition U_1 can be restated as: For given k and A, $k \notin A$, we can find weights $\theta_j^{(k)} \geq 0$, $j \in A$ such that

$$\frac{\alpha_{iA}^*}{\alpha_{hA}^*} \geq \frac{\alpha_{ik}}{\alpha_{hk}} \quad \text{for} \quad i \in A, \quad h \notin A, \tag{18-57}$$

[25] See condition (IV) of [36].

with strict inequality for $h = k$, whenever α_{ik}/α_{hk} is defined. In other words, this condition corresponds to the factor intensity condition. Uekawa's theorem is a generalization of Kuhn's theorem when n is not necessarily restricted to 2.

REMARK   Suppose that J_g is row stochastic and that condition Γ is satisfied. Then Uekawa [36] has also shown that condition U_1 (which is equivalent to the strong S-S criterion under the circumstance) implies that J_g is a P-matrix![26] If J_g is a P-matrix, then, due to the Gale-Nikaido theorem, g is globally invertible so that the factor price equalization theorem holds. This corresponds to the 2 × 2 case discussed in Chapter 3. Suppose that $[\alpha_{ij}]$ be a non-singular, non-negative square matrix, *not* necessarily stochastic. Let $B = [\beta_{ij}]$ be its inverse, and let the definition of the strong S-S criterion be changed: $[\alpha_{ij}]$ satisfies the *modified strong Stolper-Samuelson criterion*, if $\beta_{ij} \leqq 0$ for all $j(\neq i)$ and $\beta_{ij} < 0$ for some $j(\neq i)$, $i = 1, 2, \cdots, n$. Under this definition of strong S-S criterion, we can strengthen the above theorem as follows.

THEOREM   If $[\alpha_{ij}]$ is a non-negative square matrix with condition Γ, then condition U_1 is necessary and sufficient for $[\alpha_{ij}]$ to satisfy the modified strong Stolper-Samuelson theorem.

Note that if $[\alpha_{ij}]$ satisfies the modified strong Stolper-Samuelson criterion, then we can easily show that $\beta_{ii} > 0$ for all i.[27]

An important application of the above condition is the *generalized Rybczynski's theorem* (cf. McKenzie [20]). Let α_{ij} be the quantity of jth factor used to produce one unit of the ith good at minimum cost when w prevails. Let y_i be the output of the ith good. Let r_j be the amount of the jth factor available in the economy, which is assumed to be independent of w. Then we have

$$\sum_{i=1}^{m} y_i \alpha_{ij} = r_j, \quad i = 1, 2, \cdots, n.$$

Assuming that $[\alpha_{ij}]$ is non-singular, we obtain

$$y_j = \sum_{i=1}^{m} r_i \beta_{ij}, \quad j = 1, 2, \cdots, n,$$

where $[\beta_{ij}] \equiv [\alpha_{ij}]^{-1}$.

Now consider an increase in the endowment of the factor endowment keeping all prices and all the other factor endowments constant. Then we obtain

$$\partial y_j/\partial r_k = \beta_{kj}, \quad j = 1, 2, \cdots, n.$$

---

[26] To obtain this conclusion, simply combine his theorem 6 with his theorem 2.

[27] To see this, suppose the contrary so that $\beta_{ii} \leqq 0$ for all i. Let σ be the n-dimensional (column) vector whose elements are all equal to one, and consider $\sigma = (B^{-1}B)\sigma = B^{-1} \bar{\sigma}$ where $\bar{\sigma} \equiv B\sigma$. Then $\bar{\sigma} < 0$ by assumption, which is a contradiction since $B^{-1} \equiv [a_{ij}] \leqq 0$.

Then the modified strong Stolper-Samuelson criterion says that $\beta_{kj} \leq 0$ for all $j \neq k, \beta_{kj} < 0$ for some $j \neq k$, and $\beta_{kk} > 0, k = 1, 2, \cdots, n$. This is nothing but the generalized Rybczynski theorem. In other words, the output of the kth good must increase, while the output of no other good can rise and the output of at least one of them must decline absolutely.

We now turn to the weak Stopler-Samuelson theorem. First recall equation (18-51). In order to indicate the assumption $d\pi_j = 0$ for all $j \neq i$ which underlies (18-51), we replace d in (18-5) by ∂, and rewrite (18-51) as

$$\partial\omega_k/\partial\pi_i = a_{ki}, \quad k = 1, 2, \cdots, n. \tag{18-51'}$$

Now we can come to the result, which is central in Uekawa [36].

DEFINITION   Let J_g be a non-singular $n \times n$ stochastic matrix and let $J_g^{-1} \equiv [a_{ij}]$. J_g is said to satisfy *the weak Stolper-Samuelson criterion*, if $a_{ii} > 1$ *and* $a_{ki} < a_{ii}$ for all $k \neq i, i = 1, 2, \cdots, n$.[28]

REMARK   Compared with the usual Stolper-Samuelson theorem, the above condition imposes the additional restriction $a_{ki} < a_{ii}$ for all $k \neq i$. The above criterion, due to Uekawa [36], is a modification of Chipman's weak Stolper-Samuelson criterion.

REMARK   Consider the three factor model—land, labor, and capital—with three goods produced (say, wheat, textile, and machinery). Assume that this country imports wheat. Consider the imposition of a tariff on wheat (for example, the Corn Laws). Suppose further that the imposition of tariff increases the domestic price of wheat, and assume, for the sake of simplicity, that the prices of the other goods are fixed. Then Uekawa's restriction $a_{ki} < a_{ii}$ for $k \neq i$ means that capitalists as well as landlords may benefit from the tariff, but the capitalists' gain must be less than the landlords' gain.

Let A be the subset of the index set $\{1, 2, \cdots, n\}$ and consider the following condition.

CONDITION U_2 For any non-proper A, there exist θ_j (which depends on A), $j \in A$ such that $\theta_j > 0$ and

$$\sum_{j \in A} g_{ij}\theta_j > \sum_{j \in A} g_{kj}\theta_j \quad \text{for any } i \in A \quad \text{and} \quad k \notin A.$$

We are now ready to state the following theorem.[29]

THEOREM (Uekawa)   Let J_g be a row stochastic matrix. Suppose conditions Γ and U_2 hold. Then J_g is a P-matrix *and* J_g satisfies the weak Stolper-Samuelson criterion.

[28] Again condition Γ will be required for $a_{ii} > 1, i = 1, 2, \cdots, n$ to be meaningful.
[29] See theorem 3 of [36].

REMARK Uekawa [36] has also shown that if J_g is row stochastic with conditions Γ and U_1, then condition U_2 is satisfied (cf. his theorem 6). Hence, if J_g is row stochastic with conditions Γ and U_1, then both the weak and the strong Stolper-Samuelson criteria hold. We may schematically describe the above situation, assuming J_g is row stochastic and satisfies condition Γ, as follows:

$$(\text{Strong } S\text{-}S) \Leftrightarrow (U_1) \Rightarrow (U_2) \Rightarrow (\text{Weak } S\text{-}S)$$
$$\Downarrow$$
$$(J_g \text{ is a } P\text{-matrix}) .$$

THE CASE OF COBB-DOUGLAS PRODUCTION FUNCTIONS

In this section we shall consider a special case of the above analysis. We shall be concerned with the case in which the production function for each industry is of the Cobb-Douglas type. Using this simple case we would like to illustrate our consideration of the cost minimization, the Shephard-Samuelson theorem, the factor price equalization theorem, and the Stolper-Samuelson theorem. Let us write the production function for a certain industry as

$$f(x) = \left[k \prod_{i=1}^{m} x_i^{\gamma_i} \right] \quad \text{where} \quad k \equiv \prod_{i=1}^{m} \gamma_i^{-\gamma_i}, \ \sum_{i=1}^{m} \gamma_i = 1 \ \text{ and } \ 0 < \gamma_i < 1 \text{ for all } i.$$

The restriction of k as above is not really a restriction, for we can choose the unit of measurement of the output properly so that we can choose k as above.

Assume the cost minimizing behavior (the minimization of $\sum_{i=1}^{m} w_i x_i$ subject to $f(x) \geq 0$, $x \geq 0$ for a given $y > 0$). Then, assuming an interior solution, and others, the following first order conditions give necessary and sufficient conditions for this minimization problem:

$$w_i = v f_i(x) \quad \text{and} \quad y = f(x) .$$

Here the superscripts such as (*), which indicates the optimality of x, are omitted. Also $f_i \equiv \partial f / \partial x_i$ evaluated at the optimal value of x. Since $f_i(x) = \gamma_i y / x_i$ by definition of f, we can obtain the following relation from the above conditions:

$$v = \prod_{i=1}^{m} w_i^{\gamma_i}, \ \sum_{i=1}^{m} \gamma_i = 1 , \ \sum_{i=1}^{m} w_i x_i = v y ,$$

$$v = C/y , \quad \text{where} \quad C = \sum_{i=1}^{m} w_i x_i .$$

This confirms the Shephard-Samuelson theorem which we discussed in the second section.

Next we shall examine the factor price equalization theorem using the above relation. Let v_j denote the above v for the jth industry and γ_{ij} denote the above γ_i for the jth industry. Then we have

$$v_j(w) = \prod_{i=1}^{m} w_i^{\gamma_{ij}}.$$

We assume that $m = n$ and note the following relation:

$p_j = v_j(w)$, or $p = v(w)$, where p_j denotes the price of the jth good.

Define $\pi_j \equiv \log p_j$ and $\omega_i = \log w_i$, $i = 1, 2, \cdots, n$. The above relation can be rewritten as:

$$\pi_j = \sum_{i=1}^{n} \gamma_{ij}\omega_i, \quad j = 1, 2, \cdots, n.$$

Let π and ω be n-vectors whose jth element is, respectively, π_j and ω_j. Let $G = [\gamma_{ij}]$, $n \times n$ matrix. Then

$\pi = G'\omega$, where G' is the transpose of G.

Since $\sum_{i=1}^{n} \gamma_{ij} = 1$, G' is a row stochastic matrix. This confirms a relation

obtained in connection with the Stolper-Samuelson theorem. The factor price equalization occurs if G' is non-singular. *Assuming G' is non-singular*, we can obtain ω.

$\omega = [G']^{-1}\pi$.

The non-singularity of G' corresponds to Pearce's condition, and it is certainly required by the Gale-Nikaido condition. In fact, for the factor price equalization theorem to be economically meaningful, we require more than the non-singularity of G'. We should require the non-negativity of the factor prices, w. Hence, ω must be greater than 1. Suppose that all the goods prices are positive, so that $p_i > 0$ for all i or $\pi_i > 1$ for all i. Can we deduce that all ω_i are greater than 1? It is clear that the mere requirement that G' is a non-singular stochastic matrix is not sufficient to conclude this. It may so happen that some elements of $[G']^{-1}$ can be less than one or even negative, as the above Chipman's example of a 3×3 stochastic matrix shows.

Now we can realize immediately the relevance of our consideration of the Stolper-Samuelson theorem. This theorem, as remarked in the previous section, requires that all the diagonal elements of $[G']^{-1}$ be greater than unity. This is not necessarily the case, as mentioned before.

REFERENCES

1. Afriat, S., "Analytical Theory of Production," *Lecture Note,* Purdue University, Spring 1968.
2. Apostol, T. M., *Mathematical Analysis* (Reading, Mass.: Addison-Wesley Publishing Company), 1957.
3. Arrow, K. J. and Enthoven, A. C., "Quasi-Concave Programming" *Econometra,* 28, October 1961.
4. Arrow, K. J., Hurwicz, L. and Uzawa, H., "Constraint Qualification in Maximization Problems," *Naval Research Logistics Quarterly,* 8, June 1961.

5. Chipman, J. S., "Factor Price Equalization and the Stolper-Samuelson Theorem," *International Economic Review*, 10, October 1969 (abstract in *Econometrica*, 32, October 1964).

6. ———, "A Survey of the Theory of International Trade: Part 3, The Modern Theory," *Econometrica*, 34, January 1966.

7. Fleming, W. H., *Functions of Several Variables* (Reading, Mass.: Addison-Wesley Publishing Company), 1965.

8. Gale, D., and Nikaido, H., "The Jacobian Matrix and Global Univalance of Mappings," *Mathematische Annalen*, 159, 1965.

9. Inada, K., "The Production Coefficient Matrix and the Stolper-Samuelson Condition," *Econometrica*, forthcoming.

10. James, S. F., and Pearce, I. F., "The Factor Price Equalization Myth: Mathematical Appendix," *Review of Economic Studies*, XIX, 1951–52.

11. Kemp, M. C., and Wegge, L. F., "On the Relation between Commodity Prices and Factor Rewards," *International Economic Review*, 10, October 1969.

12. Kuhn, H. W., "Factor Endowments and Factor Prices: Mathematical Appendix (to an A. H. Land article)," *Economica*, XXVI, May 1959.

13. ———, "On Two Theorems in International Trade," *Economica Mathematia*, Rome, 1967.

14. ———, "Lectures on Mathematical Economics," in *Mathematics of the Decision Sciences*, Part 2, ed. by Dantzig, G. B. and Veinott, A. F. (Providence, R.I.: American Mathematical Society), 1968.

15. Kuhn, H. W., and Tucker, A. W., "Non-linear Programming," *Proceedings of Second Berkeley Symposium on Mathematical Statistics and Probability*, ed. J. Neyman (Berkeley: University of California Press), 1951.

16. McKenzie, L. W., "Equality of Factor Prices in World Trade," *Econometrica*, 23, July 1955.

17. ———, "Matrices with Dominant Diagonals and Economic Theory," *Mathematical Methods in the Social Sciences*, 1959, ed. by Arrow, Karlin, and Suppes (Stanford: Stanford University), 1960.

18. ———, "The Inversion of Cost Functions: A Counter-Example," *International Economic Review*, 8, October 1967.

19. ———, "Theorem and Counter-Example," *International Economic Review*, 8, October 1967.

20. ———, "The Theory of International Trade: II. Mathematical Theory," in *The International Encyclopedia of the Social Sciences* (New York: The Free Press), 1969.

21. Meade, J. E., "The Equalization of Factor Prices: The Two-Country Two-Factor Two-Product Case," *Metroeconomics*, 2, December 1950.

22. Nikaido, H., *Convex Structures and Economic Theory* (New York: Academic Press, Inc.), 1968, especially Chapter VII.

23. Pearce, I. F., "The Factor Price Equalization Myth," *Review of Economic Studies*, XIX, 1951–52.

24.   ———, "A Further Note on Factor-Commodity Price Relationships," *Economic Journal*, 49, December 1959.

25.   ———, "More about Factor Price Equalization," *International Economic Review*, 8, October 1967.

26.   ———, "Rejoinder to Professor McKenzie," *International Economic Review*, 8, October 1967.

27.   ———, "Rejoinder to Professor Samuelson's Summary," *International Economic Review*, 8, October 1967.

28.   Reiter, S., "Efficient International Trade and Equalization of Factor Prices," *International Economic Review*, 2, January 1961.

29.   Samuelson, P. A., "International Trade and the Equalization of Factor Prices," *Economic Journal*, LVIII, June 1948.

30.   ———, "International Factor-Price Equalization Once Again," *Economic Journal*, LIV, June 1949.

31.   ———, "Prices of Factors and Goods in General Equilibrium," *Review of Economic Studies*, XXI, 1953–54.

32.   ———, "Prices of Factors and Goods in General Equilibrium: 1965 Postscript," in *Collected Scientific Papers of Paul A. Samuelson*, ed. by Stiglitz (Cambridge, Mass.: M.I.T. Press), 1966, p. 908, Vol. 2.

33.   ———, "Summary on Factor-Price Equalization," *International Economic Review*, 8, October 1967.

34.   Shephard, R. W., *Cost and Production Functions* (Princeton: Princeton University Press), 1953.

35.   Stolper, W. F., and Samuelson, P. A., "Protection and Real Wages," *Review of Economic Studies*, IX, November 1941, reprinted in *Readings in the Theory of International Trade*, ed. by Ellis and Metzler, 1949.

36.   Uekawa, Y., "On the Generalization of the Stolper-Samuelson Theorem," *Econometrica*, forthcoming.

37.   Uzawa, H., "Duality Principles in the Theory of Cost and Production," *International Economic Review*, 5, May 1964.

38.   ———, "Prices of the Factors of Production in International Trade," *Econometrica*, 27, July 1959.

39.   Wegge, L. F., and Kemp, M. C., "Generalizations of the Stolper-Samuelson and Samuelson-Rybczynski Theorems in Terms of Conditional Input-Output Coefficients," *International Economic Review*, 10, October 1969.

Index